Political Science at the University of Wisconsin–Madison

Political Science at the University of Wisconsin–Madison: A Centennial History

Edited by Crawford Young

Production and design, University Communications, University of Wisconsin–Madison

ISBN 0-9748952-2-9

To the 190 past and present faculty,
the 593 doctoral alumni,
and the 11,000 living undergraduate alumni
of the University of Wisconsin–Madison
Department of Political Science

Contents

Appendixes

Preface

As the centennial of the Department of Political Science approached, Emeritus Professor Clara Penniman suggested that a history of the department should be undertaken, and provided a generous contribution to make the project possible. Penniman, the first woman to hold a faculty appointment in the department, served from 1953 till 1984, and celebrated her 90th birthday during the centennial year of 2004. Without her catalytic initiative, this history would remain unwritten.

There had been some earlier steps toward assembling a history. Llewellyn Pfankuchen, who taught from 1932 to 1972, had gathered data on the approximately 300 doctoral alumni from 1896 through 1975. Capsule biographies were published as a brochure in 1976. Pfankuchen had also carefully saved department minutes and other documents covering the years of his active service, a precious archive. Booth Fowler had worked with Pfankuchen in gathering historical material, but the vision of a full history fell dormant until the Penniman gift.

After some delay in defining ways and means of achieving the goal of a department history, Chair Mark Beissinger in fall 2001 formed a committee of emeritus faculty resident in Madison to move the project forward. In March 2002, Crawford Young agreed to assume responsibility for this task, with Leon Epstein and Booth Fowler serving as a steering committee to provide ongoing guidance.

A preliminary survey of sources for the history revealed a rich body of material to supplement the major archive collections of papers from Richard T. Ely, Paul Reinsch, Frederic Ogg, John Gaus, and a number of others. Oral histories were conducted with all emeritus faculty and former chairs. The oral history office of the University Archives, whose assistance was invaluable, had earlier recorded a number of oral histories; a few had been done by the oral history project of the American Political Science Association. The University Archives serves as the permanent depository for this valuable data source.[1]

Extended interviews were conducted in 2003 and 2004 with all department faculty with at least 10 years of service, and some former colleagues as well (notably Susan Pharr and Barbara Stallings). John Armstrong and Leon Epstein have written extended memoirs, which are to be deposited in University Archives.

Another major venture was a survey of the more than 400 living doctoral alumni. The survey, the oral history collection, and the archival research benefited from the able assistance of four talented project assistants: Matthew Dull, Rachel Girshick, Deryk Pankratz, and Mark Schrad. The abundant documentary materials included in the 28 appendixes to this volume are mostly the work of the four project assistants. Schrad in addition created a Web site for the project, assembled the photographs, and prepared the material in the digital form now required for publication.

The discovery early in our research that the actual foundation date of the Department of Political Science as a self-standing unit was 1904, and not 1901 as previously believed,[2] prompted plans for a centennial celebration. Happily so: curiously, the 2001 date had slipped by without a solitary soul remarking on its centennial significance.

Thus the rectification of a historical error permitted appropriate observation of a signal moment in the life of the department. On 26–27 March 2004, a conference took place in Madison, devoted to the past, present, and future of the department. Several hundred alumni, present and former faculty, students and guests attended the event. Drafts of seven chapters were presented at the conference, which also featured presentations by a number of distinguished alumni, such as Senator Russell Feingold (B.A. 1975) and Representative David Obey (B.A. 1960, M.A. 1968).

A number of other departmental histories exist or are in preparation: anthropology, atmospheric and oceanic sciences, chemical engineering, chemistry, economics, electrical and computer engineering, geology and geophysics, history of science, journalism and mass communication, mathematics, music, philosophy, physics, Scandinavian studies, Slavic studies. Of these, only economics, and electrical and computing engineering produced book-length volumes comparable in scope.

The project has benefited from the generous assistance of a number of university staff. The University Archives provided constant assistance, especially Barry Teicher of the oral history project. Bernard Schermetzler of the University Archives staff gave invaluable help with assembling the photographs. University Historian John Jenkins extracted from his vast files a number of invaluable leads, including not least the correct founding date for the department. Judith

Photo courtesy University of Wisconsin–Madison Archives

Clara Penniman

Craig of the College of Letters and Science and Lois Beecham of the Graduate School unearthed important materials, as did Paula Gray of the Secretary of the Faculty office. Former Letters and Science Dean Phillip Certain gave vital support to the centennial conference, and he deserves credit for insisting upon (and funding) an official photographer, many of whose pictures appear in these pages.

Although the Penniman gift provided the bulk of the financial support for the project, acknowledgment is also due to the department for partial funding of two project assistants, office space, and other staff support. Two of the project assistants were supported by remaining research funds attached to the H. Edwin Young Chair of international studies held by Crawford Young.

Few of the present faculty, including the editor of this volume, had any familiarity with the early history of the department. Yet the remarkable achievement of high national recognition and esteem in the first years of the 20th century created a reputational capital that permitted the department to retain its ranking among the top departments nationally despite nearly complete faculty turnover in the wake of World Wars I and II. The names of Frederic Ogg and John Gaus live on among young generations, but many other key figures of the early decades, such as Pitman Potter and Arnold Hall, and even founding leader Paul Reinsch, are all but unknown. Perhaps the most enduring contribution of this volume is to preserve the memory and record of the contribution of so many faculty whose teaching and scholarship cumulatively constitutes the core legacy of Wisconsin Political Science.

Notes

1. The University Archives have oral histories for the following: David Adamany, Bernard Cohen, Melvin Croan, Jack Dennis, Dennis Dresang, Peter Eisinger, William Farber, Booth Fowler, Joel Grossman, Henry Hart (2), Charles Jones, Herbert Kritzer, Leon Lindberg, Richard Merelman, Clara Penniman, Virginia Sapiro, James Scott, David Tarr, Crawford Young, William Young (2). The American Political Science Association oral history holdings, at the University of Kentucky Library, include Leon Epstein, Matthew Holden, and Clara Penniman.
2. The 1901 date was imprinted in public memory by the centennial history of the university, Merle Curti and Vernon Carstensen, *The University of Wisconsin: A History 1848–1925* (Madison: University of Wisconsin Press, 1949), II, 338.

CHAPTER 1

Toward the Creation: Lathrop, Parkinson, and the Ely School of Economics, Political Science and History (1849–1904)

Crawford Young

Prehistory: Forerunners to Political Science before the Ely School

The centennial history of the University of Wisconsin, by Merle Curti and Vernon Carstensen, situates the creation of a separate Department of Political Science in 1901.[1] However, the record shows that the Letters and Science Faculty on 18 January 1904, in response to a proposal from President Charles Van Hise and Letters and Science (L&S) Dean Edward Birge, voted to break up the School of Economics and Political Science into self-standing departments, as part of a larger reorganization. The University of Wisconsin Board of Regents approved the official establishment of a separate Department of Political Science the following day.

Yet the ancestry of Political Science extends more than a half century beyond the formal foundation. The first chancellor of the university, John Lathrop, named at the initial meeting of the board of regents on 7 October 1848, arrived in Madison in October 1849 to take up his duties as founding leader and also as "professor of ethics, civil polity, and political economy." When he was forced out as chancellor in 1858, he was consoled with a professorship of "Ethical and Political Science."[2] This designation of his chair came only a year after what discipline historians cite as the first American professorship in political science: the Columbia Chair of History and Political Science awarded to Francis Lieber in 1857.[3] In 1858 a reorganization of the fledgling university provided for a "department of Science, Literature and the Arts," with a school of "polity" (along with schools of philosophy, philology, natural science, civil and mechanical engineering and agriculture).[4] There were only a half dozen faculty; Lathrop taught the "polity" courses to last-year students. As with all colleges of the time, there was a fixed four-year curriculum for all students. Lathrop organized the senior recitations in Ethics, International Law, Civil Polity, Constitutional Law, Political Economy, and the History of Civilization.[5] Thus, although the elements of what were to become organized political science entities by the 1880s were clearly visible in the Lathrop portfolio, there was little sense of clear field boundaries, much less of specialized scholarship. The scholar could still claim cosmopolitan intellectual reach, which Lathrop exhibited by resigning his professorship of ethical and political science in 1859 to join the University of Missouri faculty as professor of English literature (and later to become Missouri president).

The first permanent faculty member to carry the banner of what would become political science was John B. Parkinson, himself an example of the scholarly versatility of those years. His initial appointment in 1867 was in mathematics, and only in 1872 was his appointment redesignated as professor of "civil polity and political economy." Further evidence of his multivalent profile was his selection as official Poet for the 1865 commencement.[6] Parkinson as a youth took part in the California gold rush from 1853 to 1856, spending three years in the mines with only modest returns.[7] He enrolled at Wisconsin in 1856, earning one of the first B.A. degrees in 1860, followed by an M.A. in 1863. The Civil War years were spent on the home front,[8] where he rose to prominence rapidly; he was named superintendent of public instruction in 1863, then appointed as a regent in 1866, a post he resigned to take up the faculty appointment in mathematics. After an interlude from 1874 to 1876 as part owner and editor of the *Madison Democrat*, and chair of the state Democratic Party, Parkinson returned to the university, now as professor of "civil polity and international law." In 1885, he became vice president, a position he held until his 1908 retirement. The post was at the time merely ceremonial; Parkinson stood in for the president on public occasions when the latter was absent. With the retirement of Parkinson, the position disappeared until 1948.[9] His name was touted as a presidential prospect at the successions leading to appointments of John Bascom (1874) and Charles Adams (1892).[10] A contemporary appraisal of Parkinson provides a generous portrayal:

> Professor Parkinson's style of writing is clear and forcible, simple and concise. It exhibits pruning and trimming—characteristics of culture. His reasoning is apt to be correct; and it is enforced with a vigor quite refreshing to the reader. . . . His periods are usually short; his thoughts, lucid; his conclusions, convincing.[11]

Curti and Carstenson offer a more nuanced portrait: "A zealous and efficient friend of the University, Parkinson . . . was a skillful teacher and loyal friend of youth as well as a public-spirited citizen, but he lacked profound scholarship and had little contact with many of the new developments in the field." He never published his lectures or any scholarly works. During much of his long career, Parkinson and his family resided in a house on the present site of the University Club.

John Bascom as Social Scientist

Beyond Parkinson, in the period before the 1890s, one other important figure who belongs in the intellectual lineage of political and other social sciences deserves mention: John Bascom, president from 1874 to 1887. Bascom embodied what remained during his tenure as a widely accepted older model of the ideal scholar: "a cultured man as one at home in all fields of learning," in the words of Curti and Carstenson.[13] His instruction was in the field of philosophy, but his interests and published work spanned the social sciences. Reared and educated in a Calvinist-tinctured environment of evangelical piety,

Photo courtesy University of Wisconsin–Madison Archives

Top row: Charles Haskins (history), David Kinley (economics); *middle row:* Frederick Jackson Turner (history), Richard T. Ely (economics), John B. Parkinson (political science); *bottom row:* William A. Scott (economics), John M. Parkinson (political science).

his synthesis of Protestant Christian ethics with new intellectual stirrings of empirical spirit and social concern reflected an antipathy to nascent trends of specialization. Bascom wrote:

> The most serious evil, associated with the present tendency in education to special departments, is that the immediate uses of knowledge are allowed to take the place of its widest spiritual ministrations. The mind is made microscopic in vision and minute in method, rather than truly comprehensive and penetrating.[14]

His first book, *Political Economy* (1859), was a comprehensive text summarizing British economic theory from Adam Smith to David Ricardo. He wrote on psychology, most notably *Principles of Psychology* (1877), then turned to sociology, a topic he began to develop through Sunday afternoon lectures at Wisconsin (with young Robert La Follette frequently in the audience).[15] Sociology, wrote Bascom, is an integrated field "so wide and fertile" that it "overwhelms one with the multitudinous processes of reaping and of storing the harvest. All culture of mind and heart, all gains of science and faith, all inherited forms of law, and all renewed forces of life are united and completed in sociology."[16] He drew together his sociological reflections at Wisconsin to formulate, in his 1887 book, *Sociology,* a moral philosophy of the state as a beneficent force organizing social power to combat destructive and ruthless material forces abroad in the land. Although political science was the only major social science not graced with a Bascom treatise, his theory of the state as agency of social power closely paralleled the intellectual preoccupations of the emergent discipline of politics.[17] In its moral component, Bascom's philosophy was an important early source of the social gospel movement. A further sociology treatise, *Social Theory,* appeared in 1895; over a third of this volume is devoted to the state. His commitment in an 1874 passage to empiricism foreshadows the early understandings of the vocation of political science:

> . . . investigation can only proceed securely as it limits the causes which it considers and explains. The possibility, then, of a science of Political Economy—indeed, of any social science—will depend on the question, whether there are causes underlying its phenomena so few, as to be within the reach of inquiry; so controlling, as to render that inquiry safe in its practical deductions; and so traceable, as to give us their law, and also prepare us for the exceptions.[18]

These summations of social science knowledge came in addition to his books on his core concerns of ethics, philosophy, and theology.[19]

Letter and Science (L&S) Dean Edward Birge, memorializing Bascom in 1911, declared, "I question whether the history of any commonwealth can show so intimate a relation between the forces which have governed its social development and the principles expounded from a teacher's desk, as that which exists between Wisconsin and the classroom of John Bascom." No social influence was more potent in his time than that of Bascom, argued Birge. The ideas radiating from the Bascom classroom shaped "the temper of the people of the state."[20]

University Transformation and the Birth of Political Science

By the time of the Bascom resignation in 1887, momentous changes were in course both in the nature of the American university, and in the rapidly coalescing social science disciplines. The introduction of the elective system, initially at Harvard, freed the curriculum from its narrow classical definition, and permitted a rapid diversification of subject matter. The emergence of graduate programs at the leading universities, beginning with the award of the first Ph.D. by Yale in 1861, opened the door to a research vocation, with Harvard, Columbia, Cornell, and Michigan as early leaders. The large-scale importation of a German research university model was a powerful influence, mediated above all by the creation of Johns Hopkins University in 1876 as a primarily graduate institution. The social base of student enrollment expanded to take in much of the middle class, and college began to be seen as a necessary route to social mobility by those below. A spirit of innovation was in the air, reflected in the cult of progress, and a strengthening faith in science. The university began to perceive a mission of engagement in progressive social reform.[21] Bascom reflects this ethos of the times in his 1893 summary of social theory, attributing his motivation to write the volume as "prompted by a progressive temper," which "it is hoped, will awaken, correct, and guide the same temper in others."[22]

These national stirrings resonated powerfully at the University of Wisconsin. At the time of the Bascom departure in 1887, the university enrolled a mere 500 students. In the next 15 years, under presidents Thomas Chamberlin (1887–92), Charles Adams (1892–1900), and Edward Birge (1900–03), enrollment grew sixfold, a research mission for the university was defined, and advanced graduate study was introduced as a core activity. At the beginning of this period, Wisconsin was a small regional university of modest standing. By its end, the university had achieved national rank as a leading public institution.

Political science began to take clear form as a discipline nationally in the last two decades of the 19th century, separating out from the parent fields of philosophy, law, and history, and cognate spheres of sociology, economics, and psychology. Leading discipline historians, such as John Gunnell, James Farr, and Anne Haddow, are unanimous in citing the 1857 appointment of Lieber, a German exile, to a newly created Chair of History and Political Science at Columbia as a foundational moment. Lieber in his inaugural address identifies political science as a middle road between a historical school merely valorizing the past and a philosophical school postulating laws of social evolution. Political economy he swept into political science as a mere branch.[23] John Burgess, who replaced Lieber in the Columbia chair in 1876, founded the first Faculty of Political Science in 1880 at Columbia, drawing upon faculty in public law, history, and philosophy. Burgess launched the first discipline journal, *Political Science Quarterly,* in 1885.

Other institutions began creating separate schools, faculties, or departments of political science in the 1880s. In 1881, future Wisconsin President Charles Adams created a School of Political Science at Michigan. Adams, who studied political philosophy with Andrew White at Michigan, had replaced the latter that year when White left to become president of Cornell University. Adams introduced a German model of graduate study of political science which he had observed while studying at Bonn, Berlin and Leipzig.[24] Adams succeeded White as Cornell president, and then became Wisconsin president in 1892. Although he is conventionally identified as a historian, political science can lay claim to at least part of his academic identity.

The most important early seedbed of political science was Johns Hopkins University. This newly created university exercised enormous influence in the emergence of social science during the latter years of the century. The Johns Hopkins wholesale adoption of a German model was a seminal moment in American university history. The Department of History, Politics and Economics created at Johns Hopkins in the late 1870s trained three crucial figures in Wisconsin social science (John R. Commons, economics; Frederick Jackson Turner, history; and E. A. Ross, sociology), in addition to such other early luminaries as Albion Small, Woodrow Wilson, Henry Carter Adams, Edward Bemis, and John Dewey. Among the key Johns Hopkins faculty during those extraordinary years was Richard T. Ely, a Columbia product appointed in 1881.[25]

In final decades of the 19th century, political science was still historically focused and weakly bounded. When the American Historical Association was created in 1884, it attracted membership from political scientists and economists as well as historians. Herbert Adams posted in his Johns Hopkins seminar room the slogan "History is past Politics and Politics present History." Economics was widely termed "political economy," a title retained by the Wisconsin Department of Economics until 1918. The strong German influence reverberated in a central place for the state as defining core of the nascent field. The 1885 translation of the Johann Bluntschli opus, *The Theory of the State,* provided one of the early basic texts. The Burgess Faculty of Political Science at Columbia defined its curriculum as "the history of *institutions,* the origin and development of the State through its several phases of *political organization* down to the modern constitutional form" and "the history of the philosophic theories of the State."[26] Treatises on the state were standard fare for the early generation of political scientists (for example, W. W. Willoughby, *The Nature of the State* [1896]; Woodrow Wilson, *The State: Elements of Historical and Practical Politics* [1899]).

The Ely School of Economics, Political Science and History

The ambiguous boundaries between history, economics, and political science by the 1890s help explain the decision by President Chamberlin in 1892 to launch a bold new venture in social science as a school combining the three (and subsuming sociology and commerce), and to recruit as director Richard T. Ely of Johns Hopkins at the unheard-of salary of $3,500 (higher than any other professor or dean at the time).[27] Chamberlin assumed office in 1887 with an audacious vision of building a research university. He swiftly recruited a former student of William Allen (the pioneer of history at Wisconsin), Frederick Jackson Turner, who had recently completed graduate training at Johns Hopkins. Turner shared the Chamberlin ambition to create a research-based social science, and urged the recruitment of his former Johns Hopkins mentor, Ely, for this purpose. Turner was aware that Ely was frustrated at Johns Hopkins, which had refused his promotion to full professor, and was open to alternatives. At first, the Ely appointment was envisioned to energize economics by removing it from the Parkinson portfolio. In the difficult negotiations to recruit Ely, a more ambitious design of a School of Economics, Political Science and History took shape, an idea Ely attributes to Turner.[28]

The political science component was important to Ely in substance, though apparently not in terminology. President Chamberlin circulated a query to Ely, Turner, and Parkinson asking preferences among possible titles for the school. Ely listed as first choice "Economics, Civics and History," and as second preference "Economics, Civic Science and History," with the name eventually chosen as only a third option.[29] Whatever the debate over terminology, a more substantive issue concerning the place of political science in the Ely School at once confronted Ely: the role of Parkinson, long a popular university fixture with a broad network of political connections and warm ties with a number of regents. Parkinson necessarily became a part of the school, but Ely regarded the form of scholarship Parkinson embodied to be an artifact of the past. Parkinson, still vice president, accepted the loss of his economics title and the Ely appointment, but resented the Ely prerogative of bringing a young assistant professor and a graduate assistant from Johns Hopkins with him as junior partners. Parkinson insisted that he also be provided an assistant, and when Chamberlin demurred, went directly to the board of regents to secure such an appointment. The regents bestowed upon the Parkinson nominee—none other than his son, John M. Parkinson—the title of "assistant professor," apparently unaware of the distinction between "assistant" and "assistant professor." Ely was furious, believing with good reason that the younger Parkinson had inadequate qualifications for a faculty appointment. In fact, J. M. Parkinson had just earned an M.A. in 1891 at Johns Hopkins, so Ely undoubtedly knew him, and must have held an unfavorable opinion.[30] When Ely then learned that Chamberlin intended to resign to accept a Chicago professorship, leaving uncertain the promises of funding for books and development of his school, he angrily wrote Chamberlin that "as nearly as I can gather, you leave me in the hands of Parkinson . . . and you have had no provision made for books and facilities for advanced work. What a mortification for me! What am I to say to students who come to Madison with enthusiasm and high expectations? They will feel that they have been deceived."[31] Chamberlin tried to soothe Ely by assuring him that the appointment of the younger Parkinson would be brief (he left by 1894), and that some of the board "are not educated up to the point of granting a new and unknown man unlimited control of a school into which was to be put one or more of the Faculty of long standing."[32] At the same time, he denied Ely the title of dean which he desired, suggesting the title of "director" instead, apparently to minimize conflicts with Parkinson.[33]

On his departure from the university to join the University of Chicago geology department in mid-1892, Chamberlin gave vent to the frustrations which Ely's inflexible stance regarding Parkinson had caused him. "I do not think," Chamberlin wrote, "you are wise in making life a burden to those who would gladly help you but who have to be constantly on their guard lest they shall be construed to agree to something they do not or be dragged into some unexpected responsibility only to be whipped up with it in season and out of season. Your methods of treating your friends and those of whom you seek aid are the worst I have ever encountered in similar correspondence."[34]

The maneuvering over the younger Parkinson notwithstanding, the elder Parkinson wrote a gracious letter of welcome to Ely when the appointment was announced, expressing his "gratification" that Ely was to head the "Department of Economics and Social Science." Parkinson added, "I have long felt the necessity of a division of my Chair, and was the first to suggest it. I know of no one whom I would prefer to see take up the work offered you here." However, he added the request that he "be permitted—temporarily at least—to retain some little organic connection with the work in Political Economy—a lectureship for instance on some of its practical applications."[35]

Ely was perhaps the most visible young economist in the nation at the time of his appointment. He had completed a B.A. in 1876, and his doctorate in 1879, both at Columbia. It is interesting that he spent the entire period from 1876 to 1879 studying in Germany, suggesting that Columbia required no residency and only a thesis at the time.[36] He then joined the Johns Hopkins faculty. He played a leading role in the founding of the American Economics Association in 1885, and served as its secretary till 1892. He was a vigorous critic of classical economics and its deductive master premise of a universal law of self-interest driving economic man; Ely advocated a more inductive, empirical science acknowledging the altruistic side of human behavior, and the possible evolution of a morally improved human actor open to cooperative endeavor and normative solidarity. He and his fellow founders of the AEA, which in its early years included historians and political scientists among its members, adopted a platform including the affirmation that "we regard the state as an educational and ethical agency whose positive aid is an indispensable condition of human progress."[37] Ely's Christian socialist orientation (which he listed on his letterhead)[38] in his early career included an idealistic view of labor union potential for uplift, temperance, and education. The vision of advanced social science training, for Ely, included not only expanding the frontiers of knowledge, but the training of skilled public servants imbued with ideals of social reform (perhaps the explanation for his preference for "civics" or "civic science" rather than "political science" in the school title).[39] In coming to Wisconsin, Ely frequently expressed his aspiration for a role for the school comparable to that of West Point in military science and engineering: training for careers in journalism, law, civil service, and work with reform institutions.

The social agenda that Ely brought to his task of creating the School of Economics, Political Science and History soon led him into deep trouble. Oliver Wells, superintendent of public instruction and ex officio regent, roundly denounced Ely in a letter widely reprinted in the media. Wells accused Ely of having entertained a Kansas City strike organizer, and having threatened a local printer with loss of business unless the shop was unionized, in addition to teaching "socialist cant." "Only the careful student will discover [the] utopian, impracticable and pernicious doctrines [advanced by Ely], but their general acceptance would furnish a seeming moral justification of attack on life and property such as the country has already become too familiar with," Wells wrote.[40] A regent committee was appointed to study these allegations, which gave a resounding endorsement to Ely; the statement adopted on the occasion, probably drafted by President Adams, supplies the text for the ringing celebration of academic freedom recorded in the "sifting and winnowing" plaque on Bascom Hall: ". . . In all lines of academic investigation it is of the utmost importance that the investigator should be absolutely free to follow the indications of truth wherever they may lead. Whatever may be the limitations which trammel inquiry elsewhere we believe the great state University of Wisconsin should ever

Photo courtesy University of Wisconsin–Madison Archives

Richard T. Ely

encourage the continual and fearless sifting and winnowing by which alone the truth can be found."[41]

Ironically, the Ely defense was not on academic freedom grounds, but rather on the baseless nature of the allegations. The key Wells charges collapsed on inspection, and the Ely lawyer quoted from his writings to show that he was not really a socialist, was against labor violence, and had a growing tendency to conservatism. Indeed, Ely stated that, "if true, the allegations unquestionably unfit me to occupy a responsible position as an instructor of youth in a great university."[42]

Ely was provided $5,000 for books for his school; Wisconsin was the first western university to offer some graduate fellowships.[43] From the outset, the primary mission of the Ely School was graduate training. Turner, in an 1892 letter, expresses his cordial accord with the Ely view that the new school be primarily a graduate school, though noting this might be politically difficult. However, Turner concluded, "it is well understood here now that we are to have an advanced graduate school, and they will see that they cannot expect that such a school will cripple itself by doing an undue amount of undergraduate work."[44] Despite the apprehensions of Ely over the departure of President Chamberlin, his replacement, Charles Adams, with his history and political science background, was a strong supporter of the school. Undergraduates and graduates were attracted in large numbers; the 1894 biennial report of the president to the regents noted its classes were the most attractive on campus. President Adams in his 1896 report declared that "we are entitled to feel that in no institution in the country, unless it be in the School of Political Science at Columbia College, is more thorough and comprehensive work done that we are now giving in this important department of the University." From its founding till 1900, the Ely School awarded half of the total number of doctorates granted by the university. A board of visitors report at the time concluded that the abundant publications, the placement success of its alumni, and the distinction of its staff made the school a jewel in the crown of a university just rising to national prominence.

Political science during this period evidently contributed much less to the standing of the school than did economics (Ely) and history (Turner and Charles H. Haskins, another Johns Hopkins product). Parkinson remained the primary political science faculty member through the 1890s. The 1895–96 Political Science report submitted by Parkinson lists only Parkinson and a graduate student assistant, Samuel Sparling, as instructors; earlier, a couple of lecturers had supplemented the Parkinson offerings. The latter taught courses in elementary law, constitutional law, comparative constitutional law, Roman law, and international law, and offered a "Political Science Seminary" (not, one may note, the political economy course he had plaintively requested). Sparling taught a pair of courses on public administration and municipal government. The following year Paul Reinsch contributed as an assistant. In 1896, Sparling received the first doctorate in political science, and the following year was named to the faculty. Reinsch completed his degree in 1898, and joined the faculty in 1899.

One may note in passing that both these first political science doctorates were awarded without direction by a political scientist. Parkinson appears to have had little or no role in the supervision of Sparling and Reinsch. The former wrote a dissertation on municipal administration in Chicago, apparently with Ely as primary mentor. The Reinsch dissertation examined English common law in the early American colonies, under the direction of Frederick Jackson Turner. The Ely School also produced the first doctorate in anthropology in 1896, without benefit of any faculty closely connected to the field.[45]

Some insight into the content of graduate instruction at this time is found in the transcript of Charles McCarthy, later to become a lecturer for the department, who will make an extended appearance in the next chapter. McCarthy completed a doctorate in the Ely School in1901, with a history focus, though including substantial work with Reinsch. The dissertation dealt with the anti-Masonic movement. His academic program is listed in table 1.1.[46]

One may note that Sparling and Reinsch do not appear to have followed as extensive a program of courses at Wisconsin. During a good part of their respective doctoral years, they were studying in Europe, especially Germany. One may also note that during part of the fall semester of 1898 for which he was registered, McCarthy was coaching the football team at the University of Georgia, a position that collapsed when one of the players was killed and the season was canceled.[47]

By 1900, the Ely School had gained national renown for Wisconsin. In 1900, the school had a faculty of 14, who offered 72 courses, and enrolled 72 graduate students.[48] According to Curti and Carstenson, the school "represented the first real graduate program at the university," adding that "the greatness of the university largely rested on the achievements and reputation of the School of Economics, Political Science and History."[49]

Table 1.1 Doctoral Program of Charles McCarthy, 1898–1901

Course Title	*Professor*
Semester I, 1898–99	
Constitutional History of England	Charles H. Haskins
History of the West	Frederick J. Turner
Theories of Value	George W. Scott
Semester II, 1898–99	
Constitutional History of England	Charles H. Haskins
History of the West	Frederick J. Turner
Theories of Production and Consumption	George W. Scott
Semester I, 1899–1900	
Europe during the Middle Ages	Charles H. Haskins
History of French Institutions	Charles H. Haskins
Economic and Social History of the United States, 1789–1850	Frederick J. Turner
Seminary in American History	Frederick J. Turner
Historical Conference	Charles H. Haskins
Semester II, 1899–1900	
History of Political Thought	Paul S. Reinsch
Seminary in Political Philosophy	Paul S. Reinsch
Economic and Social History of the United States, 1789–1850	Frederick J. Turner
Theories of Production and Consumption	George W. Scott
Semester I, 1900–01	
History of Europe in the 19th Century, 1815–1900	Victor Coffin
The Distribution of Wealth	Richard T. Ely
Colonial Politics	Paul S. Reinsch
Semester II, 1900–01	
History of Political Thought and the Philosophy of the State	Paul S. Reinsch
The Distribution of Wealth	Richard T. Ely
History of Europe in the 19th Century, 1815–1900	Victor Coffin

Source: Edward A. Fitzpatrick, *McCarthy of Wisconsin* (New York: Columbia University Press, 1944).

The Demise of the Ely School

From the outset, Ely sought to maximize his authority as school director. At the time of his appointment, he fought hard to secure the title of dean, which President Chamberlin refused to concede. However, he did win the right to independent status for the school, not directly subject to L&S, whose first dean, Edward Birge, was named in 1891. Birge chafed under the Chamberlin

Photo courtesy University of Wisconsin–Madison Archives

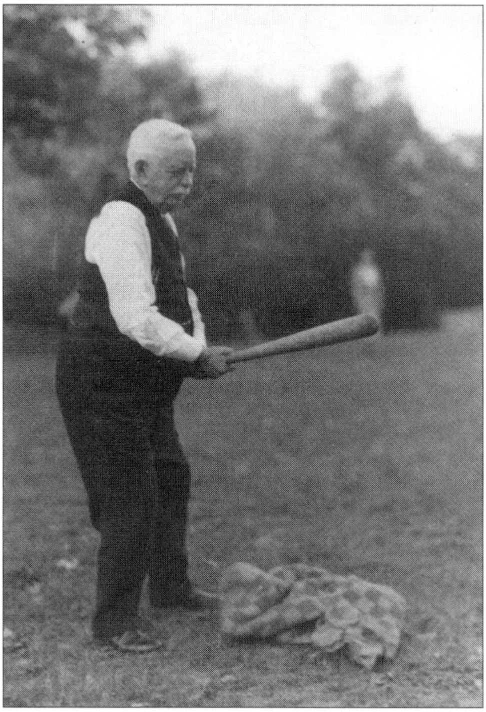

Richard T. Ely steps up to the plate.

vision of his role as essentially a dean of students. When President Adams fell seriously ill in 1900, Birge was for the first time able to assert his authority over departments.

In 1900, the Ely School began to break apart. By this time, the Ely relationship with President Adams had soured. Ely had repeatedly sought greater autonomy, arguing that the school should be responsible only to the regents and school faculty, not to the overall faculty. In an 1897 report, Ely complained that he had been promised on coming that his school would have "a large measure of independence," but his administrative work not only increased but was dependent on the decision of other executives.[50]

When Adams was forced from office by declining health in 1900, Birge as interim president soon found an opportunity to cut the Ely School down to size. Turner had an attractive offer from the University of Chicago to chair the history department; to dissuade him, Birge approved creation of a School of History under Turner's direction, with the grudging agreement of Ely.[51] The latter was even more unhappy when about the same time, a School of Commerce was formed, appropriating the business offerings in the Ely School.[52] With political science beginning to acquire under Sparling and Reinsch a more vigorous profile, and new President Charles Van Hise by 1903 determined to reorganize the university on departmental lines and end the proliferation of autonomous schools, the final splintering of the Ely School became inevitable, consummated in 1904. Ely, disappointed by this outcome, began fishing for other opportunities. None of his overtures for a return to Johns Hopkins, a Harvard position, or a top government post bore fruit; however, Ely, who remained chair of the Department of Political Economy until 1911, could find justifiable consolation in subsequent recruitment of other distinguished Johns

Hopkins products: John R. Commons to his political economy staff in 1904, and E. A. Ross in 1906[53] to launch instruction in sociology. Ely remained at Wisconsin until 1921, when at age 71 Northwestern lured him with an endowed chair and princely salary. He died in 1943 at the age of 89.[54]

Notes

1. Merle Curti and Vernon Carstensen, *The University of Wisconsin 1848–1925* (Madison: University of Wisconsin Press, 1949), II, 338.
2. C. W. Butterfield, *A History of the University of Wisconsin from its First Organization to 1879; With Biographical Sketches of its Chancellors, Presidents, and Professors* (Madison: University Press Company, 1879).
3. James Farr, "The History of Political Science," *American Journal of Political Science,* 32, 4 (1988), 1174–95.
4. Stephen H. Carpenter, *An Historical Sketch of the University of Wisconsin from 1849 to 1876* (Madison: Atwood & Culter, 1876), 30.
5. J.F.A. Pyre, *Wisconsin* (New York: Oxford University Press, 1920).
6. Carpenter, *An Historical Sketch,* 38.
7. Parkinson in an 1892 paper read to the Twentieth Century Club provides fascinating detail on his California gold rush adventures. John B. Parkinson, "California and Her Golden Fleece," 1892. Wisconsin State Historical Society Archives.
8. Over 90,000 Wisconsin men served in the Civil War, or a fifth of the total male population. Of the 50 graduates of the university up to 1864, 28 joined the Union army. The 1864 commencement was canceled because all male students were in service. The disappearance of male students was one of the factors in the first admission of women in 1863. Pyre, *Wisconsin,* 144; Curti and Carstensen, *The University of Wisconsin,* I, 194–96; Carpenter, *An Historical Sketch,* 38.
9. Ira I. Baldwin, *My Half Century at the University of Wisconsin* (Madison: Omnipress, 1995), 181.
10. Curti and Carstensen, *The University of Wisconsin,* I, 247, 561.
11. Butterfield, *A History,* 93.
12. Curti and Carstensen, *The University of Wisconsin,* I, 345.
13. Curti and Carstensen, *The University of Wisconsin,* I, 281.
14. Cited in Laurence R. Veysey, *The Emergence of the American University* (Chicago: University of Chicago Press, 1965).
15. La Follette in his autobiography pays a warm tribute to Bascom, writing, "The guiding spirit of my time, and the man to whom Wisconsin owes a debt greater than it can ever pay, was its President John Bascom." The Sunday Bascom lectures to students, La Follette recalled, "were among the

most important influences in my early life." Bascom, continued La Follette, "was in advance of his time in feeling the new social forces and in emphasizing the new social responsibilities." In this sense, La Follette suggests that Bascom was the true originator of the Wisconsin Idea. Robert M. La Follette, *La Follette's Autobiography: A Personal Narrative of Political Experiences* (Madison: University of Wisconsin Press, 1963), 12–13.

16. John Bascom, *Things Learned by Living* (New York: G.P. Putnam's Sons, 1913), 176.
17. See the interesting intellectual portrait of Bascom in J. David Hoeveler, "The University and the Social Gospel: The Intellectual Origins of the 'Wisconsin Idea,' "*Wisconsin Magazine of History,* 59, 4 (Summer 1976), 282–98.
18. John Bascom, *Political Economy: A Text-book for Colleges* (Andover: Warren F. Draper, 1874), 9–10.
19. Curti and Carstensen devote an entire chapter to "the mind of John Bascom"; *The University of Wisconsin,* I, 275–95.
20. Charles McCarthy, *The Wisconsin Idea* (New York: Macmillan Company, 1912), 24.
21. Valuable histories of the American university and the rise of social science within it include, in addition to Veysey, *American University,* Dorothy Ross, *The Origins of American Social Science* (Cambridge: Cambridge University Press, 1991); Frederick Rudolph, *The American College and University: A History* (New York: Alfred A. Knopf, 1962).
22. John Bascom, *Social Theory: A Grouping of Social Facts and Principles* (New York: Thomas Crowell & Company, 1893), preface.
23. John G. Gunnell, *The Descent of Political Theory: The Genealogy of an American Vocation* (Chicago: University of Chicago Press, 1993); Anne Haddow, *Political Science in American Colleges and Universities 1636–1900* (New York: D. Appleton-Century Company, 1939); James Farr, "The History of Political Science."
24. Gunnell, *The Descent of Political Theory,* 37.
25. Gunnell, *The Descent of Political Theory,* 32–39.
26. Gunnell, *The Descent of Political Theory,* 52.
27. Benjamin G. Rader, *The Academic Mind and Reform: The Influence of Richard T. Ely in American Life* (Lexington: University of Kentucky Press, 1966), 111.
28. Curti and Carstensen, *The University of Wisconsin,* I, 633–35; Richard T. Ely, *Ground Under our Feet: An Autobiography* (New York: Macmillan Company, 1938), 179. One may note that this was also the structure at Johns Hopkins.
29. University history project data set, Chamberlin memorandum, 30 January 1892.
30. J. M. Parkinson held an appointment as instructor in 1891–92, following his Johns Hopkins M.A. *Wisconsin Badger,* 1894.
31. Curti and Carstensen, *The University of Wisconsin,* I, 634–35.

32. University history project data set, Chamberlin to Ely, 22 April 1892.
33. John Frank Cook, "A History of Liberal Education at the University of Wisconsin 1862–1918," PhD diss., University of Wisconsin, 1970, 174.
34. Cook, "A History of Liberal Education," 176.
35. Ely papers, State Historical Society, Parkinson to Ely, 29 January 1892.
36. According to the brief biography in *Wisconsin Badger,* 1894.
37. Richard T. Ely, *Ground Under our Feet: An Autobiography* (New York: Macmillan Company, 1938), 136.
38. Veysey, *American University,* 80.
39. See the excellent biography by Rader, *The Academic Mind.*
40. Ely, *Ground Under our Feet,* 220.
41. Curti and Carstensen, *The University of Wisconsin,* I, 525. This robust statement of academic freedom may be compared to a more qualified declaration by the Johns Hopkins University trustees, also in 1894: "[We] regard the discussion of current political, economic, financial and social questions before the students of the University as of such importance that the lessons should be given only by the ablest and wisest persons whose services the University can command. . . . The Trustees are of the opinion that no instruction should be given in these subjects unless it can be given by persons of experience, who are well acquainted with the history and principles of political and social progress. . . . The Trustees recommend great caution in the selection and engagement of lecturers and other teachers." Veysey, *American University,* 411.
42. Curti and Carstensen, *The University of Wisconsin,* I, 516. On this episode, see also Rader, *The Academic Mind,* 135–53.
43. Rader, *The Academic Mind,* 111.
44. State Historical Society, Ely papers, Turner to Ely, 23 February 1892.
45. According to historical remarks at a celebration of the 50th anniversary of the Department of Anthropology in 1989.
46. Edward A. Fitzpatrick, *McCarthy of Wisconsin* (New York: Columbia University Press, 1944).
47. Fitzpatrick, *McCarthy,* 23–24.
48. Robert J. Lampman (ed.), *Economists at Wisconsin* (Madison: University Publications, 1993), 15.
49. Curti and Carstensen, *University of Wisconsin,* I, 641.
50. Cook, "A History of Liberal Education," 178–80.
51. Cook, "A History of Liberal Education," 181. Turner eventually left for Harvard in 1909.
52. The School of Commerce lost its autonomous status in 1904, when newly appointed President Charles Van Hise brought it under the authority of the College of Letters and Science, along with the School of History. Curti and Carstensen, *The University of Wisconsin,* II, 29–30.

53. Ross was summarily fired at Stanford in 1900 at the demand of the sole trustee, the widow of Leland Stanford, founder and primary benefactor of the university. The Ross sin was a speech at the Oakland socialist club, opposing Asian immigration and seemingly advocating municipal ownership of utilities. The Stanford railway trust employed many Chinese workers, and owned a number of streetcar lines. Ross approached Ely, with whom he had studied at Johns Hopkins, for a position after his dismissal, but Ely replied that the case was too hot. Ross finally found interim employment at Nebraska, whose President, E. Benjamin Andrews, had been earlier fired as Brown University leader for advocating free silver. Eventually Ely was able to recruit Ross as the first sociology instructor in 1906, within what was now the Department of Political Economy. Sociology and anthropology did not acquire separate departmental status until 1929. On the Stanford episode, see especially Veysey, *American University,* 385–410. On the Ross career, see his autobiography, Edward Alsworth Ross, *Seventy Years of it: An Autobiography* (New York: D. Appleton-Century Company, 1936), and Julius Weinberg, *Edward Alsworth Ross and the Sociology of Progressivism* (Madison: State Historical Society of Wisconsin, 1972). The latter two sources provide full detail of the academic freedom episode involving Ross at Wisconsin in 1910, when he was censured by the regents (though not dismissed, as some urged) for escorting anarchist Emma Goldman around campus and announcing her lecture to his class.
54. Rader, *The Academic Mind,* 163–233.

CHAPTER 2

Paul Reinsch and the Founding Years (1904–1918)

Crawford Young

Official Creation of the Department of Political Science

The official birth of the Department of Political Science must be dated 19 January 1904, when the board of regents gave their imprimatur to creation of a departmental unit separate from the former Ely School of Economics, Political Science and History. The term *department* appears from time to time in 19th-century university history, but without the formal meaning the term had acquired by 1904. An 1858 university reorganization, for example, established a "Department of Science, Literature and the Arts," with a half-dozen "schools," including "polity."[1] The university catalogues from 1888 to 1892 listed a "Department of Civil Polity and Political Economy," whose sole member was John B. Parkinson; there were a number of other instances of one-person "departments." When the Ely School of Economics, Political Science and History was launched in 1892, catalogues referred to political science as one of the "departments of instruction." Thus the term *department* lacked stable meaning; for the most part, it appeared to reference categories of instruction, rather than organized administrative units.

As suggested at the close of the previous chapter, several factors flowed together to give the concept of a department its contemporary meaning: an administrative and budgetary unit responsible for organizing instruction within a defined disciplinary sphere, enjoying substantial internal autonomy but subject to the hierarchical tutelage and control of a college dean, and ultimately the president. Edward Birge, College of Letters and Science (L&S) dean from 1891 until 1918, was determined to assert authority over the programs within his domain, and had found Ely a particularly frustrating adversary. When geologist Charles Van Hise became president in 1903, he was determined to reorganize the university to free the presidency of detailed responsibility for managing the entire campus. Van Hise preferred to delegate to the college deans authority for the supervision of the faculty and academic programs within their domains, which dovetailed neatly with the Birge desire to achieve clear authority over Ely; the organizational principle was departmentalization of the campus. On 13 November 1903, Van Hise addressed the L&S faculty, suggesting that the various schools such as that directed by Ely were anomalies which should be discontinued in favor of departmentalization, and proposing that political science should be among other fields constituted as separate departments.[2] There was some speculation that Van Hise, beyond the search for more efficient organization, was also motivated by a desire to placate Birge, who had been narrowly passed over in the selection of the president.[3] Finally, with a pair of promising young scholars, Samuel Sparling and Paul Reinsch, to supplement the aging Parkinson, there was enough of a faculty core upon which to erect a department.

Sparling, Reinsch, and the Early Department

The elaboration of a post-Parkinson political science came from within; the kernel of a full-fledged department consisted of the first two Wisconsin doctorates in the field, Samuel Sparling (1896) and Paul Reinsch (1898). Both of these young scholars swiftly assumed leadership; Parkinson, who retired in 1908, died in 1927 at the age of 93. Sparling and Reinsch both had graduate careers including extended periods of study in Germany and elsewhere in Europe, and acquired early visibility in their field. Beginning in 1895, first Sparling, then Reinsch began to expand the available instruction in political science, initially as assistants.

Sparling, an Indiana native, was a student of municipal administration. He may have begun graduate study with the launching of the Ely School in fall 1892; by early 1894 he was already in Germany, first at Jena, then Halle, Leipzig, and eventually Berlin. At most, he could have had three semesters of residence taking courses and seminaries before departure for Europe. His period of individual study abroad, attending diverse lectures, was completed with some months in Paris. His primary Wisconsin mentor was Ely, with whom he maintained a regular correspondence while in Europe; Sparling sought assurance of an instructorship to permit completing his doctorate, which Ely provided for the 1895–96 year. The Sparling correspondence refers to applications to other universities, which apparently would have provided a doctorate on the basis of a dissertation. During 1895–96, Sparling taught principles of administration and municipal administration, while also completing his thesis. The Parkinson report for 1895–96 observes that "the degree of Ph.D. was conferred upon Samuel E. Sparling, A.B. University of Indiana, Fellow in Public Administration. His major was Public Administration, his minors Economics and American History; his thesis subject 'The Municipal Government of Chicago.'"[4] The nature of doctoral requirements at the time was presumably in process of definition; the Charles McCarthy transcript reproduced in the previous chapter suggests that a formal set of course requirements was in place by the time the department was officially constituted.

Sparling wrote Ely from Germany expressing some indignation that American students at Halle University were able to complete a doctorate in one year, compared to the three or four required in America.[5] But his German study was an important influence; in his correspondence with Ely he describes in some detail the current state of German academic analysis of municipal administration, combined with Sparling's own observation of urban institutions in the cities where he studied. His comparative reflections on German and American higher education are interesting; although he considers the American university system superior, he admires the depth of German scholarship. "At best, in an American university, we can only become acquainted with the standard works. Back of these greater systematic works stands a field of literature which, it seems to me, is scarcely less valuable to the young student. In administration there have opened to me innumerable works of value that I never could have hoped to know in America."[6]

Sparling, the 1900 president's report notes, "has performed an important service to the state by the part he has taken in aiding to organize the Wisconsin League of Municipalities, and in establishing, as its organ, the monthly publication,—'The Municipality.'" The municipalities league quickly became an important voice of urban policy concerns, which it remains to this day. Sparling was also an active participant in city affairs, even serving as an alderman.

Sparling was also a catalyst for the Madison Women's Club engagement in civic reform. In a speech to this group delivered in 1900, he cited a long roster of conditions needing to be "perfected." Madison "schools are crowded, her streets are dirty, her lake shores provide no public baths, her garbage is not systematically collected, her children unattended roam the streets late into the night, no adequate hospital, no kindergartens, no branch libraries." According to Madison historical chronicler David Mollenhoff, Sparling's "clear and forceful presentation of what in the women's movement came to be called the 'modern civic agenda' proved to be terribly exciting to Women's Club members, the keynote address for a brilliant decade."[7] Sparling earned mention in the six-volume *History of Wisconsin* for his activism in promoting municipal garbage collection.[8] Despite his high visibility in the field of municipal reform, his name never figures among those who like Reinsch, Ely, and John R. Commons were close academic advisors to Robert La Follette and the state progressive movement.

The one major Sparling publication, *Introduction to Business Organization* (1906), was a text intended for commerce students. A work on marketing published as recently as 2000 cites the Sparling book as a path-breaking contribution in which "early marketing and its organizational principles began to take shape."[9] His correspondence with Ely refers to substantial personal expenses incurred in collecting material for this treatise, and a keen interest in its sales and possibilities for a revised edition. The book was even translated into Japanese. However, by this time his commitment to an academic career was waning, perhaps because in contrast to his colleague Reinsch, who was advanced to the rank of full professor within two years of his assistant professor appointment in 1899, Sparling never moved beyond the level of associate professor by the time of his 1908 departure.

The Sparling career shift at that time was especially ironic, in view of his specialization in municipal administration. He returned to his native Indiana, and took up farming. He remained in occasional correspondence with Ely, who encouraged him to consider returning to academic life. However, Sparling in a 1914 letter replied that he was far too prosperous in his new pursuits to consider reviving his professorial career. By this time, he had abandoned Indiana for Alabama, where he had a 750-acre estate worked by 85 African-American field hands producing cotton and alfalfa.[10] Sparling died in 1941.

Though Sparling preceded him in faculty appointment, the real driving force in the building of a Department of Political Science of national rank was Reinsch. Through his precocious achievement of an international scholarly reputation, and the nature of his published work, he also imprinted upon the fledgling department an enduring international orientation. Like Sparling, Reinsch augmented his graduate experience with study in Europe; he spent two summers and the year following his 1898 doctorate visiting Bonn, Leipzig, Berlin, Paris, and Rome, attending lectures and establishing intellectual connections.

Reinsch was born in Milwaukee of German immigrant parents, who provided him a strict Lutheran upbringing; German was his first language. The family moved to Madison in 1888 to facilitate Reinsch's enrollment at the university. He found particularly inspirational some of his history professors, especially Turner and Haskins. After his undergraduate degree in 1892, he acquired a law degree at Wisconsin in 1894, and briefly practiced law. When President Adams offered him a post as assistant in history in 1895 in the Ely School, he eagerly returned to the university.[11]

Photo courtesy University of Wisconsin–Madison Archives

Paul Reinsch, about 1905

After the year in Europe in 1898–99, he began his faculty career in 1899. His first major work, *World Politics at the End of the 19th Century as Influenced by the Oriental Situation*, appeared in 1900 in a Macmillan series edited by Ely. The thrust of his scholarship owes much to its temporal context. Imperialism was at flood tide, with the United States becoming a major participant following the 1898 Spanish-American war. He embraced the open door doctrine as an alternative to colonial conquest, which Reinsch saw as a threat to peace. However, the forceful American assertion of the Monroe Doctrine which defined the international politics of Latin America met with Reinsch approval. These themes all run through his numerous early publications, which reflect a special interest in East Asia and secondarily Latin America. These concerns explain the early appearance in the political science curriculum of courses on colonial, Asian, and Latin American politics. Also they explain an early influx of Asian students to study with Reinsch, at a time when at most eastern universities save Harvard, Chinese students in particular were unwelcome.[12]

After his *World Politics* book, other volumes swiftly followed, dealing with colonial administration, American rule in the Philippines, and imperialism.

Two years after his initial appointment as assistant professor (he had earlier been an instructor in history), he was promoted to the rank of full professor in 1901, then became the first chair in 1904. He served as department head until 1908, then again in 1910–11 and 1912–13.

Reinsch was also among the founders of the American Political Science Association (APSA). He took part in a preparatory committee formed in 1902, under Jeremiah Jenks of Cornell; until that time, many political scientists participated professionally through the American Historical Association or the American Economics Association. He was named second vice president at the inaugural APSA meeting in New Orleans in December 1903, and subsequently, well after his departure from Wisconsin, became APSA president in 1920. A recent intellectual history of the field of international relations by Brian Schmidt devotes a number of pages to his "illustrious career in political science, a discipline he would do much to establish in the United States."[13]

The first Reinsch book, *World Politics*, was an innovative study that offered a broad overview of the political, economic, and intellectual forces shaping international politics. The erudition of this volume, and that of his second major work, *Colonial Government: An Introduction to the Study of Colonial Institutions* (1902), is astonishing, given that his dissertation on the English common law in the early American colonies was entirely unrelated. The bibliographies of these two works include a great range of scholarship, including many titles in French and German; not least intriguing is where he found many of these sources, since a good fraction of them were unlikely to have been available in the still extremely modest holdings of the University of Wisconsin Library.[14]

Schmidt highlights the intellectual significance of the Reinsch contribution:

> . . . it is crucial to note that the account Reinsch provided was informed both by the theoretical discourse of the state and by an empirical assessment of the underlying forces currently shaping world politics. It was within the framework of this discussion that one of the early substantive components of the discourse of international relations can be discerned. There was for the first time, at least within the emerging discipline of political science, an autonomous discourse specifically focused on the issues and concerns arising from the political and economic interactions of states.[15]

Following the success of the *World Politics* volume, Ely urged Reinsch to take on the issue of colonial rule. In this equally seminal work, Reinsch cast a critical eye on the tide of imperial expansion then in course. He argued that the push for political sovereignty over vast tracts of Asian and African territory was driven by the desire of capital for safe places for investment. A better alternative, for Reinsch, was commercial expansion through trade: thus his affinity for the "open door" policy. However, once colonial rule existed, it should be defined by the nature and needs of the indigenous population.[16] His comparative treatment of early colonial policies was lucid, critical, and informed.

Reinsch was a pioneering figure in yet a third realm of analysis: international organization. His 1911 treatise, *Public International Unions: Their Work and Organization*, "must be regarded," writes Schmidt, "as a foundational text in the history of the field."[17] Public international unions were defined as associations of states sharing common interests in particular spheres of regulation and cooperation. These were far from distant ideals, but an active manifestation of the growing interdependence of states, whose significance Reinsch was one of the first to discern. Although the study of international organization became a major subfield only after World War I and the creation of the League of Nations, Reinsch was once again a prescient forerunner. In his 14 years on the faculty, Reinsch published five books, a high school civics text, dozens of articles, and many magazine essays; his publications were unusual in their day for their degree of reliance on primary materials. Reinsch was a prototype of what later became known as the "public intellectual."

Reinsch used an attractive offer from Stanford in 1902 as leverage to obtain a substantial salary improvement, flexible teaching loads, frequent leaves and a pledge of university support for a diplomatic post, which he was already assiduously pursuing. He was a major presence on campus; his weekly public lectures on international politics were regularly covered in the *Daily Cardinal.* His biographer describes him as an imposing, handsome figure, with well tailored European clothes—"charming, witty, gregarious—a pleasant companion and good conversationalist."[18]

Reinsch participated actively in the exciting years of university development and state progressive reform which marked the Charles Van Hise presidency (1903–18), and the moment of Progressive Republican dominance at the state level from 1900 to 1914 under governors Robert La Follette, James Davidson, and Frances McGovern.[19] Reinsch was among the numerous faculty in the public eye. He was a regular at the Saturday noon lunch conversations which Governor La Follette organized, along with such other participants as Van Hise, Commons, Ely, and E. A. Ross.[20] He was in thrall, his biographer suggests, to the theories of Dr. William Ostler at John Hopkins, which held that the main creative work of a person of exceptional talent was completed by age 40. Therein perhaps lies the explanation for the frenetic pace of his activity in his Wisconsin years. Financial pressures may have entered the picture as well; beyond public service lectures, some of his itinerant speaking engagements, and remunerated articles for popular magazines, helped augment an income which, although by university standards generous, was inadequate to sustain his train of activity. Like Ely and Parkinson, he also dabbled in Madison real estate.[21]

In 1909, Reinsch played a key role as faculty leader in a confrontation with the regents over purported excessive interference into faculty affairs, a practice that was both intrusive and undermining academic freedom. The loss of Turner to Harvard at that time was blamed on regent meddling. In a tense meeting of some leading faculty, led by Reinsch, and several regents, an accord was reached which vindicated the faculty position. As summarized by Reinsch, the regents declared:

> The regents have no intention of interfering with the customary methods of educational administration by the faculty; . . . they will continue to allow to the faculty the initiative in formulating educational policies; . . . they desire appointments to be made through the regular channels as developed in the custom of the University.[22]

In spite of his towering reputation, Reinsch was not without his critics. President Van Hise and L&S Dean Birge felt Reinsch was inclined to operate the department as a one-man show, and was slow to build its ranks. He was also accused of traveling too much, and reckless spending. Some in the department, according to his biographer, believed that Reinsch failed to create a balanced, integrated faculty.[23] Also worth noting is that, despite the Reinsch reputation as a magnet for students, very few doctorates were completed in this period. The first doctorate after that of Reinsch in 1898 was James Barnett in 1905, and only six others finished before 1914. Of these, only three were in the international field.

Still, his remarkable accomplishments, as scholar and as public intellectual, played no small part in catapulting the fledgling department to national prominence. Reinsch made Wisconsin an early leader in international relations and in Asian and Latin American politics. His creed is summarized in a statement published in the 1923 *Wisconsin Badger* at about the time of his death:

> The broadening view of human relationships, the idea of the State as a big family, the devotion of the best talent therein to

work for the good, the resting of all human rights by their just subservience to human welfare, the aims so clearly expressed in the Wisconsin Idea, helped me beyond words, in facing the difficulties and responsibilities of an arduous time.[24]

From 1902 on, Reinsch lobbied for a diplomatic appointment, seeking both university backing and help from the Wisconsin congressional delegation. He missed out on ambassadorial vacancies in Tokyo, an attorney-general post in Puerto Rico, and the Hong Kong consulship, then narrowly failed in a bid for the China embassy in 1909. He was named to the American delegations to the third (Rio de Janeiro, 1906) and fourth (Santiago, 1910) Pan-American Conferences, as well as a 1909 Pan-American Scientific Congress, also in Santiago. When Woodrow Wilson, with whom he had worked in launching APSA, was elected president in 1912, the Reinsch campaign went into overdrive, and he did land the nomination as ambassador to China (winning out over Wisconsin rival E. A. Ross). He became an advocate for Chinese resistance to imperial encroachment, particularly Japanese pressures, and fought hard within the walls of American diplomacy to win support for Chinese concerns in the Versailles peace settlement. He helped persuade China to declare war on Germany in April 1917, although he was unable to convince Washington to come up with a $200 million loan, for which China offered to provide 500,000 troops for the Western front.[25] Reinsch, however, was unaware of a secret American accord with Japan, which acknowledged the Japanese "special interests" in China that were so bitterly resented by the Chinese. In a prophetic passage, Reinsch notes that China had concluded that the United States was an unreliable ally; if a new world war was to come, he suggested, it would begin in China (as it did with the 1937 "Nanjing incident").[26] Disappointed by what he regarded as a betrayal of China in the Versailles Peace Treaty, Reinsch resigned his ambassadorship in 1919.

The Wisconsin Democratic Party nominated him as senatorial candidate in 1920; he was traveling in the Philippines at the time, and apparently unaware of the initiative. He dutifully campaigned, and lost badly, coming in third in a very poor year for Democrats, as the nation turned away from Wilsonian internationalism. In his final months, he served as a consultant for the Chinese government, dying in China in 1923.

From the time of his faculty appointment, Reinsch had excellent contacts in the Chinese and Japanese intellectual worlds. In 1902, he arranged a faculty appointment for a leading young Japanese scholar, Toyokichi Iyenaga, who spent two academic years on the staff. Iyenaga, trained at Johns Hopkins, later a regular visiting lecturer at the University of Chicago, had published one of the first English language studies of the Meiji restoration, *Constitutional Development of Japan, 1853–1881* (1891).

Reinsch recruited his best former student, Stanley Hornbeck, to replace him when he took the China post. Hornbeck, who had taught five years in the Chinese Government College, published a major treatise on Asian politics, *Contemporary Politics in the Far East* (1916). Hornbeck left in 1917 for diplomatic service, mostly as an East Asian specialist, finishing his career as ambassador to the Netherlands from 1944 to 1947.

Another possible Reinsch impact may be seen in the striking flow of Chinese doctoral students to the department in the interwar years. Between 1929 and 1936, seven of the 28 doctorates awarded went to Chinese scholars. The hefty payments imposed on China as Boxer Rebellion indemnities were in good part commuted after World War I into student fellowships; the Reinsch connections may have encouraged intending Chinese scholars to choose Wisconsin.

Formative Influences: Emerging Notions of Political Science

In assessing the foundational years of the department, two contextual dimensions require consideration. The early years of the discipline were marked by both a quest for more systematic study of politics and the belief that the improved knowledge base thus generated could find quick translation into ameliorative reform of government. The impulses of progressive reform evident in many regions as well as nationally reinforced its proponents' belief that the accumulation of knowledge about government served larger public purposes than filling the library shelves. Within the state and university, the "Wisconsin Idea" appeared as a codification of the linkage of reform aspirations with the emergent research mission.

To find a self-conscious summation of the nature of the emergent discipline of political science at the turn of the 20th century, one may turn to an APSA statement announcing the launching of the association:

> . . . political science has to deal with all that directly concerns political society, that is to say, with societies of men effectively organized under a supreme authority for the maintenance of an orderly and progressive existence. . . .

> The definite field thus marked out for the political scientists is divisible into three parts. First, there is the province of political theory or philosophy, the aim of which is the analysis and exact definition of the concepts employed in political thinking, and which thus includes the consideration of the essential nature of the state; its right to be; its ends; its proper functions and its relation to its own citizens, and the nature of law. Secondly, there is the domain of public law, including as its subdivisions constitutional, international and administrative law. Thirdly, there is the general study of government, its different forms, the distribution of its powers, its various organs—legislative, executive and judicial, central and local—and the principles governing its administration.

The close affinity with history and economics was acknowledged, citing the dictum of Sir John Seeley that "politics without history has no root, and history without politics has no fruit," and adding that the "connection between economics and politics is, if anything, even more intimate."[27] Henry Jones Ford in a definition of discipline scope the following year distanced the field from an earlier John Burgess view of Hegelian resonance that "only Europe and North America have succeeded in developing such political organizations as furnish the material for scientific treatment." Ford asserts a kinship with the natural sciences in methodological aspiration, and a broader view of the political:

> . . . [political science] must take for its subject-matter the nature of public authority whatever forms it may assume, elucidating their genetic order and formulating the laws of their growth and development. . . . In fine, political science can not be held to be constituted as such until it is put upon an objective basis. It must experience the reconstruction which the general body of science has undergone at the hands of inductive philosophy, and take its place in orderly connection with natural history.[28]

Ford concludes with an affirmation of the ultimate ameliorative purposes: "Doubtless it will take the labors of generations of scholars to bring political science to a position of authority as regards practical politics, but certainly no undertaking could be more important or more inspiring to effort, since success means attainment of the power to give rational determination to the destinies of nations."[29]

In contemporary terms, the predominant mood of the field might be characterized as "historical-institutionalist." A number of the most visible political scientists, such as William Dunning (Columbia), were historians of political thought. The Dunning 1902 treatise, *A History of Political Theories*, was authoritative for several decades. Dunning was mentor to Charles Merriam, whose own initial book (*History of American Political Theories*, 1903) was in this field. Another key figure was W. W. Willoughby at Johns Hopkins, a seminal contributor to state theory. The state as idea and institution stood at the core of early political science. In its institutional manifestation, the study of public administration took root, suffused with the notion that scientific study pointed the way to the perfectibility of the bureaucratic instances of the state. Indeed, Woodrow Wilson argued that public administration was more susceptible to genuine scientific study than any other domain of politics.[30] Municipal government emerged as a challenging field of study, in which Sparling was an early leader; the industrial age was producing urban agglomerations of a new size and kind.

Rogers Smith frames the early history of the discipline as the first act in a continuing tension between the aspiration to a truly scientific politics and a normative commitment to improving democratic practice. The faith in science and democracy having a joint destiny was robust in the progressive era.[31] Dennis Mahoney suggests a somewhat different summation of early 20th century political science as an uneasy synthesis of the statist heritage of German political thought, the pragmatism of John Dewey, and progressivism. "Human society," wrote Mahoney, "was envisaged as capable of permanent and perpetual improvement, and the state was the chosen instrument for accomplishing that improvement." However, reform ambitions needed filtering through the pragmatics of practical reason.[32]

The most prolific contributor to discipline intellectual history, John Gunnell, draws these themes together in insisting upon the uniquely American nature of the political science practiced in the United States.

> Notwithstanding its universal scientific aspirations, . . . and the waves of foreign influence that have contributed to shaping it, political science bears a unique relationship to American political life and ideology. And its concerns have been practical as well as scholarly. While political science gives a descriptive and explanatory account of the nature of the American democratic polity, affecting democratic thought and behavior was, from the beginning, a principal goal of the discipline. It was committed to creating a truly scientific study of politics, but despite

> changing images of science, there has been a persistent search for a discipline that would contribute to realizing and enhancing democratic values and institutions.[33]

The dominant mood of the discipline was reflected in the reform engagement of Sparling and Reinsch; Charles McCarthy, who was a lecturer for the department from 1905 to 1917, was deeply immersed in the politics of progressive reform in the state, and viewed citizenship training as a core function of the field. Ford MacGregor, who joined the faculty in 1909, was a specialist in tax administration, and devoted most of his energies to extension work. Of the dozen dissertations completed from 1904 to 1918, two-thirds dealt with practical issues, with a social improvement and reform imprint. One finds such topics as state administration of taxation (James Barnett, 1905); reform of state health administration (Ulysses Dubach, 1912); social legislation in the industrial field (Selden Lowrie, 1912), and civil service reform (Ben Arneson, 1916).

Political Science and the Wisconsin Idea

The faith that science and democracy had a joint destiny, realized in progressive reform, found crystallization in the "Wisconsin Idea," which took form in the early years of the 20th century, and found expression above all in the speeches and writings of President Van Hise and McCarthy. This concept was especially central to the department in the period under review in this chapter, but became embedded in the informal premises of the departmental community. The ethos underpinning the Wisconsin Idea was well expressed by presidential candidate Adlai Stevenson in a Madison campaign appearance on 8 October 1952:

> But the Wisconsin tradition meant more than a simple belief in the people. It also meant a faith in the application of intelligence and reason to the problems of society. It meant a deep conviction that the role of government was not to stumble along like a drunkard in the dark, but to light its way by the best torches of knowledge and understanding it could find.[34]

President Charles Eliot of Harvard University in 1908 declared Wisconsin to be "the leading state university," praise which some believe was not simply tribute to academic excellence but a recognition of university service to the state. In an introduction to the McCarthy book, *The Wisconsin Idea*, Theodore Roosevelt wrote that Wisconsin "has become literally a laboratory for wise experimental legislation aiming to secure the social and political betterment of the people as a whole. . . . All through the Union we need to learn the Wisconsin lesson of scientific popular self-help, and of patient care in radical legislation."[35] Frederick Rudolph, in a standard history of higher education, concluded that such an encomium found justification in "the success with which it incorporated in its rationale two curiously conflicting currents of Progressivism: the resort to an *expertise* in the affairs of state, and the development of popular nontechnical lectures which carried the university to the people."[36]

The Wisconsin Idea has several sources and multiple meanings. One primary author of the idea, Legislative Reference Library (later Bureau) founder and political science lecturer Charles McCarthy, gave it a political cast, describing it as "various ameliorative activities of the Wisconsin progressive movement, including the University." For others, especially after the progressive era ended in 1914, the notion was more narrowly defined as university public service to the state. In popular understandings, the Wisconsin Idea is embodied in the slogan, which apparently emerged later, that "the boundaries of the University are the boundaries of the state." Stark, in a thorough and thoughtful history of the Wisconsin Idea, proposes as definition "the University's direct contributions to the state: to the government in the forms of serving in office, offering advice about public policy, providing information and exercising technical skill, and to the citizens in the forms of doing research directed at solving problems that are important to the state and conducting outreach activities."[37]

McCarthy attributes the origins of the Wisconsin Idea to Ely and the German ancestry of an important part of the populace. Certainly the form of institutional economics pioneered by Ely provided some basic premises: rejection of laissez-faire; protection of labor rights; regulation as a means of taming capitalism, and more broadly incorporating the ethos of the social gospel movement. Though Stark disputes the significance of Ely, the Ely School in its many publications did examine a range of policy issues, and its founder viewed preparation of experts for public service as a core mission. In his autobiography, Ely quotes approvingly the German example of professors occupying high public positions; he adds, "My experience in Germany had first brought to my attention the importance of linking book knowledge and practical experience."[38]

McCarthy argued that the first generation of German immigrants, the 1848 cohort, brought high ideals and an insistence upon orderly, careful government. Later German achievements in the science of government showed the possibilities of conscious state action: "once a country of poor peasants, shot over by every conquering swashbuckler, transformed by the might of intelligence, noble philosophy and keen foresight into a shining example for the rest of the world."[39] The German impact is less evident as a derivative of their numbers in the state at the time; an ethnic map of the La Follette Progressives would give more weight to Scandinavian stock. But the powerful influence of the German university figured indirectly, mediated especially through Johns Hopkins and the impact of graduate study periods in Germany of many leading social scientists of the day, such as Ely, Sparling and Reinsch. Whatever cogency the McCarthy thesis of German antecedents to the Wisconsin Idea may have had, assertions of German ancestry to the concept were erased in 1917, when the anti-German hysteria which accompanied World War I swept over Wisconsin.

Frederick Jackson Turner cites a populist tradition particular to the Midwest, writing:

> Nothing in our educational history is more striking than the steady pressure of democracy upon its universities to adapt to the requirements of all the people. From the State Universities of the Middle West, shaped under pioneer ideals, have come the fuller recognition of scientific studies, and especially those of applied science devoted to the conquest of nature.[40]

Another historian of the Wisconsin Idea links the concept to the social gospel movement, whose ideals were formative for Bascom, Ely and Commons, each of whom "found in the new role of the University the logical and critical vehicle of their ideals: the perfection of the Christian state."[41]

The crucial vehicle linking political science to the Wisconsin Idea was Charles McCarthy, a former football hero, part-time Wisconsin assistant football coach, and doctoral alumnus of the Ely School. McCarthy created the Legislative Reference Library (LRL) in 1901, which developed into what Curti and Carstenson call a "brilliantly successful" agency, supplying legislators with information and aid in drafting bills.[42] As a research service on policy issues, the LRL was an innovation copied in many other states, and by the Library of Congress at the federal level.[43] From 1905 to 1917, McCarthy also served as a lecturer for the Department of Political Science, a popular and influential teacher. Deeply engaged in the progressive reform movement,

McCarthy was a prime figure in the Saturday luncheon groups with La Follette that Reinsch attended. Like Ely and Reinsch, McCarthy dreamed of replacing such ad hoc "brain trusts" with a more permanent system of embedding expertise in policy making and application through a skilled cadre of trained civil servants, on a German model.[44] At the same time, his faculty colleagues often disappointed him, through their reluctance to join the fray. Professors, regretted McCarthy, wait until they are asked before offering their views; "indeed, they are generally afraid of criticism, and it sometimes requires a good deal of urging upon the part of the legislature to obtain their help."[45] In a 1916 letter to Ely, McCarthy was even more critical, suggesting that the faculty were now fleeing public engagement like scared jackrabbits, in the wake of the ouster of the Progressive Republicans in 1914.[46]

In his autobiography, McCarthy provides a list of the 46 faculty who gave active service to the state in 1910–11. His roster included five names associated with political science: Reinsch, newly appointed faculty Chester Lloyd Jones and Arnold Hall, an LRL staff member who has an unpaid lecturer for the department, Matthew Dudgeon, in addition to McCarthy himself.[47]

Indeed, the progressive affinities of even those faculty active in public affairs are easily exaggerated. Ely in his later years became very conservative. John R. Commons in his autobiography suggests that as many as 90 percent of the faculty are "on the conservative or reactionary side," and that Wisconsin was never "a university that governs a state."[48] But Commons pays high tribute to McCarthy: "his versatility, ingenuity, determined will-power and sympathy for the underdog typified to me the Irishman the world over."[49]

Another product of the reform era was the creation of a series of commissions: the Wisconsin Tax Commission (1899); the Railway Commission (1901); the Public Utilities Commission (1907); the Insurance Commission (1907); the Industrial Commission (1911). The excesses of unbridled capitalism were to be curbed by regulation, not socialism.[50] A McCarthy colleague in the LRL, Edwin Witte, later professor of economics and political science, was appointed to the Industrial Commission.[51] To assure an expert and impartial bureaucracy appointed by merit, Commons helped La Follette draft a civil service act in 1904. However, when a Civil Service Commission was created to implement the reform, Commons declined nomination, and notes that an unnamed political science professor was named instead. This can only have been Sparling, since the other two professors at the time were Reinsch and Parkinson, for different reasons unsuitable nominees.[52] Another link between the LRL and political science was Matthew Dudgeon, a legal specialist who held occasional lecturer appointments in the department.

In the web of commissions McCarthy helped design, the embedded premise was the necessary role of professionals in directing social amelioration. The experts staffing the network of commissions had an undoubted impact on social policy. At the same time, the active and visible role of the array of commissions helped catalyze a reaction which by 1914 drove the Progressives from power for a generation.[53]

McCarthy beyond doubt added substantially to the national visibility and reputation of the department. Although he never held a regular faculty appointment, as a permanent lecturer he was often perceived to be a professor. He was responsible for and involved in an APSA Committee of Five on Practical Training for the Public Service.[54] In a 1912 letter, he wrote that "I am in an ideal situation here; I believe I do not overstate it when I say that I have the confidence of the people in Wisconsin, and as professor at the University I am surrounded by young students who are constantly being taught to take a place in public life—public service."[55] His earthy Irish humor was revealed in a reproach to a legislator who asked a professor how many (classroom) hours he worked (taught) a week. McCarthy retorted that this was entirely the wrong question to ask; for a stud horse, what was important was the product, and not the number of hours a week worked to create it.[56]

Wisconsin historian John Buenker, in a chapter examining the Wisconsin Idea, concludes that it rested on three pillars. The first was the Legislative Reference Library; the second, the university. The third was the impressive array of regulatory commissions created between 1899 and 1914.[57] McCarthy was in many respects the connecting link between the three: as head of the LRL; as lecturer in the department; and as designer and drafter for much of the legislation creating the commissions. One of his final contributions was to stimulate the adoption of a 1917 statute authorizing the university to create a Training School for Public Service.[58] Although no action followed immediately, this provision decades later provided the statutory basis for the establishment of the Center for the Study of Public Policy and Administration in 1967 (see chapter 10).

Beyond Reinsch: The World War I Interlude

The 1913 departure of Reinsch marked the end of an era. Political science as a field was gaining coherence and strength nationally. One measure is the growth of APSA membership from 214 in 1904 to 1,462 in 1915. By that time, 38 departments of political science existed across the country. The number of doctorates awarded increased dramatically: 34 from 1885 to 1900; 610 from 1900 to 1910; 1,015 from 1911 to 1915.[59] By 1900, the doctorate had become established as a prerequisite for academic appointment, though few from earlier generations held the degree (for example, Parkinson). Wisconsin was not yet a major contributor to the flow of doctorates; of the 1,625 awarded from 1900 till 1915, only nine were from Wisconsin. Yet, especially thanks to Reinsch and McCarthy, Wisconsin already enjoyed national respect.

The faculty roster before 1914 never numbered more than a half dozen. Several taught briefly in this period; two served as interim chair during Reinsch absences (Robert Scott 1908–10, Harold McBain 1911–12). MacGregor, a municipal government and tax specialist (perhaps recruited as a replacement for Sparling), was a department member from 1909 till 1934. In this period, three appointments of lasting significance were made: Arnold Hall and Chester Lloyd Jones[60] in 1910, and Frederic Ogg in 1914. Their real impact fell in the interwar period, and will be examined in the next chapter.

On the eve of World War I, the university was roiled by a hostile inquiry directed by William V. Allen, whose published report in 1915 was inspired by Taylorist "scientific management" theories, proposing among other things a 48-week academic year to ensure fuller plant utilization. The investigation was partly motivated by conservative resentment at university faculty involvement in the progressive reforms of the La Follette era, but also had some Progressive support. Enormous energies were consumed in responding to the barrages of questionnaires launched by the Allen team, and rebutting its allegations. Ely, in a 1914 letter to Sparling, vented his frustration with the Allen team harassment: "One investigation follows another and I dare say that there is more than one who would feel inclined to congratulate you upon the fact that you are not subject to investigation with the result that you are sure to be damned if you do and damned if you don't for it all seems to make little difference."[61] In the end, the excesses of the report doomed it to irrelevance; not even critics of the university found its conclusions useful.[62]

World War I was less disruptive to the university than the second war. The relatively brief duration of American participation meant that its impact was mainly felt in only two academic years. The conscription drained male students, but there was not a comparable loss of faculty to war service. The most noteworthy aspect was the war fever which swept the campus, manifested in a collective letter to Senator La Follette to "protest against those utterances and actions . . . which have given aid and comfort to Germany and her allies in the present war; we deplore his failure to support the government in the prosecution of the war." La Follette had strenuously opposed the drift to war in 1916, and was one of six to vote against the declaration of war. Though he had been a steadfast friend of the university, some 93 percent of the faculty signed the letter, including all political scientists save newly appointed instructors Pitman Potter and Graham Stuart.[63] Ely in January 1918 became president of the newly formed Wisconsin Loyalty League, another measure of the psychosis of war. Yet another example was the publication of a "War Book" consisting of a number of shrill papers by faculty members on the causes of the war. Among the contributors was Ogg, whose chapter avers:

> *These, then, are the ideas that of late have dominated the Empire's governing classes. The Germans are superior to all other peoples. They are fittest to rule. God intended that they should rule. Therefore they will rule. Their rule is to be established by the sword. And it is to be world-wide* [italics in original].[64]

L&S Dean George Sellery later confided his embarrassment at having signed the round-robin letter denouncing La Follette.[65] The War Book authors as well may have later regretted passages composed in the context of war fever, and intense pressure on faculty to exhibit their loyalty.

The war marked a clear moment of transition. A major turnover occurred immediately preceding and following the war; a new generation of faculty emerged as the leading figures. Perhaps emblematic of this transitional moment was the acquisition of a departmental home in South Hall in 1917. Before that time, the handful of department faculty were housed in different buildings, mainly Bascom (then University) Hall and the State Historical Society (which had become by 1900 the University Library). From 1910 till 1917, the chair had an office in Bascom. Assembling the faculty in one location was an evident landmark in building an institutional identity. At war's end, personnel turnover posed a formidable challenge to the young faculty newly housed together in South Hall.

Notes

1. Stephen H. Carpenter, *An Historical Sketch of the University of Wisconsin from 1849 to 1876* (Madison: Atwood & Culter, 1876), 30.
2. University history project data set.
3. John Frank Cook, "A History of Liberal Education at the University of Wisconsin 1862–1918," PhD diss., University of Wisconsin, 1970, 189–91.
4. Report of the Department of Political Science, 1894–95, University Archives.

5. Ely papers, State Historical Society, Sparling to Ely, 8 May 1894.
6. Ely papers, Sparling to Ely, 26 August 1894.
7. David V. Mollenhoff, *Madison: A History of the Formative Years* (Dubuque: Kendall/Hunt Publishing Company, 1982), 371. Mollenhoff adds that "Sparling's message was no less popular among Madison's male leadership, identifying what a number of men perceived as a secondary domain of civic action which could be allocated to female civic energies."
8. John D. Buenker, *The History of Wisconsin: The Progressive Era, 1893–1914* (Madison: State Historical Society of Wisconsin, 1998), 159.
9. David Parmerlee, *Preparing the Marketing Plan* (New York: McGraw Hill/Contemporary Books), 2d ed., xii.
10. Ely papers, Sparling to Ely, 27 March 1914.
11. The biographical information on Reinsch is mainly drawn from the biography of Noel H. Pugach, *Paul S. Reinsch: Open Door Diplomat in Action* (Millwood, NY: KTO Press, 1979). Pugach was a student of former University President Fred Harrington, who prior to his absorption in administration contemplated a biography of Reinsch. Harrington managed to assemble the scattered Reinsch papers at the State Historical Society.
12. Laurence R.Veysey, *The Emergence of the American University* (Chicago: University of Chicago Press, 1965), 288.
13. Brian C. Schmidt, *The Political Discourse of Anarchy: A Disciplinary History of International Relations* (Albany: State University of New York Press, 1998), 71.
14. In preparing *The African Colonial State in Comparative Perspective* (1994), I had occasion to consult the major works regarding imperialism and colonialism from this period, and can attest that Reinsch was encyclopedic in his research.
15. Schmidt, *Political Discourse*, 71.
16. See the extended appraisal in Schmidt, *Political Discourse*, 131–38.
17. Schmidt, *Political Discourse*, 118.
18. Pugach, *Paul S. Reinsch*, 19.
19. "Progressive" in this chapter refers at once to a reform political movement, for which lowercase is used, from the 1890s till 1934 a major faction of the Republican Party, associated especially with the La Follette family, and from 1934 to 1946 a separate political party, led by Philip La Follette. "Progressive" when referring to the wing of the Republican Party or the separate party is capitalized.
20. Robert M. La Follette, *La Follette's Autobiography: A Personal Narrative of Political Experiences* (Madison: University of Wisconsin Press, 1963), 15.
21. Pugach, *Paul S. Reinsch*, 50. In a 1906 letter to Ely, Parkinson asks what "his *very lowest price* might be for the corner lot at Lathrop Street and Summit Avenue"; State Historical Society, Ely papers, Parkinson to Ely, 28 March 1906.

22. Curti and Carstensen, *The University of Wisconsin*, II, 59–62.
23. Pugach, *Paul S. Reinsch*, 22.
24. Pugach, *Paul S. Reinsch*, 49.
25. Paul S. Reinsch, *An American Diplomat in China*, Garden City, NY: Doubleday, Page & Co, 1922), 303. In this volume, Reinsch records his experiences as American ambassador to China.
26. Reinsch, *An American Diplomat,* 328.
27. W. W. Willoughby, "The American Political Science Association," *Political Science Quarterly*, 19, 1 (1904), 107–10.
28. Henry Jones Ford, "The Scope of Political Science," *Proceedings of the American Political Science Association*, 2 (1905), 198–206.
29. Ford, "The Scope of Political Science," 206.
30. Rogers M. Smith, "Still Blowing in the Wind: The American Quest for a Democratic, Scientific Political Science," *Daedalus*, 126, 1 (1997), 256.
31. Smith, "Still Blowing in the Wind," 253–87.
32. Dennis J. Mahoney, *Politics and Progress: The Emergence of American Political Science* (Lanham, MD: Lexington Books, 2004), 13.
33. John G. Gunnell, *Imagining the American Polity: Political Science and the Discourse of Democracy* (University Park: Pennsylvania State University Press, 2004), 3–4. Other valuable sources on the history of the discipline include David Easton, John G. Gunnell, and Michael B. Stein (eds.), *Regime and Discipline: Democracy and the Development of Political Science* (Ann Arbor: University of Michigan Press, 1995); John G. Gunnell, *The Descent of Political Theory: The Genealogy of an American Vocation* (Chicago: University of Chicago Press, 1993); James Farr, John S. Dryzak, and Stephen T. Leonard (eds.), *Political Science in History: Research Programs and Political Traditions* (Cambridge: Cambridge University Press, 1995); James Farr and Raymond Seidelman (eds.), *Discipline and History: Political Science in the United States* (Ann Arbor: University of Michigan Press, 1993); Bernard Crick, *The American Science of Politics: Its Origins and Conditions* (Berkeley: University of California Press, 1959); David M. Ricci, *The Tragedy of Political Science: Politics, Scholarship, and Democracy* (New Haven: Yale University Press, 1984); Dorothy Ross, *The Origins of American Social Science* (Cambridge: Cambridge University Press, 1991); Raymond Seidelman, *Disenchanted Realists: Political Science and the American Crisis, 1884–1984* (Albany: State University of New York Press, 1986).
34. Quoted in Jack Stark, "The Wisconsin Idea: The University's Service to the State," in State of Wisconsin, *1995–96 Blue Book* (Madison: State Department of Administration, 1997), 101.
35. Charles McCarthy, *The Wisconsin Idea* (New York: Macmillan Company, 1912), vii-x.
36. Both quoted in Stark, "The Wisconsin Idea," 101. On the history of the Wisconsin Idea, see also John Witte, "Wisconsin Ideas: The Continuing

Role of the University in the State and Beyond," in Lynn H. Levery and David R. Colborn (eds.), *Understanding the Role of Public Policy Centers and Institutes in Fostering University Government Partnerships* (San Francisco: Jossey-Bass, 2000), 7–16.

37. Stark, "The Wisconsin Idea," 102.
38. Richard T. Ely, *Ground Under Our Feet: An Autobiography* (New York: Macmillan, 1938), 187.
39. McCarthy, *The Wisconsin Idea*, 10.
40. Stark, "The Wisconsin Idea," 105.
41. Hoeveler, "The University and the Social Gospel," 282–98.
42. Curti and Carstensen, *The University of Wisconsin*, I, 437.
43. A clipping from the *Trenton Times* dated 24 December 1906 reports a visit by McCarthy to the Governor of New Jersey to explain the virtues of the LRL; Governor Stokes was impressed by the McCarthy presentation, and intended to propose establishment of a New Jersey equivalent. The LRL model had already been adopted by California, Nebraska, and Indiana, and proposals for its establishment were pending in a dozen other states. The current director of the Congressional Reference Service of the Library of Congress told me in September 2004 that the memory of McCarthy's inspiration remains a central part of the founding narrative of the service.
44. On McCarthy and the importance of the Legislative Reference Library, see Buenker, *The History of Wisconsin*, IV, 596–98.
45. McCarthy, *The Wisconsin Idea*, 137.
46. Edward A. Fitzpatrick, *McCarthy of Wisconsin* (New York: Columbia University Press, 1944.
47. McCarthy, *The Wisconsin Idea*, 313–17.
48. Commons, *Myself*, 110.
49. Commons, *Myself*, 107.
50. Especially in this sphere, the reform ideas of the progressive movement go beyond the 1880s "Mugwump" agenda of good government and social reform. The Industrial Commission was identified by La Follette's biographer as the "most famous feature of the Wisconsin Idea." Inspired by Commons, the Commission mandate was to foster a safe, healthy working environment for workers through labor codes proposed by experts. David P. Thelen, *Robert M. La Follette and the Insurgent Spirit* (Boston: Little, Brown and Company, 1976), 109.
51. Witte, "Wisconsin Ideas," 10.
52. Commons, *Myself*, 102–3.
53. Thelen, *Robert M. La Follette*, 117–19.
54. Fitzpatrick, *McCarthy*, 132.
55. Fitzpatrick, *McCarthy*, 68.
56. Fitzpatrick, *McCarthy*, 238.
57. Buenker, *The History of Wisconsin*, IV, 569–610.

58. Fitzpatrick, *McCarthy*, 133. Fitzpatrick provides the date of 1915 for this statute, but when rediscovered in 1965 it was listed as 1917.
59. Mahoney, *Politics and Progress*, 11.
60. In many records, Lloyd Jones is listed as if it were a hyphenated compound surname. However, in university records, and in library catalogs, his index name is Jones, which we retain in this volume.
61. Ely papers, Ely to Sparling, 4 April 1914.
62. See the stinging summary by Curti and Carstenson, *The History of Wisconsin*, II, 267–83. See also G.C. Sellery, *Some Ferments at Wisconsin* (Madison: University of Wisconsin Press, 1960), 6.
63. Chester Lloyd Jones and Stanley Hornbeck did not sign, but appear to have been away at the time.
64. *War Book of the University of Wisconsin: Papers on the Causes and Issues of the War by Members of the Faculty* (Madison: University of Wisconsin, 1918). History project assistant Mark Schrad located a set of the War Book pamphlets on eBay, for $3.95.
65. Sellery, *Some Ferments*, 7–8.

CHAPTER 3

Ogg, Gaus, and the Interwar Years (1918–1945)

Crawford Young

New Currents in Political Science

World War I marked a turning point for the department. The founding figures (John B. Parkinson, Samuel Sparling, Paul Reinsch) had passed from the scene for some time. The roster, always small before 1920, shrank during the war years, from seven in 1914–15 to four in 1919–20. Ogg became acting chair in 1917, then chair in his own right in 1919, a post he occupied until 1940, then again from 1942 to 1944. During this period, the department was entirely rebuilt, and somewhat expanded, peaking at a strength of ten.

In the 1920s, a new mood was taking shape in political science nationally, perhaps best captured and incarnated by Charles Merriam at Chicago. Merriam, in a seminal summons to a more scientific study of politics in 1923, called for more systematic methods, more effective measurement, and more extensive engagement with theoretical advances in the related fields of psychology, sociology, and economics.[1] Merriam praises in passing the kind of systematic "fact collection and analysis" pioneered by Charles McCarthy and the Wisconsin Legislative Reference Library (LRL), and the commitment to unite theory at the actual practice of government.[2] But a scientific approach was the key. The development of the survey, the increasing appreciation of statistical method, and incorporation of political psychology are all key advances. Merriam concludes with a rather apocalyptic warning of the perils of ignoring scientific method:

> It is easy to scoff at the possibilities of scientific research in the field of government, but unless a higher degree of science can be brought into the operations of government civilization is in the very gravest peril from the caprice of ignorance and passion. . . .

> As custodians of the political science of our time, the responsibility rests upon us to exhaust every effort to bring the study of government in its various stages to the highest possible degree of perfection, to exhaust every effort to obtain effective knowledge of political forces, to bring to bear every resource of science and prudence at our command.[3]

Merriam is widely viewed as the inspiration for what later became the behavioral movement. His influence was in large measure mediated through his students, many of whom became leaders in their subfields: Harold Lasswell, Quincy Wright, Harold Gosnell, V. O. Key, Herbert Simon, David Truman, Leonard White, and many others; 80 doctorates in political science were awarded by Chicago from 1920 to 1940. The "Chicago school" had a huge impact upon the field.[4]

For his biographer, the Merriam call for a more scientific study of politics was inseparable from its political end: a more rational polity, reformed of its abuses. Such a conviction informed his own sustained political immersion as a Chicago alderman and reform mayoral candidate. His leading role in the creation and operation of the Social Science Research Council (SSRC), founded in 1923, was dedicated to mobilizing the resources of social science in the service of a vision of scientific progressivism. So also was his presence among the teams of academic advisors recruited by President Franklin Delano Roosevelt.[5]

In the years preceding Roosevelt and the New Deal, the dominant mood in the country was hostile to policy activism from the academic community. Strong currents of anti-intellectualism flowed in the 1920s, accompanied by the Red Scare of the early postwar years. In some respects, the turn to a vision of strengthening political science by reinforcing its scientific methodology replaced earlier engagement in "good government" or social reform policy reform.[6]

Given the prominence of Chicago political science during this period, the standing of its department as the leading center of the new political science, and for that matter its proximity, its influence upon Wisconsin was surprisingly modest. Of the 13 faculty recruits from 1920 to 1940, only one held a Chicago doctorate (Joseph Harris, 1923–30). The primary Wisconsin vehicle for the Merriam vision of a reformed political science at Wisconsin was Arnold Hall, who joined the faculty in 1910 from Northwestern, after a graduate degree at Chicago in 1907. Although his degree was a J.D., he had studied with Merriam, and maintained a close association with him. At Wisconsin, Hall had a joint appointment in the Law School but in his political science role he became imbued with a mission to foster a more scientific study of politics.

On home terrain, his evangelical message fell upon stony ground. Neither of the two giants of the interwar period, Frederic Ogg and John Gaus, shared this enthusiasm, although their papers show no trace of open opposition to it. Those of primarily international interests, such as Pitman Potter, Grayson Kirk, Walter Sharp, or Llewellyn Pfankuchen, found difficulty relating the new methodological preoccupations to their own research. Scanning the titles of the 51 dissertations completed in the department from 1918 to 1940, one is hard-pressed to detect the slightest influence of the Merriam school, or for that matter any discontinuity with the types of topics chosen in the earlier years. One might interpret a resolution, proposed by Sharp in 1933, that all graduate students be required to take a course in statistics as a gesture toward the developing scientific mood; the motion passed unanimously.[7]

National Ranking of Wisconsin Political Science

By the time the first national rankings of academic departments were published in 1925, the department ranked fourth, behind only Harvard, Chicago, and Columbia (see appendix 12). This precocious high ranking merits some exploration. Like subsequent rankings, the method employed was reputational. Conducted by R. M. Hughes at Miami University (Ohio), a survey was carried out, based upon names suggested by Miami faculty as leaders in the different fields, with at least half the names from colleges rather than major universities. In each discipline surveyed, 40 questionnaires were sent; in the case of political science, 19 responded, of whom only two (Ben Arneson and James Barnett) were Wisconsin doctoral alumni. Seven of the 19 ranked Wisconsin first, and only four placed the department lower than fifth.

This high reputation rested upon a rather slender foundation at the moment of the survey. Of the seven Wisconsin faculty listed at that moment, in 1923–24, only three had any national standing. Hall had exceptional visibility at the juncture, through his role as leader in organizing the first of three National Conferences on the Science of Politics, examined later in the chapter. Ogg, though still early in his career, had already published extensively. Potter, who joined the faculty in 1920 after completing a Harvard doctorate in 1918, had published a book on international organization and won tenure promotion in just three years. The other four faculty, however, were then little known. Ford MacGregor, a municipal government specialist who was first appointed in 1909, was still only an associate professor when he left the faculty in 1934. He directed the Extension Division municipal reform bureau, and as long-serving secretary of the Wisconsin League of Municipalities was visible to the state public but not to the discipline nationally. Harris, Allen Saunders, and Walter Sharp were all newly appointed instructors in 1923, though Sharp and Harris had achieved national prominence by the end of the decade. The department ranking possibly reflected in part a shadow effect from the distinction of its first years, reinforced by the standing of the three key faculty. A lingering aura of the Reinsch era may also have drawn upon the continuing fame of Wisconsin scholars in neighboring social sciences whose published work overlapped political science: Richard T. Ely, John R. Commons, E. A. Ross, Frederic Jackson Turner, among others. Charles McCarthy, widely perceived to be a departmental professor although he held only a lecturer appointment, was a nationally known publicist and public intellectual before the war, whose notoriety may have reflected upon department prestige. In numerical strength, the department was not much smaller than its main competitors. The three top-ranked departments, Harvard, Chicago, and Columbia, had faculty strength of nine, eight, and eleven, respectively. Illinois, which placed fifth, had only five.[8]

Another survey of department graduate training quality was conducted in 1934 by the American Council on Education, somewhat more systematically.[9] The secretary of the American Political Science Association (APSA) was asked to provide a list of a hundred top scholars, to whom the survey was sent, including data on current faculty and numbers of doctorates awarded in the previous five years. Respondents were asked to identify departments with acceptable quality, and star those of the highest rank. From this survey there emerged a roster of eight political science departments rated as distinguished, listed only alphabetically (Columbia, Harvard, Princeton, California, Chicago, Illinois, Michigan, and Wisconsin). At this juncture, the Wisconsin claim to distinction was far more compelling. Of the ten faculty listed on the 1933–34 roster, six were of national stature (Ogg, Chester Lloyd Jones, Sharp, John Gaus, Grayson Kirk, and Edwin Witte, the latter primarily an economist but holding a joint appointment in political science). Two were recently appointed instructors (Llewelyn Pfankuchen and John Lewis). Another, John Salter, had been recruited at tenure level in 1930 from Oklahoma, and was then known for his work on boss politics in Philadelphia. The tenth, MacGregor, was in his final year on the faculty; as noted earlier, his work was mainly in extension and municipal government service. Wisconsin was then one of 20 universities offering doctoral training in political science. Of the 210 doctoral degrees awarded nationally in the discipline from 1928 to 1932, 16 came from Wisconsin. Of the 62 responding to the survey, only five were doctoral alumni (Arneson, Barnett, Harold Bruce, Harold Quigley, Graham Stuart); thus the ranking cannot much reflect institutional loyalty or nostalgia for graduate years. The success in sustaining the quality of the department in the interwar years speaks well for the leadership of Ogg, whose virtually permanent role as chair during this period undoubtedly assured a decisive influence in appointment decisions.

The emergence of published rankings of departments may be seen as part of a process of institutionalization of the discipline nationally, along with the consolidation of a national association and discipline journals. The first faculty at Wisconsin were produced from within. By the 1920s, most new recruits had advanced degrees from other institutions, an interpenetration of formative intellectual experiences which was part of a larger process of nationalizing the field.

Arnold Hall and the National Conferences on the Science of Politics

At the 1922 APSA annual meetings, Hall convened a meeting of 17 political scientists, most notably Merriam, A. N. Holcombe and Luther Gulick, to plan a National Conference on the Science of Politics. The six-day conclave met in Madison in September 1923, with 93 participants from 42 institutions. Hall was convinced that the great advances in the natural sciences could be replicated in the political sphere, through an adaptation of their methods. Most political theory, Hall lamented, is really only literature; "true theory is a generalization that accurately explains the facts of political behavior."[10]

In his introductions to the reports of the 1923 conference and its two annual successors in 1924 and 1925, Hall enlarges upon themes which echo the Merriam *American Political Science Review* article:

> The marvelous technique of [the natural] sciences has proved of incalculable benefit to civilization. But who will deny that the perfection of social science is indispensable to the very preservation of this same civilization.
>
> Some system of social control which will guide humanity by its intelligence rather than by its passion, by which the true course of social progress may be more prophetically discerned; in short, which causes mankind to become the creator rather than the helpless creature of destiny is essential if civilization

> is to survive the caprice of ignorance and passion. However humble the present achievements may be in developing a technique of politics, the significance of this technique cannot be ignored, and the hope of the future lies in a continuous and insistent struggle to devise a technique adequate to the tremendous problems of modern life.[11]

In the 1924 Report, Hall returned more insistently to the improved social control theme as discipline teleology:

> The need of today is for developing the power-controlling sciences until they equal the efficiency of the power-creating disciplines, to the end that mankind can become the conscious arbiter of its own destiny. We must evolve a system of social control by which reason rather than passion will be the dominating power. . . . Our civilization is unable to control itself, to realize its ideals, to accomplish its most cherished ends. The only hope seems to lie in the development of the power-controlling sciences, until mankind can devise the means by which its noblest aspirations can prevail.[12]

The conferences broke down into eight roundtables, each of which presented its conclusions on the application of scientific method to its field to a plenary for adoption. The topics of the roundtables provide an interesting profile of the sectors of the discipline most influenced by the scientific aspiration. Though there was a slight variation in roundtable labels over the three conferences, the basic format remained similar to the 1923 Madison assembly. The most important theme was psychology and politics, chaired by Merriam. The other seven were problems and methods in civil service with special reference to efficiency ratings, public finance, legislation, political statistics, public law, nominating methods, and international organization. The conferences discovered a privileged affinity to psychology; in 1924, the organizers resolved to attach at least one psychologist, as well as one statistician, to each roundtable. One may note the essentially American focus of the proceedings; only one roundtable was devoted to international affairs. Participants in this last roundtable, in the 1925 report, expressed some frustration in the lack of cumulative progress over the three years, and a degree of ambivalence toward its purposes. The question of method, in itself, "is not inexhaustible," they concluded, adding that "the use of statistical methods and quantitative measurements in this field, where it proves feasible, could only be estimated at its true value by a comparison with methods obtained by what for convenience may be called the older philosophical method." Nonetheless, they conclude, "it has seemed to members surprisingly practicable to adopt a strictly scientific method in the treatment of problems of international organization on a par with problems outside the fields of social science, that it has seemed possible to recognize and define the main features of that method, and that the results promise to be more reliable than any obtained by a less objective and critical mode of treatment."[13]

The very modest Wisconsin involvement in the conferences also stands out. Potter served as rapporteur for the international organization roundtable; the League of Nations was his special sphere of inquiry. Future Wisconsin faculty Salter and Gaus are mentioned by the reports as participants in at least one conference. Wisconsin psychology professor Clark Leonard Hull took part; so also did Katherine Klueter (later Wood), who must have been early in her Wisconsin doctoral studies. She completed her doctorate in 1929, the first woman Ph.D. in political science. Her academic career was spent at Bryn Mawr, where she directed the School of Social Work and Social Research, with periods of government service.

Hall sought funding without success for a continuation of these conferences, and asked for university backing. However, he was disappointed in his quest, partly because Merriam and others threw their weight behind a different formula, a series of smaller meetings under the sponsorship of the newly created SSRC, beginning at Dartmouth in 1925.[14] Ogg, in a lukewarm letter of support for the Hall project for a 1926 conference in Madison, addressed to President Glenn Frank, noted the competing Dartmouth initiative:

> Some of the leaders in our field with whom I have talked in recent weeks are inclined to believe that, for this particular year at all events, the conference of the sort held annually since 1923 ought to give way to a conference of a smaller group . . . probably to be held at Dartmouth.

Ogg indicated that he tended to agree with this view, adding that if the larger conference were to take place there was no reason not to hold it in Madison.[15]

Another obstacle was a 1925 board of regents resolution that "no gifts, donations, or subsidies shall in the future be accepted by or on behalf of the University of Wisconsin from any incorporated Educational endowments or organizations of like character." Introduced by a Progressive member of the Board, its sponsors claimed that the action was necessary "to protect colleges and universities from the selfish dictates of corporate wealth."[16] Untainted money from the state, they argued, would readily provide for worthwhile research. Among other effects, this resolution blocked substantial Rockefeller funding for John R. Commons research. Possibly it contributed to the Hall decision the following year, to the consternation of Ogg,[17] to accept the presidency of the University of Oregon. For Hall, this was a perhaps surprising leap to the academic summit, since he had no apparent prior administrative experience; to boot, he soon found himself embroiled in controversy over his advocacy of repeal of prohibition. After a six-year stint at Oregon, he became director of the Institute for Governmental Research at the Brookings Institution in 1932; he met an early death at age 55 in 1936.

Pitman Potter and Others: The Reinsch Legacy in International Affairs Preserved

Potter, Hall's Wisconsin partner in the National Conferences on the Science of Politics, had joined the department in 1920 after a 1918 doctorate at Harvard and brief service at Illinois. During the 1920s, he was one of the most visible, active, and popular faculty members, and a frequent spokesperson for the League of Nations and international cooperation. Brian Schmidt observes that Potter "assumed the role that Reinsch had occupied earlier as the preeminent scholar of international relations. The study of international organization throughout the interwar period was essentially synonymous with the work of Potter," adding the cogent observation that he is "one of the forgotten figures from the past."[18]

In a 1923 article in the *American Political Science Review*, Potter chastised the discipline for ignoring the field of international organization. He blamed this in part on the disposition to abandon deductive analysis for inductive methods more compatible with new aspirations for scientific method. The consequence of this change in methodological orientation, Potter held, was that political science was "concerned primarily with the description of facts, the formulation of principles of interpretation and explanation to fit those facts in retrospect, not with the declaration of rules of action to be followed in the future."[19] He further argued that political science gave excessive deference to the doctrine of sovereignty as an insuperable barrier to meaningful international organization, pointing out that in innumerable treaties and international regulatory mechanisms, states voluntarily accepted some restriction on the scope of their sovereignty for the sake of mutually beneficial international cooperation. Whereas 150 universities offered courses in international law, only a handful provided instruction in international organization. Yet the traditional study of international law, Potter believed, had contributed next to nothing to world peace. In his article on international organization in the 1933 edition of the *International Encyclopedia of the Social Sciences*, he suggested that international law specialists held "absurd pretensions to their own importance and their own scientific soundness and have insisted on frightening the common layman away from the study of international affairs."[20]

The field of international organization, for Potter, divided into two elements: institutions and practices. The former dealt with organizational features, while the latter concerned the mechanisms of diplomacy, arbitration, conferences, and other procedures through which structural international cooperation was transmitted. His two most influential books, *An Introduction to the Study of International Organization* (1922) and *The World of Nations: Foundations, Institutions, Practices* (1929), were landmark works in the interwar period. A powerful current of progressive reform commitment is visible throughout his writings. The Schmidt history of international relations, in placing Potter in the pantheon of original and foundational scholars, underlines the Potter conviction that the anarchic state system "was susceptible to a certain degree of progressive reform," and that "modification in the relations of states was possible even in the absence of a global sovereign."[21]

Potter gave frequent public lectures in support of his theses on international cooperation, and the need for the United States to take part in its summit venue, the League of Nations. Such views were heretical to currents of isolationist sentiment strong in Wisconsin, particularly among La Follette circles. In March 1926, Regent John Cashman, a Progressive Republican, called for the firing of Potter and two other prominent faculty accused of similar views (William G. Rice of Law, Carl Russell Fish of History). The League, for Cashman, was nothing more than a sinister plot hatched by perfidious Albion. Britain under the cover of the war had seized vast new areas in Africa and Asia, and now wanted to lure America into guarding the booty through the League Covenant. Britain, wrote Cashman, "has always had rich imperialists, like Cecil Rhodes and Andrew Carnegie, to set aside their millions to extend the British Empire and undermine patriotism in other lands; and she has always had puppets ready to do her dirty work."[22]

Potter forcefully rebutted the allegations that he was a British hireling, and pledged to continue to uphold his views that the United States should join the league as the best instrument for peace. President Frank ignored the

Cashman attack, and no action was taken by the regents.[23] Potter left Wisconsin for the Graduate Institute of International Studies in Geneva, Switzerland, in 1932.

However, there were by now other hands to carry on the international studies tradition. At the time of the Potter resignation, of the nine faculty in the department, five were primarily international in their interests (two, Potter and Grayson Kirk, in international relations, and three, Ogg, Lloyd Jones and Sharp, in comparative politics). Kirk was appointed an instructor in 1929, while he was completing his Wisconsin doctorate (1931); his thesis dealt with French policy in Alsace-Lorraine since these lost provinces were recuperated from Germany after World War I. Kirk soon achieved national visibility, publishing work on the domestic factors in American foreign policy, a Latin America study, *The Monroe Doctrine Today* (1941), a 1936 book on *Philippine Independence*, and an influential text on international relations (co-authored with colleague Sharp), *Contemporary International Politics* (1940). Kirk was a popular teacher, and frequent public lecturer. William Farber, reminiscing on his doctoral years in Madison 1932–35, notes that Kirk popularity was perhaps surprising since he had a pronounced stammer in class.[24] Eldon Johnson, a 1939 doctorate and subsequently President of the University of New Hampshire, in his autobiography lists Kirk first among the "particularly distinguished lot" of faculty mentors he recollects.[25] William Young shares the Farber recollection of Kirk as a popular instructor, despite the speech impediment. He describes Kirk as a handsome figure, with the demeanor of a sophisticated Ivy League professor.[26] Indeed, Kirk soon fulfilled his image, departing for Columbia in 1940. After wartime government service, he returned to an administrative leadership role, serving as Columbia President from 1951 to 1968, when he fell victim to the wave of student antiwar protest.

Walter Sharp was an Indiana native, whose undergraduate degree was earned at Wabash College. He pursued doctoral study in France, completing a doctorate at Bordeaux in 1922. After a year at Washington and Lee, he joined the Wisconsin faculty as an instructor in 1923. His primary research focus was French politics, concerning which he published two important books during his Wisconsin career, *The French Civil Service: Bureaucracy in Transition* (1931), and *The Government of the French Republic* (1938). He also coauthored with Ogg a treatise on *The Economic Development of Europe* (1926), and the 1940 text on international politics with Kirk noted earlier. When Sharp almost left in 1931, Gaus made an urgent appeal to Dean Sellery for a generous counteroffer, stressing his importance to the international field.[27] Sharp also taught American politics, and authored one book on Wisconsin government, *The Chief Executive and Auxiliary Agencies in Wisconsin* (1936). He was a regular contributor to campus debates on current international issues; the columns of the *Daily Cardinal* make frequent reference to Sharp lectures. He also collaborated with Kirk and Lloyd Jones in launching a new international relations major in 1938.[28] He left in 1940 for the City College of New York at a salary of $6,100, compared to $4,650 at Wisconsin; Dean Sellery would promise no more than $5,000.[29] By 1943 Sharp was engaged in wartime and international service, holding an important post in the United Nations Educational, Social and Cultural Organization (UNESCO) from 1948 to 1950. He returned to the academy in 1951, teaching at Yale until his retirement in 1964.[30]

Photo courtesy University of Wisconsin–Madison Archives

Llewellyn Pfankuchen, about 1940

Llewellyn Pfankuchen was recruited by Ogg in 1932, primarily as a specialist in international law. His career falls mostly in the postwar period, but he became a significant player in the department by the beginning of World War II, and served as chair from 1944 to 1948. When a tenure decision was due in 1938, Dean Sellery expressed concern about the slender research record; the major Pfankuchen publication, a *Documentary Textbook in International Law,* appeared in 1940. Pfankuchen's colleagues sprang to his defense, urging at the same time that a salary gesture be made to meet an attractive offer ($4,200) from the U.S. Department of Agriculture; his Wisconsin salary was $2,750.[31] Gretchen Pfankuchen, his wife, recalls that shortly after their arrival he received a notice that he had agreed to waive 10 percent of his $2,000 salary in response to the fiscal emergency.[32] The department promotion recommendation did win approval, with a modest raise, and Pfankuchen completed his long career at the university in 1971.[33]

Pfankuchen spent a year in Washington 1935–36 with the Department of Agriculture, an opportunity arranged by Gaus. He was a popular undergraduate teacher. Mary Lewis, department secretary in the early 1930s, reported that long lines of students were always to be found in front of his door. His postwar career is covered in chapter 4.

The other long-serving figure in the international and comparative sphere, in addition to Ogg, was Chester Lloyd Jones. From a Wisconsin rural background, Lloyd Jones completed a B.A. at the university in 1902, then earned a doctorate at the University of Pennsylvania in 1906, where he stayed on as an instructor until invited to Wisconsin in 1910. He replaced Reinsch as chair in 1913 when the latter left for China, remaining in that post until 1917. From 1914 to 1917, he served as secretary and treasurer for the APSA. He then entered diplomatic service for a decade, serving in Madrid, Paris, and Havana. In 1928, according to his memorial resolution, "it became desirable to make better provision at the University for instruction and research in the increasingly important Latin American field,"[34] and Lloyd Jones was brought back to Wisconsin. His appointment now was joint in political science and economics. In 1930, he became dean of the School of Commerce, still within Letters and Science (L&S), but since 1926 fully separate from the Department of Economics. He remained dean until 1935, then returned to his faculty role in political science until his death in 1941. He was the author of several books on the Caribbean, Mexico, and Guatemala. "Not only was he an earnest and patient teacher, but his first-hand knowledge imparted reality to all that he taught . . . one of the most beloved members of the University faculty, both among his colleagues and in his relations with students," concluded the memorial resolution.

A final prewar appointment in comparative politics was William Ebenstein, an Austrian emigre who completed a Wisconsin doctorate in 1938. He belongs to the generation of brilliant Jewish refugee scholars from Germany and Austria whose impact on American intellectual life was enormous.[35] He was appointed that year as instructor, the first Jewish member of the department. He published a pair of books on fascism in the Axis powers, *Fascist Italy* (1939) and *The Nazi State* (1943). He left for Princeton in 1946, then the University of California–Santa Barbara in 1964; in his later career his research interest shifted to political thought (see chapter 7).

Frederic Ogg, Pillar of the Department

The two scholars of the interwar years whose impact upon the department was most profound were beyond doubt Ogg and Gaus. Ogg, one may recall, was chair from 1917 till 1940, and Gaus replaced him from 1940 to 1942. Ogg served a final brief term from 1942 to 1944. Ogg, of Indiana farm background, completed a Harvard doctorate in 1908. After teaching at Simmons College for a few years, he joined the Wisconsin faculty in 1914. He had already published two books, *Social Progress in Contemporary Europe* (1912) and *Daniel Webster* (1914). Fifteen other books were to follow. His scholarly work bridged the comparative and American fields; he contributed widely used, basic texts to both areas. He is perhaps best remembered in the academic world for his writings on European governments; Curti and Carstenson identify him as a comparative government specialist, "who gave the Wisconsin department an international reputation as his texts became ever more widely used."[36] He also taught courses on East Asian politics.

But the memorial resolution adopted after Ogg's 1951 death identifies his classic American government text, *Introduction to American Government and Politics* (with slightly varying titles in different editions) as his most famous work (with coauthor P. Orman Ray in a clearly secondary role). The book, read the resolution, was a "monumental textbook which is now a national college and university institution in the United States. Grayhaired professors brought up on the early editions of Ogg and Ray (the first appeared in 1922) are now requiring their students to read the Tenth (1951)."[37] This exceptionally successful text, which made Ogg a comfortably prosperous scholar, continued after Ogg's death through several editions with William Young replacing Ogg as primary author.

In recent decades, the highly competitive market for American government texts is met by volumes designed to win attention through their graphic content, photographs, and sidebars; the Ogg and Ray volumes had none of these cosmetic features. In nearly a thousand pages of plain text, there was a comprehensive and authoritative institutional and historical description of American government, with extensive bibliographic suggestions for each chapter. As a summary of contemporary knowledge about American institutions, Ogg and Ray had no peer in the interwar period. In successive editions, one can see a significant evolution of content; by the time of the 1951 edition, extensive sections were devoted to public opinion, parties, nominating conventions, and other topics that had little coverage in the first edition.

Conversely, the long section in the initial text dealing with theories of the state redolent of turn-of-the-century political science had disappeared.

The abundant Ogg corpus of published work is noted for its solidity and influence through classroom use rather than conceptual or interpretive originality. According to William Young, many, and perhaps Ogg himself, considered his 1936 book, *English Government and Politics*, to be his finest work. This erudite study, cast in a historical-institutional mold, was inspired in part by Ogg's sense that the remarkable tradition of representative democratic government, which Britain embodied, was under growing threat from the spread of fascism and communism.

He was a leader in political science nationally, serving as *American Political Science Review* editor from 1926 to 1949, a strategic position from which the evolving profile of the discipline can be shaped. The memorial resolution attests that the *Review*'s "pages faithfully reflect his concern with every major development, and with every faint stirring of new promise."[38] In 1941, Ogg was elected APSA president.

Ogg chaired a major L&S curriculum review committee in 1944–46, a process marked by sharp divergences on educational philosophies extending over innumerable meetings. The memorial resolution characterizes the final report as "a magnificent educational document," attributing its wholehearted faculty acceptance to the skillful brokering and crafting by Ogg. One of the eventual outcomes of the report was the creation of the Integrated Liberal Studies Program, an initiative that Ogg viewed with some skepticism. Earlier, Ogg was one of a handful of faculty who organized what became the Social Studies Divisional Committee in 1920; in the late 1920s he served as its chair.

Ogg was a strong leader of the department, but sustained an ethos of collegiality which carried on in subsequent decades. "Among the strong men who served with him there were significant differences of opinion; but these, due largely to his character and influence, were patiently worked out, and differences never led to factions," the memorial resolution read. "His sense of justice was felt by all who knew him, and he had a rare understanding of how human procedures, patiently pursued, could bring agreement and improvement from conflicting views deeply and strongly held." Farber recollects hearing as a graduate student occasional snide comments about "what the old man wanted," which he felt unfair; he made Ogg the model for his own 38 years as department head at the University of South Dakota.[39] Although faculty rules requiring an annual election of the chair were adopted in 1920, one may doubt whether such procedures operated at a time when not only Ogg but many other department chairs had virtually permanent tenure. President Clarence Dykstra had occasion to remind departments of this rule in 1940, and there is reference in a Gaus letter to Dean Sellery to a 1940 balloting in the department.[40]

Before the 1937 death of his wife, Emma Ogg, Ogg and his wife regularly hosted Sunday afternoon social events, as well as meetings of the Political Science Club and diverse colloquia. He was a generous mentor to young colleagues; Gretchen Pfankuchen recalls how graciously the Oggs eased their adjustment to Madison, and how frequently Ogg invited Llewellyn Pfankuchen for dinner after the death of Emma Ogg, when Ogg normally dined out.[41] Indeed, in his will he left small sums to the two Pfankuchen children.

William Young recollects Ogg as "a very decent gentleman—very kind, considerate, but not at ease with young people." He was heavyset, methodical, unusually industrious, but not given to many "flights of fancy." He

Photo courtesy University of Wisconsin–Madison Archives

Frederic Ogg enjoys a birthday party with graduate students, about 1947. Henry Hart is fifth from the left among those standing.

Exterior of Ogg House at 1711 Kendall Avenue

seemed the incarnation of a New England gentleman, invariably wearing a vest and a pocket watch. "He was the only member of the department that confessed to being a Republican and listed it in *Who's Who*."[42] Even after the death of his wife, Ogg continued to invite occasionally small groups of graduate students for dinner. For the students, Young recalls, sustaining conversation could be a problem; Ogg was known for two passions outside of political science: football and opera. Most students knew too little about the latter to risk this subject, and raising the football topic at an Ogg dinner appeared intellectually unseemly (see appendix 26).

In his final years, after the death of his wife, he was a lonely, very self-contained man. James McCamy, in a letter to Gaus shortly after the 1951 Ogg death, remarks on the "amazing" persona of Ogg, abundantly kind, generous, and erudite, yet leading an isolated inner life within an outwardly Victorian manner.[43] Perhaps this partly mirrored his total commitment to his work. His productivity was made possible by a stern regimen, beginning with arrival at his South Hall office at 8 a.m., where he remained until 6 p.m. After dinner, he resumed work, ending at midnight. His study at home had five separate desks, one for each of his major scholarly functions. After retirement, he continued to

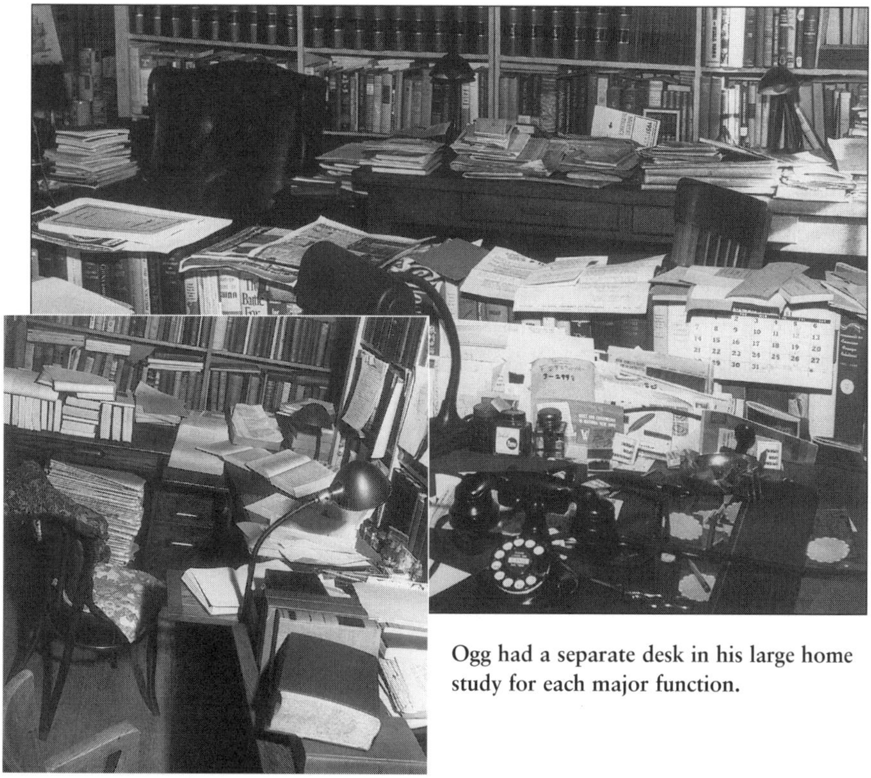

Ogg had a separate desk in his large home study for each major function.

come regularly to his office, and department minutes record his continuing attendance until shortly before his death. When he died, he had nearly completed the revisions for the tenth edition of his American government text.

In his last years, with no children or other immediate relatives other than a sister in Fort Wayne, Ogg adopted his housekeeper and her family as his own, dining with them every Sunday evening, and lavishing affection on their small daughter. To general astonishment, he left much of his $250,000 estate to them; "none of us knew," McCamy wrote, "about his attachment to the Wicks until the funeral."[44] He did bequeath $15,000 to the department for the Emma Ogg graduate fellowships, as well as his personal library; in addition, he left $25,000 to the university for scholarships, and $10,000 to the APSA.[45]

Ogg devoted his prodigious professional energies primarily to the department, his prolific writing, and service to the profession as *American Political Science Review* editor. He was not active in public policy issues, nor involved in state political affairs. Neither did he enjoy a relationship of influence with top campus administrators. But by building upon the Reinsch foundations, broadening the scope of the department, and consolidating its national distinction, his impact was immense and his legacy lasting.

Ogg as chair can be remembered as a shrewd and successful judge of faculty potential in the 14 faculty appointments on his watch. Five (Potter, Sharp, Gaus, Kirk, and Pfankuchen) gave long and praiseworthy service. Three others, Allen Saunders, John Lewis, and Herbert Wengert, were Wisconsin doctoral students appointed as instructors for a few years, presumably to help them complete their doctoral work and find permanent positions. Harris, a public administration and American politics specialist, began his teaching career at Wisconsin in 1923, moving on to Washington (Seattle) in 1930, then later to California-Berkeley. James Grant, a Stanford Ph.D., taught in international relations and American politics from 1927 till 1930, then returned to his native California to join the newly created department at UCLA. Jacob Jacobson, a Brown Ph.D., served as instructor in 1927–30, then vanished from the political science lists. Ebenstein served eight years after his 1938 doctorate, before departing for Princeton in 1946. The last appointment for which Ogg must have had primary responsibility, William Beard (son of Charles Beard) in 1940, served only briefly, leaving for wartime civilian, then military service and never returning.

The only serious personnel miscalculation by Ogg was the 1930 tenure appointment of John Salter. At the time of his appointment, there was reason to see promise in Salter; he had attracted attention for his research on boss politics in Philadelphia, innovative in its day for the stress on a quasi-anthropological direct observation and extensive interviewing of actors in the Philadelphia Republican machine. Some publications issued from this research, including *Boss Rule: Portraits in City Politics* (1935), *The Pattern of Politics: The Folkways of a Democratic People* (1940), and *The People's Choice: Philadelphia's William S. Vare* (1971), and three articles in the *American Political Science Review* (1933, 1935, 1940), the latter perhaps benefiting from a gentle boost from *Review* editor Ogg. In 1931–32, Salter won a fellowship from the SSRC.[46] Later, at the beginning of World War II, he was invited to Stanford University for a year as visiting professor. Near the end of the war, he served as historian for the Air Force; after the war, he held visiting professorships in the Philippines and Taiwan.

However, at Wisconsin he quickly lost the respect of his colleagues. Farber, a doctoral student in the early 1930s, recollects that a view was already widespread that Salter research did not measure up to Wisconsin standards, describing him as an unusual personality, long-haired and bohemian in his habits.[47] William Young is more direct, suggesting that Salter had retired the day he completed his dissertation.[48] By the postwar years, he had ceased participating in department meetings; his teaching was limited to some introductory American politics courses. He was constantly but a half step ahead of his many creditors; the hot plate in his office was a frequent source of warnings to the department by the fire marshal.[49]

His two enthusiasms, recalls William Young, were guns (of which he had an impressive collection) and photography.[50] In 1945, Chair Pfankuchen wrote Dean Ingraham pointing out that Salter had come with a salary promise of $3,750, but owing to the Depression salary "waivers" his stipend had never reached this level, still lagging at $3,637.[51] By the time of his 1968 retirement, his salary was less than that of newly appointed assistant professors. McCamy, in a 1951 letter to Gaus, suggests that the impecunious Salter lived on meager rations. McCamy confided that he had recommended no salary increase for Salter, which McCamy reports Salter accepted with good grace, but added that his wife, Kathryn Salter, was in a mood to shoot McCamy, Gaus and Dean Ingraham.

The Enduring Impact of John Gaus

The recruitment of John Gaus to the department took place through the vehicle of the Alexander Meiklejohn Experimental College, a major and controversial venture in radical educational reform. Gaus, a native of upstate New York, attended Amherst College, completing his undergraduate degree in 1915 at a time when Meiklejohn was serving as president. He pursued doctoral study at Harvard, completing his doctorate in 1924. While still a doctoral candidate, he was appointed to a faculty post at Amherst in 1920 by Meiklejohn. In 1923, the latter was ousted by the Amherst trustees, hostile to his radical political and educational ideas. Gaus left Amherst in protest, and joined the faculty at the University of Minnesota; he rose from assistant to full professor in just three years.

Meiklejohn was tapped by President Glenn Frank (1925–37) in 1926 to implement a transformative vision of undergraduate education. An Experimental College under his direction, established in 1927 in the face of considerable faculty skepticism, and quiet opposition from L&S Dean Sellery, called for a select group of about a hundred freshmen to follow a two-year interdisciplinary program in place of the regular college curriculum. The first year was devoted to intensive study of Periclean Athens, and the second to a contemporary civilization. Several specially recruited faculty would provide the instruction. The

Meiklejohn college was presented as an experiment, to show the pedagogical possibilities of a radically reshaped undergraduate education. The object, for Meiklejohn, was to instill in students a broad intellectual culture; college, he had written earlier, "is not primarily to teach the forms of living, not primarily to give practice in the art of living, but rather to broaden and deepen the insight into life itself, to open up the riches of human experience, of literature, of nature, of art, of religion, of philosophy, of human relations, social, economic, political, to arouse an understanding and appreciation of these, so that life may be fuller and richer in content."[52]

Meiklejohn drew heavily on former Amherst associates for his enterprise; Gaus was the first recruited. The several Meiklejohn faculty recruits were not all welcome in the departments invited to house them, in part because their salaries were far above university norms. Political Science, however, happily welcomed Gaus to its ranks. The Meiklejohn faculty were expected to contribute to departmental instruction as well as to the Experimental College.

Gaus was a key member of the Meiklejohn college faculty during its brief existence; it was terminated in 1932. In particular, Gaus gave body and content to the second-year format, which university historians Cronon and Jenkins argue was the most successful aspect of the program:

> The most important Gaus contribution was the major research project each student was assigned to begin over the summer after the freshman year: a wide-ranging study of the development of some American region or community—usually the student's home town—to be completed as a sophomore thesis by the beginning of the following spring semester under the direction of one of the advisers. The regional study was an imaginative attempt to sharpen the students' research skills and have them apply their general knowledge of the unfolding of the Athenian and American civilizations to the development of a particular American community.

For most students, this project proved the most valuable part of the Meiklejohn curriculum.[53]

Another Gaus contribution to the Experimental College program was the placement of *The Education of Henry Adams* as core text for the second year. Gaus remained attached to this work as a unique pedagogical resource throughout his long career, assigning it in many courses. The better part of the spirit of the Experimental College lived on with Gaus, in his wide-ranging

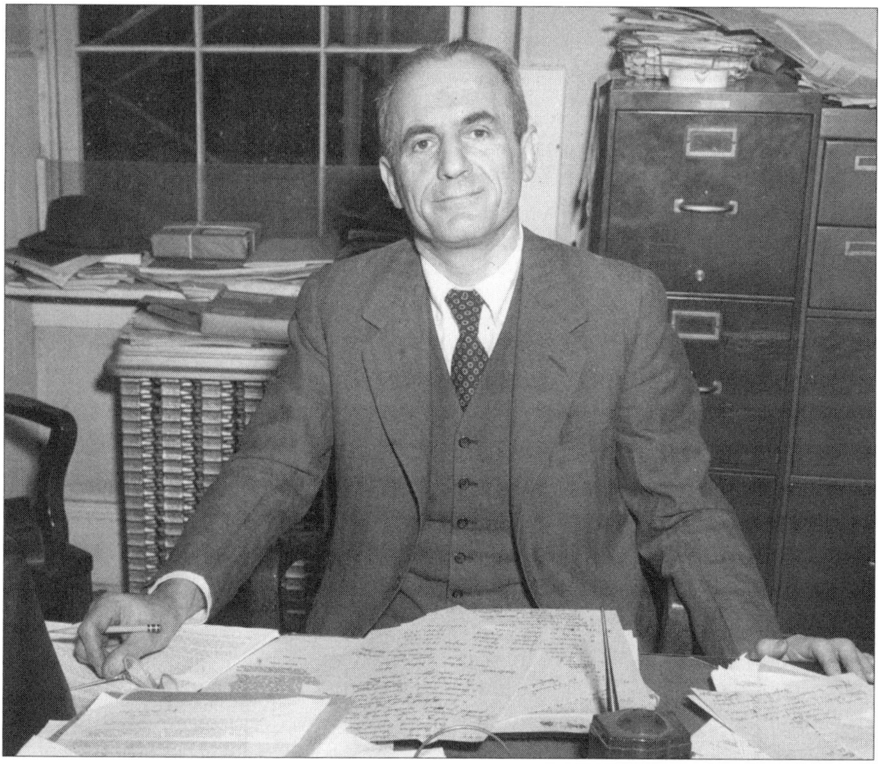

John Gaus, about 1940

interests, and his capacity to draw upon his vast erudition for insightful commentary on contemporary affairs.

The network of connections from Gaus ran in many directions. He was a close friend and confidant of presidents Frank (1925–37) and Clarence Dykstra (1937–45), though not President E. B. Fred (1945–58). The 27 boxes of Gaus correspondence in the archives include regular exchanges with many leading political scientists. At the time of the Frank dismissal, Gaus was among a list of 28 possible candidates for the presidency which appeared in the press.[54]

During the La Follette years, he was actively engaged in policy discussions on regional planning and the rural sector. He worked closely with Governor Philip La Follette in finding restorative uses for the cutover area of northern Wisconsin, identifying creative public utilization of the large tracts of tax delinquent land that had escheated to the state. With a shrewd political skill, he cooperated both with conservation interests and the paper industry for sustainable forestry. In a memorial service eulogy in Cambridge in 1969, McCamy wrote:

> In a sense, John Gaus in all his life was a combination of the best of rural America and the Ivy League. His hardheaded, pragmatic approach to the study of government was the best of rural America. His style, his manner, his personality were urbane, assured, individualistic, and interesting, hence the best of Ivy League.[55]

His instructional style was idiosyncratic, and not to the taste of those expecting highly structured presentations. His lectures and conversations were strewn with wise reflection and illuminating insights, unconstrained by any intrusive ordering principle. On Saturday afternoons, he and his wife held informal open house for graduate students for conversations on current issues of public policy or political science; many years later those who had attended recalled these sessions as high points of their doctoral experience. Eldon Johnson recollects the advice in the 1930s to incoming graduate students: "you ought to take a course with Gaus no matter what: it's not the course, whatever it is; it's John Gaus." He added that the "free-wheeling style" could be baffling to undergraduates looking for organized coverage of the text material.[56] Farber describes him as an exacting mentor, viewed with awe by his students.[57] William Young also remembers the Saturday afternoon sessions as especially valuable experiences, noting Gaus's erudition; Young adds that "it would be hard to describe his teaching as political science in any strict definition of the word."[58]

Gaus was best known for his major study of the Department of Agriculture, *Public Administration and the United States Department of Agriculture* (1940, with Leon Wolcott) and a pair of basic treatises on public administration, *Frontiers of Public Administration* (1936, with Leonard D. White and Marshall Dimock) and *Reflections on Public Administration* (1947). He was a specialist in agricultural policy, regional planning, and public administration. However, his interests were always wide-ranging, and never confined within the boundaries of particular topics or subfields.

Harvard had begun courting Gaus several years before he returned to his doctoral alma mater in 1947. Some Wisconsin developments seem to have contributed to his departure. Gaus was displeased with the 1945 departure of Dykstra, to take on the provost position at the University of California-Los Angeles (UCLA). More important, however, was the bitter dispute with the board of regents over the proposed appointment of Howard McMurray to a tenured position in the department in 1947. The McMurray case is examined in full detail in chapter 4; here I sketch only the basic elements. After his 1940 Wisconsin doctorate, he had lectured for political science extension in Milwaukee, and in 1945–46 was a very popular instructor for the department, teaching basic American government courses. He had served a term in Congress in 1942–44, and ran unsuccessfully as Democratic Senate candidate in 1944 and 1946. In November 1946, McMurray was proposed by the department for a tenured faculty post. The regents vetoed the appointment in January 1947, claiming that McMurray merely wanted the faculty post as a launching pad. Gaus and his departmental colleagues were deeply angered by the regent action, which they regarded as a fundamental violation of academic freedom.

Harvard then renewed its courtship. Although Gaus had rejected an earlier formal offer, Harvard now found Gaus willing to quit Wisconsin. He told the *Milwaukee Journal* in explaining his choice to depart that "the McMurray affair certainly was a factor in my decision to leave."[59] The department made a couple of subsequent efforts to woo him back, but to no avail.

His Harvard years until his 1961 retirement, many believe, were less happy than the two decades in Madison. No major publications followed his 1947 book. The Harvard environment did not permit the kind of unique role he played at Wisconsin, as teacher, policy consultant, and faculty leader. He was only a secondary figure at Harvard, and did not play a significant part in the factional fights that split the Harvard department at the time. The brilliant years of his career belonged to Wisconsin.

Gaus left a portion of his library to the Wisconsin department. McCamy managed to raise sufficient funds to establish it as a special collection in the University Library, now housed at the Helen C. White Undergraduate Library. The nature of the collection provides interesting insight into the intellectual profile of Gaus. It consists entirely of poetry works; Gaus reportedly found relaxation in reading poetry, and his last act before retiring at night was to read a poem.

The Second Reform Era: The Wisconsin Idea Revived

The election of a Progressive Republican governor in 1930, and President Roosevelt in 1932, opened a renewed era of faculty policy engagement in progressive reform. Gaus, as noted above, was very close to the La Follette family, especially Governor Philip La Follette (1931–33, 1935–39). In 1932, Gaus headed an Executive Council in the office of the governor, and after La Follette's reelection in 1934 was one of a small group of faculty who served on an advisory group; others included Witte, Law Dean Lloyd Garrison, Max Otto (philosophy), John R. Commons, and several of the latter's former students: Harold Groves, Elizabeth Brandeis, and Paul A. Rauschenbush.[60] The Gaus role in forestry and conservation in northern Wisconsin was described in the preceding section.

Witte was particularly important in the policy realm; just before leaving the LRL in 1933 to take a position in economics and political science at the university, he had played a key role in formulating the 1931 Wisconsin unemployment compensation act. He joined the faculty as a full professor, succeeding to the economics chair held by Commons.[61] Although the economics history suggests that no formal record of a joint appointment in political science has been uncovered, department minutes show that Witte regularly attended department meetings until after World War II, actively participated in departmental curricular and other affairs, taught a course in political science, was listed in the political science rosters in the catalogues, and supervised several doctorates in the department.[62] Thus, though his primary affiliation was economics, he acted as a full member of the Department of Political Science. Witte, grandfather of current faculty member John Witte, had replaced McCarthy at his death in 1921 as LRL head. Less aggressively partisan than McCarthy, he was equally engaged in the policy process and sustained the special reputation of the LRL as not only the pioneer but also the continuing leader in state policy analysis. His policy engagement was especially strong on labor issues, and the regulation of women's and children's work. He followed in the Commons tradition of backing the control of the abuses and excesses of capitalism through a network of regulatory commissions.[63] What his biographer terms his lifetime major work, *The Government in Labor Disputes* (1932), clearly overlaps institutional economics and political science.

The most remarkable Witte policy role was service in 1934–35 as executive director of the President's Committee on Economic Security, which prepared the 1935 Social Security Act.[64] The design of this landmark act involved complex compromises, and adjudication of a host of competing visions. President Roosevelt began with a more ambitious design for "cradle to grave" social insurance. Witte, with his long experience of legislative crafting and political navigating in his many years with the LRL, had the skills necessary to push to the outer limits of congressional possibility, but not beyond. Then-Secretary of Labor Frances Perkins, under whose mantle he served, pays high tribute to Witte in her introduction to the posthumously published Witte account of the drafting of the Social Security Act. Her encomium merits extended quotation:

> It was a strange assignment that Edwin Witte had when he came to Washington in mid-summer of 1934 to act as director of the work of studying the possibilities and drafting an acceptable scheme for a social security act. . . . The Committee on Economic Security had been appointed by the President and consisted of five Cabinet members close to him and clearly sympathetic to him and responsive to his desires. . . .
>
> Witte came to do the hard, laborious, intensive work which these five Cabinet officers had no time or opportunity, or even the training, to do. We set up a technical committee, which proceeded to take on a lot of experts, and this was where Witte's headaches began. It was like driving a team of high-strung unbroken horses. The patience, the intelligence, the level-headedness, the amiability of Ed Witte was all that made possible a report and a set of recommendations based upon consideration of all of the facts as well as the actuarial and tax problems involved. The result was a plan which has proved itself practical and effective and yet amenable to amendments and administrative changes as they have been necessary. . . .

Witte's memorandum reflects some of the confusions which rose as the violent differences of opinion among the experts and advisors made themselves felt, but it does not entirely reveal his cool-headed understanding of human nature, his success as a mediator, and his constant drive and ability to get the facts translated into works of a bill which could go before Congress.[65]

Witte served a pair of terms as chair of the Department of Economics, from 1936 to 1941, and from 1946 to 1953.[66] His second term in particular was difficult, as Witte was increasingly at odds with dominant trends in the discipline, and within his department. The institutional economics which he represented was increasingly contested by a new generation of economists, committed to theoretical and econometric approaches. Witte in turn could offer acid criticism of such visions of economics, closer in his view to "medieval scholasticism" than to modern intellectual activity.[67]

Notwithstanding his trenchant defense of institutional economics, to his surprise he was elected president of the American Economics Association in 1956, just before his 1957 retirement at Wisconsin. He used the occasion of his presidential address to roil the disciplinary waters with a stinging attack on the theoretical and mathematical turn of the field. "Believing as I do that the original concept of economics, expressed in the old term 'political economy' sound,

I inquire why economists have so little influence in public affairs. Among these reasons, I believe is the more recent attitude of looking upon government as belonging within the domain of the political scientist, and only on the periphery of economics." Contemporary economists, Witte regretted, are apologetic about advising policy makers; they "greatly prefer to deal with universal truths which lend themselves to model building and mathematical reasoning."[68]

The second Witte term as economics chair marked his withdrawal from active involvement in political science. Until after World War II, department minutes record his faithful attendance at department meetings, and his full participation in departmental affairs. Witte was a political economist in every sense of the term.

Political science in this second progressive reform era was less visible than economics, but nonetheless engaged. Beyond Witte, the most important figure in a renewal of the Wisconsin Idea was Gaus. The reformist disposition of Pitman Potter in the international arena was noted earlier. Another significant figure was Ford MacGregor (1909–34). As mentioned above, the MacGregor professional contribution lay especially on the extension side, both as director of an Extension municipal reform bureau, and especially as secretary of the important Wisconsin League of Municipalities. In 1926, MacGregor was in the eye of a political storm, when Governor John Blaine called for the regents to fire him because of an offending text from his pen on tax issues. The pamphlet in question, "A Taxation Catechism," was a playful attack upon the state claims of fiscal rectitude achieved by shifting financial burdens to the municipalities, presented in the form of a question-and-answer dialogue.[69] Newly arrived President Frank spoke strongly in MacGregor's defense: "A teacher's opinions, however widely they may differ from prevailing policies and beliefs at the moment, cannot, with my consent, be made a subject of university discipline."[70]

Clarence Dykstra, World War II, and Interregnum

The defenestration of Frank orchestrated by Governor La Follette in 1937 brought another political scientist to the helm, Clarence Dykstra; if we may lay claim to Lathrop and Adams, five of the 27 presidents or chancellors of the Madison campus have been political scientists.[71] The new president had pursued doctoral study at the University of Chicago, after an undergraduate degree at Iowa. He then taught at Ohio State (1908–09), Kansas (1909–20), and became a founding member of a Department of Political Science at

UCLA in 1922. During his Los Angeles period, he directed the City Club for several years, an organization dedicated to local government affairs.[72] A specialist in municipal government, he was invited in 1930 to assume the post of city manager in Cincinnati. His forceful style earned him the moniker "dictator of Cincinnati," which sent shivers of apprehension in some faculty quarters. However, most were won over by his academic background, and his continuing active membership in professional associations such as the APSA, the American Academy of Political and Social Sciences, and the American Association of University Professors, betokening a commitment to faculty rather than merely managerial values.

Dykstra as president from 1937 to 1945, moreover, proved very respectful of faculty governance and institutional procedures. One of his first acts was to remind faculty of the rule calling for annual election of chairs.[73] The board of regents that made the appointment was dominated by La Follette supporters, and Dykstra was on excellent terms with the governor. However, shortly after his appointment La Follette was defeated in the 1938 elections, replaced by Stalwart Republican Julius Heil. The new governor stung the university with a severe budget slash in 1939, reducing the appropriation below that of 1922 when student enrollment was only half as large.[74] By 1944, the La Follette regents who appointed Dykstra had all been replaced, and Dykstra, many believe, sensed that he had lost the confidence of the board. In October 1944, he announced his departure effective January 1945 to return to UCLA as provost. Officially the departure was cordial.[75]

Although Dykstra held an appointment in political science, he played no role in departmental affairs. He did, however, offer in 1940 to contribute to the teaching of the basic American government course, an offer eagerly accepted. However, he at once went on leave to head the Selective Service System, making fulfillment of the promise difficult. His political science credentials were burnished by election as president of APSA in 1938. Gaus was doubtless his closest department contact; beyond the shared link to Governor La Follette, they had common interests in the field of public administration. One other department member was in frequent touch with Dykstra through an administrative connection: Harold Stoke, appointed in 1940 to the department and also as assistant dean of the Graduate School. With Graduate School Dean E. B. Fred away much of the war years directing the national biological warfare program, Stoke and two fellow assistant deans ran the school. Apparently he was not much involved in department service. He left in 1944 to become president of the University of New Hampshire, later holding presidencies at Louisiana State and Queen's College.

The war years were very disruptive to the university and to the department. Male students evaporated to the draft, a number to reappear in one of the military training programs that became housed at the university. A number of women students diverted their energies into war-related activity or employment. Most of the faculty were also drawn into war service of some description, at least for periods of time. By 22 July 1942, a department memorandum reported an imminent crisis in staffing, with Gaus, Ebenstein, Beard, Salter, Pfankuchen, and Ebenstein all expected to be away. Several courses would need to be combined, and the basic courses in political theory, constitutional law, international law, public administration, and comparative government could not be taught.[76] In addition, special courses had to be created for armed forces training programs on campus. A December 1944 department newsletter noted that, although there were many fewer military students, the smaller wartime classes were mainly populated by women.[77] Then, immediately following the war, the deluge of veterans for whom the GI Bill opened college opportunity appeared on the scene, well before the faculty had been reconstituted. Some degree of normality returned only about 1947.

The modest scale of the department by the war years is reflected in the table below. The budget figures include not only faculty salaries, but also teaching assistants and office staff. At the end of the war, the total department budget was less than two-thirds of the starting salary of a new assistant professor by the end of the century.

Table 3.1 Profile of the Wartime Department

Year	*FTE*	*Enrollment*	*Budget*
1941–42	8.5	1,764	$31,912
1942–43	6.75	1,454	$26,937
1943–44	5.5	959	$27,398
1944–45	6	1,724	$30,685

Source: Department of Political Science Biennial Report, 1944–46.

Another measure of the limits of department resources was the salary scale by the end of the war, implicit in the budget totals in the table above. The highest paid department member was Stoke at $6,300, followed by Gaus at $6,200, and Ogg at $6,000. Pfankuchen received $4,200, Salter $3,750, Ebenstein $3,250, and newly appointed Gordon Skilling $2,850. One may recollect that Ely was recruited in 1892 at $3,500. Pay did not merely stagnate in the long Depression years, but draconian salary recisions occurred in two stages in 1932 and 1933, culminating in faculty reductions ranging from 17 to 25 percent. These salary waivers remained in full effect for three years, and were only gradually modified, finally ending a decade later.[78] So severe was the university fiscal crisis in the Depression years that typewriters and telephones vanished from the offices of younger faculty.[79]

Worth recollecting is that not only were salaries meager, but there was little provision for retirement. Beard in a 1945 letter to Gaus inquires about recovery of $250 deducted from his salary for a retirement fund, which he hoped to recuperate. An arresting fact is that between the 1908 retirement of Parkinson, and the 1948 retirement of Ogg, not a single member of the department retired from the university. Thus when Lloyd Jones died at the age of 59 in 1941, in declining health his last years, he had clung to his appointment even though by 1940 he was unable to continue teaching.[80]

By the advent of World War II, the undergraduate curriculum was stabilized. As appendix 20 shows, there is little change in the list of courses offered in 1920 and 1940. The graduate program as well was institutionalized. With the exception of a single graduate seminar, devoted to scope and method, graduate students took the advanced undergraduate courses for the first couple of years; armed with an M.A. from Pittsburgh, William Young was able to complete his doctorate in just two years. A copy of the 1942 "bible" (statement of requirements for advanced degrees) notes that preliminary examinations were offered three times yearly. Candidates were required to take four six-hour written examinations at a single session, with at least one from each of three categories (political theory, American, comparative and international). The theory field had a single examination, while in the American area one could choose among public administration, public law, American institutions, and public opinion, parties and policy; the international category included international law and institutions, international relations, and comparative government.[81] French and German language examinations were obligatory, a source of some friction. This basic structure remained in place until the mid-1960s.

An issue that came to a head during the war was the department responsibility for Extension, the program of adult education short courses and lectures organized around the state. During the war years and for a time thereafter, University Extension managed the correspondence courses offered by the United States Armed Forces Institute (USAFI). A memorandum at this period indicated that "we have abandoned the idea of caring for extension teaching largely through appointments of staff members who would customarily serve on both L&S and the Extension Division. Extension was invited to build its own staff; department members found it impossible to do extension and resident teaching the same semesters, and the obligation to commit an entire semester to the itinerant labor of extension service was unattractive to many. On 4 April 1944, the department expressed its approval for the creation of an Extension Department of Political Science.[82] MacGregor, one may recall, for many years had a largely extension role, and one finds references of departmental extension work extending back to the annual reports of Parkinson in the 1890s. For a time, Lorentz Adolfson was the link between the department and Extension. He completed a Wisconsin political science doctorate in 1942, and had served as an Extension political science instructor since 1938. From 1942 to 1944, he held a regular faculty appointment in the department, shifting entirely to Extension in 1944 to become its dean until 1964.

In the department, the turnover at the end of the war was almost complete. The salary figures above are surely part of the explanation, as well as the reason for losing several key faculty years before the war (Kirk, Sharp, Potter, among others). Ebenstein left for Princeton in 1946, Gaus departed for Harvard in 1947, Skilling left for Dartmouth in 1948, Ogg retired in 1948, and Witte withdrew to economics. Of the prewar faculty, by 1948, only Salter and Pfankuchen remained. Thus when the war ended in 1945, the department faced a mammoth challenge of complete reconstruction, a challenge that was also a great opportunity.

Notes

1. Charles Merriam, "Recent Advances in Political Methods," *American Political Science Review*, 17 (1923), 274–295, reprinted in James Farr and Raymond Seidelman (eds.), *Discipline and History: Political Science in the United States* (Ann Arbor: University of Michigan Press, 1993), 129–46.
2. Farr and Seidelman, *Discipline and History*, 143.
3. Farr and Seidelman, *Discipline and History,* 146.
4. For a convincing argument to this effect, see Heinz Eulau, "Political Science," in Bert F. Hoselitz (ed.), *A Reader's Guide to the Social Sciences* (Glencoe: Free Press, 1959), 89–127.
5. Barry D. Karl, *Charles E. Merriam and the Study of Politics* (Chicago: University of Chicago Press, 1974).
6. This interpretation is found in Bernard Crick, *The American Science of Politics: Its Origins and Conditions* (Berkeley: University of California Press, 1959), 133–139.

7. Department minutes, 3 May 1933.
8. R. H. Hughes, *A Study of the Graduate Schools of America* (Miami, OH: Miami University Press, 1925).
9. American Council on Education, *Report of the Committee on Graduate Instruction* (Washington: American Council on Education, 1934).
10. Quoted in John G. Gunnell, *The Descent of Political Theory: The Genealogy of an American Vocation* (Chicago: University of Chicago Press, 1993), 98.
11. Arnold Bennet Hall, "Report of the National Conference on the Science of Politics," *American Political Science Review*, 18, 1 (1924), 121–22.
12. Arnold Bennet Hall, "Reports of the Second National Conference on the Science of Politics," *American Political Science Review*, 19, 1 (1925), 110.
13. Arnold Bennett Hall, "Reports of the Conference on the Science of Politics," *American Political Science Review*, 20,1 (1926), 169–70.
14. Karl, *Merriam*, 130–34.
15. Ogg papers, University Archives, Ogg to Frank, 17 December 1925.
16. E. David Cronon and John W. Jenkins, *The University of Wisconsin: A History 1925–1945: Politics, Depression, and War* (Madison: University of Wisconsin Press, 1994), III, 67–68.
17. Ogg papers, Ogg to Frank, 24 April 1926.
18. Brian C. Schmidt, *The Political Discourse of Anarchy: A Disciplinary History of International Relations* (Albany: State University of New York Press, 1998), 201. My own inquiries among current faculty confirm this point; in spite of the importance of his contribution, few had heard of Potter.
19. Pitman B. Potter, "Political Science in the International Field," *American Political Science Review*, 17, 3 (1923), 381–91.
20. Cited in Schmidt, *Political Discourse*, 206.
21. Schmidt, *Political Discourse*, 209.
22. *Madison Capital Times*, 12 March 1926.
23. Cronon and Jenkins, *The University of Wisconsin*, III, 128.
24. William Farber, oral history, 1984.
25. Eldon L. Johnson, *Stranger in the World* (Urbana: Prairie Publications, 1999), 88.
26. William Young, oral history, 17–18 June 2002.
27. Gaus papers, University Archives, Gaus to Sellery, 9 March 1931.
28. *Press Bulletin*, 28 September 1938.
29. Gaus papers, Sharp to Gaus, 7 December 1939.
30. Interestingly, there is no mention of Sharp in the portrait of the Yale Department of Political Science at the height of its leadership of the behavioral movement and pluralist theory from 1955 to 1970 by Richard M. Merelman, *Pluralism at Yale: The Culture of Political Science at Yale* (Madison: University of Wisconsin Press, 2003). Sharp clearly did not share the dominant orientations at Yale at the time. However, he did contribute a

chapter to one of the seven volumes on political development sponsored by the SSRC Committee on Comparative Politics.

31. Ogg papers, Ogg to Dykstra, 29 August 1938.
32. Gretchen Pfankuchen, oral history, 1983.
33. Pfankuchen also declined an offer from Brooklyn College in 1951 to chair the department.
34. Minutes, University Faculty Meeting, 3 February 1941.
35. An excellent account of their wide-ranging influence on social science is provided by Lewis A. Coser, *Refugee Scholars in America: Their Impact and Their Experiences* (New Haven: Yale University Press, 1984). The roster includes Herbert Marcuse, Theodor Adorno, Franz Neumann, Erich Fromm, Ludwig von Mises, Paul Lazersfeld, as well as Coser himself, among others.
36. Merle Curti and Vernon Carstensen, *The University of Wisconsin: A History 1848–1925* (Madison: University of Wisconsin Press, 1949), II, 339.
37. Faculty document 1027, University Faculty Meeting, 3 December 1951. The composition of the memorial resolution committee is interesting; such ad hoc bodies are constituted by colleagues of long-standing and close association. Chaired by Pfankuchen, it included L&S Dean Mark Ingraham (unusual), Merle Curti, and Edwin Witte.
38. By the time Ogg left his editorship of the *American Political Science Review*, there were growing calls for his ouster by the young generation. Ogg, they argued, was no longer attuned to new currents in the discipline; the Review, according to Austin Ranney, had become a "fuddy-duddy" journal. Austin Ranney oral history in Michael A. Baer, Malcolm E. Jewell and Lee Sigelman (eds.), *Political Science in America: Oral Histories of a Discipline* (Lexington: University of Kentucky Press, 1991), 227.
39. Farber oral history.
40. Gaus papers, Gaus to Sellery, 5 March 1940.
41. Gretchen Pfankuchen oral history.
42. William Young oral history, 2002.
43. Gaus papers, McCamy to Gaus, 13 April 1951.
44. Gaus papers, McCamy to Gaus, 3 November 1951.
45. *Wisconsin State Journal*, 31 October 1951.
46. Department minutes, 6 April 1931.
47. Farber oral history.
48. William Young oral history, 2002.
49. McCamy to Gaus, 13 April 1951, Gaus papers, University Archives.
50. Interview with William Young, 2 April 2004.
51. Pfankuchen to Ingraham, 17 February 1945, Pfankuchen papers, North Hall.
52. Laurence R.Veysey, *The Emergence of the American University* (Chicago: University of Chicago Press, 1965), 210–11.
53. Cronon and Jenkins, *The University of Wisconsin*, III, 170–71.

54. Cronon and Jenkins, *The University of Wisconsin*, III, 340.
55. Gaus papers, McCamy talk at Ogg memorial service, Cambridge, 18 November 1969.
56. Johnson, *Stranger in the World*, 89.
57. Farber oral history.
58. William Young oral history, 2002.
59. *Milwaukee Journal*, 20 October 1947.
60. Paul W. Glad, *The History of Wisconsin: War, a New Era, and Depression, 1914–1940* (Madison: State Historical Society, 1990), IV, 378.
61. For additional detail on the Witte career, especially his role in the Department of Economics and his embodiment of the "Wisconsin Idea," see David B. Johnson, "Edwin E. Witte's Years on the Faculty, 1933–1957," in Robert J. Lampman (ed.), *Economists at Wisconsin: 1892–1992* (Madison: University Publications, 1993), 106–17.
62. Johnson, "Edwin E. Witte's Years," 108.
63. Interview with John Witte, 11 September 2002.
64. Theron F. Schlabach, *Edwin E. Witte: Cautious Reformer* (Madison: State Historical Society of Wisconsin, 1959). Schlabach focuses particularly on the Social Security Act, and does not mention his political science role.
65. Edwin Witte, *The Development of the Social Security Act: A Memorandum on the History of the Committee on Economic Security and Drafting and Legislative History of the Social Security Act* (Madison: University of Wisconsin Press, 1963). Witte wrote this detailed account, based on the careful diary he kept, in 1936, but never found the occasion to turn the manuscript into a book. His economics colleague Robert Lampman, with the help of Wilbur J. Cohen, then Assistant Secretary of Health, Education and Welfare, saw the manuscript to publication after the Witte 1960 death.
66. He also served an interim year in 1955–56.
67. Schlabach, *Edwin E. Witte*, 223.
68. Edwin E. Witte, "Economics and Public Policy," *American Economic Review*, 47, 1 (March 1957), 1–21.
69. Ford H. MacGregor, "A Taxation Catechism: Some Pertinent Questions Relative to the Taxation Situation Asked and Answered," Wisconsin League of Municipalities, n.d. [1926].
70. Cronon and Jenkins, *The University of Wisconsin*, III, 128–29.
71. The others are Bernard Cohen (1987), and Donna Shalala (1987–93).
72. Winston W. Crouch, *A History of the Department of Political Science: University of California, Los Angeles 1920–1987* (Los Angeles: Department of Political Science, UCLA, 1987), 3–4.
73. An important Dykstra innovation which later became one of the cornerstones of faculty governance was to invite a few faculty to screen candidates for vacant deanships, and to recommend a few names; over time this practice became formalized and entered the statutes as the search and screen committee procedure,

mandatory for top administrative appointments. Ira Baldwin, *My Half Century at the University of Wisconsin* (Madison: Omnipress, 1995), 132.

74. Cronon and Jenkins, *The University of Wisconsin*, III, 372–76.
75. Cronon and Jenkins *The University of Wisconsin*, III, 453–55, interpret the Dykstra departure as entirely cordial and voluntary. Others, however, believe that friction with the Regents played a part. Interview with William Young, 2 April 2004. Ira Baldwin suggests that a bitter struggle with the Regents over the establishment of an independent School of Commerce, which Dykstra opposed, may have hastened his departure. Baldwin, *My Half Century*, 211.
76. Pfankuchen papers, North Hall.
77. Pfankuchen papers, North Hall.
78. Cronon and Jenkins, *The University of Wisconsin*, III, 232–35.
79. Interview with William Young, 16 July 2004.
80. Faculty Minutes, 3 February 1941.
81. Pfankuchen papers, North Hall.
82. Pfankuchen papers, North Hall.

CHAPTER 4

Remaking the Department: Turnover, Expansion, and the Campus Crisis Years (1945–1975)

Crawford Young

World War II ended just before the fall semester of 1945 was to begin. American involvement in the second war had lasted much longer, and mobilized far more of the energies of the university and department than the first world war. The transformations in the wake of the war were far more consequential. A virtually reborn department emerged out of the nearly complete turnover of personnel by the 1950s.

This chapter and the next will cover the main aspects of overall postwar departmental history. After 1945, subfields of the department became much more sharply delineated, and generated their own historical itineraries. Chapters 6 through 11 provide detailed narratives for each major subfield. The purpose of this and the following chapter is to trace developments affecting the department as a whole.

The evolution of the department was shaped in important ways by the larger university, state, and discipline contexts within which it was situated. Thus I begin by examining these broader parameters. In analyzing the state political scene, I will consider important faculty contributions to the Wisconsin policy arena, and the impact of major political episodes upon the department (the McMurray affair, McCarthyism).

The Changing Face of the University

By 1943, university enrollment had dropped by half from its prewar peak of 12,000. However, at war's end the campus welcomed a growing flood of war veterans, whose university enrollment was made possible by the GI Bill of

Rights. The generous provisions of this legislation opened college doors to a far broader cross-section of the American population than ever before, in the process creating expectations of college enrollment for a much larger portion of America. At the time of the department's creation, only 2 percent of college-age cohorts pursued higher education; by 1975 the proportion was one-third.[1] Despite stringent university restrictions on out-of-state enrollment during the immediate postwar enrollment crunch, by 1946 student numbers reached 18,598, doubling in one year.[2] Enrollment expansion then slowed, and contracted for a time in the first half of the 1950s when the veteran bulge had worked its way through the system, and the small birth cohorts of the early depression years reached university age. By 1954, a steady expansion resumed, reaching over 30,000 by the mid-1960s, and its recent level of over 40,000 by 1985–86.

Initially, campus infrastructure was overwhelmed. No significant new buildings had been erected since Mechanical Engineering in 1929. For some years after the war, the several hundred students enrolled in the introductory American politics course (Political Science 7, subsequently renumbered as 104) held class in the First Congregational Church. The University Library was squeezed into the north wing of the State Historical Society building; not till 1949 was an appropriation secured for the construction of Memorial Library, finally opened in 1953. In the department, a number of faculty relied on a single shared telephone on each floor of South Hall until into the 1960s.

In the university, the cautious leadership of bacteriologist President E. B. Fred, who replaced Clarence Dykstra in early 1945, and the short-lived presidency of biochemist Conrad Elvehjem (1958–62) gave way to what Cronon and Jenkins term the "imperial presidency" of historian Fred Harrington (1962–1970).[3] Harrington took office in 1962 at a time of extraordinarily swift expansion; the faculty, who numbered only 809 in 1945, increased to 2,324 by the end of his presidency.[4] Harrington played a key role in fostering the development of the social sciences and humanities. Of particular importance to the department was broadening the use of Wisconsin Alumni Research Foundation (WARF) funds provided to the Graduate School Research Committee beyond the natural sciences, a move which Harrington sponsored as vice president under Elvehjem.[5] Harrington also held an expansive view of the international mission of the university, and fought hard for Ford Foundation funds to build the various area studies programs on campus, a major boost for comparative politics (see chapter 6).

Harrington firmly believed that only by aggressive expansion could the university maintain and enhance its position as a leading research university.

In 1962, he predicted that the university would enroll over 100,000 students by the end of the century. In 1964, plans were announced (but soon abandoned) to build a second 20,000-student undergraduate campus in southwest Madison, on a university farm site that is now the University Research Park.[6]

The university became a multicampus institution in the postwar years, first through the establishment of what eventually became 13 two-year University Centers, then by the creation of the Milwaukee campus in 1957, followed by Green Bay and Parkside in the late 1960s, and finally by merger with the Wisconsin State University (WSU) System in 1971. Harrington revived the office of chancellor as Madison campus head in 1964, appointing Robben Fleming, who left in 1967 to become president of the University of Michigan. He was replaced briefly by sociologist William Sewell, then from 1968 to 1977 by former Letters and Science (L&S) Dean and economist H. Edwin Young.

The Changing State Political Environment

The state political environment impinged directly upon the university, and indirectly upon the department. At several junctures, department members played important roles at the state level. In briefly summarizing major changes at the state level in this chapter and the next, I will highlight points at which department faculty were important actors.

During and immediately following the war, there was a major reconfiguration of partisan alignments. The old Progressive movement intimately associated with the La Follette family, with which a number of political scientists from Paul Reinsch to John Gaus had close associations, went into terminal decline. In their early years, Progressives formed a wing within the Republican Party; in 1934, Governor Philip La Follette established a separate Progressive Party. Senator Robert La Follette (the younger) was reelected to the Senate on a Progressive ticket in 1940.

However, by 1944 the Progressive Party was in advanced decomposition; it was little more than the personal machine of the La Follette brothers. Robert La Follette—after prolonged hesitation—chose to abandon the Progressive label in 1946 and run on a Republican ticket. He faced primary opposition by a little-known Fox Valley judge, Joseph McCarthy. Political science lecturer Howard McMurray was the undisputed Democratic nominee. "The Democratic strategy," writes state historian William Thompson, "was to . . . hold as many voters as possible in the Democratic primary so as to deny them to La Follette in the Republican primary." Conventional wisdom held McCarthy to be a less potent opponent than anyone bearing the storied La Follette name. McMurray during the primary campaign launched ferocious attacks against La Follette. "La Follette spent five years before the war voting for Hitler," McMurray told the university Young Democratic club in May 1946. "If a man had to sell out his civilization to get votes he should not represent a free people in a democratic society," McMurray added.[7] McCarthy did narrowly upset La Follette, but foiled the Democratic strategy by crushing McMurray in the November election, a national Republican landslide, winning 61 percent of the votes; McMurray carried only Dane County. The Progressive followers of La Follette did not forgive McMurray for his attacks on their leader.

McMurray had been an effective and highly popular lecturer in American politics courses in 1945–46, at a moment of desperate staff shortages; he was also an active participant in departmental affairs. Previously, after completing his Wisconsin doctorate in 1940, he had been an Extension lecturer in Milwaukee, then won election to the House of Representatives from a Milwaukee district in 1942. In 1944, he ran unsuccessfully as the Democratic challenger to incumbent Senator Alexander Wiley. Following this defeat, he had been named to a lecturer post in the department.

The department wished to make his appointment permanent, although agreeing to defer action until the outcome of the 1946 senatorial campaign was known. Immediately thereafter, the department proposed to give McMurray a regular tenured faculty appointment. Although Dean George Sellery and President Fred endorsed the department recommendation, the regents at their December 1946 meeting were reluctant, inviting the department to reconsider and to explore alternatives. The department vigorously reaffirmed its proposal, in a letter that found its way into the press. By the time of the January 1947 regent meeting, which rejected the McMurray candidacy, the issue generated heated press coverage, and national academic attention.

The reason advanced by the regents for the McMurray rejection was their assumption that he would use the faculty post as a mere trampoline for public office. The McMurray supporters indignantly rejoined that his intimate familiarity with the real world of politics was a qualification for teaching American government. As all regents at the time were Republican nominees, McMurray backers and part of the press, especially the *Madison Capitol-Times*, suspected political motives.[8] The department and many in the university community perceived the action as a violation of academic freedom.

In fact, there were possible grounds for regent reticence, though not the ones publicly stated. McMurray at the time had no significant publications, calling into question his qualification for a tenure appointment. Nor did his subsequent career at the University of News Mexico produce important scholarly work. Llewellyn Pfankuchen, then chair, years later confided that he believed regents probably had been right, though at the time he fought for the unanimous departmental recommendation. Such is also the verdict of Dean Sellery in his memoirs (see appendix 24). However, as reported in chapter 3, amongst the fallout from the McMurray affair was the departure of John Gaus for Harvard, a major blow to a department already decimated of its prewar cadres.[9]

The 1946 election marked the end of the Progressive Party. An era of Republican ascendancy, which began in 1938 with the defeat of Philip La Follette, continued until 1957 when William Proxmire won in a special election the Senate seat vacated by McCarthy's death.[10] None of the three Republican governors during the immediate postwar period were cut from the cloth of the arch-conservative Governor Julius Heil (1939–43). Walter Goodland (1943–47), Oscar Rennebohm (1947–51), Walter Kohler (1951–57), and Vernon Thomson (1957–59) all governed as moderates, as did Warren Knowles, Republican governor from 1965 to 1971.[11]

The national image of Wisconsin Republicans, in the early 1950s, was shaped by Senator McCarthy. He remained an obscure freshman senator until January 1950, when in Wheeling, West Virginia, he launched his campaign of allegations that an ever-shifting number of Communists had penetrated the upper reaches of the State Department and other sensitive government agencies. The anxieties of the Cold War provided fertile soil for the relentless McCarthy demagoguery. From 1950 until he overreached in 1954 by attacking the Army, McCarthyism was synonym for a tide of anti-Communist hysteria which swept the country.

Though the university might have seemed a tempting target, McCarthy refrained from including liberal or leftist Wisconsin faculty among his roster of alleged subversives. Those who recollect the period share the conclusion of Thompson: "there were too many loyal Badgers—and too many Republicans on the Board of Regents—to take the chance."[12] Had McCarthy chosen to attack the university, the department could well have provided a target: Henry Hart, who was appointed to the faculty while completing his doctorate in 1948. Hart had been a Communist Party member for 18 months around 1936, while working with the Tennessee Valley Authority (TVA).[13] He was summoned to appear before the House Un-American Activities Committee in 1939,[14] then subpoenaed in 1947 by the Senate Atomic Energy Committee chaired by the once redoubtable but aging Senator Kenneth McKellar of Tennessee. The real target for McKellar was former TVA head David Lilienthal, who had been nominated by President Harry

Truman to head the Atomic Energy Commission. Hart was implicated through a forged letter, purportedly signed by Hart and published in Knoxville newspapers, claiming that Lilienthal provided valuable cover for Communist activity in TVA. Hart, though acknowledging his brief party membership, effectively rebutted the false charges.[15]

The department rallied to his defense, and named him to the faculty at a moment when this background would have damaged his appointment prospects elsewhere in the anti-Communist paranoia then prevailing. However, Hart's brief party membership was never an issue within the university. Nor was it a basis for external attacks by McCarthy or others who mimicked his anti-Communist witch-hunt. The dark cloud of McCarthyism did cast its shadow on the university and the department in indirect ways, as it did the nation as a whole. But emeritus faculty who lived through the period agree that the inner workings of the department were not affected.

These were years of major change in Wisconsin state government: expansion, professionalization of the executive and legislature, reform on several fronts. Political scientist William Young played a key role in the design of several major policy innovations. Young, who joined the faculty in 1947, was recruited by Governor Rennebohm in 1949 to serve in his office as director of departmental research, a position transformed by Young into a role as executive assistant.[16] Among the reforms whose design he helped shape was the 1949 creation of a State Building Commission as a mechanism for facilitating crucially needed state infrastructure, which had been blocked by constitutional provisions prohibiting state borrowing for internal improvements. The solution for overcoming the huge backlog of state building needs was recourse to dummy corporations to engage in the borrowing on behalf of the State Building Commission (the state constitution was later amended to permit capital borrowing). This paved the way for a wave of campus construction, including a number of buildings heavily used for department classes (Humanities, Social Science, Commerce, Van Hise, Van Vleck).

William Young was also instrumental in reorganizing the university budgetary review process. Rather than have the Legislature scrutinizing individual faculty budget lines or numbers of typewriters purchased, Young developed a system for calculating per-student costs, which could be used as a formula for budgeting. At the same time, student fee income became incorporated into the budgeting process. The resulting enrollment-based funding helped the university meet the challenge of swelling student numbers from 1954 onward.

Other important reforms whose design Young helped fashion included consolidation of the public school districts, reducing the number from 5,000

(1,800 nonoperating) to 500. At the time, the dysfunctional school organization had as one serious consequence a ranking next to the bottom among states in percentage of pupils completing high school. In the process, the one-room schoolhouse disappeared (a sentimental icon for many), and a more effective program of state aids became possible. Other areas of reform in which Young was involved included welfare and provision for the mentally ill.[17]

Young continued in this role for the remainder of the Rennebohm governorship, then for most of the first year of the Kohler administration in 1951. The *Milwaukee Journal*, in a 1950 profile of Young, portrayed him as "the key man in the administration of Wisconsin's state government."[18] This account of his role, though fully accurate, was an embarrassment to Young in seeming to overshadow the governor, though Rennebohm never complained. Young's experience in the State Capitol permitted him to develop a network of relationships in both the executive and legislative branches that made him an invaluable negotiator on behalf of the university from 1953 till 1963 as budget director.

The election of Democrat Gaylord Nelson as governor in 1958 marked the opening of a new era of two-party competition in state politics. The Democratic Party had been a feeble competitor to the Republicans most of the time since the Civil War; prior to Nelson, the Democrats had won the governorship only once in the 20th century, when they were swept into office for one term on the coattails of the Roosevelt landslide in 1932. Paul Reinsch as Democratic Senate nominee in 1920 had finished a distant third, behind the Republican winner and an independent candidate. From 1923 to 1927, the Democrats held not a single State Senate seat, and only one in the Assembly. The party was a vestigial assemblage of patronage seekers, "Post Office Democrats" as they were scornfully known.

The party revival began in 1944, partly as part of a realignment caused by the demise of the Progressive Party. The tireless organizational efforts of Patrick J. Lucey built a party structure on the ground during the 1950s, and a new generation emerged amongst party leadership. Democrats began to be competitive in state and local elections, and by 1958 were able to win a Senate seat and an Assembly majority as well as the governorship. Thus Wisconsin took on its present profile as a state with pendulum swings in relative party dominance. A number of university and department faculty were active in the rejuvenated party; Gretchen Pfankuchen (wife of Llewellyn) nearly won a legislative seat in 1962 as Democratic candidate in a Madison west side district.[19] David Fellman was a frequent speech-writer for Nelson in his two gubernatorial terms (1959–63),[20] and for his Democratic successor, John Reynolds (1963–65).[21]

The administrations of Nelson and Reynolds were marked by bitter struggles over tax policy. By 1958, state budget analysts had concluded that the swiftly growing expenditure needs, especially for higher education, highways, and welfare, could not be met through existing revenue sources, mainly income and corporate taxes. A sales tax seemed the only solution. Nelson named a "blue ribbon" commission of university faculty to examine the issue, which identified the various options. Among the members of the committee was political scientist Clara Penniman; her major 1959 book, *State Income Tax Administration* (co-authored with Walter Heller), had just appeared, establishing her as a nationally respected specialist in the taxation field. After a bitter struggle, a limited sales tax was adopted in 1961. Reynolds campaigned in 1962 on a pledge to repeal the sales tax, but after election had to accept its permanence and even its expansion. Reynolds offered Penniman the position of commissioner of revenue in 1963, but she felt obliged to decline the invitation, because she had already agreed to chair the department beginning that year.[22]

The Republicans regained power under Warren Knowles in 1965, with a swing back to the Democrats in 1971 under Patrick Lucey. Among the staff assistants to Knowles was political science graduate student and future Vice President Richard Cheney (see appendix 25). An important initiative of Governor Knowles affecting the department was provision in the 1965–67 budget for establishment of a graduate training program for state public servants. The university, which had not requested this item, happily accepted the proposal. A committee co-chaired by political scientists Clara Penniman and James Donoghue was appointed to formulate a program, which in 1967 became the Center for the Study of Public Policy and Administration (CPPA, subsequently the La Follette School; see chapter 10 for details).[23]

The Democrats returned to state office in 1971, with the election of Lucey as governor (1971–77), followed by Martin Schreiber (1977–79). An intimate associate of and advisor to Governor Lucey was David Adamany, a 1967 Department Ph.D., and faculty member from 1972 to 1978. The role of Adamany in the university merger legislation will be discussed later in the chapter. One may note that Lucey inadvertently damaged the Adamany cause as a candidate for a public law position in the department by suggesting through intermediaries that he would be pleased by an Adamany appointment.[24] Lucey resigned as governor in 1977, to accept appointment by President Jimmy Carter as ambassador to Mexico.[25]

Changing Orientations in the Discipline

World War II was a watershed in the evolution of political science as a discipline, as well as for the university and the state. The field became far more self-conscious of its identity as a scientific discipline, and its theoretical grounding. The immersion in governmental realities of many political scientists through wartime service brought to postwar political analysis the empirical intuitions of the participant-observer. One result was more demanding research expectations in both concept and data; long gone were the days when Woodrow Wilson could write his 1885 classic, *Congressional Government*, without ever visiting Capitol Hill. The large contingent of outstanding emigre scholars brought a fresh infusion of continental intellectual culture, including Weberian political sociology, Marxist political economy, and a critique of positivism.[26]

Of the competing paradigms in the wake of war, what became known as the behavioral persuasion (or for its more ardent advocates "revolution") became the dominant orientation. In 1945, Social Science Research Council (SSRC) Director Pendleton Herring led a Committee on Political Behavior which took the first steps in defining a new approach. This became a standing committee in 1949, chaired by V. O. Key until 1953, then by David Truman until 1964. The SSRC committee played a catalytic role in defining the behavioral movement, whose seminal figures included Heinz Eulau, as well as Key and Truman. Major centers devoted to behavioral research were created at Michigan (Institute for Social Research) and Stanford (Center for Advanced Study in the Behavioral Sciences).

The characterization of the movement by a number of its participants as a revolution illuminates one motivating element: a rejection of the dominant orientation of earlier political science. Among the flaws cited were an excessive preoccupation with formal institutions of government, deficient theoretical awareness, and weak methodologies. Older scholarship was stigmatized as "traditional," producing only description. A crucial foundational text for the new political science was the 1953 David Easton work, *The Political System*, setting forth the premises of behavioralism. Discoverable uniformities in human behavior could be confirmed by empirical inquiry using rigorous methods in data collection, privileging quantification. Greater conceptual sophistication could be achieved by empirical theory construction and value-free inquiry.[27] The ultimate goal was supremely ambitious: a science of the entire political process. Gunnell provides a useful summary of the behavioral revolution:

> [Behavioralism] introduced an unprecedented metatheoretical consciousness about scientific theory and scientific explanation.

> Second, much of the energy of the behavioralists went into calling for, creating, and applying what they took to be theories. Third, there was a distinct emphasis on pure or theoretical science and a turning away from the idea of liberal reform and social control as the rationale of social science.[28]

During the 1950s and 1960s, many of the most influential works were inspired by the behavioral orientation, perhaps above all in the field of voting behavior where the survey method could be used with such fruitful effect. One of the most influential products of the movement was the conceptualization of the polity as a political system, importing an organic analogy. In its fully developed form, this became structural-functionalism which for a time shaped comparative politics (see chapter 6). The elevation of political system as master concept required banishing the core concern of early political science, the state. According to Easton, a critical contemporary mind "might conclude that the word ought to be abandoned entirely. . . . In fact, clarity of expression demands this abstinence."[29] Indeed, a withering away of the state was a noteworthy feature of most scholarship in this period.

In his 1961 American Political Science Association (APSA) presidential address, Robert Dahl—often associated with the behavioral orientation—suggested that the movement had so fully conquered that its particularity would disappear.

> . . . the behavioral mood, considered as a movement of protest . . . will gradually disappear. By this I mean only that it will slowly decay as a distinctive mood and outlook. For it will become . . . incorporated into the main body of the discipline. . . . As a separate, somewhat sectarian, slightly factional outlook it will be the first victim of its own triumph.[30]

In reality, behavioralism never enjoyed such complete hegemony. From the outset, there were many skeptics, reticent before some of its more ambitious claims of a coming scientific theory of the polity. Doubts were expressed as well about the possibility of a value-free science of politics. Among the most outspoken critics were some of the refugee scholars, whose intellectual formation was in a different cultural universe.[31]

The emergence in the later 1960s of a radicalized mood in the intellectual world in general, and the discipline in particular, placed the behavioral orientation on the defensive from another front. The cry arose from graduate students (see appendix 19) and many faculty, especially among the younger, that, far from being value-free, behavioralism was essentially conservative, impervious and irrelevant to the great crises of the day: the Vietnam War, the wave of racial riots in many of the great American cities. The citadels of the APSA were shaken by the 1967 emergence of the Caucus for a New Political Science, which challenged the leadership and demanded an activist stance for the discipline.

A turning point came at the 1969 annual meetings, when Easton used his presidential address to proclaim an end to the behavioral revolution, which had been "overtaken by the increasing social and political crises of our time." Easton, often seen as an early proponent of behavioralism, now called for a postbehavioral revolution, a future-oriented perspective that aimed at transcending rather than denying the behavioral past. He conceded the central critique of its adversaries, acknowledging that behavioralism "unwittingly purveys an ideology of social conservatism tempered by modest incremental change." Research needed to be relevant to social conditions, and could not be evaluatively neutral. The political scientist had an intellectual obligation to uphold humane values, and put knowledge to work for social betterment.[32] Karl Deutsch used the same platform two years later to confirm and extend the message, calling for a "big tent" inclusive discipline, renewing its vocation as a policy science committed to upholding democratic government.

Initially, the advent of the behavioral persuasion had only limited effects on the department; conversely none of the major figures who defined behavioralism were Wisconsin political scientists. The initial departmental declarations as to its concept of the discipline contain no premonition of new currents in the field. A War Manpower Commission had developed a definition of "the Profession of Political Science," which Chair Pfankuchen incorporated into his 1944–46 biennial report as an "authoritative and nationally recognized description of the field."[33] The commission distillation of the discipline declared:

> Political Science deals with what government does and how it does it—with function and institution. As the principal coordinating agency and process in society, the government transmits and interprets pressures, enacts laws, executes and judicially applies them. The political scientist prepares men to enter all branches of the public service; he studies, synthesizes, and recommends programs and policies applicable to this institution and to its function.

This synthesis reasonably captures a prewar mainstream view of political science, but contains no hint of the behavioral transformation about to emerge. Until the 1950s, there was little impetus from within the department to reconsider it.

Of the early postwar recruits, none could be classified as ardent behavioralists, though some—notably Ralph Huitt and Leon Epstein—were attuned to the new movement, and shared a number of its premises. Henry Hart in his later work became a convinced follower of a number of its axioms.[34] However, even without strong partisans within the walls, by the middle 1950s the department was clearly aware of the need to link itself to the emerging behavioral trends in the discipline. A Committee on the Future reporting to a department meeting on 24 February 1956 noted the inadequacy "in the area of statistical-psychological-'behavioral' research and teaching. . . . This type of analysis of political behavior was mentioned as one of the trends in this field."[35] Recruitment of a candidate in the "behavioral study of politics" was identified as the top priority. With some delay, faculty of such orientation did join the department: Harry Scoble in 1958 (departing in 1963), Lewis Froman in 1960 (departing in 1965), Rufus Browning (1961, departing in 1967), and Herbert Jacob (1962, departing in 1969). A permanent representative of the behavioral persuasion awaited the 1963 appointment of Jack Dennis (see his analysis of behavioralism in the department in chapter 12).

A measure of the slow move of the department into behavioral political science was its minimal role in the Social Systems Research Institute (SSRI). The SSRI was created in 1960, as an interdisciplinary body devoted to the promotion of Wisconsin social science research. A distinguished econometrician, Guy Orcutt, was recruited from Harvard to direct the SSRI, which was launched with high hopes. The ambition for the SSRI was to serve as an organizing stimulus for interdisciplinary social science research whose political science mode was behavioralism, and to raise external funds in its support. Though at one moment the SSRI claimed association of 67 faculty members from 11 departments, the financial resources failed to materialize, and SSRI never took off. In 1967, Orcutt abandoned hope in SSRI, and left for the World Bank.[36]

In chapter 12, Dennis reflects on some reasons for the limits on departmental commitment to the behavioral orientation. At the moment of the movement's maximal impact on the discipline, the most ardent Wisconsin advocates were junior faculty, several of whom stayed only briefly. As well, the size and strength of comparative politics, less influenced by behavioralism than the American field, partly explains the slow absorption of the orientation.

Interestingly, neither the delay in internalizing behavioralist currents, nor the almost total postwar turnover in personnel, to which I turn next, appeared to affect departmental prestige. Between 1945 and 1975, departmental rankings (see appendix 12) were published on four occasions, 1957 (Kenniston), 1963 (Somit and Tannenhaus), 1964 (Cartter), and 1975–76 (Roettger).[37] Department reputation exhibited a remarkable stability: eighth in 1957, tied for eighth in 1963, tied for seventh in 1964, and eighth in 1975. The 1957 status is especially intriguing; though some of the postwar additions to the department, such as Leon Epstein, Ralph Huitt, and John Armstrong, were beginning to win national recognition, they were still early in their careers. The only more senior scholars of national rank were James McCamy, whose prize-winning 1950 book, *The Administration of American Foreign Affairs*, won high praise, and David Fellman, already known for his writings on civil liberties (though his first major book was published only in 1957). The explanation may be a repetition of the 1925 pattern analyzed in chapter 3, where the shadow effect of earlier distinction played some part in the high ranking. By 1963 the ranking seems solidly grounded, as several of the postwar generation had built national reputations. The 1962 addition of Austin Ranney solidified the department's standing, further enhanced by senior recruits Murray Edelman (1966), Matthew Holden (1969), and Barbara Hinckley (1972).

One striking feature of the 1963 Somit and Tannenhaus ranking emerges from their analysis of the methodological predispositions of those contributing to the evaluations. Somit and Tannenhaus identified among their respondents a number who were either strongly pro-behavioralism or markedly hostile to it. Far more than any other top ten institution, outliers who were anti-behavioralists gave Wisconsin especially high ratings, with correspondingly weak backing from strong behavioralists.[38] Possibly the high rankings partly reflected sheer productivity across the board; a 1979 study of publication volume ranked Wisconsin seventh.[39] Moreover, the perceived strength of the department was not an artifact of star power. Though Frederic Ogg was listed as one of the top ten most important contributors for the prewar period, no Wisconsin political scientists figured among the ten most influential for 1945 to 1960, or 1960 to 1970.[40]

Although the department was slow to embrace behavioralism as a staffing priority, there was no pronounced opposition to seeking recruits with such a specialization. At the time, Yale and Northwestern were the leading departments fostering a behavioral orientation in graduate training.[41] Harry Scoble (1958), Bernard Cohen (1959), Rufus Browning (1961), and Herbert Jacob (1962) all had Yale doctorates, and Lewis Froman (1960) came from Northwestern. Perhaps the most skeptical toward the behavioral orientation were David Fellman and John Armstrong; the former bemoaned in his oral history what he perceived as the growing illegibility of the *American Political Science Review* and doubtful achievements of quantifiers, and the latter expressed reservations in his memoir about "extreme behavioralists" in some parts of the American field.[42] In some other departments at the time, the most outspoken opposition to the positivism associated with behavioralism came from political philosophy scholars such as Leo Strauss, or Sheldon Wolin at the University of California-Berkeley; this subfield did not yet exist at Wisconsin. Perhaps the Dahl presidential address cited above best characterizes the quiet assimilation of behavioralism into the department. Particularly in the American field, a substantial number of younger faculty identified to varying degrees with the behavioral orientation. This, however, flowed into the consensual currents that had become a hallmark of departmental culture, without coalescing into factional conflict.

Remaking the Department: Turnover and Expansion

Chapter 3 closed with a summary of the several departures and Ogg retirement which decimated the department at the close of World War II. By 1948, only Llewellyn Pfankuchen and John Salter of the prewar faculty remained. The financial circumstances of the university limited rebuilding by senior recruitment at that time. Of the fourteen faculty recruited in the first postwar decade, from 1945 to 1955, nine pursued their entire careers with the department (David Fellman, James McCamy, and William Young, added in 1947; James Donoghue, Leon Epstein, and Henry Hart in 1948; Ralph Huitt in 1949; Clara Penniman in 1953; and John Armstrong in 1954). Of this list, Donoghue, who for years directed the Extension Institute for Governmental Affairs, then still linked to the department, was visible mainly at the state level. Young, whose remarkable accomplishments in the state policy sphere were noted earlier in the chapter, served as department chair from 1952 to 1960, budget director for the university from 1953 to 1963, then created and directed the Center for Development for the balance of his career; he also assured several additional editions of the storied Ogg & Ray American government text, following the 1951 death of Ogg. All the others, however, achieved national distinction in their specializations. By the mid-1950s, the department had regained its strength under a new generation of postwar leadership.

In rebuilding the department, a consensus took hold that preservation of departmental standing required a firm commitment to a research expectation for promotion and merit salary increases. This required some painful decisions in the 1950s, in particular the nonrenewal of John Thomson in 1957. Thomson was a very popular undergraduate teacher, and well connected in the faculty community.[43] Research expectations could not yet be as high as they later became; funding for research internally was all but inexistent until the Graduate School Research Committee opened to social science in the later 1950s, and external funds were much scarcer than they became by the 1960s. But the day when the department could unanimously recommend McMurray for a tenure appointment, with no publications to his record, was now past.

When Epstein became chair in 1960, the pace of expansion quickened. Three new junior appointments were made in 1961, four in 1962, and four in 1963. In addition, in 1962 Epstein recruited an established star in the American (and behavioralist) field, Austin Ranney. Although only Leon Lindberg of the 1961 and 1962 recruiting classes gave extended service to the department, the 1963 cohort (Jack Dennis, Joel Grossman, David Tarr, and Crawford Young) proved of exceptional durability. All four remained at Wisconsin until their retirements; between 1969 and 1987, the recruiting class of 1963 chaired the department for all but three years (Young from 1969 to 1972, then again from 1984 to 1987; Tarr from 1972 to 1975; Grossman from 1975 to 1978; and Dennis from 1978 to 1981). In 1945–46, the department had merely nine faculty. A decade later, the figure had slowly increased to 14. By 1965–66, the effects of expansion were clearly visible; the faculty had more than doubled to 31. In 1975–76 the roster count was 37; thereafter it fluctuated, from a low of 34 in 1983–84 (following a university budget crisis) to a peak of 45 in 1994–95,[44] averaging around 40.

Not all subfields benefited equally from expansion. The greatest number of additions were in the American and comparative politics areas (for detail, see chapters 6 and 9). As chapter 8 argues, the accidental pattern of international relations courses being covered mainly by specialists in American foreign policy (Bernard Cohen, James McCamy, David Tarr), international law (Pfankuchen), or comparative politics in retrospect inadvertently impeded development of a distinctive international relations subfield. Also, those appointments made before 1976 of faculty whose primary specialization was international relations (Constantine Menges in 1964, David Kay in 1966, Ellen Seidensticker in 1975) served relatively briefly in the department.

Political theory for the first time became staffed by specialists with the 1959 appointment of Thomas Thorson; earlier most faculty were presumed capable of teaching theory courses (see chapter 7). The 1956 committee on the Future chose not to make recruiting in the theory field a priority. The Committee reasoned that theory was a product of government at work in society, and it was thus "customary to have the subject taught in a variety of courses by a variety of political scientists." Further, the committee argued, a philosophy specialist would not feel at home, and undergraduates could find such courses in other departments, such as philosophy. After all, ran the conclusion, they know of no political science department which was really strong in "philosophic concerns."[45] These objections dissolved during the 1960s. Though Hannah Pitkin, a theorist recruited in 1964, departed in 1966, as did Thorson, with the 1967 appointment of Booth Fowler and Donald Hanson, theory acquired a permanent rooting in department staffing.[46]

Adaptations to Expansion

With a department by 1975 more than four times its 1945 faculty strength, a number of organizational adjustments became necessary. The first major alteration in department mores was the introduction of a rotational chair. Although Pfankuchen and McCamy did not seek extended tenure as chair, William Young served for eight years. The conscious choice of Epstein to limit his tenure to a three-year term (though he could easily have been elected for a more extended period) set a firm precedent. Across the campus as well, rotation in department leadership was becoming an expectation. By the end of the 1960s, the precedent was irrevocably established.

Particularly in the 1960s, the rapid pace of expansion created an unusual demographic pyramid, with the executive committee (tenured ranks) constituting less than half the total faculty (14 of 31 in 1965). In earlier periods, at any given moment there would be only a tiny handful of assistant professors. Some generational tensions were implicit in this unusual bulge in the junior ranks. One consequence was turning to a younger generation for leadership; Crawford Young became chair in 1969 only six years after completion of his doctorate, followed by Tarr in 1972 of the same age set.[47]

Another product of the expansion years, and of a period in the 1960s when output of doctorates fell behind market demand for new faculty, was a faster pace of promotion. Elevation to tenure rank after three probationary years became possible (Charles Anderson, David Tarr, Crawford Young, James Scott), and most who ultimately earned tenure in these years did not linger in assistant professor rank for the full six years. The counterpart to this market response was that tenure expectations were not as stringent as they became in later decades. Nor was scrutiny as close at higher levels, by the divisional committee and dean; the tenure promotion recommendation for Tarr in 1966 discovered in the department files was only two pages, in sharp contrast to the bulging documents to justify tenure promotion currently required.

A different form of adjustment to market pressures came in a change in the teaching load in 1969, negotiated by Chair Bernard Cohen. The three-course-per-semester load became an increasing recruiting handicap, as most leading institutions expected two courses per term. The formula negotiated with Letters and Science (L&S) Dean Epstein called for an increase in the number of credit hours per undergraduate course from three to four; thus, the total number of credit hours per faculty member changed only marginally. The "fourth hour" was intended to be either a discussion session, or some other form of contact in lieu of a fourth lecture. The periodic legislative curiosity about faculty teaching loads required that some defensible explanation of the fourth hour be sustained.

A striking example of the tensions generated by expansion is provided by an unusual proposal developed by McCamy in January 1963. Competitive pressures produced a sharp increase in the entry-level stipends ($8,000 by 1963), causing pronounced salary compression at senior levels. McCamy evidently devoted much time and thought to his elaborate scheme, whose purpose was to restore a reasonable salary range and appropriate incentives for senior faculty. His proposal was framed to be budget-neutral, and thus in his view administratively feasible. The improved incentive structure consisted of a teaching load limited to one graduate and one undergraduate course each semester, a year of guaranteed research time every third year, and salary improvements for existing meritorious faculty. To achieve these ends without budgetary increases, McCamy proposed halting almost all new recruitment, cutting back the undergraduate curriculum to one basic course in each subfield (which would provide enough credits for the major), and eliminating the staff-intensive, giant introductory American government course. Needless to say, so far-reaching a proposal failed to gain traction within the department; the minutes of 25 January 1963 laconically note that the department "discussed James McCamy's proposals relating to salaries, staffing and research time." Epstein, then chair, has no recollection of the proposal, which evidently found its way quietly into the archives.[48] However unrealistic, the proposal bears witness to discontent bubbling beneath the surface, generated in part by rapid expansion.

Until the mid-1960s, the department administrative infrastructure consisted of only the department chair and department secretary, aided by a handful of secretarial staff. The tension generated by greater faculty, graduate, and undergraduate numbers forced changes on several fronts. The first adjustments came during the Penniman years as chair (1963–66), involving undergraduate advising and graduate student placement.

Until 1964, undergraduate advising for political science majors was carried out entirely by faculty, each being assigned a number of advisees. Well into the 1950s, this system functioned well; those like Epstein who both remembered this advising pattern as a prewar undergraduate, and later as a faculty member, attest to the effectiveness of this service at that time. However, by the 1960s undergraduate advising was eroded on two fronts: the sheer numbers of students on the one hand, and the influx of new junior faculty not yet familiar enough with the campus or the curriculum to be effective advisors.[49] Students found ways of evading the requirement that registration forms bear the signature of the advisor, presumably by simply forging them.

To repair a system in shambles, Penniman created the position of undergraduate advisor, an innovation which soon spread to other large departments. The first incumbents were faculty spouses with an academic background and familiarity with the university. Over time, recruitment to this post extended to a broader pool. Ann Nelson (1965–70) gave initial definition to the position, but its institutionalization as a full-time function owes to Ernestine Vanderlin, who served for two decades (1971–90) (see appendix 15). At the graduate level, Penniman also innovated, delegating the placement function to a faculty member.

When Crawford Young became chair in 1969, while also serving as associate dean of the Graduate School, he proposed that an associate chair be established, with responsibility for the graduate program; Melvin Croan was the first incumbent.[50] Such an office was a novelty at the time, but over time became a normal component for larger departments across the university. A member of the office staff became designated as graduate program assistant, a position that soon became an indispensable service function.

Since 1917, the department had been housed on two floors of South Hall for most of the period, squeezed between the L&S offices and journalism and mass communication. The completion of several new campus buildings, including the Social Science Building, permitted a move to more spacious accommodations. Although some in the department hoped for inclusion in the Social Science Building completed in 1962,[51] in the end this was reserved for economics, sociology, and anthropology. Instead, when Van Vleck Hall became available for the previous North Hall occupant, mathematics, the department in late 1963 moved to its present location. The historic charms and ample space of North Hall soon won over whatever doubters remained, especially after the building was air-conditioned in 1972, and some of the dysfunctions of the newer campus buildings became apparent over time. As the oldest building on campus, North Hall had an unusually rich history. The board of regents minutes of 7 January 1966 record its placement on the National Register of Historic Places. The minutes noted that this recognition did not come at the request of the university, but that it was a great honor; relatively few such sites are located at universities (see appendix 23).

Finally, expansion compelled a formalization of many practices and procedures. Both in the university at large and at the department level, greater size and the rapid influx of new faculty compelled a more thorough codification of rules. In 1963, after completing a term as University Committee chair, David Fellman wrote President Harrington expressing frustration at the lack of any organized compilation of university rules; the faculty and administration somehow operated on the basis of what was known as the Red Book, a potpourri of sometimes contradictory regent resolutions and faculty decisions adopted over the years. Harrington rewarded Fellman for his identification of an urgent need by appointing him chair of a small group which over the next six years engaged in the first systematic codification.[52] The restatement and modernization of .the rules created a far more thorough compilation of regulations relating to faculty status and department procedures, which necessarily produced a marked formalization of university process, a more rule-bound university than had ever existed in the past. The rules which Fellman and his colleagues drafted for approval by the faculty, subsequently labeled *Faculty Policies and Procedures*, became a veritable constitutional document. The new university legislation adopted in implementation of the 1971 merger required further adaptations, and there have been subsequent updatings, most recently in the early 1990s. Penniman recalls that in her first years in the department all decisions on hiring and promotion were taken by informal consensus; there were never formal votes.[53] By the end of this era, a recorded vote was mandatory on personnel issues.

Curricular Changes

In the postwar years, important changes took place at both the undergraduate and graduate levels. A striking development was the steady increase in enrollments; by 2004 political science was the largest major in L&S, and since the 1970s it has consistently been one of the top two or three. In 1952, by contrast, political science had only 147 majors, ranking far behind English, with 348, and trailing history (242), sociology (190), zoology (162), and speech

(154).[54] A number of factors explain this development, including the rising attraction of law school, the major's lack of extensive quantitative requirements, and the appeal of a public service career. Among the explanations, however, figure a flexible and attractive set of offerings, and a positive teaching reputation of department faculty; a 2004 analysis of overall course evaluations over the previous 10 years yielded an average score of 4.42 on a five-point scale.[55] In the 1960s, department faculty won university teaching awards in 5 of the 10 years (Thomas Thorson, Charles Anderson, Herbert Jacob, Kenneth Dolbeare, Booth Fowler); until 1963 there were only two such awards each year, a number that increased only slightly over the decade (see appendix 11).

A much larger faculty made possible a broader range of specialized courses, catering to a wide variety of interests. As well, more extensive staffing meant that faculty could teach more courses within their specialization; in prewar years, instructors needed to maintain a diverse teaching portfolio. Undergraduate instruction remained an important commitment for most faculty. When the department shifted from a three- to two-course teaching load, a rule was established requiring that, of the four yearly courses, only one could normally be a graduate offering, and one should be a large introductory course.[56]

At the graduate level, there was a de-emphasis of the M.A. degree by the 1960s. As a preparation for public service, the departmental M.A. was supplanted from 1967 by the degree awarded by the CPPA. The M.A. thesis requirement was abandoned in the mid-1960s.[57] Earlier, this thesis had been important in providing guidance to graduate candidates as to prospects for successful completion of a doctorate. However, the heavy burdens on faculty for supervising M.A. thesis work when graduate enrollments rose rapidly by the 1960s made the requirement impossible to sustain. In its place, a seminar paper was required as part of an oral examination to determine whether the candidate could continue.

At the end of the 1960s, the Graduate School, responding to pressures from a number of departments, ended the requirement of two foreign languages. In practice, the requirement—a feared obstacle in prewar oral histories—had become so minimal that surveys showed that few actually achieved a usable level of proficiency for research purposes. Further, survey data also demonstrated that in many fields scholars never had occasion to use a foreign language; in political science, Americanists had no real need for mastery of other languages. Definition of a language requirement was delegated to departments; in turn, the department attributed this prerogative to subfields and individual faculty. The result was the retention of language requirements only in most comparative politics fields, no longer the traditional French and German but those languages necessary for research in the region of specialization. The increased importance of methodological skills, quantitative and other, forced such issues of rational priorities of doctoral training needs onto the agenda.

Before World War II, graduate students enrolled in the courses in the upper-level undergraduate curriculum; only a couple of seminars were available for graduate students. Gradually beginning in the 1950s, a separate graduate curriculum emerged. The aspiration was to provide core graduate courses in the major subfields, and to pair these offerings with research seminars in the student's field of concentration.

The prewar structure of preliminary examinations remained intact until the mid-1960s. The requirements were undeniably rigorous: four, six-hour written examinations, all of which had to be taken within the same compressed time frame of little more than a week. By the later 1960s, preliminary examinations were a chronic subject of graduate student friction and agitation. In incremental steps, the scope of the examination burden was reduced: from four fields to three, with a "write-off" by two graduate courses; from six hours to four, with the option of creating one specially tailored field. Beyond graduate student discontent, aggressively expressed in the radicalized mood of the late 1960s, rethinking of preliminary examination requirements was also driven by departmental participation in a major Ford Foundation program whose funding was intended to facilitate a norm of completion of doctoral work in four years (or five, if extended overseas research was required). Preliminary examinations were a crucial choke point which needed attention. As well, the deepening specialization characteristic of the discipline was in tension with the desirability of a broad sweep of knowledge, which the earlier preliminary examination requirements were designed to encourage.

Finally, exploding graduate enrollments by the later 1960s, partly driven by the deepening unpopularity of the Vietnam War and attendant desire for student deferments, compelled the department to impose more restrictive admission policies. Until the 1960s, the key requirement was a 3.0 undergraduate grade point average, although any hope of a first-year fellowship necessitated a more competitive record. In 1968, this relatively open admission policy produced an entering class of 75, which overwhelmed department capacities for supervision and course staffing. For the first time, a quantitative target was set in 1969, at 50, in the event 60 matriculated. By 1970, new factors entered the equation. Studies of demographic trends in production of doctorates and prospective student enrollments showed that the era of rapid expansion of the latter would soon end, and that the market scarcity of new doctorates in the

1960s was turning into a Ph.D. glut.[58] In the case of political science, more doctorates were awarded nationally between 1960 and 1970 (3,836) than in the entire period between the first political science Ph.D. in 1880 and 1960 (3,700).[59] For the department, the output in the decade of the 1960s matched the total between 1896 and 1948. By 1970, the department was beginning to face some difficulties in placing the doctoral class for the first time in many years. Thus a more restrictive target for the entering graduate class was set, aiming at a cohort of 30–35.

Diversity

The early generation of department faculty came from relatively homogeneous backgrounds. Of those for whom we have background information, most came from midwestern or upper New York small-town or rural origins. None to our knowledge came from wealthy families. All but a handful of German descent bear names of English or Scottish resonance.[60]

The first to break this mold was William Ebenstein, a young member of the distinguished generation of mostly Jewish refugee scholars who fled Nazism. He had an advanced degree from the University of Vienna, but enrolled as a doctoral candidate in the department, completing his Ph.D. in 1938. He was immediately hired, becoming the first Jewish member of the faculty. Ebenstein remained on the faculty through the war years, departing for Princeton in 1946; at the time, Ebenstein was a rising star in the discipline.

In contrast to Ivy League universities, Wisconsin had never restricted Jewish student enrollment. However, Cronon and Jenkins observe that the strict curbs on out-of-state enrollment at the time of the veteran deluge immediately following World War II gave rise to whispered charges of anti-Semitism, which they regard as untrue.[61] Similar suspicions arose in the later 1960s when some members of the State Legislature, infuriated by the perceived excesses of the student protest movement, suggested similar restrictions.

By the postwar years, Jews on the faculty ceased to be a rarity. In political science, three of the critical postwar additions to a rejuvenated department were Jewish: David Fellman in 1947, Leon Epstein in 1948, and Bernard Cohen in 1959.[62] A number were to follow in subsequent years, superfluous to identify. Those with long departmental memories cannot recall any occasion when Jewish identity was ever a publicly or privately discussed issue in personnel policy.

However, this was not be taken for granted in 1945. Prior to his Wisconsin appointment, Fellman recollects a hostile chair at Nebraska and exceedingly slow promotions, for which he suspected religious bias.[63] Epstein in his oral history recalls that entering academic life "was not an easy decision for a Jew to make. There was a feeling, that in addition to the other constraints of the job market, that it might be harder for a Jew to get a job. I am not sure of how much evidence there was of overt discrimination, there must have been some." In making up his mind, Epstein contacted one of his undergraduate teachers, Selig Perlman in economics:

> . . . when I was trying to make up my mind, while still in Britain in the army. . . I remember writing Perlman about this; and telling him that in trying to make up my mind, I wondered whether I should take this into consideration though I was not a person who had felt in my life discriminated against. . . .

Perlman replied that there might be some disadvantage, but not an insuperable one that should be a reason for avoiding an academic career. Perlman added that he thought Epstein "had some advantage in being a small town Jew and somehow might look different."[64] Perlman believed himself a victim of anti-Semitism during his academic career at Wisconsin.[65]

On another dimension of diversity, John Armstrong in his memoir makes the arresting statement that he believed himself to be the first Catholic appointment in the social sciences at the time of his recruitment in 1954. Intrigued by this claim, we have pursued the issue with Armstrong, and parsed earlier faculty rosters. Although we lack information on religious affiliation of most earlier faculty, the predominance of English and Scottish names of unlikely Catholic antecedents makes the Armstrong thesis as it applies to the department possible, though not proven. More certain is that until the 1950s, undercurrents of anti-Catholic sentiment still lingered in some nooks and crannies of the university. Armstrong recalls that some older faculty had "a scornful attitude toward Catholicism," and that he overheard one remarking that "an excellent Catholic Ph.D. candidate would 'get over that religion.'"[66]

Women were also scarce in academic ranks until the 1960s. Clara Penniman was the first female department faculty member, appointed in 1953. From a modest family background in a small Wisconsin town, following high school she entered the state civil service in 1937. After a decade of state service, she decided to seek a higher education, completing a B.A. and M.A. at Wisconsin. Following doctoral study at Minnesota, she joined the Wisconsin faculty in 1953 with degree nearly in hand; she managed to progress from college entry to doctorate in only six years. She recalls that, at the time of her graduate study, there were only a couple of other women doctoral candidates at both Wisconsin and Minnesota. Only one woman completed a department doctorate before World War II, and merely four between 1945 and 1960 (see appendix 17).

At the time Penniman was seeking an academic position, she recollects the response received by one of her mentors who recommended her to the University of New Hampshire:

> I have your letter recommending Miss Penniman for this position. Unfortunately, we here at New Hampshire have never heard of women's emancipation, and (being hard of hearing) we couldn't consider a women for our position. Somehow, there is a feeling here that women get married. Now, it's true that men also get married, but this inconsistency has never affected our policies.[67]

At the time of the Penniman appointment, women were still rare in the Wisconsin faculty ranks, located mostly in English and the language departments. Large departments such as history, Penniman noted, were years away from adding their first woman, and still were "notorious" for their attitudes in this domain. She points out that she did not belong to the generation of "ardent feminists," and never felt handicapped by her gender in her own career; she reached full professor rank seven years after her appointment, and won election as chair within a decade.[68] She credits William Young in particular for a supportive role; he had been her undergraduate advisor, and hired her as an assistant while he worked in the governor's office. She recalls a conversation during her student years when Young urged her to ask for whatever she needed, even if it were contrary to university rules. Rules are made for the norm, he said, "but you are the kind of person for whom an exception is in order."[69]

However, academic opportunity for women on any scale began only in the 1960s. More than a decade passed before another woman joined the department faculty (Hannah Pitkin in 1964, departing 1966). Barbara Hinckley, hired in 1972, was the next woman with extended service in the department (till 1988). Female graduate numbers began to grow substantially only in the 1960s (see the recollections of Barbara McClennan and Margaret Turner in appendix 26), and not till 1975 did recruitment of women faculty become frequent.

Awareness of a need to extend diversity on the racial front did not emerge until the aftermath of the 1968 assassination of Martin Luther King. A militant black student movement took form later that year, culminating in a February 1969 strike discussed later in the chapter. Among the "non-negotiable demands" was hiring of African-American faculty, all but absent from the instructional corps. A sensed urgency of taking some steps to meet the concerns expressed by the strike organizers elevated recruitment of black faculty to a priority. Thus the climate was propitious for the department to pursue in 1969 a highly regarded African-American scholar, Matthew Holden, then at Wayne State.

As well, beginning in 1969, "affirmative action" became a conscious objective in the graduate program. There had been a couple of African-American graduate students in earlier years, but none had completed a degree. The Graduate School at this time received a major grant from the Danforth Foundation in support of African-American doctoral training, which phased into the Advanced Opportunity Program that still continues, extended to other targeted racial minorities. A modest influx of African-American graduate students began in 1969; the first to complete his doctorate was Edmond Keller in 1974. Keller went on to a distinguished academic career at Indiana University, University of California–Santa Barbara, and UCLA; in the early 1980s the department made an unsuccessful effort to recruit him at a senior rank (see his recollections of graduate student life in appendix 26).

Linkages

Extension instruction had always figured amongst the roster of departmental responsibilities. Chapter 3 records the desire of the department, by the time of World War II, to disengage from direct Extension responsibilities. Increasingly, the ties became more tenuous; separation became all but total with the reorganization of Extension by President Harrington in 1964. Links continued primarily through two important Extension leaders with departmental ties.

The first, Lorentz Adolfson, completed a 1942 Wisconsin dissertation on the office of the county clerk. Though he served on the department faculty from 1942 to 1944, his specialization pointed to Extension. In 1944, he left the department to become dean of University Extension. Under his leadership, what had begun as Extension centers in various midsize communities were transformed into two-year University Centers, offering credit instruction to help meet the postwar enrollment boom; center graduates could transfer to Madison in their junior year. Initially the centers were to operate under the loose tutelage of Madison departments, which helped with screening personnel and reviewing curricula; political science was among the 23 university departments involved, a role that had ended by the 1960s. Adolfson was one of four finalists for the presidency in 1958, when Elvehjem was named.[70] However, he was moved from Extension by Harrington to become chancellor of a University Center System in 1964.[71]

The other postwar connecting link with the extension mission was James Donoghue (1948–84), the last member of the department with primarily Extension responsibilities. Under Donoghue's leadership, a Bureau of Governmental Affairs was launched in 1948, erected on the memory of a Municipal Information Bureau, which operated from 1909 until about 1930, providing assistance to local governments. The department, according to the bureau, "provided support and advice, but had no formal responsibility for the Bureau." In 1964, the organization was reframed as the Institute of Governmental Affairs.[72] Under the direction of Donoghue and his successor Edward Schten, a 1959 Wisconsin doctorate, for a number of years the institute had an active program of short courses for county officials and other public servants, applied research for governmental units, and advisory services. During the 1970s it had over 30 staff. By the 1980s, many of its functions became absorbed by the agencies themselves, and it shrank back to a tiny remnant.[73] Donoghue for many years contributed to the biannual *State of Wisconsin Blue Book*, and was a tireless compiler and analyst of Wisconsin electoral data.

For some years following the creation of the University of Wisconsin–Milwaukee (UWM), the department played a part in helping its Milwaukee counterpart establish personnel practices and quality control. This task was made delicate by the assimilation into UWM of the staff of the former Milwaukee State Teachers College, tenured under the rules of a different institutional mission. By the mid-1960s, the tutelary role had diminished to an annual dinner with UWM political science faculty, at some restaurant midway between the two cities. By 1970 this tradition had ceased as well.

A final linkage deserving mention extended overseas. At the initiative of Chair Cohen, an annual exchange was established with the counterpart department at the University of Essex, in the United Kingdom. Although the Essex department was in its infancy when the exchange began, it swiftly rose to prominence in Britain. At first the costs not covered by the simple exchange of personnel were provided by the Graduate School; at this point the exchange at times included graduate students as well as one faculty member in each direction. When the funding support ended, the practical difficulties posed by salary-level differentials and health insurance costs made the exchange impossible to sustain; as well, the candidates for the exchange were thinning out. But for nearly two decades it brought a steady flow of eminent British scholars to the department, and the opportunity for a number of Madison faculty to spend a year overseas. One of the Essex visitors, Graham Wilson, became a permanent member of the Wisconsin faculty in 1984, and chair in 2004 (see appendix 22).

Some Major Figures

The careers and intellectual portraits of many of the leading faculty of this period are profiled in chapters 6 to 11, or elsewhere in this chapter. For career profiles of John Armstrong, Leon Epstein, Charles Anderson, Crawford Young, and James Scott, see chapter 6; William Young and Clara Penniman are covered elsewhere in this chapter, and in chapter 10. David Adamany is briefly covered at the close of this chapter. In the paragraphs which follow, I will examine the careers of faculty whose department services fell mainly in this period.

The first postwar chair (1944–48) was Llewellyn Pfankuchen, whose prewar phase is described in chapter 3. His tenure as chair included the tumultuous and traumatic period in 1946–47 of the McMurray affair, examined earlier. By the time he stepped down in 1948, some degree of stability had returned. Before the war, he had taught courses in constitutional and international law, and had some interest in rural local government; chapter 3 notes his year of service with the Department of Agriculture, arranged by John Gaus. The most dramatic episode in his professional life was the opportunity to participate as an international law specialist on the American delegation to the spring 1945 San Francisco conference, which drafted the United Nations (UN) Charter. This experience pushed him more completely into the orbit of international relations, and made him a tireless advocate of the UN on campus and in lectures around the state. For many years he taught the introductory course in international relations.

In the early postwar years, Pfankuchen played a significant role in university affairs, serving on two of the most powerful (and time-consuming) faculty committees, the University Committee (1945–48) and the Social Studies Divisional Committee (1944–49). He long helped direct the international relations major, and in the late 1960s organized, jointly with UWM, a summer seminar on the UN in New York, which continued annually long after his retirement. His major publication, *A Documentary Textbook in International Law*, appeared in 1940. Through the 1950s, he and a geography colleague,

Richard Hartshorne, worked on a text on the geopolitics of international relations, which was never completed. Until his retirement in 1972, he maintained the course in international law which dates back to John B. Parkinson; this offering then (to his regret) disappeared from the department curriculum.

Earlier in the chapter, the signal importance of the McCamy and Fellman appointments was stressed. At the time of his appointment, McCamy enjoyed a reputation built upon influential positions during the war years, which also shaped much of his research career. Of Texas antecedents, he earned his doctorate at Chicago in 1938. He was a top aide to Henry Wallace in the Department of Agriculture (which probably brought him into contact with Gaus), and a manager of the lend-lease program and postwar reconstruction funding in Europe. He was one of the drafters of the International Trade Organization charter, then had a top post in the occupation administration in Austria.

The year after arriving in Madison, he became department chair, a post he skillfully held for four years. His prizewinning 1950 book on the administration of foreign policy established his reputation; through the 1950s, assuming salary is a measure, he was regarded as the senior member of the department in national standing. He became one of the early specialists in the emerging field of science and government, publishing an influential book on this subject in 1960, *Science and Public Administration.* He was especially close to Gaus, though they overlapped on the faculty for only one year; the University Archives contain an extended correspondence between them, and McCamy was invited to offer a memorial speech at the Gaus funeral in 1969.

David Fellman grew up in Omaha, where his immigrant father managed a small grocery. His father had fled the Russian Empire in 1905 to avoid conscription for the Russo-Japanese war, and wound up in Omaha where a pair of uncles were located. A deeply religious man, the father was reluctant to see young David attend university, fearing an erosion of religious commitment. Fellman worked his way through the University of Nebraska teaching in Hebrew school. After a brief flirtation with law school, Fellman completed a political science M.A. at Nebraska in 1930; his department kept him on as an instructor. The following year, he won a fellowship at Yale, completing his doctorate in 1934.[74] He returned to Nebraska as a faculty member, but progressed slowly; after 13 years, Fellman was only an associate professor. Thus the Wisconsin invitation in 1947 was a welcome opportunity; Harold Stoke, a former Nebraska colleague and Graduate School assistant dean during the war years, had arranged a visiting appointment in Madison for Fellman in 1942, so his name came at once to mind when a permanent vacancy occurred in public law.[75]

Fellman was already known for his work in the area of civil rights. For a number of years, he contributed to the *American Political Science Review* an annual review of important developments in constitutional law, which to his dismay the *Review* discontinued after 1961. From 1957 a rapid flow of influential Fellman books began: *The Censorship of Books* (1957), *The Defendants Rights* (1958), *The Limits of Freedom* (1959), *The Constitutional Rights of Association* (1963), and *Religion in American Public Law* (1965). This remarkable burst of scholarship qualified Fellman for one of the first rounds of Vilas professorships, the most prestigious chair awarded by the university.[76]

Fellman was a major campus figure. Beyond his codification of university regulations noted above, he served on the University Committee, was first chair of the Committee on Faculty Rights and Responsibilities, and for many years led the Honorary Degrees Committee. In national professional life, he was active in the leadership of the American Association of University Professors (AAUP), particularly in the work of Committee A on Academic Freedom and Tenure, and served as AAUP president from 1965 to 1967. He was also the first editor of what is now the *American Journal of Political Science*.

Another memorable Fellman role was his leadership of a campaign to eliminate boxing as a university sport. A member of the Wisconsin boxing team received a fatal injury in the ring. Fellman knew the young man, who was a close friend of his daughter; this led him to organize a Faculty Senate move to abolish the sport. His campaign was successful, and boxing was dropped from the Athletic Department roster of intercollegiate teams.[77]

Ralph Huitt, recruited in 1949, came from a comparably modest background. He grew up in Beaumont, Texas, attending a small nearby college (Southwestern). After his 1934 graduation, he worked for eight years as a YMCA secretary, before a brief stint teaching at Lamar College in Beaumont, then military service. Not till 1946, at the age of 33, did he begin graduate study at the University of Texas–Austin.

In his scholarship, Huitt combined a sensitivity to the new behavioral currents in the discipline, and the acute insights of the practitioner. He was a staff aide to Senator Lyndon B. Johnson in 1953–54, then legislative assistant to Senator William Proxmire in 1959. The analytical gaze of the political scientist was sharpened by the intimate familiarity with congressional process of the insider. Although his publications were not numerous, his four major articles on the Senate had exceptional impact. In the words of his memorial resolution, "he established what can fairly be called the Huitt school for the study of Congress."[78]

Huitt put his legislative knowledge to practice in an extended tour of duty in Washington from 1965 to 1978, serving first as assistant secretary for legislation in the Department of Health, Education and Welfare in the Johnson administration, and next as executive director of the National Association of State Universities and Land-Grant Colleges from 1970 to 1978, with the initial encouragement of the university administration. He then returned to teaching for a final five years. The extended 13-year leave he received precipitated a review of policy in such matters. Thereafter the department permitted only two consecutive years of leave at a time, and required that faculty be on instructional status at least half the time over the years.

The addition of Austin Ranney to the faculty in 1962 was a major success. As a specialist in political parties, joining Epstein, Ranney gave the department exceptional strength in this field, and—added to Huitt—distinction in the American politics field more broadly. After a Northwestern undergraduate education, and an Oregon M.A., Ranney completed a Yale doctorate in 1948, early in the period when Yale political science was achieving preeminence as a center for behavioralism. His initial standing as a party specialist was assured by his first major publication, the 1954 book *The Doctrine of Responsible Party Government.* Ranney offered a critical challenge to a number of the premises of an early postwar APSA committee report urging a more centralized two-party system modeled on the British pattern. He returned to the topic of party reform in his 1975 book, *Curing the Mischiefs of Faction.* By now his analysis was informed by participation in several Democratic Party commissions regarding the delegate selection process for national conventions, notably the McGovern-Fraser Commission, whose report was completed in 1971. En route he made a comparative detour to examine the candidate selection process in the United Kingdom; his 1965 work, *Pathways to Parliament*, subverted conventional wisdom by demonstrating that constituency influence was more consequential than commonly believed.

During his years in the department (1962–76), Ranney enjoyed great influence in departmental affairs, and was an intellectual lodestar for younger faculty and graduate students. He was equally influential for an extended period in the life of the APSA, editing the *American Political Science Review* from 1965 to 1971, also serving as book review editor for a time, and winning election as president in 1974–75. The presidential year, Ranney observed, was the summit of his career, though it was a contentious moment in association history. The leftist Caucus for a New Political Science, which ran a competing list of candidates for APSA office, nearly had a majority on the council, the apex of their representation. The major decision for the year was selection of a new editor for the *Review*; Ranney made good on his determination to outwit the caucus in the designation.

Ranney left Madison in 1976 for a research position with the American Enterprise Institute. In 1986, he joined the faculty of the University of California-Berkeley, where he completed his career. Wisconsin was fortunate to share some of the years of his most influential work.[79]

Matthew Holden likewise was a critical addition to the faculty, even though his active teaching service was briefer than that of Ranney. Holden, of Mississippi family background, spent his secondary years in Chicago. He won early admission to the University of Chicago, but initially floundered, finding himself after transfer to Roosevelt University. There he was particularly influenced by Africanist St. Clair Drake. The African interest partly explained his enrollment at Northwestern for graduate study in 1953; Northwestern then boasted the leading African studies program, and a department in transition to a strongly behavioral commitment.[80]

Though the African interest lingered, Holden became a well-rounded specialist in American politics. He joined the Wayne State faculty in 1961, remaining there with a two-year Pittsburgh interlude until the 1969 Wisconsin appointment. In 1975, he was named by Governor Lucey to the Wisconsin Public Service Commission (energy regulation), then in 1977 appointed as a commissioner to the federal Department of Energy, a post he retained until 1981. At that time, he resigned his Wisconsin position to take a senior post at the University of Virginia.

In an APSA oral history, Holden indicates that "Wisconsin by all odds was from my point of view intellectually the most favorable experience." His explanation merits citation, since it captures an important quality of the department, its breadth of interest and diversity of orientation:

> The reason is that the Wisconsin department was a big department with a large number of active people and I was able to take advantage of the fact that in the department there were people of considerable ability who had some interest in almost any question you asked.

Holden described circulating a memorandum explaining core concepts of his current work, and receiving a substantial number of responses, ranging from Patrick Riley and Charles Anderson on the philosophic dimension to Barbara Hinckley on congressional aspects. Years later, reviewing the responses, he found them still valuable. Holden stressed the value of "a collegial atmosphere in the sense on the whole people were friendly and in addition were able to be helpful intellectually . . . on the matters of pertinence."[81]

Brief mention is appropriate for two faculty of the early postwar years, who both departed to join the newly created Department of Urban and Regional Planning in 1962, Fred Clarenbach and Coleman Woodbury. Clarenbach joined the department at its hour of greatest need, in 1945. A specialist in rural local government, his appointment was joint with agricultural economics and regional planning. Following a 1941 Cornell doctorate in public finance, during the war years he had served in the Department of Agriculture. Though Pfankuchen in his 1944–46 biennial report describes the appointment as opening unique and exciting possibilities for the department, these expectations were not fulfilled. The nature of Clarenbach's specialization placed him at the margins of the discipline, and he was an outlier in the department.

The Woodbury recruitment occurred in a very different context. A 1930 Northwestern Ph.D., Woodbury was a specialist in urban planning. He had extensive experience in urban affairs, particularly in the areas of housing, urban redevelopment and planning. He had served for a time on the Harvard faculty, and was Ford Foundation advisor on urban issues.

By the late 1950s, there was a growing sense of impending urban crisis, as suburbanization was transforming inner cities. A vision of the university as an instrument of urban social action took form in the mind of Harrington as vice president in 1958. With his characteristic energy and drive, he aspired to combine the resources of University Extension and the social science skills of the resident faculty into an agency for engagement with the urban challenge. Woodbury, as Ford Foundation advisor on these issues, appeared to be a potential strategic asset; this led Harrington to ask the department to accept Woodbury as a tenured colleague, with the promise that it was an extra position.

Woodbury thus joined the faculty in 1958, and the following year Harrington won a million dollar grant from Ford for what he gave a catchy acronym: TRUE (Teaching, Research, Urban Extension). No sooner was Woodbury on board than Harrington decided that his new recruit did not correspond to his urban reform vision. According to Cronon and Jenkins, Harrington quickly concluded that "Woodbury's approach was too scholarly and his outlook too conservative; he was more interested in commissioning broad scholarly background studies than in developing bold action programs."[82] Harrington shunted Woodbury aside in the management of the Ford grant, and took the lead himself. In contrast to the impressive accomplishments and enduring impact of the Harrington promotion of international engagement, the urban reform venture had only modest accomplishments.

One of the spinoffs of the urban initiative was the creation in 1962 of the Department of Urban and Regional Planning. Both Clarenbach and Woodbury transferred completely to the new department, without objection from political science. Neither fell within the evolving disciplinary identity of political science. The unease of their situation in the department perhaps reflected a larger pattern of sharpening discipline boundaries.

The Student Protest Years

The last half of the 1960s was an extraordinary moment in university life. Deepening waves of protest swept over the campus, culminating in the traumatic bombing of Sterling Hall on 24 August 1970. In this crescendo, multiple discontents interacted, escalating into the utter disorder of spring 1970. Above all the Vietnam War cast its darkening shadow. Black anger at racial oppression overflowed, with the April 1968 assassination of Martin Luther King unleashing accumulated tides of discontent. In the wake of the civil rights revolution, gender inequality came under vigorous challenge. Teaching assistants engaged in militant mobilization. And the discipline establishment—like all others—was contested by a radical vision of a politically engaged political science.

I recollect leaving Madison in August 1965 for a visiting professorship in Uganda during 1965–66. On my return, the atmosphere was dramatically changed; the escalation of the war was now in earnest, and the draft beginning to bite. In early 1965, the *Daily Cardinal* still supported the war. I remember a petition of similar substance circulating in the department, which most of us signed; the only faculty member who conspicuously declined was Pfankuchen.

The first major episode occurred in October 1967, when a crowd of demonstrators tried to block Dow Chemical recruiters from conducting interviews in the Commerce (now Ingraham) building. The Madison police were asked to clear the building, whose corridors were choked with protesters. They did so, with billy clubs and tear gas, an action that proved a detonator for radical activism. A brief student strike followed, in which a number of department teaching assistants participated.[83]

In a steadily escalating climate of tension, the next major episode was the black student strike in February 1969. The depth of student unrest found illustration in the many thousands who participated in support of the Black Peoples Alliance demands for more black faculty, students, support services, and a black studies department.[84] The strike, which lasted over a fortnight, disrupted many classes and produced militant crowds far too large for the

Photo courtesy University of Wisconsin–Madison Archives

Black student strike, February 1969

university and Madison police forces to manage. For nine days, nearly 2,000 National Guard troops were mobilized on campus to help contain disorder and violence, an utterly disconcerting sight.[85]

Meanwhile, extreme factions of the Students for a Democratic Society (SDS) made their appearance; the Mother Jones Revolutionary League left its signature on various disruptions. Trashing windows of university buildings and nearby stores entered the repertoire of protest. North and South halls were targets; expensive, rock-resistant screens were installed. In early 1970, firebombing of buildings began; the Old Red Gym, the Primate Laboratory, and a temporary building housing ROTC offices were targets. The flames did extensive damage to the Old Red Gym. The stage was set for the surreal Cambodia spring of 1970.

Within the department, student mobilization took place on two tracks: the Political Science Association of Students (PSAS) and the Teaching Assistants Association (TAA). Both were animated by a belief in the therapeutic energy of student power. During the course of 1968, activist student associations like PSAS emerged in a number of large social science and humanities departments.

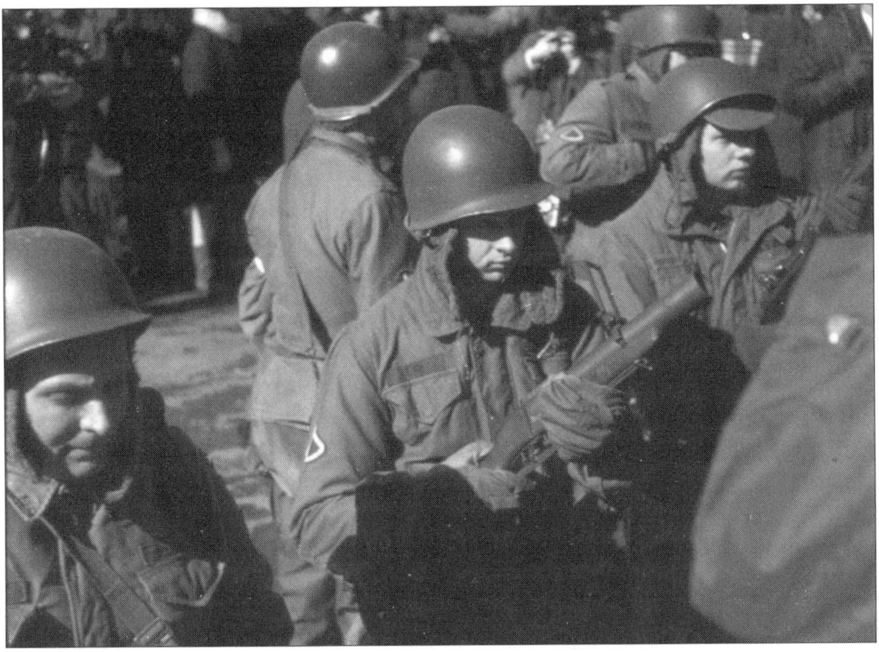

National Guard troops summoned during black student strike, February 1969

Cronon and Jenkins attribute this to a coordinated venture of the Students for a Democratic Society (SDS) to use the departmental social universes of graduate students and, more indirectly, undergraduate majors as an efficacious mechanism for mobilization. They pursue in detail the History Student Association, whose leadership was considerably more radical than that of PSAS.[86] Whatever the affiliation of some PSAS activists, the organization had no evident external link. The radicalized mood on campus, to which graduate students were especially sensitive, provided the context; the themes of student power and discipline reform defined the agenda (see appendix 19 for extracts from PSAS publications). PSAS emerged as an active voice in the last year of Cohen's tenure as chair; after an incandescent moment of vocal activity in 1968–69, by late 1970 it had disappeared.

Former PSAS leaders interviewed[87] indicated that the dynamics of the organization revolved around a given pre-dissertation generation; doctoral students already immersed in their dissertations were much less involved. The general principles of the association included a critical perspective toward established political science, the right of students to participate in defining

Photo courtesy University of Wisconsin–Madison Archives

TAA strike, spring 1970. The tear gas canister was emblematic of that turbulent era.

their education, and to equal representation on all department committees. Perhaps the zenith of student activism was a mass meeting summoned by students (though not explicitly PSAS) in May 1970, which was intended to speak for the department, with majors, graduate students, and faculty all having a single vote. The meeting, which David Fellman agreed to chair, had few faculty in attendance, though a large number of students. A set of resolutions was passed reflecting the fevered emotions of the moment, among other things calling for a referendum on immediate closure of the university and a two-week suspension of classes before the November elections to permit students and faculty to campaign for antiwar candidates.

Student activism was by no means universal. A number of graduate students, like Richard Cheney, remained on the sidelines. But the protest climate was so strong that those students who still sympathized with the war chose to remain silent.

Photo courtesy University of Wisconsin–Madison Archives

TAA strike picket line, spring 1970

The student power motif was also central in the emergence of the TAA and the 1970 strike. The TAA first took form in June 1966.[88] At first the union grew slowly; organizing in political science was initially difficult, as compared to departments like English with armies of TAs and less direct contact with faculty.[89] However, at the time of the black student strike, the threat was made in the Legislature to rescind out-of-state tuition remissions for TAs; though the punitive action was not pursued, the menace to TA status hit home, and organization gained momentum. Though there was no statutory provision for teaching assistant unionization, Chancellor Young, whose specialty was labor relations, chose to enter into a structure agreement and have an election for TAA recognition as bargaining agent in May 1969. The threat of a strike for recognition was in the air; Young was apprehensive about a second student strike in the inflamed atmosphere following the black student strike. Many faculty were highly critical of the choice to recognize; though he believed in collective bargaining, Young later came to feel that he might have been mistaken.[90]

The TAA won recognition by 931 for, 278 against, with about two-thirds of those eligible to vote taking part. By this time the TAA leadership had a determined radical core, on a collision course with the university.

The union girded for a strike, but recognized that it could be effective only if undergraduates participated. Thus the bargaining agenda included a number of student power issues, which contributed to the impasse. The most critical was the demand that students and teaching assistants bargain at the department level to gain decision-making roles in "educational planning" of all courses involving TAs.

The strike began 16 March, and continued until 7 April 1970. The picket lines around major classroom buildings were often confrontational, as the strike wore on. At first, participation was substantial in most of the humanities and social science departments. Faculty were reminded of their obligation to maintain instruction, and TAs were warned that strikers would not be paid. In the department, most courses continued with reduced attendance; some smaller ones moved off campus. To my recollection, about two-thirds of the department TAs took part when the strike began.

The TAA made a major tactical error in beginning the strike soon before spring break. This meant for the strikers 10 days of lost wages during a period when the strike had no effect. After the break, student participation in the strike began to wane; TAA hope for faculty backing on the educational planning issue ended when a two-day mass faculty meeting by a 530 to 256 vote insisted on the "ultimate responsibility of the faculty for curriculum and course content."[91] The TAA then accepted the university contract offer, which did include provisions for meaningful TA participation in educational planning, though not bargaining over course content.

Even under the pressures of the larger climate of student protest, relations between political science graduate students and faculty had remained mostly congenial, especially at the individual level. Many faculty, particularly among the younger, shared student anger and anguish over the Vietnam War, and a number identified with some of the agenda for radical change. The strike strained momentarily but did not inflict lasting damage on faculty-student relations. By the last days of the strike, several department TAs who had originally participated had quietly returned to work.

Following the strike, departmental bargaining took place over the application of the contract provisions. A committee for this purpose composed of Crawford Young, Leon Epstein, and Donald Hanson for the faculty, and Stephen Zorn, Fred Rynhart, and Jules Steinberg for the TAA. (The following year, Zorn became president of the campus TAA.) In the end, agreement was reached on a careful definition of TA workload, and on a procedure for evaluation of TA performance including faculty, TAs, and undergraduates. The reform of workload definitions was long overdue, and in my view highly beneficial to the department. Previously, there had been gross disparities in the actual work requirements, with a number of teaching assistants in the vague category of "non-teaching TAs."

The tensions associated by the strike had barely subsided when a new crisis exploded. On 30 April 1970, President Richard Nixon escalated the Vietnam War, by ordering American troops into Cambodia, to attack North Vietnamese supply routes. The *Daily Cardinal*, whose new editorial staff was led by far left radicals Rena Steinzor and James Rowen, warned that a revolutionary moment was coming:

> Nixon had better begin arming for a new kind of war in this country, civil war. He has lied, he has cheated, he has escalated. And the time of reckoning is at hand.[92]

The campus, inflamed by this new escalation, experienced a further wave of protest, now more militant and violent. A further strike was called by the activist leadership on 5 May, after National Guard troops had fired on demonstrators at Kent State, killing four. That evening, protestors tossed firebombs into several university buildings, and the Kroger supermarket near campus was burned to the ground. A half-dozen homes of leading faculty were also firebombed, although none suffered real damage.[93]

There followed daily mass protests with thousands of participants swarming over Bascom Hill. The National Guard was again summoned, and faced more hostile crowds than during the Black Peoples Alliance strike. Repeatedly tear gas was used on Bascom Hill; one grenade exploded inside North Hall. For a number of days, by midafternoon North Hall was uninhabitable, and office staff had to be sent home. The radical underground paper *Kaleidoscope*, then widely circulated on campus, captures the mood of the extreme left fringe of the protestors:

> GET A GUN AND LEARN TO USE IT! Dig it! There's no excuse not to have at least one, and to have a good hiding place for it in your pad. The Community gotta become an armed camp, an armed OUTLAWS OF AMERIKA camp![94]

Photo courtesy University of Wisconsin–Madison Archives

Cambodia invasion protest, May 1970

One of my vivid recollections of the protest days was the swarm of blue-denim-clad demonstrators surging up Bascom Hill, chanting "The Revolution has begun! It's time to get your gun!"

Many faculty tried to maintain their classes, in numerous instances by converting them into forums for discussion of the war and the campus crisis. On 11 May, Chancellor Young declared a "Day of Concern," instructing departments to organize gatherings, drawing together faculty and students. The department created a week of such activities, featuring discussions led by faculty, local political figures, journalists, and others on the theme of effective political organization to effect change. The university intent was to draw students off the streets and into dialogue. Those attending were graduate students deeply distraught over the war, but not from the radical fringe.

Between the TA strike and Cambodia protests, the semester had become a shambles, particularly for large undergraduate courses. Many student voices called for ending the semester early, with a universal pass-fail system. Such an extreme action was not acceptable to many students who had continued to attend classes, and wanted full academic credit and grade recognition for their work. The department took the lead in proposing a compromise formula.

Photo courtesy University of Wisconsin–Madison Archives

Cambodia invasion protest, May 1970

John Armstrong surprised his colleagues at a 12 May department meeting by proposing that examinations take place as scheduled, but that all students have the option of waiving the final and receiving an S (satisfactory) grade if they had been previously attending and completing required work.[95] The department proposal was presented to a reluctant Dean Stephen Kleene, who would have preferred massive use of incompletes. However, for too many students the semester was beyond salvation, and the department proposal became the basis for L&S policy.

In calmer times, it is difficult to appreciate the depth of passion surrounding these events. In Cambodia spring, no one could see the end of the campus crisis. I recollect despairing comments from various colleagues; one senior professor felt that the only avenue open was to close the university for a year. But a further, even more traumatic, event was to transform the psychological environment: the powerful truck bomb which exploded at 3:30 a.m. on 24 August 1970, inflicting massive damage on its target, Sterling Hall, home to the Army-supported Mathematics Research Center, and shattering windows in all surrounding buildings.[96]

The profound shock of the bombing decompressed the explosive pressures of the spring. The senseless nature of symbolic destruction appalled many; even more dismaying was the death of a physics student. The bombers planned their attack for a moment they assumed the building would be empty; they failed to calculate on the presence in Sterling Hall of the computer center, then operating around the clock. The self-appointed revolutionary fringe, always small in number, which planned and implemented the bombing, lost its ties to the much larger moderate-to-left spectrum which abhorred the war but deplored violence. The mood when classes resumed just after the bombing was subdued.

Coda: University Merger

Soon another major issue absorbed the faculty, though not the students: merger of the existing University of Wisconsin (Madison, Milwaukee, Green Bay, Parkside, and the Centers) with the nine campuses of the Wisconsin State University System. Although the question was mentioned only once during the 1970 gubernatorial campaign, newly elected Governor Lucey unveiled the merger proposal as a centerpiece of his biennial budget proposal in early 1971.[97]

Beginning in the 19th century, normal schools for teacher training were created in several locations. With the dramatic expansion in student numbers after World War II, the teachers colleges sought expanded missions, first as state colleges in 1951, then as state universities in 1964. With state capacity to finance higher education finite, beginning in 1947, proposals emerged to integrate the different campuses. Governors Goodland, Rennebohm, and Kohler all introduced merger plans, but in the face of strong opposition, especially from the Madison campus, the proposals stalled. Instead, in 1955 a Coordinating Committee for Higher Education (CCHE) was created to screen budgets and degree proposals. Although the CCHE was initially effective, by the 1960s direct budgetary competition in the Legislature between the two systems intensified.

Although Lucey made oblique reference to consolidation of higher education at a 12 June press conference, campus unrest was a far more visible issue during the campaign. On 3 September, Lucey declared that, "Another semester of violence and disruption will surely kill [the university] as a great public university."[98]

Thus the public and the faculty were taken by surprise by the Lucey proposal in February 1971 to abolish the CCHE, dissolve the two boards of regents, and replace them with a single board, including some existing members both from the University of Wisconsin Board of Regents and the WSU board, plus new appointees and a couple of officio members. Two aspects of the merger proposal alarmed most Madison faculty—especially equalization of undergraduate instructional costs across the system and cutbacks in graduate education. At first many believed that, with Republicans still in control of the Senate, the complexity of the issue and diversity of interests involved would sink the scheme as in the past. They did not count on the unbreakable determination of the governor to force the measure through. In the wake of Cambodia spring, the negative image of the university left by the mayhem on campus meant public skepticism toward faculty dismay regarding merger.

The campus administration and faculty leadership, through the University Committee, were caught in a bind. An overly public campaign against merger could easily backfire into a final version much more unfavorable to Madison. Yet engaging in bargaining on the terms made its consummation more inevitable. Through the long spring and summer months, sparring continued; until the end many hoped and believed that no merger bill would pass. However, in September 1971 the die was cast, and Lucey by a narrow margin won his victory.

The department had a dual link to the merger issue. David Adamany played a prominent role in the origin of the proposal. Once adopted, Clara Penniman was an important player in the implementation provisions, particularly as they related to faculty governance.

Adamany, after Harvard undergraduate and law degrees, began doctoral study in Madison in 1961. He quickly became active in Democratic politics, becoming an assistant to then Lieutenant Governor Lucey in 1965.[99] While completing his doctorate, he was an instructor at the Whitewater campus of the WSU System. After finishing his doctorate in 1967, he joined the Wesleyan faculty as an undergraduate dean. During these years, he became a staunch advocate of the primacy of undergraduate education.

When Lucey entered the gubernatorial race in 1970, Adamany returned to Wisconsin in May to spend the summer on the Lucey campaign, writing speeches and policy papers. He returned to Wesleyan for the fall semester, but came back in January to help with the budget process, then again returned to Wesleyan for the 1971–72 academic year. As noted earlier, he was invited to join the department in 1972.

Many believe that Adamany was the prime architect of merger. Cronon and Jenkins state that the merger plan "had been worked out" by Adamany.[100] Adamany, however, denies paternity in his oral history, conceding only that he played some role, but was far from the exclusive promoter.[101] Rather, he argues, Lucey as lieutenant governor was shocked by the UW–WSU budgetary rivalry, and by a perception that President Harrington intended to build four doctoral campuses in the UW System. He believed as well that the WSU campuses deserved the cachet of a "University of Wisconsin" degree. One may conclude that Adamany was an influential advocate, but that no initiative as complex and politically perilous as merger would be undertaken on the advice of a single advocate.

The merger legislation left a number of details for resolution by an implementation committee. Penniman, who began a term with the University Committee at the time of merger passage, was designated as the faculty member representing the old University of Wisconsin System in the Governor's Merger Implementation Committee. The object was to preserve as much autonomy for the Madison campus as possible, to protect the robust faculty governance provisions, and to cope with issues arising from the WSU efforts to secure System standing for their union. In these aims Penniman was very successful. The bitter antipathy to merger among many faculty has subsided over the years, especially after the UW System was led from 1985 to 2004 by two able presidents (Kenneth Shaw and Katharine Lyall) who recognized the importance of acknowledging and preserving the unique status of Madison within the system as a top-ranked comprehensive university.

Concluding Reflections

By 1975, the era of expansion was clearly over. A more normal balance between younger and senior faculty had emerged. After the Ogg retirement, no others occurred until Salter became emeritus in 1968. McCamy followed in 1971, then Pfankuchen in 1972. The last link with the prewar years was severed.

The department had been entirely refashioned. Comparative politics had become a major strength, especially in developing area studies. The American field had fully regained its prewar eminence, and a small but strong theory contingent was taking form. International relations faced an ongoing challenge of defining itself as a subfield. Meanwhile, the growth of the CPPA was beginning to redefine the role of public administration, by moving M.A. training out of the department.

The overall portrait drawn here draws heavily on my own recollections, and those whose memories of these years are recorded in oral histories. Perhaps some others might perceive darker hues: a higher level of tension between younger and older faculty, especially during the late 1960s; possibly a decline in standards, reflected in the undeniable grade inflation; an arguable negative impact upon undergraduate education produced by the deteriorating faculty-student ratios. Those who left for other institutions might have a more critical stance.

Yet I believe that in the face of transformation those important dimensions of department culture which reproduced themselves merit stress. The value of consensus remained paramount, combined with a tradition of collegiality. Although the student protest era brought strains within the faculty, the mischief of faction remained alien to departmental mores. Finally, the much larger faculty included a broader diversity of methodological orientations and conceptual perspectives, but the ethos of inclusiveness and eclecticism remained dominant.

Notes

1. Andrew Delbanco, "Colleges: An Endangered Species?" *New York Review of Books*, 10 March 2005, 18.
2. E. David Cronon and John W. Jenkins, *The University of Wisconsin: A History, 1945–1971: Renewal to Revolution* (Madison: University of Wisconsin Press, 1999), IV, 7–19.
3. Cronon and Jenkins, *The University of Wisconsin,* IV, 163–224.
4. Cronon and Jenkins, *The University of Wisconsin*, IV, 228.
5. Before this change, in the middle 1950s, WARF was providing a million dollars annually to the university, none of which went to social science. Mark Solvey, "Shattered Dreams and Unfulfilled Promises: The Wisconsin Social Systems Research Institute and Interdisciplinary Social Science Research, 1945–1965," MA diss., University of Wisconsin, 1960, 73.
6. Cronon and Jenkins, *The University of Wisconsin*, IV, 171.
7. William F. Thompson, *The History of Wisconsin: Continuity and Change, 1940–1965* (Madison: State Historical Society, 1988), VI, 449–53.
8. Stalwart Republican Governor Julius Heil abolished the existing Board of Regents in 1939, replacing it with a new Board of nine members, eight of whom were conservatives. *Madison Capital Times*, 27 January 1947. Vacancies between 1939 and 1946 would have been filled either by Heil, or his Republican successor, Walter Goodland.
9. The McMurray case was examined by the Wisconsin Chapter of the American Association of University Professors (AAUP), which concluded that, since McMurray was not a faculty member, in terms of AAUP rules the case was moot. The chapter went on to discuss the issues raised by the case, acknowledging the right of the regents to use their own judgment, but yet defending the value of faculty active participation in the public square as a civil right and duty, not a privilege. The AAUP chapter report was drafted by

Charles Bunn, H. L. Ewbank, and Richard Hartshorne. The university faculty, in meetings on 3 and 10 February 1947 devoted to the McMurray affair, declined to ask the regents to reconsider, but endorsed the position of President Fred that the regents should accept faculty recommendations unless clearly in error. The faculty added that "practical experience in his field enhances the value of a teacher and scholar." Dean Sellery, in a 26 January 1947 statement, said that the regents had made a mistake, but had the right to do so. However, he recalled that "when my friend, the late Paul S. Reinsch, was increasingly taking leave of absences to go on diplomatic missions for the federal government . . . my chief and I, the dean, ruefully observed that Prof. Reinsch was in effect using the university as a perch to rest upon momentarily between diplomatic flights." *Madison Capital Times*, 26 January 1947. These documents are contained in a file on the McMurray affair kept by Pfankuchen, now in possession of his son, David Pfankuchen.

10. Progressive Orland Loomis was elected as Governor in 1942, but died before taking office. His place was taken by the Republican lieutenant governor, Walter Goodland.
11. William Young in a 1984 oral history interview identifies Rennebohm and Kohler as tied to the Stalwart wing of the Republican Party; from the early Progressive period until the 1940s there was a bi-factional rivalry pitting Progressives against more conservative "Stalwarts." William Young, Oral History, November 1984. Thompson, *History of Wisconsin*, VI, characterizes the substance of their gubernatorial role as belonging in the moderate camp.
12. Thompson, *History of Wisconsin*, VI, 581.
13. According to Hart, he was suspect to the party because his wife, Virginia, had a tainted class background, as daughter of a real estate broker. Henry Hart oral history, University Archives, December 2002.
14. Nothing came of his appearance before a 1939 House Un-American Activities Committee investigator in Chattanooga, Tennessee. Hart believes the inquiry into his background was not pursued because the investigator seemed to think that, as a Vanderbilt University graduate, Hart could not have knowingly been a Communist. Hart oral history, 2002.
15. McKellar asked Hart where he had been born. When Hart identified Lucknow, India, as his birthplace, McKellar then asked where his parents were at the time. When Hart explained and showed that the signature on the letter was a forgery, McKellar then asked, "If you did not sign the letter, who did?" According to Hart, McKellar was by this time somewhat senile. A primary reason for the McKellar vendetta against Lilienthal, according to Hart, was the construction by TVA of a couple of dams which flooded large landholdings of one of McKellar's principal contributors; herein the old adage that "all politics is personal" finds vindication. Hart oral history, 2002.
16. The centrist policies of Governor Rennebohm are illustrated by his appointment to what became such an influential post of a faculty member whose private partisan attachment was Democratic.

17. For further detail on the advisory role of William Young, see his 1984 oral history, as well as a subsequent one conducted in June 2002, both in University Archives.
18. University News Service, press release, 27 June 1983.
19. Gretchen Pfankuchen gives an interesting account of her campaign, as well as reflections on the life of a faculty wife in the difficult depression years. Gretchen Pfankuchen oral history, University Archives, 1983. Unfortunately, there is no oral history for Llewellyn Pfankuchen.
20. Fellman also recruited his colleagues to ghostwrite Nelson speeches. Bernard Cohen recalls a pair of such occasions in 1959–60; on the second instance, the speech was poorly received, and Nelson scolded Cohen by denying him the opportunity for further speech writing. Cohen, of course, was grateful to escape this chore. Cohen, personal communication.
21. David Fellman oral history, University Archives, 1982.
22. Clara Penniman oral history, American Political Science Association, December 1989. A separate oral history was conducted for University Archives in 1981.
23. The university statutes contained a provision dating from 1917 calling for a training program for public servants; however, it had never been pursued. In the mid-1950s, William Young tried to introduce an M.A. program within the department aimed at present or prospective civil servants, but encountered opposition led by David Fellman on quality grounds; Young quietly dropped the scheme. Interview with William Young, 3 March 2005.
24. As chair at the time, I well recollect the resentment caused among several department members by what they felt was inappropriate Lucey interest in the issue. There was, however, no direct pressure placed upon the department. The public law group strongly supported the appointment, as did a substantial majority of the department.
25. Thompson, *History of Wisconsin*, VI, 563–666, portrays Lucey as an organizational genius who played a pivotal role in building the party organization which made the Democrats competitive. His ambassadorship, a reward for organizing Wisconsin for Carter, was a disappointment; his intimate knowledge of Wisconsin politics and executive skills as governor proved inadequate preparation for a difficult diplomatic post. A controversial coda to a brilliant political career in party-building was his acceptance of the vice presidential nomination with John Anderson in a quixotic 1980 campaign as an independent ticket.
26. Of the abundant works evaluating the conceptual evolution of political science in this period, I found most helpful Gabriel A. Almond, *A Discipline Divided: Schools and Sects in Political Science* (Newbury Park, CA: Sage, 1990); James Farr and Raymond Seidelman (eds.), *Discipline and History: Political Science in the United States* (Ann Arbor: University of Michigan Press, 1993); Ada W. Finifter (ed.), *Political Science: The State of the Discipline* (Washington: American Political Science Association, 1993); Ada W. Finifter (ed.), *Political Science: The State of the Discipline* (Washington:

American Political Science Association, 1983); John G. Gunnell, *The Descent of Political Theory: The Genealogy of an American Vocation* (Chicago: University of Chicago Press, 1993); Richard M. Merelman, *Pluralism at Yale: The Culture of Political Science in America* (Madison: University of Wisconsin Press, 2–3); Raymond Seidelman, *Disenchanted Realists: Political Science and the American Crisis* (Albany: State University of New York Press, 1985); Albert Somit and Joseph Tanenhaus, *American Political Science: A Profile of a Discipline* (New York: Atherton Press, 1964); Heinz Eulau, "Political Science," in Bert F. Hoselitz (ed.), *A Reader's Guide to the Social Sciences* (Glencoe: Free Press, 1959), 89–127.

27. David Easton, "Political Science in the United States: Past and Present," in Farr and Seidelman, *Discipline and History*, 291–309.
28. John G. Gunnell, "Political Theory: The Evolution of a Sub-Field," in Finifter, *Political Science* (1983), 12.
29. David Easton, "The Idea of a Political System and the Orientation of Political Research," in Farr and Seidelman *Discipline and History*, 229–46.
30. Robert Dahl, "The Behavioral Approach in Political Science: Epitaph for a Monument to a Successful Protest," in Farr and Seidelman, *Discipline and History*, 261.
31. One particularly acerbic critic of behavioralism was Leo Strauss. See his polemic, "An Epilogue," in Herbert J. Storing (ed.), *Essays on the Scientific Study of Politics* (New York: Holt, Rinehart and Winston, 1962), 305–27. Strauss and his disciples had their own legion of fierce critics.
32. David Easton, "The New Revolution in Political Science," *American Political Science Review*, 63, 4 (December 1969), 1051–52.
33. Pfankuchen papers, North Hall.
34. Hart is not usually remembered by his colleagues as a follower of the behavioral movement. However, in his oral history, he explained that he had come to the conviction in his later Indian research that the rigorous empiricism and hypothesis-testing associated with the behavioralist school was a necessary research orientation. Henry Hart oral history, December 2002.
35. Department minutes, 24 February 1956.
36. Solvey, "Shattered Dreams," 98–101. Cronon and Jenkins, *The University of Wisconsin*, IV, 285–286, give 1970 as Orcutt's departure date.
37. These are reproduced in Naomi B. Lynn, "Self-Portrait: Profile of Political Scientists," in Finifter, *Political Science* (1983), 95–123. The 1957 and 1964 rankings were part of larger studies of the reputational standing of departments in different fields. The Somit-Tannenhaus and Roettger rankings covered only political science. In addition, in the table of rankings provided in the appendices, there is also a 1969 survey which also ranks the Department eighth. See appendix 12.
38. Somit and Tannenhaus, *American Political Science*, 39.
39. John S. Robey, cited by Lynn, "Self-Portrait," 102.

40. Walter B. Roettger, cited by Lynn, "Self-Portrait," 106. The same source, in a ranking of the top twenty political scientists from 1970–79, as measured by the number of their citations, listed Ira Sharkansky as the twentieth.
41. See Merelman, *Pluralism at Yale*, for an interesting account of theoretical currents at Yale, and their influence on the graduate student community.
42. Fellman oral history; John Armstrong memoir, University Archives, 156.
43. Thomson left the academic world and had a successful career in the State Department, mostly as an Asian specialist.
44. This figure needs some deflation to account for the substantial number of faculty (ten) who held joint appointments, especially with the La Follette School. Until the 1970s, split appointments were much less frequent.
45. Department minutes, 24 February 1956.
46. Franklin Bonn, an instructor from 1962 to 1965, was a specialist in theory and Latin American politics.
47. Leon Epstein and Bernard Cohen had earlier become chair at the relatively young age of 40.
48. McCamy papers, University Archives.
49. I recollect on arrival in 1963 receiving a list of a dozen or so students who were my advisees; only one ever came by.
50. Before this time graduate admissions were a responsibility of the chair. By the time that Cohen held this office (1966–69), the rapid rise in application numbers made this duty very onerous.
51. The initial plan for the Social Science Building in 1953 envisaged housing the Law School along with sociology and anthropology (still a single department). However, Law acquired funds for its own building, and construction of the Social Science Building was delayed for years by a heated controversy over its placement in Bascom Woods.
52. Fellman oral history.
53. Penniman oral history, 1989.
54. Department minutes, 2 December 1952.
55. Mark Beissinger, address to department centennial conference, 27 March 2004.
56. The first year of the reduced course load, Chair Crawford Young discovered that an expectation which built in the 1950s that faculty could normally include one graduate offering amongst the three offerings translated into an implicit belief that the same rule would apply to the two course arrangement. The discovery that the resulting academic program for 1969–70 had a serious shortage of undergraduate offerings led to the imposition of the new rule limiting graduate offerings to one per year. This regulation, introduced by memorandum from the chair, was applicable across the board, regardless of seniority; it won acceptance as equitable and necessary, and in its basic outline remains in force to this day.
57. When the M.A. thesis requirement was abolished, the department wrote to all those who had recently completed all requirements save the thesis, offering

the opportunity to claim the degree. Among the grateful beneficiaries was Congressman David Obey.

58. As Graduate School associate dean at the time, I recollect that we spent anxious hours parsing these figures, finally choosing to warn departments that caution in doctoral admissions was now prudent. Allan Cartter of the American Council of Education had written extensive and persuasively on this topic; his data was influential for us.
59. Lynn, "Self-Portrait," 107.
60. One will recollect the exception of Japanese scholar Toyokichi Iyenaga, briefly appointed by Reinsch in 1902–04, described in Chapter 2.
61. Cronon and Jenkins, *The University of Wisconsin*, IV, 18.
62. In their oral histories, neither Fellman nor Cohen mention encountering any handicaps at Wisconsin because of their Jewish background. Fellman does speak at length of his Jewish upbringing in Omaha, in a very orthodox and religious family. By the time he was 15, he had read the Old Testament in Hebrew. David Fellman oral history, 1982, University Archives.
63. Fellman oral history, 1982.
64. Leon Epstein oral history, American Political Science Association, May 1989, 80–82.
65. Perlman was asked by his chair, Richard T. Ely, to revise Ely's badly dated text on the labor movement. Displeased by Perlman's revisions, Ely blocked a promotion. Perlman desperately sought academic employment elsewhere, and was rejected by both Cornell and Arkansas explicitly on grounds of his Jewish identity. E. A. Ross and John R. Commons then came to his rescue, and the Ely veto was overturned. Julius Weinberg, *Edward Alsworth Ross and the Sociology of Progressivism* (Madison: State Historical Society of Wisconsin, 1972), 228–229. Subsequently, the chair in economics held by John R. Commons was given to newly recruited Edwin Witte rather than Perlman, though the latter was the senior specialist in labor economics. According to Perlman's son, Mark Perlman, his father believed that "unadulterated anti-Semitism" was the reason for the Commons preference for Witte as the successor to his chair. David B. Johnson, "Edwin E. Witte's Years on the Faculty, 1933–1957," in Robert J. Lampman, *Economists at Wisconsin 1892–1992* (Madison: University Publications, 1993), 107.
66. Armstrong, Memoir, 101.
67. Penniman oral history, 1989.
68. Bernard Cohen reports that, during his term as chair (1966–69), the dean of the School of Business asked for the name of a faculty member to attend a dinner Business was organizing in honor of Walter Heller. Cohen proposed the obvious choice, Clara Penniman, coauthor of a book with Heller, and his former student. The Business dean rejected the proposal, and asked for a male name. Cohen then designated Penniman a second time, which Business finally accepted.
69. Penniman oral history, 1989.

70. Cronon and Jenkins, *The University of Wisconsin*, IV, 301–28.
71. Interview with William Young, 3 March 2005.
72. "The Institute of Governmental Affairs," brochure, 1964.
73. Interview with Edward Schten, 28 March 2003.
74. Fellman oral history.
75. Fellman oral history.
76. The failure of the department to elect him as chair was a source of disappointment to Fellman. He nearly accepted an offer from the State University of New York–Stony Brook to come as dean of the Graduate School, but in the end remained in Madison.
77. Fellman oral history.
78. Faculty document 684, Memorial Resolution on the Death of Emeritus Professor Ralph K. Huitt, 2 February 1987.
79. "Austin Ranney," in Michael A. Baer, Malcolm E. Jewell and Lee Sigelman (eds.), *Political Science in America: Oral Histories of a Discipline* (Lexington: University of Kentucky Press, 1991), 214–30.
80. As chapter 6 documents, Holden was one of a number of faculty, beyond the Africanist contingent, who began doctoral study as intending Africa specialists (Donald Emmerson, Paul Hutchcroft, Susan Pharr, John Witte).
81. Matthew Holden oral history, American Political Science Association, November 1993, 60–63.
82. Cronon and Jenkins, *The University of Wisconsin*, IV, 257–59.
83. For detail on the student protest era, see Cronon and Jenkins, *The University of Wisconsin*, IV, 450–520; David Maraniss, *They Marched into Sunlight: War and Peace Vietnam and America October 1967* (New York: Simon & Schuster, 2003); Tom Bates, *Rads: The 1970 Bombing of the Army Math Research Center* (New York: HarperCollins Publishers, 1992).
84. Cronon and Jenkins, *The University of Wisconsin*, IV, 479–86. Several department members became involved in the university response to the strike. Michael Lipsky, who had good contacts among some of the activists, was named as a special assistant to the chancellor to advise on racial issues. Fred Hayward, only in his second assistant professor year, was a key intermediary in the arduous negotiations of the university administration with the Black Peoples Alliance which organized the strike. In the wake of the strike, the university agreed to create a Department of Afro-American Studies; Crawford Young chaired the steering committee appointed to draft a proposal for regent approval establishing the department and creating a degree program.
85. University and Madison police were limited in numbers, and overwhelmed by angry crowds of many thousands of demonstrators. The alternative to the National Guard was inviting the Dane County sheriff to deputize large numbers for this purpose. Given the lack of training of such a force, this option was not appealing.

86. Cronon and Jenkins, *The University of Wisconsin*, IV, 472–78.
87. Michael Kirn and Jules Steinberg.
88. For details on the history of the TAA, see Judith S. Craig, "Graduate Student Unionism: The Teaching Assistants Association at the University of Wisconsin–Madison, 1970–1980," PhD diss., University of Wisconsin–Madison, 1986.
89. Craig, "Graduate Student Unionism," 96.
90. Craig, "Graduate Student Unionism," 119.
91. Cronon and Jenkins, *The University of Wisconsin*, IV, 504.
92. *Daily Cardinal*, 2 May 1970, cited in Cronon and Jenkins, *The University of Wisconsin*, IV, 508.
93. Cronon and Jenkins, *The University of Wisconsin*, IV, 509.
94. Bates, *Rads*, 241.
95. Department minutes, 12 May 1970.
96. The most thorough account of the Sterling Hall bombing and its perpetrators is found in Bates, *Rads*.
97. See the detailed discussion of merger in Cronon and Jenkins, *The University of Wisconsin*, IV, 521–96.
98. Cronon and Jenkins, *The University of Wisconsin*, 555.
99. Lucey was elected Lieutenant Governor in 1964, at the time that Republican Warren Knowles narrowly won the gubernatorial election. The ballots for governor and lieutenant governor in Wisconsin are separate.
100. Cronon and Jenkins, *The University of Wisconsin*, 555.
101. David Adamany oral history, University Archives, 1985.

CHAPTER 5

Fluctuations around a Steady State (1975–2004)

Crawford Young

Historians normally leave a comfortable cushion of time between the time of publication and the cutoff date for their narrative. David Cronon and John Jenkins, in their final volume of the history of the university, published in 1999, stop at 1971. The State Historical Society six-volume history of Wisconsin suspends analysis in 1965, in the tome devoted to the contemporary period, published in 1988. However, since I am a mere trespasser in the historical discipline, the convention may be set aside for this volume. Not, however, without some hesitation and trepidation: historians have good reason for their reticence to tiptoe up to the boundaries of the present. Some temporal distance provides important perspective on the nature of events. Like the fog of war, the mists of immediacy may inhibit clarity of view.

But a centennial history shorn of a quarter of its substance would fall short of serving its purposes. Too many important contributions would fail to win notice; too many consequential trends would pass unexamined. Thus this chapter will venture into the terrain of the last three decades. As with the previous chapter, this discussion will avoid duplication with chapters 6–11 covering the major subfields.

Expansion, by 1975, was clearly over. University enrollment by the mid-1980s stabilized at just over 40,000. The last three decades were not marked by the dramatic changes of the previous three. Rather, one may characterize the epoch as fluctuation around a mostly steady state. Nonetheless, there were more gradual changes, in faculty composition, in the graduate program, in departmental orientation, and in the larger political and discipline environments.

State Environment and the Wisconsin Idea

State politics since the 1970s are characterized by two extended pendulum swings. Beginning in 1970, when Democrats won the gubernatorial election and the lower legislative house, a shift to Democratic predominance for the first time since the Civil War began. During the 1980s, the Democrats controlled both houses of the Legislature, at times with a two-thirds majority in the Assembly. Democrat Patrick J. Lucey served as governor from 1971 to 1977, succeeded by Martin Schreiber from 1977 to 1979. The colorful, red-vested Republican Lee Dreyfus, holder of a Wisconsin doctorate in communications and former chancellor of the University of Wisconsin–Stevens Point (1967–79), held gubernatorial office from 1979 to 1983, though faced with a Democratic Legislature. Democrats returned to the top office under Anthony Earl from 1983 to 1987. Then began the record-setting, fourteen-year gubernatorial tenure of Republican Tommy Thompson; no previous governor had served more than seven years. When Thompson left for a cabinet post in Washington in 2001, he was replaced by his Republican lieutenant governor, Scott McCallum.

During the Thompson years, there was a steady Republican trend in legislative elections. Both houses were captured by 1995. Democrat James Doyle won the governorship in 2002, but by the department centennial year Republicans neared a two-thirds majority in the Assembly. At the same time, Wisconsin politics drifted in a more polarized direction, shaped by a markedly more conservative Republican caucus, with the Christian right an increasing component. Thompson, an alumnus of the university law school and a Madison political science major, was favorably disposed toward the university; as a legislative leader, he had been a crucial ally in the mid-1980s struggle for faculty "catch-up" pay increases. But after his departure, the contentious political environment posed difficult challenges for those managing university relations with state government.

Not least of the difficulties was the steady erosion of state budgetary support. At the beginning of the 1970s, state general-purpose revenue appropriations for the university operating budget covered close to half the costs. In 1973–74, the state contribution to the university budget was 44 percent. By 2004–05, the figure had dwindled to 19.5 percent. The heightened phobia regarding taxes introduced into the public realm beginning in the Reagan years hemmed in the state on the revenue side. On the expenditure part of the ledger, swelling obligations for corrections, state aids, and Medicaid constrained choices. Three decades ago, the university appropriation far exceeded prison costs. At the present time, prisons cost the state far more than the outlay for the Madison campus.

Two major consequences ensued from these state budget trends. Each time a recession hit state revenues, which occurred in the early 1980s, early 1990s, and just after 2000, virtual salary freezes were imposed. Although in the mid-1980s, after a tough campaign by the university and its faculty representatives, a catch-up pay package was achieved, the political cost of this success was high, and it could not easily be repeated. This placed at risk the capacity of the department to retain its midcareer faculty with high national reputations. The second consequence was continuing escalation in tuition rates; the implicit bargain with the state was offsetting the budget shortfalls with higher student fees to meet instructional costs. A large increase in federal and other research funds, and gifts, also partly compensated for declining relative state-funding support. Whereas tuition revenues accounted for only 10.7 percent of the university budget in 1973–74, by 2004–05 the figure had risen to 15.7 percent.

The Wisconsin Idea retained its vitality; several faculty members had significant policy involvement during these years. Dennis Dresang, although recruited in 1969 as a specialist in African bureaucracy, had an opportunity to apply his knowledge to the American scene when Governor Lucey concluded that a comprehensive review of the state public service was needed. Dresang had shared views on the issue with David Adamany, then a faculty member and an informal advisor to Lucey. Adamany recommended Dresang to the governor, who asked him to direct a comprehensive study of the state personnel system. This required a year of full-time endeavor by Dresang in 1976–77; the commission he headed proposed several important changes. Some artificial barriers to affirmative action were identified and removed. Ways of making union contracts more compatible with effective personal management were proposed. The Department of Employment Relations was to replace the Department of Administration as manager of the civil service. Though the legislation resulting from the commission labors at first stumbled, eventually most of the recommendations were adopted.

The visibility acquired by Dresang as a specialist in civil service reform caught the eye of a presidential commission on civil service reform created by President Jimmy Carter. Dresang served as a resource person for the commission, undertaking research assignments and offering recommendations. By 1982, he had become a campaign advisor for gubernatorial candidate Anthony Earl.[1] When Earl took office, he asked Dresang to chair a commission dealing with the issue of comparable worth (equity of compensation for female-dominant employment categories). This proved a very contentious issue, particularly within the university. The "academic staff" category covered a wide variety of functions and many specializations, which were difficult to structure in a way permitting comparable worth methodology in assigning salary scales. Among those offended by the Dresang commission proposals was Republican legislative leader Tommy Thompson. When Thompson became governor in 1987, he made his displeasure regarding Dresang known to the university, and sought his removal, at least as director of the La Follette Institute.[2] Although Dresang did step down as he had planned from heading La Follette in fall 1987, the incident left Dresang with an even greater appreciation of the value of tenure.[3]

John Witte became drawn into a contentious issue of state and national policy in 1989, "school choice" and voucher programs. What began as a modest study of racial disparities in the Milwaukee school system evolved into a much more ambitious evaluation of voucher programs that consumed a decade of his academic career. The final act was the 2000 publication of a definitive treatise on this theme.[4]

Witte, after a Wisconsin undergraduate degree, completed a doctorate at Yale in 1978. After a brief flirtation with African politics under David Apter, he switched to the study of industrial democracy, initially in Yugoslavia. With Robert Dahl as mentor, he spent two years in dissertation research working with a California firm which was ostensibly committed to workplace democracy, as a participant-observer. The experiment was a clear failure, as were the Yugoslav examples he studied. His book on the subject was widely read, and remained on the publisher's list for almost two decades. He was also the author of a classic monograph on the American taxation system, *The Politics and Development of the Federal Income Tax* (1985). The review in the *American Political Science Review* praised the work as "seminal."

He joined the department in 1977, with a developing interest in policy studies. Meanwhile, tensions over racial disparities in the Milwaukee school system were intensifying. The Milwaukee School Board threatened to sue the county to force countywide school integration in early 1984. Governor Earl was not eager to see this issue forced, nor was his African-American secretary of employment relations, Howard Fuller (a Milwaukee North graduate), though the Millikin (1974) precedent blocking metropolitan integration in Detroit suggested such a suit would fail. Thus Earl turned to Witte to direct a study of the racial disparity issue in Milwaukee.[5]

Witte directed a staff of 17, which began its work in 1984. By the time the report was complete, Earl had been defeated for reelection. The report made a number of proposals, of which only a few were adopted, including teacher assignment policies, bolstering leadership of problem schools, focusing resources on the poorest schools, and creation of magnet schools. The issue of metropolitan integration was not addressed. Nor was school choice part of the study; thus the report did not cover the voucher issue (entitlement to draw upon a sum equivalent to public school per pupil cost for use in private schools). Various commission members then continued studies on different aspects of the issue.[6]

After the Earl defeat, Fuller became superintendent of the Milwaukee school system. In this role, he was a strong advocate of vouchers for low-income parents for use in designated private schools. A voucher bill was defeated in 1988, but passed on a limited, experimental basis in 1989. Included in the legislation was provision for a study of the impact of vouchers. Witte became a logical candidate to direct the study; he was strongly encouraged by Chancellor Donna Shalala to accept the mission. She pledged assistance in acquiring Spencer Foundation funding, and made good on her promise by helping obtain a $400,000 Spencer grant supporting the study, which began in 1990.

As site of the first voucher program, Milwaukee was the crucible for a national debate over such policies. The more ideological adversaries on each side of the issue took starkly opposed positions. Doctrinal conservatives argued for universal school choice, claiming a therapeutic impact of market forces in education, with public schools forced to compete for pupils. Some liberal opponents and teacher unions argued that vouchers threatened the very survival of public education.

The Milwaukee experiment was limited in scope, and ambiguous in result. Initially participation was capped at 1 percent of the Milwaukee school enrollment, later raised to 1.5 percent. A handful of private schools took part, at first mostly former Catholic schools. In 1995 the program was opened to Catholic schools, an expansion which narrowly passed court challenge. Witte concluded that school choice may have some benefits, in helping salvage some good private schools, and providing alternatives for some children. But unless choice schools are selective, there is not dramatic test score improvement. Advocates of universal school choice, Witte suggests, in reality are proposing a large middle class subsidy. School choice alone cannot alter the environment of widespread poverty and social disorganization within which inner city schools function, nor can they contribute to the goal of integration. The Milwaukee choice schools encountered many of the same problems as their public counterparts: high staff turnover, inadequate resources, student attrition. Indeed, the magnitude of student turnover posed formidable methodological problems in carrying out the study. In the end, Witte concluded that school choice could not reduce black-white disparities very much, but neither was it a clear failure. The vouchers were valued by a number of participating black parents.[7]

The angry debates swirling around the issue placed Witte at the eye of a hurricane. A fervent academic-voucher advocate, Paul Peterson of Harvard, used the Wisconsin open records law to gain access to the Witte data well before the study was complete. He and his allies used various forums for sharp attacks on the Witte study, claiming their reanalysis of the data produced different conclusions. In his 2000 book, Witte notes that he was "subject to vicious attacks on my character and my work by voucher advocates."[8] Although the Witte study could not resolve the dispute over the wisdom of vouchers, the careful, nuanced data and conclusions supplied invaluable material for more informed policy reflection.

Donald Kettl, a faculty member from 1990 to 2004, was another important contributor to public policy formulation. His involvement began with the Clinton administration; Vice President Albert Gore was assigned the mission of "reinventing government." The Kettl name was suggested to Gore by the Brookings Institution. Kettl was invited to brief Gore, an assignment which expanded into an association with the commission, then eventually a book.[9] As an exercise in identifying what works in government, and what does not, Kettl felt the Gore commission deserved an A for effort, and B for substance. A working group in the Bush administration continued the work, though dropping the term "reinventing government." Kettl was consulted, and felt that his work and the Gore commission had provided a useful intellectual framework for the Bush group.[10]

At the state level, Governor Thompson, following the 1996 election, approached Kettl to lead a commission on campaign finance reform. During the campaign, Thompson had taken a beating on campaign finance. The bipartisan commission (which included David Adamany) provided a unanimous set of recommendations in May 1997. By this time, with the storm passed, Thompson lost interest in the issue, and never put his weight behind the proposals (substantial public funding of campaigns, restrictions on spending and contributions, disclosure on issue ads). As a consequence, nothing in the end was adopted.[11]

However, when Thompson had another commission idea in 2000, he again turned to Kettl. This time the assignment was state and local finance, a source of widespread discontent. The unhappiness arose over application of the state commitment to fund two-thirds of the K–12 school costs, with a number of accompanying restrictions. By the time that this Kettl commission, after arduous deliberations, produced a unanimous report in January 2001, Thompson was packing his bags for a new post as secretary of health and human services in Washington. His successor, Scott McCallum, was not interested in the recommendations, so the report vanished into the archives. When Kettl announced his resignation to accept a chair at the University of Pennsylvania in 2004, Governor James Doyle issued a statement calling Kettl "an example of the success of the Wisconsin Idea, and the tremendous contributions the university makes to our state."[12] (For other examples of the Wisconsin Idea on the state, national, and international levels, see chapters 6 and 10.)

The University: Stable Leadership and Fiscal Pressures

During the last three decades, the university has enjoyed a period of stable leadership, at the campus and college level. Edwin Young was elevated from the chancellorship to the University of Wisconsin System presidency in 1977. He was replaced as chancellor by chemist and former Provost Irving Shain. Shain resigned in 1987, with political scientist and Provost Bernard Cohen serving a year interim term as acting chancellor until a successor, Donna Shalala (also a political scientist), took office in January 1988. Shalala served five years, until she was called by newly elected President William Clinton to serve as secretary of health and human services. Provost David Ward, a geographer, moved up to the chancellor post. When Ward departed to head the American Council on Education in 2000, his provost, John Wiley, an engineer and physicist, stepped into the top post in 2001.

The deanship of the College of Letters and Science (L&S) was equally stable. Historian David Cronon, who became dean in 1974, continued until 1989. After the brief tenure of philosopher Donald Crawford, from 1990 to 1992, and an interim year with Crawford Young, chemist Phillip Certain served from 1993 until 2004.

During these years, the department contributed remarkably to campus administration and faculty governance; one may safely assert that no other department produced such a wide range of university leaders (see appendix 8). Perhaps political science by its nature has a special affinity for governance. Cohen, in addition to his brief interim role as chancellor, served as vice chancellor for academic affairs from 1984 to 1989. In an earlier era, Leon Epstein served as L&S dean during the difficult years of 1965 to 1969. When Dean Crawford suddenly left in 1992 for a top administrative post at the University of California–Santa Barbara, Crawford Young, who had been a finalist in the previous search, was asked to step in for a year; he removed himself from the search for a permanent successor. From 1982 to 1990, department members Fred Hayward and Jack Dennis successively occupied the post of L&S associate dean for social science. The position of social science associate dean in the Graduate School was held by three political scientists: Crawford Young (1968–71), Cohen (1971–75), and Barbara Stallings (1987–90). Hayward was acting dean of International Studies and Programs in 1989; Stallings, Leigh Payne, and Aili Tripp also served in international studies administrative posts. Many department faculty served a term as chair of one of the area studies programs: Young, Hayward, and Michael Schatzberg for Africa; Stallings for Latin America; Donald Emmerson for Southeast Asia; John Armstrong, Melvin Croan, Mark Beissinger, and Kathryn Hendley for Russia and Eastern Europe. Charles Anderson and Booth Fowler served terms as head of the Integrated Liberal Studies Program. Jack Dennis, Kenneth Mayer, and Herbert Kritzer served long terms as directors of the Data and Program Library Service, and Virginia Sapiro a shorter one. Sapiro also chaired the Women's Studies Program from 1986 to 1989, and was named associate vice chancellor in 2002. Department faculty leadership of the La Follette School is detailed in chapter 10.

The highest-ranking political scientist during this period was Chancellor Shalala. After World War II an expectation had taken root that university leaders would normally arise from within the ranks; Clarence Dykstra (1937–45, see chapter 3) was the last previous campus head recruited from the outside without prior Wisconsin service.[13] Further, an explicit rule was now in place requiring that the chancellor qualify for faculty tenure in a university department. Such a provision had not existed before the second war; Glenn Frank (1925–37) had no academic credentials. As chair of the search and screen committee to identify a few candidates for chancellor deemed qualified by a faculty-majority group which also included academic staff, student, and administration representatives, I recollect retiring Chancellor Shain indicate that, in his view, no suitable available internal candidates existed (Cohen declined to seek the post).

Thus the search committee focused on external candidates. Shalala emerged as one of four recommended by the committee, and informally the top preference; she also had a network of support on campus, especially from some women faculty. She had served as assistant secretary for housing and urban development in the Carter administration, then as president of Hunter College of the City University of New York. Previously, she had taught at Columbia

Teachers College. At an early stage in her career, she had attracted notice as an energetic and talented policy analyst. Governor Nelson Rockefeller of New York had tapped her for a policy advising role, and she served with the commission led by Felix Rohatyn in the mid-1970s to devise a way for New York City to escape bankruptcy.

Because she had taken on government and academic leadership roles early in her career, her research record, though respectable, was modest in quantity. Much of her publication was in the field of educational policy. She did enjoy the distinction of a Guggenheim Fellowship in 1975–76. When she became a finalist in the chancellor search and the question of tenurability was posed, the first approach was to the Department of Educational Policy Studies, which was eager to include her among its faculty ranks.

However, late in the negotiations she insisted on tenure in political science as well. The initial reaction was hesitant. However, after extended informal discussion in the corridors, and careful scrutiny of the overall record, the department without dissent agreed to extend a tenure invitation as part of the terms by which she accepted the chancellor post. Although she played no part in departmental affairs, she did teach a freshman seminar on a couple of occasions. She also demonstrated her appreciation by hosting the departmental holiday parties at the elegant Prospect Avenue official residence during her period as chancellor.

She was an early supporter of William Clinton in the 1992 Democratic primary campaign, and a friend and committee colleague of Hillary Rodham Clinton; she was an obvious cabinet choice when Clinton won election. She departed in January 1993 to become secretary of health and human services, then, when Clinton left office, she became president of the University of Miami in Florida in 2001. The regents had placed her on leave status for national service during the first Clinton term; when he was re-elected, she resigned her department position. No one had expected that she would return to take up a regular faculty position.

Political scientists were equally evident in the major committees which serve as apex to the system of faculty governance. The most important is the University Committee, a six-member body elected in all-campus balloting which serves as the executive committee for the Faculty Senate. From 1971 to 1994, four political scientists occupied seats on this committee nearly half the time, all serving as chair their final year (Clara Penniman, Bernard Cohen, Crawford Young, and Joel Grossman). During the period covered in this chapter, nine political scientists were elected to the crucial Social Studies Divisional Committee, which among other duties reviews all tenure recommendations.

Crawford Young chaired three major search and screen committees: System Academic Vice President in 1985, Chancellor in 1987, and Provost in 1995 (those eventually appointed were Eugene Trani, Shalala, and John Wiley, respectively). Bernard Cohen served on the search and screen committees that identified Katharine Lyall as a prospective University of Wisconsin System vice president in 1981, and later Kenneth Shaw as president in 1985. Leon Epstein headed the search and screen committee from whose list of finalists Cohen was chosen as provost in 1984.

Fiscal Constraints and Downsizing

The financial stress placed upon the university by the slow erosion in the relative level of state funding became visible in various ways. Since state general-purpose revenue is a crucial element in meeting instructional costs, its effect on faculty numbers is direct. By 1992, the campus administration had concluded that over time the size of the faculty roster (then about 2,400) was not sustainable, and that it had to be reduced, if possible by attrition, by more than 10 percent (100 positions in L&S). The fiscal crisis affected not just Madison, but public higher education across the country. In September 1992, former Wisconsin vice chancellor and then president of the American Council on Education Robert Atwell had declared "that higher education is in its most dire financial condition since World War II is almost unarguable. Two-thirds of the states have revenue shortfalls, and total state appropriations for higher education actually declined in 1991. . . . I do not think things will get better until sometime after the year 2010."[14] By 2004, faculty numbers had shrunk to just over 2,000. L&S was by some distance the largest unit, accounting for nearly half the operating budget. Also, since less of its faculty was supported on federal or other research funds, L&S was slated to take the largest hit.

When Crawford Young became acting dean in 1992, L&S was just beginning the "downsizing" exercise. There was general agreement that reductions should not be accomplished by simple across-the-board cuts. Rather, rational and broadly accepted criteria needed to be applied, legitimated by extensive faculty consultation, especially through the elected College Academic Planning Committee. The three core criteria adopted were quality, need, and efficiency. The L&S Strategic Plan elucidated these notions:

> Quality was measured above all in national standing, and distinction brought to the University by the recognition and

> achievement of a given program. Need could be evaluated in numbers of students served, contribution to the central curriculum of the College, and centrality of the program to the mission of the College. Efficiency was understood as effectiveness in use of resources made available to the unit; a useful measure was the instructional personnel required currently to instruct a given number of students as compared with other similar departments and as compared with a decade ago.[15]

Political science fared well in the strategic planning review, which employed a wide variety of indicators developed to apply the three broad criteria. The evaluation of the department merits extended quotation:

> This department displays many high-quality indicators: it is highly ranked nationally (8th in 1989); it is composed of productive faculty who are also industrious teachers; it has been cooperative with a variety of departments in making joint hires (and has had many successful hires in recent years). It is the largest major in the College, with well over a thousand majors each year since 1988–89. For many years it housed the International Relations major, but in 1990–91 that program moved both physically and academically out of Political Science. However, Political Science still provides a significant amount of instruction for IR majors.[16]

Despite the favorable evaluation, the department was asked to contribute its share to the downsizing exercise, and to reduce its roster by one position in relation to its 1992–93 roster, or three in terms of the prospective 1993–94 faculty numbers. The strategic plan mandate imposed tight limits on recruiting for a couple of years. As budgetary pressures somewhat eased in the later 1990s, Dean Certain gradually relaxed then abandoned the plan.

Another implication of the fiscal unease was the active venture of the department into fund-raising. Since World War II, gift funds had slowly accumulated, but by passive accretion. The University of Wisconsin Foundation became more aggressive in its search for funds by the 1980s, at which time a major capital campaign was launched. Gifts and grants were only 6 percent of the university budget in 1973–74, but had increased to 19.6 percent by 2004–05. In 1982, an annual political science alumni newsletter was launched, including an appeal for funds. By 1984, Chair Hayward could announce that $35,000 had been raised.[17] At the turn of the century, a UW Foundation staff member had special responsibility for the department; at foundation urging, by 2000 the department had created a Board of Visitors (shared with the La Follette School), whose advisory role included fund-raising. By the time Graham Wilson assumed the chair in 2004, fund-raising travel was considered a component in the job description, an unheard-of responsibility a couple of decades ago.

Changing Orientations in the Discipline

At the centennial moment for political science as a discipline, if we arbitrarily date its formal existence from the 1903 founding of the American Political Science Association (APSA), a survey of the debates concerning the direction of the field in APSA publications and among discipline historians reveals two main interpretations. No effort is made here to resolve the debate. I merely endeavor to present the contending views, by way of situating trends and tendencies in the Wisconsin department.

On one side, the primary trend perceived is the pluralization of perspectives. In this view, with the arrival of the post-behavioral moment about 1970, a pronounced diversification of concept and method took place.[18] The editors designated by APSA to take a reading of discipline trends in 2002, Ira Katznelson and Helen Milner, interpret the orientation of the field broadly, concluding that the "diverse elements in political science have formed a single broad family with recognizable features and distinguishing characteristics: a pragmatist orientation to the modern state that makes the analysis of power and choice a constitutive feature; attention to the nature and stability of liberal political regimes and, increasingly, to democracy; and a dedication to study the state and liberal democracy in ways that are transparent and systematic." Political science may be seen as "an organized professional enterprise with contested yet real boundaries, and a common state of mind."[19]

Distinctive theoretical pathways defined the major subfields. In political theory, the rise of communitarian theories and the Rawls recasting of liberalism created new cross-currents. In comparative politics, state theory returned to the agenda, through the influence of Theda Skocpol, Charles Tilly, and others. Particularly in third world studies, for a time various currents of dependency and neo-Marxist theory challenged earlier orthodoxies. The cultural context of political choice entered the analytical arena; neither liberalism nor democracy could be presumed. In international relations, the discipline struggled with the defining condition of anarchy; idealism, realism, and more recently, constructivism jostled for primacy as theoretical orientations. In American politics, the unfolding debate between structure and agency as core determinant found reflection in a revived historical-institutional current on the one hand, and rational-choice theorists on the other.

Gabriel Almond suggested a different classification of disciplinary trends, organized along two axes, ideology and methodology; his stress on difference reinforces the pluralization thesis.[20] On the ideological side, he situated neo-Marxists, and dependency and world systems theorists on the left, with critical theorists of the Frankfurt School as a softer version. On the right, he placed the Straussians with their assault on the enlightenment and positivism on the soft edge, and the public-choice movement associated with William Riker, James Buchanan, and Gordon Bullock on the hard right, which takes "the most intractable elements of political processes—the individual and collective choices of political actors—and try to treat them deterministically."[21] On the methodological axis, the variation extended from interpretivists deploying a Geertzian "thick description" to those reading politics through formal mathematical models.

Those reading the trend as pluralization would add other dimensions of the diversity of orientations within the elusive boundaries defining political science. Indeed, the frequency with which discipline analysts seek to erect a fence around the field by taking stock of "the state of the discipline" bears witness to the stubborn diversity of its practitioners.[22] Various strands of post-structuralism and post-modernism, influenced by Michel Foucault and Jacques Derrida among others, crept inside the gates, at least rhetorically. "Discourse" has become a standard analytical term. At another edge, some advocate experimentalism as the key to analytical progress.[23] Others see a paradigmatic convergence, a marriage between institutionalism and rational choice.[24] Still others, such as Robert Bates and Margaret Levi, advance the analytical narrative as integrative touchstone. Yet others discover a lodestar in the constellation of metatheoretical themes: "liberalism, democracy, the state, capitalist economy, human rights."[25]

The alternative view is that rational or public-choice theories are clearly ascendent; their leading practitioners claim that rational choice has become mainstream political science. A key founder, William Riker, wrote that the paradigm is "the one that by its success is driving out all others."[26] Elsewhere, he asserted that rational choice was the only genuine advance to ever occur in political science.[27] The approach rests upon the core axiom that, as stated by two of its disciples, S. M. Amadae and Bruce Bueno de Mesquita, individual decision-making is "the source of collective political outcomes," and that "the individual functions according to the logic of rational self-interest. Individuals are thought to rank their preferences consistently over a set of possible outcomes, taking risk and uncertainty into consideration and acting to maximize their expected payoffs." Through the use of formal language, mathematical models, statistical analysis, and game theory, rational-choice theorists seek "to build models that predict how individuals' self-oriented actions combine to yield collective outcomes."[28] Above all, rational-choice theory in its pure form lays claim to a universal theory of politics. Among its canonical texts are Kenneth Arrow, *Social Choice and Individual Values* (1951), Anthony Downs, *An Economic Theory of Democracy* (1957), and William Riker, *The Theory of Coalitions* (1963).

The premise that behavior is driven by interests rather than attitudes differentiates rational choice from behavioralism, which implied a kinship with psychology analogous to the affinity of public-choice theory with neo-classical economics. The emergence of a claim to paradigmatic ascendancy by the 1970s took place in the wake of acknowledgment of a post-behavioral era by a number of the pioneers of behavioralism. Under Riker's leadership, the University of Rochester department became a leader in the training of a new generation of rational-choice theorists.[29] In a number of leading departments, such as UCLA, the University of Texas at Austin, and Harvard, rational-choice theorists have become a dominant force. If one accords analytical primacy to agency in understanding political process, and accepts the axioms of the paradigm, then its explanatory powers are beyond dispute. Many, however, are unwilling to set aside historical, institutional, structural, and cultural vectors.[30] In a number of departments, painful factional splits have occurred between advocates and adversaries of the approach.

In spite of the claims of rational-choice theory to mainstream standing, the forces of pluralization are potent. One measure was the discovery in a 1998 American Political Science Association (APSA) survey of membership to ascertain satisfaction with Association services that the greatest target of discontent was the *American Political Science Review*.[31] An anonymous political scientist employing the pseudonym of "Mr. Perestroika" disseminated a stinging tract attacking the *Review* for its heavy tilt toward formal modeling, quantitative, and rational-choice-oriented articles, with "technicism" trumping substance. An open letter in 2000 signed by 222 political scientists, including a number of the most eminent, joined in querying why the *Review* and "other prominent professional fora seem so intensively focused on technical methods, at the expense of the great, substantive political questions that actually intrigue many APSA members, as well as broader intellectual audiences?"[32] Although APSA President Robert Jervis defended the *APSR* drift as a product of self-selection of contributors rather than editorial design, nonetheless major changes were made in response to the discontents. Lee Sigelman was named editor of the *Review* in replacement of Ada Finifter (a 1967 Wisconsin Ph.D.), during whose term the trends decried by the Perestroika movement had become most pronounced. Sigelman pledged an active effort to attract more submissions based on qualitative research, and from subfields such as comparative politics underrepresented in recent years. A new APSA journal, *Perspectives on Politics,* was planned, launched in 2003 under the editorship of Jennifer Hochschild, one of the signers of the Perestroika open letter. *Perspectives on Politics* is dedicated to policy-relevant and problem-oriented scholarship, in addition to absorbing the book review section of the *APSR*.[33]

In navigating between these two trends, the historic disposition to eclecticism places the department predominantly within the pluralization camp. Recruiting patterns have reflected the established commitment to diversity of orientation; methodological preference of candidates in my recollection has always been secondary to their substantive qualifications. In setting staff priorities, field needs trump consideration of paradigm. However, over time the increasing influence of rational-choice theory is reflected in a slowly growing contingent of scholars to a greater or lesser degree attracted to a public choice orientation. In 2004, their number would include Scott Gehlback, Melanie Manion, Mark Pollack, and David Weimer, as well as, during his brief stay, William Howell, plus some others significantly influenced by this perspective.

As with the incorporation of behavioralism in the 1950s, the department was doubtless slow to adapt to the major impact the rational-choice approach was having on the profile of the discipline, particularly in the American field, and to a lesser extent in international relations. Charles O. Jones in his chapter on American politics concludes that "perhaps the most glaring omission in accommodating to change in the discipline is the failure to have incorporated the rational choice perspective in the Department's American offerings" (see chapter 9). One possible explanation is the relative salience of comparative politics in the department; Amadae and Bueno de Mesquita observe with dismay that comparative "was slowest among substantive fields of study to utilize, if not embrace, the theoretical advances that positive political theory had brought to the study of American politics and international relations." They add that "this is the most surprising and disappointing aspect of the efforts to spread the Rochester school's focus on rational action."[34] The pattern established in the departmental encounter with behavioralism thus appears to repeat. There is already visible assimilation by a number of faculty, particularly in the American field, of elements of the rational choice perspective which they find valuable, without implying an intellectual commitment to the paradigm as a universal theory of politics.

Evolving Departmental Profile

Beyond the rational-choice theory issue, there were occasional ventures into paradigms less central to mainstream American political science, but important internationally and in some related fields, such as history and anthropology. In the 1960s, neo-Marxism began to escape the stifling orthodoxies of Stalinism. In the radicalized environment of the late 1960s, some undercurrents of criticism were heard regarding the failure of the department to include a Marxist in its ranks, or to adequately prepare doctoral students conducting thesis research in the third world for the ideological perspectives often dominant amongst intelligentsias in their field research sites. Some new faculty had views well to the left of their colleagues. Edward Friedman, recruited in 1967, had such an image, and endeavored in his Chinese politics instruction to help students understand Maoism, though never as an advocate. But he was a disciple of the class theories of Barrington Moore, not Marx. Barbara Stallings, whose early work was influenced by dependency theory and neo-Marxism, had a higher commitment to empiricism, which led her to shift to a more liberal international political economy in her later scholarship. The collapse of "really existing" state socialism and the Soviet bloc by 1991 was a deadly blow to the intellectual attraction of diverse currents of Marxism, and this issue vanished from view.

The other paradigm that achieved a strong foothold in a number of anthropology and history departments, and dominated much of literary theory, was post-modernism in its various guises (post-structuralism, postcolonial and subaltern studies, cultural studies). The deconstructive premises of the post-modern orientation, with its pronounced hostility to empiricism and scientific modes of explanation, was much more inimical to the political science mainstream than neo-Marxism, which accepted scientific method within its own framework of dogma. When the Murray Edelman retirement in 1990 was imminent, the department resolved to find a replacement who might preserve his intellectual legacy as a unique and original voice of interpretive political science, open at the margin to some of the post-structuralist reasoning.[35] Diane Rubenstein, a Yale student of David Apter in his post-Weberian phase, was chosen for this role in 1987. As Rubenstein in her postdoctoral scholarship plunged more deeply into deconstructive discourse, and in other respects was at odds with the department, her Madison stay was brief.

There were other consequential changes in the departmental profile. Though as chapter 3 notes, the need for graduate training in statistics was recognized as early as 1931, many years passed before the growing importance and sophistication of quantitative research was reflected in faculty staffing. For a time, faculty trained in the behavioral school assured the graduate methodology offerings, but by the 1970s the need for instructors with advanced skills in the field was recognized. Development of a methodology subfield was slowed by some unsuccessful hires, initially of young faculty with a major second field beyond advanced quantitative skills; Michael Leavitt (1970–73), Richard Li (1973–75), Raisa Deber (1974–78), and Robin Marra (1983–87) had only brief careers in the department. A long-term capability in this field began to develop only with the addition of Herbert Kritzer in 1978.

Kritzer grew up in Dayton, Ohio; his father, a civil servant, lacked a college education, though his mother had a University of Georgia degree and some graduate study. During his senior year at Haverford College, he was invited to join a major sociological study on nonviolent political action directed by Paul Hare; the funding came and the project began after his graduation. This was during the peak of the Vietnam War, for which Kritzer was a conscientious objector, but failed the physical examination and thus was not required to do alternative service. During his doctoral study at the University of North Carolina, he specialized in political elites and mass political behavior. He began to recognize his own qualifications as a methodologist only when, while serving on a North Carolina search committee in this field, he realized his credentials exceeded those of many in the applicant pool.

Still, he did not yet regard himself as a methodologist; indeed, on the job market he had difficulty articulating just what his specialization was. After brief stints at Indiana and Rice, Kritzer joined the department in 1978 to fill a methodology position. Early in his career, most of his publications were in this area. However, soon after joining the faculty he became a partner in a very large project directed by David Trubek of the Law School, with several other collaborators, including Joel Grossman. This research venture, funded by a $2,000,000 grant from the Department of Justice, examined patterns of civil litigation; Kritzer joined the project as methodologist, but became attracted to its substance, which shaped much of his subsequent scholarship. Several major books ultimately resulted from his civil litigation research: *The Justice Broker: Lawyers and Ordinary Civil Litigation* (1990), *Let's Make a Deal: Negotiation and Settlement in Ordinary Litigation* (1991), *Legal Advocacy: Lawyers and Nonlawyers at Work* (1998), and *Risks, Reputations, and Rewards: Contingency Fee Legal Practice in the United States* (2004).[36] Though part of his teaching contribution fell in the judicial politics area, Kritzer remained the early backbone of department methodology instruction. He conducted an initial overhaul of the offerings in the field in

1984.[37] But a more comprehensive upgrading awaited the addition of a full-time methodologist, Charles Franklin, who arrived in Madison in 1992.

Franklin was one of the few department faculty whose adolescent years were spent in the South. His childhood home was Alabama, where his father, a naval officer, had retired. Franklin came of age at the peak of civil rights tensions in the Deep South. The Methodist church his family attended split in 1962, with the minority sympathetic to racial equality then meeting in the library basement. A Franklin letter published in the local newspaper protesting the refusal of the town cemetery to permit burial of a black soldier killed in combat in Vietnam resulted in a cross-burning on the family lawn.

Franklin first displayed his political science potential in high school, with a prizewinning paper surveying primary school pupils at several grade levels to study their evolving political socialization. A small but inspiring political science faculty at Birmingham Southern University encouraged his interests and graduate school application to Michigan. Although his doctoral study concentrated on American politics, increasingly his focus fell on methods.

Franklin joined the department after beginning his career at Washington University. This permitted a significant expansion in methodology offerings, and by 1995 Franklin felt able to propose the introduction of methods as a new preliminary examination field. Although the first initiative failed, by the following year departmental assent was won. His success in winning recognition for a methodology field was a far cry from the 1950s, when quantitative instruction had to be subcontracted to Burton Fisher of the sociology department.

Beyond the emergence of a distinctive methodology field, a primary objective in faculty recruiting during the last three decades was protection of the areas of acknowledged strength, American and comparative politics. There was a continuing struggle to strengthen international relations, a field in which the department had recruiting difficulties. The drift of Cohen into administrative roles, the transfer of much of Neil Richardson's professional energies into serving college and campus advising services; the 1995 retirement of David Tarr; and the loss of a pair of promising and productive additions, Michael Barnett (1990–2004) and Emanuel Adler (1992–95), were all setbacks. The future will lie in the hands of Jon Pevehouse (2000–) and other subsequent recruits.

Political theory, as chapter 7 explains, enjoyed a golden age in the 1980s, when Booth Fowler and Patrick Riley were joined by Charles Anderson, gradually shifting his focus from comparative politics, and James Farr for five years. The theory group was further strengthened by Marion Smiley (1989) and Bernard Yack (1991). However, by the centennial year, the theory area was in flux. Anderson retired in 1996, Fowler in 2002, Smiley and Yack departed the same year, and the Riley retirement was imminent. The addition of Richard Boyd (2002) and Eric MacGilvray (2003) is intended to begin rebuilding theory.

Affirmative action, which first became an explicit goal only at the end of the 1960s, slowly increased. In 2004, eight of the 41 department faculty were women, though only three of the 22 full professors. Although a dramatic contrast with the 1950s, change on this front, rapid in the 1970s, was subsequently only gradual. Indeed, in 1990 and 2004 the numbers of female and total faculty were identical. In the expansion years of the 1960s, only one of 42 faculty hired was female. In the 1970s, six of 21 new faculty were women; for the 1990s, the comparable figures were nine of 26.

On the racial minority front, progress was less evident. Matthew Holden during his department years (officially 1969–81, though his active teaching service ended in 1977) was the first African American.[38] No replacement for the teaching niche in African-American politics Holden had created was found till 1984, when Franklin Gilliam joined the faculty; his loss to UCLA in 1988 was a major setback. The next in this lineage was Hawley Fogg-Davis, who joined the faculty in 1999. Two Asian Americans, Richard Li (1973–75) and Kelly Chang (1998–2002), had brief stays, and Aseema Sinha joined the department in 1999; none, however, were specialists in Asian-American politics. Jack Dennis (1963–2001), though not commonly perceived in diversity terms, is a registered member of the Cherokee tribe. Mark Pollack, a Cuban American, served from 1995 to 2004. Benjamin Marquez, who earned his doctorate in the department in 1983 and returned as a faculty member in 1991, introduced instruction in Chicano politics and expanded teaching in American cultural pluralism more broadly.

The Hawkins Chair and Cluster Hiring

Another dimension to the faculty staffing equation was the surprise bequest from Glenn Hawkins, a 1927 Wisconsin history Ph.D., which funded a distinguished chair for the department. Hawkins spent most of his career at Oklahoma State University, where he taught political science when it separated from the history department. The $1,100,000 bequest was originally intended for Oklahoma State, but diverted to Madison when he could not agree to terms at Stillwater (for details, see appendix 10).[39] The department agreed that the Hawkins Chair would be reserved for a senior scholar from outside, with some preference (though not absolute) for the American field. Although the chair, which became available in 1982, was very attractive (permanent half-time research appointment, significant research funds), recruitment of a senior scholar whose distinction matched departmental hopes proved more difficult than expected. Two years were required to find the first incumbent, Herbert Jacob, whose early career (1962–69) flourished in Madison. To great disappointment, Jacob made definitive a decision to return to Northwestern in 1986. Another two years went by marked by unsuccessful searches, until word reached North Hall that Charles O. Jones, then at Virginia, might be available. The successful recruitment of Jones was a master stroke; he proved a superb incumbent, and a permanent role model for the chair. Although he held the Hawkins professorship only nine years, until his 1997 retirement, his impact was immense.

Jones spent his adolescent years in a small South Dakota town; his father was a Congregationalist minister. Modest family circumstances pushed toward undergraduate study at the University of South Dakota, which proved a happy choice. His primary mentor was William Farber, a loyal Wisconsin doctoral alumnus who sent a number of his best undergraduates to Madison for doctoral study. Farber encouraged student research, and as an undergraduate Jones completed studies on turnover in the South Dakota legislature and local town governance.

Jones held an ROTC commission, at the time of the Korean War. He was chosen to join a history project on the testing of the hydrogen bomb in the Marshall Islands in 1954. When his military service was completed, he chose Wisconsin over Michigan and Yale for graduate training. Leon Epstein and Ralph Huitt were his most important doctoral mentors. As a disciple of the Huitt school of congressional studies, he completed a dissertation on the House Agricultural Committee, with a particular eye to grasping the mechanisms of representation. The Huitt influence shaped his commitment to stress interviewing in his research, as well as the search for quantitative measures upon which his M.A. thesis was based. After completing his dissertation in 1959, he accepted a teaching position at Wellesley College. In 1962–63, he spent a formative year at the National Center for Education in Politics, an opportunity for extensive travel and valuable contacts. His teaching career then took him to Arizona, Pittsburgh, and finally Virginia, before returning to Wisconsin as Hawkins Professor.

Jones was a remarkably productive scholar, and earned recognition as a leading congressional specialist; he has a dozen books to his credit. His research also included important contributions to policy studies and, in his most recent books, on the presidency. His early books included *Party and*

Policy-Making: The House Republican Policy Committee (1965), *Every Second Year: Congressional Behavior and the Two-Year Term* (1967), and *The Minority Party in Congress* (1970). During his Hawkins years, he published *The Trusteeship Presidency: Jimmy Carter and the United States Congress* (1988), *The Presidency in a Separated System* (1994), *Passages to the Presidency: From Campaigning to Governing* (1998), and *Clinton and Congress 1993–1996: Risk, Restoration and Reelection* (1999). Jones regarded his 1975 work, *Clean Air: The Policies and Politics of Pollution Control,* as the "best book he had ever written."[40]

Jones was a scholar of deep professional loyalties—to his profession, to the discipline, to his department. He served APSA as editor of the *American Political Science Review* from 1975 to 1981, and as president in 1994. He was generous to his students, quietly drawing upon his research funds to finance student research assistantships and travel to APSA meetings. He benefited from a wide network of Washington contacts in Congress, in the White House, and among political journalists; his thoughtful reflections on current politics were—and still are—frequently cited in the quality press. His congenial personality, wise judgments, and moderate sensitivities commanded the highest respect in the department.

Two key Jones statements, his 1994 APSA presidential address, and a 1998 inaugural lecture at the University of Oxford, give interesting insight into his scholarly orientation. In the latter, he summons a "speculative imagination" as indispensable to law-making. This is especially true in what he terms the "separated system" of powers in the United States, at a moment when the coming entitlements crisis will impose difficult and painful major adaptations. "It should be the scholar's purpose to locate and mark the conditions for doing so."[41] In his APSA address, Jones concludes:

> It is this fascinating process by which the laws follow the growth in knowledge that should stimulate our research impulses. Ultimately, any government will be tested by its capacity to make laws of a quality to meet the needs of its citizens. To the extent that we as political scientists are prepared to explain and predict the procession of laws, we justify our professional craft and create a need for what we have learned.[42]

The Jones retirement in 1997 gave rise to another repeated series of searches and unsuccessful courtships for a Hawkins successor. Finally, in 2001, a distinguished replacement for Jones was found, Byron Shafer. After his 1979 University of California–Berkeley doctorate, Shafer had spent most of his career at the University of Oxford; he was perhaps the senior Americanist in the United Kingdom. With eight books providing elegant empirical analysis of American politics to his credit, he is a worthy successor to Jones. His most recent book, *The Two Majorities and the Puzzle of American Politics* (2003), is a subtle and sophisticated untangling of the conundrum referenced in his title.

In 1998, the university embarked upon a new mode of hiring. The governor and Legislature were persuaded to allocate some new positions to the university, provided that new criteria be utilized in the recruitment. The initial argument for what became known as "cluster hiring" was the rapid reconfiguring of the biological sciences, as research findings transgressed extant departmental boundaries. Thus the invitation was extended to interdisciplinary groups united by a research theme to constitute themselves as a "cluster." Through a competitive application process, "clusters" would win attribution of two or three recruitment slots. Successful candidates, however, would need to find approval from one or more departments that would serve as tenure homes.

The cluster concept was then extended to other fields. In several competitions over the period from 1999 to 2003, dozens of clusters won allocation of more than 100 positions. Although at first the cluster concept applied to what appeared to be new positions, over time the process necessarily competed with regular openings created by resignations or retirements. Departments were encouraged to cooperate with the cluster hiring process by the promise that those added to their ranks through this mechanism would not "count": that is, enter the calculus on whether a recruiting request would be honored by the school or college. In reality, such a pledge over time can hardly have contractual force; nonetheless, departments could hardly afford not to participate. By 2004, Melanie Manion, Joe Soss, Helen Kinsella, and Tamir Moustafa had been recruited through the cluster mechanism.

Curriculum and Instruction

The most important changes in the instructional mission of the department during this period occurred at the graduate level. The perennial issue of preliminary examinations was the principal matter at stake. These examinations are not only the primary hurdle, or choke point, in the doctoral program; their structure and content by retroaction shapes and defines the student course and seminar selection. An offering lacking instrumental linkage to the preliminary examination seems, for many, an unaffordable luxury.

Over the years, in response to the recurrent graduate student calls for preliminary examination reform, incremental adaptations occurred, several of which were noted in the preceding chapter. There had been a slow proliferation of examination fields, and a gradually increasing use of the specially designed fields constructed to meet individual needs. In 1989, however, a committee led by Richard Merelman was appointed to consider more far-reaching reforms.

The Merelman committee undertook a survey of recent doctoral alumni to elicit their retrospective evaluation of the program, and to collect suggestions for change. The responses closely coincided with those received in a doctoral alumni survey conducted for the history project (see appendix 18). In their communications to the committee, those responding "praised this department for its intellectual vigor, its eclecticism, its openness to new ideas, and the quality of its scholarship."[43] The most substantial reform proposed by the Merelman committee was the restructuring of department subfields into four: American, comparative, international relations, and theory. In the process, a number of long-established preliminary examination fields disappeared, among them politics and the legal order, and political psychology and sociology. Each major subfield was then asked to redefine itself in light of the newly broadened examination areas, especially American politics. As noted above, six years later, methodology was added as a fifth field.

Other changes introduced by the Merelman committee included the creation of a new course required of all entering graduate students, Political Science 800, intended to serve as a comprehensive conceptual orientation to the discipline. The examination structure was altered to require six-hour examinations in two of the redefined major fields, followed by a "dissertation examination" based upon a paper that served as conceptual formulation and literature review for the prospective dissertation. By this means, the preliminary examination cycle would more closely link with the dissertation itself.

A further major reform of the doctoral program took place under the leadership of Associate Chair John Coleman in 2002. The preliminary examination was again modified into a "first field," the area of the prospective thesis, and a "second field," drawn from the five extant areas growing out of the Merelman reform. The process of developing and formally defending a dissertation proposal was made more explicit. The minor field requirement also has been somewhat modified, making provision in some cases for an internal minor, and the scope and ambition of Political Science 800 was narrowed.

Another important change at the graduate level took place in 1996–97, under the impetus of Associate Chair Diana Mutz. Since the 1960s, the department was normally able to assure financial support for nearly all doctoral candidates beyond the first year, within the limits of "normal progress" doctrines. Particularly after new rules governing teaching assistant employment resulted from the first labor contract in 1970, which included multiyear guarantees for those appointed as TAs, the department was reluctant to offer TA positions to new incoming students. There needed to be an opportunity to evaluate their performance as graduate students, and to assess their readiness for classroom teaching, before making such a commitment. Thus to receive financial aid, first-year students had to qualify for one of the competitive University Fellowships, awards available through the area studies programs, research assistant appointments, or one of the handful of department awards. This meant that only a part of the first-year class was assured of financial aid.

Increasingly, other leading institutions guaranteed support for those admitted, and competing for the most promising applicants became more difficult. Mutz and Chair Herbert Kritzer, by creative budget redesign, developed a plan by which all incoming students could be guaranteed four or five years of financial aid. To achieve this goal, the size of the entering class had to be further reduced, from the target of approximately 25, which had prevailed in recent years, to about 16. In addition, a weekend of hospitality for top prospective students became part of the spring ritual. The sharpening competition for incoming students was in some respects paradoxical, since it was not matched by ease of placement of the doctoral classes; on the whole the 1990s were a difficult decade in this respect, with a completed degree and even publications becoming a necessary credential, and a number of the doctoral class forced to accept temporary positions initially.

The reduction in the size of the entering class necessarily made admission more selective. Although this assured intakes with impressive, even dazzling grade-point averages and Graduate Record Examination scores, the goal of diversity became more difficult. On the gender front, the gradual increase in the number of women students continued, although far from parity; in the 1990s, 27 of the 126 doctorates awarded were earned by women. However, in terms of African Americans and Latinos, progress stalled, even regressed in comparison to the 1970s. Between 1974 and 1990, six African Americans completed doctorates (and all began their doctoral study in the 1970s).[44] Since that time, only Calvin Brutus (of Caribbean origin) won a Ph.D., in 1996. In addition, in the last three decades, ten Africans completed doctorates. During that same period, there were only six Latino doctorates.[45] Asians and Asian Americans were more numerous, eight and five respectively during the 1990s.

On the native American side, one may cite Haunani-Kay Trask (1981), recently a leading figure in the Hawaian sovereignty movement.[46]

Although there were no major changes in the undergraduate curriculum, the steady increase in the attraction of the political science major, already noted in chapter 4, merits further examination. The attractions of the field to undergraduates were several. Certainly the excellent teaching reputation of the department faculty was a significant factor; a 2004 analysis of overall course evaluations over the previous 10 years yielded an average score of 4.42 on a five-point scale.[47] During this period, a remarkable number of faculty won all-campus distinguished teaching awards (Patrick Riley and Donald Emmerson 1985, Melvin Croan 1986, James Farr 1987, Joel Grossman 1988, Donald Downs 1989, James Coleman 2001). Credit is also due to the excellent undergraduate advising services under Ernestine Vanderlin and her successors (and predecessors). The value of a political science major as preparation for law school or a public service career played a part. Doubtless the intrinsic interest of the subject matter, its generic utility as a liberal arts major, and the lack of extensive quantitative requirements all had some influence. But table 5.1 makes clear the growing popularity of the political science major.

Table 5.1 Comparative L&S Major Enrollments, 1954–2003

	1954–59	1959–64	1964–69	1969–74	1974–79	1979–84	1984–89	1989–94	1994–99	1999–2003*
Political Science	414	952	1880	1592	1632	2047	3459	5206	2475	2534
Sociology	325	493	986	1397	1301	1765	2194	1736	977	1174
Economics	1647	1421	1629	1077	1503	1384	1870	2222	2055	1625
Psychology	537	1079	2193	2293	1203	1308	1711	2576	2051	1429
Zoology	376	778	1451	1610	1188	691	738	1020	1688	1975
International Relations**								412	1493	1297

* Covers only a four-year period. The figures are a total for the period indicated.

** The international relations major was housed in political science until 1990–91, and not counted separately until after that time.

Source: UW–Madison Enrollment Reports, 1954–55 to 2002–03.

Some of the increase in the last two decades in political science enrollments derives from the dramatic rise in the international relations major. This was created in 1938, and since that time has virtually always been directed by political scientists. Although the requirements were by no means identical with those of the department major, the political science content was always substantial. Perhaps because of the political science leadership (since the second war, Llewellyn Pfankuchen, Bernard Cohen, Neil Richardson, Leon Lindberg, and Michael Barnett), and its housing in the department until 1991, the university statistics subsumed international relations under political science. As well, during this period political science provided the advising services. Until the 1980s, the major enrolled small numbers, no more than a few dozen. But then its numbers exploded, increasing from 50 to 500 during the 1980s, for reasons that are not entirely clear. Although over time there was a gradual increase in the interdisciplinary content of the program, there were no other changes to the major.[48] But as table 5.1 shows, in the most recent period, international relations added to political science totals more than twice the number of majors of the next largest social science.

A major new responsibility devolved upon the department in the early 1990s was delegated responsibility for budget management. Previously, budgetary operations were centralized in L&S. Dean Certain decided to delegate budget operation to a modest number of larger departments that had been historically well governed, and had the potential administrative capacity to assume this responsibility. Political Science was among those so chosen. This major new charge required reshuffling staff responsibilities in the office, and necessitated a new skill for chairs; the reform was first implemented under Virginia Sapiro, but ended under Mark Beissinger. Though budget delegation meant new burdens, it also provided greater flexibility. One may doubt whether the Mutz-Kritzer initiative on guaranteed graduate student funding would have been otherwise feasible.

The 1980 Teaching Assistant Strike

The most conflictual episode in the last three decades was the 1980 strike by the Teaching Assistant Association (TAA). Although in the early aftermath of the 1970 initial labor contract with the TAA relations were reasonably civil, as the decade wore on they became increasingly adversarial. One basic flaw in the bargaining process was the difficulty in defining an appropriate university negotiating team. Because issues placed on the table often involved educational policy and faculty prerogatives, faculty representatives needed to participate, but in the process became locked into the structurally adversarial role of the labor contract bargaining process. On the TAA side, the constant leadership turnover inhibited the accumulation of bargaining experience. There is little doubt that labor bargaining is facilitated when both sides deploy experienced and professional negotiators. As well, some faculty involved in the bargaining relationship came to feel that the TAA was a distinctive kind of union, some of whose leaders perceived their goals to be restructuring the university through militant labor action, as a first step toward a larger goal of societal transformation.[49]

As the 1970s progressed, the strike threat began to arise during the bargaining, and some strike votes were taken, though the strike option was theoretically foreclosed by no-strike clauses in the successive contracts.[50] At the same time, the TAA adopted an aggressive stance on grievances, filing several against the department which most faculty felt were ill-founded.[51] By early 1980, negotiations were at an impasse, and a strike was clearly in the air. This time, the TAA made much more careful preparations for an extended strike. An active campaign of building undergraduate support was undertaken; the larger context of 1970 of student disaffection and antiwar sentiment was absent, and the TAA faced the task of persuading students that a strike was intended to improve undergraduate education, to which, they argued, many faculty lacked commitment. As well, graduate students in the social sciences and humanities were exhorted to boycott the graduate offerings. The spring break trap that undermined the 1970 strike was avoided; the walkout would begin only after the March recess.

The strike began on 1 April 1980, and was suspended only on 5 May. The educational impact was substantial in our department and many others in the social sciences and humanities. Undergraduate attendance was sharply reduced, and the boycott of graduate courses and seminars was very effective. In political science, 13 of 14 TAs participated in the strike, a substantially greater percentage than in 1970.[52] In the end, the strike was halted before reaching a point where suspension of pay would have triggered loss of tuition remissions.[53] As well, an L&S faculty meeting expressed support for the university bargaining stance, ending all hopes the strikers may have held for faculty support for the TAA demands. Although there was no repeat of the general pass-fail option on this occasion, in many courses so much of the semester was lost that the final examinations and grading process were difficult; the policy enunciated was not to punish students for their participation in the strike.[54]

The issues that produced the strike remained unresolved.[55] In August 1980, Chancellor Shain gave an ultimatum to the TAA to accept university terms by 22 September, or face an end to university recognition. The TAA demurred, and the university carried out its threat to abrogate its contractual accord with the union. The TAA continued to exist, and with important support from other unions, turned to a legislative effort to secure adoption of a law that would authorize collective bargaining for TAs. Extant laws, dating from 1959, made provision for state employees to bargain collectively, but university faculty, academic staff, and teaching assistants were excluded. The university and its faculty representatives, the University Committee, lobbied strenuously against such legislation, but in 1985 an enabling law was passed.[56] However, there was a crucial difference with previous arrangements: collective bargaining for the state would be conducted by the Department of Employment Relations (DER), and not by the university. This removed the faculty and the university from the adversarial frictions of the bargaining process. Successive contracts were negotiated through this mechanism until 2003, when a new impasse occurred over the state insistence that all employees, including TAs, make some co-payment on health benefits. The TAA offered to accept an offsetting reduction in wage increase, but the DER was adamant. On this occasion, in contrast to the previous strikes, the department faculty expressed its unanimous support for the TAA position. In the fall of 2004, the TAA carried out a brief work stoppage, and threatened to withhold final grades for the semester, a menace later withdrawn. As the centennial passed, the impasse continued.

Some Major Figures

To complete the narrative, I profile some faculty whose contributions were not fully treated in chapters 6 through 11, or elsewhere in this chapter or the previous one. Only those whose departmental careers covered more than a decade are included. Clara Penniman and William Young, whose careers fell primarily in the earlier period, are discussed in chapters 4 and 10. Leon Epstein, Henry Hart, John Armstrong, Charles Anderson, Barbara Stallings, Leigh Payne, Crawford Young, Fred Hayward, Aili Tripp, James Scott, Donald Emmerson, Paul Hutchcroft, Edward Friedman, Susan Pharr, Melvin Croan, Mark Beissinger, Kathryn Hendley, Leon Lindberg, Graham Wilson, and Mark Pollack are profiled in chapter 6 (in that order). Dennis Dresang, John Witte, Donald Kettl, Herbert Kritzer, Charles Franklin, and Charles O. Jones are reviewed elsewhere in this chapter. Brief details about several former members of the department faculty, who served for more than a decade in this period, but for whom we have neither oral histories nor extended interviews, are found in other chapters: Marion Smiley and Bernard Yack in chapter 7, Michael Barnett in chapter 8, Diana Mutz in chapter 9, and William Gormley and Ira Sharkansky in chapter 10. I begin with a pair of original scholars—Murray Edelman and Richard Merelman—whose contributions resist classification by the conventional subfields, then group the profiles by field.

Murray Edelman was a unique figure in departmental annals, the very embodiment of the intellectual eclecticism which characterizes the department. Impossible to categorize, Edelman drew conceptual inspiration from a transdisciplinary universe that included symbolic interactionism, phenomenology, post-structuralism, social psychology, linguistic theory. His eclecticism, he explained, is rooted in his view that none of the basic theories used by political scientists originated in the discipline of political science.[57] His theoretical influence on the field was great; however imperfect a measure the *Social Science Citation Index* may be, there is surely indisputable significance in the fact that in 2000, a decade after his retirement, he had nearly three times as many citations as the next highest department member (Charles Jones). Another critical vehicle for his enduring influence was the graduate course he taught for many years on empirical political theory (Political Science 820), a course cited by many doctoral alumni for the significance of its impact.

Edelman grew up in the coal country of eastern Pennsylvania in an Orthodox Jewish family; both parents were committed socialists, and his father once ran for a minor New Jersey office on a socialist ticket. Years later, Edelman encountered long-time Socialist Party leader Norman Thomas, who remembered Edelman's father. The latter died when Edelman was a child; his mother supported the family by managing a variety store in Wilkes-Barre. As a child, he contracted scarlet fever, which apparently did permanent heart damage. Just before coming to Madison in 1966, he fell victim to rheumatic fever and was hospitalized for six weeks. In 1977, he had his first major heart attack, and was warned that he did not have long to live.[58] In spite of the heart condition which continued to plague him, he survived for another quarter century, until 2001.

After a Bucknell B.A., and a Chicago M.A. in history, Edelman did military service during the war, then earned a doctorate at the University of Illinois in 1948. He stayed on with the Illinois faculty. His first book grew out of his thesis on radio licensing, a topic suggested by his dissertation supervisor. His initial Illinois appointment was three-quarters in the Institute of

Labor and Industrial Regulation, a location that determined his next research on labor relations. During the course of this work, he became intrigued with the degree to which the process of industrial bargaining was highly stylized and ritualized. From this epiphany came the arrestingly original insights that shaped his 1964 classic, *The Symbolic Uses of Politics*, through which he found his authorial voice. The book in its epistemology stood in antithesis to the then-ascendent behavioral orientation of political science, and initially received a polarized reception. Indeed, Edelman notes that his intellectual sources came mainly from outside political science, especially from social psychology and the philosophy of science, represented by such iconic figures as George Herbert Mead and Ernst Cassirir. However, as time passed, the work achieved increasingly positive recognition as a major conceptual innovation. In its pages, Edelman inaugurated the themes that would find further development in his subsequent work. "Not only does systematic research suggest that the most cherished forms of popular participation in government are largely symbolic," he wrote, "but also that many of the public programs universally taught and believed to benefit a mass public in fact benefit relatively small groups."[59] This core insight shaped his subsequent work, which pushed the symbolic dimension of political action in a number of different directions: *Politics as Symbolic Action: Mass Arousal and Quiescence* (1971), *Political Language: Words that Succeed and Politics that Fail* (1977), *Constructing the Political Spectacle* (1988), and *From Art to Politics: How Artistic Creations Shape Political Conceptions* (1995). Of these, Edelman considered *Political Language* and *Political Spectacle* his finest works.[60]

His skeptical and critical posture toward the "official story" of democratic politics often cast him as a pessimist: in his own eyes, however, he was a "cheerful pessimist."[61] The categories created by political discourse in turn shape and constrain public reflection. Edelman notes the singular impact of some masters of the public metaphor, such as Ronald Reagan or Martin Luther King.

Edelman was at his best in graduate courses. His quiet style did not electrify large undergraduate classes. Nor did he seek roles in academic leadership. The Illinois department conscripted him as chair shortly before his departure for Madison; he found the role distasteful and stressful, and was delighted to escape its servitudes.[62]

Richard Merelman, like Edelman, resists consignment to conventional categories of scholarship. He also draws upon a wide range of intellectual sources. More than Edelman, his research has wandered into diverse realms, always offering unusual insights. His methodological iconoclasm is perhaps measured by his postretirement avocation as a poet, just reaching publication stage.

Merelman grew up in Washington, in the family of a civil servant. The peculiar nature of Washington, as the northernmost part of the South and southern edge of the North, introduced him through adolescence in a marginal arena "to the contradictions and paradoxes of power."[63] He attended George Washington University, first challenging convention by participating in a student action group seeking greater breadth in the intellectual and political atmosphere, well before the age of student protest. This timid assertion, Merelman felt, may have compromised his standing with potential faculty references; in his graduate applications, he was admitted only to Illinois. A happy development: his work there with Ranney and Edelman fired his ambitions, and he transferred to Yale in 1960. In his doctoral training, Robert Lane and Robert Dahl were especially influential.

Merelman joined the department in 1969, after teaching at Wesleyan and UCLA. By then, he had concluded that his mark upon the profession would not be in the behavioralist mainstream, based on a natural science model. Eventually he returned to some of the classic sociological grand theorists, Max Weber and Emile Durkheim, and the major structural anthropologists, in particular Claude Levi-Strauss, Clifford Geertz, Edward Leach, and Mary Douglas, who had a profound influence upon his subsequent work.[64]

His first book, *Political Socialization and Educational Climates: A Study of Two School Districts*, followed the conventions of that field. However, his next major work, *Making Something of Ourselves: On Culture and Politics in the United States* (1984), reflected the new influence of structural anthropology. He went further in seeking a grasp of political culture in what he regards as his finest work, *Partial Visions: Culture and Politics in Britain, Canada, and the United States* (1991). In this monograph, Merelman combines the tenacious empiricism of his Yale training with his dogged unconventionality in the pursuit of evidence. He traces the sources of popular culture in television soap operas, magazine advertisements, corporate publications, and civics texts. The political messages embedded in these everyday sources construct a popular culture yielding only "partial visions" of democracy and polity. Although he finally concluded that a fully articulated theory of culture was not obtainable, the book was a fruitful venture in making it legible as a whole structure.

His last two books go in very different directions. In *Representing Black Culture: Racial Conflict and Cultural Politics in the United States* (1995), he ventures into the field of race theory. In his final major work, *Pluralism at Yale: The Culture of American Political Science* (2003), the enigmas of culture are tracked into the womb of a single academic department at a maximal moment of its influence.

In the theory area, two profiles need expansion, those of Booth Fowler and Patrick Riley (see also chapter 7). Fowler grew up in Niagara Falls; his father was a metallurgist for a large corporation, and his mother a community activist, whose commitments first awakened his interest in politics, and whose friendship with early feminist leader and League of Women Voters founder Carrie Chapman Catt later inspired him to write her biography. His undergraduate study took place in the congenial environment of Haverford College, where he did a senior thesis on the political thought of Mao Tse-Tung.

At Harvard for graduate study, Fowler began as a student of V. O. Key in American politics, but switched to theory when Key passed away after his first year. His dissertation advisors were Michael Waltzer and Louis Hartz. Equally stimulating were a pair of talented fellow graduate students, Doris Kearns and Barney Frank. The Harvard intellectual environment was formative, but provided inadequate training in professional culture: for example, the urgency of publication. When Fowler joined the department faculty in 1967, his extraordinary teaching gifts were evident at once, but the publication record was slow to develop. But over time his scholarship gained momentum, and by the time of his 2002 retirement he had more single-authored books to his credit than any other active member of the faculty.

Fowler brought broad and distinctive interests to his scholarship and teaching. His primary field was contemporary American political thought, but he had a fine command of the classics and intellectual history generally. Fowler was particularly concerned with the interpretation of American political culture. He worked then not only with the studies of political theorists, but also with the writings of public intellectuals, civic and religious leaders, novelists and essayists as he tried to capture the underlying spirit of an historical period or of the present moment. Much of his theory writing was in the field of religion and politics, where he achieved considerable distinction. His writings include *Believing Skeptics: American Political Thought 1945–64* (1978); *A New Engagement: Evangelical Political Thought 1966–1976* (1982); *Religion and Politics in the United States* (1985); *Carrie Chapman Catt: Feminist Politician* (1986); *Unconventional Partners: Religion and Liberal Culture in the United States* (1989); *The Dance with Community: The Contemporary Debate in American Political Thought* (1989); *The Greening of Protestant Thought: 1970–90* (1995); and *Enduring Liberalism: American Political Thought since the 1960s* (1999). In his final work, *Enduring Liberalism*, Fowler describes his own intellectual commitment as a synthesis of opposites: "part Enlightenment liberal, part Burkean conservative, part Emersonian anarchist, part religious existentialist."[65]

From the beginning of his career to its end, Fowler was one of the best and most beloved teachers in the department. He was warm and friendly with individuals, dramatic, often spellbinding in the classroom. He was equally well received by freshmen, advanced undergraduates, and graduate students. He supervised or participated in supervising most of the theory dissertations written during his career at Madison, and his students include some of Wisconsin's most distinguished alumni.[66]

Patrick Riley has been the other political philosophy mainstay during the entirety of the period under review. His abundant corpus of publication, reviewed in chapter 7, stands in counterpoint to the contemporary theme of the Fowler oeuvre. Riley strides in the footsteps of the classical historians of political philosophy.

Riley grew up in Los Angeles where his father was an auto dealer, and his mother a secondary school Shakespeare teacher, a major early intellectual influence. One grandfather bequeathed a large library, which Riley as an adolescent devoured avidly. As an undergraduate at the Claremont Colleges, he was introduced to political philosophy by T. M. Greene. Before doctoral study at Harvard, he spent a year at the London School of Economics, working with Michael Oakeshott, who had a profound influence on the young Riley. At Harvard, he benefited from an extraordinary array of mentors: Carl Friedrich, Louis Hartz, Judith Shklar, John Rawls. According to Riley, his three best thesis chapters examined Leibniz, Kant, and Rousseau; these three theorists have provided the core of his research ever since. With retirement near in 2004, he has contracts with Chicago, Yale, and Princeton for further books on each.

Riley had a joint appointment with philosophy, where his intellectual affinities are closer than with many of his political science colleagues. Although he finds no hostility to theory on the part of the department as a whole, graduate students, advised that classical political philosophy is a difficult specialization for job placement, avoid the field for dissertation purposes. Thus his dissertation supervision has been mainly at Harvard, where he often has taught summer school, and in philosophy.[67]

The pattern of leadership in the law and politics field established by David Fellman in the 1950s was sustained by Joel Grossman and Donald Downs as well as Kritzer, whose contribution was reviewed earlier in the chapter. Grossman spent his early years in New York; his parents, the children of immigrants, both had M.A. degrees, and pushed hard on the importance of education. His father was an accountant, and his mother a teacher. He attended the academically demanding Stuyvesant High School, then Queen's College. After a brief and boring job with Prudential Insurance Company, Grossman enrolled in the Columbia graduate program. The key faculty at Columbia seemed to him past their prime, and he accepted an invitation from Iowa to come as a teaching assistant. At the time, some young rebels had just succeeded in overthrowing an encrusted department gerontocracy, and an exhilarating spirit of change was in the air. Vernon Van Dyke was the key figure in departmental renovation, but there were several stimulating young faculty, and an excellent mentor in John Schmidhauser in judicial politics. Grossman was strongly influenced by the applications of the behavioral orientation to the law and politics field, and attracted to the possibilities for quantitative study of judicial decisions.

Placing a doctoral candidate at Wisconsin in 1963 was a moment for celebration for Iowa. Grossman's first book, *Lawyers and Judges: The ABA and the Politics of Judicial Selection* (1965), established his national reputation, consolidated by a 1972 constitutional law text, coauthored with Richard Wells, *Constitutional Law and Judicial Policy Making*. Grossman was present at the creation of the Law and Society Association, which drew together social scientists and the several Law School faculty drawn to the sociology of law. Out of this group came an important journal, the *Law and Society Review*, which Grossman edited from 1976 to 1982. Another major venture, in collaboration with Jack Ladinsky in sociology, was the creating of the Wisconsin Law and Behavioral Science program, which provided a popular major.

An active faculty leader, Grossman was department chair from 1975 to 1978, and later chaired the University Committee. He followed the trail blazed by Fellman in an active concern for academic rights and for due process in university procedures. His initial attraction to jurimetrics began to fade, and his substantive research interests shifted to the analytical and normative dimensions of judicial studies. The massive Civil Litigation Research Project (CLPP), in which Grossman was a leading figure, was discussed earlier in the chapter. In 1996, Grossman took early entry into the emeritus ranks, to accept a position at Johns Hopkins University, where he still teaches full time.

In his 33 years at Wisconsin, Grossman taught constitutional law to well over 5,000 undergraduate students, and supervised numerous doctoral theses. In 1988 he was awarded the Emil Steiger campuswide teaching award. He has also won the 2005 Lifetime Achievement Award presented by the Law and Courts Section of the APSA.

Donald Downs has been not only a crucial addition to the law and politics group, but an important contributor to political theory, and a storied figure on campus with relation to academic freedom and ethics issues. He is also a masterful lecturer, teaching large public law classes. His principled willingness to adopt unpopular positions, his continuous process of self-reflection and willingness to change his positions on the basis of new evidence, and his articulate persuasiveness make him a campus citizen of exceptional worth.

He was born in Canada; his father's forebears were loyalists during the American Revolution who fled to Canada. However, his adolescent years were spent in Chicago. His undergraduate study at Cornell coincided with the peak of the student protest movement in 1969, when Cornell was a violent epicenter. An armed group of African-American students along with some other participants occupied the Cornell Union; the ensuing crisis forced the resignation of President James Perkins, and posed existential threats to academic freedom at the university. During the crisis, Downs particularly admired the intellectual courage of Walter Berns, a political scientist of Straussian orientation with an uncompromising insistence on upholding academic freedom in the face of the nihilistic passions of the moment. As a history major at Cornell, Downs enjoyed an excellent faculty; Walter Lefeber and Donald Kagan were especially influential.

Downs began his graduate study at Illinois, where he studied political philosophy with John Schiller; he came to political science via philosophy. He then transferred to the University of California–Berkeley, where he specialized in American government, public law, and political philosophy. Robert Kagan, Michael Rogin, and Hannah Pitkin were all important influences. Kagan, who supervised his dissertation on Nazis in Skokie, implanted three principles in Downs: look at politics and law from different perspectives; be intellectually fair and honest in research and teaching, without shying away from uncomfortable truths; and take empiricism seriously.

After four years at Notre Dame, Downs joined the department in 1985. His five books each address major dilemmas in defining the boundaries of freedom. *Nazis in Skokie: Freedom, Community, and the First Amendment* (1985) asks whether the right to demonstrate for those espousing doctrines most find hateful can be abridged. *The New Politics of Pornography* (1989) and *More the Victims: Battered Women, the Syndrome Society, and the Law* (1996) explore the normative, psychological, and criminal law interactions in issues understood as the victimization of women. In *Cornell '60: Liberalism and the Crisis of the American University* (1999), he revisits the traumatic events of his undergraduate years, sifting through the failures of will among many liberals confronted with crisis. His most recent book, *Restoring Free Speech and Liberty on Campus* (2005), addresses the political and normative issues associated with the status of free speech and liberty on campus nationwide. The book includes two chapters on Wisconsin.

Downs has been tireless in offering guidance and wise counsel in a succession of campus issues implicating the boundaries of free speech. After much reflection in 1992, he decided to oppose passage of a revised student speech code in the Faculty Senate. The code passed, but was rejected by the regents based on a new Supreme Court ruling. In 1993, Downs publicly supported the *Badger Herald* when it was under fire for publishing a cartoon which he believed was falsely interpreted as racist. In 1995, finding that a faculty speech code had been misapplied, he took part in a movement to combat the code. By 1999, the code was effectively abolished by the Faculty Senate. In 1996, he became secretary of a newly formed group of about 20 members, the Committee for Academic Freedom and Rights, which has supported several faculty and staff on issues of academic freedom and due process. In 2000, he led a campaign to dismantle a program establishing 35 boxes around campus for deposit of anonymous complaints about individuals; the evidence of abuse was substantial, and Chancellor Wiley agreed to stop the process. In 2001, he supported the *Badger Herald* again, this time for refusing to apologize for publishing an advertisement from conservative activist David Horowitz. Since 2001, he has been involved in organizing protest on academic freedom grounds against the firing by the board of regents of Professor John Marder at the University of Wisconsin–Superior. Many of these positions required real courage; Downs has always been willing to swim against the currents of opinion when he is convinced of the principle at stake. This boundless energy in support of academic freedom in his campus activity, as well as his scholarship, bears witness to the unique role played by Downs.[68]

The contributions of several Americanists merit further examination, in order of arrival on the faculty. Jack Dennis grew up in Oklahoma City in modest circumstances; his father worked in the circulation department of the main newspaper. His first enthusiasm, to which he returned in retirement, was art. Though he held jobs throughout his high school years, he finished at the top of the class. His adolescent ambition was to study commercial art at Pratt Institute, but family finances would not permit. Thus he took up a scholarship at the University of Oklahoma. Though his family initially pushed him to a pre-medical major, he soon switched to an interdisciplinary "letters" major, based entirely on honors courses. His program was a peculiar mix of natural science and philosophy, though the latter was his most influential field.[69]

Dennis won a Rhodes Scholarship, and pursued the "PPE" (politics, philosophy, and economics) option at Oxford. The Rhodes years sharpened his intellectual faculties; the thrust of the Oxford training was historical and philosophical. Though Dennis had acquired some awareness of the behavioral approach, it was entirely absent from Oxford.

After military service, Dennis chose Chicago for doctoral training. He was attracted by its image as in the vanguard of the discipline; he had been particularly drawn to the critique of the field put forward by David Easton in *The Political System*. Though his doctoral study included fruitful work with Duncan McRae, Morton Kaplan, and David Apter, Easton became his major influence. Dennis was a research assistant on an ambitious project directed by Easton, examining child political socialization, then a nearly unexplored subject. Dennis canvassed relevant sociological and psychological sources, and took part in the huge survey, involving 12,000 subjects, including parents and siblings in eight major cities in the United States. He helped develop the methodology for the study, in the process acquiring a thorough familiarity with survey and data analysis methods. This research provided the basis for the landmark 1969 book, *Children in the Political System: Origins of Political Legitimacy*, coauthored with Easton.

After completing his doctorate in 1962, Dennis stayed on at Chicago for a year as a research associate of Easton, then joined the Wisconsin department in 1963. Through his long career he retained his commitment to the behavioral study of politics, for which he provides a forthright defense in chapter 14. Behavioralists, Dennis notes, were always a minority in the department, but he and those such as Donald McCrone, Charles Cnudde, Austin Ranney, Wendy Rahn, and Diana Mutz, who over the years shared his perspectives, worked to nurture this orientation. On arrival, he found allies in Rufus Browning and Herbert Jacob; with them, he persuaded the department to introduce a required course in empirical methods (Political Science 817), which he initially taught. But he always considered himself a user of methodology, and not a methodologist; when other hands became available to offer this and other methods courses, he transferred his instructional energies to the behavioral curriculum: elections and voting behavior, political psychology, political socialization, and political communication. In his scholarship, Dennis viewed himself as a comparativist, not just an Americanist.

His research themes always had political socialization as a core element. After *Children and the Political System*, his abundant research contribution came through articles in leading journals. He was involved in the national election studies carried out by the Michigan Survey Research Center, and a close collaborator in the Wisconsin surveys carried out by Harry Sharp and his survey laboratory. He helped found what became the Data and Program Library Service, which he directed for several years.

Dennis also played an important role in L&S, serving as an associate dean from 1987 to 1990 under Dean Cronon, whose leadership Dennis greatly admired. At the end of his tenure, frustrations grew as frictions grew between the college and Chancellor Shalala, especially over issues of college autonomy.[70] In 1992, Dennis headed a review committee examining the L&S administration; his thorough report provided a manual for reform under interim Dean Young. The perspective gained from his portfolio of managing well over a dozen social science departments, plus more than two dozen other programs, reinforced his appreciation for the culture of the department, which he found the most collegial of those with whom his deanship brought him into close contact.

After retirement, Dennis returned to his youthful passion for art. His paintings and prints won a place in a number of exhibitions. He also followed in a family tradition of owning a hobby farm, occasionally dabbling in cultivation and holding a tobacco allocation. Somehow Dennis looked as much at home seated on a tractor as he did behind a computer.

Peter Eisinger joined the faculty six years after Dennis, in 1969. His childhood household was academic; his father taught English at Purdue. The home was lined with bookshelves, and television was banished. His father's red pen sharpened the writing skills of the young Eisinger. A Fulbright took his father to Austria, where Eisinger learned French and German.

As a Michigan undergraduate, Eisinger chose a political science major as an intending law student. Frank Grace in political thought was one major influence; Eisinger's senior thesis on Charles Maurras and *Action Française* was written under James Meisel. But the critical impact was a course on scope and method by Samuel Barnes. This pushed Eisinger to graduate study at Yale. Here Eisinger flourished under Robert Dahl, James David Barber, William Muir, and Karl Deutsch; as well, his contemporaries were a remarkable generation.[71]

His doctoral study took place in the politically charged environment of the late 1960s. Eisinger was struck by how little the discipline had to contribute on issues of poverty and protest; he thus embarked on a dissertation on community action organizations stimulated by the poverty program. Eisinger turned down other offers, including one from Michigan at a higher salary, to join the department in 1969. This was a baptism under fire; teaching very large courses on the politically volatile subject of urban politics, Eisinger felt the brunt of the prevailing campus turmoil. Several times his classes were interrupted by outside activists who barged into his lectures, demanding the classes be suspended to discuss oppression of racial minorities and the Vietnam War.[72]

The first major Eisinger project at Wisconsin was a survey of race issues in Milwaukee, leading to his 1976 book, *The Patterns of Interracial Politics*. He then turned to explore how white political and business elites responded to black electoral control of the mayor's office in Detroit and Atlanta, the first two major cities to come under black leadership. Eisinger framed his analysis in *The Politics of Displacement: Racial and Ethnic Transitions in Three American Cities* (1980) by the comparison with earlier patterns of ethnic succession, when Irish, Italian, or Eastern European mayors displaced the earlier Yankee elites. Eisinger was intrigued by the degree to which black mayors in Detroit and Atlanta had to commit political capital to the search for investment and promotion of building projects. Service on an advisory committee to the state Strategic Development Commission in the mid–1980s convinced Eisinger that the conscious pursuit of state economic development was a major new sphere of public policy, which he explored in *The Rise of the Entrepreneurial State: State and Local Economic Development Policy in the United States* (1988).

The balance of the Eisinger career at Wisconsin was committed mostly to administrative leadership. He chaired the department from 1987 to 1990, then the La Follette Institute from 1991 to 1996. The following year, his wife, Erica, a legal scholar, was invited to join the faculty at Wayne State University. To permit her to seize this opportunity, Eisinger also accepted a faculty post at Wayne State, taking early retirement from Wisconsin.

Eisinger joins many others in underlining the enduring importance and value of the departmental culture of collegiality. His reflections on this theme merit citation:

> That tensions over the war, the TA strike, and the demonstrations never tore the department apart was testimony to the strong norm of civility and restraint that governed the North Hall community during my 28 years. Of course there were instances when the norms were violated, but for the most part I always marveled at how different life in our department was from the turmoil that plagued places like Indiana or Stanford and other schools where young and old, liberal and conservative, behavioralists and traditionalists did not speak to one another or worse.[73]

At the same time, Eisinger notes with regret some loss of community: more solitary sandwiches in the office rather than shared sack lunches; dwindling of dinner gatherings or other social gatherings. "People blamed this on women entering the workforce," Eisinger said, "but I think it was just a general inward-turning that afflicted households where only one spouse worked as well as those with two people working."[74]

Virginia Sapiro is a third-generation teacher. A New Yorker, she attended the High School of Art and Music in Harlem, but knew from the start of her Clark University undergraduate study that she wanted to major in political science. Clark, she found, was a perfect match; she developed a lasting attraction to political philosophy, and did a senior thesis on classical Jewish political thought. During the Cambodia spring season of student strikes and attendant turmoil in Madison, Sapiro was among the organizers of a student strike at Clark. The strike was the moment for a feminist epiphany for Sapiro; in defining their objectives, strikers enthusiastically applauded statements against imperialism and racism, but laughed when someone wanted to add a declaration against sexism. Sapiro and 30 other women walked out in disgust.

She chose Michigan for graduate study, majoring in political behavior and minoring in political thought. She served as a research assistant on a political socialization study conducted by Kent Jennings, and particularly flourished in the environment of the Institute for Social Research, with its strong culture of mentorship. She was also one of five founding members of the Michigan Teaching Assistant Union, though she dropped out of the leadership because she felt the other leaders tried to make too many issues subject to collective bargaining.[75]

At the time of her 1975 employment search, gender discrimination persisted in the academy. Women were frequently interviewed, but infrequently hired; they were discouraged from pursuing topics related to gender. At Wisconsin, Sapiro was appointed at a salary lower than that offered to males, and remained the lowest paid department member almost until she won tenure.[76] However, she recalls with appreciation that she was free to pursue her research on gender and politics; she is, she believes, the first political scientist at a top institution to earn tenure exclusively on works relating to gender.

Her appointment was joint with the recently created women's studies department. Because women's studies was newly established, its procedures were fluid and its governance demands on young faculty very great. More broadly on campus, the service burdens on women faculty were heavy. Nonetheless, Sapiro quickly made her mark upon the profession. Her first book, *The Political Integration of Women: Roles, Socialization and Politics*

(1983), helped define the field of women and politics, and the basic text on women's studies she completed soon after provided the first major synthesis of this subject. She then returned to her early interest in political philosophy, publishing a prizewinning study in 1992 of the political thought of Mary Wollstonecraft, an 18th-century pioneer of feminism.

Sapiro served as principal investigator of the American National Election Studies at the University of Michigan from 1997 to 2000. She was the only scholar from outside the Michigan faculty ever to do so. She discovered, first as chair of the Women's Studies Program during 1986–89, then as political science chair from 1993 to 1996, that she not only had administrative talents, but thrived in the role of academic leadership. During her term leading the department, L&S embarked on a decentralizing reform, delegating budgetary autonomy to a small number of large and well-managed departments. Superintending this critical transformation was a major challenge. In 2002 she became associate vice chancellor, a role that gave wide latitude for her energy and gifts for innovative initiative. By this time she had concluded that she would commit the balance of her academic career to higher levels of administrative leadership.

Kenneth Mayer (1989), David Canon (1991), Benjamin Marquez (1991), and John Coleman (1992) are more recent additions to the Americanist contingent, achieving national recognition early in their careers. Mayer, whose early years were spent in California, attended the University of California–San Diego, initially with medical or bioengineering ambitions. Political science soon captured his imagination, and during his last undergraduate year he had an internship with the Democratic Congressional Campaign Committee. This experience confirmed his interest in politics, but convinced him to abandon plans for a legal career. Restless to leave California, he chose Yale for graduate study, attracted to its high reputation rather than its methodological orientation. Particularly influential were Edward Tufte in political economy, David Mayhew in American politics, and Bruce Russett in national security issues. Yale in the second half of the 1980s had its painful moments, with a prolonged strike by the clerical and custodial staff, whom Mayer and many others believed received shabby treatment from the university.

Before completing his degree, Mayer found employment as a civilian contract specialist in the Navy, a fascinating insight on the inner workings of a bureaucracy, which housed some very able people. Though he was never tempted to pursue a Washington career, the experience pointed to a dissertation on defense contracting. This developed into his first book, *The Political Economy of Defense Contracting* (1991).

After a Harvard fellowship in 1987–88, and a Brookings year in 1988–89, Mayer joined the Wisconsin faculty in 1989. The vacancy was listed as American politics, but he was hired as a specialist in Congress and national security studies. However, the beginning of his teaching career coincided with the end of the cold war, which led Mayer to conclude that foreign policy and security studies would have diminished appeal as a research focus. He thus shifted entirely to the domestic political scene, and found a fertile new field for inquiry in the study of executive orders, then a seldom examined topic but now an exploding field of interest. His research took him to several presidential libraries, and led to a book breaking new ground in 2001, *With the Stroke of a Pen: Executive Orders and Presidential Power*. His current research continues in the presidency field, an inquiry into presidential power. He also is collaborating with Howard Schweber, a public law specialist who joined the department in 1999, in erasing the boundary between political and legal studies.[77]

David Canon grew up in the heart of Indiana. His political interests were fashioned from an early age by a family strongly engaged in public affairs, his father a humanities professor at Indiana State, and his mother a school librarian. At age nine, he was an active participant in the Hubert Humphrey presidential campaign, and was a child participant in anti–Vietnam War protests. As an undergraduate at Indiana University, his interests had already congealed on congressional politics. His senior thesis studied the Farmer–Labor Party in Minnesota, a state where his family had ancestral roots.

This background perhaps had some incidental impact upon his choice of Minnesota for doctoral study. The faculty he found most influential included John Aldrich, Frank Sorauf, and Dennis Simon. At Minnesota his interests broadened to encompass political behavior and American political institutions, focusing increasingly upon the latter. His thesis, however, returned to Congress, examining the role of political amateurs (subsequently published as *Actors, Athletes, and Astronauts: Political Amateurs in the United States Congress*, 1990).

His first position was at Duke University, a location that had a pair of important impacts upon his career. Being situated in a department with an unusually strong rational-choice contingent put Canon in close quarters with this orientation; through this experience, he gained a deepened appreciation for its value, without accepting it as a conceptual lodestar. Second, his Duke period coincided with an epic battle over the role of race in North Carolina congressional redistricting, an issue that made repeated trips to the Supreme Court and gave rise to landmark cases (*Shaw v. Reno* 1993 and successor decisions). Canon plunged into the vexed issue of the appropriate use of race in redistricting, which led to a major 1999 book, *Race, Redistricting, and Representation: The Unintended Consequences of Black-Majority Districts.*[78]

Canon and his family, steeped in midwestern culture, were not entirely comfortable in North Carolina, where some negative strains of the Old South still persisted. Thus Canon was open to an invitation to join the Wisconsin faculty in 1991; Charles O. Jones was an especially compelling recruiter. Canon proves a worthy heir to the Wisconsin tradition of leadership in congressional studies, extending from Ralph Huitt through Barbara Hinckley to Jones. By the centennial year, fellow congressional specialists listed Canon as one of the top half-dozen in the nation in this field.[79] His present work explores the historical evolution of congressional candidates. He is among the editors of a multivolume compilation of the history of all congressional committees. His leadership potential was displayed in an excellent term as associate chair, 1999–2001.

Benjamin Marquez, of Mexican-American ancestry, grew up in El Paso, Texas. Some of his ancestors trace their lineage to preannexation Texas; most are more recent immigrants. His household was bilingual, though the parents insisted on speaking English to the children. His father repaired washing machines, and his mother was a garment worker; only one uncle had a college degree. His high school years in the early 1970s were a period of intense Chicano mobilization. An activist environment also prevailed during his undergraduate study at the University of Texas–El Paso; his own political engagement influenced his choice of a political science major. Wisconsin was the only graduate school to offer a fellowship, which determined his migration to a distant and very different environment, although he did not feel culturally at odds with his classmates. Some faculty, Marquez recalls, were initially intimidating in their erudition (Murray Edelman, Richard Merelman); others, in particular Booth Fowler, Virginia Sapiro, and Melvin Croan, were especially supportive. After temporary positions at San Jose State and Kansas, Marquez found a permanent one at the University of Utah, before responding to the invitation from his doctoral alma mater in 1991.

Marquez achieved national standing in the Chicano studies field with a pair of important books, *LULAC: The Evolution of a Mexican American Political Organization* (1993), and *Constructing Identities in Mexican-American Political Organizations: Choosing Issues, Taking Sides* (2003). He accepted a difficult assignment from L&S from 1995 to 1997 to bring order into the deeply troubled Chicano Studies Program, torn between activism and scholarship.[80]

John Coleman came of age in a working-class family near Worcester, Massachusetts; both parents had been factory workers. The family background, Coleman feels, had a lasting impact upon his outlook, leaving a special sensibility regarding issues of class and representation.[81] Excellent high school teachers awakened his intellectual ambitions; his first dream was to become a high school principal. Proximity to Worcester shaped his choice of Clark for undergraduate study; at the time, he was but dimly aware of the historic role of the university as a pioneer of graduate study on a German model, along with Johns Hopkins. He also did not realize that Clark had no educational administration program, which ended his hopes of managing a high school. Clark did have a very open curriculum, with few requirements, permitting him to pursue his natural curiosities with a large component of government and history courses, though in later years he regretted being able to avoid hard-science subjects. For Coleman, the immersion in a peer group mostly of more privileged background required some adjustment. A formative undergraduate opportunity was participation in survey research projects. Since there were few graduate students, undergraduates had the opportunity to serve as research assistants. Involvement with survey preparation and data analysis were fascinating experiences. Coleman identified some other pivotal moments: a high school teacher who told him he had excellent writing skills; a Clark instructor who encouraged him to revise a paper for publication; a lecturer who in an inspiring way wove together history, politics, and political economy.

Coleman chose the Massachusetts Institute of Technology for graduate study. After completing his preliminary examinations, he served as a research associate for over three years at the Harvard Business School, writing cases and helping with research. Though some encouraged him to stay, he could see that, though attractive in the short run, this was not a good long-run choice.

After a year at Brookings, he joined the faculty at the University of Texas–Austin in 1990. Not long after his arrival, Anne Khademian, a department member 1990–97, and a Coleman colleague at the Brookings Institution, called to urge his application for a Wisconsin opening in political parties, a delayed replacement for Epstein. The persuasive appeals of Jones and Khademian, along with a number of others, helped make the 1992 department invitation appealing for Coleman. Though Austin had its attractions, Coleman like Canon felt difficulty in identifying as a southerner.

His first book, *Party Decline in America: Policy, Politics, and the Fiscal State* (1996), tied together his two passions: political parties, and political economy. Coleman regards his research as weaving together historical institutionalism—a political development perspective—with political economy in unconventional ways. His work on parties continues with an exploration of the notion of party strength, looking for relations between legislative productivity and party cohesion, and organizational strength on attitudes. He also plans research on the politics of income distribution, asking why 30 years of deepening inequality in America does not translate into political change, a study joining class and political culture. The resilient mythologies of mobility in the face of its diminishing reality are a puzzle inviting inquiry.

Coleman gave yeoman service as associate chair from 2001 to 2004. His signal impact on graduate program reform is detailed earlier in the chapter. Especially gratifying to Coleman was finding the means to add a fifth year of financial support for doctoral candidates.

Finally, I turn to the long-serving members of the international relations field, Bernard Cohen, David Tarr, and Neil Richardson. Cohen is of New England family background; his mother was the first Jewish graduate of Mount Holyoke, and his father, though lacking in formal education, had an intense interest in public affairs. Thus the pathway to political science was natural.

Cohen did his undergraduate study at Yale, interrupted by wartime military service, majoring in international relations. He then continued at Yale in 1948 with doctoral study in international relations, at the time a program entirely distinct from political science. His graduate faculty contacts had little overlap with the undergraduate study; the most senior faculty had little involvement with undergraduate teaching.

His most important mentor and lifelong close friend was Gabriel Almond, at that stage especially interested in public opinion and foreign policy; his book on this theme remains a classic, and the topic an enduring interest for Cohen. By his third year, he became a research associate in the Yale Institute of International Studies. The Carnegie Endowment for International Peace asked the institute to undertake a study of organizations active in citizen education in world affairs; this eventually became the basis for his dissertation, published in a monograph series by the Center for International Studies as *Citizen Education in World Affairs* (1953).

In 1951, Princeton lured the institute to relocate on its campus, renamed as the Princeton Center for International Studies. Soon thereafter, the Department of State requested a study of the Japanese peace treaty, signed in 1951. Cohen examined the domestic influences upon the treaty, which led to his first major book, *The Political Process and Foreign Policy: The Making of the Japanese Peace Settlement* (1957). Although he never had status in the Princeton politics department, he eventually received a nontenured faculty appointment in the Woodrow Wilson School of Public

Affairs. With George Kennan and Robert Oppenheimer at the Institute for Advanced Study nearby, and a constant flow of leading figures from the policy world, the intellectual environment was shaped by the proximity to Washington, and a concern with contemporary foreign policy issues. Cohen later regretted that the international relations doctoral program, and his early professional experience, did not adequately expose him to the full range of political science.[82] By 1957, some of the key faculty of the Princeton Center began leaving: Lucien Pye went to MIT in 1956, Almond to Yale in 1957. Cohen began to consider the search for a permanent home as well. Before he did, however, a joint seminar with Almond at the Wilson School supplied some of the initial material that grew into his landmark 1963 book, *The Press and Foreign Policy*.

In 1959, Cohen was invited to join the department, initially as an assistant professor; the unhappy precedent of the tenure appointment of John Salter in 1930, sight unseen, apparently still haunted the department. Once in Madison, Cohen was quickly promoted, and swiftly became a central figure in departmental affairs; in 1966 he was chosen as chair to succeed Clara Penniman. Cohen was recruited as an international relations specialist, with a mission to develop this field. He at once found the environment at a public university crucially different from that of a private university, a breath of fresh air. One dramatic contrast was in the student relations with faculty; at Princeton, students never came to see professors, and indeed would not acknowledge them on the street. Another was the introduction to lecturing to large classes; most of the courses Cohen taught during his instructional years were sizable.

Cohen completed another major book in 1972, *The Public's Impact on Foreign Policy*. Shortly thereafter, he embarked on a study taking his research in a new direction, extending his career-long concern with public impact upon diplomacy into the realm of comparative foreign policy. Repeated extended forays into academic leadership long delayed completion of this project; the book, *Democracies and Foreign Policy: Public Participation in the United State and Netherlands*, appeared only after his retirement in 1995.

Not long after completing his term as department chair, Cohen succeeded Crawford Young as associate dean of the Graduate School, a position he retained until 1975. Then, in 1984 he became vice chancellor for academic affairs (later retitled as provost), an entirely absorbing post which he held until 1989, briefly serving as interim chancellor in 1987. In between, he served on the University Committee from 1978 to 1981, and chaired it in 1980–81. Cohen was a meticulous administrator, combining a carefully reflected judgment on large issues with an attention to detail, operating with innate fairness and openness.[83] These roles of academic leadership left little time for intensive research.

Like many others, Cohen in his oral history remarks upon the unusual civility of the department.[84] However, he feels that over time there has been a loss of social cohesion, in part a reflection of the growing size of the faculty. But the mutual respect and self-restraint remains, with little tension over methodological differences.

David Tarr is another Massachusetts native, from a family of modest means. Though neither parent had gone beyond high school, both had strong interests in politics. The family was democratically organized; major decisions were made by a family council, in which children had participation rights. Tarr was active in various extracurricular activities in high school: a lead actor in a school play, a member of several singing groups. He was also a star football player for a state championship team; the football reputation, Tarr believes, helped win him admission to the University of Massachusetts–Amherst.[85]

At Massachusetts, Tarr was active in campus organizational life, though he abandoned football. At first his grades were indifferent, but by his junior year a couple of inspiring courses awakened his motivation, and he never received another B grade. Tarr graduated as the Korean War was winding down in 1953. As an ROTC officer, he was posted to an armored unit on the East German border. With the cold war at its peak, this was a formative experience in directing his interests toward security studies. The war games in which he was involved, with their mock nuclear attacks, stimulated reflection upon the impact of nuclear weapons upon foreign policy. The immersion in the military culture also informed his subsequent understandings of the patterns of thought within the national security community.

After release from the army, Tarr enrolled at the University of Chicago. At the time, the behavioral orientation was not dominant. Particularly influential in his doctoral study were Quincy Wright, Hans Morgenthau, and especially his thesis supervisor, Robert Osgood, whose limited war theories Tarr found valuable. After a brief stop at Mount Holyoke and Amherst College, teaching political behavior, Tarr found a position as defense analyst with the Library of Congress Legislative Reference Service (now Congressional Research Service). For a time he drafted speeches for Senator John Kennedy on defense topics, then was assigned to the Senate Armed Services Committee, especially the Preparedness Subcommittee then chaired by Senator Lyndon Johnson.

The experience, knowledge, and contacts within the national security community which Tarr thus derived were of lasting value. He then obtained a Rockefeller Foundation grant for further national security research, based at the School of Advanced International Studies of Johns Hopkins University and the Center for Foreign Policy Research in Washington; Arnold Wolfers was the leading figure. This placed Tarr close to the nerve centers of government at the moment of the 1962 Cuban missile crisis.

Tarr was recruited as a specialist in national security studies and American foreign policy, not international relations. With Llewellyn Pfankuchen nearing retirement, other international relations recruits at this period serving only briefly, and Cohen increasingly absorbed in administrative responsibilities, for extended periods of his career major responsibility for leadership in the field and for management of the international relations major fell to Tarr. He extended his teaching repertoire to include international relations courses.

When Tarr joined the department in 1963, the war in Vietnam was on a gradual trajectory of escalation. By 1965, the first organized protest calling for an end to the war began; Donald Carlisle, then a department member, cooperated with a number of undergraduates to form a committee which took the name Students and Faculty in Support of the People of South Vietnam, which doubtless at this time and for a couple of years thereafter still represented the majority opinion, though not the most vocal.[86] Solicited to make public engagement in support of this group and their backing for the war, Tarr concluded that as a specialist in defense policy studies his obligation was to explain government policy, but not to serve as advocate. Instead, he organized a visit by State and Defense Department representatives to explain Vietnam policy; the tense session in a jammed, large Social Science lecture hall, overflowing with protesters, was the first major campus event that made evident the growing polarization on the war issue, and the deepening anger of the antiwar group.

Classes dealing with American foreign policy and security issues which Tarr gave in the inflamed environment of the Vietnam War drew huge enrollments. Tarr's specialization in national security studies made him a target for attack from radical left circles. For some years his classes were subject to disruption by activists, and he endured hostility from the more radicalized currents of student opinion.

His published work dealt especially with the policy challenges posed by nuclear weapons. This was the theme of his first book, *American Strategy in the Nuclear Age* (1966). He regards his 1991 volume, *Nuclear Deterrence and International Security: Alternative Nuclear Regimes*, as his finest intellectual achievement. Tarr characterizes this monograph as his best book, published at the wrong time, coincident with the transformation in global strategic parameters resulting from the collapse of the Soviet Union.[87]

Tarr participated in a national network of security studies specialists, to promote well-grounded instruction in this field. The group operated a summer workshop at Colorado College which operated for a number of years in the 1970s into the 1980s. He also took part in an ongoing armed forces and society seminar in Chicago.

Tarr contributed his share to the unusually strong departmental involvement in campus governance. His most absorbing service was chairing the Athletic Board from 1979 to 1986. Athletic policy is always in the public eye, and a number of contentious issues arose during this period. The scope of faculty responsibility for the athletic program is a distinctive feature of Wisconsin, matched by no other Big Ten university, and few anywhere else. Mediating between the intense pressures for winning teams and financial solvency, and the imperatives of academic control, required of Tarr a high order of diplomatic skill and careful judgment. Tarr notes that, during this extended period, his Athletic Board responsibilities inadvertently separated him from the department; the heavy time requirements forced a reduced teaching load, and board meetings conflicted with department meetings.

After leaving the Athletic Board, Tarr returned to full-time teaching and research. He was director of the Center for International Cooperation and Security Studies for several years; the center sponsored a number of important conferences. On the research front, he turned to the relations between the Joint Chiefs of Staff with civilian leadership in the Pentagon, a project that yielded a number of articles and book chapters.

Neil Richardson joined the department as an international relations specialist in 1979. His undergraduate degree was earned in his native Ohio at Miami University, followed by an M.A. at Ohio State. He completed his doctorate at Michigan in 1974, then began his career at the University of Texas–Austin.

His Michigan training schooled him in quantitative approaches to international relations, as well as international relations theories. His 1978 book, *Foreign Policy and Economic Dependence*, is an important venture in empirical testing of dependency theory. At the time of his study, dependency theory had an important following, especially among the intelligentsias and many political leaders in Latin America and Africa. The claims of the *dependentistas*, asserted in their more extreme form by authors such as Andre Gunder Frank and Samir Amin, were always freighted by their reliance on structural premises of Marxist derivation. The task of empirical testing of the master hypotheses of dependency theory was an important challenge in its time, well met by the Richardson work.

Shortly after his arrival in Madison, with his tenure prospects still uncertain, Richardson was asked by incoming Chair Fred Hayward to serve as associate chair. Notwithstanding the career risks, Richardson accepted the responsibility, serving from 1981 to 1984. Subsequently, as noted earlier, he directed the international relations major for a half-dozen years in the 1980s, and also gave signal service to the college faculty advising office. Richardson displayed special talent in this role, which was formalized in 1996 as a half-time responsibility. Since that time, he has played a leading role in advising services, and won the L&S Advising Award for 2005.[88]

Concluding Reflections

By way of closing this chapter, one can do no better than cite the reflections on the evolution of the department by one of its leading figures, Leon Epstein. In his memoir, he notes that expansion in itself is not a major accomplishment, nor had the department done more than maintain its position in the lower part of the top ten. He continues:

> A more plausible source of pride lay in the manner of our departmental development. It was not so abrupt or revolutionary as to disturb relatively amiable relationships. Behavioral political science did not threaten to supplant traditional political science. Not all of our new and younger faculty members were behaviorally trained as were most of the Americanists whom we appointed. We recruited broadly. In foreign area studies, new Ph.D.s tended to have historical, cultural, and language training rather than quantitative or other skills that went with the behavioral persuasion. So, of course, did newly added specialists in political philosophy. In thus maintaining a balanced and eclectic department, we did not marginalize any old-timers or newcomers. This is not to say that there was a complete absence of generational tensions, linked to methodological differences. But the tensions were not sharply divisive. We had no enduring feuds, or even well-defined factions contending that only one kind of political science was legitimate.[89]

Over the years, there has been a slow diversification in the origins of department faculty, illustrated in table 5.2, analyzing geographic provenance and doctoral institutions for those faculty for whom data are available. In the earliest years, there was a heavy midwestern cast; even today, the great majority hail from the Northeast or the Midwest. In doctoral training, until the most recent decades, faculty were recruited exclusively from a small number of doctoral institutions. In the contemporary period, a larger number of doctoral institutions have the standing and quality to produce competitive candidates. As well, the formalization of recruiting procedures by the end of the 1960s, with national advertisement of all positions and search committee scrutiny of all dossiers, has brought a wider ranger of candidates and institutions into the field of vision. Until the middle 1960s, much recruiting was through informal channels, and restricted to a handful of top universities.

Table 5.2

Patterns of Faculty Origins

	Region of birth	**Doctoral training**
Northeast	41	74
Midwest	42	71
South	8	5
Pacific coast	3	20
Mountain	6	0
International	20	6

There have been some important achievements during the last three decades. The National Research Center departmental rankings listed Wisconsin as eighth in 1983, and tenth in 1993, in the face of sharpening competition from a number of institutions, such as University of California–San Diego, never previously of high rank. Mark Beissinger was the first department member to win the most prestigious APSA award, the Wilson prize for the best book in a given year, for his seminal 2002 work, *Nationalist Mobilization and the Collapse of the Soviet State*; this remarkable volume won two other prizes (see chapter 6 for details). Four department faculty were inducted into the American Academy of Arts and Sciences: Leon Epstein (1981), Charles O. Jones (1989), Crawford Young (1998), and Virginia Sapiro (2002), an honor achieved by only three former faculty in earlier days (Austin Ranney, John Gaus, and Grayson Kirk). In 2004, APSA prizes and awards were won by a half-dozen younger faculty (Charles

Franklin, Scott Gehlbach, Kenneth Goldstein, Helen Kinsella, Benjamin Marquez, and Tamir Moustafa), a promising omen for the second century.

On two occasions during the period covered in this chapter, the department was subjected to L&S reviews by a college committee drawn from outside the department, in 1980 and 1997 (see appendix 28 for extended excerpts). Both review committees passed very favorable judgment upon the department. The 1980 report concluded:

> Our discussions with individuals within the Political Science Department, and with those in the discipline at other universities, have led to an overall favorable view of the academic strength of the department. In most of the important fields there is a strong senior person with an ongoing research program and a national reputation. This is particularly true in the comparative fields and certain of the more traditional areas in political science. In these areas of strength, research productivity has been steady and at a high level.

The 1997 report echoed these words:

> Over the past several decades, the College of Letters and Science and the University have been very well served by its Political Science Department. Its faculty has been productive in scholarship, respected in the profession, superb in its classroom teaching, willing to teach its share of student hours, serious about its graduate and undergraduate programs, unstinting in its service to the College and University, and humane and civil in its everyday life. The continuity of these characteristics may be seen quite clearly from the last review of the Department. . . . Despite the passing of nearly two decades, much of what was said in that report could be said again today.

Both reports made a number of suggestions for improvement, and identified some weaknesses. Here and there was a note of apprehension regarding sustaining these standards of excellence. But, remarkably, the department greeted its centennial year in robust condition.

Notes

1. Dresang again served as Earl campaign aide in the unsuccessful campaigns for reelection as governor in 1986, and for the Senate seat eventually won by Herbert Kohl in 1988.
2. This account is based upon the Dennis Dresang oral history, University Archives, March 2003.
3. Another incident placing Dresang in the eye of a storm took place in 1981. Former Governor Lucey, after leaving the Mexico ambassadorship in 1979, expressed an interest to Dresang in offering a one-time course for the La Follette Institute. L&S Dean Cronon demurred, initially on budgetary grounds, but when Dresang found other funds for the Lucey invitation Cronon vetoed the course on policy grounds. The dean feared the precedent of offering teaching posts to former politicians without academic credentials, on the grounds that other political figures would demand the same opportunity. The affair became public, and stirred up some legislative unhappiness, as well as leaving an uneasy relationship between Dresang and the L&S administration. Dresang oral history.
4. John F. Witte, *The Market Approach to Education: An Analysis of America's First Voucher Program* (Princeton: Princeton University Press, 2000).
5. Interview with John Witte, 9 June 2003.
6. Growing out of a 1989 conference organized as part of the study was a volume examining the school choice issue nationally; William H. Cline and John F. Witte (eds.), *Choice and Control in American Education* (Bristol, PA: Falmer Press, 1990), 2 vols.
7. Witte, *The Market Approach to Education*, 150–51.
8. Witte, *The Market Approach to Education*, xiv.
9. Donald F. Kettl, *Reinventing Government: Appraising the National Performance Review* (Washington: Brookings Institution, 1994).
10. Interview with Donald Kettl, 16 June 2004.
11. Kettl interview.
12. Toni Palmeri, "Deconstructing Don Kettl," *Wisconsin Political Scientist*, 2004, 3.
13. Robben Fleming, chancellor from 1964 to 1967, came from Illinois but had previously served on the Madison faculty. The same was true of Irving Shain, recruited from the University of Washington to serve as chancellor from 1977 to 1987.
14. Quoted in College of Letters and Science, *Strategic Plan 1993–1998*, June 1993, 1.
15. L&S, *Strategic Plan*, 19
16. L&S, *Strategic Plan*, 69.
17. Department Minutes, 1 March 1984.

18. For particularly valuable summaries of contemporary debates about the nature of the discipline, see Ira Katznelson and Helen V. Milner (eds.), *Political Science: State of the Discipline* (New York: W.W. Norton & Company, 2002); John G. Gunnell, *Imagining the American Polity: Political Science and the Discourse of Democracy* (University Park: Pennsylvania State University Press, 2004); Benno C. Schmidt, *The Political Discourse of Anarchy: A Disciplinary History of International Relations* (Albany: State University of New York Press, 1998).
19. Ira Katznelson and Helen V. Milner, "American Political Science: The Discipline's State and the State of the Discipline," in Katznelson and Milner, *Political Science*, 2.
20. Gabriel A. Almond, *A Discipline Divided: Schools and Sects in Political Science* (Newbury Park, CA: Sage, 1990), 7–31.
21. Almond, *A Discipline Divided*, 48.
22. John G. Gunnell, "Handbooks and History: Is It Still the *American* Science of Politics?" *International Political Science Review*, 23, 4 (2002), 339–54.
23. Donald P. Green and Alan S. Gerber, "Reclaiming the Experimental Tradition in Political Science," in Katznelson and Milner, *Political Science*, 805–32.
24. Barry R. Weingast, "Rational-Choice Institutionalism," in Katznelson and Milner, *Political Science*, 660–92.
25. Katnelson and Milner, "American Political Science," 26.
26. Cited in S. M. Amadae and Bruce Bueno de Mesquita, "The Rochester School: The Origins of Positive Political Theory," *Annual Review of Political Science*, 1999, 291.
27. Donald P. Green and Ian Shapiro, *Pathologies of Rational Choice Theory: A Critique of applications in Political Science* (New Haven: Yale University Press, 1994), 2.
28. Amadae and Bueno de Mesquita, "The Rochester School," 270.
29. Amadae and Bueno de Mesquita, "The Rochester School," 269–95, provide an impressive roster of major figures in this field trained by Riker in the department he built around the rational choice concept.
30. For a careful critique of rational choice theory, see Green and Shapiro, *Pathologies of Rational Choice Theory.*
31. Stephen Earl Bennet, "'Perestroika' Lost: Why the Latest 'Reform' Movement in Political Science Should Fail," *PS: Political Science & Politics* 35. 2 (June 2002), 177–79. More than 40 percent of current members responding to the APSA survey expressed discontent with the *APSR*. On this issue, see also Jennifer Hochschild, "On the Social Science Wars," *Daedalus*, 133, 1 (Winter 2004), 91–94; Suzanne Hoeber Rudolph, "The Imperialism of Categories," *Perspectives on Politics*, 3, 1 (March 2005), 5–14.
32. "An Open Letter to the APSA Leadership and Members," *PS: Political Science & Politics*, 33, 4 (December 2000), 735–37.

33. Five past, present, or future members of the department, in addition to a large number of doctoral alumni, signed the Perestroika letter: Kenneth Mayer, Tamir Moustafa, James Scott, Marion Smiley and Aili Tripp. The solicitation of signatures was not systematic; a number of others agreed with its content.
34. Amadae and Bueno de Mesquita, "The Rochester School," 286–87.
35. Murray Edelman oral history conducted by Lance Bennett, November 1992. I am grateful to Bacia Edelman for making available the tapes of this extended interview exploring the Edelman scholarship. They are now on deposit at the University Archives.
36. Herbert Kritzer oral history, University Archives, 10 April 2003.
37. Department minutes, 1 March 1984.
38. The absence of an African-American voice from the discipline had significant effects in the sociology of knowledge. Ralph Bunche was the first African American to earn a doctorate, at Harvard in 1934. Despite the singular importance of race in American politics and history, the topic was all but ignored by political scientists until the 1960s. A content analysis of the *American Political Science Review* from 1906 to 1963 identified only 13 articles with the words "Negro," "Civil Rights," or "race." Paula D. McClain and John A. Garcia, "Expanding Disciplinary Boundaries: Black, Latino, and Racial Minority Group Politics in Political Science," in Ada W. Finifter (ed.), *Political Science: The State of the Discipline* (Washington: American Political Science Association, 1993), 247–79.
39. The Hawkins bequest sufficed not only to endow the Hawkins Chair, but to support several smaller awards to more junior faculty.
40. Charles O. Jones oral history, University Archives, October 2002.
41. Charles O. Jones, "The Speculative Imagination in Democratic Lawmaking," Inaugural Lecture delivered before the University of Oxford on 30 November 1998, Oxford University Press, 1999, 24.
42. Charles O. Jones, "A Way of Life and Law," *American Political Science Review*, 89, 1 (March 1995), 9.
43. Report of the Ad-Hoc Committee on the Graduate Program, 1990, 2.
44. Edmund Keller (1974), KC Morrison (1977), Brenda Hart-Boyne (1979), Bai Akridge (1979), Joseph Reed (1985), and Mary Coleman (1990).
45. Jose Vadi (1977), Benjamin Marquez (1983), Isabel Souza (Brazilian, 1985), Jorge Benitez-Nazario (1989), Enrique Arias (2001), and Sharon Navarro (2001).
46. For a review of the graduate student diversity issue, see Appendix IIIb.J of the Department of Political Science Self-Assessment, August 1998.
47. Mark Beissinger, address to the Department centennial conference, 27 March 2004.
48. Interview with Neil Richardson, 22 March 2005.

49. Judith S. Craig, "Graduate Student Unionism: The Teaching Assistants Association at the University of Wisconsin–Madison, 1970–1980," PhD diss., University of Wisconsin–Madison, 1986, 76. She cites Arlen Christenson of the Law School as an example.
50. On the TAA strike, its impact and its legal dimensions, I have benefited from information supplied by Judith Craig, David Cronon, and university legal services head, Vice Chancellor Melanie Newby.
51. I was the target for one of the TAA grievances. One of our African-American graduate students, specializing in Africa, had lacked the opportunity for teaching experience during her graduate work, having always won fellowships. I designed with her a teaching internship tied to the small African politics course, whose enrollment fell far short of justifying a TA. The experience was so structured that she did not replace me in any instructional obligation. To my disappointment, the university declined to contest the grievance, and I was instructed to end the internship. The student in question, Linda Thomas Greenfield, completed her preliminary examinations, and field research in Liberia, but then chose to pursue a successful career in the foreign service.
52. Craig, "Graduate Student Unionism," 346.
53. To qualify for a tuition remission, the graduate student had to hold at least a one-third time appointment. Had the strike persisted, the portion of the semester would have fallen below the one-third mark, calling into question legal entitlement to the tuition waiver. Whether the university would have carried out the threat to dun strikers for the tuition bill may be doubtful, but the pressure this placed upon the union to suspend the strike was certain.
54. The strike was a costly experience for some undergraduates. Two of our daughters were enrolled in the university in 1980; both respected the picket lines, and as a consequence missed so much of the semester that they felt it necessary to withdraw to avoid compromising their academic records, thus forfeiting their tuition.
55. The major issues were class size, participation in university budget planning and policy, role and authority of the faculty, and bargainability of wages.
56. Craig, "Graduate Student Unionism," 2.
57. Edelman oral history.
58. Edelman oral history. Interview with Bacia Edelman, 9 June 2004.
59. Quoted in his memorial resolution; Faculty Document 1605, Memorial Resolution of the Faculty of the University of Wisconsin–Madison on the Death of Professor Emeritus Murray J. Edelman, 4 February 2002.
60. Bacia Edelman interview.
61. Edelman oral history.
62. Bacia Edelman interview.
63. Richard Merelman oral history, University Archives, 26 March 2003.
64. Merelman oral history.

65. Booth Fowler, *Enduring Liberalism: American Political Thought since the 1960s* (Lawrence: University Press of Kansas, 1999), 243.
66. Charles Anderson contributed part of the text for the Fowler profile.
67. Interview with Patrick Riley, 20–21 September 2004.
68. Interview with Donald Downs, 27 September 2004, supplemented by several e-mail elaborations.
69. This profile is based upon an oral history interview with Jack Dennis, 17 April 2003, available in University Archives.
70. Dennis oral history.
71. See Richard M. Merelman, *Pluralism at Yale: The Culture of Political Science in America* (Madison: University of Wisconsin Press, 2003) for detail on this period. Included in the Eisinger network were Robert Putnam, Robert Axelrod, Edward Tufte, Daniel Levine and Bruce Berman, among others.
72. Peter Eisinger oral history, University Archives, 12 February 2003.
73. Eisinger oral history.
74. Eisinger oral history.
75. Virginia Sapiro oral history, University Archives, 1 April 2003.
76. Sapiro oral history.
77. This is based upon an interview with Kenneth Mayer, 1 October 2004.
78. Interview with David Canon, 29 September 2004.
79. Mayer interview.
80. Interview with Benjamin Marquez, 27 September 2004.
81. Interview with John Coleman, 18 October 2004.
82. Bernard Cohen oral history, University Archives, 1992.
83. I recall that in visiting his spacious office as vice chancellor, one found a huge table covered with carefully sorted piles of current documents relating to the many issues on the forefront of the agenda.
84. In comments upon this manuscript, Cohen remarks that civility has a downside. Civility can be a behavioral norm creating pressures for consensus which suppress discussion of issues on which divided opinions existed. In such instances, traditional practice dictated that advocates of a proposal that would encounter dissensus would forebear from raising the issue. In the absence of open discussion, persuasion and education could not be attempted. Instances of topics not raised for formal discussion, in spite of significant support from some quarters, were the decisions not to seek placement in the new Social Sciences Building, and not to cosponsor an honorary degree for Martin Luther King.
85. David Tarr oral history, University Archives, 31 March 2003.
86. Tarr oral history.
87. Tarr oral history.
88. Interview with Neil Richardson, 2 July 2004.
89. Leon Epstein, memoir, typescript, 164–65.

CHAPTER 6

The Expanded Role of Comparative Politics

Crawford Young

Changing Patterns in Comparative Politics

Comparative politics was a major source of strength for the Wisconsin Department of Political Science in the final decades of the twentieth century. The contingent of comparativists was unusually large, compared to distributions of specializations in most major departments. At the turn of the century, more than a third of the faculty were comparativists.

This relative weight of comparative politics was also reflected in graduate student specializations and undergraduate enrollments. During the quarter century between 1970 and 1995, 134 of the 307 doctorates awarded fell in the comparative area; in the fall of 1970, of a total enrollment in undergraduate courses of 3,664, 1,247 were in comparative offerings. The strength of several area studies programs contributed substantially to preserving the high national ranking of the department.

This striking role of comparative politics had little to do with strategic planning at the beginning of the postwar period. Rather than a calculated architecture, the latter 20th-century dimensions of comparative politics resulted largely from unanticipated consequences of pathways pursued by a handful of key young faculty and sudden opportunities seized in the 1950s. Leon Epstein, Henry Hart, and John Armstrong were crucial actors, but only Armstrong was actually trained for the role played.

The nature and content of comparative politics was transformed after World War II, reflecting national trends in the discipline. However, the departmental lineage of comparative politics traces from the restless spirit of inquiry of the founding chair, Paul Reinsch. Indeed, early 20th-century generations of undergraduates could choose from courses covering a surprising range of world regions: not only Europe, but also Asia, Latin America, and even Africa. However, before World War II, at Wisconsin and elsewhere, "comparative politics" lacked a fully developed identity as a field. Its early practitioners were knowledgeable students of "foreign governments" or colonial administration; some, like Reinsch, Stanley Hornbeck, and Chester Lloyd Jones, pursued part of their careers in diplomatic service.

In the interwar period, highly visible scholars such as Frederic Ogg and Walter Sharp made Wisconsin a major center for the study of comparative government. In a 1931 appeal to Letters and Science (L&S) Dean George Sellery for a generous counteroffer to retain Sharp, John Gaus argued that "the department has particular prestige for its advanced work in comparative government, a prestige unusual for an inland institution especially, and notable beyond the United States."[1] Sharp was retained (until 1940); in 1931, of the nine faculty members, three were comparative specialists (Ogg, Lloyd Jones, in addition to Sharp), and two others wrote on international politics (Pitman Potter and Grayson Kirk). Of the 47 doctorates awarded from 1920 to 1940, 14 involved comparative government dissertations (and 10 others international politics); one may speculate (though not prove) that these figures were unusually high compared to other doctoral departments nationally.

Still, though the study of world affairs, international organization and law, and foreign governments was well rooted in the department, comparative politics as a conceptual field was less developed. An interesting measure of the lack of a field identity is found in the important series of national conferences devoted to promoting the scientific study of politics, which began in Madison in 1923, with Wisconsin political scientist Arnold Hall (1910–26) the primary organizer. The conference broke into eight subcommittees, covering the different areas of political science; of these, none dealt with comparative politics, and only one (international organization) was outside the American politics field.[2]

The post–World War II era witnessed a complete reconfiguration of comparative politics, both nationally and locally. On the national scene, the quest for a more theoretically driven and methodologically self-conscious comparative politics captured the intellectual energies of the postwar generation of scholars, partly as a product of the behavioralist movement in the discipline at large. The received tradition of comparative government was viewed as too preoccupied with formal structures and constitutional formalities.

On the Madison scene, the early postwar years were marked by a total turnover in personnel, the rise of a third world focus, and a period of explosive growth. These transformations were driven by some unusual university budgetary factors, as well as national trends in political science. Doubtless, embedded expectations from the past of an international orientation played some part in the emphasis given to comparative politics in the postwar period.

In the same way that the Reinsch discovery of international politics was triggered in large measure by the global context of imperialism at flood tide, the subfield of comparative politics was profoundly reshaped by the postwar environment dominated by the emergent cold war. Not only was state socialism as a mode of rule poorly understood, but decolonization brought dozens of new states into the international arena, whose political processes awaited discovery. New ideological currents surged through the world, their impact difficult to understand or predict. In the domestic public arena, the imperatives of national security made comparative politics seem a more practical endeavor; for the first time, comparative political research was not merely an intellectual pursuit, but a "national need." Vastly increased resources, foundation and federal, became available for graduate training and faculty research.

Simultaneously, major transformations in the concept of comparative political study appeared. The field counts a distinguished ancestry, conventionally traced to Aristotle, and including such luminaries as Ibn Khaldun, Machiavelli, and Montesquieu. In the 19th and early 20th centuries, a number of grand masters contributed analytical categories, concepts, and methods which continue to serve as theoretical sources for contemporary scholarship: Max Weber, Karl Marx, Emile Durkheim, Vilfredo Pareto, Gaetano Mosca, Roberto Michels, among others. But the rise to ascendancy of what may be loosely termed the behavioral persuasion, in its many inflections, in the discipline at large shaped the perspectives of the most influential scholars of the postwar generation. The quest for a more scientific study of politics included more rigorous theoretical formulation, the search for measurement, incorporation of theory and substance from cognate disciplines, and a shift away from a focus on formal institutions and constitutional arrangements. In reality, in the United States by the 1940s, comparative politics had been merely an empty label applied to the study of "foreign governments," invariably taken individually; thus also at issue was a rediscovered vocation to give real meaning to the term *comparative*.

These larger currents gave rise to a wave of introspection and search for new paradigms within comparative politics. The Social Science Research Council (SSRC) convened a summer seminar at Northwestern in 1952, to reflect on the challenge to comparative politics, chaired by Roy Macridis.[3] A larger conference followed in 1953, bringing together a number of members of the SSRC Committee on Political Behavior,[4] with leading comparativists.[5] For reasons to be elucidated later, none of the participants came from Wisconsin, though one, William Ebenstein, had been in the department from 1938 to 1948. The SSRC then selected a Committee on Comparative Politics, led by Gabriel Almond. From its labors and under its sponsorship there emerged a series of highly influential volumes, beginning with *The Politics of the Developing Areas*, edited by Almond and James Coleman in 1960.[6] This work provided the seminal statement of a structural-functional theory of comparative politics, which for a number of years influenced the conceptual debates as model and foil.

In the following decades, a number of candidates for paradigmatic ascendancy rose and fell: modernization theory of various types; neo–Marxist; dependency; state-centered; historical institutionalist; culturalist; rational choice. Over the years, a series of classificatory schemes were superimposed upon the evolving conceptual debate: nomothetic vs. ideographic; modernization vs. underdevelopment; structure vs. agency; state vs. society. The evolving epistemologies are well reflected in the contrasting appraisals of comparative politics in the successive collective dialogues on the state of the discipline sponsored by the American Political Science Association (APSA).[7] Gabriel Almond sorts the contending paradigms into cleavages of ideology and methodology: from the orthodox Marxists through the soft left of critical theory over to neoconservatives, on the ideology dimension, and from the hard methods of formal modelers to the soft modes of Geertzian "thick description."[8] Mark Lichback and Alan Zuckerman develop an influential contemporary categorization identifying the three major analytical streams as rational choice, political culture, and structure.[9] Rational-choice theorists depart from the premise of the calculating, self-interested human agent. Culturalists privilege ways of life, systems of meaning, and values. Structuralists are drawn to historical institutionalism, state as prime actor, and state-society interactions. Once influential approaches such as structural-functionalism and most other versions of modernization theory have long since faded into the background. So also has dependency theory. Intellectual Marxism in its various versions suffered severe collateral damage from the collapse of state socialism. However, elements of these earlier approaches, even though no longer advanced as paradigms, may often be detected in current perspectives. Not all conceptual currents fit neatly into the threefold classification, nor can all or even most comparativists be placed solely within one of these boxes. Indeed, as will be apparent at the end of this chapter when I return to this taxonomy, such classificatory schemes fail to capture the eclectic ethos that governs a good deal of the most influential comparativist scholarship here and elsewhere.

The other national development that profoundly shaped comparative politics at Wisconsin was the rise of area studies. This development in the 1950s found reinforcement in the sputnik shock of 1957, and its accompanying tremors of apprehension of losing ground in the global competition with the Soviet Union.[10] The Ford, Rockefeller, and Carnegie Foundations, followed by the federal government with the passage of the National Defense Education Act (NDEA) in 1958, began to offer generous financial backing for the support of area study programs at major universities. The area studies concept implied a much more explicitly interdisciplinary approach to graduate training. As well, the insistence upon field research at the dissertation stage, training in the regional languages, and immersion in the cultures altered doctoral programs in important ways. Selection committees for faculty and graduate student research were interdisciplinary in membership, implying different criteria for success than would apply in a discipline-centered screening.

Wisconsin was an especially active university in the development of area studies. The panoply of Wisconsin area studies programs and the larger international studies structure that housed them drew heavily on the leadership talents of department comparativists. Across the board, Wisconsin area studies programs achieved distinction, measured in their exceptional success in competing for NDEA Title VI funding; in the 2003–06 funding cycle, seven Wisconsin area studies programs won nearly $12 million.[11]

The field of comparative politics was unevenly affected by the rapid expansion of area studies by the end of the 1950s. Western Europe was not initially included in the area studies focus, and did not at first benefit from the new funding opportunities linked to federal and foundation sponsorship of area studies. Western European specialists at the time tended to focus on a given country; there was presumed to be an adequate pool of such specialists, and no security imperative compelled additional funding.

Another consequence of the area studies approach was an insistence upon training in regional languages and usually dissertation field research. For those specializing in Asia, Africa, and the Americas, the field research cachet became a prerequisite for scholarly credibility. In the case of the Communist world, until the 1980s, field research was difficult, and severe restrictions limited its scope even where entry was granted to the country of study.[12]

The concept of "area studies" came under attack from some quarters in the 1990s. SSRC Vice President Stanley Heginbotham in 1994 criticized area studies as outmoded, calling for a more thematic transregional approach, a preference at once reflected in SSRC as well as other foundation funding patterns. The controversy also pitted area studies against discipline-oriented approaches, a dispute that intensified in the later 1990s. Critics claimed that area studies specialists were hostile to broader social science theory, and that their work lacked rigor. Advocates retorted that the discipline-based approaches were overly formal, abstract, and remote from real world situations.[13]

The national debate was not matched by comparable controversy within the comparative contingent locally. Most comparativists shared a commitment to the area studies approach without denying the possible value of transregional research or a basic identification with the discipline that is their ultimate intellectual as well as administrative home. The fundamental necessity of research and instruction grounded in a deep understanding of the states and societies studied in terms of cultural heritage, historical experience, and social structures is axiomatic; the political cannot be stripped from its context. The examination of the scholarly contributions of Wisconsin comparativists which follows will demonstrate that there is no singular commitment to the ideographic; contributions to broader social theory are numerous, and there is no reticence before the canons of empirical rigor, contextually applied.

One important consequence of the importance of area studies at Wisconsin, and the strength of the major programs, is that many of the comparative contingent find an important part of their intellectual company amongst their area studies colleagues. Most of the programs have more active calendars of colloquia and visiting lectures than does the department. As noted elsewhere in the chapter, many department comparativists have played active roles in the leadership of area studies programs. Arguably this diversion of collegial energies comes at some cost to departmental associations. But the comparative contingent has also contributed five chairs since 1960 (Leon Epstein, Crawford Young twice, Fred Hayward, Mark Beissinger, and Graham Wilson), or six if Dennis Dresang, hired as a comparativist, is counted, and plays its full share in departmental governance and affairs generally.

The Postwar Period 1948–60: Turnover and Transformation

These national developments would have compelled a recasting of comparative politics at Wisconsin under any circumstances. But the disruptive effect of World War II on university staffing, for comparative politics as for other fields, resulted in a virtually complete faculty turnover. As did the department as a whole, comparative politics faced the challenge of a total rebuilding of its staff. At the moment of the Japanese surrender, there were only three comparativists on the faculty, Ogg, Ebenstein, and Gordon Skilling. Ogg was at the end of a long and distinguished career, stepping down from the chair post he had held for 25 years in 1944, and retiring in 1948. Ebenstein was an

Austrian emigre who completed his doctorate at Wisconsin in 1938, then was kept on as a faculty member. Although later in his career his interests shifted to political theory, during his Madison years he was primarily a comparativist, publishing works on *Fascist Italy* in 1939, and *The Nazi State* in 1943. Ebenstein left for Princeton in 1946. Skilling was a young Canadian scholar specializing in the Soviet Union and Eastern Europe; he joined the faculty in 1943, and left in 1948.

The first comparativist to be recruited after the war was William Stokes, a 1943 UCLA doctorate appointed at tenure rank in 1946. Stokes, a Latin Americanist, had a regular radio program in Chicago which absorbed a portion of his time and energy. Of a conservative orientation unusual for postwar Latin Americanists, he published two monographs on Honduras and a text on Latin American politics, but never became a leading figure in the field. Charles Anderson, who chose Wisconsin for doctoral study, intending to work under Stokes, recollects that he was one of the first Latin Americanists to go beyond formal institutionalism. He was a popular lecturer, and for years gave the huge introductory American government course, then given in the First Congregational Church for want of campus instructional space. He left for the Claremont Colleges in 1958.

The resurrection of comparative politics really began in 1948, with the recruitment of Leon Epstein and Henry Hart. Ironically, though both have played a capital role in restoring comparative politics to its earlier high rank, neither was trained in the field, nor was their subsequent commitment immediately apparent.[14] Epstein was a Wisconsin native, growing up in Beaver Dam where his father was a store owner. After completing an undergraduate degree (1940) and an M.A. (1941) in economics at Wisconsin, followed by military service, Epstein began graduate study in political science at the University of Chicago in 1946, determined to complete his degree as quickly as possible. By the end of the year, he passed preliminary examinations in political theory, public administration, and public law. His dissertation topic, chosen in good part to permit speedy completion, was a judicial biography of Justice William Douglas. Although he had no formal training in comparative politics, he had an autodidactic link to British politics. While in military service, he was stationed for over two years in the United Kingdom (UK), and took the opportunity by avid observation of British politics through the press and available books to acquire a good working knowledge. He was able to spend a term at Oxford University in a student status, offering the opportunity for exposure to academic knowledge about Britain.

Notwithstanding the absence of formal training in comparative politics, Epstein was invited to join the faculty in 1948, in part to take over courses in British and continental European politics previously taught by Ogg, as well as to contribute to political theory instruction. On arrival, Epstein asked outgoing Chair Llewellyn Pfankuchen, "of these two fields which are somewhat different, which one am I expected, if any, to specialize in, develop graduate courses, and do my own work in." Pfankuchen replied, "either one." Epstein adds that "I was not interviewed for the position; and I don't think anybody here read my dissertation."[15] He had no enduring aspiration to focus on political theory, much less public law, then covered by David Fellman. He was not asked to teach public administration, in which he had significant graduate training at Wisconsin and Chicago. Conversely, he found the opportunity to teach British politics very appealing, though he was more apprehensive about European politics, in which he lacked the self-taught background he had developed for the UK.

In his first year or so, Epstein faced the necessity of making a clear choice. Under the leadership of James McCamy and William Young, the department was intent in establishing a clear research standard for promotion, and Epstein did not wish to pursue the Douglas topic beyond two articles in the *Wisconsin Law Review*. He chose comparative politics as initial primary professional identity, with a focus on Britain. At the same time, Epstein adds, "as a comparativist, . . . I was an Americanist. Always in my mind was the notion that British politics ought to be taught, ought to be studied for that matter, even in research, with the American comparison in mind."[16] His first articles on British politics appeared in the *American Political Science Review*, the *Political Science Quarterly*, and the *Public Administration Review* in 1951. These served to win tenure in 1951. In 1952, he won a Ford Foundation award for study in Britain; this opportunity for field research led to his first book, *Britain—Uneasy Ally* (1954), which established his reputation as an emergent figure in the field.

Epstein developed the first formal graduate instruction in comparative politics; although he was not senior enough at the time that the SSRC Committee on Comparative Politics was formed to be selected as a member, he was engaged in the national comparative politics movement. However, he was cautious about some of its theoretical enthusiasms; Epstein describes himself as "a middle range generalizer," and felt that "some of the conceptualization was broader and looser; and I must say more abstract than appealed to me."[17] After a return to American politics and his Wisconsin roots through the 1958 book *Politics in Wisconsin*, Epstein contributed a second major study of British politics in 1964, *British Politics in the Suez Crisis*. During his tenure as L&S Dean (1965–69), he published his most broadly comparative work, *Political Parties in Western Democracies* (1967), which remains a classic. In this conceptually innovative study, he fulfills his long-term commitment to incorporate the American political experience fully into comparative politics. His comparative commitments were reflected in his teaching as well; he broadened the British politics course into a comparative offering including the politics of the old Commonwealth.

Epstein very quickly became a core figure in the department; his leadership played a crucial role in the building of comparative politics at Wisconsin. In 1960, he became chair, at a time of rapid expansion; four of the thirteen faculty recruited on his watch were comparativists (Aristide Zolberg, Donald Carlisle, Leon Lindberg, and Crawford Young). During his 1965–69 deanship, he was supportive of the ambitions of the rapidly expanding area studies programs, all of which had at least one political science member. By the time that he returned to the department at the beginning of the 1970s, the central focus of his research and teaching interest shifted to American politics, though always informed by a comparative perspective. By that time, there were ample numbers of faculty to cover the comparative courses, though Epstein continued to teach the British politics course until his 1988 retirement.

Henry Hart spent his early childhood in India, where his father was a YMCA secretary. His family returned to Tennessee during his adolescence; after an undergraduate degree in psychology at Vanderbilt in 1936, he finally found a job as a messenger at the Tennessee Valley Authority (TVA), then imbued with the ethos of a great social experiment. Those years left an enduring fascination with regional planning and river valley development. After military service, he began graduate study at Wisconsin in 1946, initially under John Gaus, then McCamy after Gaus left for Harvard.

While still working on his dissertation, Hart received a faculty appointment as instructor in 1948, then remained on as assistant professor on completion of his thesis in 1950. Like Epstein, Hart's graduate study included everything but comparative politics: public administration, political theory, public law, American politics. His earlier work with the TVA led to the choice of the Missouri valley development schemes as a dissertation topic. Hart discovered that Missouri valley developments could not fit into the then widely admired TVA model; his findings found publication in 1957 as *The Dark Missouri*.

A serendipitous combination of Hart's family background and his interest in river valley development brought an early shift in his primary focus to South Asian politics. His interest in comparative river valley development, initially focused on Colombia, was redirected to India by the Ford Foundation, which offered financial support for field research there in 1952. The Damodar Valley Authority appeared an apt parallel with TVA, which had influenced the Indian design. He was able to stay on a second year thanks to a Fulbright award, and was thus a charter member in a new cohort of comparative scholars specializing in South Asia, a standing cemented by his 1956 book, *New India's Rivers*.

During his research stay in India, his interests broadened to encompass larger issues of India's development, and the immense challenge of political integration in this vast laboratory of cultural diversity. However, neither Hart nor the department believed in the mid-1950s that there would be sufficient enrollment for a course in Indian politics. But Hart at once became a central figure in a dynamic that led to the emergence of area studies on campus.

The roots of the development of South Asian studies lay outside the department. Murray Fowler (linguistics) taught a course in Sanskrit, and was interested in developing study in Indian religion and culture. The College of Engineering was actively engaged in government-sponsored technical assistance programs in India, and School of Education Dean John Guy Fowlkes (1947–54) served as advisor to the Indian Minister of Education, involving several other education faculty. Regular meetings began in 1955, seeking a framework for campus activity regarding India. In 1957, Hart and Fowler introduced an interdisciplinary course on the civilization of India, a radical innovation at the time. William Young, then chair, did not oppose Hart diverting a portion of his teaching load into this cross-listed but interdisciplinary course.

In 1959, Fowler overcame the skepticism of Hart and Dean Mark Ingraham in pushing through a Department of South Asian Studies, bringing together linguists and specialists on Indian religion, literature, and culture. At the same moment, the planets were aligning in a remarkable moment of expanded resources for area studies more broadly. The NDEA provisions seemed likely to provide $15 million annually to third world studies, which was 10 times the amount that foundations were then investing.[18] The Rockefeller Foundation had provided funds for introduction of language instruction in Hindi/Urdu and Telugu. The aggressive intervention of Academic Vice President Fred Harrington (soon after president) by 1962 had added Wisconsin to a small roster of elite universities receiving a major, multiyear Ford grant ($1.2 million) for the development of third world area studies. The Carnegie Corporation about the same time made a substantial grant for a comparative tropical history program, under the direction of Philip Curtin.[19]

South Asia, with an established interdisciplinary structure in place, was uniquely situated to take the lead, although its strength was then in the humanities. Vice President Harrington approached Hart in 1959, asking him to take charge of preparing a grant request under the NDEA program, which would develop the social science component. Four new appointments were made, and Hart became the first director of a South Asian area studies program (distinct from the Department of South Asian Studies). Other area studies quickly followed: Russian and East European (1959), Africa (1961), and Latin America (1962), followed by the East Asian, and later Southeast Asian, Middle Eastern, and European programs.

Hart's leadership role in area studies and comparative politics was especially salient in these early years. Although he maintained his links with his original specialization in river valley development and regional planning, he continued throughout his career to teach Indian politics, to take part in the Indian civilization course, and to contribute to graduate instruction in comparative development administration and politics. Like Epstein, he was attracted by the premises of the behavioral movement, though he never felt adept in applying its methods.[20] In their very different pathways, he and Epstein were central to the building of a new comparative politics.

The third pivotal figure in this process was John Armstrong, who joined the faculty in 1954, after graduate training at Chicago and Columbia. Of Irish-Hispanic (Minorcan) ancestry, his early years were spent in Jacksonville, Florida, where his father was a railway employee. He undertook undergraduate study at Chicago, but completion was interrupted for four years of military service. After a Chicago M.A., he completed doctoral training at Columbia, with Philip Mosely and John Hazard as influential mentors. Unlike Epstein and Hart, Armstrong was trained in comparative politics, as a Soviet specialist. However, Armstrong recalls that the academic literature was still painfully thin at the time of his doctoral study; the landmark Merle Fainsod monograph, *How Russia Is Ruled,* appeared only in 1953. Like Epstein and Hart, Armstrong quickly won recognition as a leading figure in his field, with early publication of his dissertation research as *Ukrainian Nationalism* (1955), and influential monographs on the Soviet system: *The Soviet Bureaucratic Elite* (1959), *The Politics of Totalitarianism* (1961), and *Ideology, Politics, and Government in the Soviet Union* (1962), all but one of which went through multiple editions. This remarkable early productivity assured swift promotion from beginning assistant professor to full professor in six years.[21]

Armstrong was committed to high research expectations for the department, and felt a satisfactory career depended upon the ability to provide thorough training to graduate students in Soviet studies. By 1958, he helped Michael Petrovich in history set about securing appointments for established scholars in key social science departments; a long-established Slavic languages department already assured linguistic and literature instruction. Through their efforts, by 1958 a Russian Area Studies Program was launched, with key appointments in economics (David Granick), sociology (Kent Geiger), anthropology (Chester Chard), and geography (Robert Taafe). The Armstrong-Petrovich success in rapidly building a distinguished Soviet studies program benefited much less from access to external funding than did the third world programs. Through the 1960s, Armstrong was a key leader for the Russian and East European Studies Program (recently renamed Center for Russian, East European and Central Asian Studies, or CREECA), serving for a time as its chair.

Armstrong, like Epstein and Hart, became fully responsive to new currents in comparative politics well after completing graduate training; these perspectives were especially slow to reach the Soviet field, given the nature of available data and the impossibility of empirical research on the ground. "Towards the middle of my preoccupation with organizing Sovietological studies," he writes, "I became aware of the growing concern of the political discipline for more rigorously defined approaches. Instead of loose, almost journalistic analyses, or straight historical narratives, by the early 1960s the discipline was insisting on sharply defined categories, clearly stated assumptions and models, and testable hypotheses."[22] These called to mind his exposure during his Chicago graduate days to anthropologist A. R. Radcliffe-Brown's views on a scientific perspective to analyzing behavior in a social system. Armstrong by the 1960s was turning to more comparative research, finding special value in the works by anthropologists like Fredrik Barth and linguists like Horace Lunt. The collective volumes produced under Almond's leadership by the SSRC Committee on Comparative Politics were regarded by Armstrong as a "splendid series" which were a model of comparative scholarship. His admiration for Almond increased after the latter took the "historical cure." Karl Deutsch was also an important influence, in the skill he showed in adapting concepts like nationalism to quantitative indicators. At the same time, Armstrong was resistant to what he termed the "extreme behaviorists" in some parts of the American field; he made up his mind to refuse "to relinquish my increasing number of Ph.D.'s to the extreme behaviorists."[23]

Armstrong in the latter phases of his distinguished career turned to broad, historically informed, conceptually and methodologically rich comparative studies, each of which required years of research and extensive field inquiry. A scholar of exceptional erudition, Armstrong also had the polyglot skills (fluency in French, German, Russian, and Ukrainian) to make research of such scope possible. His landmark monograph on *The European Administrative Elite* appeared in 1973, followed by a volume even more ambitious in historic and geographic scope, his magnum opus, *Nations before Nationalism*, in 1982.

His national stature in the Soviet field brought periodic overtures from other institutions. In 1961, Armstrong actually accepted an offer from the University of California–Berkeley, and had sold his house to Seymour (zoology) and Shirley Abrahamson (now chief justice of the Wisconsin Supreme Court). California at the last minute reneged on the offer, and to the immense benefit of comparative politics and the department, Armstrong completed his career at Wisconsin.

In his memoir, Armstrong singles out a number of his doctoral advisees who have left their mark: Monte Palmer, Sylvia Margulies, James Oliver, Trond Gilberg, Donald Schwartz, John Swanson, Arnold Krammer, Gilbert Mathieu, Donald Pienkos, Alfred Evans, Joel Moses, Brian Silver, Jeffrey Chinn, Kenneth Farmer, Joan de Bardeleben, and Peter Stavrakis.[24] He also emphasizes his engagement with Catholicism as a defining moral compass.[25] Another constant was the enduring conviction that state socialism and the Communist ideology upon which it rested was profoundly flawed, even an "evil empire."

Beyond the substantial number of graduate students he supervised, Armstrong contributed pedagogically not only through helping cover the Soviet politics courses, but also through regularly teaching the large American foreign policy course (for a number of years alternating with a parallel offering by radical historian William Appleton Williams), and the introductory comparative politics course. In his first years, he also taught the basic American government offering. His mark on the comparative politics field is indelible.

Other comparativists were on the staff for short periods during the 1950s, but only Epstein, Hart, and Armstrong had an enduring impact. Jaroslav Mayda, a Czech emigre, for a short time covered the Soviet bloc, from a rather legal point of view, preceding Armstrong. John Thomson, a Columbia Ph.D. specializing in Chinese and Southeast Asian politics, served from 1951 to 1957. Thomson, who grew up in China of missionary parents, was a popular teacher, active in organizing the annual model United Nations which was a major undergraduate event at the time. However, his publication record was too thin for tenure, and he left for a rewarding career in the State Department and the Central Intelligence Agency (CIA) as a China and Burma specialist.[26] Carr Donald briefly replaced Stokes in the Latin American field (1958–60), but then left to pursue a career on the staff of the Organization of American States.[27] The gap between the virtual demise of comparative politics in the immediate aftermath of World War II, and its vigorous renewal by the end of the 1950s, is illustrated by the decline in the relative number of comparative doctorates awarded. Between 1950 and 1960, only nine of 49 doctorates were in the comparative field, of which one was hired (Charles Anderson).

Explosive Growth: The 1960s

The phase of explosive growth of comparative politics (and the department overall) began in the late 1950s, and had essentially ended by 1970. From the later 1950s until the mid-1960s, state budgets for the university were based upon an enrollment-funding formula; this meant that the rapidly expanding student numbers translated into a flow of new revenue. The enactment of a sales tax in the early 1960s contributed to a state revenue stream that for a brief period sustained university budget growth.[28] As well, during this period the impact of the wave of new foundation and federal funding was felt, and in important part translated into new appointments. At an earlier stage of declining postwar enrollments and very tight budgets, longtime L&S Dean Mark Ingraham perforce was extremely reluctant to permit faculty recruiting based upon soft money.[29] His successors, Edwin Young (1961–65) and Epstein (1965–69), could take a more expansive view, and assume that the pace of state budgetary expansion would suffice to absorb appointments initially based at least partly upon external funding. Many departments as well adopted an aggressive expansion perspective, and could be persuaded that externally funded area studies appointments were "free," and would not count against the unit in advancing its established priorities.

The new wave of comparative politics began in 1958 with the appointment of Fred von der Mehden, the first Southeast Asia specialist, followed by Anderson in 1960. The first Africanist recruited was Aristide Zolberg (1961); though on the faculty for only two years, he swiftly earned a national reputation through his first book (*One-Party Government in the Ivory Coast*, 1961). Zolberg, along with Curtin and Jan Vansina (history), and Fred Simoons (geography), was a founding member of the African Studies Program. A second Soviet specialist, Carlisle, came in 1962, and Leon Lindberg was recruited in the field of European studies the same year. Crawford Young replaced Zolberg in 1963, then became chair of the African Studies Program the following year.

These appointments were all at the beginning level; those recruited had pursued doctoral training in the midst of the ferment in comparative politics and the rise of area studies. Most swiftly published major books and earned national recognition. Lindberg carved out a national role in theoretical interpretation of European integration with his 1963 work, *The Dynamics of European Economic Integration.* Anderson, von der Mehden, and Young established the department as a leader in comparative third world studies. Anderson published a pair of books in 1963, *The Political Economy of Mexico* (coauthored with William Glade of the School of Business) and *Latin American Political Systems*, followed by *Politics and Economic Change in Latin America* (1967). Von der Mehden, also in 1963, authored *Religion and Nationalism in Southeast Asia*, followed by *Politics of the Developing Nations* in 1964. The Young[30] monograph on the turbulent transition to independence of the former Belgian Congo, *Politics in the Congo* (1965), was long a standard work on that sprawling country. Anderson, von der Mehden, and Young during the 1960s became close collaborators in research and teaching; they jointly authored the 1967 volume *Issues of Political Development*, which attracted considerable attention at the time of its publication. All three pursued their area specializations in a comparative vein, as evidenced by the titles of the Anderson and von der Mehden books. Young had begun the projection of his early instrumentalist exegesis of Congo ethnicity to a comparative canvas, which eventually led to his 1976 work, *The Politics of Cultural Pluralism.* Their shared, broadly comparative commitment left an enduring imprint on the study of third world politics in Madison.

Anderson was the last Wisconsin doctorate hired directly on completion of graduate study, a practice frequent in the early years of departmental history, beginning with the first two doctorates, Samuel Sparling and Paul Reinsch. Of Wisconsin antecedents, Anderson grew up in suburban Chicago, his father a midlevel Sears employee and his mother a part-time journalist. During his Grinnell undergraduate years, he absorbed a college ethos suffused with social commitments originating in its role as a seedbed of abolitionism, and later as a center for the social gospel movement. He began his Wisconsin doctoral program after an M.A. at Johns Hopkins, drawn naturally to the Wisconsin Idea and a progressive heritage dating from Richard T. Ely and John R. Commons. These normative influences shaped his enduring attachment to philosophic pragmatism, social Christian beliefs, and political economy interests.[31]

When Anderson began his doctoral study in 1957, the departure of Stokes left the department briefly without a Latin Americanist. Epstein assumed responsibility for his supervision, and Anderson swiftly completed his doctorate in 1960. In his first years with the department, Anderson was absorbed in institutional development as well as his first books. He worked closely with Glade and Robert Mulvihill in launching the Ibero-American Studies Program, and was the key political science member of the team that built the Land Tenure Center (LTC), which initially specialized in land reform studies in Latin America with substantial funding from the Agency for International Development. The LTC at the time, led by Raymond Penn (agricultural economics) among others, embodied in its land reform commitments the Ely-Commons heritage. By the 1970s, Anderson began to shift his focus from Latin American politics to public policy, comparative political economy, and eventually political theory; his important role in that field is examined in chapter 7. During his Latin American phase, Anderson supervised an unusually large number of graduate students; among those who became respected scholars in the field were Gary Wynia, Howard Handelman, Elsa Chaney, and Reid Reading.

There were some new arrivals and departures in the late 1960s, but by 1970 an enduring framework of comparative politics was in place, preserved in part by an important degree of staff continuity. Epstein, Anderson, Hart, Armstrong, Lindberg, and Young spent their entire careers at Wisconsin, though as noted above, the first two eventually shifted their focus away from comparative politics. Edward Friedman, recruited in 1967 as the first postwar China specialist, Melvin Croan, wooed from Harvard in 1967 to introduce East European politics, and Dennis Dresang, added in 1969 as a comparative development administration specialist with an African focus, were all career members of the department, though Dresang within a few years shifted his primary focus to public administration in the United States. Von der Mehden was lost to Rice in 1968, but the loss was cushioned by the addition of James Scott in Southeast Asian politics in 1967. Carlisle, whose research career eventually blossomed at Boston College, left in 1967. Constantine Menges, a Latin America and international politics specialist later to win visibility at the Hudson Institute and in the Reagan administration, was briefly on the faculty in 1964–67.[32] Donald McCrone, recruited from North Carolina in 1965 as a Latin Americanist of more behavioralist bent, left in 1971 to continue his career at Iowa and Washington. Alexander Wilde was added as a Latin Americanist whose research focused on Colombia in 1969.[33] He left in 1976, eventually joining the Ford Foundation Latin America staff. Stuart Scheingold, also recruited in 1965, shared the Berkeley background and Lindberg interests in political integration and the European community. They coauthored the influential book, *Europe's Would-Be Polity: Patterns of Change in the European Community*, in 1970. Scheingold was lost to the

University of Washington that same year. Another West Europe specialist, Rodney Stiefbold, briefly served from 1966 to 1968. Fred Hayward was added as a second Africanist in 1967, and swiftly became an important administrative leader; until his resignation in 1991, he was a significant player in the comparative contingent.

During the post-1970 period of consolidated strength in comparative politics, the field was sustained by a number of key additions, whose contributions will be examined later in the chapter. Donald Emmerson, also a Yale product, reinforced Scott in the Southeast Asian field in 1970, remaining until his 2001 retirement. Graham Wilson, a specialist in American and European politics, especially British, bridged the American and comparative fields when he came to the department as a senior appointment from Essex (UK) in 1984. Leigh Payne, a student of Juan Linz at Yale, joined the faculty in 1991 to reinforce Latin American politics. The gap in African politics left by the Hayward resignation was filled by Michael Schatzberg, a 1977 doctoral alumnus, and also Aili Tripp, recruited as a women and development specialist jointly with the women's studies department. Two other permanent comparativists were added in 1993, Kathryn Hendley in Russian political economy and Paul Hutchcroft in Southeast Asian politics. Mark Pollack, a Harvard doctorate who straddled the comparative and international relations fields, joined the department in 1995, continuing the Lindberg/Scheingold tradition in European integration studies. Preservation of Wisconsin strength in comparative politics seems guaranteed by an array of excellent appointments of promising younger scholars in the last half-dozen years: David Leheny, a Japan specialist in 1998; Aseema Sinha, South Asian politics, in 1999; Melanie Manion, a China specialist and Jason Wittenberg, East European politics, in 2000, and Scott Gehlbach (primarily Russian politics) and Tamir Moustafa (Middle East politics) in 2003. All but Manion were beginning assistant professors.

Six other comparativists served briefly during this period. T. J. Pempel, a Japan specialist, was recruited at a senior level in 1993 to direct the East Asian Studies Program, whose reinforcement was then a major campus priority. However, he remained only two years, moving on to the University of Washington, then to California-Berkeley. James Bjorkman, whose work in policy studies included both health politics in the United States and South Asian studies, served from 1976 to 1985. His career subsequently flourished at the International Institute of Comparative Government in Lausanne, Switzerland, and since 1990 at the prestigious Institute of Social Studies, The Hague, Netherlands. Ayesha Jalal (1987–90) also a South Asia specialist, was to become a major figure in that field.[34] Charles Gillespie (1988–91), another

Yale Ph.D. of high promise, died prematurely at the age of 33. Stephen Lewis (1985–94) and Stephen Anderson (1987–93) were Western Europe and Japan specialists, respectively; the latter switched to government service overseas, posted in Japan and China.

Until the 1960s, there were only area and country courses. Epstein initiated a new pattern of more broadly comparative offerings, both at the introductory level (106, Introduction to Comparative Politics) and for graduate students (850, Politics of Advanced industrial Societies). Von der Mehden followed with comparable courses at both levels (653, 852) on the politics of developing areas. In keeping with a larger department-policy evolution, increasingly graduate students were encouraged to enroll primarily in courses numbered 700 and above, reserved to graduate students (with a few exceptions for gifted seniors). An array of core courses, covering broadly defined regions (advanced industrial societies, developing areas, Communist states) or key themes (political economy, cultural pluralism), were completed by more specialized seminars. The structure of the comparative politics preliminary examination encouraged a mastery of theoretical literature extending beyond a region of specialization, and within the area of focus a general substantive knowledge of at least the major countries within the region. This stress on broad comparative training was reinforced by the reforms instituted by the Merelman committee at the beginning of the 1980s, which identified a half dozen broad themes (such as political psychology, political economy, political culture, political development, or state and society) from which three had to be chosen However, the great majority of doctoral candidates specialized in a given region, and were generally expected to fulfill their minor field requirement through the relevant area studies offerings; of 164 dissertations completed in comparative politics from 1970 to 1998, all but a dozen focused on a single region.[35] The requirements of language competence and resources make multiregion fieldwork-based dissertations all but impossible. The area specialization emphasis through the 1980s reflected the structure of the employment market, with comparative vacancies normally identified by region. With the attack on the "area studies" concept as antithetical to an integrated political science, which emerged in some quarters of the discipline in the 1990s, there were some signs of change in field definition patterns at the national level in recruitment.

At the undergraduate level, large enrollments were driven by several factors, especially the remarkable number of majors in political science and international relations, the broad appeal of some topics, a campuswide "ethnic studies" requirement imposed in the late 1980s, and a School of Business curricular reform in the early 1980s funneling large numbers of intending business students into the introduction to comparative politics (106). The interdisciplinary area survey courses, often coordinated by a member of the department faculty, and courses such as the politics of revolution (654, introduced by Scott and Friedman at the peak of antiwar protest at the end of the 1960s), and the politics of multicultural societies (230, introduced by Young to help meet the ethnic studies requirement) always drew large enrollments. At the same time, the size of the comparative faculty made possible a wide range of upper-division offerings with much smaller numbers and closer faculty contact.

Particularly noteworthy in the comparative politics field was the high level of engagement of department faculty in leadership roles in area studies programs and international studies more broadly. The crucial contributions of Hart and Armstrong to the launching of South Asian, and Soviet and East European studies, respectively, was noted earlier. Young was the second chair of the African Studies Program, and led the effort to secure support under the NDEA Title VI program, backing the program has maintained ever since. Hayward subsequently served a term as African Studies chair (1973–76), then as acting dean of International Studies in 1989–90, a position many expected he would retain before his resignation. Stallings was briefly head of the Latin American Studies Program (1985), before joining the Graduate School as associate dean, then later became the first director of the newly launched Global Studies Research Program, a post later held by Payne. Croan served a decade as head of the Russian and Eastern European Studies Program (1972–79, 1989–92), a role played by Hendley at the turn of the century, and Emmerson led the Southeast Asian Studies Program for several years in the 1980s. Pempel, as noted earlier, during his brief Madison tenure directed the East Asian Studies Program.

Intellectual Itineraries and Portraits: Latin America

In turning to the intellectual contributions of Wisconsin comparativist scholars, we will find the area structure of the field a convenient organizational guide. The major works of the postwar pioneers of comparative politics (Epstein, Hart, Armstrong, and Anderson) have already been reviewed. In the Latin America field, following Anderson, whose work was also examined earlier, the next to win national recognition was Stallings. Although her earliest perspectives reflected the orientation of a moderately prosperous and very conservative family in Phoenix,[36] at Mount Holyoke an intellectual environment she found liberating transformed her outlook. She was a student activist, much involved with the National Student Association (NSA). Her first stop after graduation was to work in a national student press association linked to NSA in 1966–67, the year the CIA covert funding of the NSA international program was exposed. Added to the Vietnam War, the radicalizing impact of this revelation was great. The following year, she was at the Inter-American Graduate Program in Santiago, Chile; dependency theory, then still novel and just reaching its zenith of influence, totally dominated the intellectual environment. One of her mentors was Fernando Cardoso, later president of Brazil, but then architect of the most enduringly influential strand of dependency theory. Stallings then returned to Chile in 1972–74 for her Stanford dissertation research, a pregnant historic moment that spanned the radicalization of the socialist Salvador Allende regime, then its brutal liquidation by the military junta led by General Augusto Pinochet. This research led to her first major book, *Class Conflict and Economic Development in Chile, 1958–1973*. The volume, which earned excellent reviews, marked her as a coming leader in the field, drawing flexibly upon dependency and Marxist theory.

Her strong Stanford record won an SSRC postdoctoral award, which she used to pursue a second doctorate at Cambridge University in economics, training she felt indispensable to pursue her engagement with political economy as the key to understanding Latin American development. The Cambridge dissertation evolved into her celebrated book, *Banker to the Third World: U.S. Portfolio Investment in Latin America 1900–1986* (1987), where she deftly demonstrates the sharp differences in prewar and postwar debt structure and traces the political consequences. Stallings notes that, although the Chile book could be read as Marxist in inspiration, *Banker to the Third World* is rooted in a different set of perspectives, and an emerging commitment to international political economy.[37]

In campus far-left quarters, a standard criticism of the department was its alleged refusal to diversify ideologically and methodologically by appointing candidates of Marxist persuasion. Thus the Stallings job interview attracted wide attention, and her formal presentation took place in tense circumstances with a large crowd, whose student component longed for their ideological appetites to be satiated, while the faculty voting on the appointment expected a performance consistent with professional canons. Somehow Stallings won over the latter without antagonizing the former.

Although the period of administrative immersion beginning in 1985 slowed her research production, she had already earned the international reputation that led to her recruitment by the United Nations Economic

Commission for Latin America (ECLA) in 1993 to carry out a multimillion-dollar appraisal of the 1990s continent-wide effort to replace the "lost decade" of the 1980s with a renewed development momentum in the 1990s based upon the "Washington consensus" of market-oriented reform. The final product of this massive project, which sought to tease out the micro-linkages of macroeconomic policies, coauthored with Wilson Peres, was published in 2000 after her 1996 departure from Wisconsin (*Growth, Employment, and Equity: The Impact of the Economic Reforms in Latin America and the Caribbean)*. The study concludes that the results fell far short of what market enthusiasts touted, but the modest gains exceeded the forecasts of antimarket critics. Growth rates improved over the 1980s, but fell short of the 1950–80 benchmark; trade deficits grew a little, and employment-generating impact of growth was disappointing. However, inequality did not increase sharply as critics predicted. Beyond its academic value, this richly documented monograph is a major contribution to a crucial global-policy debate.

Leigh Payne, who joined the department in 1991, has maintained the tradition of distinction in Latin American politics. Born in Korea of missionary parents, her adolescent years were spent at an alternative New Hampshire Quaker high school on a working farm; "Granola High," she recollects, was its nickname.[38] Her father had left mission work to pursue an academic career, teaching at New York University; the free tuition determined her college choice for NYU. She abandoned pre-medical study for a double major in history and political science.

Her Latin American interests took form during a study abroad program in Madrid. Her two years in Spain came at an electric moment: the final demise of long-serving dictator Francisco Franco, and the transition to democracy. Her history teacher was leader of the socialist party, and introduced her into democratic left circles. As well, she developed contacts with the large networks of Chilean and Argentine exiled intellectuals. She chose Yale for graduate study (over Wisconsin, which also offered her a fellowship) to work with Alfred Stepan, who immediately left, leaving her in the hands of Juan Linz, an intellectually rewarding advisor. Scott was an important informal mentor, as was Stallings, who spent a visiting year at Yale.

At Wisconsin, Payne's first book, *Brazilian Industrialists and Democratic Change* (1994), dealt with business elites in Sao Paulo, Brazil. She explains the apparent paradox that these private-sector leaders had backed authoritarian intervention in 1964 but welcomed democratization in the late 1980s; the key was changing perspectives on how stability was best assured. Her national standing was cemented by an ambitious second book, *Uncivil*

Movements: The Armed Right-Wing and Democracy in Latin America (2000). This work drew upon extensive interviews with leaders of such movements in Argentina, Brazil, and Nicaragua. Not only was the research original; also, as her tenure review committee noted, it was dangerous. Those she contacted, the review noted,[39] included assassination among their repertoire of interpersonal skills. But she shows that violent right-wing movements also contain peaceful opponents of elected rulers, and to a large extent make use of democratic processes. Her research has important policy lessons on how uncivil movements can be contained within a democratic framework. The long-standing interest in democratic transitions and legacies of authoritarianism led to her third major project, probing the traumatic memories of the repressive brutality associated with dictatorial rule, and mechanisms by which the demons of an ugly past may be exorcized.

South Asia

In the South Asian field, the Hart retirement left a gap. Bjorkman, only partly in the South Asian field, made some contribution to its maintenance until his 1985 departure. Jalal was too brief a faculty member to leave an impact. Sporadic searches for a South Asian specialist proved unsuccessful until the appointment of Aseema Sinha in 1999. Of Indian origins, she completed her doctoral training at Cornell, and pursued a comparative inquiry into state level economic policy differences in India, resulting in a 2004 book, *Regional Roots of Developmental Politics in India: Leviathan Divided.*

Africa

In the realm of African studies, the Wisconsin program would figure on most rosters of the top three nationally. Young, during his long tenure (1963–2001), was a mainstay. Of academic parentage (father an economist at the University of Pennsylvania, later research director at the Federal Reserve Board, mother an English professor at American University), he was active in international student politics (like Scott, Stallings, and Emmerson). A doctoral student of Samuel Beer and Rupert Emerson at Harvard, his African specialization drew upon his experiences with student leaders from many parts of the continent. His thesis research in the immediate post-independence turmoil in Congo-

Kinshasa, originally cast as a study in federalism debates, forced him to confront the realities of an ethnicity-saturated political environment. Ethnicity was then almost exclusively understood as a primordialist phenomenon; in his revised dissertation, *Politics in the Congo* (1965), and then more systematically and comparatively in *The Politics of Cultural Pluralism* (1976), Young contributed to the introduction of an instrumentalist and constructivist reading of ethnicity. Subsequently, his 1982 book sponsored by the Council on Foreign Relations, *Ideology and Development in Africa*, identified three major ideological streams (Afro–Marxism, populist socialism, and African capitalism), and examined the developmental policy consequences and impacts of these policy preferences. The book was widely used as a text until the fall of the Soviet Union eviscerated socialist orientation as an alternative pathway. His return to Congo-Kinshasa (then Zaire) in 1973–75 as dean of the Social Science Faculty at the Lubumbashi campus of the national university permitted initiation of a second major Congo study in collaboration with former student Thomas Turner. This book, long an authoritative summation of the Mobutu Sese Seko regime, was published in 1985 (*The Rise and Decline of the Zairian State*). His last major work, *The African Colonial State in Comparative Perspective* (1994), delineates the logic of the imposition of European rule in Africa, and portrays the pathologies bequeathed to postcolonial African states by the structural requirements of imperial domination in the particular economic and social circumstances of Africa. *The Politics of Cultural Pluralism* won major prizes from both the African Studies Association and APSA; *The African Colonial State* earned an award from the APSA Comparative Politics section.

Hayward, a Princeton product whose mentor was Manfred Halpern, did extensive research in several smaller West African states (Sierra Leone, Ghana, and Senegal). Though he never published a major book, his valuable survey research, a challenging methodology to apply in Africa, led to several influential journal articles, including three in the *American Political Science Review*. The surveys in Ghana and Sierra Leone, repeated at different periods, not only produced striking insights on the surprising levels of political information available to rural publics, but also captured the growing pessimism about politics and future prospects.

Dennis Dresang, who grew up in a paper mill town in the Fox Valley, was attracted to African politics by an undergraduate course at Wisconsin, and by a 1962 summer internship at the Department of State. The high point of the internship was preparation of a briefing for President John Kennedy for a meeting with the Somali ambassador. The ambition to specialize in African politics shaped the choice of UCLA, then the leading African studies center, for doctoral study; there his mentors included James Coleman and Richard Sklar. On returning to Madison as a faculty member in 1969, he originally was a member of the African politics contingent. His first book, *The Zambian Civil Service: Entrepreneurialism and Development Administration* (1975), identified episodes of innovation within the Zambian bureaucracy, before its morale and ethos were devastated by an extended period of economic decline which set in just after the research was completed. He then, with Ira Sharkansky (1968–85), undertook a study of public corporation performance in Kenya, sponsored by the Wisconsin Center for Development. However, by this time he was shifting his focus to public administration and civil service reform in the United States. His field change partly reflected a view that, with Young and Hayward, the African teaching needs were met.[40]

The 1991 Hayward resignation was offset by the addition of Michael Schatzberg and Aili Tripp. Schatzberg grew up in Brooklyn; his family, of modest circumstances, ran a small business. His father died the year he finished high school, but had made insurance provision for college for the two children, and his mother struggled to keep the enterprise alive until Schatzberg and his sister completed their university education. Initially intending a legal career, Schatzberg was inspired by Robert Legvold at Tufts to shift to a Soviet specialization. However, his aspirations changed when a Peace Corps assignment to Cameroon immersed him in village Africa. He chose Wisconsin for doctoral study because of its African studies strength, with Young as primary mentor. He identified a small up-river town (Lisala) in Congo-Kinshasa (Zaire) for his dissertation research in the mid-1970s, a moment when conditions were propitious for access to local archives as well as extensive interviews. His rich trove of materials served as source for two books, *Politics and Class in Zaire: Bureaucracy, Business and Beer in Lisala* (1980) and *The Dialectics of Oppression in Zaire* (1988). His captivating representation of the nexus linking the state apparatus and its repressive organs, the local political and business operatives, and the astonishing patterns of beer marketing and consumption won him national recognition. After stops at Dalhousie, the Virginia Polytechnic Institute, and the Johns Hopkins School of Advanced International Studies, he returned to his doctoral alma mater in 1991. His research focus evolved from political economy to culture, marked by the 2001 publication of his strikingly original comparative opus, *Political Legitimacy in Middle Africa: Father, Family, Food.* In this work, Schatzberg probes the basic understandings of legitimacy in popular culture, rooted in metaphors of ruler as father figure, to be judged by his role as provider for the subject, a richly documented and compelling analysis. His predilection for unusual domains of inquiry continues with his present research on the politics of football (soccer), the national sport everywhere in Africa.

Tripp was destined from childhood for an African specialization. She grew up in Tanzania; her Finnish mother was an anthropologist, and her father (originally a Wisconsin native) was involved in refugee work. As a secondary-school student, enrolled in correspondence courses, she served as an informal research assistant for her mother. Her family was well connected to the young nationalist elite; top figures such as President Julius Nyerere had been household guests, and their vision of an African communal socialism had great appeal. She then went to the United States for university education, first at Luther College, then Chicago; the latter had a rich array of exceptional comparative politics faculty, including Zolberg and Leonard Binder, plus other outstanding Africanists such as Ralph Austen (history) and John and Jean Comaroff (anthropology). She continued for an M.A. at Chicago, at first with an Arab world focus by way of differentiation from her parents. She transferred to Northwestern for her doctorate, raising an unusual sum ($150,000) for dissertation research on the Tanzanian informal economy, in collaboration with two Tanzanian economists, Bernard Ndulu and Mboya Bagachwa. This inquiry, which provided the basis for her first book, *Changing the Rules: The Politics of Liberalization and the Urban Informal Economy in Tanzania* (1997), was not originally focused on gender, though close scrutiny of the explosion of the informal sector and corresponding decline of the official economy brought gender issues to the fore. Important changes were occurring in household dynamics, as women petty traders became the main income source, while their state employee husbands saw their real wages shrivel through inflation. Her book makes clear why by the mid-1980s there was little resistance to the abandonment of the visionary Nyerere socialism; in reality, the state ideology was by then a hollow shell, which collapsed of its own weight. Her subsequent research then shifted explicitly to gender; her second major book examined *Women & Politics in Uganda* (2000). In this work, she shows how the political opening beginning in 1986 permitted the rise of an array of vigorous and effective women's organizations in which gender solidarity trumped ethnic or religious difference. The commitment to gender studies, Tripp recalls, was a natural outgrowth of the findings of her first major research project, and was not simply shaped by her joint appointment at Wisconsin with the Women's Studies Program.[41]

The numbers of doctoral alumni in African politics are exceptionally large—50 from 1967 to 2001, 10 of them from Africa. Frequent note is made at national Africanist meetings of the exceptional numbers and influence of

Wisconsin alumni. Some who achieved prominence in the field include Joel Samoff, Catharine Newbury, Georges Nzongola-Ntalaja, Okello Oculi, Edmond Keller, John Harbeson, Thomas Turner, K.C. Morrison, Louis Picard, Gretchen Bauer, Gregory White, William Reno, Joshua Forrest, Linda Beck, Timothy Longman, Jimmy Kandeh, Stephen Orvis, Bruce Magnusson, Kathleen Staudt, and Stephen Morrison.

Southeast Asia

The Southeast Asian field, after the 1968 departure of von der Mehden, was anchored by Scott (1967–78), Emmerson (1970–2001), and Paul Hutchcroft (1993–). Scott was drawn to the field by a Rotary fellowship in Burma (Myanmar) in 1958–59, following his Williams undergraduate study. At Rangoon University at the time, diverse Communist factions were in bitter struggle to control the student organization. This exposure to student politics led to a period of involvement in the international program of NSA, followed by doctoral study at Yale. At that time, in the early 1960s, Yale was the epicenter of the behavioral revolution and pluralist theory.[42] Though Scott observes that he had never heard of behavioralism before enrolling at Yale, he was deeply influenced by it during his doctoral studies.[43] His first book, *Political Ideology in Malaysia: Reality and the Beliefs of an Elite* (1968, based on the dissertation), reflected a behavioral orientation that Scott quickly abandoned. This volume had only modest impact, and Scott soon left behind the elite focus for a commitment to subaltern politics and peasant society.[44] His new engagement embodied a populist streak which marked his subsequent scholarship. A penchant for framing complex realities around a seemingly simple but compelling theme became evident in his very influential 1976 book, *The Moral Economy of the Peasant: Rebellion and Subsistence in Southeast Asia*, where he shows that rural rebellion is not caused by the social fact of inequality alone, but rather triggered by acts of landowners that violate the implicit contract of reciprocity with the peasantry by increasing their impositions. His research after his 1978 return to Yale pursued similar themes, exploring the subtle and hidden ways in which peasants resist their exploiters, and how state projects of high modernity are undermined by the fatal simplifications governments impose upon complex social realities by their codified reading of society. Consultation of *Social Science Citation Index* figures for past and present faculty in 1985 and 2000 revealed remarkably high figures for Scott, reflecting the core insights about peasant politics and state behavior for which his work is an obligatory reference; among then-current department faculty, only Murray Edelman had comparable figures.[45]

Scott joined the faculty as the crescendo of antiwar protest was growing. A vehement critic of the Vietnam War, he was at once drawn into faculty debates when the protest against Dow Chemical recruiting on campus in October 1967 led to an angry riot in Ingraham Hall (then Commerce Building), pitting protesters against police and leading to a number of injuries. Scott was a frequent orator at the massive faculty meetings held in the wake of this crisis, and his outspoken criticism of the university administration irritated a number of older faculty, leaving in its wake some lingering, mutual ill will.

Donald Emmerson grew up in a diplomatic family, with a cosmopolitan childhood influenced by the successive postings of his father, John Emmerson: Japan, Peru, Soviet Union, Pakistan, India, Lebanon, France, Nigeria. His father took part in a mission to China in 1944, to assess the strength and prospects of the Chinese Communists. Those involved were subsequently pilloried by an aggressive China lobby tied to the Chiang Kai-shek regime, as well as McCarthyites, for "losing China"; though John Emmerson suffered less than some other members of the mission, the episode probably foreclosed any possibility of an ambassadorial appointment. The family, however, was always shielded from this unpleasantness. The precocious international experience ingrained upon Emmerson a desire to be different, even a contrarian strand in his thinking.

Emmerson was a Princeton undergraduate, an experience that failed to ignite his intellectual energies.[46] Despite a mediocre undergraduate record, and rejection by the Foreign Service, he won admission to Yale after an interlude of international student politics. Here he became an enthusiastic convert to behavioralism. At the same time, a growing attraction to area studies, influenced by Southeast Asia historian Harry Benda, pulled Emmerson in a different direction.

However, his first area attraction was to African politics. His original dissertation proposal, a survey-based study of anticolonial insurgencies in Guinea-Bissau, Mozambique, and Angola, was encouraged by the department but rejected by all funding agencies. Momentarily at intellectual loose ends, an opportunity for summer Indonesian language study at Cornell opened, which led to the eventual choice of an Indonesia thesis topic. A "Cornell school" of Indonesian studies at Cornell, associated with Benedict Anderson and George Kahin, competed unsuccessfully with Yale specialists such as Benda in the shaping of his perspectives. Eventually he chose to work on political culture, leading to his first major book probing this theme in Indonesia, *Indonesia's*

Elite: Political Culture and Cultural Politics (1976). He later became a little uneasy with the notion of a "national culture," and his next major field inquiry was in a Javanese fishing village, which led to a lasting fascination with maritime politics.

Emmerson helped to organize the now widely admired Center for Southeast Asian Studies (CSEAS), beginning in the 1970s. He later strengthened the center by helping organize successful applications for Title VI NDEA funding, with an unbroken record of winning this funding. As CSEAS director in the late 1980s, he led a successful campaign for a multimillion dollar endowment of the center by obtaining a Mellon Foundation challenge grant with matching support from the university and multiple other sources, including faculty members and his own mother.

Emmerson was an influential contributor to national and international debates on politics and policy in Southeast Asia. His important edited volume, *Indonesia Beyond Suharto: Polity, Economy, Society* (1999), was an influential appraisal of a regime whose earlier image of success was tarnished by the circumstances of its fall soon after. He summed up his work on low-income fishing communities in Asia in a monograph published by the World Bank in 1980. In 1999, he helped the Carter Center monitor East Timor's vote for independence from Indonesia before Jakarta's violent reprisal forced his evacuation.

He also was an important contributor to debates about "Asian values" and the Southeast Asian development model. Perhaps more than any other comparativist, his influence was felt less through major works than in his role as a public intellectual, author of frequent opinion essays directed to the policy community as well as the academic world. Although the mastery of Indonesian politics remained his forte, all of Southeast Asia was his intellectual realm, and a gadfly role runs throughout his career.

A final Emmerson legacy was his part in identifying Paul Hutchcroft as an additional Southeast Asian specialist in 1993. After an unsuccessful search for a South Asian expert, Emmerson persuaded the department to redefine the vacancy to include Southeast Asia, which proved a happy choice. Hutchcroft came from an academic family, his father an agronomist at Iowa State. His political and international interests took early shape; he served as a page in the State Legislature, and was a full-time staff member of the 1976 campaign of former Representative Tom Harkin. A high school summer in Denmark and family travel opened his eyes to the world beyond the borders.[47] He completed his undergraduate degree at Macalester College, which had a strong international program. A study abroad program took him to

Stirling University in Scotland, where work with Africanist historian Robin Law incubated an ambition to specialize in African politics.

The accidents of career development, however, took him in a different direction. He participated in a Methodist third world outreach program; rather than the African assignment he requested, he was dispatched to the Philippines, where he arrived in late 1980 as opposition to the authoritarian rule of Fernando Marcos was growing. This year of travel around the archipelago, meeting with church groups, was transformative, and provided an initial network of Filipino contacts.

After a couple of years working with Clergy and Laity Concerned in support of the opposition to the Marcos regime and American bases in the Philippines, Hutchcroft pursued graduate study at Yale, no longer dominated by a pluralist and behavioral ascendancy; his mentors included Scott, Susan Woodward, Margaret Keck, and David Apter. His dissertation research led to his influential first book, *Booty Capitalism: The Politics of Banking in the Philippines* (1998). In this signal contribution, Hutchcroft develops the notion that the oligarchy-centered patrimonialism of Filipino politics engendered a distinctive form of capitalism, where the state, rather than serving as regulator of a market economy, was merely an accomplice in the draining of its funds. "The government," wrote one of his reviewers, "emerges as little more than the getaway driver for a long line of professional thieves who make notorious American bank robber Willie Sutton look like a neophyte Ermita pickpocket." Drawing effectively on Weberian theory, Hutchcroft shows convincingly why the Filipino postwar economic development performance has been so meager.[48]

The influence of *Booty Capitalism* extended far beyond the academic realm. General Jose Almonte, a leading collaborator of former reformist President Fidel Ramos, wrote that he had reproduced "dozens and dozens of the two-volume manuscript copies" for distribution to key leaders in Congress, the cabinet, and the judiciary. Related work was widely distributed in Association of Southeast Asian Nations (ASEAN) nations as well, establishing Hutchcroft as the leading American political scientist working on the Philippines. His further work is moving in a comparative direction, as well as toward the exploration of capital and countryside linkages and colonial heritage. He has also been tireless in service roles, both locally, and nationally and in the Philippines.

East Asia

Chinese politics, which loomed so large in the first days of the department with Reinsch and Hornbeck, went into a prolonged relative eclipse, though Ogg regularly offered a seminar on Chinese politics during the interwar years, and Thomson included China in his realm of specialized knowledge in the 1950s. However, for a decade before the arrival of Edward Friedman in 1967, the department had no instruction in Chinese politics. Friedman grew up in an Italian and Jewish Brooklyn neighborhood in the very modest circumstances typical of an earlier generation of faculty, but less prevalent in recent years. His father, who worked in the garment industry, had left school after third grade. The socialist and progressive ideas frequently encountered in the recent-immigrant milieux of the day animated household political conversation. Friedman spent many long afternoons in the Brooklyn Public Library, working his way through the journals, especially moved by the liberal Catholic publication, *Social Justice*.[49]

As a Brandeis undergraduate, he took courses with a number of well-known scholars: Herbert Marcuse, Lawrence Fuchs, John Roche. He was introduced to China by Milton Sachs, and was strongly influenced by a course on European utopianism and its dangers by Frank Manuel. Although he began college as an intending science major, he graduated as a prospective China specialist.

As a Harvard doctoral student, his mentor in Chinese politics was Benjamin Schwartz, a meticulous, historically oriented scholar. However, his key advisor was Barrington Moore, who along with Judith Shklar, shaped his commitment to a progressive liberal orientation. A course with Talcott Parsons provided a negative pole of reference; Friedman found him dogmatic and insensitive.

Friedman in his student days took part in the Student League for Industrial Democracy, which led to his attendance at the second meeting of Students for a Democratic Society (SDS). After this gathering, SDS fragmented, some factions mutating into the "Weathermen" and other far-left cliques whose extremism repelled Friedman. He characterized his orientation at that time as a progressive liberal with a strong civil liberties and human rights commitment, beliefs which have remained his lodestar.[50]

His dissertation explored the 1911 Chinese revolution, and his first book, *Backward Toward Revolution: The Chinese Revolutionary Party* (1974), examined the early postrevolution years in the Canton area, based upon archival materials not yet available for more recent periods. The beginning of a political opening in China in 1978, after the devastation of the Cultural Revolution years, provided the first opportunity for field research in China. With a team of four scholars, Friedman began a series of visits—eventually 25 over 33 years—to the same north central China community. The intimate familiarity with the village, the time depth achieved by repeated observation over many years, and the development of a web of key informants, made his 1991 book (with three coauthors), *Chinese Village, Socialist State*, a landmark monograph, profoundly revelatory of ground-level politics under Communist rule. This volume, which was translated into Chinese, won the Association for Asian Studies prize in 1991 for the best book on modern China. A further volume, *Revolution, Resistance and Reform in Village China*, is scheduled for publication by Yale University Press in 2005, covering the 1960–2000 period.

Triggered by the "democracy wall" in Beijing in 1978, Friedman developed a lasting interest in the glacial process of democratic opening in China. He became closely involved with many of the leaders of the democracy movement. In his teaching and writing, he developed a powerful critique of what he termed "Leninist regimes," whether of Maoist, Titoist, or Stalinist inspiration. In his first Madison years, he was uncertain as to how Maoism should be appraised; his initial approach was through suggesting four different approaches. Subsequently, the Chinese Communist regime was interpreted through the lens of Leninism. With the "third wave" of democratization sweeping many parts of Asia and the developing world by the 1980s, Friedman introduced both graduate and undergraduate courses on this theme.[51]

An accidental supplementary theme of recent Friedman publication was the nationality issue. This first struck him during a 1984 lecture tour of China, when the different cultural worlds of north and south China caught his attention. This led to a number of publications on this theme, including his 1995 book, *National Identity and Democratic Prospects in Socialist China.*

Friedman is also a major contributor to Taiwan studies. He has written widely on this theme, and is respected on the island for his contribution to the democratization movement. He was active in the campaign more than two decades ago to save the lives of the political prisoners of the opposition party; they and their party are now in power.

An important influence in the Friedman career itinerary was his three years of service on the staff of the House of Representatives Foreign Affairs Committee, then chaired by fellow Brooklynite Stephen Solarz. Subsequently he served for two years on a Department of Defense panel on democracy and peacekeeping. This immersion in Washington policy debates, and associated extensive travel to global trouble spots, Friedman suggests, brought a strong dose of realism to his policy perspectives.[52] He has also been an active participant in rural development and poverty alleviation projects for the United Nations Development Program, the Land Tenure Center, and other bodies in such far-flung locations as Nicaragua, El Salvador, Sumatra, and Albania. He is part of a large Wisconsin and Chinese team engaged in a long-term project on sustainable development in the Himalayas.

The East Asian studies group provided less of a congenial extra-departmental association than did its other area counterparts. The program divides sharply into its China and Japan components; although Japan specialists Pharr and John Dower (history) were once close intellectual companions, Friedman found no comparable associations on the China side. Scott, Emmerson, and Young shared many interests, but Friedman felt himself somewhat of a "loner."

An additional China specialist, Melanie Manion, joined the faculty in 2000. Jointly appointed with the La Follette School, Manion studied at McGill and London before completing her doctorate at Michigan. She has worked on party cadres, local elections, and bureaucratic corruption, from a rational-choice perspective. She is the author of a pair of books, *Retirement of Revolutionaries in China: Public Policies, Social Norms, Private Interests* (1993) and *Corruption by Design: Building Clean Government in Mainland China and Hong Kong* (2004).

On the Japan side, Pharr was the pioneer. She grew up in Atlanta; her parents divorced when she was five, compelling her mother to find work for the first time as a secretary. On this meager income, she managed to provide for her two children. After attending a public high school in Atlanta, Pharr enrolled at Emory, initially as an English major. She noticed an announcement on a bulletin board about a Georgetown graduate summer institute on francophone Africa, and succeeded in gaining special permission to participate as an undergraduate. She developed stimulating contacts with the francophonic African diplomats in Washington, and spent the following summer as a Crossroads Africa volunteer working outside Dakar, Senegal. These experiences decided her to pursue graduate study in African politics at Columbia.

However, like Emmerson and Hutchcroft, circumstance drove her in a different direction. Her African politics mentor, L. Gray Cowan, she found pedestrian, but she was inspired by a course with Dankwart Rustow, a Middle East specialist fresh from coediting a volume on Japan-Turkey comparative modernization. Soon thereafter, on a whim, she joined a Sunday judo group, mostly Japanese, whose descriptions of Japanese culture captivated her. She switched her language study from Hausa to Japanese, and her advisor from Cowan to James Morley. Her eventual dissertation topic on political women in Japan was chosen not in response to the emergent feminist movement, but through a curiosity aroused by friendships with Japanese women students in her Tokyo dormitory while she attended an intensive Japanese language program. Many of these young women were involved in radical student politics. After two years on the staff of the SSRC, she joined the Wisconsin faculty in 1976.[53]

Her first major work, *Political Women in Japan: The Search for Place in Political Life* (1981), broke new ground in illuminating the various pathways into political roles women constructed. Pharr also completed a study of the gender dimension of the postwar Japanese constitution, drafted with the strong influence of American occupation authorities. The novel standing and rights opened to women in this document were the consequence of the determined efforts of a tiny knot of women, made possible by the relatively low profile of this issue.

Her second major project explored status politics, using as cases such low-status groups as burukumin (outcasts) and tea-pourers (indispensable office subalterns, invariably female). The anthropological nature of her field research was a new departure. Although the research was completed during her Wisconsin stay, the well-received book, *Losing Face: Status Politics in Japan,* was published in 1990 after her departure for Harvard. The nearly simultaneous loss of Pharr and historian Dower was a lethal blow to Japanese study at Wisconsin, damaging its standing for many years. By the time of Pharr's resignation, only a tiny handful of Japanese politics specialists matched her standing.

Her immediate replacement, Stephen Anderson, and thereafter Pempel, failed to take root. Hopes for the field were renewed with the 1998 addition of David Leheny, from Cornell. His first book, *Rules of Play: National Identity and the Shaping of Japanese Leisure* (2003), used the tourist industry as a prism for inquiry into Japanese culture.

Russia and Eastern Europe

In the Russian and Eastern Europe area, Melvin Croan replaced Carlisle as a second specialist in 1967, and became the architect of East European studies. Croan's early years were spent in Boston, of modest family circumstance (father in the automobile trade, mother a secretary), in a house devoid of books. The rigors of Boston Latin School molded his study habits in preparation for

Harvard, destination of choice for Boston Latin products. Two key influences in his undergraduate days were McGeorge Bundy, later national security advisor to Presidents John Kennedy and Lyndon Johnson, and Merle Fainsod, the leading Sovietologist of his generation. Croan remained at Harvard for his doctoral study, and the first seven years of his career, though no permanent position was in sight. Particularly influential in shaping his political science perspective was Carl Friedrich: informed by history, elucidating and defending philosophical values, then examining how institutions and processes realize those values.[54] Close associates during his Harvard years included a number of leading figures: Zbigniew Brzezinski, Samuel Huntington, Henry Kissinger.

Within the larger field of Soviet bloc studies, the Croan concentration on East Germany was shaped partly by ancestral heritage. He had a special interest in German culture and literature, and held a Fulbright fellowship in Germany in 1953–54 following his 1953 Harvard B.A. Croan was to become a national leader in East Germany studies.

Opportunity was plentiful for young and well-recommended doctorates in the early 1960s. While at Harvard, he received offers from California-Berkeley, UCLA, Swarthmore, Washington University, and Rice; only the last he came close to accepting, but declined because he was then unable to drive, a necessity for survival in Houston.[55]

No fewer than five Harvard doctorates came to Madison in 1967 (in addition to Croan, Friedman, Booth Fowler, Donald Hansen, and Theodore Marmor). Croan was especially drawn to Madison by historians Thomas Skidmore and George Mosse. Throughout his career, he traveled widely in East Europe, and had an extensive network of contacts with intellectuals from the region. He wrote extensively on East German politics and foreign policy, and taught political theory courses as well as introducing courses on East European politics. He regularly taught the large course on Soviet foreign policy. One of the department's most gifted teachers, he won a campus Distinguished Teaching Award in 1986.

Croan also introduced and defined the office of associate chair in 1969. Young, when designated as chair at that time, asked that this position be created, in view of the rapid growth in the department, the swelling graduate enrollments, and the tensions created by the Vietnam War. Croan tailored the responsibility as director of graduate study, a position definition which has endured. Though most larger departments now have such a post, at the time it was a novelty.

On the occasion of his seventieth birthday, a number of his former doctoral students organized a special panel in his honor at the annual meetings of the American Association for the Advancement of Slavic Studies. In attendance were David Ost, Robert Evanson, Stephen Burant, Roman Laba, and Matthew Rhodes. Croan's oratorical skills won him invitation as Wisconsin commencement speaker in 1991. After some delay, following the 1996 Croan retirement, he was replaced by another East European specialist, Jason Wittenberg, an MIT Ph.D. whose initial research was on Hungarian politics.

In replacement of John Armstrong, Mark Beissinger was recruited from Harvard in 1988. His childhood years were spent in a Philadelphia suburb; his father was an accountant, and his mother active in school board service. His attraction to Soviet studies began in his Duke undergraduate years, sparked by courses with Sheridan Johns (also an Africanist) and Werner Lerner (history of socialism and communism). As a Harvard graduate student, he was especially influenced by Adam Ulam and Thane Gustafson; the latter drew his attention to the use of policy studies as prism to discover who holds power. Two young comparative scholars important to his intellectual development were Joel Migdal and Robert Putnam. But his main intellectual associations took place in the Russian Research Center rather than the department. After completing his dissertation in 1982, he remained at Harvard till 1987.

His initial field of inquiry was scientific management as an instrument of social control in the Soviet Union; this was the theme of his first book, *Scientific Management, Socialist Discipline and Soviet Power* (1988). However, by 1984 his interest was beginning to shift to nationalism, initially his involvement as the main organizer of a coedited study, *The Nationalities Factor in Soviet Politics and Society* (1990), in which he had a prescient coauthored essay. The growing evidence of nationality unrest by the late 1980s led him to undertake the monumental study which eventuated in his book, *Nationalist Mobilization and the Collapse of the Soviet State* (2002). This volume won no less than three 2002 prizes: the Mattei Dogan Award of the Society for Comparative Research; the Organized Section on European Politics and Society of the APSA award for best book on European politics; and above all, the APSA Woodrow Wilson Prize for the best book on government, politics, or international affairs. The Wilson prize, inaugurated in 1946, is the top award of the APSA, and Beissinger is the first winner from the department faculty.

This landmark volume stands out both for its methodological innovation— quantitative as well as qualitative—and for its theoretical depth and scope. Encyclopedic data, garnered from the regional Soviet press and other sources, subjected to sophisticated statistical exegesis, brought to light key patterns in nationalist mobilization. Above all, Beissinger illuminates the dynamic by which the tide of nationalism swept away the seemingly impregnable Soviet state, whose demise was forecast by almost no one. Yet in a compressed time frame the impossible became inevitable, as a powerful interaction of events, processes, and nationalist protest action undermined the Communist colossus. The Wilson prize citation concludes that the "importance of the question, the scope of coverage, the quality and depth of the research, the integrated use of quantitative and qualitative methods, and the clear and compelling writing—all of these factors make this a model for books in comparative politics and political science in general. Beissinger masterfully weaves detailed historical knowledge of a series of events to show their connectedness and interaction in a convincingly argued dynamic analytical framework."[56]

The Beissinger agenda now turns in a more comparative direction. The reconception of the Soviet regime as an empire-state rather than a socialist commonwealth in its late stages leads to a comparative inquiry into the persistence of empire in the minds of many in a postimperial age. This was an important theme in the major international collective volume coedited with Young in 2002, *Beyond State Crisis? Postcolonial Africa and Post-Soviet Eurasia in Comparative Perspective*. Beissinger chaired CREECA from 1992 to 1998, and served as department chair in 2001–04, organizing the March 2004 centennial celebration.

Kathryn Hendley joined the faculty in 1993 as a second Russian specialist, jointly appointed with the Law School. She grew up in Pittsburgh, where her father was a nuclear engineer with Westinghouse. Her first ambition was to become a professional musician (flute and piano); this directed her to Indiana University, noted for its strength in humanities. But like many of her future colleagues, her interests changed during her undergraduate study, leading to a history major and then law school at UCLA—not a fully reflected choice, she later noted.[57] The major eastern law firms did not interview at UCLA; she did not want to remain in Los Angeles, and so took employment with a Dallas partnership. This proved an unhappy location; her three years as a law firm associate attached to a difficult partner were boring and circumscribed. As an escape hatch, she enter an M.A. program at Georgetown, during which a fascinating tour of the Soviet Union redefined her career options. She committed to a Soviet specialization at Georgetown, then entered the doctoral program at California-Berkeley. Although Gail Lapidus and George Breslau were valuable advisors, her greatest influence was Robert Kagan in public law, who introduced her to a "law and society" approach which has shaped her subsequent career.

Her first book, *Trying to Make Law Matter: Labor Law and Legal Reform in Russia* (1996), offers a ground-level exploration of the interaction between enterprises and trial courts. She achieves novel insights in the empirical examination of how law actually operates in practice in the Russian setting. Her Law School associations, especially with Stewart Macaulay, have been valuable in showing how law and society interact in the field of contractual relations; her Law School courses examine contracts in a comparative perspective. Her recent research explores inter-enterprise relations, and how courts are used to ensure contracts; the planned publications will be the first broad view of enterprise-level behavior in post-Soviet Russia. She succeeded Beissinger as head of CREECA from 1998 to 2001.

An additional Russian (and East European) specialist, Scott Gehlbach, joined the faculty in 2003. A California-Berkeley Ph.D., Gehlback spent 2001–03 as a visiting scholar with the Moscow Center for Economic and Financial Research. He adds a rational-choice perspective and quantitative disposition to the comparative contingent.

Western Europe

Although European studies at Wisconsin has less of an "area studies" identity than the others, many distinguished faculty in other social science departments, especially history, as well as political science have been European specialists. Beyond the key department faculty in the field whose careers are reviewed here (Leon Lindberg, Graham Wilson, and Mark Pollack), other comparativists have made some transatlantic research connection. The Epstein role was noted earlier; the Armstrong book on *The European Administrative Elite* covers France and Germany as well as Russia. One Anderson book, *Political Economy of Modern Spain*, dealt with a less-frequently studied European state; for a time, he worked closely with Lindberg on international political economy. Stallings wrote on International Monetary Fund stabilization programs in Portugal, Britain, and Italy. Americanist Austin Ranney, just after joining the Wisconsin faculty, wrote a monograph on British politics, *Pathways to Parliament* (1965).

Lindberg's parents immigrated only in the late 1920s. They had been radical journalists with far-left Swedish newspapers. Some of his school years were in Sweden; after high school, he worked for a year on a Swedish freighter, plying the waters of Asia and East Africa. These formative experiences helped shape a normative orientation inspired by Swedish social democracy.[58]

He grew up in San Francisco, making California-Berkeley a logical destination for undergraduate and graduate training. His undergraduate study gravitated toward political theory; Sheldon Wolin and John Schaar were a strong influence. So also was his tutor, Peter Odegaard. His doctoral study began in sociology, then shifted to political science. Particularly influential were Philip Selznick, an exponent of the symbolic interactionism associated with George Herbert Mead, and Reinhard Bendix, who deepened Lindberg's understanding of Weber and Durkheim.

His dissertation advisor, Ernest Haas, encouraged his interest in European integration, the focus of his first books, *The Political Dynamics of European Economic Integration* (1963) and *Europe's Would-be Polity* (with Scheingold, 1970). The first offered a functionalist theory of European integration, a dynamic sidestepping particular nationalisms by proceeding sequentially in the economic realm, propelled by spillover effects at each step. By the time of the second book, he had become convinced that the first wave of integration energies were spent, and that changing international realities and domestic contexts required a new theoretical approach. Reflecting on his intellectual journey in 2001 on the occasion of receiving an award from the European Community Studies Association for lifetime contributions to the field, Lindberg felt that critics of his initial integration theory helped him see its limitations: a naively technocratic, pluralist theory of industrialization, a debatable implicit premise that integration was a positive-sum game in its distributional consequences, an unexplained assumption that market agents pursuing profit maximization would necessarily push integration forward, and an unexamined belief that the United States would have a benign role.[59]

Lindberg then turned to a focus on the stresses and contradictions in advanced capitalism. His subsequent research drew heavily on close collaboration with political scientists and sociologists in both America and Europe; he spent several years at different research centers in Europe. Several major Lindberg edited works emerged under his leadership: *Stress and Contradiction in Modern Capitalism* (1975), *Politics and the Future of Industrial Society* (1976), and *Governance of the American Economy* (1991). His intellectual focus and teaching role by the 1980s was almost exclusively in international political economy, concentrating on advanced capitalist states including the United States and Japan as well as Western Europe. In his final faculty years in the 1990s, he returned to the theme of European integration, as the Maastricht accords and expansion seemed to give new momentum. He forecasts a Europe increasingly based on concentric circles of integration, facing difficult dilemmas of distributional consequences between nations and classes, and ongoing tension between a European social model of capitalism and invasive neoliberal currents from the United States and Britain. The dynamic interplay of economic integrative forces and nationalism, he argues, requires situation in a much longer time frame than merely the founding of the European Economic Community; the temporal boundary needs to be extended back to the early 19th century.

Lindberg attracted a large number of graduate students drawn by his approach to international political economy. Teaching, he reflected, was the most rewarding aspect of his academic career. Among his political science students with a strong reciprocal impact he mentioned Alberta Sbragia, Kenneth Bickers, John Woolley, and Brigitta Young; he also served on a number of sociology doctoral committees. Sbragia, in presenting the 2001 ECSA award, cogently observed that a "significant portion of the 'mental map' that we bring to the study of the EU was drawn by Leon Lindberg."[60]

Graham Wilson, like Epstein, bridged the American and comparative fields. As well, like Epstein, Lindberg, and others, his work reflects a rejection of the artificial separation of the American political experience from comparative politics. Born near Liverpool in a family of very modest means, his parents—though neither had a higher degree—clung to a middle-class status. His state secondary school, though staffed by excellent teachers, found reason to rejoice when one of its graduates broke through to win Oxbridge admission. Wilson was admitted to Oriol College at Oxford, one of the less prestigious units attracting the bottom end of the public (British version) school products, many, he recalls, of modest intellectual talent.[61] Oriol sought upgrading by leading the way in admitting women, whose first cohorts clearly raised academic standards. On completion of his first degree, Wilson almost chose a public service career in the Bank of England, but finally opted for graduate work at Essex. Philip Williams, a distinguished expert on French politics, urged him to continue doctoral study at Nuffield College Oxford, which proved a superb intellectual environment.

After completing a dissertation on comparative agricultural subsidies in the United States and United Kingdom, he had the opportunity to return to Essex, as an American specialist (thus a comparativist in the British mode). At the time, the study of British politics seemed stale and stagnant, founded on a premise of the stable and unchanging nature of the system. American politics seemed more fluid and changing. Hugh Heclo and his comparative bureaucracy and policy formulation research was an important influence at Essex. So also was Jean Blondel, through whom Wilson became involved with the Essex-based European Consortium for Political Research. Another formative experience was attendance at a seminar directed by Philippe Schmitter and Gerhard Lehmbruch on neocorporatism, which broadened his comparative vision.

His most extensive contribution lies in the field of comparative interest groups, especially US and UK, the focus of five of his eight books. The first, *Special Interests and Policymaking: Agricultural Politics and Policies in the United States* (1979), grew out of the dissertation. Other comparative interest-group works include *Business and Politics: A Comparative Introduction* (1985) and *Interest Groups* (1990). His works on regulatory politics (*The Politics of Safety and Health*, 1985) and the British bureaucratic model (*The End of Whitehall: Death of a Paradigm*, 1995, with Colin Campbell) reflect a repertoire extending beyond interest groups, as does his engaging recent work, *Only in America? American Politics in Comparative Perspective* (1998). The study of American politics, Wilson reflects, tends to be technically sophisticated but substantively narrow, locked in a faulty premise of American uniqueness. A comparative frame for American politics is indispensable, he feels, invoking the adage that American politics has the evidence and comparative politics the ideas.[62]

Wilson joined the Wisconsin faculty in 1984, after an earlier year in Madison as a participant in the Essex Exchange. He has played a major role as administrative leader, serving a term as associate chair from 1990 to 1993, chair of the European Studies Program 1992–95, then three and a half years directing the La Follette School beginning in 1999. In the latter role, he led the way in internationalizing La Follette, partly through absorbing the Center for Development. He became department chair in 2004.

The most recent addition to European studies was Mark Pollack; like Lindberg, his work and teaching falls on the boundary between comparative and international relations. His parents fled Cuba in 1960; the Castro regime stripped the family of its wealth, and his parents achieved only moderate prosperity in their adopted New Jersey home. His family was tightly integrated into a right-wing Cuban exile community, fiercely anti-Castro. He went to the state university at Rutgers, where his interests became focused on political science, especially international relations and European unification. His Rutgers mentors pushed him toward top graduate schools; he enrolled at Harvard for his doctorate.

He arrived in Cambridge at a moment of intense struggle between rational choice theorists and others termed "traditionalists." Robert Putnam, then Pharr, as chairs during his graduate study, maintained an equilibrium, but their successor, Kenneth Shepsle, pushed the department strongly in a rational-choice direction. Stanley Hoffman, viewed by the rational-choice advocates as a major adversary, served as Pollack's advisor. This made impossible Shepsle's participation in the dissertation supervision; he refused to serve on the same committee with Hoffman. Another key mentor was Robert Keohane.

The new momentum on European integration at the beginning of the 1990s, leading to its expansion, deepening, and currency integration, created a renewed excitement to European Union (EU) studies, and shaped his dissertation choice. His first book, *The Engines of European Integration: Delegation, Agency, and Agenda Setting in the European Union* (2003), draws on both comparative and international relations theory. His current research examines structures of governance in the transatlantic marketplace with the complex interdependence of the United States and the EU; also on the agenda are studies of structural rules for aid to poorer EU regions, and the mainstreaming of gender in the EU since the 1995 UN Beijing conference on women.

Pollack describes his methodological approach as "soft rational-choice theory." Some of its evangelical advocates, he suggests, give the appearance of claiming that analysis informed by rigorous adherence to the canons of rational choice can proceed without detailed contextual knowledge or "real world" awareness. This perhaps unwarranted impression creates a resistance among graduate students to the contribution that contextually informed, flexibly applied rational-choice theory can make.[63] Pollack left for Temple University in 2004, in order to pursue his career where his wife could also find faculty employment.

Concluding Reflections

Of the 20 comparative politics faculty who served a decade or longer after World War II, oral histories or interviews were conducted with all but two (von der Mehden and Hayward), inquiring about family background, perspectives about the department and the role of comparative politics, and their contributions. A broad similarity in backgrounds is notable; none grew up in very wealthy households. Only Dresang and Friedman might be classified as of working-class antecedents, though several others had parents of very modest circumstances (Armstrong, Croan, Lindberg, Pharr, Pollack, and Schatzberg). Four had academic parents (Hutchcroft, Payne, Tripp, and Young). Three had missionary or international nongovernmental organization backgrounds (Hart, Payne, and Tripp). The Epstein and Schatzberg parents operated small businesses; Anderson, Beissinger, Emmerson, Hendley, Scott, and Stallings had fathers with professional careers (accounting, middle-rank executives, diplomacy, law). Interestingly, in addition to the four Africanists (Hayward, Schatzberg, Tripp, Young), four others had initially intended an African specialization (Emmerson, Hutchcroft, and Pharr, as well as John Witte in the American field).

The attraction to comparative politics in most instances arose from a formative international experience before doctoral study. Several had been involved in international student affairs (Emmerson, Scott, Stallings, Young). Others had particularly influential overseas study experiences (Payne, Scott, Stallings); Schatzberg served in the Peace Corps, and Hutchcroft with an international church program. Tripp grew up in Tanzania, the early Hart years were in India, and Lindberg spent some school years in Sweden. Wilson immigrated from Britain; Armstrong and Epstein spent army years in Europe.

The comparative group held doctorates from a small number of leading institutions. Yale led with four (Emmerson, Hutchcroft, Payne, and Scott). Harvard (Croan, Pollack, and Young), California-Berkeley (Hendley, Lindberg, and von der Mehden), and Wisconsin (Anderson, Hart, and Schatzberg) came next with three each. Columbia had two (Armstrong and Pharr), and Chicago (Epstein), Princeton (Hayward), UCLA (Dresang), and Northwestern (Tripp) each had one. Regional backgrounds tilted toward the Northeast (seven) and Midwest (five). Three came from the South, three from California, and one from the Southwest.

Unanimous was the preference for a commitment to eclecticism. The strong attachment to the department and its comparative contingent expressed by all faculty interviewed was grounded in the conviction that diversity of methodological orientation and theoretical perspective was essential to a spirit of comity and collegiality. The range of interests and breadth of coverage likewise contributed to the strength of comparative politics.

These faculty views were echoed in doctoral alumni responses to a survey conducted for the department history in 2003. Of the 137 responses, 44 were identifiable as comparative politics specialists. A handful expressed regret at inadequate quantitative training, though of these most were concerned about capacity to evaluate work of others rather than preparation for their own research. But there was virtually no dissent from the robust praise for the eclectic orientation of the program, and the breadth of preparation it provided. The commitment to critical inquiry and insistence on field research were also frequently mentioned. Appreciation for the engagement with research and the model provided by the publication quality of leading faculty members also ran through the comments.

If one endeavors to apply the Lichbach and Zuckerman classification scheme (rational choice, culturalist, structuralist) referenced earlier in the chapter, the eclecticism again stands out. The categories may be clear, but the placement of individuals within them is not; most would make a reasonable claim to multiple placement. Pollack, and among newer additions, Melanie Manion and Scott Gelbach, fall in the rational-choice field. At least part of the work of Emmerson, Payne, Pharr, Schatzberg, Tripp, and Young might be classified in the culture and identity category. In the structuralist and historical institutionalist frame, one might place Armstrong, Croan, Epstein, Hutchcroft, Lindberg, Scott, Stallings, Wilson, and Young, though not without some difficulty. Above all, classification founders on the commitment of most to drawing upon diverse theoretical resources in their work, and reticence before engagement to a single paradigm.

In terms of the ideological spectrum suggested by Almond, referenced earlier, neither the neoconservative right nor the far left are represented. However, there is a range of perspectives, doubtless cohering around a middle ground of center left, ranging from the populism of Scott, the strong human rights engagements of Friedman and Payne, and the social democratic perspective of Lindberg to the moderate conservatism of Armstrong. Although the area studies imprint remains strong, cross-regional comparison stands out in the work of Anderson, Epstein, Lindberg, Scott, Wilson, and Young.

Whatever the classificatory difficulties, the importance of the theoretical contributions of Wisconsin comparativists is beyond dispute. Perhaps the most striking single domain with a unique imprint is the comparative politics of cultural pluralism, a theme with multiple Wisconsin contributors. For more than a decade, beginning in 1992, Young and Beissinger organized a continuing interdisciplinary workshop on this theme, which attracted a number of distinguished visiting speakers. Armstrong delved into the distant roots of the idea of nation across Eurasia; Beissinger brilliantly dissected the role of nationalism as engine of demolition of the Soviet empire. Young in his wide-ranging comparative work on ethnicity helped redefine its conceptual focus. Friedman dismantles the notion of a monolithic Han nation. A new generation of doctoral alumni, who participated in this collective endeavor, promise to build upon its influence: Edward Schatz, Laura Jenkins, Hakan Yavuz, Linda Beck, Virginia Tilley, Kathleen Graney, David Green, Stefanie Nanes, among others.

Other noteworthy theoretical contributions of lasting influence include Epstein on comparative political parties, Armstrong on comparative European bureaucracies, Lindberg on the political economy of advanced capitalism, Stallings on the international political economy of Latin America, Schatzberg on African concepts of legitimacy, and Young on the imperatives shaping African state behavior. Many of the monographs authored by Wisconsin comparativists have important conceptual resonance: Hutchcroft on crony capitalism in the Philippines, Tripp on the gender dynamics of informal economies, Pharr on status politics in Japan.

Notably missing until the Gehlback appointment in 2003 are comparativists whose research rests primarily on quantitative methods, though many from Armstrong to Manion and Beissinger have made important use of statistical data. Also missing is the cross-polity survey mode of inquiry, which relies upon comparative analysis of quantitative indicators profiling different countries. Another important gap was Middle East politics, until the 2003 recruitment of Tamir Moustafa. Jalal had taught courses on Islamic politics, and some visiting staff or lecturers had offered occasional courses on one or another aspect. But there had never been a regular faculty appointment in the field, reflecting in part the difficulties in creating a viable Middle East studies program at Wisconsin.

An academic prophet contemplating the department in 1945 could hardly have forecast the scale and significance of comparative politics in the last four decades of the century. The leadership, vision, and entrepreneurial energy of a few key figures in the 1950s gave a basic shape to the field which has been preserved. The rapid rise to prominence of a number of junior appointments made in the 1960s gave the program stability. So also did the ability of the department to retain its core comparative faculty: only a few major losses over five decades, in the face of a Wisconsin salary scale that lags most of its competitors. The department policy of relying on entry- or junior-level recruitment, coupled with a high standard for tenure,[64] finds vindication in the stability and standing of comparative politics. Several successful appointments were made at the younger but tenured level (Croan, Schatzberg, Wilson, and most recently Manion), but the only clearly senior recruit, Pempel, had a disappointingly brief stay.

The very success of comparative politics may have unintentionally inhibited until recently the development of international relations, a point also made in chapter 8. International political economy evolved as a subfield within comparative politics. Comparativists taught a number of international relations courses, especially those dealing with regions (such as African international relations, Latin American international relations, Japan and the world order, Soviet foreign policy). In a subliminal way, over the years the need to sustain comparative politics perhaps competed with the imperatives of building international relations. Arguably as well, the attractions of a strong comparative politics faculty may have drained some graduate students of international bent from international relations.

Nonetheless, the postwar practitioners of comparative politics have preserved and built upon a heritage dating from Reinsch and the creation of the department. They have also transformed it, and made what Gaus termed "an inland university" with no natural destiny as a major center of international studies into an academic endeavor in comparative politics of world renown. The roots are now deeply implanted; there is reason to believe that the distinction of the comparative politics field will continue to survive the periodic budgetary vicissitudes that beset the university.

Notes

1. John Gaus to Dean George C. Sellery, 9 March 1931.
2. Arnold Hall, "Reports of the National Conference on the Science of Politics Held at Madison, Wisconsin, September, 3–8, 1923," *American Political Science Review*, 18, 1 (1924), 119–66; "Reports of the Second Conference on the Science of Politics," *American Political Science Review*, 19, 1 (1925), 104–62; A. B. Hall et al., "Reports of the Conference on the Science of Politics," *American Political Science Review*, 20, 1 (1926), 124–70.
3. Those attending the 1952 seminar included Samuel Beer, Harry Eckstein, George Blanksten, Karl Deutsch, Kenneth Thompson and Robert Ward.
4. David Truman, Conrad Arensberg, Angus Campbell, Alfred de Grazia, Oliver Garceau, V. O. Key, Avery Leiserson, M. Brewster Smith.
5. Gabriel Almond, David Apter, Ralph Braibanti, William Ebenstein, Lloyd Fallers, G. Lowell Field, Pendleton Herring, George Kahin, Joseph La Palombara, Marion Levy, Roy Macridis, William Marvell, Guy Pauker, Lucien Pye, Kenneth Thompson, Bryce Wood and Roland Young.
6. For a valuable study of the SSRC Committee on Comparative Politics, see Suzanne Duval Jacobitti, "Political Theory and Comparative Politics: A Critique of the Political Theory of the Committee on Comparative Politics," PhD diss., University of Wisconsin–Madison, 1967. Interestingly, none of the contributors to the Almond-Coleman volume, and only two of the 61 chapter authors in the seven SSRC political development volumes which followed had Wisconsin connections: Walter Sharp, who left in 1938, and Kemal Karpat (History). At the time these volumes were planned, most of the new generation of Wisconsin comparativists had not yet established national reputations. Leon Epstein attended a couple of the conferences Almond organized in the development of this project.
7. See the essays by Joel S. Migdal, "Studying the Politics of Development and Change: The State of the Art," in Ada W. Finifter (ed.), *Political Science:*

The State of the Discipline (Washington: American Political Science Association, 1983), 309–31; David Collier, "The Comparative Method," in Ada W. Finifter (ed.), *Political Science: The State of the Discipline* (Washington: American Political Science Association, 1993), 105–19, and David D. Laitin, "Comparative Politics: The State of the Subdiscipline," in Ira Katznelson and Helen V. Milner (eds.), *Political Science: State of the Discipline* (New York: W.W. Norton & Co, 2002), 630–59.

8. Gabriel A. Almond, *A Discipline Divided: Schools and Sects in Political Science* (Newbury Park, CA: Sage, 1990).
9. Mark Irving Lichbach and Alan S. Zuckerman (eds.), *Comparative Politics: Rationality, Culture, and Structure* (Cambridge: Cambridge University Press, 1997).
10. The model for area studies actually traces to crash programs during World War II, mounted by the military. Civil affairs training schools were created at 10 universities, including Wisconsin. In addition, 55 language and area programs were created at colleges and universities, again including Wisconsin. Of the 55, only two (Indiana and Stanford) offered more languages than Wisconsin. Richard D. Lambert, *Beyond Growth: The Next Stage in Language and Area Studies* (Washington: Association of American Universities, 1984), 6.
11. The funded centers were African Studies Program, Center for Russia, East Europe and Central Asia, Center for East Asian Studies, Center for South Asia, Center for Southeast Asian Studies, Center for European Studies, and Latin American, Caribbean and Iberian Studies Program. The titles of some programs have varied over the years. Only the Middle East program failed to qualify.
12. For assessments of the evolution and impact of area studies, see Mark Tessler (ed.), *Area Studies in Political Science: Strategies for Understanding Middle East Politics* (Bloomington: Indiana University Press, 1999), and Lambert, *Beyond Growth.*
13. For a review of the controversy, see Robert Bates, "Area Studies and the Discipline: A Useful Controversy," *PS Political Science & Politics*, 30, 2 (1997), 165–69, and Mark K. Tessler, Jodi Nachvey and Anne Banda in their edited volume, *Area Studies and Social Science*, vi-xxi.
14. For detail on the career of Leon Epstein, see the 1989 oral history conducted on behalf of the APSA by Samuel Patterson, on deposit at the University of Kentucky library. As well, he has completed a memoir, not yet available for consultation. Two oral history interviews have been conducted with Henry Hart, by Laura Smail in 1982, and Crawford Young in 2002. Unless otherwise indicated, all oral history tapes are on deposit with the University of Wisconsin–Madison Archives, Steenbock Library.
15. Leon Epstein oral history, American Political Science Association, 1989, 115.
16. Epstein oral history, 123.
17. Epstein oral history, 168.
18. Henry Hart oral history, University Archives, 1982.

19. E. David Cronon and John W. Jenkins, *The University of Wisconsin: A History, 1945–1971—Renewal to Revolution* (Madison: University of Wisconsin Press, 1999), 119, 132–33, 259.
20. Henry Hart oral history, University Archives, 2003.
21. A richly detailed 310 page memoir completed in 2000 by John Armstrong is on deposit at the University of Wisconsin–Madison Archives.
22. Armstrong memoir, 144.
23. Armstrong memoir, 156.
24. Armstrong memoir, 242–46.
25. Armstrong memoir, ix-x.
26. Marjorie Harris, longtime administrator with the African Studies Program and close friend of the Thomson family, provided career details. Thomson died about 1999.
27. Anderson interview.
28. William F. Thompson, *The History of Wisconsin: Continuity and Change, 1940–1965*, Vol VI (Madison: State Historical Association, 1988), 183.
29. Hart oral history, University Archives, 1982.
30. Hereafter, in this chapter "Young" without first name indication refers to Crawford Young, not William Young.
31. Anderson interview.
32. Menges later became identified with a very conservative stance not fully evident during his Madison years. He authored regular columns in the *Washington Times* warning of a Brazil nuclear threat. During the 2002 Brazilian presidential election campaign, he wrote that the election of Luiz Inacio Lula de Silva was the "largest intelligence failure since the end of World War II," and that unless Lula were stopped George Bush "will have lost Latin America."
33. His book was eventually published in Colombia: Alexander Wilde, *Conversaciones con caballeros: la quebra de la democracia en Colombia* (Bogota: Ediciones Tercer Mundo, 1982). An abbreviated version was included in Juan Linz and Alfred Stepan (eds.), *The Breakdown of Democratic Regimes* (Baltimore: Johns Hopkins University Press, 1978).
34. Notably for her several influential books, *The Sole Spokesman: Jinnah, the Muslim League, and the Demand for Pakistan* (1985), *State of Martial Rule: The Origins of Pakistan's Political Economy of Defence* (1990), *Democracy and Authoritarianism in South Asia: A Comparative and Historical Perspective* (1995), and *Self and Sovereignty: Individual and Community in South Asia since 1850* (2002).
35. The exceptions: Robert Jackman, *Politics and Social Equality: A Cross-National Analysis*, 1972; Phil Arnold, *Political Integration in Culturally Plural States: A Comparison of Political Preferences in Canada, Belgium, and Argentina*, 1974; Richard Flannery, *Civil-Military Relations in Wartime U.S. and Soviet Union, 1940–1945*, 1974; John Seitz, *The Gap Between Expectations and Performance: An Exploration of American Foreign Aid to Brazil, Iran, and*

Pakistan, 1950–1970, 1976; Okello Oculi, *Colonial Capitalism and Malnutrition: Nigeria, Kenya, and Jamaica*, 1977; Kathleen Peroff, *A Times Series Analysis of Health and Social Welfare Expenditures Policy in Canada, United Kingdom and the United States*, 1977; Joan Debardeleben, *Theoretical and Ideological Discussion of Environmental Problems in the Soviet Union and East Germany 1965–77*, 1979; Robert Evanson, *Political Terror in Czechoslovakia and the Soviet Union: A Study of Comparative Communism*, 1979; Jung-Il Gill, *Preadult Learning of Democratic Orientations in Three Nations, the United States, Korea and Japan*, 1996; Jon Honeck, *Industrial Policy in Older Industrial Regions: A Comparison of Ohio and the Basque Region*, 1998; Laura Jenkins, *Identity and Identification: Affirmative Action in India and the United States*, 1998. One may note that four of these use the United States as one pole of comparison, and that two involve the Soviet Union and Eastern Europe, sometimes considered as one region. Only the Oculi and Jenkins theses involved field research.

36. Stallings recalls that her father, a lawyer, had been a major contributor to the 1964 Goldwater campaign; her mother had sought the dismissal of a high school American history teacher who suggested alternative perspectives. Barbara Stallings interview, 28 May 2003.
37. Stallings interview.
38. Leigh Payne interview, 11 July 2003.
39. Report to the Executive Committee, Crawford Young and Edward Friedman, 1998.
40. Dennis Dresang oral history, University Archives, 27 March 2003.
41. Aili Tripp interview, 13 June 2003.
42. For a detailed inquiry into the Yale Department of Political Science and its impact on the discipline, see Richard M. Merelman, *Pluralism at Yale: The Culture of Political Science in America* (Madison: University of Wisconsin Press, 2003).
43. James C. Scott oral history, University Archives, 1976.
44. I recollect a rather patronizing review of the first book in the *Economist*, which concluded with the observation that "really, Yale, this simply will not do."
45. Although *The Moral Economy of the Peasant* first established Scott as a widely cited author, most of the citations in the 1985 and 2000 volumes of *Social Science Citation Index* were to his major works after leaving Wisconsin: *Weapons of the Weak: Everyday Forms of Peasant Resistance* (1985); *Domination and the Arts of Resistance: Hidden Transcripts* (1990), and *Seeing Like a State: How Certain Schemes to Improve the Human Condition Have Failed* (1998).
46. In his oral history interview, he playfully characterized his main achievement as avoiding expulsion. Donald Emmerson oral history, University Archives,12 September 2002.
47. Paul Hutchcroft interview, 9 July 2003.
48. The citation is from the department tenure recommendation, 27 March 2000.

49. Edward Friedman interview, 11 June 2003.
50. Friedman interview.
51. The term was coined by Samuel P. Huntington, *The Third Wave: Democratization in the Late Twentieth Century* (Norman: University of Oklahoma Press, 1991).
52. Friedman interview.
53. Susan Pharr interview, 23 June 2003.
54. Melvin Croan oral history, University Archives, October 2002.
55. The long delay in learning to drive was a product of a fatal accident his father experienced, leading him to permanently abandon driving.
56. *PS: Political Science and Politics*, 36, 4 (October 2003), 900.
57. Kathryn Hendley interview, 12 September 2003.
58. Leon Lindberg oral history, University Archives, 22 October 2002.
59. "Acceptance Remarks by Leon Lindberg," ECSA's Second Lifetime Contribution to European Union Studies Award, ECSA's 2001 7th Biennial International Conference. Typescript. See also Lindberg oral history.
60. "Introduction by Alberta Sbragia," Lifetime Contribution Award for Leon Lindberg, ECSA 7th Biennial International Conference. Typescript.
61. Graham Wilson interview, 18 June 2003.
62. Wilson interview.
63. Mark Pollack interview, 3 October 2003.
64. Of 32 tenure-track comparative politics faculty recruited between 1950 and 1997, 10 were either denied tenure, or left when such an outcome appeared likely. Seventeen were promoted to tenured rank.

CHAPTER 7

Political Theory and the Enduring Spirit of John Gaus

Booth Fowler

Political theory as a field in the Department of Political Science at the University of Wisconsin–Madison dates to its very beginning. But from the start, political theory was a something of sidelight, classes on the topic offered on an occasional basis by scholars who were specialists in others areas of political science. Under the influence and self-conscious philosophy of John Gaus (1894–1969), the Wisconsin department practiced the view that political theory was important enough for most department faculty to know something about it and that a good number should teach it on a part-time basis. Through the 1930s, 1940s, 1950s, and beyond this was the way political thought took place in the department. There were no professional political theorists among the faculty and thus there were no scholars who devoted their main writing, publishing, or teaching endeavors to political theory. The tradition in the Wisconsin department was thus for professors whose teaching specialties and research lay elsewhere to undertake the instruction in political thought. One consequence was that political theory became central to the department in terms of the number and range of people who taught it but was distinctly less central than the other fields in that no scholarly work in the field occurred at Wisconsin. Predictably, before the 1960s, the department granted few graduate degrees in the field.

Beginning with the hiring of the first professional political theorist (Thomas Thorson in 1959), the department gradually, but not without doubts, moved to create a political thought subfield, staffed by professionals in political theory. In the 1970s and 1980s, in particular, the department appointed a considerable number of political theorists, so a vigorous program of graduate education and scholarly research in the field flourished. This continued somewhat in the 1990s, but by 2004 the field was in a period of reconstruction and redefinition. What did not change, however, was the endurance of the older tradition, the Gausian ideal. What continued is a practice of openness in the department, openness to colleagues with a variety of specialties who from time to time wish to teach political theory. Today political theory at Wisconsin is both a professional specialty for a few professors and a broader interest for many political science faculty, to the benefit of the field of political thought.

The Early Years

Political theory was taught only a little in the first years of the department. There was definitely no systematic program at the graduate or undergraduate level. Few courses considered political theory, even if it were defined broadly. Ideas about what ought to be done in politics or in specific political settings, however, were considered in courses, then as now. Paul S. Reinsch's course on "the philosophy of state" was one of the early courses. Reinsch, a Wisconsin Ph.D. (1898), taught at Wisconsin from 1897 to 1913. As a founder of the Wisconsin department, Reinsch's sometime interest in political theory foreshadowed what became the traditional Wisconsin approach: political theory as a valued sideline for many political science professors. Reinsch's special subfields, as we have seen elsewhere, were comparative politics and international relations, China in particular. Thus from the department's origins, a comparative perspective proved congenial for reflection on what ought to be in political life.

Reinsch was an active scholar and writer not only on China, but also on other subjects, including American legislatures, Chile, Wisconsin, and even common law (the subject of his thesis), but not on political theory. Like so many other early Wisconsin political scientists, Reinsch was devoted to policy activism and served as an advisor to state officials and then in and with the national government, serving as ambassador to China from 1913 to 1919. For him, pursuing what ought to be in politics was a matter for both the classroom and the "real" world beyond the classroom.

By the middle of the twentieth century's second decade, political theory was a regular part of the course program in political science at Wisconsin. Its two principal teachers were specialists in other subjects but true to an already established Wisconsin tradition, nonetheless also were interested in political thought. One was Stanley K. Hornbeck, who received his Wisconsin Ph.D. in 1911 and whom Paul Reinsch considered his best student. Hornbeck, like Reinsch, was a China and international relations expert who went on to a distinguished government career, serving in the U.S. State Department and as U.S. Ambassador to the Netherlands. While teaching at Wisconsin (1908–09,

1914–17) he created and taught regularly what became the department's standard course in the history of political thought. It was one of 20 or so courses that were then offered each year. It was open only to graduate students since, then as now, political thought was widely believed to be a difficult subject for most undergraduates. Hornbeck did no publishing in political theory, but his *Contemporary Politics in the Far East*, first published in 1921, was being republished as late as 1970, several years after his death.

Hornbeck was followed by Frederic Ogg in teaching political thought in the 1920s. Ogg, who was to serve as a professor at Wisconsin from 1914 to 1948, received his Ph.D. from Harvard in 1908 and was a comparativist. He obtained considerable reputation in the political science profession over his career, serving as a longtime editor of the *American Political Science Review* and as president of the American Political Science Association. He was a very active publisher, especially of textbooks which went through many successful editions. These included *Governments of Europe*, *European Governments and Politics*, and most famously, his *Introduction to American Government* with P. Orman Ray. His most highly regarded book was *English Government and Politics*. Ogg also published a number of other monographs such as *The Reign of Andrew Jackson*. He did not publish in political thought.

Ogg did not teach theory in the beginning of his Wisconsin career but he began teaching the main course in the 1920s and continued to do so for several decades, always as a sidelight to his main interests. As an instructor, Ogg was a disciplined, hardworking, and informed, but hardly dynamic, teacher. He was known for his somewhat remote kindness and as one who tried to get to know his students. He regularly had students over to his house for formal Sunday socials. His approach to teaching theory was historical, concentrating on "the greats" of the Western political philosophical tradition.

While Ogg did most of the theory teaching at Wisconsin throughout much of the 1920s, he did not work alone. Others who shared the work were not primarily political theorists, but some came closer than others. Perhaps the closest was Allan F. Saunders, who came up through the Wisconsin system and received his Ph.D. from the department in 1927. Saunders had a wide range of interests including political theory, public law, and comparative politics. He began teaching at Wisconsin in 1923, well before he received his degree, but moved on in 1928, first to Minnesota and eventually to the University of Hawaii where he remained on the faculty into the middle 1960s. Saunders's theory focus was the history of American political thought, a course in which he taught to undergraduates with sophomore standing and above. He was the first at Wisconsin to emphasize American political thought and also the first to open the door to undergraduates. These expanded roles for theory in the department were to remain.

The Era of John Gaus

John Merriman Gaus established the tone for and carried on the practice of political theory at Wisconsin for many years. His influence, albeit seldom recognized, endures today. Receiving his Ph.D. at Harvard in 1924, Gaus taught at Amherst and Minnesota before coming to Wisconsin, initially recruited by Alexander Meiklejohn to teach in the Experimental College, but with a joint appointment in political science. His primary field of teaching and research was public administration. His coauthored *Frontiers of Public Administration* went through many editions from the 1930s through the 1960s, although his 1947 *Reflections on Public Administration* best reflected his mature analysis in his field.

Gaus began teaching political thought at Wisconsin from his beginning here, during the 1927–28 academic year, which Ogg and Saunders were already doing. He continued to work and to teach political philosophy at Wisconsin most years until 1947 when he left Wisconsin for Harvard.

From the start Gaus advanced the philosophy of theory teaching for which he became known. His view was that every political scientist ought to know theory and that a good many of them should be teaching the subject as a sidelight to their primary professional specialty. Over the years, Gaus lived out his approach by teaching several different political thought courses, including the history of European political thought, American political thought, and contemporary American political theory. His favorite text was *The Education of Henry Adams*, still an illuminating book about both American political theory and larger themes in political thought. His sympathies lay toward the value of government in a democracy as an agent of popular will. But Gaus was no text teacher, nor indeed someone noted for his systematic lectures on any topic. He was an informal teacher, more interested in offering observations and reflections on a given thinker, period, or topic, and this Gaus did with a success that many former students remembered as affectionately as they did their despair at taking notes from him. Gaus also pursued his topics with his students at lively Saturday coffees held at his home, an activity that in his case greatly strengthened his appeal as a teacher.

Though Gaus himself was not always in residence, the Gaus era in terms of political theory lasted from the late 1920s through the war years.

During this period, offerings in political theory expanded. Ogg continued to teach theory in the late 1920s as did Saunders until his 1928 departure. At times graduate students and instructors rather than regular faculty taught political thought. Thus from 1927 to 1931 Jacob Jacobson, who received his Brown Ph.D. in 1929 but who held the rank of instructor at Wisconsin, taught American political thought by focusing on classic documents. He published *Development of American Political Thought* as a text in 1932, and it was still being reprinted as late as 1961. John D. Lewis, who later became a well-known political theorist at Oberlin College, was another example, teaching here from 1930 to 1935 while he pursued his Ph.D. His Ph.D. thesis on aspects of Otto von Gierke's ideas was one of the very earliest dissertations at Wisconsin that touched on anything remotely connected with the history of political thought.

Llewellyn Pfankuchen, an authority in international organization and law and longtime chair of the department, did much of the theory teaching along with Gaus during the middle and later 1930s. Pfankuchen began his 40-year career at Wisconsin in 1932 after receiving his Ph.D. from Harvard the previous year. Like the rest, Pfankuchen did not really have scholarly interest or publications in the theory field, though he certainly had an interest in normative aspects of international politics and international law. He had an affection for political theory, however, and a willingness to teach it. Thus he was an almost perfect expression of the Gausian ideal for the teaching of political thought.

Beginning in the early 1940s, David Fellman was another Wisconsin professor who undertook this Gausian role, in his case teaching American political thought, and he continued to do so off and on for about 20 years. Fellman, who received his Ph.D. from Yale in 1934 and came to Wisconsin from the University of Nebraska in 1947, was a constitutional law scholar. Like many others in this subfield, he was able and at first willing to teach the history of American thought, a subject that some argue is inextricably part of the constitutional law and history in the United States anyway. Not surprisingly, Fellman's emphasis was distinctly on legal and constitutional matters and the normative and policy issues that arose from them. The First Amendment was his particular interest, including free speech, religious liberty, and defendants' rights.

By far the most well-known teacher of political theory who was at Wisconsin before the 1960s, however, was William Ebenstein. A refugee from Austria, Ebenstein received his Ph.D. from Wisconsin in 1938. He was a comparativist, but also taught some theory during his years (1938–46) at Wisconsin, where he received tenure in 1943. He left Wisconsin for Princeton and later went on to the University of California, Santa Barbara. His research interests were not in political thought, but rather in subjects as disparate as German politics and public housing policy in the United States.

Ebenstein became arguably the most famous "political theorist" ever in the Wisconsin department, because of his widely used and decidedly influential textbooks on political theory, despite the fact that he was neither primarily a theorist nor a scholar of theory. Among his texts were *Great Political Thinkers, Plato to the Present*, *Introduction to Political Philosophy*, *Modern Political Thought: The Great Issues*, and *Today's Isms*. These works were all published beginning just a few years after he left Wisconsin, and were often republished in revised editions. Perhaps the most famous of his texts was *Great Political Thinkers,* which contained selections from "the great thinkers" of the Western political tradition accompanied in each instance by a lucid discussion by Ebenstein of their ideas and their significance. It covered the whole sweep of Western political theories from Socrates and Plato to contemporary thought.

The Years from the Gaus Departure to 1960

The departure of Gaus to Harvard did not mean teaching political theory ended in the department. Far from it. The Gausian tradition was well established, and it lasted long after John Gaus moved on from Wisconsin. Thus when Leon Epstein was hired in 1948, after receiving his Ph.D. from Chicago the same year, it was understood in the Gausian spirit that he would do part of the theory teaching, though his areas of greatest specialty were to be American political parties and British politics. Since Epstein was well grounded in political theory from his graduate work and at that time interested in the subject, this arrangement worked smoothly in his early years in the department.

Epstein's long and successful career at Wisconsin lasted until 1988. He emerged as a major scholarly figure in political science in British and American politics with numerous and influential publications. He also became president of the American Political Science Association. While Epstein's interest in teaching and research in political thought proved short-lived, he was only one of a number of new faculty who arrived with specialties in areas other than political philosophy who nonetheless, in the Gausian manner, sometimes gave courses in the subject.

This was especially true of William Young, who had received his Ph.D. in 1941 from Wisconsin and taught at the University of Pennsylvania before arriving back in Madison in 1947. Like Gaus, Young was an expert in the theory—and practice—of public administration, but from the onset of his service at Madison he taught the graduate political theory course (as did Epstein at times). At both the graduate and undergraduate levels, Young and Epstein followed a consistently historical approach, focusing on Western theorists from Plato to Marx. Both used thinkers' original writings as well as the classic secondary account of George Sabine.

In American political thought, the continuing work of David Fellman was supplemented by another new hire, again a nonspecialist in political thought, Fred Clarenbach. An American government and planning specialist with a 1941 Ph.D. from Cornell, Clarenbach was to serve in the Wisconsin department from 1945 to1962, when he switched to the Department of Urban and Regional Planning. Clarenbach published widely in regional planning and related topics, not political theory. While Fellman's approach emphasized the legal dimension in American thought and practice, Clarenbach was quite taken with John Dewey and related left-liberal themes of political thought of that day.

By the 1950s Henry Hart was also teaching American political thought from time to time. Hart joined the faculty in 1948 as an instructor while completing a Wisconsin Ph.D. (1950). Before World War II military service, he had worked with the Tennessee Valley Authority. His specialties were India, where he was born, as well as water policy and American politics, and he wrote several scholarly works, including the classic, *Dark Missouri.* He retired in 1982. For Hart, another example of Gausian ideal in practice, American political theory was about teaching civic responsibility in a democracy as well as grappling with such American values as the individual and equality in the contemporary context. But in addressing such issues, Hart employed classic texts in American political thought that engaged these concerns. A favorite was de Tocqueville's *Democracy in America.*

Finally, Ralph Huitt, a Congress expert who came to Wisconsin shortly before receiving his Ph.D at Texas in 1950, also provided some instruction in American political thought in the mid-1950s. A master storyteller, his approach reflected in his own unique fashion the characteristic Wisconsin approach to teaching political theory.

Indeed, by the 1950s a large number of political scientists at Wisconsin at times offered a course in political thought. There was nothing strange about this practice in those years. Quite the contrary: the Gausian model was very much alive. In this era, moreover, every graduate student was required to take the political theory preliminary examination, and so the considerable number of part-time teachers of political theory made for a wide choice of paths to satisfactory negotiation of the exam. Of course this did not mean there was any research in political theory or philosophy in the department. No such research was taking place.

Wisconsin, then, was a lively and expansive center for the Gausian model of teaching theory, but it was not at all a location for scholarship in political theory. Wisconsin offered nothing to the debates and discoveries in this subfield in the 1950s, or earlier, which was obvious when Wisconsin is compared to the theory scholarship at other ranked departments in that era.

The Emergence of Professional Political Theory

Thomas Thorson's teaching of political theory at Wisconsin beginning in 1959 marked a major change, one which turned out to be permanent. The age of professional political theorists had arrived. Thorson, who received his Ph.D. from Princeton in 1960, was not only the first political theory specialist hired as a regular member by the department, but he was also employed with the specific idea that he would build this subfield. He taught theory at Wisconsin until his 1966 departure.

In part, Thorson's hiring reflected a decision that it was time for Wisconsin to join the rest of the discipline and turn to full-time professionals in political theory. As much or more, it reflected the force of circumstances, that those who had taught political theory as a sideline were no longer available because of other duties or loss of interest. It also acknowledged the limitation of an exclusively Gausian approach to political philosophy in the department—that is, if everyone was supposed to (be able to) teach political theory, then in a sense, no one would (as a main focus), a reality no longer acceptable. In any case, the decision was important. As it turned out over the next 40-some years, Thorson was only the first of a good number of other professionals in this subfield who taught and did research at Wisconsin in political thought.

Through the early and mid-1960s Thorson *was* political theory at Wisconsin. His definition and defense of liberal democracy in his work *The Logic of Democracy* became well known as did his later research and arguments on nature and politics, especially his *Biopolitics*, as well as his revised edition of Sabine's influential *History of Political Theory.*

Thorson's interests were distinctly contemporary, which was another major reason he was hired. He shifted the direction of political thought at

Wisconsin from its longtime historical moorings toward contemporary thought—for example, toward normative issues concerning liberal democracy as well as toward questions of social science methodology. Under his direction, for the first time, a serious graduate program in political theory emerged, as opposed to a course or two for graduate students.

In 1964 the department proceeded to hire yet another theorist, this time a Berkeley Ph.D. Hannah Pitkin was destined to achieve considerable prominence as a scholar in political theory. Her stay at Wisconsin was short, however, and after only two years she moved on to Berkeley where she developed a fine reputation and became known as a leading political theorist in the 1970s and 1980s. Pitkin's influential scholarship on representation, justice and modern language, and Machiavelli, was all published after her time at Madison, but her hiring at Wisconsin represented a significant expansion of the department's commitment to professional political theory. Her presence expanded the program's focus because she was interested primarily in continental thought at the time.

At the same time, however, the Gausian tradition was alive on a parallel path, greatly enriching the extent of political theory that was available for interested students to pursue—at both graduate and undergraduate levels. In the early 1960s Hart, Young, Epstein, and Fellman were all still teaching a theory course from time to time; while their political theory course offerings steadily declined, other political scientists took up and continued the tradition. This included Franklyn Bonn, who taught from 1962 to 1965 as an instructor and concentrated on American political thought; Donald Carlisle, a comparativist who taught a number of honors theory courses from 1962 to 1967; and Kenneth Dolbeare, an Americanist who came in 1965 and taught contemporary American political thought. During the five years Dolbeare was at Wisconsin, he was closely associated with the New Left student movement. None of these individuals, except for Dolbeare, did significant research in political theory, but they made a serious intellectual contribution to the theory program through their various teaching directions.

Dolbeare was a highly effective instructor who related well to radical students, and although he was not a scholar in political theory, he was a major author and coauthor of left-leaning textbooks on American political thought both during and especially after his years at Wisconsin. These included his *Directions in American Political Thought*, which was published while Dolbeare was at Wisconsin. He left for the University of Washington in 1970.

The departures of Thorson and Pitkin from Wisconsin in 1966 raised the question of whether there should be a professional field of political theory at Wisconsin. More broadly, this raised the issue as to whether the department should continue with political theory in any form. After all, there was no tradition of political theory as a faculty path at Wisconsin, and few graduate students had ever obtained a Ph.D. here with a dissertation on a theory topic. Department faculty struggled with this matter and eventually resolved it by the decision made during the 1966–67 academic year to hire replacements for Thorson and Pitkin. In large part this decision flowed from the simple recognition that political thought was part of the political science profession and if Wisconsin was going to remain a top department, it had to have professional political theory and theorists.

What followed over the next 20 years was a flowering of political philosophy at Wisconsin. While the process began slowly, it picked up considerable speed as more and more theorists were hired, and it was supplemented as in the past by a Gausianlike participation of other colleagues in teaching and scholarship in political theory. It was to be the golden age of political theory in Wisconsin political science.

The first two people hired were Harvard Ph.D.'s, Donald Hanson and Booth Fowler. Hanson was a historian of political thought who, while at Wisconsin, published his impressive, revised thesis, *From Kingdom to Commonwealth: The Development of Civic Consciousness in English Political Thought*. He remained at Wisconsin for only four years. Fowler's dissertation was also a historical project and he was to continue at Wisconsin for 35 years until he retired in 2002. Over that span of years his research work in political theory, as distinct from his research in religion and politics, proved to be largely in contemporary American political thought. He eventually published a number of works such as *Believing Skeptics: American Political Intellectuals 1945–1964*, *The Dance with Community: The Contemporary Debate in American Political Thought*, and *Enduring Liberalism: American Political Thought since the 1960s*. During his last years in the department, Fowler shifted to full-time teaching in the Integrated Liberal Studies Program (ILS), which he chaired from 1999 to 2002.

Hanson and Fowler were a team that worked well together professionally, intellectually, and personally and they developed a program of political thought at Wisconsin. They significantly revised the theory preliminary examination for graduate students toward more current professional concerns in the field. The exam, like the program in theory, continued to honor the long tradition of "great" thinkers from the Western European past, but also concentrated on contemporary issues and theorists while ending any concern with past thinkers' empirical claims and contemporary social science findings.

Moreover, given their conviction that political theory at Wisconsin badly needed more emphasis on contemporary thought, Hanson and Fowler created a new introductory course that concentrated on current normative and analytical political theory. Over the next 35 years this course came to be for many undergraduates the one course in the subject they took, and it served as the primary training ground for political philosophy graduate students in the actual teaching of political theory.

At the same time, these new theorists welcomed the Gausian example of nonspecialists also teaching political thought. For example, Murray Edelman, an Americanist who came to Wisconsin in 1966 from the University of Illinois where he had received his Ph.D. in 1948 and subsequently taught, created a graduate course in empirical political theory that often involved normative concepts. It became an integral and valued part of the graduate program in political thought. Edelman continued at Wisconsin until he retired in 1990. His scholarly work outside the theory subfield was distinguished and influential in political science, as it explored the psychological dimension of politics and political manipulation, most famously in his *Politics as Symbolic Action.* His devotion to graduate students, including those working on theory dissertations, was outstanding as was his unusually supportive role to female graduate students who began to enter the profession in large numbers in the late 1960s.

From the start of the professional era, another pluralistic aspect of political theory at Wisconsin was central. This was the field members' commitment to the idea that approaches to the teaching of political theory should be diverse—in terms of areas of focus, method, ideology, and much more. This idea, reflecting a longtime principle of Wisconsin political science, was that intellectual diversity creates the best learning environment for students, including graduate students, and also for professors. The assumption was that a genuine congeniality—would provide field unity, an assumption that proved true for several decades.

The 1970s and 1980s were a time of great growth and prosperity for political theory at Wisconsin. By the 1980s, theory had reached a high point in its Wisconsin history. The field attracted many students and offered many courses, at both graduate and undergraduate levels, and a spirit of cooperation and diversity permeated the field. Personnel also changed, and the total effect greatly strengthened the theory program.

The first and most long-lasting was the arrival of Patrick Riley in 1971. Riley was to serve with distinction at Wisconsin through our centennial year. He was an active and highly respected scholar whose contributions were in the area of traditional Western political philosophy. He was the author of many books, articles, and editions of thinkers' works. Among his publications were *Kant's Political Philosophy*, *Leibniz's Universal Jurisprudence: Justice as the Charity of the Wise*, and *Will and Political Legitimacy: A Cultural Exposition of Social Contract Theory in Hobbes, Locke, Rousseau, Kant, and Hegel.*

Riley, much admired by committed students, gave the basic history courses, especially the "modern" course covering Machiavelli to Nietzsche. He also undertook a variety of other undergraduate classes, most often exploring political philosophy and philosophers rather than intellectual history or normative and analytic theory. He also offered quality graduate courses on some of his favorite philosophers, above all Kant, Rousseau, and Plato.

In coming to Wisconsin, Riley succeeded Hanson, who left, lured by the University of Utah and weary of New Left protests at Wisconsin. But Riley was not the only new theorist to arrive in this era. During the following decade or so, Diane Rubenstein (also a comparativist) came from the University of Cincinnati (in 1986). A Yale Ph.D., she brought a postmodern view to the department before moving to Purdue in 1991.

James Farr joined the faculty in 1984, recruited from Ohio State University. During his five years at Wisconsin Farr had a huge impact as an assistant professor and then associate professor in the political theory field. Farr attracted immediate, widespread, and richly deserved attention as a skilled and popular teacher at both undergraduate and graduate levels. His teaching interests were broad, ranging from the introductory theory course to American political thought, to the study of modern social science and political science, and more. His diverse research contributions reflected his commitment to meticulous and closely argued scholarship. Farr left Wisconsin to continue his career at the University of Minnesota in 1989.

At the same time, Charles Anderson became also the perfect embodiment of the Gausian ideal, moving from being the Ibero and Latin American specialist in the department to teaching more and more political thought, indeed eventually becoming a full-time political theorist. His special emphasis was on issues of policy and political economy. While Anderson began teaching at Wisconsin in 1960, his book *Statecraft,* published in 1977, served notice that he was very much engaged in the field. Anderson had received his Ph.D. from Wisconsin in 1960, and had an already well-established reputation as a teacher and scholar. It was no wonder that department theorists welcomed his entrance into the field. Anderson was to continue to play an active role in the subfield for 20 more years. He published actively, guiding Ph.D. students in theory to their degree, and successfully teaching political thought to many hundreds of pleased students both in the department and in ILS until his 1996 retirement.

Anderson's interests tended to be contemporary and policy-driven, and he led the way in fashioning and teaching a new course, Ethics and Values in Policy-Making, during this period. His interest in educational policy was especially strong and was manifested in his devotion to the Integrated Liberal Studies Program, the descendent of Alexander Meiklejohn's Experimental College. It also appeared in a busy lecture schedule all over the country and in his writing, particularly the influential *Prescribing the Life of the Mind: An Essay on the Purpose of the University*. Anderson, however, also cared about the classic Western historical tradition in political thought, and he taught it in both political science and ILS. His range was as impressive as his enthusiasm and insight.

Anderson also gave graduate courses especially devoted to issues of contemporary liberalism, and he attracted many graduate students and directed a number of theses that addressed aspects of this concern. His passion for the combination of pragmatism and liberalism was deep and resulted in his work of original political argument, *Pragmatic Liberalism*.

In the 1980s and beyond, the tradition of theory remaining open to whoever wanted to teach a course in the field was as strong as ever, and the field was enriched by the efforts of a long list of Wisconsin political scientists who took the plunge. During the late 1970s and earlier 1980s, Melvin Croan, who came to Wisconsin in 1967 and was an accomplished Russian and East European specialist and superb instructor, repeatedly gave the introduction to political theory course with great success. Murray Edelman continued to teach empirical political theory, and Richard Merelman, an Americanist with extensive interests and major research accomplishments, also taught social theory at the graduate level.

Merelman came to Wisconsin in 1969 from a post at UCLA, and some of his work directly addressed American political culture with theoretical insights and empirical evidence as well as normative perspectives. These perspectives appeared in such books as *Making Something of Ourselves: On Culture and Politics in the United States* and *Political Visions: Culture and Politics in Britain, Canada, and the United States*. Merelman's other theoretical interests included the ideas of Weber and Durkheim, and his course on these theorists as well as his undergraduate course in literature and politics proved valuable for many theory students and the political thought program as a whole.

The theory field was also particularly blessed from the 1980s through the beginning of the 21st century by the presence of others who had a real interest in theory in addition to their main specialties. These included Virginia Sapiro, a 1976 Michigan Ph.D. who came to Wisconsin the same year and was a multitalented scholar, teacher, and administrator. At times she offered feminist political theory as a separate course, though she also addressed theory issues in her women and politics courses. She was also active with theory graduate students. Her scholarship, too, touched many areas having to do with political thought. For example, her *Introduction to Women's Studies*, which has gone through several successful editions, engaged many issues of political thought and public policy, and her splendid *Vindication of Political Virtue: The Political Theory of Mary Wollstonecraft* was a classic essay on that pioneering thinker.

Another important example was Donald Downs, a 1983 Berkeley Ph.D., who came to Wisconsin from Notre Dame's faculty in 1985. Downs was a constitutional law scholar, schooled in contemporary normative and policy issues in connection with criminal law and other issues affecting the law and contemporary society. His impressive and intellectually stimulating scholarship always included consideration of normative issues, dilemmas, and paradoxes as illustrated in such books as *More Than Victims: Battered Women, the Syndrome Society, and the Law* and *Cornell '69: Liberalism and the Crisis of the American University.* He was also known for his interest in some aspects of the tradition of Western political thought, notably the ideas and analysis of de Tocqueville and Nietzsche. Like Sapiro, Downs was a strong supporter of the political philosophy field and often helped out with graduate advising and with theory Ph.D. dissertations.

From the 1990s to the Future

The 1990s brought both change and stability to the theory section of the department. Marion Smiley, a Princeton Ph.D., began teaching at Wisconsin in 1989. Bernard Yack, who had been teaching at the University of Michigan, joined her in 1991. Both were active teachers and committed to creating a highly professionalized theory graduate program under their direction. Yack taught all levels of students from the introductory theory course to the most advanced graduate seminars. Smiley preferred small junior-senior and graduate courses. Their subjects for teaching ranged widely from contemporary topics to historical surveys, with Smiley more oriented toward contemporary theory and Yack somewhat more historical. Both were excellent scholars.

Smiley was especially interested in moral and political issues from the perspective of her version of pragmatism. She published her revised Ph.D. dissertation as *Moral Responsibility and the Boundaries of Community: Power and Accountability from a Pragmatic Point of View* early in her career at Wisconsin.

Yack published widely and extensively during his time at Wisconsin. Perhaps his most influential book was *Problems of a Political Animal: Community, Justice, and Conflict in Aristotelian Political Thought*, a stimulating and reflective exploration of the possible implications of Aristotle's ideas in the contemporary era. In his most recent work, Yack has contributed importantly to theories of nationalism, by highlighting the central importance of the doctrine of popular sovereignty in evolving discourses of nation.

By the later 1990s, Hawley Fogg-Davis, a 1998 Princeton Ph.D., began her career in the department. She taught in a number of areas, including political theory. Among the courses she brought her talents to were African-American political thought, feminist political thought, and the established ethics and values course. Her main research interests were in the area of public policy and American politics.

The decade also saw a revision of the theory preliminary exam for graduate students, opening options for both legal thought and for contemporary political theory, while maintaining the requirement that all theory prelim students had to be versed in the classic Western European "greats." This decade saw the creation, too, of a number of new courses in the theory area, especially at the junior-senior level, as the program expanded. These included courses in feminism, Marxism, and conservatism, all of which were offered a number of times during the decade.

In this era, too, others undertook to teach courses much involved with political thought in the spirit of the old, Gausian tradition. Some continued to do so as they had in the past, as was true of Downs and Sapiro. But there were new examples, such as Edward Friedman, a distinguished senior China specialist whose classes often focused on "the challenges of democracy" from a distinctly comparativist perspective. His many publications often focused on this theme, as in his *Politics of Democratization: Generalizing East Asian Experiences.*

The arrival of the first years of the new century produced, however, serious changes in the department's theory situation. Booth Fowler retired in 2002, Smiley and Yack left, and the retirement of Patrick Riley was imminent. The department hired one new theorist, assistant professor Richard Boyd, a historian of English political thought, in 2002. It then hired a second junior theorist, Eric MacGilvray, a pragmatist concerned with contemporary political theory, who began teaching in fall 2004. These hirings are the start of what will necessarily be a long journey back for theory at Wisconsin, but one that should prove as promising as it is challenging.

John Lathrop, Chancellor 1849–58, and Professor of Civil Polity

John Bascom, President, 1874-87

Robert M. La Follette, future governor and senator, as a student

Chester Lloyd Jones, 1910–19, 1929–41

John T. Salter, 1930–68

Harold Stoke, 1940–44

William Young, Ph.D. 1941, Faculty 1947–81

Ralph Huitt, 1949–83

L. H. Adolfsen, Ph.D. 1942; Faculty 1942–44; Chancellor UW Center System, 1944–72

Photos courtesy University of Wisconsin–Madison Archives

Fred Von der Mehder, 1958–68

Stanley Hornbeck, Ph.D. 1911; Faculty 1909–10, 1914–18

David A. Kay, 1966–75; Chief, CIA Iraq Weapons Search, 2003–04

Matthew Holden Jr., 1969–81

Austin Ranney, 1962–76

John A. Armstrong, 1954–86

David W. Adamany, 1972–78

David Tarr, 1963–95

David Fellman, 1947–78

Photos courtesy University of Wisconsin–Madison Archives

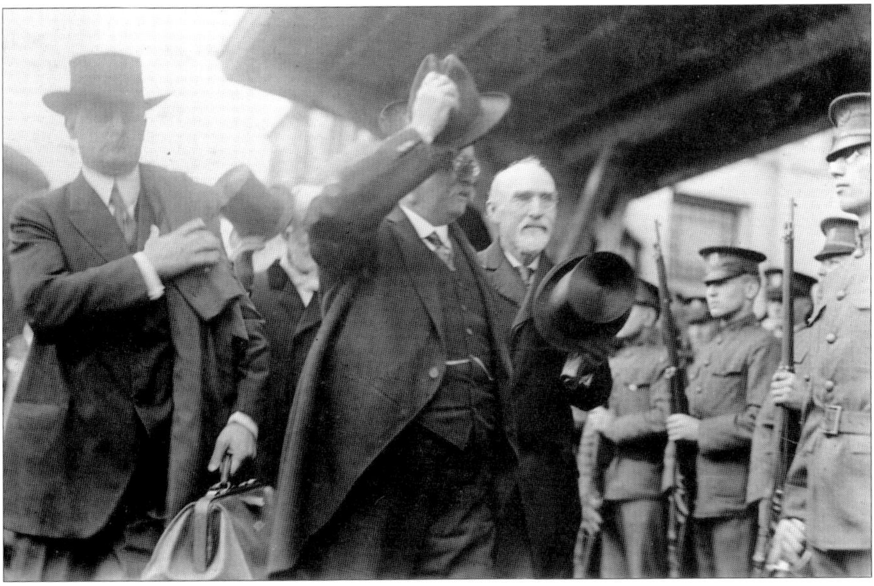

Foreground: President Theodore Roosevelt with University President Charles Van Hise, 1903–18

President Harry Truman addressing the university community, circa 1948

Photos courtesy University of Wisconsin–Madison Archives

Senator Joseph McCarthy visits campus, circa 1950.

Martin Luther King Jr. visits campus, circa 1960.

Photos courtesy University of Wisconsin–Madison Archives

Franklin Gilliam, 1983–87

Henry C. Hart, 1948–82

Charles W. Anderson, 1960–96

Murray Edelman, 1966–90

Dennis Dresang, B.A. 1964; Faculty 1969–

Leon Lindberg, 1962–97

Fred Hayward, 1968–91

Peter Eisinger, 1969–98

Bernard Cohen, Faculty 1959–90; Provost, 1984–89

Photos courtesy University of Wisconsin–Madison Archives

Donald K. Emmerson (top) and Patrick T. Riley (bottom) receive distinguished teaching awards from Chancellor Irving Shain, 1985.

Photos courtesy University of Wisconsin–Madison Archives

Edward Friedman, 1967–

Melvin Croan, 1967–96

Mark Beissinger, 1987–

Benjamin Marquez, Ph.D. 1983; Faculty 1991–

Michael Schatzberg, Ph.D. 1977; Faculty 1991–

Byron Schafer, 2001–

Donald Downs, 1985–

Debbie Bakke, Office Staff, 1992–

Paul Hutchcroft, 1993–

Photos, top row, courtesy Univeristy of Wisconsin–Madison Archives

Orfeo Fioretos, 1999–2005

Richard Merelman, 1969–2001

Susan Pharr, 1977–87

R. Booth Fowler, 1967–2002

John Witte, 1977–

Crawford Young, 1963–2001

Photos courtesy University of Wisconsin–Madison Archives

Donald Kettl, 1991–2004

Jack Dennis, 1963–2001

Herbert Kritzer, 1978–

Alumnus Senator Russell Feingold, Department Centennial

Courtesy University of Wisconsin–Madison Archives

Alumnus and former Governor Tommy Thompson, Chancellor (1987–93) Donna Shalala, and Arlie Mucks (Wisconsin Alumni Association)

Courtesy University of Wisconsin–Madison Archives

Chancellor Donna Shalala, Provost Bernard Cohen, Graduate School Dean Robert Bock, and L&S Dean David Cronon, 1988

Jack Dennis, Mary Grossman, Alexander Wilde, and Joel Grossman at McCamy retirement, 1971

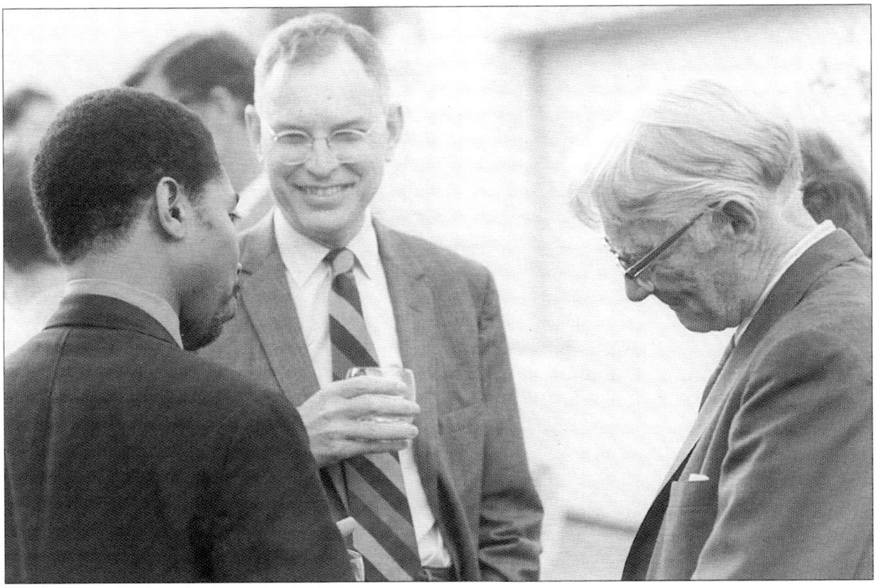

Matthew Holden, John Armstrong, and James McCamy at McCamy retirement, 1971

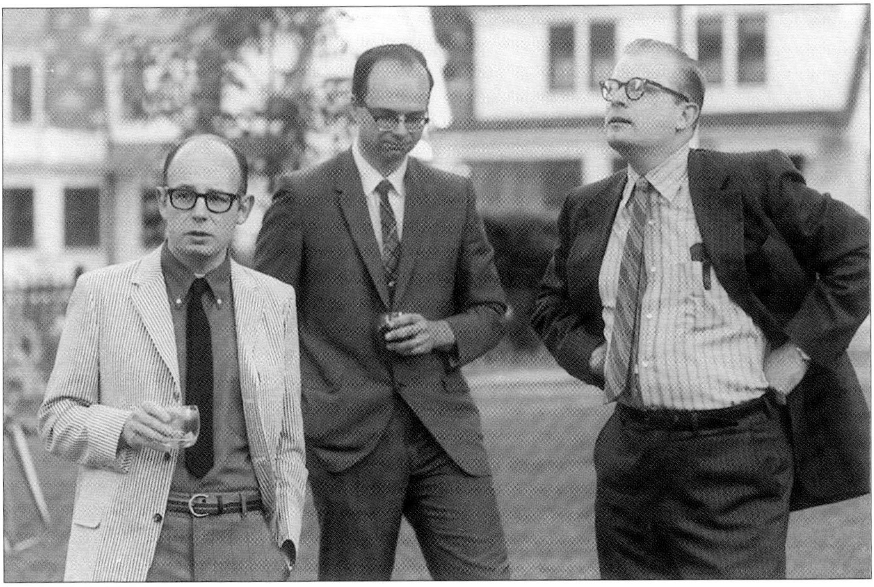

Ira Sharkansky, Charles Anderson, and Crawford Young at McCamy retirement, 1971

Mark Beissinger, Dean Phillip Certain, Department Centennial

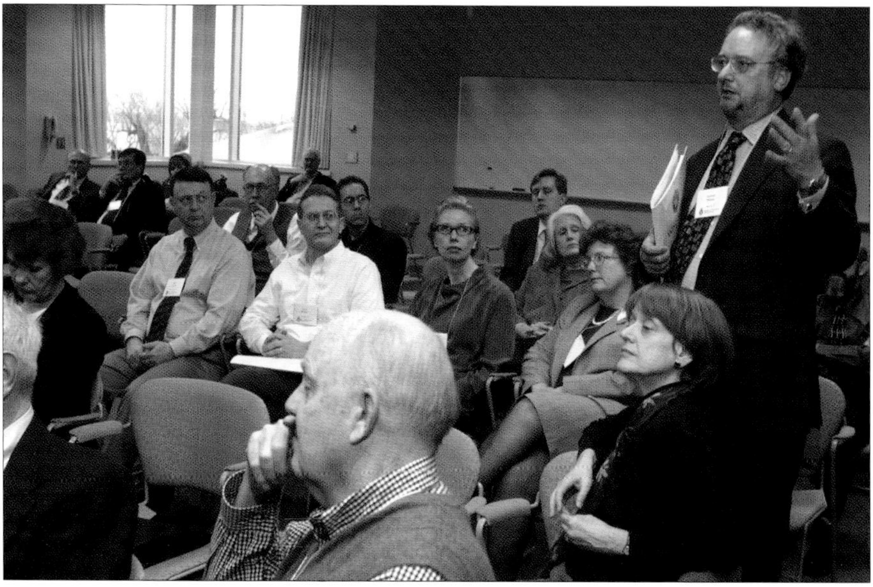

Graham Wilson holds the floor, Department Centennial. In the foreground are John Bibby (Ph.D. 1963) and Barbara Stallings.

David Adamany, William Young, Department Centennial

Kenneth Mayer, Mark Beissinger, John Bibby (UW–Milwaukee), Department Centennial

Foreground: Tom Loftus (La Follette alumnus, former Speaker of State Assembly, current University Regent), Representative David Obey, at Department Centennial

Mark Schrad, Assistant for the History Project, and Elizabeth Smith, Assistant to Chair, at Department Centennial

Charles O. Jones, Leigh Payne, at Department Centennial

Melanie Manion, Barbara Stallings, Mark Beissinger, at Department Centennial

Center and right: Edward Friedman, Herbert Kritzer, at Department Centennial

Ernestine Vanderlin (Undergraduate Advisor 1971–90) and Leon Epstein, at Department Centennial

Hawley Fogg-Davis, 1999–2005

David Weimer, 2000–

Stephen Morrison, Ph.D. 1987

David Obey, B.A. 1960; M.A. 1962; Member of Congress 1969–

Chartles O. Jones, 1988–97

Leon Epstein, 1948–88

Charles Franklin, 1991–

David Canon, 1991–

Neil Richardson, 1979–

Joel Grossman, 1963–96

David Leheny, 1998–

John Coleman, 1992–

Michael Barnett, 1990–2004

Virginia Sapiro, 1976–

Joe Soss, Ph.D. 1996; Faculty 2003–

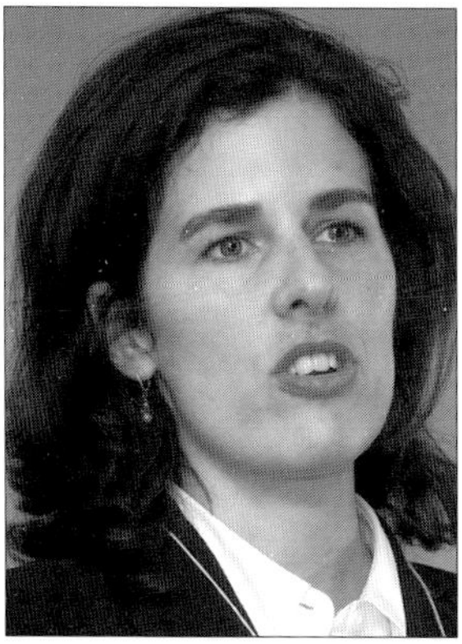
Katherine Kramer-Walsh, B.A. 1994; Faculty 2000–

Kenneth Goldstein, 2000–

Jon Pevehouse, 2000–

Governor Robert M. La Follette in campaign mode

Edwin Witte, Economics and Political Science, 1933–57

Photos courtesy University of Wisconsin–Madison Archives

Charles R. McCarthy, Founding Director, Legislative Reference Service; Lecturer in Political Science, 1905–17

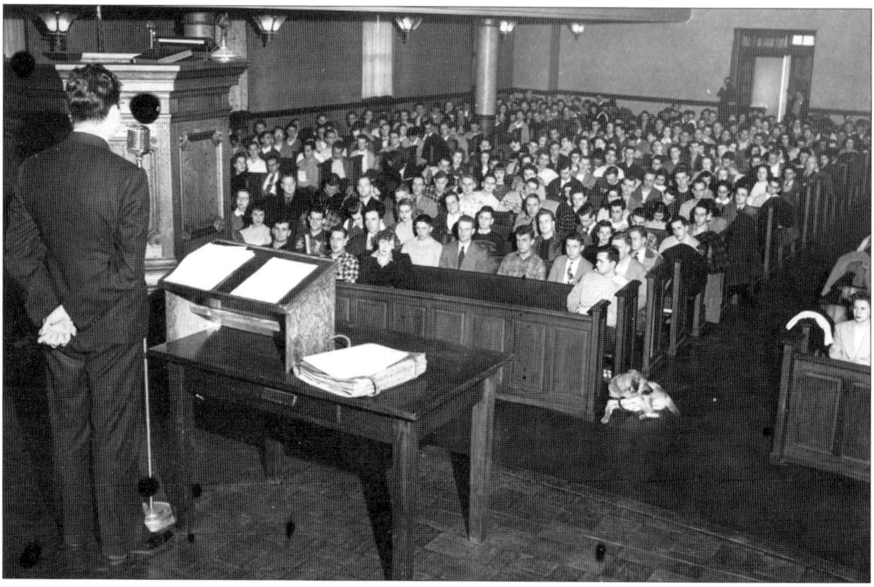

William Stokes, 1946–58, lecturing to Political Science 7 (now 104) in First Congregational Church, circa 1947

CHAPTER 8

International Relations and Wisconsin, 1945 to the Present

David W. Tarr

Attempting to construct a history of the international relations subfield of Wisconsin's political science department presents several conceptual difficulties. The first problem is field definition. How distinctive a "field" was and is international relations? Which faculty and what courses "count" as international relations? How does one distinguish the international field from the comparative field, whose specialists often include in the latter case country-specific foreign policies and regional international relations in their teaching and research agenda? Another, but lesser problem concerns the role and identification of American foreign policy within the rubric of international relations rather than that of American politics. The history that follows tracks two clues in our records: the subject matter of course offerings, evidenced by title, and the identity and work of the scholars involved.

In the Beginning

The department was founded by Paul S. Reinsch, a Wisconsin Ph.D. (1898), whose subfield specialization could be regarded as international relations (he taught courses in international law and international relations—but also many other topics). The record indicates that political science courses were offered from the earliest years in such generic international topics as "international law," "international politics," "international relations," and "world politics." International relations and international or world politics were probably synonymous terms for much of our history, even though a theoretical distinction was to become important by the middle of the 20th century. During the same early period more specialized courses appeared with titles such as "Colonial

Politics," "European Governments," "Consular Services" and "American Diplomacy." In later decades we find such additional titles as "Contemporary International Relations," the "Foreign Service," the "League of Nations," "Far Eastern Politics," and the "British Commonwealth," while at the same time the older standbys of "International Relations," "International Law," and "International Organization" continued to be offered.

Looking back from today's perspective, we recognize these topics as falling within three overlapping clusters: international politics or relations [either of which I will refer to by the standard shorthand, "IR"]; comparative politics; and American foreign policy. But such specialized field distinctions in fact emerged quite slowly, changing almost imperceptibly until the expansion of the department in the 1960s.

In more recent times a theoretical distinction arose within the political science discipline between two contrasting conceptions—"international *relations*" on the one hand, and "international *politics*" on the other. To complicate matters, a distinction also developed between international and *comparative* politics (and relations). Finally, while American foreign policy courses are usually thought to reside properly within the IR field, the foreign relations of other states and regions (e.g., Latin America, Africa) have tended to be categorized as falling within the comparative field. Moreover, an argument can be made as well (though seldom asserted) for locating *American* foreign policy courses within the American politics subfield, especially as foreign policy studies began more consistently to include domestic factors rather than exclusively to focus on diplomatic activities, and as American politics began to include other policy issues.

These distinctions thus reflect differing perspectives on what constitutes the proper range and focus of interrelated subject matters by the scholars who teach them. At Wisconsin, so long as the department remained small, the course obligations large, and the discipline undifferentiated, such distinctions mattered little. In particular, there was no apparent difference between international *relations* and international *politics*. These terms were used interchangeably and apparently still are. Similarly, IR and comparative distinctions among the courses offered and the fields and faculty they represent were not always apparent.

During our department's first half-century, a handful of faculty had to contend with the political universe as best they could. They offered an astonishing array of courses (by today's standards). This meant that faculty members were obligated to participate in sharing the large burden of covering not only the obvious basics (e.g., political theory, national politics), but also the rest of the world, so to speak. Each faculty member taught courses outside his (there was no "her" in those days) primary specialization. American foreign policy, comparative politics, and international politics and relations ultimately emerged as subfields out of the experience of expanding the range and depth of political coverage by the department.

From a national perspective, as the discipline matured, one can see that two fundamental approaches contended for acceptance during the refinement of field specializations. The first argued that political science should focus its research and analyses primarily on international *political* relationships—the study of international law, organization, and diplomacy, and of other institutional and government-to-government relationships, including the balance of power between and among nations. Note that many departments were initially called "government" rather than "political science" departments (and some still are, under the supposition, I presume, that this is what we primarily study). In any case, early tendencies were to focus research and teaching on governmental relationships, meaning institutions, power factors, the diplomatic relationships among states, and international law and organizations, as the core understanding of that which is "political."

The second approach argued for more inclusive, interdisciplinary foci, encompassing a host of political, economic, legal, social, cultural, psychological, geographic, and other factors. Initially, political science departments typically embraced the more exclusive political definition on the understandable grounds that the essence of political science was about "politics," however one defined it. Moreover, the ambition to be so inclusive as to embrace all international relationships in a field of study to be called international relations, while both commendable (and, for the advancement of the social sciences) necessary, seemed beyond the reach and training capacities of most political science departments during their fledgling years. They needed to become disciplinary before they could afford to become interdisciplinary.

This latter comment is certainly true of the Wisconsin situation, where the very few who offered instruction in international relations (qua politics) did whatever they could to cover the subject. Courses appeared with some frequency on international law, international organization, and American foreign relations, as well as on the diplomatic relationships among states of various regions of the world. But lacking the theoretical power and perspective of such a scholar as Quincy Wright (University of Chicago), the Wisconsin "IR" contingent stuck to its more basic task—teaching international relations, international law and organizations, and, occasionally, the foreign policies of various powers, especially that of the United States. Regional international relations were occasionally taught by comparativists. Few scholars could be expected to address the whole corpus of international relationships beyond the introductory and intermediate levels, even in the restricted sense of *political* relationships, unless they specialized in IR theory, or authored comprehensive texts on international relations, and no one at Wisconsin had done that since Walter Sharp and Grayson Kirk (*Contemporary International Politics*, 1940).

In any case, political science departments throughout the United States largely resisted the broader conception of international relations pioneered by Quincy Wright and some of his students. As a result, in a number of cases separate international relations departments or programs were formed to permit or encourage interdisciplinary approaches. Something of the sort occurred at Wisconsin via the development of an undergraduate major in international relations, spearheaded in 1938 by Walter Sharp, Grayson Kirk, and Chester Lloyd Jones. But a separate department never emerged. The undergraduate IR major simply constituted a cluster of courses offered by various departments (primarily political science, history, economics, and geography, plus several foreign language departments) that together defined an undergraduate concentration or "major." Today this major is called "international studies," and the choice of the word "studies" reflects the absence of any disciplinary focus.

Though not of the theoretical power of Wright, two early Wisconsin faculty did win credit as foundational figures in international relations as a field. A recent history of the IR field, Brian Schmidt (*The Political Discourse as Anarchy: A Disciplinary History of International Relations*, 1998) cites Paul Reinsch as the pioneer whose 1900 treatise on world politics for the first time established an explicit focus on the issues and concerns arising from the political and economic interactions of states. The same author describes Pitman Potter (1920–31) as the preeminent IR scholar of his day, leading the way with his study of international organizations, especially the League of Nations.

At the national level, when the American Political Science Association was founded (with Reinsch among the founders), a subcomponent of international politics and international relations was part of that development. Many years later, some scholars felt that APSA was not sufficiently hospitable to IR. The International Studies Association was created in 1964 to enhance a more inclusive and interdisciplinary approach and indeed, to argue for a distinctive "field" of international relations. But this movement had only a limited impact on the development of the IR field nationally and virtually none locally. To this day most universities locate their international relations (politics) specialists in political science departments; only a few have separate programs.

At Wisconsin, until the expansion that began in the 1960s permitted greater specialization, international relations as a field had not achieved a tradition of strength and identity, or even focus. Of course, after the Second World War, the fundamental changes that had occurred in the structure of the international system and in the orientation of American power had their inevitable impact upon Wisconsin's political science department in terms of the direction of student interests, personnel recruited, research agendas pursued, and therefore, in the range of curriculum offered. In the early postwar years, for example, it became clear that the United States would remain a major world power, and indeed, within a few years become engaged in a "cold war" with the Soviet Union. What did that mean in terms of curriculum and research agendas? As we shall see, the department's response was at first simply to do what it could with the personnel it had.

Early Postwar Years

In the years following the departure of Grayson Kirk and Walter Sharp in 1940, Lewellyn Pfankuchen served as the anchor for the IR field, insofar as it could be called such, offering a series of courses related to international law, relations, and organization. Pfankuchen, born in Oshkosh and educated at Minnesota and Harvard, came to Wisconsin in 1932. His primary interest was international law. In 1945 in San Francisco, he was witness to the process that created the United Nations. For several years thereafter Pfankuchen pretty much stood alone as our IR specialist, unless one counts comparative as part of IR. If so, we can include such comparativists as William S. Stokes (1946–58), known primarily for his work on Latin American affairs, and even Frederic A. Ogg (1914–48), who because of his famous, multi-editioned American government textbook, might be thought of as an Americanist, but published and taught comparative subjects as well; his extraordinary teaching repertoire included occasional IR courses. This was a characteristic of the early postwar years: the department teaching faculty had to contend, inter alia, with the rapid influx of students on the GI Bill of Rights, and with the multitude of issues arising from postwar international relations that attracted student interest, so everyone chipped in, field specialist or not.

The first significant addition for IR was James L. McCamy (1947–71), who joined the department in 1947 (Ph.D., University of Chicago, 1938), bringing his own prewar and wartime governmental experience and expertise to both the fields of public administration and of foreign policy. He soon began offering courses on the "Administration of American Foreign Affairs" (publishing an influential book by that title in 1950). While we can assert that

McCamy was Wisconsin's first foreign policy specialist, we could as easily classify him as an Americanist with teaching and research interests in public administration and in science and government.

Similarly, other "international" courses of that period might well be classified as comparative courses (by today's standards). To wit: the "British Commonwealth," "Far Eastern Politics," and the "International Relations of Latin America." One must conclude that during those early postwar years the notion that American foreign policy was located in the *field* of international relations was no more obvious than that comparative politics was not. The faculty of the political science department was simply too small and the discipline too immature to allow for the distinctions and specialization that were to come about in years to follow. In the nationwide discipline of political science such refinements and definitions of subfields were just beginning to develop.

In the early postwar years, when such monumental changes were occurring as the founding of the United Nations, the onset of the cold war, the implementation of the Marshall Plan, the blockade of Berlin, the establishment of the North Atlantic Treaty Organization, and outbreak of war in Korea, there were, sequentially, only two Soviet bloc specialists, and their services were brief: Gordon Skilling (1943–48) and Jaroslav Mayda (1951–54). The former, with B.A degrees from the University of Toronto and Oxford, and Ph.D. from the University of London, was a comparativist who specialized in the Soviet Union and Eastern Europe; the latter, with legal training at Masaryk University, was a Czech exile and an Eastern European scholar.

In short, the two mainstay scholars in those years who presented teaching and research interests that were most directly relevant to IR were Pfankuchen and McCamy. From 1951 to 1957, John Thomson also contributed to IR instruction, though he was primarily a comparativist specializing in Southeast and East Asian politics. Nine years after the war, well after the departure of Skilling and Mayda, the department finally added an expert on the Soviet Union and Eastern Europe to its ranks, John Armstrong. Not until 1959, when Bernard Cohen came on board, did it add a second scholar to its American foreign policy ranks.

On the national scene, the emergence of international relations theorists and/or IR textbook writers in a number of major political science departments (e.g., Quincy Wright, Hans J. Morgenthau, and Morton Kaplan, Chicago; Harold and Margaret Sprout, Princeton; A. F. K. Organski, Michigan) had already had a significant impact on the emergence of, and debates about, international relations as a field. No Wisconsin scholar was among those shaping the field. While the department had for many years a

Ph.D. preliminary examination "field" of international relations (sometimes identified more restrictively as "international politics"), until the expansion of the department in the 1960s and 1970s a substantial field specialization in international relations, per se, was not supportable at the graduate level. The small number of faculty available did not permit it.

Oddly enough, the "field" of American foreign policy became the inadvertent focus of the department's international relations offerings, perhaps by default. Another American foreign policy specialist, David Tarr, joined the faculty in 1963. Like McCamy earlier, the two new American foreign policy specialists of that period—Cohen and Tarr—were regarded by the department as located in the international relations "field," even though for both of us, research and self identities placed us as comfortably within the field of American politics as well. Indeed, both Cohen and Tarr elected to teach the introductory American government course on occasion as their contribution to the basic course curriculum. The introductory IR course usually fell to Pfankuchen, though Cohen in his first years in the department also contributed. Toward the later years of his career, McCamy had more successfully identified with public administration, especially the subject of science and government. As a result, in his last years he infrequently participated in IR subfield responsibilities such as curriculum development or the construction of preliminary examinations for the graduate program.

A scholar's field identification is to some degree adventitious. In most political science departments today, country and area specialists see themselves as comparativists, rather than as international relationists, even though many teach, research, and publish about subjects that deal with the power factors, diplomacies, or other international relationships of their respective regions. But while comparativists began to see themselves as outside the purview of IR, American foreign policy types generally speaking did not distance themselves from IR by, as a parallel example, emphasizing their connection with the American subfield. For whatever reasons that might account for these developments, those political science departments in the United States that did not have one of the more general IR theorists or textbook writers among their faculty tended to rely upon American (and occasionally Soviet) foreign policy specialists to anchor their international relations field curricula. This may, indeed, have been an artifact of America's rise to superpower status, as American foreign policy analysts had, by the nature of American power and interests, to deal with global considerations, leaving other country specialists to deal with their own geographically defined regions. This was certainly the case at Wisconsin.

Thus, from 1945 until 1990 there were, sequentially, but four members of the department who carried responsibilities for the broadly defined field of international relations: Lewellyn Pfankuchen until his retirement in 1972; David Kay from 1966 to 1975, Neil Richardson, from 1979 forward, and (more briefly) Ellen Seidensticker from 1975 to 1979. The rest chose to focus upon particular countries (e.g., American foreign policy) or regions (e.g., Western Europe). Pfankuchen's course offerings on international law and international organization were the foundations of the department's IR field for a considerable period of time, certainly until the 1960s, when additional faculty arrived on the scene. Gradually, other faculty were to teach introductory and advanced international relations courses as Pfankuchen neared retirement.

As already indicated, the department's only American foreign policy specialist of the early postwar period was James L. McCamy (1947–71). He had a distinguished career in government service during World War II and leveraged that experience to become a notable scholar of American public administration. Two of his most influential books addressed the administrative aspects of the conduct of American foreign affairs, *The Administration of American Foreign Affairs* (1950) and *Conduct of the New Diplomacy* (1964). He was identified, therefore, not only as an American foreign policy specialist but also as an expert in public administration. McCamy's expertise in foreign affairs established a tradition of departmental strength in American foreign policy, the mainstay of what was regarded as international relations, as ethnocentric as that might have been.

Cohen and Tarr were to be the two remaining principals of that subfield for most of the rest of the 20th century although many others with shorter tenures contributed. Cohen joined the department in 1959 and I arrived in 1963. In the meantime, as noted, John A. Armstrong arrived in 1954. He became a scholar of the first rank within the field of Soviet, European studies, and nationalism. I leave further comment on his contributions to those areas to the chapter on comparative politics, but I must mention his impact also on the international relations field within the department. Armstrong taught in both Soviet and American foreign policies at the undergraduate level and Soviet and Eastern European relations at the graduate level. He frequently served on the international politics preliminary examination committee as well as with dissertation committees that worked with students in the international relations and American foreign policies fields. His was a significant intellectual presence so far as the IR subfield is concerned.

Bernard C. Cohen (1959–90) earned his Ph.D. at Yale in international relations and was associated with the Princeton Center for International

Studies prior to his appointment at Wisconsin in 1959. He established a career-long scholarly interest in public participation in foreign policy formation as reflected in his major publications and in most of the courses he offered during his long tenure at Wisconsin. His two most important publications in this area were *The Press and Foreign Policy* (1963) and *The Public's Impact on Foreign Policy* (1974), each of which greatly enlarged our understanding of the nature of the participants and of the processes of foreign policy making in the United States.

Throughout Cohen's career, he offered undergraduate and graduate courses that focused on the formulation of American foreign policy, placing it in the context of the larger American political experience, as well as international relations. His extensive involvement in university administration—three years as department chair, four years as associate dean of the Graduate School, over five years as vice chancellor for academic affairs, and one year as acting chancellor—indicated the value of his administrative talent to the department and to the university, but that also meant his administrative duties attenuated his involvement within the department. In 1995 Cohen culminated his contributions to the scholarship of policy formation with the publication of *Democracies and Foreign Policy: Public Participation in the United States and the Netherlands.*

Expansion

As noted in each of our reports, the 1960s ushered in profound changes as the university and the department underwent significant expansion. For the international relations component, that expansion really began with Cohen in 1959, then continued with two new hires: Leon Lindberg in 1962 and David Tarr in 1963. Lindberg (Ph.D. U.C.–Berkeley, 1962) was hired to teach international relations but his research and teaching inclinations from the beginning were in European integration and integration theory more broadly. In the years to come, Lindberg pioneered the development of the IR subfield of international political economy. So while Leon Lindberg's training and interests were definitely in IR, in most respects he identified himself, and was regarded by others, as a member of the cohort of comparativists. His substantial scholarship and teaching addressed Western European integration, the European Union, and increasingly the international political economy. He contributed in significant ways to the graduate and undergraduate international relations curriculum, particularly by vitalizing and emphasizing the international political economy component. Lindberg served many dissertators in the IR field, helped shape the IR curriculum and prelims, and was clearly a major contributor to the department's IR field, however defined, throughout his career. He also served as chair of the Council for European Studies, among many other notable career accomplishments.

Chronologically speaking, David Tarr was the next "IR" appointment, joining Bernard Cohen and James McCamy as the department's third resident specialist in American foreign policy in 1963. Tarr's graduate training was in political science (Ph.D. University of Chicago, 1961). His focus was on national and international security matters, while Cohen's work emphasized domestic political factors. In terms of both scholarship and teaching, Tarr's field identification was essentially that of an American foreign policy specialist, with emphasis on national security issues, institutions, and political processes. He found himself frequently the department's default position for the international relations field, for example, serving often as chair of the international politics prelim committee. His first book, *American Strategy in the Nuclear Age*, marked him as a security specialist. In the 1970s he worked on a number of national programs to train scholars in the security subfield, most particularly, during several summer months at Colorado College (National Security Affairs Seminar, 1977–79). In the 1980s he turned his attention in terms of both scholarship and teaching to the nuclear weapons and arms control dilemmas of the time, publishing a book on that subject, *Nuclear Deterrence and International Security* (1991). In the 1990s, he returned to the subject of American military leadership, publishing a number of articles on that subject in the years following my retirement. Over the course of his tenure, Tarr was also drawn into university service and away from teaching: he served as chair of the department, as director of the Center for International Cooperation and Security Studies, and not incidentally (given the eight years of service and turmoil), chair of the university's Athletic Board.

To continue the narrative on department expansion, as noted earlier, the department grew at a substantial pace in the 1960s. While Pfankuchen continued to offer the introductory and intermediate courses in international relations, in the first five years of that decade four more faculty members with research and teaching interests in international relations joined the department: I have already mentioned Leon Lindberg (1962–97). The appointment of Donald Carlisle, 1962–67 (Soviet politics and foreign policy), doubled our Soviet contingent, and Russell Edgerton, 1965–68 (American foreign policy), suggested departmental strength in numbers in IR with notable emphasis on the American foreign policy field. Indeed, counting Pfankuchen, Cohen, and myself, that made for an IR core of eight faculty (Pfankuchen, McCamy, Armstrong, Cohen, Lindberg, Carlisle, Tarr, Edgerton), four of whom were foreign policy specialists (McCamy, Cohen, Tarr, and Edgerton). During this period enrollments in IR courses increased dramatically, fueled in part by student interest and concern about both the cold war and the war in Vietnam.

During the next few years Carlisle and Edgerton departed. There followed four significant additions—David Kay (1966–75), an international organizations specialist and the first international relations generalist since Pfankuchen; Melvin Croan (1967–96), a specialist on the Soviet Union and Eastern Europe; Edward Friedman (1967 to the present), our resident China specialist; and Donald Hanson (1967–71), political theory and international relations. But only one of these identified IR as his primary field (Kay). Hanson's major field was political theory.

So while Melvin Croan effected a significant presence within the field of international relations, as had Armstrong, his main work and course offerings were technically classified as in the comparative field. A leading scholar on the politics of East Germany, Croan also chaired the Russian Area Studies Program for many years. His courses on such subjects as totalitarian political systems, Eastern and Western European politics, Soviet foreign policy, and the like were without exception of direct relevance to the field of international relations.

Edward Friedman, arriving in the department in 1967, had a similar relationship to the IR program. A specialist on Chinese politics, Friedman was an accomplished area specialist. He has contributed importantly to the international relations program not only by his emphasis on China's role in regional and international relationships, but also by teaching courses on revolution, democratization, and the politics of human rights. He has also regularly taught a large undergraduate course on the politics of the world economy, a long-standing scholarly interest of Friedman. As a staff member of the House Foreign Affairs Committee for three years, and a regular consultant to the departments of State and Defense, Friedman has been a practitioner as well as a notable scholar in the field.

In any case, this apparent strength in the late 1960s in international relations, however one defined the field, quickly dissipated. Hanson departed in 1971. At about the same time, McCamy and Pfankuchen retired. David Kay left in 1975, eventually achieving national prominence after the first Gulf War as a UN weapons inspector, and more recently as the CIA's chief weapons inspector in Iraq. The department added Michael Leavitt (1970–73) who offered courses both in methods and international relations for a short period, but the department nevertheless struggled to maintain cohesion in the field throughout the decade.

In summary, the mainstays for advanced and graduate instruction from 1960 through 1975 were Cohen, Lindberg, Kay, and Tarr, augmented by several comparativists, notably Armstrong, Lindberg, Croan, and Friedman. Note that *none of these except Kay regarded international relations as their primary field.* Ellen Seidensticker (1975–79), an international organization specialist, joined the department briefly, followed by two substantial additions, Barbara Stallings (1977–96), and Neil Richardson (1979 to the present). After that the department could not make much further progress in international relations until the 1990s.

Stallings and Richardson added breadth and depth to the international political economy group. Stallings (Ph.D. Stanford and Cambridge) joined the department in 1977. While she classified herself as a Latin Americanist, her many publications and her consistent offering of the department's graduate seminar on international relations made for a notable contribution to the department's IR program, particularly from the perspective of the international political economy. As was the case with so many other members of the IR field, Stallings was drawn into administrative service for the university. In 1985 she became director of the Latin American and Iberian Studies Program and soon thereafter was named associate dean of the Graduate School. Subsequently she was appointed director of the Global Studies Program. She departed in 1996 after an extended period of leave from the department.

Neil Richardson (Ph.D. Michigan) joined the department in 1979 shortly after publishing his book titled *Foreign Policy and Economic Dependence.* He eventually replaced Lewellyn Pfankuchen as the principal international relations generalist of the department, offering with some consistency the introductory undergraduate courses in international relations. The focus of his work and his advanced offerings have most frequently dealt with the international political economy, the politics of international trade, and global business. In recent years Richardson took on the additional administrative post of director of the L&S Advising Center.

In the 1980s the department continued its effort to expand its IR contingent. Robin Marra, 1983–87 (methods and international relations); Steven Greffenius, 1987–89; and Robert McCalla, 1987–97 (American foreign policy) joined our ranks for short periods. But not until the arrival of Michael Barnett in 1990, and the heady but brief addition of Emmanuel Adler (1992–95), did the international relations field begin to gain strength.

Recent Developments

The appointment of Michael Barnett in 1990 (Ph.D. Minnesota) marked the beginning of a transition of both faculty and focus in the IR subfield. The old-timers who had been hired during the expansion years were nearing retirement. Barnett, trained in international relations and identifying himself readily as "IR," also functioned comfortably as a regional specialist (our first Middle East expert), for he was both. His teaching and research ranged across a wide spectrum of international and regional considerations, from the "power and pathologies" of international organizations to the power struggles in the Middle East. As senior IR faculty departed, Barnett became the established anchor of the department's IR program.

At the time of the Rwanda genocide in 1994, Barnett held a fellowship at the Council on Foreign Relations; in this role he served as intern on the staff of the United States delegation to the UN, assigned to the Rwanda issue. The experience was a powerful lesson on the singular power of "group-think" in bureaucratic politics, inhibiting staff challenge to the American policy of opposing forceful UN action to halt the genocide. Barnett offered thoughtful reflections on this calamitous policy failure, for which President Bill Clinton publicly apologized to Rwanda, in a 1997 article in *Current Anthropology*. The participant-observer experience provided the basis for the critical examination of the failings of the UN Secretariat in responding to this tragedy, in a volume titled *Eyewitness to a Genocide: The United Nations and Rwanda* (2002). Subsequently, Barnett turned to issues of global governance; an early product of this new orientation was *Rules for the World: International Organizations in Global Politics*, coauthored with Martha Finnemore (2004). He left for Minnesota in 2004.

In 1995 the department added Bruce Cronin (1995–2003) and Mark Pollack (1995–2004) to the IR contingent, but by then Armstrong, Cohen, and Tarr had retired, and Stallings and McCalla had departed. Pollack, like Barnett, has both IR and regional interests (comparative, Western Europe), but left for Temple in 2004. Other recent IR appointments include: Orfeo Fioretos (1999), international relations and political economy; and John Pevehouse (2000), now the sole expert on American foreign policy.

Conclusions

As the department moves into the 21st century, the IR subfield continues a pattern established long ago of interminable struggle to establish and sustain strength in its quality and numbers against the limited resources available and the competing needs of the other subfields of the department. Competition for scarce resources is, of course, a normal condition across all the subfields. No field component should take the quality of its people and programs for granted. That said, my subjective view of the overall record is that, except for the short-term gains made in the mid-to-late 1960s, the IR component of the department was somewhat less successful than the other major components, and the one area of strength, even if we measure strength just in numbers—American foreign policy—has been left with but one scholar standing. This has been the case despite the fact that international relations courses have consistently remained popular choices among students—most especially, American foreign policy courses.

What explains the failure of the university and of the department to build and sustain a more robust IR subfield? Surely the demand has been there, in terms of student interest and of the serious political and intellectual challenges that international affairs have posed for political scientists over the past 100 years, spanning two world wars and a host of smaller conflicts, the rise of the United States to superpower status, the ascent and demise of the cold war, the rapid development of global economic interdependence, and the post-cold-war spread of terrorist activities. I am sure that among the reasons that we have fallen short of our aspirations in this field are some that are simply unintentional outcomes of short-term considerations. But there may also be some systemic explanations. Let me suggest consideration of several interrelated hypotheses for the potential insights they might provide.

Perhaps the IR specialists were less effective bargainers in the endless struggle for recruitment priorities within the department. But why would this be the case for so long a period of time? And why wouldn't those very people who profess to understand strategy, bargaining, and the balance of power be more successful? Do we have only ourselves to blame? One factor may have been that the IR program had fewer assets to draw upon in terms of institutionalized research programs, such as the NDEA Title VI resources that the established area studies programs offered to comparativists.

Some observers have suggested, not entirely in jest, that environmental factors, such as the politics, culture, and geographic location of the University of Wisconsin—specifically, Madison liberalism, prairie progressivism, and midwestern isolationism—tended to undercut support for the study of foreign affairs and international, making it less likely that IR could flourish in this environment. Isolationism was a declining factor after World War II, but liberals and progressives have tended quite consistently to be critical of the foreign policy agenda of the United States, and while they professed to support "peace studies," they also tended to opposed the study of war (which is part of the research agenda of most international relations scholars). Such attitudes came to bear more heavily during the denouement of the Vietnam conflict, but may have been a factor before and since.

But if such environmental and intellectual biases played a role, how does that account for the fact that during the same period the comparative politics subfield became so robust? One possible environmental answer lies in the intellectual agenda of the area studies programs, especially those of the third world, which were more compatible with liberal and progressive ideologies; their approaches may have been perceived as more compatible with prevailing intellectual orientations than were those of the IR field.

In any case, the very strength of comparative may explain IR's weakness. Comparative undercut the departmental need to enhance IR, as all the comparativists have served supporting roles in the IR curriculum and training programs. Comparative certainly supplemented our IR curriculum. Moreover, it is fair to note that over the years a number of our best incoming IR graduate students migrated to one or another of the area or country studies, where research opportunities and financial support were substantially better.

Finally, some have suggested that a partial explanation arises out of certain alleged conditions and biases of the political science discipline itself. Is it a fair observation that international relations never gained the respect and consideration of the more dominant subfields within the American political science profession? Certain critics of this persuasion have pointed, for example, to the *American Political Science Review*, claiming that our most prestigious journal has not and does not give IR a fair shake (suggesting thereby that the journal reflects the bias of the discipline as a whole). In return, some defenders of the faith have alleged that IR lagged behind the other subdisciplines in its professional development, in particular in failing to embrace fully the "behavioral revolution." Some have also claimed that, across the nation, too many IR specialists failed to exploit the application of quantitative methods to their research schemes and graduate training programs. Still others have complained that too many scholars in the IR field have been "policy oriented." In short, some critics argue that IR has been less scientific in its approach than have the other subfields of the discipline.

While these assertions are overly broad (I have certainly overstated them in the interest of brevity), perhaps they have some pertinence. However, they certainly do not account for why the IR components of some other major political science departments have been more successful than our own.

Having made these observations, however, I must nevertheless end on a positive note. The IR subfield has made notable strides, especially over the second half century of our department's existence. With the support of our comparative colleagues, IR has been able to develop and sustain high-quality teaching and a substantial record of research and public service. But with more resources, it could have accomplished much more. A first-ranked university such as ours will, one hopes, attend to this deficiency in the years ahead.

CHAPTER 9

The Study of American Government and Politics at the University of Wisconsin–Madison

Charles O. Jones

The study of American government and politics at the University of Wisconsin–Madison has a long tradition of strength by almost any measure one wishes to employ. In the formative period of the Department of Political Science, many if not most faculty had some level of expertise in the subject, a feature also true of political theory. Faculty had diverse professional interests by today's standards, typically writing and teaching in several fields (though often with a core concentration on law and administration). In this age of faculty teaching loads of two or fewer courses per semester, consider that Paul S. Reinsch offered five courses in the first semester of 1899–1900, eight in the second semester. Frederic A. Ogg, a coauthor (with P. Orman Ray) of the leading text on American government until well after World War II, wrote widely about foreign governments, mostly European. He taught a broad range of courses: law (domestic and international), comparative government and administration, party government, British politics, Far Eastern politics, municipal government, and even the "Political Status of Women" in 1931. His normal course load was three and three during the time that he was chair and editor of the *American Political Science Review* (*APSR*).

John M. Gaus was a leading scholar of public administration. But as with other leaders in that field at the time—for example, Leonard White, William Anderson, Luther Gulick—Gaus took an expansive, even ecological, approach to the subject. One can identify in Gaus's work the roots of a post-World War II emphasis on public policy. Accordingly, much of what he wrote and taught had relevance for the study of American government and politics. And, in fact, he served as president of both the American Political Science Association (APSA, 1944–45) and the American Society of Public Administration (1951–52).

Perhaps the first purely "Americanist" (that is, by contemporary standards) to join the department was John T. Salter. Hired in 1930, Salter taught political parties, political leadership, public opinion, and legislation. During the 1930s, he published well-received books, especially *Boss Rule,* an empirical study of Philadelphia politics. He then ceased research and significant publication and remained an associate professor for the rest of his career.

Post–World War II Developments

The post–World War II period witnessed a substantial increase in specialization and, with that development, a marked increase in the size of the department. Faculty came to be identified with one of the four general areas: American government, comparative politics, political theory, and international relations, and increasingly with a more specialized sub-field within those categories. Americanists came to specialize in national political institutions (typically one—Congress, the Presidency, political parties, interest groups), public opinion, voting behavior and elections, federalism, public administration and the bureaucracy, public policy, state and local politics, urban politics, political parties, political psychology and sociology, and a whole series of processes (legislative, administrative, judicial, leadership, policy, and intergovernmental relations, to cite several of the most common concentrations). Eventually, the department recruited on the basis of specializations, seeking, for example, to hire a "Congress," "political parties," "elections," or "Presidency" scholar. The curriculum naturally followed this trend as well. After all, a Congress scholar would likely want to teach a course in his or her area of specialization—typically a course called "The Legislative Process," but one mostly concentrating on Congress.

One consequence of these developments for this history is simply that the concentration on American government and politics became substantially more multifaceted than before. Had a history been written 50 years ago, one essay would have been written for tracking the American field. Now several essays are required to treat various specialized subfields within the American rubric. Specialization has also had effects on judging the quality of a department. The Wisconsin department has strengths and weaknesses among the subfields, making the tasks of hiring faculty and of rating programs more challenging than in the past. The department has consistently received high rankings, as has the American program. But there has been little improvement in that ranking over the years.

Faculty Expansion

Tables 9.1–9.3 provide data on the postwar faculty growth: faculty hired by decade and by subfield, longevity of service in the department and whether service was completed at UW or is still pending, and the mean years of service by subfield. Placing faculty into subfields of American government and politics is not a simple exercise. The categories overlap in many respects. They mask the specialties within the category (e.g., on voting within "political behavior" or a particular issue within "public policy"); several faculty have multiple subfield interests; methods are employed in every subfield (the label so often associated primarily with quantitative work); and the concentration is on a process, e.g., administration, but at a particular level of government, perhaps a city or state. It is also the case that some faculty interests span fields. For example, administration and law may be more comparative or international, theorists may concentrate on political institutions, and comparativisits often include American government in their analysis. An effort was made to include those with a primary scholarly emphasis on American topics.

The six categories relied on here are these: administration (those traditionally associated with public administration and bureaucracy); judicial/constitutional law (faculty concentrating on the judiciary, judicial process, Supreme Court, and public and constitutional law); political behavior/methods (a broad category of faculty specializations in voting behavior, campaigning, elections, political participation, sociological and psychological aspects of politics, and research methods as a discrete subject); political institutions/leadership (primarily those faculty concentrating on the Congress, the Presidency, political parties, and interest groups); public policy (those focusing on specific policy issues, singly, comparatively, or historically, and on decision-making processes related to policy matters); and state/local/urban politics (faculty concentrating on state and local governments and politics and the special area of urban politics that expanded in the postwar period). I am not including here the foreign policy area, which is treated in the international relations chapter.

Faculty teaching American-related topics in the period immediately following World War II (1945–1950) numbered eight: John Gaus (administration), John Salter (political institutions), Fred Clarenbach (regional planning), David Fellman (constitutional law), William Young (administration), Henry Hart (administration and resource development), James Donoghue (state and local governments), and Ralph Huitt (legislative process). The focus on administration and law carried over in the immediate postwar period, with five of the eight so concentrated. By comparison in 2003, the number of

Table 9.1 American Government and Politics Faculty (by subfields and decade hired) 1945–2003

Faculty	*Subfield*	*Decade Hired*
	Administration (13)	
Gaus		1920s
Clarenbach, W. Young, Hart		1940s
Penniman		1950s
Browning, Davis, Dresang, Holden		1960s
Miller		1970s
Meier		1980s
Khademian, Kettl		1990s
	Judicial/Constitutional Law (9)	
Fellman		1940s
Jacob[1], Grossman		1960s
Adamany, Feeley, Kritzer		1970s
Downs		1980s
Schweber, Fogg-Davis		1990s
	Political Behavior/Methods (14)	
Scoble		1950s
Froman, Dennis, Clausen, Cnudde, Edelman, Merelman		1960s
Sapiro, Page		1970s
Mutz		1980s
Franklin, Rahn		1990s
Goldstein, Walsh		2000s
	Political Institutions/Leadership (15)	
Salter		1930s
Huitt		1940s
Ranney, Manley, Dolbeare		1960s
Wolanin, Hinckley		1970s
Wilson, Champagne, Jones, Mayer		1980s
Canon, Coleman		1990s
Howell, Shafer		2000s
	Public Policy (10)	
Marmor		1960s
Sharkansky, Rosenbaum, Witte		1970s
Gormley, Gilliam, Johnson		1980s
Marquez, Kronebusch		1990s
Weimer		2000s
	State, Local, and Urban Politics (3)	
Donoghue		1940s
Lipsky, Eisinger		1960s

1. Note that Jacob was also hired in 1980s.

Table 9.2 American Government and Politics Faculty, Longevity, and Career 1945–2003

Faculty Member	*Years at UW*	*Completed at UW?*	*Still at UW?*
Salter	38	Y	
Dennis*	38	Y	
Young*	36	Y	
Donoghue	36	Y	
Huitt[1]	34	Y	
Dresang**	34	-	Y
Hart	34	Y	
Grossman*	33	N	
Fellman	32	Y	
Merelman	32	Y	
Penniman*	31	Y	
Clarenbach[2]	27	Y	
Eisinger*	27	N	
Sapiro*	27	-	Y
Witte	26	Y	
Kritzer*	25	-	Y
Edelman	24	Y	
Gaus	20	N	
Wilson	19	-	Y
Downs	18	-	Y
Hinckley	16	N	
Ranney	14	N	
Sharkansky	14	N	
Mayer	14	-	Y
Canon	13	-	Y
Kettl	13	-	Y
Holden	12	N	
Mutz	12	N	
Franklin	12	-	Y
Marquez	12	-	Y
Jacob[3]	11	N	
Coleman	11	-	Y
Jones	9	Y	
Feeley	8	N	
Wolanin	7	N	
Khademian	7	N	
Scoble	6	N	
Froman	6	N	
Browning	6	N	
Adamany	6	N	
Johnson	6	N	
Clausen	5	N	
Dolbeare	5	N	
Manley	5	N	
Cnudde	5	N	

Table 9.2 (continued)

Faculty Member	*Years at UW*	*Completed at UW?*	*Still at UW?*
Miller	5	N	
Gormley	5	N	
Champagne	5	N	
Kronebusch	5	N	
Davis	4	N	
Lipsky	4	N	
Rosenbaum	4	N	
Gilliam	4	N	
Meier	4	N	
Rahn	4	N	
Schweber	4	-	Y
Fogg-Davis	4	-	Y
Marmor	3	N	
Goldstein	3	-	Y
Walsh	3	-	Y
Weimer	3	-	Y
Page	2	N	
Howell	2	N	
Shafer	2	-	Y

*Served as Chair. **Served twice as Chair.

1. Huitt was on leave, 1963–1978.

2. Completed service in the Department of Urban and Regional Planning, 1962–72.

3. Jacob served at two different times: 1962–69; 1984–88 (second stint as Hawkins Professor).

Americanists was eighteen. Administration and law continued to be important components of the program but several other specialties were then included. The breakdown was: administration—2 (Dennis Dresang and Donald Kettl); judicial/constitutional law—4 (Herbert Kritzer, Donald Downs, Howard Schweber, Hawley Fogg-Davis); political behavior/methods—4 (Virginia Sapiro, Charles Franklin, Kenneth Goldstein, Katherine Cramer Walsh, with several others also suited to this category); political institutions/leadership—5 (Graham Wilson, Kenneth Mayer, David Canon, John Coleman, Byron Shafer); and public policy—3 (John Witte, Benjamin Marquez, David Weimer). State/local/urban politics had no one with that primary specialization, though Dresang taught state politics, and Kettl's and Witte's policy interests spanned the levels of government. Accordingly, instead of nearly two-thirds of the faculty, administration and law combined had one-third, with political institutions and political behavior the most numerous (9 of 18). Therein lies the story of the study of American government and politics during the last half of the twentieth century—expansion of the program

Table 9.3 American Government and Politics Faculty, Average Service by Subfield, 1945–2003

Subfield	*Mean Years of Service*
Administration[1]	16.9
Constitutional Law/Judiciary	15.7
Political Behavior/Methods	12.9
Political Institutions/Leadership[2]	10.4
Public Policy	8.2
State, Local, and Urban Politics	22.3

1. Does not include Gaus, who carried over from the prewar period; Clarenbach's service includes his service in the Department of Political Science (17 years).
2. Does not include Salter, who carried over from prewar, or Huitt's 13 years of leave.

beyond the more traditional subjects to the specializations reflecting developments in the discipline.

Among the immediate postwar faculty, Gaus and Salter carried over from the prewar period, the only Americanists to do so. Gaus left for Harvard in 1947 and his significant impact on the department and the university came to an end. Because of his limited service in the postwar period, Gaus is not included in tables 9.2–9.6. Salter stayed on until his retirement in 1968, but he had only the most limited role in departmental development.

It is evident from table 9.1 that administration and judicial/constitutional law continued to be major strengths in American governmental study. Of the 63 faculty listed, 21 are associated with these two subfields. Beginning in the 1970s, and in line with trends at other major universities, a public policy subfield emerged that was closely related to administration. Further enhancing this strength in administration and the growing subfield of public policy was the creation in 1969 of a Center for the Study of Public Policy and Administration that then became the La Follette Institute (now School) of Public Affairs in 1983. Clara Penniman was a founder and first director of the center. She was also the first woman to chair the department (and also the first female faculty member). Several faculty with interests in administration, public policy, and state, local, and urban politics have had joint appointments in the department and La Follette. Four—Dresang, Peter Eisinger, Kettl, and Witte—have served as directors, others as associate directors. It is notable as an indication of department–La Follette relations that two of these directors served as department chairs (Eisinger and Dresang twice) and one as associate chair (Witte). Also striking is the number of center, then La Follette School, faculty called upon by governors and other state officials to participate in commissions and other study groups, all very much in the University of Wisconsin tradition. Another likely effect of the existence of La Follette was the shift of state, local, and urban political study from the department to the institute (later school), at least as focused on Wisconsin.

Political behavior/methods and political institutions/leadership were the growth subfields during the 1960s and beyond. Harry Scoble was the first political behavior hire in the late 1950s, followed by Lewis Froman. Neither stayed at Wisconsin. The anchors of the program were Jack Dennis (1963), Murray Edelman (1966), and Richard Merelman (1969), later joined by Virginia Sapiro (1976), each with quite different perspectives, methods, and research interests. These four remained to provide stability of personnel (average service of 30 years—see table 9.2), if not a uniform concentration. Most notably, as Dennis points out in his chapter, he and Sapiro were more devoted to the application of social science and quantitative methods, while Edelman and Merelman regularly questioned the reliability of these methods. Diana Mutz and Wendy Rahn later contributed substantially to this emphasis but neither remained at Wisconsin. However, Mutz stayed for 12 years, the last three in distinguished service as associate chair. Her specialties were political communication and psychology, fields to which she contributed many articles, and a well-received book, *Impersonal Influence: How Perceptions of Mass Collectives Affect Political Attitudes* (1998).

As with political theory, it was long believed that methods was a subject associated with each of the subfields. All political scientists were theorists, all methodologists (though that term was not typically used in earlier times). In the 1950s, students desiring training in statistics or survey methods had to take courses outside the department (Burton Fisher, sociology, was relied on during this period for survey methods). With the development and use of increasingly sophisticated techniques, it became necessary to hire specialists trained in research methods. Many in the political behavior subfield were qualified to teach methods, as were some outside that subfield (e.g., Kritzer and Witte). Aage Clausen and Charles Cnudde were, perhaps, the first hires with primary responsibility for methods, though Scoble had worked with survey data. No one of these three hires stayed at Wisconsin beyond six years. Kritzer was relied on to teach methods for several years before Franklin became the anchorperson assuming responsibility for training in methods. Franklin also served as associate chair, 1993–96.

Rational-choice theory and methods has been a notable slight within the department, as contrasted to most other top-level departments. Efforts were made to hire persons specializing in that approach but with limited success. William Howell (Stanford) was hired in 2000 but stayed only two years, leaving for Harvard. David Weimer, who came in 2000, offers instruction in the social-choice field, and a couple of comparativists have a rational-choice orientation (see chapters 5, 6). It is said that rational-choice scholars require associates, a department can't have just one. Perhaps so. It has been the case at some universities that several hires were made at the same time. The Wisconsin department has not been willing to expend resources on that strategy, ever sensitive to maintaining the balance among existing subfields. It may well be that graduate study has been deficient at Wisconsin for not having had a sufficient presence of persons devoted to rational choice available to students.

The responsibility for the political institutions and leadership subfield was mostly that of Huitt through the 1950s and until the arrival of Austin Ranney in 1963. Huitt came to be known as the father of the contemporary study of Congress, attracting students at Wisconsin and followers elsewhere. He directed the APSA Study of Congress project during the 1960s. Huitt's own method was that of participant observation. He encouraged students to observe legislators at work and to conduct interviews. As with Richard E. Neustadt's influence on presidential studies, Huitt's insights on congressional (mainly Senate) behavior were broadly influential. His research as a participant often took him away from Madison. He worked for Senator Lyndon B. Johnson (D-Texas), then Senate Majority Leader, 1953–54, for Senator William Proxmire (D-Wisconsin), 1959, and for President Johnson, 1965–69, as assistant secretary for legislation, Department of Health, Education, and Welfare. He then served as executive director of the National Association of State Universities and Land Grant Colleges, 1970–78. As one would expect, the longer Huitt served in Washington, the more he was a participant, not a participant-observer, and the less he published.

The interruption in Huitt's service (he was on leave for a record 13 years) meant that there was no core group to provide continuity as with Dennis, Edelman, Merelman, and Sapiro for political behavior. Both with national reputations, Huitt and Ranney, serving together, would have been a most impressive duo in the national institutions subfield. As it was, however, Ranney had left by the time Huitt returned in 1978.

Ranney stayed at Wisconsin for 14 years, Barbara Hinckley for 16 years (five years overlapping with Ranney). Both had fine scholarly records at Wisconsin and attracted a number of graduate students. As well, Ranney had impressive service to the profession during his time at Wisconsin, as editor of the APSR (1965–71) (and earlier as book review editor), as well as APSA

Table 9.4 American Government and Politics Faculty, 1945–2003: Ph.D., Hired From, Left For (by decade and subfield)

Faculty Member (subfield)	*Ph. D. From*	*Hired From*	*Left For*
1940s (6)			
Clarenbach (1)	Cornell	Fed. Gov't.	Other UW Dept.
W. Young (1)	UW	Penn	—
Hart (1)	UW	UW*	—
Fellman (2)	Yale	Nebraska	—
Huitt (4)	Texas	Lamar College	—
Donoghue (6)	UCLA	Penn	—
1950s (2)			
Penniman (1)	Minnesota	Minnesota*	—
Scoble (3)	Yale	Boston University	UCLA
1960s (18)			
Browning (1)	Yale	Yale*	Mich. State
Davis (1)	Michigan	Michigan*	Wash. Univ.
Dresang (1)	UCLA	UCLA*	—
Holden (1)	Northwestern	Wayne State	Fed. Gov't.
Jacob (2)	Yale	Tulane	Northwestern
Grossman (2)	Iowa	Iowa*	JHU
Froman (3)	Northwestern	Northwestern*	Irvine
Dennis (3)	Chicago	Chicago*	—
Clausen (3)	Michigan	Michigan*	Ohio State
Cnudde (3)	North Carolina	Irvine	Mich. State
Edelman (3)	Illinois	Illinois	—
Merelman (3)	Yale	UCLA	—
Dolbeare (4)	Columbia	Columbia*	Washington
Ranney (4)	Yale	Illinois	AEI
Manley (4)	Syracuse	Syracuse*	Stanford
Marmor (5)	Harvard	Harvard*	Minnesota
Lipsky (6)	Princeton	Princeton*	MIT
Eisinger (6)	Yale	Yale*	Wayne State
1970s (11)			
Miller (1)	Michigan	Michigan*	?
Adamany (2)	UW	Wesleyan	Long Beach (Provost)
Feeley (2)	Minnesota	Yale	UCLA
Kritzer (2)	North Carolina	Rice	—
Sapiro (3)	Michigan	Michigan*	—
Page (3)	Stanford	Chicago	Chicago
Wolanin (4)	Harvard	Harvard*	Congress
Hinckley (4)	Cornell	Cornell	NYU
Sharkansky (5)	UW	Georgia	Hebrew Univ.
Rosenbaum (5)	Chicago	Chicago*	Connecticut
Witte (5)	Yale	Yale*	—

1980s (11)			
Meier (1)	Syracuse	Oklahoma	Milwaukee
Jacob (2)	Yale	Northwestern	Northwestern
Downs (2)	Berkeley	Notre Dame	—
Mutz (3)	Stanford	Stanford*	Ohio State
Wilson (4)	Oxford	Essex	—
Champagne (4)	Indiana	Indiana*	Law School
Jones (4)	UW	Virginia	—
Mayer (4)	Yale	RAND	—
Gormley (5)	North Carolina	Stony Brook	Georgetown
Gilliam (5)	Iowa	Parkside	UCLA
Johnson (5)	Michigan	Michigan*	Williams
1990s (10)			
Khademian (1)	Michigan State	Michigan State*	Michigan
Kettl (1)	Yale	Vanderbilt	—
Schweber (2)	Cornell	Cornell*	—
Fogg-Davis (2)	Princeton	Princeton	—
Franklin (3)	Michigan	Wash. Univ.	—
Rahn (3)	Minnesota	Ohio State	Minnesota
Canon (4)	Minnesota	Duke	—
Coleman (4)	MIT	Texas	—
Marquez (5)	UW	Utah	—
Kronebusch (5)	Harvard	Fed. Gov't.	Fed. Gov't.
2000s (5)			
Goldstein (3)	Michigan	Arizona State	—
Walsh (3)	Michigan	Michigan*	—
Howell (4)	Stanford	Stanford*	Harvard
Shafer (4)	Berkeley	Oxford	—
Weimer (5)	Berkeley	Rochester	—

*Denotes that UW was a first job—26, 42% of total.

Note: Subfields: 1=Administration; 2=Judicial/Constitutional Law; 3=Political Behavior/Methods; 4=National Political Institutions/Leadership; 5=Public Policy; 6=State, Local, and Urban Politics

president (1974–75). Ranney's editorship returned the *APSR* to UW, Ogg having had the job for a record 23 years (1926–49). Ranney also joined Ogg as one of the few political scientists to serve as both editor of the journal and president of the association.

The situation for the political institutions/leadership subfield stabilized in the late 1980s. A core group emerged with full coverage of the political institutions and diverse ancillary interests. Wilson (19 years), Mayer (14 years), Canon (13 years), and Coleman (11 years)—all full professors—were joined

Table 9.5 American Government and Politics Faculty, 1945–2003: Source of Ph.D. and Retention Rates (by decade and subfield)

Decade	Source of Ph.D.			Retention Rates
	*Big 10**	*Ivy*	*Other*	
1940s	2	2	2	6/6=100%
1950s	1	1	-	1/2=50%
1960s	7	8	3	4/18=22%
1970s	6	3	2	3/11=27%
1980s	4	2	5	4/11=36%
1990s	5	5	-	7/10=70%
2000s	2	-	3	4/5=80%
Totals	27 (43%)	21 (33%)	15 (24%)	29/63=46%
Subfield				
Admin.	7	3	2	6/12=50%
Judicial	3	5	2	5/10=50%
Behavior	9	2	3	7/14=50%
Institutions	3	6	5	7/14=50%
Policy	5	3	2	3/10=30%
State/Local	-	2	1	1/3=33%

Note: Jacob is counted twice for purposes of this table, given that he was hired twice and left twice.
*Chicago is counted in the Big 10 for purposes of this table.

in 2001 by the Glenn B. and Cleone Orr Hawkins Professor, Byron Shafer, formerly Andrew Mellon Professor of Government, Oxford University (see tables 9.1 and 9.2). This group is as impressive as any in the nation in this subfield, offering outstanding coverage at the senior level of the range of institutional specialties, with Wilson and Shafer providing comparative perspectives as well.

The last category in table 9.1, state/local/urban politics, shows no hiring after Eisinger in 1969. As noted, La Follette took over much of the responsibility for research on Wisconsin issues, including urban areas and with comparison to other states. Courses are still offered at the undergraduate level, with enrollments sufficient to justify a partial hire in this subfield, but it has not been a priority for expansion within the department, regardless of its importance.

Table 9.3 displays the variation in the mean years of service for the six subfields. Leading is state/local/urban politics, due to the long service of Donoghue (36 years) and Eisinger (27 years). Administration and judicial/

Table 9.6 Advancement of Tenured American Government and Politics Faculty, 1945–2003

Hired as Professor (9)
Edelman, Fellman, Holden*, Jacob**, Jones***, Kettl, Ranney*, Shafer***, Weimer

Associate Professor (8)
Adamany*, Hinckley*, Neier*, Merelman, Sharkansky*, Wilson, W. Young

Assistant Associate Professor (17)
Canon, Coleman, Dennis, Donoghue, Downs, Dresang, Eisinger*, Franklin, Gormley*, Grossman*, Huitt, Jacob**, Kritzer, Marquez, Mayer, Sapiro, Witte

Instructor Assistant Associate Professor (2)
Hart, Penniman

Assistant Associate (5)
Dolbeare*, Feeley*, Goldstein, Manley*, Mutz*

* Did not complete career at UW.
** Jacob had two terms of service at UW, 1962–69 and 1984–86.
The second term was as the Glenn B. and Cleone Orr Hawkins Professor.
*** Serving as Glenn B. and Cleone Orr Hawkins Professor.

constitutional law show impressive average longevity—17 and 16 years, respectively. Turnover by this measure has been highest in the public policy field (average longevity just under 10 years) and marginally greater in the political institutions/leadership and political behavior/methods subfields (10.6 and 12.8 mean years of service, respectively). The latter is particularly interesting because the four mainstays, Dennis, Edelman, Merelman, and Sapiro, had an average of 30 years, indicating the high turnover among others in that subfield.

Perhaps the most exciting period of growth was that during the early 1960s. Undergraduate and graduate enrollments were increasing rapidly, behavioralism was having its effect, research funds were plentiful, and the job market was excellent, with newly minted Ph.D.s much in demand. The department chair during this time, 1960–63, was Leon Epstein. A true comparativist, Epstein had strong research interests in American government and politics. As a consequence he attracted a number of graduate students whose research interests were primarily in American government and politics with a comparative perspective. Several students, like myself, also profited greatly from his critical and timely reading of manuscripts. Epstein has written about the growth period of the early 1960s:

> The first several years of the 1960s, before the full impact of Vietnam and urban riots later in the decade, were the most promising that I experienced in higher education. Our enrollments, virtually doubling in a decade following the late 1950s, provided most of the basis for increasing faculty numbers. Greater federal research funds were helpful too. At the same time, student performance seemed to be higher than at any other time that I taught before or after the early 1960s (except perhaps in the late 1940s). Academic standards became temporarily more rigorous as the nation responded to the challenge posed by the Soviet Union's successful launch of sputnik during the late 1950s. (Leon Epstein memoir, 152–53)

Epstein identified an optimism regarding the discipline of political science and its future. "I had a sense of belonging to a generation, now in its forties, that was asserting academic leadership and doing so when prospects were especially bright. Hence I welcomed the opportunity to chair the Department in 1960." (Epstein, 153)

Recruiting in the period of expansion was a much less elaborate process than it became later. The department chair personally managed most of the tasks. According to Epstein, as described in his memoir, there was no public advertising of openings, nor were applications typically submitted. The APSA employment service newsletter developed some years later. For lower level positions, inquiries were made to major university departments (often to an acquaintance), a leading prospect was identified, and that person was then invited to the campus. "For the less frequent senior appointment, the process was even less openly competitive; the department simply approached an individual in whom it was interested." (Epstein, 155)

Tables 9.4 and 9.5 provide an overview and summary of recruitment and retention of Americanists in the department, from 1945 to 2003. Several observations are relevant. First, it is striking that the department has recruited heavily from Big Ten and Ivy League universities. Combined, these schools have produced 48 (76 percent) of the Ph.D.'s in the American area. Southern and southwestern universities supplied just four Ph.D.'s (6 percent)—three from the University of North Carolina and one from Texas. Western universities offered eight Ph.D.'s (13 percent)—three each from Berkeley and Stanford, two from UCLA.

Four universities supplied 28 of the 63 Ph.D.'s (44 percent)—Yale 10 (11 if Jacob is counted twice), Michigan 8, Wisconsin 6, and Minnesota 4. Five other universities—Cornell, Harvard, University of North Carolina, Berkeley, and Stanford supplied three Ph.D.'s each. Interestingly, no one of the three Harvard Americanist Ph.D.'s achieved tenure in the department (though those in other subfields did). Yale Ph.D.'s, on the other hand, have been very successful in achieving tenure and status within the department—eight of the ten. Among these Yale products is a department chair (Eisinger), an associate chair (Witte), three directors of La Follette (Eisinger, Witte, and Kettl), holder of the Hawkins Chair (Herbert Jacob), and Vilas Professor (Fellman).

As with many departments in major graduate institutions, the Wisconsin department has been reluctant to hire its own Ph.D.'s fresh from completing graduate study. Just one of the six Americanists—Henry Hart—began his teaching career at UW. Of the rest, Ira Sharkansky returned after four years, David Adamany after five, Young after six, Marquez after eight, and Charles O. Jones after 28. All but Marquez were hired with tenure.

The record supports Epstein's observation regarding the level at which faculty have been hired. In the American area, 62 percent of those hired, 1945–2003, were new Ph.D.'s. Of the rest, nine were hired at the full professor rank (three of these as the Hawkins Professor) and eight at the associate professor rank (see table 9.6). Yale Ph.D.'s are also the most numerous among those hired with tenure—four of the nine at the full professor level; another at the associate level. UW is next with one at the full and three at the associate level. There is no discernible "raiding" pattern in hiring at advanced levels. The only double hire from a single institution was that of Ranney (1963) and Edelman (1966) from Illinois, both at full professor.

Tables 9.4 and 9.5 also fail to show any pattern of Wisconsin being raided by other institutions. Of course, several of those leaving were forced to do so for lack of attaining tenure. Of those at advanced levels, personal circumstances appear to explain most of the changes. In several cases—Matthew Holden (federal government), Ranney (American Enterprise Institute), Adamany (university administration), Feeley (Law School faculty)—faculty members left for positions outside academic political science. Sharkansky moved to a foreign university. Grossman and Eisinger moved after 33 and 27 years, respectively, at UW, actually retiring in each case to accept a position at another university. These seven moves constituted half of those among tenured faculty in American government and politics.

Still, the retention rates, as shown in table 9.5, show high turnover during the decades of the sixties, seventies, and eighties. The overall retention rate for this period was just over one-fourth of those hired. The rate is higher for the 1990s, though it is early to make a final accounting. The retention rate for those hired in the 1960s illustrates the volatility during that time. The low percentage should be modified, however, by the fact that Grossman and Eisinger left after lengthy service at Wisconsin. The rate among subfields does not vary significantly, apart from public policy, a condition evident as well in table 9.3.

Periods of expansion and turnover in a department can easily foster factionalism and discord. That has not happened at Wisconsin. One of the most frequently cited features of the department is that of congeniality. "A congenial academic home," is the way Epstein described the department during his 40 years of service. What explains the relative harmony? Epstein is likely correct in this assessment: "It [departmental development] was not so abrupt or revolutionary as to disturb relatively amiable relationships." (Epstein, 164)

Citing Epstein's recollections invites one final and important topic in reviewing the American field of study at UW. Nominally a scholar of British and European politics, Epstein has been critically important in developing the American government and politics program at UW. His comparative studies of political parties are standard works in the field and have been influential in work on American politics. In the early 1970s, Epstein shifted to American politics, while still teaching the British politics course. In Huitt's absence, Epstein and Ranney were mainstays for the political institutions subfield, with Ranney also doing work on British politics during this time. Throughout his career at Wisconsin, Epstein was deeply involved in the American program. He chaired the department during the expansion period of the early 1960s. He directed the dissertations of some of the most outstanding American graduate students. I can testify that graduate students relied heavily on him for advice, whether or not he was directing their dissertations. He taught political parties and state politics. A strong case can be made for including him as an Americanist, one with an admirable devotion to treating American politics in a comparative context. Few, if any, faculty have contributed more to the development of the department and the congenial relationships characterizing it.

Other faculty members too have contributed to the growth and development of the American government and politics program. Notable among these was Booth Fowler. His undergraduate teaching skills are legendary. But he also directed many dissertations in the American area. He developed a religion and politics program that attracted graduate students and received national recognition. Nominally a political theorist, Fowler taught and advised in a manner that encouraged the practice of empirically testing American political ideas.

Curriculum

There is, perhaps, no more dramatic illustration of change in the political science curriculum than to compare the course offerings from the close of the 19th century to the start of the 21st. In the fall semester of 1899 (five years before the official creation of the department), a political science faculty of three offered 14 courses. John B. Parkinson taught constitutional and international law (3 courses); Paul S. Reinsch taught elementary law, contemporary and colonial politics, and political philosophy (5 courses); and Samuel E. Sparling taught the rest—mostly administration but including courses on party government and elements of political science. Reinsch and Sparling had Ph.D.'s, Parkinson had an M.A. from Wisconsin and an honorary law degree. Students interested in studying American government and politics seemingly had to extract their learning from courses with broader themes and concepts, as interpreted by a limited and busily occupied faculty. Of the 31 courses offered in 1899–1900, 13 had "law" or "jurisprudence" in the title; another 6, "administration" or "administrative."

Fast forward to the fall semester of 2000. Well over 40 faculty members offered more than 60 courses, seminars, and special topics. Offerings in the American government and politics area alone, excluding foreign policy and American political theory, numbered more than 20. Students of American government had a very different problem in 2000 than in 1899—that of choosing among specializations: presidency, constitutional law, legislative process, public opinion, socialization, Mexican-American politics, women in politics, policy making, and methods. Typically the challenge of integrating specialized knowledge so as to develop an understanding of governing in America, a strength of the earlier program, was left to students. The general American government course was offered as an introduction, not as a capstone.

Much of this proliferation of courses occurred after World War II. Even as late as the fall semester of 1940, the curriculum had not grown greatly—21 courses offered by eight faculty. Specialized courses in American government numbered about four or five, with a heavy emphasis still on law and administration. And, in fact, one must move ahead to the 1970s to see the full impact on the curriculum of the expansion of the postwar period, especially that in the 1960s. By the fall semester, 1970, the curriculum offered a number and variety of courses that would become commonplace for the rest of the century.

The growth of more fully articulated graduate seminars was also a notable development during the 1960s, though seminars appeared as early as 1899. Earlier graduate students typically enrolled in upper division

Table 9.7 American Government and Politics Dissertations, 1945–2001 (By decade and subfield)

Subfield / *Decade:*	*1940s*	*1950s*	*1960s*	*1970s*	*1980s*	*1990s*	*2000s*	*Total*
Administration	4	5	2	0	0	2	0	13 (6%)
Judicial/Law	0	5	7	12	6	13	2	45 (21%)
Behavior	0	0	6	13	7	4	3	33 (16%)
Institutions	1	2	9	11	14	6	0	43 (20%)
Policy	1	2	3	10	6	11	0	33 (16%)
State/Local/Urban	2	10	5	15	6	7	0	45 (21%)
Total	8 (4%)	24 (11%)	32 (15%)	61 (29%)	39 (18%)	43 (20%)	5 (2%)	212

Source: Compiled from Llewellyn Pfankuchen, Virginia Sapiro (with David Green and Paul Martin), and Herbert Kritzer, "Careers in Political Science."

undergraduate courses, then wrote papers as an added assignment and met individually with faculty. A few general seminars were offered, mostly to read and critique literature in the subfield. By 1970, a number of specialized seminars were offered, many suited to the research interests and expertise of faculty. An effort was made to offer several of these seminars at least once every second or third semester (e.g., on the presidency, political parties, legislative process, etc.). Methods seminars also became standard.

At the undergraduate level, a full complement of institutional courses came to be supplemented by a variety of topics suited to the emergence of political and policy issues, as well as the expertise of faculty. In addition, research methods, internships, and seminars or special topics courses began to appear, along with honors programs that fostered independent research. Some undergraduate students were also hired to assist in faculty research projects.

Impact on the Profession

What has been the impact on the profession of the program of American government and politics at the University of Wisconsin? In part a response to that question has to be subjective, dependent on how one views strengths and weaknesses. There are, however, a few more objective criteria, notably the quality of the faculty as measured by scholarly and professional achievements, the ratings of the program by outside evaluations, teaching and course assessments and awards, the quality of the graduate students, and the placement of Ph.D.'s, as well as their achievements as scholars and teachers.

First I will venture a subjective view of the American government program. The basis of my judgment is my experience as a graduate student, comparison with three other Ph.D.-granting state universities in which I taught, acquaintance with faculty who received their graduate degree from Wisconsin, continuing contact with department faculty, and nine years of serving on the Wisconsin faculty (1988–97). My comments are directed to the American program but are heavily influenced by the broader intellectual climate that permeates the university and the Department of Political Science. My experiences at Wisconsin and with others so associated influenced my entire professional life. I sought to teach the way I was taught, to observe as well as study politics and politicians, to take seriously the "public" part of a public institution, to accept the responsibilities as well as the benefits of the profession, and to guard against the narrowing effects of specializing. These were the values that I have associated with Wisconsin and the department. I venture to state that other Wisconsin faculty and Ph.D.'s would subscribe to these same goals. The department has preserved these canons of performance because they are worth saving. They undoubtedly influence recruitment and have prevented narrow, often competing, specializations. The cost of this approach may be criticism that new methods are not sufficiently incorporated into the program, and that charge has been leveled. It is a mark of the impact of the department and the American program that so many of its products seek to emulate how it was, and is, done at Wisconsin.

What of the more objective indicators? National reputations in the subfields of American government and politics would be one important test. Several American faculty have attained leadership positions in the profession—three as presidents of the APSA (Gaus, Ranney, and Jones). Epstein also served as APSA president, as did Holden after he left UW. Several have had positions in Washington, D.C., think tanks, directing programs and publishing important policy studies. Kettl's work with The Brookings Institution and Ranney's with the American Enterprise Institute are especially noteworthy. Many have edited journals, including the two leading publications in American government and politics: the *APSR* and the *American Journal of Political Science*. Some developed national followings because of their pioneering research. Many have received awards for books written and have been invited to lecture, to accept visiting appointments, and to spend a year at the Center for Advanced Study of the Behavioral Sciences. Three Wisconsin

Americanists are members of the American Academy of Arts and Sciences (Ranney, Jones, and Sapiro), as are Epstein and another who left Wisconsin (Holden). There has been less of a tendency at Wisconsin compared to other peer institutions to develop research centers or to seek large grants for team research, though such grants have been received and research conducted (as with Goldstein's Wisconsin Advertising Project and directorship of the Center for the Study of Politics and Communication). Rather distinction in scholarship has been commonly achieved more by individual contributions. It is also characteristic of the American program that each specialization has consistently had nationally recognized faculty.

Rankings of the department have been rather uniform in recent decades, always in the top ten, never higher than eighth since 1925 when it was ranked fourth behind Harvard, Chicago, and Columbia. The steady state in ranking probably reflects the feature noted earlier, that of maintaining distinguished, solid, and respectable programs but reluctance to endorse new methods, especially rational choice. Unfortunately there are very few rankings of specific subfields. The one ranking that does rate subfields, *U.S. News and World Report*, is not held in high regard. The 2001 ranking of the American politics program at UW was 13th, tied with Duke University. One study ranked universities by book production of graduates and current faculty. The results showed Wisconsin to be a book-writing department. UW Ph.D.'s ranked eighth in books, current faculty ranked third. Rankings for journal articles were lower in both cases (Rice, McCormick, and Bergmann, *Political Science and Politics*, December 2002, 752).

Perhaps least measurable, yet most important, is the impact faculty have in the classroom. Thousands of undergraduate and graduate students are enrolled in American government and politics courses each semester—often a thousand just in the introductory course. Teaching has traditionally been taken very seriously at Wisconsin generally and by the Department of Political Science in particular. The curriculum is a frequent topic of discussion in faculty meetings. Changes in the curriculum are invited and carefully evaluated. Serious efforts are made to judge teaching performance. Several American government faculty members have won teaching awards. The success of Downs in a classroom of 500 students is legendary. Unfortunately there is no method for tracking undergraduates so as to determine the impact of their training, nothing more than anecdotal evidence. The most that can be done is to support experimentation and to evaluate the curriculum on a continuing basis.

Somewhat easier to judge are the effects of graduate training, at least by inference. Table 9.7 categorizes the American government and politics dissertations from 1945 to 2001 (the most recent update). Several observations are appropriate. Note that just under a third of all dissertations were completed in the 1970s. The explanation surely lies in the problems of hiring during the high-demand 1960s. Supply sought to meet demand.

As regards the subfields, the decrease in the number of dissertations in administration is striking. The explanation is found in the increases in dissertations in public policy and state/local/urban politics. As noted in the discussion of faculty expansion, much of what earlier was categorized as public administration came to be labeled policy studies. Also, many of the dissertations on state, local, or urban areas concentrated on administrative or policy issues. Taken together, it is interesting that administration, public policy, and state/local/urban politics constitute 43 percent of the dissertations. Add judicial and constitutional law, and the total is 64 percent of the postwar dissertations in the subject areas that were dominant in the prewar era—administration and law, though relying on very different methods.

The number of political behavior dissertations reflected the development of that emphasis in the 1960s. As categorized here, they include those concentrating on elections, campaigning, and more sociological or psychological topics. Of course, none of these categories is discrete. Behavioralism is also viewed as a method or a perspective. Accordingly, other subfield dissertations were clearly influenced by the behavioral approach. Other observations on table 9.7: the strength of the judicial/law subfield in production of dissertations in the 1990s, the significant number of dissertations concentrating on various environmental issues (in the policy subfield) during the 1990s, and the nearly 60 percent of the institutions dissertations written during the 1970s and 1980s.

It is difficult to provide specific data on the impact of graduate students on the profession and the study of American government and politics. General impressions and anecdotal evidence must be relied on. Placement data are available, of course, but it is hard to assess their meaning over time. Apart from the most elite institutions, rankings of programs vary over time. Thus, placing a student at a particular university at one time may be more impressive than at another time. Or a student placed at a lower-ranking institution may have been influential in upgrading the program. Others move from lower-ranking schools to higher-ranking schools through their careers; some go the other direction. Wisconsin American government and politics Ph.D.'s have either started at or moved to Harvard, Yale, Michigan, Minnesota, Ohio State, Iowa, North Carolina, and other top-ranked programs, but many more have served on the faculties of lesser-ranked institutions. Short of comparative analysis of other institutions' placement record, the most that can be said is that UW Ph.D.'s are well placed for the good reason that they are well trained.

Citing individual cases is one means for demonstrating impact. The problem is that of failing to acknowledge someone who has had demonstrable impact in teaching, administration, or public service. Still, apologizing in advance for oversights, certain cases should be acknowledged. Three Wisconsin Ph.D.'s have won the APSA Frank J. Goodnow Award for Distinguished Service to the profession: Frank Sorauf (1953 Ph.D.), Samuel Patterson (1959 Ph.D.), and Jones (1960 Ph.D.). Several have served as presidents of major associations: Sorauf, Patterson, Jones, John Kingdon (1965 Ph.D.), Ada Finifter (1967 Ph.D.), Marjorie Hershey (1972 Ph.D.); or as APSA program chairs: Sorauf, Patterson, and Finifter. A prewar Ph.D., William O. Farber (1935), was also president of the Midwest Political Science Association in the postwar period. Three of the seven editors of the *APSR*, 1971–2003, were Wisconsin Ph.D.'s: Jones, Patterson, and Finifter. Several other UW Ph.D.'s have edited important journals: Patterson (*American Journal of Political Science*; *Legislative Studies Quarterly*); George Edwards (1973 Ph.D., *Presidential Studies Quarterly*); and Donald Kommers (1963 Ph.D., *Review of Politics*). Gary King (1984 Ph.D.) is acknowledged to have had significant influence in research methods within political science and within governments. Paul Herrnson (1986 Ph.D.) has influenced the study of political parties and campaigns.

Conclusion

This overview of the postwar development of American government and politics in the Department of Political Science portrays a consistently vibrant program, one adjusting to the changes within the discipline during a period of rapid growth. Cautious about fads, the program has opted for emphasizing traditional strengths in administration, law, and institutions, adding impressive behavioral methods and interpretations of American political life. Behavioralism has permeated most of the standard research topics in the study of national, state, local, and urban governments. It is a mark of the care and quality of recruiting that so many faculty have become leaders in the profession, as have many of the Ph.D.'s awarded in the American area.

Perhaps the most glaring omission in accommodating to change in the discipline is the failure to have fully incorporated the rational-choice perspective into the department's American offerings. The impact nationally of this approach to the study of politics has been significant but the department has not been willing to make the commitment required for robust training, accepting the possible effects of this omission in recruiting and placing graduate students.

Most exceptional to the author of this essay are the atmospherics of learning about American government and politics in the department. Without question, a large part of this attribute is due to the university and its traditions. Yet it is important that this intellectual heritage permeate all programs throughout the campus. That it does is, I believe, reflected in this review of the American government and politics program.

CHAPTER 10

Public Administration and Public Policy

David J. Fleming, John Witte, and Donald F. Kettl

When the American Political Science Association (APSA) was founded in 1903, public administration was one of the five fields forming the new discipline, along with comparative government, public law, international law, and political theory. Of the first eleven APSA presidents, five came from public administration and played important roles in framing the new discipline. From its very beginning, public administration was one of the critical foundations of political science, and political science was the natural home of public administration.

As the study of public administration and public policy has changed over the last century, so too has the field's institutional location. Political science departments gradually moved away from scholarly work in the field. Meanwhile, new schools of public policy and administration, separate from political science departments, began springing up. The movement started with public administration programs—the creation of Syracuse University's Maxwell School in 1924 was the first—and accelerated with the establishment of schools of public policy in the 1960s and 1970s; by 1982 a reputational ranking of such institutions listed no less than 50 of these graduate training programs. This trend led one of the field's great figures, Dwight Waldo, to write sadly in 1975:

> It is now unrealistic and unproductive to regard public administration as a subdivision of political science. . . . The truth is that the attitude of political scientists (other than those accepting public administration as their "field") is at best one of indifference and is often one of undisguised contempt or hostility. We are now hardly welcome in the house of our youth.[1]

This national trend was apparent in the Department of Political Science of the University of Wisconsin–Madison. In part this reflected a shift in focus of public administration toward public policy studies. As well, the 1967 creation of the Center for the Study of Public Policy and Administration (commonly shortened to "Center for Public Policy and Administration," or CPPA) over time shifted much of the graduate instruction in this area to this new program. The CPPA, ultimately renamed the Robert M. La Follette School of Public Affairs, gradually became the organizing focus for much of the university's work in policy analysis and public administration, through its large M.A. program designed to provide skilled personnel for state and other echelons of government, and an active outreach and research agenda. Undergraduate classes in public administration and policy remained within the department, while most graduate classes in this area have recently been taught through the La Follette School.

Although at many universities the study of public administration and policy has spun off into fully independent schools, at Wisconsin there has remained a strong organic connection between La Follette and the Department of Political Science. At the centennial point in 2004, Dennis Dresang, Donald Kettl, Melanie Manion, Joe Soss, David Weimer, Graham Wilson, and John Witte all held joint appointments. Moreover, partly because the department has long held to a studied eclecticism, it has tended to hire faculty who could move easily between the broader discipline and a focused study of public administration and policy. That, over time, has helped the department maintain intellectual leadership in these fields.

The Early Days

In the early 1900s, the department faculty reflected the central importance of public administration within the discipline. During the first half of the 20th century, in a given year one could find as many as 40 to 50 percent of the political science faculty listing public administration as a field of study. The first doctorate in political science was awarded in 1896 to Samuel E. Sparling, a specialist in municipal administration. After graduating, Sparling joined the faculty of the Ely School of Economics, Political Science and History, and helped to form a separate department in 1904. Sparling also helped bring to life the department's commitment to the "Wisconsin Idea," the notion that the boundaries of the university are the boundaries of the state, and that university faculty members ought to work energetically to use their knowledge to help solve the state's problems. Sparling helped found the Wisconsin League of Municipalities in 1898, and went on to become the league's executive director.

Public administration's prominent role within the prewar study of political science was evident in the seminal work by Wisconsin's Frederic A. Ogg and P. Orman Ray, *Introduction to American Government.*[2] This widely used text, first published in 1922, dominated the field of introductory works in American government until well after World War II; unlike contemporary political science basic-text authors, Ogg and Ray gave extensive coverage to public administration issues. They included long chapters on administration at the national level, as well as coverage of state and local government.

In the prewar years, the department was the home to many other prominent public administration scholars. John Gaus, who taught at the university from 1927 to 1947, is one of the most notable scholars in the history of the department. Some of his many contributions to the study of public administration include *Frontiers of Public Administration* (with Leonard D. White and Marshall E. Dimock, 1936), *Public Administration and the United States Department of Agriculture* (with Leon O. Wolcott, 1940), and *Reflections on Public Administration* (1947). The APSA recognized his contributions to the field by creating an annual lectureship in his name at the annual meeting, designed to recognize a "lifetime of exemplary scholarship in the joint tradition of political science and public administration." Ford MacGregor (1909–34) continued the labors of Sparling with the Wisconsin League of Municipalities, and worked extensively on state tax policy. Walter Sharp (1924–40) published in 1931 an influential work on bureaucracy in France, *The French Civil Service: Bureaucracy in Transition.*

The Rise of Public Policy Studies

The second half of the 20th century featured growth in the number of faculty doing work on public policy issues, while the significant increase in the total size of the department caused the percentage of public administration faculty to decrease. As a major figure in this transition, Clara Penniman played a key leadership role in both public administration and public policy studies. In addition to her crucial role in the launching of the CPPA, she was a leading scholar in the field of tax administration and policy, while assuring much of the graduate instruction in public administration. Her best-known books were *State Income Tax Administration* (with Walter Heller, 1959) and *State Income Taxation* (1980).

In the 1950s and 1960s, the Institute of Governmental Affairs, a component of University Extension, then had a close tie with the department; created in

1948, in the early postwar period the institute served as the primary extramural agency of the university in this field. Its longtime director, James Donoghue, also a member of the department faculty, for many years contributed important sections to the biennial *State of Wisconsin Blue Book*. The *Blue Book* is the basic working document and reference source for state government.

Beginning in the 1960s, a growing number of department faculty contributed to public policy studies: Dresang, Peter Eisinger, William Gormley, Wilson, and Witte, among others. Charles O. Jones, a top Americanist, published various works on public policy issues, including *Clean Air: The Policies and Politics of Pollution Control (*1975) and *An Introduction to the Study of Public Policy* (1984), long one of the core texts in the field.

While policy studies has expanded, several faculty joined Penniman in maintaining research and instruction in public administration. Faculty such as Ira Sharkansky, Dennis Dresang, Matthew Holden, and Peter Eisinger produced significant works in the field. Sharkansky, during his years on the department roster, was a remarkably prolific scholar, publishing more than a dozen books. In a 1983 volume surveying the state of the discipline edited by Ada Finifter, Sharkansky was the only department member listed among the top twenty most-influential political scientists during the 1970s, as measured by the number of journal citations. Among his books in the policy field were *The Politics and Taxing and Spending* (1969), *Policy Analysis in Political Science* (1970), *Public Administration: Policy-Making in Government Agencies* (multiple editions), and *The Maligned States: Policy Accomplishments, Problems and Opportunities* (second edition 1978). From 1975 on, Sharkansky was shared with the Hebrew University of Jerusalem, to which he increasingly shifted his primary affiliation, resigning from the department in 1985. Holden served on Wisconsin's Public Service Commission (1975–77), then left the university in 1977 to take a presidential appointment to the Federal Energy Regulatory Commission (1977–81).

Wisconsin public administration scholars have included experts on state and local politics, as well as governmental reform. Eisinger (1969–97), a leading specialist on urban government and politics, published widely on issues of race and ethnicity in city governments. Another influential Eisinger contribution was *The Rise of the Entrepreneurial State: State and Local Economic Development Policy in the United States* (1988). Dresang has also studied state and local administration, and is a specialist on federal and state civil service reform; he is the coauthor of *Politics and Policy in American States and Communities*, now in its third edition. Donald Kettl, a department member from 1990 to 2004, is a National Academy of Public Administration fellow; among his many publications are *The Transformation of Governance: Public Administration for the 21st Century* (2002) and *The Global Public Management Revolution: A Report on the Transformation of Governance* (2000).

An International Perspective

The postwar department roster has included a number of scholars with an international or comparative focus. James McCamy, a distinguished faculty member from 1947 to 1971, wrote extensively on public administration in international affairs. His seminal 1947 volume, *The Administration of American Foreign Affairs,* was a landmark contribution. Department faculty have contributed important public administration monographs on Asia and Africa. Henry Hart, an expert in South Asian politics as well as public administration and regional planning, published *New India's Rivers (*1956) and *Administrative Aspects of River Valley Development (*1961). In 1979, James Bjorkman (both a public administration and public policy scholar) wrote *Politics of Administrative Alienation in India's Rural Development Programs.* In 1975, Dresang published a book titled *The Zambian Civil Service: Entrepreneurialism and Development Administration.* Presently, Wilson has continued this internationalist tradition with his editorship of the distinguished journal *Governance,* and his 1995 book coauthored with Colin Campbell titled *The End of Whitehall: Death of a Paradigm?* Manion (2000–) has authored an important study of bureaucratic corruption in China, *Corruption by Design: Building Clean Government in Mainland China* (2004).

Center for the Study of Public Policy and Administration

By the 1960s, across the country, state governments were expanding and professionalizing, mirroring a process also evident at the federal and urban level. A growing need was felt for skilled young professionals with advanced training in public policy and administration. At the time, the Wisconsin Department of Administration keenly felt the difficulty in recruiting top budget analysts.[3]

Newly elected Governor Warren Knowles in 1965 was swiftly convinced of the urgency of this need. At a meeting of regional governors just after his election, he was taken to task by the Governor of Minnesota for Wisconsin recruitment of the best graduates of the University of Minnesota school of public administration (now the Humphrey School) with salaries Minnesota could not match; Knowles was challenged to create his own graduate training institute. According to Wayne McGown, then budget director at the Department of Administration, he was charged by the governor with exploring this possibility. A long dormant provision in the university statutes, dating from 1917,[4] was discovered, mandating such a program. On this basis, a last-minute provision for a public administration training institute was inserted into the 1965–67 budget. Although the university had not requested such an item, University President Fred Harrington readily agreed to the initiative, and it was duly adopted with the budget. Since provision for what became the CPPA was an unanticipated gift from above, no planning for the creation of such an institute had taken place. A committee led by Penniman and Donoghue was established to develop a proposal. After extensive discussions with state government officials, campus administration, and concerned departments, and surveying graduate training programs for public servants elsewhere, the committee submitted its report on 15 December 1966, recommending establishment of what was to become the CPPA, and the development of an M.A. program to be administered by the center.[5]

The center was duly established in 1967, with Penniman as its first director. The first urgent task was to develop a proposal for an M.A. degree, which required the approval of the Graduate School Executive Committee, the UW Board of Regents, and the former Coordinating Committee for Higher Education (CCHE). Initially, the 30-credit program (later raised to 36 credits) envisaged an interdisciplinary curriculum, flexibly accommodating a range of specialized student interests; however, for some time the bulk of the courses were in political science.[6] The proposal won Graduate School approval in December 1967, and was endorsed by the board of regents in February 1968. The first class of 38 students entered the program in fall 1968, with the initial degrees awarded during the 1970–71 academic year.

The CPPA soon became a budgetary unit, and a growing number of faculty held joint appointments. The center's location in North Hall in its early years helped to foster a close working relationship. At many other institutions, such as the University of Illinois, the University of Michigan, and the University of Minnesota, public administration and policy scholars split completely in separate schools and institutes, wholly separate from political science departments. This led to a divorce of the academic study of public administration and public policy from political science, a divorce that never took place at Wisconsin. Penniman remained director until 1974; after an interlude of leadership by William Young, Carlisle Runge, of urban and regional planning and the Law School, headed the program till 1981. At that time, CPPA direction returned to political science in 1981, as Dresang assumed leadership, which he retained until 1987.

The CPPA prospered and expanded. By 1980, almost a hundred students were enrolled. The 1983 program review by an L&S committee was on the whole positive, although the report noted that "the CPPA incurs some disadvantage from the frequent perception that it is merely an adjunct of the Department of Political Science."[7] However, this was already beginning to change, since at that juncture, the CPPA received a large injection of new resources, simultaneous with its renaming as the La Follette Institute (later School) in 1983.

The initiative to rename the center originated with Penniman in 1971. Robert La Follette had been a generous friend of the university as governor from 1901–05, at a moment of great expansion and transformation, yet his important contribution was nowhere memorialized on campus. Penniman secured approval from the campus administration and La Follette family, but the initiative was vetoed by then UW System Vice President Donald Percy, who felt the political climate in the state and the orientation of the Board of Regents was not propitious for such recognition of a giant of the progressive movement. The idea remained dormant for a decade, until Representative Tom Harnisch (D-Neilsville), at the behest of CPPA Director Runge, proposed a budget amendment providing for a La Follette Institute at Madison, with a $250,000 budget line.[8] Governor Lee Dreyfus used his line item veto to delete "Madison" from the budget bill, and thus the La Follette initiative at first reverted to the University of Wisconsin System. System established a committee chaired by Madison economics professor Robert Lampman, which recommended locating the institute at Madison.[9] Assembly Speaker Tom Loftus[10] in the 1983–85 budget ensured that the La Follette Institute was endorsed for Madison, with a million-dollar line item allocation. Some in campus administration were displeased by the specific La Follette line item, in keeping with a long-standing allergy to legislative earmarks. However, the new resources and name change were a boon for La Follette. The 1983 L&S review committee report was prophetic in its conclusion: The creation of the La Follette Institute is a historic turning point for the CPPA. The additional resources in prospect, and the greater sparkle and luminescence derivative from its new name, provide a remarkable opportunity for building upon its accomplishments, and transcending some of its limitations.[11]

A parallel development to the launching of the CPPA was the creation of the Center for Development (CD) at the initiative of William Young. Encouraged by the Ford Foundation to explore ways of providing advanced public policy and administration training for civil servants from developing areas, he had widely canvassed the needs and program options both here and overseas. His study convinced him that such a program had to be differentiated from American public administration, to take account of the specific circumstances of development administration. As one example, less-developed countries had no incentive to economize on personnel; the Thai budget bureau employs 1,000, as compared to 500 for the American Bureau of the Budget. The CD was established in 1967, benefiting from an $800,000 grant from the Ford Foundation and later supplemented by an additional $300,000. Although the CD program was always distinct from the CPPA, the center made use of the CPPA M.A. degree; the requirements were sufficiently flexible to be serviceable for the CD. The primary clientele for the center were third world public servants, especially from Southeast Asia. Former Ford Foundation executive George Gant, with long career experience, held a visiting professorship in the department for more than a decade. The curriculum was built mainly around political science and economics. By 1983, the CD had admitted 381 students from 51 countries, of whom a very high proportion had completed their degrees.[12]

The La Follette School of Public Affairs

The renamed CPPA with substantially enhanced resources entered a phase of expansion. A further impetus was provided by Chancellor Donna Shalala (1988–93), a strong supporter of its policy purposes and expansion of its public outreach and research. Among other changes facilitated by added resources was greater participation from policy-oriented economics faculty, two of whom (Robert Haveman and Donald Nichols) subsequently became directors. The La Follette Institute also acquired its own building, near the old observatory. In 2000, the La Follette Institute became the La Follette School of Public Affairs and added a new Master of International Public Affairs degree, succeeding the now-dissolved Center for Development.

The La Follette School pursued the same strategy as many public policy programs. It built on its traditional foundation of public administration and policy, but expanded its faculty to include contributions from a wide range of other social sciences. Thus, La Follette became more of a multidisciplinary center, with political science being one—important, but only one—discipline contributing to its work.

La Follette has escaped the strong pressures for separation from political science that have afflicted many other public policy schools. In part, this is because of the university's strong traditions for multidisciplinary research, which made it comparatively easy for faculty to continue their work in their home departments while collaborating in professional education at La Follette. In part, this is because La Follette itself has had an unusually strong commitment to balance among disciplines contributing to its work, so it was able to resist the temptation for disciplinary dominance that tilted other public policy schools in a different direction. The department has kept a strong association with the La Follette School. Currently, seven political science faculty are affiliated with La Follette. In addition to Penniman and Dresang, Eisinger, Kettl, and Witte have all served as CPPA or La Follette directors.

Strong research and first-class graduate student training has propelled La Follette to the top tier of public policy and administration graduate programs. Students can select from many field specialties, including public management and administration, social and poverty policy, city management and urban policy, and public finance and budgeting. In a 1982 ranking by the National Association of Schools of Public Affairs and Administration (NASPAA), the CPPA was ranked 19th by program administrators and 24th by practitioners (of 50 rated). In its subsequent site visit, the NASPAA team concluded that the center was stronger than they had anticipated. Although the NASPAA has done no further rankings, the comparative standing of La Follette has almost certainly improved since the 1982 survey, conducted at a time which was still very early in the life of the institute.[13]

Recent research associated with La Follette faculty has covered a wide range of issues: welfare reform, economic development, environment. Gormley (1980–91) examined a range of policy issues while at Wisconsin; his major books at the time included *The Politics of Public Utility Regulation* (1983) and *Taming the Bureaucracy: Muscles, Prayers, and Other Strategies* (1989). Witte served as the state evaluator of the Milwaukee Parental Choice (Voucher) Program, which led to a 2004 book, *The Market Approach to Education in America* (for more detail, see chapter 5). He has also written extensively on industrial democracy and tax policy, including a monograph on the income tax, *The Politics and Development of the Federal Income Tax* (1985). David Weimer (2000–), past editor of *Journal of Policy Analysis and Management*, is the coauthor (with Aidan R. Vining) of *Policy Analysis: Concepts and Practice*, a popular public policy text now in its fourth edition.

Service to the University and the Community

Throughout the history of the department, public administration and public policy scholars have actively served the university and the public in a multitude of ways, working with many local, state, and national governmental agencies. Both Hart and Harold Stoke (1940–44) worked for the Tennessee Valley Authority in the 1930s, before joining the department. Edwin Witte, an economist with a joint appointment in political science, was the major drafter of the Social Security Act (see chapter 3). McCamy served in the United States government in many capacities, including as an assistant to the secretary of agriculture, and as chief of the world trade policy staff in the Department of Commerce (1946). William Young served as special assistant to Governor Oscar Rennebohm in 1949–50, and was deeply involved in a number of key policy issues (funding capital expenditures for state building, consolidation of school districts, streamlining state legislative budgetary review through an instructional cost formula, among others; for more detail, see chapter 4). Penniman had 10 years of state service before earning her university degree. She was frequently consulted on state income tax administration (see chapter 4), and was offered the post of director of the Department of Revenue by Governor John Reynolds in 1963, which she declined because of a prior commitment to chair the department.[14]

One might suggest that, as political science shifts toward more theoretical and mathematical research, professional schools and programs, such as the La Follette School, fill a void in policy studies and public administration, bringing "the faculty in close contact with government and business, [which] often led to research, outreach and consulting relationships."[15] An example of this public service commitment is the recent role of Kettl as chair of Wisconsin governor-appointed commissions on campaign finance reform and on state and local partnerships (see chapter 5).

Public administration and policy scholars have also served the university in administrative roles. Six have served as department chairs: Gaus (1940–42), McCamy (1948–52), William Young (1952–60), Penniman (1963–66), Eisinger (1987–90), and Dresang (1990–93, 1999–2001). Penniman chaired the University Committee and played a crucial role on the committee charged with implementation of the 1971 University of Wisconsin merger legislation. She was also a member of a number of review teams for the North Central Accreditation Commission.

A Tradition of Service

The commitment of public administration and policy faculty, as well as other Wisconsin political scientists, to public service has enriched the department, the university, and the greater community. Knowledge is not just studied or taught, but department faculty have also applied their knowledge in hopes of improving government at all levels. For many public administration and policy scholars at Wisconsin, the Wisconsin Idea, which promotes cooperation between university professors and the community, is not merely an idea and a goal but also a reality.

Notes

1. Quoted in Allen Schick, "The Trauma of Politics: Public Administration in the Sixties," in Frederick C. Mosher, ed., *American Public Administration: Past, Present, Future* (University: University of Alabama Press, 1975), 160.
2. Ray at the time was a Northwestern professor. This classic work went through numerous editions, and after the death of the original authors was continued through several more editions by William Young.
3. Interview with Wayne McGown, 8 December 2004. McGown was then budget director at the Department of Administration; later he became a special assistant to the chancellor, charged with developing the Research Park.
4. According to Clara Penniman, political scientist Charles Beard, at the time a visiting professor in the Department of History, influenced the decision to insert this mandate in the statutes; interview with Penniman, 3 February 2005.
5. The text of the Penniman-Donoghue report may be found as an appendix to the Report of the Ad Hoc Committee to Review Center for Development and Center for Public Policy and Administration submitted to the College of Letters and Science, 5 July 1983. The report is available in the Graduate School.
6. Proposal for M.A. Degree in Public Policy and Administration, 12 December 1967.
7. Report of the Ad Hoc Committee, 13.
8. Interview with Tom Harnisch, 28 February 2005. According to Harnisch, he and Runge were together on a fishing trip when the topic of the need for a major, more visible school of public policy came up. They agreed that the La Follette name would add stature to the CPPA, and that special legislative provision could provide a needed boost. Runge felt that a legislative initiative was required; he feared that the campus administration could not be persuaded to make such a request. Assembly Speaker Tom Loftus, during a budget session of the Democratic caucus, offered the opportunity for amendment proposals costing no more than $250,000; Harnisch seized the opportunity to propose the La Follette item, as well as a conservation initiative.

9. There was some push at the time to locate a La Follette Institute at the University of Wisconsin–Green Bay.
10. Loftus was a CPPA alumnus. In a 21 February 2005 e-mail, Loftus confirmed this account.
11. Report of the Ad Hoc Committee, 13.
12. Report of the Ad Hoc Committee, 19. At the time, 316 had completed their degree, 28 were still in residence, 6 were non-degree candidates, 17 withdrew or transferred to other programs, and one died in residence.
13. Report of the Ad Hoc Committee, 98.
14. Clara Penniman, Oral History interview, American Political Science Association, December 1989. Interviewed by Leon Epstein.
15. John Witte, "Wisconsin Ideas: The Continuing Role of the University in the State and Beyond," in Lyn H. Leverty and David R. Colburn (eds.), *Understanding the Role of Public Policy Centers and Institutes in Fostering University-Government Partnerships* (San Francisco: Jossey-Bass, 2000), 14.

CHAPTER 11

Public Law and Wisconsin Political Science

Joel B. Grossman

Public law is an obsolete term. It was replaced in the late 1960s, and the field is now called *law and politics* (*law and courts* in the structure of the American Political Science Association), to better reflect the great expansion of the boundaries of the enterprise. But the term *public law* reflects the origins and, for most of the 20th century, its central component as well. Indeed, in 1899–1900, nearly half the political science courses offered at Wisconsin (it was not yet formally a department) were about the law. In the 1990s, law and politics, which long had been a major field in the department's curriculum, was relegated to subfield status under the American politics umbrella. An unfortunate development, to be sure, but the now *sub*field continues to prosper. Despite being a relatively small field, it also continues to prosper nationally; Law and Courts is the second largest organized section of the APSA.

Over the years, the department has offered courses in constitutional law (at both the undergraduate and graduate levels), international law, jurisprudence, elementary law, Roman law, civil liberties, administrative law, law in society, law, politics and society, the American judicial system, criminal law and justice, race discrimination and the law, the legal profession, comparative law, and law in the Middle East. No fewer than 13 faculty members, at one time or another, beginning in 1899, taught the bread and butter constitutional law course: John Parkinson, Paul Reinsch, Arnold Hall, Robert Scott, James Grant, Llewellyn Pfankuchen, David Fellman, Joel Grossman, Stuart Scheingold, Kenneth Dolbeare, David Adamany, Donald Downs, and Howard Schweber. Hall, Fellman, William Gormley, and Downs taught administrative law. Fellman, Malcolm Feeley, and now Howard Schweber have taught civil liberties. Herbert Jacob and Joel Grossman developed a number of judicial process courses (including graduate-level courses), now taught by Herbert Kritzer; and in the 1960s, for the first time, graduate courses in public law and the Supreme Court and the Constitution were offered, first by Grossman and then (and now) by Downs. Downs also has taught a course on criminal law and justice, which may hold the enrollment record for nonfreshman courses. Kathryn Hendley developed a course on comparative legal institutions; Hawley Fogg-Davis also did so on race discrimination and the law. All told, public law courses, from 1899 to 2004, were taught by 27[1] different faculty members.

The "modern" era of public law at Wisconsin began with the arrival of David Fellman from the University of Nebraska in 1947. He took over constitutional law from Llewellyn Pfankuchen and developed new courses in civil liberties and administrative law. Fellman was a nationally acclaimed constitutional law scholar, the author of many books and articles, and during the 1950s and early 1960s, author of the annual review of constitutional law in the *American Political Science Review.*

The major expansion of the field began in the 1960s. Herbert Jacob, who was hired in 1962, developed the first judicial process course. And Joel Grossman, who arrived the next year, took over the constitutional law course and also taught other law related-courses.

Three additional hires in the mid-1960s gave Wisconsin almost certainly the largest complement of public law scholars in residence at the same time. Kenneth Dolbeare and Stuart Scheingold taught sections of constitutional law (as well as other courses in other fields); John Gardiner taught law-related courses in addition to his urban politics specialty. By the end of the decade, however, Jacob, Dolbeare, Gardiner, and Scheingold had all departed.

David Adamany taught constitutional law for several years in the 1970s. Herbert Kritzer joined the department later in the decade to teach (and continues to teach) courses on the judicial process and methodology, and most recently, the legal profession. Malcolm Feeley spent several years in the department and developed our first sophomore-level course: Law, Politics, and Society. William Gormley was hired in 1980 and taught administrative law; he left the department in 1991. Donald Downs was hired in 1986 and has taught courses in administrative law, criminal law and justice, jurisprudence, and the First Amendment. Kathryn Hendley, who teaches half-time in the Law School, has taught the undergraduate law and politics course, as well as comparative legal systems, since her arrival in the 1990s. Howard Schweber also came on board in the 1990s, and teaches constitutional law, civil liberties, and courses on the First Amendment and constitutional theory. Hawley Fogg-Davis joined the department in 1998 and teaches courses on race discrimination and the law. Tamir Moustafa joined the faculty in 2003 and is a specialist in Middle Eastern and Islamic legal systems. Wisconsin continues to be at the center of law and politics teaching and scholarship in political science.

One of the factors that contributed to the strength and reputation of Wisconsin's law and politics program has been its proximity to the University of Wisconsin Law School, and its contributions to, and interactions with, the law and society program, which in 1964 formally became the Law and Society Association (LSA). The Wisconsin Law School, by the early 1960s, was already the center of sociolegal scholarship among law schools. Led by Carl Auerbach, and mostly by Willard Hurst, it provided a model that would strongly influence political scientists (as well as legal scholars, historians, sociologists, anthropologists, and a few economists).

The Wisconsin law and society community developed rapidly. In addition to the aforementioned political scientists and law professors, it initially included Lawrence Friedman, Stewart Macaulay, and Joel Handler in the Law School; Stanley Kutler in history; Robert Alford, Harry Ball, and Jack Ladinsky in sociology; and Leonard Berkowitz in psychology. Friedman, Handler, and Ball left in the late 1960s, but David Trubek, Dirk Hartog, Marc Galanter, Steven Penrod, Howard Erlanger, and Laurie Edelman (among many others) joined the program beginning in the 1970s. Jacob, Friedman, Macaulay, Handler, Galanter, Edelman, and Erlanger all served as presidents of the LSA; Galanter, Grossman, and Kritzer were all editors of *Law & Society Review*, the leading publication in the field. Grossman and Ladinsky served as directors of what was then called the Law and Behavioral Science Program at Wisconsin. Beginning in 2000, Kritzer became the director and the program was renamed Legal Studies. It would be difficult to overestimate the importance of this continuing crucial linkage between political science and law at Wisconsin. It is worth noting that when the LSA celebrated its 25th anniversary in 1989, Madison was the chosen location.

In 1960 the public law program was anchored in traditional subjects such as constitutional law, administrative law, civil liberties, international law; and at least for the first three, in traditional law school teaching methods. That began to change in the 1960s. Herbert Jacob, and then Joel Grossman, broadened the scope of the field with courses on the judicial process. Grossman introduced the department to quantitative methods of judicial behavior research. Scheingold addressed issues of the European community, while Dolbeare and Grossman wrote about political trials and political justice. Under William Gormley, administrative law was taught more from a public administration perspective. Feeley and others focused on law in society rather than on law as an autonomous and self-contained element of governance, and on the impact of courts, and not merely their pronouncements. Grossman and Kritzer wrote and taught about dispute processing and litigation. Kritzer taught advanced quantitative methods and created a separate course on the legal profession. Downs wrote not only about free speech and the First Amendment, but also about the battered spouse syndrome, and most recently, hate speech. Hendley taught (in both the department and the law school) about the Russian legal system and comparative legal institutions; Schweber about constitutional theory; Fogg-Davis about race and law; and Moustafa about law in the Middle East. Thus the law and politics field has been substantially broadened (and continues to grow) in both substance and method.

This is reflected not only in the impressive array of courses that are offered, but also in the faculty's contributions to the discipline and sociolegal scholarship. Fellman, of course, was a dominant figure of his time. Jacob published several pathbreaking books about courts in society. Before his tragic and untimely death, he edited along with Kritzer and others a leading book on the legal systems of other major democracies. Grossman wrote about the American Bar Association and judicial selection; about political justice, dispute processing, and the role of courts; and coauthored a leading constitutional law casebook. Kritzer's research related to dispute processing continues with the publication of a book on contingency fee legal practice; he has developed a research project on Supreme Court decision-making, introducing the concept of jurisprudential regime as a vehicle for understanding how law systematically influences Supreme Court decisions. Downs's writing has expanded to address more broadly the problems of free speech and civil liberties on American college campuses. Schweber has just published a book on speech and conduct, and another on the American common law is forthcoming. Hendley published a book on legal reform in Russia, and continues to write about the Russian legal system. And Fogg-Davis published a book on the ethics of transracial adoptions. She is now researching the phenomenon of black conservatism.

One of the proudest achievements of the law and politics program has been its training of Ph.D.'s. An unofficial count reveals about 75 Ph.D.'s in public law granted between 1898 and 2004.[2] Many of these students went on to have (still have) outstanding careers; there is probably no department in the nation that has produced so many Ph.D.'s in the law and politics field. Of those who have made especially significant contributions to the discipline, one might take special note of Wallace Mendelson (professor emeritus at the University of Texas), the late Clement Vose (Wesleyan University), Donald Kommers (Notre Dame), Austin Sarat (Amherst College), Lawrence Baum (Ohio State University), Charles Epp (University of Kansas), William Farber (South Dakota), Rodney Mott (Syracuse), Bradley Canon (Kentucky), and

Christine Harrington (NYU). Two of our dissertators, Phillip Dubois and Charles Epp, won the APSA's coveted Edward Corwin Award; and Sarat has been president of LSA. Space would not permit even a summary of the publications of this very distinguished group.

Notes

1. For the record, in approximate chronological order: John Parkinson, Paul Reinsch, Arnold Hall, James Grant, Pitman Potter, Robert Scott, William Carpenter, Llewellyn Pfankuchen, David Fellman, Herbert Jacob, Joel Grossman, Stuart Scheingold, Kenneth Dolbeare, John Gardiner, David Adamany, Malcolm Feeley, Herbert Kritzer, William Gormley, Donald Downs, Kathryn Hendley, Bruce Cronin, Howard Schweber, and Hawley Fogg-Davis, and Tamir Moustafa.
2. For the record (in alphabetical order): M. Glenn Abernathy, Thomas Barth, Lawrence Baum, Larry Berkson, Doris Schostal Blaisdell, Brenda Hart Bohne, Matthew Bosworth, Lisa Bower, Irwin Bromall, Sonya Brown, Don Brown, Patrick Bruer, Kristin Bumiller, Christopher Burke, Bradley Canon, Craig Coleman, Mary Coleman, Richard Cortner, Stephen Daniels, Kevin den Dulk, Phillip Dubois, William Ebenstein, Charles Epp, William Farber, Ronald Fiscus, Evan Gerstmann, Jon Goldberg-Hiller, Milton Greenberg, Christine Harrington, Donald Jackson, William Jenkins, Kristin Kelly, Lynn Khadiagala, Donald Kommers, Robert Koulish, Jay Krishnan, Robert Wheeler Lane, Daniel Levin, Orma Linford, Henry Lufler, David Manwaring, Stephen McDougal, William McLauchlan, Lettie McSpadden (Wenner), Ernest Means, Wallace Mendelson, Neal Milner, Stephen Mitchell, Rodney Mott, Samuel Nelson, Lisa Nelson, Paul Passavant, J. Mitchell Pickerill, Richard Randall, Pamela Hopkinson Rice (Rendeiro), Mark Richards, Austin Sarat, Allan Saunders, Thomas Schmeling, Harold Sprout, John Stanga, Robert Stover, Martin Sweet, H. Rupert Theobald, Clement Vose, Helen Marshall Carter Wanke, Marilyn Whisler, and Stephen Zorn.

CHAPTER 12

Behavioral Political Science at Wisconsin

Jack Dennis

Sometime around the mid-1950s, more than a quarter century after the emergence of "the Chicago School" of behavioral political science, the Department of Political Science began to get serious about moving with the times. In the "Report of the Committee on the Future" (of the department), dated 24 February 1956, is this revealing statement (under Section B, "Politics"):

> Certainly this field is now well covered for the participation of students in political parties and for the study of Congress as a social institution, both of these having been mentioned as important matters in the field. It is also well covered for training in survey research method. We are inadequate, however, in the area of statistical-psychological-'behavioral' research and teaching in Political Science. This type of analysis of political behavior was mentioned as one of the trends in this field.

The "area of statistical-psychological-'behavioral' research and teaching" is the subject of this essay. I shall try to ask, in fairly compact fashion, to what extent and in which respects has the department embraced the need to emphasize areas of statistical/psychological/behavioral research and teaching since the mid-1950s.

Before I begin that task I should note, however, that at least one now long-forgotten member of the Wisconsin department, Arnold Hall, had been representative of the "behavioral movement" in political science during the seminal period of the nineteen-teens and early twenties. Hall, who came to Madison in 1910 with a degree from Chicago, had worked with the founder of the Chicago School—Charles E. Merriam—and thus had embraced the behavioralist approach. To quote Crawford Young, whose departmental history research team unearthed the information on Professor Hall (see chapter 3): "He had worked with Charles Merriam at Chicago, and evidently shared the perspectives of his mentor in calling for a more scientific study of politics." Hall was, for example, the primary organizer of a series of three congresses in 1923, 1924, and 1925, bearing the name "National Conference on the Science of Politics." Thus, there was a prehistory of behavioralism in the department, as constituted by Hall. But he left Madison in 1926 to become president of the University of Oregon; then in 1932 he became the director of the Institute for Government Research at the Brookings Institution.

In the 30 years that elapsed from the time of Hall's departure to the "Report of the Committee on the Future," the flame of behavioralism seems to have gone out in Madison. The "Report of the Committee on the Future" may seem to us as we look back from the vantage point of the early 21st century to be the victim of a lagged disciplinary consciousness. Nonetheless, we are able to engender some sympathy for its state of awakening and rediscovery. An argument in its favor is that the Chicago School, after a decline, had itself just begun to find renewed vigor, and a second wave of disciplinary influence, in the 1950s. Chicago was aided in this revival by a new infusion of behavioral consciousness at a few other leading graduate departments, such as Yale and Michigan, at almost the same time.

Rise of Postwar Behavioralism

David Easton at Chicago, for example, published his widely influential *The Political System: An Inquiry into the State of Political Science* in 1953. Easton offered a telling critique of the forces of historicism in political theory, which he argued had slowed political science's adoption of the modes of social scientific reasoning already current in other social disciplines by that time. Easton's critique was followed by other influential statements of such intellectual descendents of Merriam, Gosnell, and Lasswell as well as Robert Dahl at Yale and Heinz Eulau at Stanford. What these various proponents of behavioralism argued was that the customary modes of reasoning about politics—philosophical, legal/institutional, and historical—while useful for many purposes, were in themselves insufficient. What was needed were some additional weapons of political analysis akin to what was being used by most other social science disciplines by the mid-1950s.

These new intellectual weapons included partisan and ideological neutrality in the conduct of political research—and thus an ability to reach conclusions that do not necessarily conform to the investigator's value, partisan or ideological premises. Second, the kind of theory sought was that of giving general explanatory accounts, rather than merely descriptions of existing states of affairs—which had become characteristic of much legal and institutional analysis of that era. Third, one needed to go beyond the tendency of the kind of historical analysis that predominated at that time, which tended to be idiosyncratic, particularistic, and impressionistic rather than nomothetic, universalistic, and based on valid statistical generalizations from more adequate samples of the phenomena in question.

Ultimately, the behavioral perspective devalued the usual intellectual practices of earlier political scientists, because it accorded them only preliminary and contextual value—in recognizing problems or in giving good definitions and descriptions of political phenomena, but not in fulfilling our ultimate need to provide verifiable and replicable causal accounts of politics and government. Some of these behavioralist critics went so far as to argue that of the existing social disciplines, political science had seemed least willing or able to upgrade its traditional modes of political reasoning that had been handed down by an endless series of political observers, beginning in the West with the pre-Socratics. Thus, by the 1950s, the new wave of behavioralists regarded the discipline of political science as much akin to an intellectual garbage dump, and thus much in need of something like a Superfund effort to clean it all up.

We could defend the 1950s Wisconsin department from some of these charges, however, on several grounds. Almost none of the other top-ten Ph.D.-producing departments at that time had moved to embrace the requisite intellectual housecleaning. Given that most tenured faculty at these institutions were part of the older intellectual traditions, it is not surprising that they successfully resisted this upstart approach except in a few places such as Yale and Michigan, and in some part, Wisconsin. The department at Wisconsin was noteworthy in that era because it lacked any distinctive emphasis on, or commitment to, political philosophy per se. Thus, it was not particularly guilty of undue historicism in the branch of the discipline that Easton had critiqued. Every faculty member was deemed worthy to teach courses on political philosophy, rather than having present a recalcitrant band of theorists who could resist any attempt to change the intellectual direction of political scholarship. And even the historically and legally/institutionally descriptive scholars who were on the scene tended to a kind of midwestern eclecticism and tolerance for those whose intellectual origins and traditions were fundamentally different from their own. Thus, by the late 1950s, the department began (again), without undue internal friction, to take a few positive steps to align itself with the new behavioral emphasis in the study of politics that had originated at Chicago some 30 years previously.

The (Re)Birth of Wisconsin Behavioralism

When I arrived here in 1963 with a Ph.D. from Chicago, and as a known collaborator with David Easton and his statistically oriented co-conspirators such as Duncan McRae, the department had already made some recent efforts to move itself toward more behavioral research. Leon Epstein, an earlier product of Chicago than myself, became a chief advocate for modernization in the study of politics in the department. Not only was he among the first here to apply statistical methods (to aggregate election and party data), but he was also instrumental in hiring and encouraging a few younger behavioral scholars such as Harry Scoble and Lewis Froman. Before that, most of the statistical and survey competence that our students gained had to come from attending courses in other departments, such as the survey methods course given by Burton Fisher in sociology. Both Scoble and Froman were able to introduce some new subject matter and approaches from a behavioral perspective. But they were relative "short-termers," and both moved on (ultimately) to the warmer clime of California, where they finished out their careers (UCLA and UC–Irvine, respectively). Other early supporters of a turn to a more behavioral orientation included Ralph Huitt and Henry Hart.

The important point is that Epstein and a few others in the early 1960s department did not give up, but persisted by bringing in some fresh recruits, especially from Yale—which had emerged by that time as an equally important source of behavioral graduate training in political science to that of Chicago. In particular, Herbert Jacob and Rufus Browning arrived on the scene; and they began to make an immediate impact on this "field." Jacob looked closely at the behavioral aspects of the judicial system, including the ordinary person's experience with it. Browning began his work with Lasswell's power-seeker personality analysis and applied it to local government officials and activists. While neither of them made their main career here—indeed, Jacob went from here to Northwestern and Browning to California State at San Francisco—both contributed some significant momentum here, and each had a distinguished career. Most significantly, Jacob and Browning, together with Epstein and a few others already here—and then aided and abetted by some 1963–64 newcomers like myself and Austin Ranney—were able to get more official departmental status for the behavioral approach. In particular, a new graduate course devoted to a general introduction to behavioral techniques of observation and analysis came into being—Political Science 817—as a requirement for all new graduate students.

What Political Science 817 was designed to do was to give all of our graduate students of that era—mid-1960s to early 1970s—an understanding of what political facts consisted of. Thus, whatever these students ended up doing in their own subsequent research, they would have at least become minimally acquainted with social science methods and approaches, as the latter had developed by that time. This familiarization meant taking more seriously the question of how political facts and generalizations are produced, which included some close attention to research design for hypothesis testing, alternative ways of operationalizing variables, alternative plans of statistical analyses, and new modes and standards of processing and interpreting political data. The latter focused especially on statistical methods as they had evolved in psychological, sociological, and econometric research by that time. The increasingly available methods of computerization—software systems, hardware configurations, data storage and retrieval, and the like—also become strong points of emphasis.

By the standards of 21st-century political methodology and substantive causal theories of politics and government, these early efforts seem outmoded and primitive. Yet, in their time, they had high utility, in that future political science professionals were introduced to the possibilities for their own conduct of more meaningful research. We should emphasize, however, that to be able to generalize reliably beyond the particular circumstances of government and politics that we see before us requires a more expensive, wide-ranging, and technologically demanding process of observation and interpretation than had been used in the seat-of-the-pants impressionism of the pre-behavioral era. As we began to take greater cognizance of the developing world of social science theories and methods from a variety of disciplines, we needed also to develop new means for political observation for which the bar had been raised significantly.

One major dimension of this increasing professionalism was the establishment, maintenance, and continuous upgrading of a behavioral political-science infrastructure. A central requirement for the Wisconsin department was bringing on board and supporting a core faculty who could serve as personal embodiments and models for this new brand of political research.

But perhaps even more basic in supporting this effort, and thus engendering a faculty who could serve as models for students and provide the necessary behavioral training, were some other expansions of infrastructure. What were the latter? Briefly, these consisted of greater financial support for faculty research by the university (especially via Graduate School Research Committee allocations); joint efforts with other social science departments to develop interdisciplinary facilities such as the Social Systems Research Institute, the Institute for the Study of Poverty, the La Follette Institute (now School), and the Data and Program Library Service (our local social science data archive); and both centralized and more localized computer centers and related services.

It also meant establishing closer connections with organizations conducting collaborative political science research of a behavioral type elsewhere, such as with the National Election Studies, centered at the Institute for Social Research at the University of Michigan. The earlier intellectual approaches, such as philosophical speculation and moralizing, legal reasoning, the conduct of historical case studies, cross-cultural and linguistic immersion studies, and the like, all had required substantial personal efforts by individual scholars. What the new social science often required was more of an interdisciplinary team effort, which demanded substantially greater organizational and financial resources. Such activities as the taking of national probability sample surveys, continuing series of interventionist experiments, or broad computer-based content analyses, for example, all necessitate significant outlays of foundation and government agency capital if they are to be successful. The economics of behavioralism entails that we get technological advances when we are able to invest the necessary technologically focused venture capital.

A major task of the new behavioral political-science core faculty then became to make these connections and to help bring to bear greater collective efforts, organization, and funding. These collective activities thus go well beyond the kind of personal attention and effort usually needed by the individual-scholar-based entrepreneurship of the traditional approaches (such as historical analysis, legal reasoning, institutional description, and philosophical speculation). For me personally this meant, as it did for my other behavioral colleagues, a recurrent yearly need to apply for substantial research grants from both private foundations and government agencies such as the National Science Foundation. Some of these applications were focused on competitions based on obtaining slices of interview time in ongoing national surveys, such as the National Election Studies (NES). Over the years, Virginia Sapiro and I, together with various younger, more recent (1990s and 2000s) colleagues such as Charles Franklin, Diana Mutz, Wendy Rahn, Katherine Cramer Walsh, and Kenneth Goldstein, all became part of this ongoing effort to obtain or make use of substantial, externally derived, and collectively oriented social science funding, which we sought individually, in connection with NES, or through other broad-based studies. To do this kind of work therefore required greater entrepreneurial effort than had usually been the case in earlier decades.

Behavioralists such as myself have also needed to develop and maintain other infrastructural resources that sustain a social scientific approach to the study of politics. One important feature of such an effort has been to join with other social scientists at Wisconsin and other institutions to establish machine-readable (computer-based, Internet-accessible) social science data archives. Such data banks became important to the cumulative gathering, storage, and retrieval of relatively expensive time-series and other large-scale surveys. They also include evidence of other types, especially contextual data that pertain to the economic, sociological, cultural, or other conditions surrounding political phenomena. Locally, this meant the establishment in the mid-1960s of the Social Science Data and Program Library, initially as part of the Social Systems Research Institute and later connected with the Data and Computation Center. More broadly, the social science data archive movement meant establishment of national archive consortia such as the Inter-University Consortium of Social Research or the Roper Center archive, in which political scientists such as those at Wisconsin, Michigan, and other Big Ten universities took an especially active role.

Another important feature of this effort was to develop institutional and in-house computing facilities that could handle large databases and apply an increasingly sophisticated set of statistical algorithms to the analyses of these data resources. At first, in the 1960s and 1970s, these were provided at UW by a highly centralized computer facility (Madison Area Computer Center). But gradually, with the improvements in personal computers, workstations, and more locally focused servers and networks, this capability improved enormously by the 1980s. We even obtained an intradepartmental computing capacity that far exceeded what had been available to us in the 1960s via the central facility, yet this was a limited capacity forerunner of the super-computers in existence today.

Another important local resource, unique among leading departments of political science of my era, was the availability of Graduate School Research Committee funds. These mainly Wisconsin Alumni Research Foundation (WARF)-originated funds were administered by all-university faculty committees that could, on a competitive basis, sponsor faculty research. The latter included the pilot projects that often proved crucial in obtaining subsequent, more substantial external funds from private foundations and government agencies such as NSF or NIH. The availability of these university-controlled funds to support social scientific endeavors of the political science behavioralists, as well as more traditional forms of political research during the past 50 years, gave us a competitive advantage, relative to most of our peer institutions and political science colleagues in other departments around the country.

Practitioners of Behavioral Research during the Second Half of Our Centenary

In his very useful chapter, Charles Jones refers to the political behavior field in terms of its role in the department's study of American politics. He focuses special attention on the "long termers" among the faculty in this field, with an implicit contrast to those who were here for shorter terms, but who may also have made significant contributions to teaching, research, and developing the requisite infrastructure. I have already referred to those such as Hall, Epstein, Scoble, Froman, Jacob, and Browning who had already been making an impact on establishing a viable behavioral offering before my cohort arrived on the scene in the early 1960s. Jones names Virginia Sapiro, Richard Merelman, Murray Edelman, and myself as the "long termers" of this subfield. There is a sense in which this characterization by Jones is true. All of the above continued over a fairly long span to offer courses in what, substantively, are courses in political behavior. Edelman taught, for example, "political communication," as did Merelman. Merelman also offered "political socialization" from time to time and other, especially political sociology, courses on how people behave as political animals. But unlike Sapiro and myself, who have remained more committed to the application of social science methodology and theories to these studies, Edelman was for the most part hostile to the behavioral movement and its methods, while Merelman seemed at best ambivalent and lukewarm about this approach, especially toward any exclusive reliance upon purely quantitatively-arrived-at generalizations. Thus, what counts here as behavioral is not entirely without ambiguity. I tend to interpret this matter a bit differently from Jones, however, as being both a substantive interest and an epistemological stance that includes a strong emphasis upon quantitatively based generalization.

We have also had across the decades a number of highly talented "shorter-termers" among the smallish number of behavioral political scientists in the department. Jones mentions in particular Wendy Rahn and Diana Mutz, who were present during the years when he had occupied our endowed Hawkins Chair from 1988 to 1997 with such distinction. Rahn and Mutz, together with the few older members of the department with a behavioral orientation such as

John Witte, were able to establish a more substantial offering of this type by the early 1990s than we had ever had before. This robustness was greatly aided by some new behaviorally oriented additions such as Kenneth Mayer, David Canon, and John Coleman in the American politics area. But before that perhaps most robust period of behavioral orientation in the department, there had been a fair number of notable "short-termers" who had contributed substantially to this emphasis. Most of these either did not attain tenure or were drawn away by other institutions and agencies that presented more attractive offers for their services. Notable among the latter who were here in the late 1960s and early 1970s were Charles Cnudde, Donald McCrone, and Aage Clausen. While Clausen dealt with a diverse set of subjects, such as congressional voting behavior and comparative political behavior, the three became very important participants in the core behavior offerings, on the side of both methods and substance.

Shortly thereafter, we hired Herbert Kritzer, who became the mainstay of the methods subfield, as well as picking up most of the burden in judicial behavior studies that had been put down earlier by Herbert Jacob. (Jacob did come back briefly to occupy the Hawkins Chair in the mid 1980s.) A few others such as Richard Li, Benjamin Page, and Raisa Deber also added, if more briefly, to the methods or other behavioral offerings in the intervening years. Kenneth Meier, during his four years as a public policy specialist here in the 1980s, also helped greatly to keep this emphasis alive. More recently, short-termers such as William Howell have added some input to a social science emphasis, but more on the theory than on the methods side. But it was Kritzer, later joined by Charles Franklin, who gave us the necessary and respectable offering in methods.

What has also contributed greatly to the continuity of this field and approach in the department has been a relatively hardy band of "fellow travelers" and clandestine supporters whose emphasis was primarily a subject matter one, rather than a behavioral approach or methods orientation per se. I am not able now to reproduce accurately just how enthusiastic about behavioralism were various members of the legions of political scientists who have been on the faculty over the nearly four decades that I was around. But I remember that from the beginning of my service here that as a group, the most enthusiastic about beefing up our behavioral emphasis were students of American politics and government.

In the early days the leaders of this support group included especially Leon Epstein, Bernard Cohen, and Austin Ranney. These were outstanding scholars (and administrators) who occasionally used quantitative methods in their own research, and who were open to more social-scientific inquiries in general. Later additions to this core group in the 1970s were people like Barbara Hinckley and Ira Sharkansky, both of whom went on to distinguished careers elsewhere. A great variety of others in the American politics and related areas were occasionally critical to keeping this offering at a respectable level—people like Peter Eisinger, Dennis Dresang, Joel Grossman, Crawford Young, Clara Penniman, and others who were, at critical moments, in key administrative positions, especially within the department, in L&S or in the Graduate School.

A few non-American-politics specialists were also highly instrumental in supporting a behavioral emphasis in the department—e.g., Fred Hayward, Susan Pharr, Graham Wilson, and Leon Lindberg in comparative and international politics, and Booth Fowler in political theory. More recent recruits such as David Weimer, Melanie Manion, and Byron Shafer have also helped to keep these traditions alive, despite their main disciplinary efforts being more institutional, policy, or comparative rather than behavioral per se.

I would argue that over the decades of my service that the main opposition to expanding the behavioral offering in the department has come from those who take more traditional approaches to the study of politics, especially some of the comparativists and theorists. Comparativists are often trained more in the language, history, and culture of particular areas of the world than in the methods of modern social science. Those whose specializations were the geographic areas where the kinds of data needed to make social scientific observations and generalizations are least likely to be present (or even very hazardous to one's health to seek) were usually the least enthusiastic about this approach to the study of politics. Equally, some of the political theorists here have been eager to protect their domain of scholarship against what they have often interpreted as the inroads of "scientism" into the study of politics, which they perceived as essentially the realm of moral concerns. Many of the theorists at Wisconsin have continued to teach political philosophy as a series of historically based intellectual developments, and they react negatively to the notion that such historicism draws our attention away from developing a systematic social scientific account of the political realm of human behavior.

Thus, we have run the gamut from those, such as American politics specialists—who for the most part have tended to support this approach, its theories, its substantive interests, and its methods—to some of those in comparative politics or political philosophy who have tended to see the whole enterprise of behavioral political science as somewhat threatening to their favorite forms of intellectual endeavor and discourse.

Contributions of the Behavioralists

It is always difficult to measure the degree of success of something as diffuse as an intellectual emphasis that stretches over many decades and encompasses the activities of hundreds if not thousands of faculty members, teaching and project assistants, other graduate students, undergraduates, and even professional staff in the department. The products of this effort might include a set of discrete courses, informal learning interactions, research projects, publications, presentations at professional conferences, releases to the mass media, outreach activities, and the formation of allegiances, and collaborations with others, both in other departments and in other institutions, and in internal infrastructure-building efforts. We have already made reference to some of the latter.

On the side of course offerings, the contribution has been fairly diverse, if never as broad as that of the department's emphasis on American politics or other diffuse fields. In terms of courses given in this area with some frequency, one would include especially the offerings in political psychology, political sociology, and political communication. At the beginning levels, we have since the early 1990s frequently provided an introductory course to undergraduates in political psychology, and an intensive writing course in the social psychology of democracy. More intermediate undergraduate-level course offerings have included the study of political elites (political leadership), elections and voting behavior, political communication, political socialization, and public opinion. At the graduate level, we have provided a wide variety of seminars and core (field) courses such as mass political behavior, electoral behavior (both American and comparative), political socialization, political sociology, political psychology, and political communication—on the substantive side. On the methods and statistics side, we have offered not simply the basic course (817) on the methodology of political science, but also a series of more advanced offerings on selected software packages and other computer methods, multivariate analysis of various types, and in recent years, some attention to more qualitative analysis of political phenomena.

Where we have perhaps been a bit different from several other leading graduate programs (referenced by Jones in his chapter) is in our fairly light treatment of rational choice and related theories derived mainly from the "formal theories" of economics. This may have something to do with the fact that most of the faculty in this area have been trained more in political psychology and political sociology than in economics. There has also been perhaps a kind of midwestern, down-to-earth resistance to highly abstract, and what often have seemed as somewhat implausible, accounts of human behavior. What the economists have discovered in the past decade is that "homo economus" is in fact more complicated than the simplifying assumptions of classical economics would lead us to believe. Thus, as politicians', activists', or voters' assumed maximizing behavior turns out to be more complex when conducted in a group-centered and media-penetrated context than rational-choice theory has assumed, we have turned more and more to the insights of other social disciplines such as social psychology, political sociology, or cultural anthropology for causal hypotheses. And these have usually seemed to have had more empirical "cash value." But even the economists, under the pressure of the new "behavioral economics," are increasingly moving in the same direction. Thus, our weakness in failing to represent adequately the rational-choice alternative may turn out to be not so fatal after all.

In terms of observational approaches, probably 90 percent of what we have done over the past 50 years, collectively, has depended upon some variant of survey research. A few of us (Dennis, Sapiro, Rahn, and Mutz) have tried (with modest success) to conduct controlled experiments, especially as a supplement to our usual survey methods. While these experiments have proved enlightening, they are nonetheless of a higher order of difficulty than the usual political survey, given that we must be in a position to intervene, if modestly, in the lives of potential political actors. There is relatively little about real-world politics that can be successfully contained, and thus controlled, within a purely laboratory-centered situation. The politicians are, however, constantly conducting uncontrolled experiments of various kinds, but with few exceptions, such policy manipulations are from a social science perspective primitively conceived and poorly documented; thus they yield relatively little useful social scientific information. This usual process of real-world experimentation does, of course, allow those in charge of initiating such social experiments never to have to take the rap for them when they go wrong! While there are probably many specific contexts in which political scientists might conduct more experimental work, such as those increasingly embedded in public opinion and electoral surveys, or in focus-group-centered political communication studies, the future of such efforts is still open to considerable debate. While the UW political science department has mounted a few efforts along these lines, experimentation, like rational-choice theory, has remained a muted, latent, or occasional theme in what we have defined as our main task.

Another marked feature of what behavioralists have typically done or not done here is contained in the pattern of conference paper presentation and publication. Unlike most of the department (by this I mean the vast majority of our faculty who have remained non- or anti-behavioralist in training, persuasion, or action over the past 50 years), the behavioralists have to a large extent resisted the main departmental tendency to be mostly book publishers, rather than frequent professional conference research paper presenters and thus largely professional journal publishers. Measured by the number of books published, the department has always ranked high (see the Jones chapter); but it has been somewhat lower on professional journal publications relative to other leading departments. It is probably the hardy, small band of behavioralists who have done most over these decades to keep the department from falling even further in the ranks of those who publish mainly in professional journals, and in the form of chapters of "readers" that put together various series of conference papers. Our more social scientifically oriented colleagues have usually taken the view, at least implicitly, that book publishing may be becoming, to some important degree, ever less professionally significant. What follows is that, as a discipline, we will gradually become, in the 21st century, more like the natural sciences. We may gradually come to confine ourselves to providing relatively brief notices in the discipline's leading journals—especially, as the latter become more purely electronic and Internet-centered. With such a new method of reporting results, it is no longer the *length* of the research report that becomes important. This has been recognized increasingly by the behavioral contingent during my years here. Indeed, we may all come to the point clearly recognized by one of my highly published friends and field-specific colleagues at Stanford University, who has remarked that he puts research findings out in book form only after the referees for the leading professional journals have rejected them as articles!

Conclusion

The behavioral revolution in political science began more than 80 years ago at the University of Chicago. A new approach to the study of politics and government began to be formulated which had a number of parts. One was a stronger emphasis upon the conduct of observation of political phenomena in a manner that could be replicated, and thus allowed such observations to be confirmed or denied by empirically valid tests. This meant the increasing use of the quantitative methods of social science, especially the advances being made by that time in psychometrics, economics, and demography. There was also an attempt to borrow from, or relate to, existing social science theories, such as those from psychology—adapted very early, for example, by Harold D. Lasswell. Thus, generalization about human behavior became a more common enterprise that spanned all of the more quantitatively oriented, theory-driven, cumulative, science-oriented social disciplines. This meant giving up much of our dependence upon the usual idiographic practices to a large degree—especially, philosophical/moral speculation and historicism, case-specific legal reasoning, or particularistic institutional description that has proceeded without any theory other than the accidents of historical sequencing, and so on. Indeed, all the traditional forms of intellectual discourse that were then in vogue among students of *res publica* were being severely challenged.

In addition, the rise of social science methodology and epistemology meant some necessary capacity for distancing the observer from his or her own moral, partisan, or ideological commitments in the conduct of research. The analogy would be that of the natural scientist whose personal convictions do not of necessity serve as an impediment to finding physical effects that are novel, surprising, or serendipitous. Because the phenomena of society are more likely to be charged with human emotion, prior political commitments, and desired states of affairs, this task of value neutrality in the conduct of research is clearly more difficult to achieve in political science than it would be in a laboratory study of microorganisms, for example (where such microorganisms' moral commitments seem as yet unknowable). But the behavioral political scientist becomes committed to never abandoning the effort to be surprised by his or her findings—however his or her questions of research may have originated, or however someone may later make use of these findings for specific political purposes.

This kind of intellectual enterprise is necessarily wider than any of the disciplinary subfields such as American, comparative, or international politics, or of political theory, since it focuses on the problem of how and what we study in general. That the department has, for organizational purposes, made the study of political behavior a subspecialty of "American politics" is symptomatic of the underlying conflicts within the discipline as a whole that have arisen from the challenge that behavioralism has represented to the more traditional forms of intellectual discourse.

The pragmatic subsuming of behavioral topics and studies under the "American politics" banner has thus been an imperfect way of accommodating behavioralists, I would argue. It is also symptomatic of the fact that the most wide-ranging series of behavioral studies of politics have been done, for the usual reasons, in this country. This emphasis has also resulted from the relatively greater numbers of numerate political scientists who study American politics relative to other fields, together with better funded, more conveniently located, safer, and more culturally compatible conditions existing for such research. But the growth of behavioral science approaches to the study of the political systems of other nations, locales, and groups of nations has also grown apace in the past few decades. As these approaches become more prominent in the 21st century, we would expect that behavior studies will no longer be specified as a subcategory of American politics, where it has been lodged during my years of service in the department.

For the committed behavioralist, the intellectual tide of increasing social science consciousness over the past century has seemed inevitably to make its mark on the political science curriculum and research. The gradual completion of the revolution that began more than 80 years ago will probably greatly increase the purview of behavioral studies as they expand beyond the confined place they had in this department during my era. Because those espousing more traditional forms of political inquiry were always in the vast majority—and thus had the votes to control faculty hiring, tenure, curriculum, and even some forms of research support—the department, until at least the 1990s, never had more than a small core of people of my hard-core persuasion. This small group was divided into those more oriented to the substantive study of political behavior and those assigned the tasks of teaching and developing political science methods of observation and analysis. But despite always being a relatively small minority, we were fortunate to have had a lot of sympathizers and occasional users from other fields, especially among the Americanist faculty. Thus, numeracy and behavioral science commitment were kept alive. Such attributes may well become more characteristic of the majority of the faculty, and thus of advanced-degree recipients in the coming century—given the success the behavioral revolution has had in the discipline more generally. The march to a perfectly social-scientific outlook and practice is not inevitable for everyone who studies the politics of the 21st century. But I foresee that behavioralism will, at some point in the not so distant future, become a considerably more robust set of intellectual orientations and concerns for those who will teach and do research in our department as the discipline and the institution evolve.

CHAPTER 13

Wisconsin Political Science in Comparative Perspective

Richard M. Merelman

Assessing Import and Impact

In this chapter I attempt to place the Department of Political Science at the University of Wisconsin–Madison within American political science. In broad strokes I assess the influence the department has had on political science. I emphasize scholarly and political influence, rather than professional or organizational influence. I render no definitive verdict on this subject. However, I will offer at least an informed perspective. No single datum, no single aspect of departmental activity, is the key to the questions I pose; indeed, each datum is incomplete and flawed. However, the totality of the material I consider compensates for the weakness of any particular datum. Put differently, I believe the whole is more than the sum of its parts. I advance my observations as simply my own interpretation—indeed, an invitation to further discussion—rather than a definitive conclusion.

Let me briefly situate this limited endeavor within intellectual history, the sociology of knowledge, and the study of political culture. I will then offer a simple conceptual framework to guide discussion: a "figure/ground/resource" model. I draw this model in part from my 2003 study, *Pluralism at Yale: The Culture of American Political Science.*

There is a relatively small literature on the intellectual history of political science (e.g., Eisenberg, 1995; Farr, Dryzek, and Leonard, 1995). There are even fewer published studies of particular political science departments or, indeed, of leading political scientists (e.g., Ware, 1998: 14–16; Karl, 1974). There is almost no systematic comparison of political science departments. The absence of a comparative intellectual history of American political science hinders my evaluation of the Wisconsin department. More important, there are conceptual limitations to intellectual history itself.

Intellectual historians typically focus upon theoretical or conceptual innovations, emergent "schools of thought," "breakthroughs," or in Kuhnian terms, "revolutions." Such research concentrates upon paradigm change, often portrayed, in Whiglike terms, as "progress," or "cumulative knowledge." For example, some writers have chronicled the behavioral revolution (Farr, 1995: 198–225). Seminal individual thinkers and their writings receive the bulk of attention. There is an implicit Hegelianism in many such works; phalanxes of ideas and theories often appear to be engaged against each other in ivory-tower battles. Some "armies"—scholars and ideas—supplant others, usually on grounds of perceived intellectual merit and explanatory power. Analysts usually diagnose influence by weighing the reaction of scholars to a particular thinker or school of thought.

A limitation of this approach is that it ignores the majority of intellectuals or academics at work at any single moment. To use the Kuhnian terminology again, intellectual history privileges scientific revolution over "normal science," i.e., the little-remarked but ubiquitous exploration of conventional ideas and theories. By definition, the great majority of academics are not innovators, imaginative theorists, "seminal" figures, or paradigm shakers. To risk analogy, no student of topology would accurately describe a mountain range by focusing only upon the highest peaks in the range and ignoring the many smaller peaks, the hills, and the valleys in the range. Why do the same in political science?

Moreover, we cannot even perceive a conceptual revolution or theoretical "breakthrough" without the presence of conventional or taken-for-granted ideas for comparison. Only by contrast with the "normal" is the "exceptional" discernible. Nor are the many scholars whose contributions promote "normal science" unimportant. To the contrary, they nourish the conceptual frameworks of most students, peers, and audiences most of the time. They also provide the necessary background against which seminal ideas stand out sharply.

The intellectual history approach also suffers from what Donald Kelley has called an "inner logic" (2002: 2), that is, a "phenomenological view which takes ideas on their own terms . . . as mental phenomena." Kelley contrasts this with "a reductionist or constructivist view which treats them [ideas] as something else—or at least as derivative of a particular cultural context" (2002: 2). Why is "inner logic" limited? To be sure, what political scientists produce is, first and foremost, ideas. These ideas need to be subjected to the tests applied to all pretenders to knowledge: coherence, comprehensiveness, parsimony, empirical validity, predictive power, explanatory persuasiveness, and so on. Nevertheless, attention to ideas solely in this form disconnects academia from culture, social structure, politics, and profession. This would be an especially grave error for political science. The study of politics is an aspect of political education, which, in turn, is part of politics itself.

Further, the Wisconsin department, like all political science departments, has become professionalized over the years. Professionalization influences departmental behavior and academic choices, even standards of scholarly merit. Finally, seminal intellectuals do not work in a vacuum. They respond not only to intellectual influences from other scholars, but also to social influences, such as departmental climate, pressures of tenure and promotion, and personal rivalries and friendships. Last, economic factors, such as available research support and publication outlets, also affect scholarship. Ignoring these contextual influences would create an incomplete picture of the generation and reception of knowledge.

The sociology of knowledge provides an alternative method for analyzing intellectuals in society. All the major classical political sociologists--Marx, Weber, Mannheim, Durkheim—investigated the connections between knowledge and social structure. More recently, Bourdieu, Foucault, Paul DiMaggio (1997: 263–87), the "strong" program in the sociology of science (e.g., Latour and Woolgar, 1986), and Randall Collins (1998) have revitalized this sociological tradition. Indeed, the concept of "epistemic community" (Miller and Fox, 2001: 668–86)—a community of policy intellectuals bound by common norms and perspectives—applies as well to a department of political science as to international organizations.

While the sociology of knowledge may be faulted for unsupported generalizations about connections between ideas and social conditions, it does offer useful guidelines for the study of our department. Let us begin by accepting Charles Camic's and Neil Gross's paraphrase of Alvin Gouldner, who argued that "support gathers behind those ideas that *resonate*, at a visceral and subconscious level, with the lived reality of the social world *as it is experienced by the intellectuals concerned*" (italics mine) (2002: 104). *Resonate*, however, is too vague a term to orient inquiry into a political science department, much less an entire discipline. It makes sense to divide resonance into two parts: *import* and *impact*.

By *import*, I refer to the relationship between the content of political science and American political culture. For example, one question we might ask is whether political science at Wisconsin supports or undermines the conventional norms and values of American political culture. By any odds, this is an important—but not the only—question about import we might address. Answering this question, I hasten to say, is not something I attempt in this chapter; nevertheless, I will suggest some possible avenues of thought. Few political scientists have distanced themselves sufficiently from their substantive scholarship to confront this question. Of those few who have, most would probably concur with Rogers Smith, who argues that political scientists have longed "to found a grand new science of politics that will make American democracy flourish" (1997: 273). I have no doubt this conclusion applies to the entire Wisconsin department; however, scholars would differ as to just what such a "new science" ought to contain. A Murray Edelman would surely offer a different answer to that question from, say, an Austin Ranney, Leon Epstein, or Leon Lindberg.

The import dimension of scholarship naturally draws attention to political ideologies versus academic "neutrality." I respect the comparative intellectual autonomy of academia (especially at Wisconsin, with its well-earned reputation of academic freedom); the conscious imposition of "scientific" (i.e., politically neutral) standards on scholarship; and the great effort of empirical political scientists—the vast majority—to present only their "findings" rather than partisan advocacy. But these qualities do not remove an ideological component from much political science research. No matter its method, topic, or intent, some portion of political science implicitly supports or criticizes the claims political authorities make. Indirectly, even the most innocuous scholarship may implicitly fortify or attack a political regime and/or its current leaders. Most research combines defense and attack in multiple variations.

Following Marx and, more recently, Althusser, some sociologists claim that academics are primarily captives of state authority, whose function it is to produce legitimating arguments for the status quo. Occasionally, a piece of empirical research supports this perspective. For example, recently Savelsberg, King, and Cleveland (2002: 327–348) demonstrated that scholarship in the field of criminology directly responds to state policy—and funding—on crime. Few would maintain a comparable view of political science. Nevertheless, Theodore Lowi and Charles Lindblom have made somewhat similar arguments. In his presidential address to the American Political Science Association in 1991, Lowi claimed, "U.S. Political Science is itself a political phenomenon and, as such, is a product of the state." For his part, Lindblom controversially argues that political science is "impaired" by a preference for social control over—rather than edification of—the masses. He characterizes as an impairment patterned reaction to "political and economic elites" who desire "hierarchy, obedience, deference, faith, inequality, and stability. Political scientists have been half-blinded to contrary or even questioning perceptions" (1997: 249).

A contrary argument is that intellectuals primarily challenge political authority. Theorists such as Mannheim and Gramsci (who foresaw working-class "organic intellectuals" opposing state ideologues) advanced such claims. Today, many neoconservatives excoriate the "tenured radicals" they suppose to have gained control of universities. They also claim that leftist elites control the media. Conservatives state that intellectuals abuse free speech to undermine American institutions. The university has become a redoubt for the engineering of major social change; scholars ridicule American political institutions, majoritarian traditions, and conventional values. For example, Alan Wolfe and Harvey Mansfield Jr. argue that, since the 1960s, academic political science has presented either willfully obscure (Wolfe in Macedo, 1997) or morally destructive (Mansfield in Macedo, 1997) attacks upon the political status quo.

One can ask the same questions about a discipline as about a political culture. Does a particular political science department's scholarship fortify existing, dominant research paradigms in a discipline, or does it challenge those paradigms? For example, a department's scholarship on Congress may conform to a dominant approach, such as a rational-choice theory of congressional committees. Or a department may pursue novel qualitative or interpretive methodologies that often challenge rational choice.

Likewise, a department's scholarship can either challenge or support conventional substantive knowledge. For example, a piece of research may provide evidence to fortify the commonly held view that social class position has less influence on American public opinion than it did during the New Deal. Or research may challenge this view, and call for a reconsideration of social class and public opinion.

Of course, neither consensus nor conventional wisdom may exist on a topic. For example, presently there is hot debate about the amount of "social capital" in the United States, as well as about the relationship of social capital to political participation. Any new piece of scholarship on social capital may fortify one of several competing positions. Such research cannot be appropriately categorized as "hegemonic" (i.e., in line with conventional wisdom) or "challenging" (i.e., opposed to conventional wisdom). An appropriate framework for the analysis of departmental scholarship needs to make room for a variety of possibilities.

Though difficult, it is easier to establish the intellectual and political import of scholarship than to measure the impact of scholarship. To make a plausible argument about import, one can rely upon the written texts themselves. By contrast, establishing impact requires evidence beyond the texts. The following questions require answers: How widely read is a scholar's work? How important do those who read the work consider it to be? Is the scholarly audience for a work actually influenced by the work? In the case of a specific political science department, the audience for scholarship is composed of students as well as researchers. What impact does a department have on its graduate students? Does the department shape the research agendas of graduates? Do other political scientists respect the members of a department? And, of course, how prolific and well-published are members of a department?

It is difficult to secure useful information to answer all these questions. But at least they pertain to specific and delimited audiences. It is more difficult to establish influence and impact beyond those in direct contact with a department, who may learn about research and teaching secondhand. To be sure, recent research (Niemi and Junn, 1998; Nie, Junn, and Stehlik-Barry, 1996) demonstrates that university teaching has a lasting effect on students. But assessing the contributions of particular pieces of scholarship, individual scholars, or entire departments is beyond the capacity of most investigations. The data gathered for our departmental history project do, however, provide some reasonable bases for informed speculation.

Organizing this information for the Wisconsin department requires a theoretical framework that synthesizes parsimoniously the considerations I have discussed. I believe a figure/ground/resource framework is the best such instrument. As part of the name implies, the figure/ground/resource framework draws upon Gestalt psychology. Gestaltists observed the simple, but profound fact that human perception combines distinctive figures (the focus of attention) and taken-for-granted grounds, which constitute the surrounding, unmarked contrast with the figure. An individual's perceptual subjectivity is that person's idiosyncratic sequence of figure/ground combinations.

By analogy, we can think of an academic discipline—or, indeed, an entire political culture—as a figure/ground phenomenon. The ground of disciplinary knowledge is that knowledge which is taken for granted. It is the conventional wisdom that "everybody knows." Any department, such as Wisconsin's, may contribute scholarship and teaching that increases or supports conventional knowledge. While it is unspectacular, conventional knowledge nevertheless provides the necessary energy to sustain a discipline over time. By contrast, the figure of disciplinary scholarship either contrasts sharply with the ground, or, in some cases, sharpens awareness of the ground itself. Figural scholarship is the landmark research, the "trendy" theory, the "breakthrough" finding, the lightning rod of debate and contestation.

Consider an example: research on political participation in the United States. For many years such research investigated individual attitudes and values. Much emphasis was placed upon the individual attributes that influenced participation. The so-called Michigan model was the heart of this paradigm. The resultant mass of research now constitutes the *ground*—the conventional wisdom—of political participation as a subfield. Then Robert Huckfeldt and

Robert Putnam offered separate new pieces of research that drew attention to the social context rather than the individual determinants of participation. Huckfeldt investigated social networks; Putnam, social capital. This research has attracted so much attention that it constitutes the figures of contemporary participation research.

Varying combinations of figure and ground—conventional and unconventional research—create the shape of a discipline. The balance between figure and ground shifts over time. In some periods conventional understandings go unchallenged: all work seemingly falls within "normal science" boundaries. The field develops new knowledge unremarkably in increments. Arguably, research on Congress fits this view. Alternatively, a subfield may be driven by so much controversy that no ground exists at all. Instead, there are competing bodies of innovative work, with much excitement and disciplinary attention. Arguably, the study of democratic transitions fits this characterization; certainly there is little conventional wisdom on the subject. Most often, however, scholarship is a combination of well-established "ground" and recurrent figural challenges. I will turn shortly to an assessment of the Wisconsin department in terms of figure and ground, summarizing my interpretation in the conclusion.

The resource component of my framework shifts the focus from the realm of scholarship and theory to the realm of economics, namely, the money available to produce research. Put simply, money matters, especially money to hire and pay staff. Wealthy academic departments obviously have an advantage over poorer departments in the production of knowledge. Therefore, a department's contribution to knowledge must be judged in relation to the resources it commands. In particular, a comparatively disadvantaged department that nevertheless performs at a high level in figure or ground deserves respect. With this observation in mind, I begin the application of the figure/ground/resource framework to Wisconsin political science by considering the resource dimension.

Resources

The University of Wisconsin–Madison is, of course, a state institution. Like most state universities, it offers lower salaries than the most prestigious private universities, especially those against which our department has traditionally competed. In addition, the state of Wisconsin lacks the tax base of its principal public university competitors, such as the University of California, Berkeley, or the

University of Michigan. Indeed, because it relies more heavily than Wisconsin on high tuition and private contributors, Michigan is a most "private" public university. These economic factors affect the capacity of the Wisconsin department to attract and retain distinguished scholars. Historically, the university has enjoyed strong state political support, reflected in relatively high tax rates. Despite this fact, even within the Big Ten, Madison offers relatively low salaries. And recently, as is well known, the state, like other state governments, has sharply reduced its portion of support for the university; today, the state directly provides less than a fourth of the university's operating funds.

Given these facts, like other Madison departments, the Department of Political Science must resemble "the little engine that could" in the famous children's story. That is, Madison scholars must work extra-hard to compensate for limited resources. Moreover, even within the Madison campus, the department has not prospered budgetarily. For example, in the 1970–71 budgetary year, there were 45 faculty in our department, as compared to 57 in sociology. By 1995 the gap between the departments in terms of numbers had widened. Our department employed 44 unclassified academic staff, as compared to sociology's 73. This disparity will obviously be reflected in scholarly production.

No doubt sociology's larger size owes something to its reliance on part-time faculty and also its capacity to exploit its #1 ranking in many studies. But sociology contains also important research centers, such as the Havens Center, and the Center for Demography programs. Our department has not generated as many such offshoots. It is not surprising that there is a large funding gap between sociology and political science. The instructional and administrative budget for sociology in 1999 was $3,143,000 for faculty and academic staff, as opposed to our $1,874,000. Indeed, our funding actually fell from 1995, while that of sociology rose in that period by over $300,000.

A comparison of our department with comparably sized departments in the social sciences is also revealing, particularly in regard to salary scales. Consider economics, for example. In 1995 for its 43 faculty and academic staff, economics spent a budget of $2,450,000; by contrast, for our 44 member faculty, the available funds were $1,940,000, over $500,000 less. Partly, this discrepancy reflects the economics department's capacity to argue that it must compete against business schools and private firms for faculty. However, in terms of national department rankings in 1995, our department ranked considerably higher than the economics department, another indication, perhaps, of the "little engine that could" phenomenon. Equally telling, as compared to anthropology—a department long known as troubled, with a weak reputation—political science was no better paid.

The available data do not permit comparisons between our department salaries and other Big Ten political science departments. Moreover, using budgetary data to make comparisons is inherently problematic. Nor am I assigning responsibility for our department's relatively low funding. The point, simply, is to support with evidence my hunch that political science at Wisconsin has not enjoyed as strong a resource base for scholarship as comparable departments in the university.

Moreover, rather than compensate for its relatively low budget by stinting on teaching, the department has instead maintained a higher undergraduate load of majors than have comparable Wisconsin departments. For example, in 1992—by which time our department already had substantially fewer faculty than sociology—there were more than 700 undergraduate political science majors, as compared to only 500 sociology majors. In the mid–1990s the gap in the number of undergraduate majors briefly vanished, but by 2001, it had increased. In 2001 there were slightly under 700 political science majors, as compared to only 400 sociology majors.

The contrast to economics is even more striking. Though the two departments had comparably sized faculties in the early 1990s, economics had only a little over 300 majors, as compared to 700 in political science. In 2001, these numbers were almost identical, even as economics enjoyed larger budgets throughout the period.

Some national data support this characterization of above-average teaching effort by Wisconsin political scientists. In 1993, of the top 18 departments according to National Research Center data, the Wisconsin department ranked behind only the University of California, Berkeley, the University of North Carolina, Chapel Hill, and the University of California, San Diego in number of political science majors. Further, Wisconsin taught more undergraduate students than did any of the top 18 departments, save Minnesota; but the latter department had only 482 majors, as compared to Wisconsin's 650. These data demonstrate that the Wisconsin department committed substantial resources to teaching at a time when, according to the National Research Center rankings of research quality, Wisconsin managed to rank tenth in the country.

The import of these data is obvious. Political science has regularly stretched itself to teach relatively large numbers of undergraduates, as compared to comparable departments. This commitment undoubtedly consumes greater time and energy for undergraduate teaching than other departments bear. The "little engine that could" apparently places a greater teaching burden on itself than do other departments. Therefore—the key point—it has less time or energy available for undertaking research than do comparable departments. In terms of resources, political science has been—and remains—quite restricted.

Publication

A department makes a national scholarly reputation first and foremost by publishing visible research. Therefore, I begin with quantitative data on publication. I recognize, of course, the crudeness and insufficiency of a quantitative estimate alone. But for practical reasons—and because there are qualitative assessments of the department's research elsewhere in this history—I concentrate on quantity. Moreover, sheer quantity is itself revealing.

A commonly voiced opinion is that the Wisconsin department is a "book," not an "article" department. This characterization is generally true, but journal publication has played a key role in department productivity during certain periods. In particular, between 1968 and 1974, the department ranked high in journal publications in the *American Political Science Review* (*APSR*), *Journal of Politics*, *American Journal of Political Science*, *Western Political Quarterly*, and *Polity*. During this period the department produced much in both behavioral and institutional research reported in journals. Among the frequent contributors were Ira Sharkansky, Barbara Hinckley, Austin Ranney, Charles Cnudde, and Herbert Jacob.

This spate of journal publication ended in the 1970s; since that time, journals have not been the principal medium for departmental scholarship. In the Miller, Tien, Peebler (1996: 73–83) analysis of *APSR* publication between 1954 and 1994, only three Wisconsin faculty (Leon Epstein, David Fellman, Richard Merelman) appear among the most-published 72. Indeed, publication in the nine most prestigious journals among political scientists between 1986 and 1996 placed the Wisconsin department 44th of the top 50 rated political science departments (in the 1993 NRC rankings of departments). The gap between the Wisconsin department's NRC 1993 ranking (#10) and its 1986–96 journal publication ranking (weighted by size of faculty) was greater than that for any of the top 50 departments save Princeton (Ballard and Mitchell, 1998: 826–29).

Many factors account for the department's relative weakness in journal publication. Journal articles tend to reflect and, perhaps, exaggerate short-term trends in disciplinary perspective and interest. For example, departments that have become bastions of rational choice and other heavily quantitative approaches to political science—the recent "cutting edge" of the discipline—

rank at the very highest levels of journal publication (Ballard and Mitchell, 1998: 826–9). Thus, California Institute of Technology, SUNY–Stony Brook, Rochester, Carnegie-Mellon, and Stanford fall within the top ten. Because the Wisconsin department has not pursued rational choice and quantitative political economy as diligently as some other departments, journal publication may have suffered.

In addition, weighted rankings of department journal publication tend to exaggerate the impact of outliers—the few particularly productive scholars in a department. Smaller departments gain from this procedure, raising their rankings relative to larger departments.

More important, perhaps, the sheer volume of submissions to premier journals has risen exponentially. Consequently, acceptance rates have declined. This phenomenon reflects growth in the number of political scientists and the pervasive spread of publication criteria for university recruitment and promotion. Wisconsin political scientists, like all others, face greater competition in journal submission than ever before. The natural consequence is lower success in journal publication.

Moreover, as we shall see, the culture of political science at Wisconsin has indeed favored book over journal publication. Colleagues over the years have commonly complained that a focus on journal publication sharply understates the research performance of the department. Until recently there were no reliable data to test this proposition for book publication. Recently, however, Rice, McCormick, and Bergmann (2002: 751–56) provided precisely the necessary evidence. The results are striking. Although they examined only a four-year period (1994–98), they confirmed that the Wisconsin department excels in book publication. Based upon total number of books reviewed in the *APSR* during these four years, the Wisconsin department ranked third in the nation, with 24. When corrected to reflect faculty size, Wisconsin still ranked fourth in the nation.

The contrast between strong book and relatively weak journal publication has implications for the figure-ground aspect of departmental impact. Journal articles typically have shorter gestation and publication cycles than do books. Therefore, they more accurately trace short-term shifts in disciplinary interest and debate. As a result, they may reflect the "figural" aspect of the discipline. But most of these "flickers of light" turn out to be transient, leaving little permanent residue.

By contrast, most book publication makes its influence felt less dramatically. Occasionally, however, a particular book may have an immediate, profound figural impact. Wisconsin faculty have, in fact, produced several such books. But most books and articles contribute to the incremental growth of the disciplinary ground. Only the occasional book—and the *very* occasional article—makes a theoretical breakthrough, a true figural impact. On balance, therefore, the Wisconsin superiority in book publishing probably does conceal some of the department's actual impact, reducing visibility and drama. Perhaps the department's scholarly production should be compared to a powerful soaking rain, rather than to a flash flood that comes and goes suddenly, with great fanfare.

Department Rankings

A second indicator of departmental influence is a department's relative ranking among all political science departments. This ranking partially reflects journal publications; as Garland and Graddy demonstrate, there is a statistically significant, strongly positive correlation between publication in three major journals and the National Research Council Rankings as of 1993. Nevertheless, a department's scholarly reputation depends on many factors, some of which are unknown, and others of which probably bear little relationship to journal publication. Arguably, this fact explains the continued strong showing of the Wisconsin department over the years, despite our relative weakness in journal publication. Indeed, most departments—including Wisconsin—display relative stability over time in national prestige assessments.

Although national rankings differ in techniques and data sources, since 1925 the Wisconsin department has maintained great consistency in relative national reputation. In 1925, Wisconsin placed fourth; in 1957, eighth; in 1963, eighth; in 1964, tied for seventh; in 1976, eighth; in 1982, seventh again. (See appendix 12.) Throughout this 50-plus years span, the competition grew dramatically, as new political science departments came into existence, a number of which possessed greater resources than the Wisconsin department. By 2004, there were 248 political science departments offering graduate study. By way of contrast, the 1925 rankings listed only 36 such departments. Thus, the department held its own, a significant—even remarkable—achievement.

The period 1983–93 appears to have been something of a watershed, however. In 1983, the National Research Center ranked the Wisconsin department eighth. However, 10 years later the Wisconsin department had declined to tenth, until then its lowest rating. By 2001, *U.S. News and World Report*—a less-well-regarded survey than the others—ranked the department eleventh, tied with three other schools. Arguably, by the 1980s the "little engine that could" was struggling, at least in the eyes of its peers.

If there is slippage, three factors may have contributed. First, the cumulative effects of relatively weak journal publication may have caught up with the department. Given the article-driven "avant garde" of quantitative political science, departmental visibility perhaps suffered somewhat. The department's strengths in comparative politics and political theory typically appeared in books or in specialized journals, not in the journals (often heavily Americanist) most visible to a broad national political science audience. Second, the department's relatively modest resource base perhaps did not support as many large, multi-investigator research projects as some of its competitors. Finally, some schools, such as Stanford, University of California, San Diego, MIT, Rochester, and the University of Chicago, focused their research and recruitment in the newly prestigious political economy and rational-choice approaches. Wisconsin may have suffered by comparison, at least so far as national perceptions are concerned.

Citation of Faculty Publications

Another indicator of a department's impact is the frequency with which its members' publications are cited by other scholars. The primary source recording citation numbers is the *Social Science Citation Index* (*SSCI*), which enumerates only those which appear in journal articles. Article writers tend to cite other articles, rather than books. Article writers also favor quantitative techniques for their compactness. Finally, journals maintain different citation norms; some journals want many citations, others few. For all these reasons, journal article citations do not provide a fully reliable picture of a department's scholarly visibility.

Nevertheless, journal citations clearly measure one kind of visibility. Indeed comparing Wisconsin citation patterns in 1985 and 2000 offers some interesting insights into departmental change. In both years, there was dramatic individual variation. In 1985 by far the most cited member of the department was Murray Edelman. His 1,486 citations were followed by a closely bunched core group of Americanists in the department, primarily behavioralists (Ira Sharkansky, Austin Ranney, Herbert Jacob, Barbara Hinckley, and Virginia Sapiro). These scholars were cited between 227 and 875 times. Despite the fact that Edelman mainly published books, he nevertheless managed to achieve significant citation visibility. By contrast, undoubtedly underrepresented, given the volume and quality of their book publications, were Leon Epstein, Crawford Young, Peter Eisinger, and Booth Fowler, many of whom published in subfields like comparative politics, which are underrepresented by journals in *SSCI*.

In terms of the figure/ground/resource model, what does this pattern of citation suggest? Edelman produced a strikingly original theory of mass political behavior that was unorthodox both methodologically and substantively. Its political implications were clearly radical. His work positioned the department within the "figural" component of the model.

The strong showing of American political behavior is more difficult to characterize. By 1985 the behavioral persuasion was the conventional approach to the study of American politics. It is probably fair to say that behavioralists in the department as of 1985 did not produce as distinctive a body of theory as Edelman. As a result, these scholars are positioned mainly within the "ground" component of the model. Grossly understated by these data is the strength of comparative politics and political theory at Wisconsin. In both subfields, scholars produced major, well-reviewed books. The theoretical contribution of these works, taken as a whole, is beyond this writer's competence, as is an assessment of their impact on comparative politics and political theory. However, the fact that most of this work did not find its way so fequently into journal citations perhaps limited its visibility.

By 2000, the picture had altered. The most cited faculty member in 2000 remained Edelman. In fact, he was cited more often (1,770 times) in 2000 than he had been in 1985 (1,486), despite the fact that his work increasingly diverged from the contemporaneous study of public opinion and mass political behavior.

By contrast, the behavioral core that was widely cited in 1985 had shrunk by 2000. Three—Hinckley, Jacob, and Sharkansky—had by then left the department. Although some department members had increased their visibility from 1985 to 2000 (Herbert Kritzer, John Witte, Peter Eisinger, Richard Merelman), the total number of their citations did not equal that of the behavioral scholars in 1985. Younger scholars, such as Kenneth Mayer, Diana Mutz, David Canon, and Michael Barnett were only beginning to attain notice through journal citations. Finally, political theorists and comparativists were infrequently cited, despite the high esteem and recognition they enjoyed among their subfield colleagues.

In figure/ground/resource terms, by 2000 Edelman remained the department's most distinctive "figural" contributor. Department contribution to ground remained respectable, but not as strong as it had been in 1985. Meanwhile, its substantial productivity of high-quality work in comparative politics and political theory was perhaps not fully reflected in journal citation.

This interpretation suggests that the department, by 2000, was assuming an idiosyncratic, almost outlier role in the discipline. After all, despite his frequent citation, Edelman did not alter the main tendencies of the discipline in ways congenial to his implicit political radicalism, nor his theoretical "constructivism." Instead, as the recent "Perestroika" movement charges, conventional political science has become increasingly quantitative, and politically liberal, perhaps neoliberal, not radical. Nor is it accidental that Edelman was prominent in the Caucus for a New Political Science in the 1960s (which failed).

Thus, frequently cited scholars are not always as dominating as might be expected. Nor is the opposite the case. Relatively uncited authors may still exert considerable influence. For example, Mark Beissinger, Michael Barnett, David Canon, Donald Downs, Charles Jones, Donald Kettl, Kenneth Mayer, Virginia Sapiro, Aili Tripp, and Crawford Young, all either current or recently retired members of the department, have written books that won APSA national prize competitions. Yet, with the exception of Jones, none rank high in the *SSCI* figures.

To be sure, had this chapter focused on policy impact, as opposed to scholarly impact, different conclusions might be drawn. For example, Paul Hutchcroft's *Booty Capitalism* influenced the anticorruption campaign of President Ramos in the Philippines. Barbara Stallings's research on international financial institutions influenced both Latin American and UN policymakers. Charles Jones and Michael Barnett have framed media discussions about such disparate topics as the American presidency and the UN role in Rwanda. David Canon's research on court-enforced "majority-minority" electoral districts has brought him into judicial and legislative policy forums. And Kenneth Goldstein's massive study of political advertising in the United States regularly receives attention in the national press. Though impossible to quantify, these contributions clearly magnify the Wisconsin department's impact.

Nevertheless, I believe the data on citations indicate that the Wisconsin scholarly influence remains primarily within the "ground" of political science. However, Wisconsin is unusual in that "figural" scholars have also flourished here (e.g., Edelman, perhaps Downs, Merelman, Crawford Young). A receptive, supportive culture of experimentation and creativity has marked the department. These aspects of departmental culture now require discussion.

Departmental Impact on Students

A salient dimension of department culture is teaching. A department's students are its most immediate, intimate, and vulnerable constituency. Moreover, the image of a department in the outside world depends, in part, on students, who are a particularly important source of information. Not only do students personally respond to the department, but they also transmit departmental influence into the academic and nonacademic settings where they later work. In so doing, they magnify or diminish the department's influence.

A telling sign of the Wisconsin department's teaching influence is the publication record of the department's graduate students. Here, the evidence is unequivocally positive. For the period 1994–98, according to Rice, McCormick, and Bergman (2002: 751–56), Wisconsin Ph.D.'s ranked eighth nationally in number of books reviewed by the *APSR*. Significantly, Wisconsin also ranked twelfth nationally in terms of publication in the five most "prestigious" political science journals. In short, through their scholarship, Wisconsin's graduates have significantly magnified the department's influence. Apparently, the department's culture of diligent scholarship "took" among an unusually large number of its graduate students.

Classes are the major vehicles for this cultural impact. In an attempt to probe this culture, we conducted a mail survey of doctoral alumni, utilizing both open-ended and close-ended questions. Students wishing to remain anonymous were free to do so. We solicited responses from 457 graduates and received 137 responses, a response rate, after accounting for the deceased and those not delivered, of 35.5 percent. Appendix 18 provides data on four aspects of departmental performance as perceived by graduate students: course quality; quality of the department; impact of the department on career preparation; and retrospective judgment about whether the respondent should have chosen Wisconsin. As the data indicate, graduate students are overwhelmingly positive in their assessments, ranking the department near the high end of seven-point scales.

Some recent graduates tend to be somewhat more critical of the department than their predecessors. We turn to the open-ended responses in order to reveal some of the grounds of their dissatisfaction.

The major discontent among recent graduates is that the department did not provide the methodological training that their later scholarship required. For example, John Portz, a 1988 graduate, commented, "My major weakness coming out of the program was in methodology, particularly statistical, but in general as well. There was no requirement in this area." A second source of dissatisfaction involves competition for funding. Traditionally, the department had not funded all of its entering class (a policy that changed in 1997–98), though nearly all received support after the first year. In some years, entering classes were quite large; new students therefore felt the funding was insecure, subjecting them to an unpleasant competition for financial aid. No doubt the increasing cost of a graduate education (during a period when the academic job market was shrinking) colors recent alumni perception of their Wisconsin experience.

Again, the absence of comparative data from other institutions prevents drawing any conclusions about Wisconsin student experiences. It may be that students in other graduate programs would respond similarly to those at Wisconsin. However, all faculty pick up anecdotal evidence about graduate unhappiness in other departments. My suspicion is that, despite their recent misgivings, graduates of Wisconsin have more positive feelings about their experience than is the norm among graduate students.

Open-ended responses identify some of the qualities that have contributed to the department's steady contribution to the "ground" of political science, and to its tolerance and encouragement of "figural" comparativists (Young, Beissinger, Wilson, Schatzberg) and Americanists (Edelman and Merelman) interested in the cultural approach to politics. Students particularly commend the eclecticism and breadth of the department. To most of the students who responded, the department seems to respect and fairly represent diverse approaches to the study of politics. For example, John Kommers, a 1962 Ph.D., remarks that in his years there was much debate among graduate students over quantitative vs. qualitative approaches to the discipline. He notes, "Wisconsin was a civil place and we, like the faculty . . . tolerated the differences and indeed most of us were committed to pluralism in the discipline." More than 30 years later, Jeffrey Lewis (1998) echoed these sentiments, singling out as the department's "most distinctive trait: eclecticism and an overall strong core of faculty rather than a particular niche or theoretical specialization."

The emphasis upon tolerance and eclecticism has produced graduates who feel they possess broader substantive knowledge and greater appreciation for diverse methodologies than graduates from other departments. For example, Eric Gorham (1990), a political theorist, although critical of the department in some respects, comments, "Whatever else can be said about UW, after receiving my doctorate, I learned that I knew a lot more about a variety of fields than I have found to be the case for graduates of other departments, save maybe Ivy League and California schools." From the perspective of American political behavior, Paul Martin (2000) writes that the "core themes" of his graduate training in the department were "the encouragement to tackle large questions, the importance of social relevance, connecting empirical research to important theoretical questions . . . and perhaps most importantly, support for methodological pluralism."

A small minority of students disputes the characterization of the department as eclectic, intellectually tolerant, and substantively diverse. And, to repeat, the absence of comparative data from other institutions prevents a judgment of Wisconsin's distinctiveness. Still, we can talk about the contribution of eclecticism, tolerance, and substantive diversity to the department's role in the figure/ground/resource model of political science. Though the department does not actively promote figural scholarship in such a way as to give Wisconsin a distinctive, strong, avant garde profile, departmental eclecticism and tolerance does reward "figural" scholarship when it serendipitously emerges. Thus, Wisconsin does not resemble a Rochester in the 1980s, a Yale in the 1960s, a Stanford today. Indeed, because—virtually by definition—conventional "ground" approaches to a discipline dominate most of the time, the Wisconsin department has primarily fortified the ground. Wisconsin provides a haven for unconventional, controversial figural approaches, but it does not intentionally champion new theoretical perspectives. It may be that this Wisconsin equilibrium between figure and ground makes the most out of the resources available to "the little engine that could."

The department's response to political turmoil on campus also, indirectly, reveals departmental norms touching on scholarship. As is well known, Wisconsin has long been among the most politically active research universities. Especially in the 1960s, protesters regularly put pressure on the university, including strikes that directly affected the functioning of the political science department.

Moreover, campus issues related to teaching-assistant unions included strife that pitted students against administrators, with department faculty caught in the middle. In some universities—Berkeley, Cornell, Columbia—outbreaks of student protest severely disrupted political science departments. In some cases, unbridgeable personal and intellectual chasms developed. What about the Wisconsin experience?

For the most part, students who took part in protests recall the department as tolerant and flexible in response. The department apparently refrained from punishing students or faculty for their strike- or protest-related action. For example, Joshua Forrest, who was active in both the 1979–80 and 1982–83 Teaching Assistant Association strikes, remarks that he appreciated the department "taking me back in after the strike and accepting me despite my radicalism at the time, and despite the fact that most professors in the UW political science department opposed the strike."

Marjorie Hershey (1972) provides a balanced, but generally positive picture of the department during the Vietnam War protests:

> There were times when a few members of the department greatly disappointed me. . . But there were many other times when faculty members and grad student colleagues offered me wonderful examples of scholars trying to live their ideals and at the same time fulfill the functions that they had contracted with the university to fulfill.

Not all *faculty* in the department shared this image of department tolerance and flexibility in the face of political strain. In his oral history interview, James Scott sharply rebukes members of the department for exerting pressures against supporters of protest. However, most oral histories reflect the views represented by Peter Eisinger:

> That tensions over the war, the TA strike and the demonstrations never tore the department apart was testimony to the strong norm of civility and constraint that governed the North Hall community all during my 28 years. Of course there were instances when the norms were violated, but for the most part I always marveled at how different life in our department was from the turmoil that plagued places like Indiana or Stanford and other schools where young and old, liberal and conservative, behavioralists and traditionalists did not speak to one another or worse.

Conclusion

This broad, eclectic, and incomplete overview of department impact yields few conclusions, but many interpretations. I suggest that the Wisconsin experience illustrates how a discipline sustains over time a particular intellectual culture, one in which the bulk of scholarship fortifies taken-for-granted knowledge.

The Wisconsin department has performed well a quite diverse set of tasks with limited economic resources. In addition to competing with other major research departments at Madison, it has devoted great effort to public service, administration, and teaching. In short, Wisconsin political science spread its limited resources widely; it has not channeled large resources to a limited, focused range of scholarly pursuits.

The Wisconsin department has also developed and maintained a politically and intellectually tolerant internal culture. There have been few exclusionary choices enforced among theoretical approaches. With but one exception, this author recalls no punishment of any faculty member for propounding an unpopular theory. The question is, "What do these patterns of high productivity, limited resources, theoretical breadth, and intellectual tolerance among peer institutions produce?"

Given the characteristic I have described, the law of averages ensures that the Wisconsin department will not leap out among peer institutions as "distinctive" or "figural." Occasionally, a few "figural" scholars have serendipitously appeared and (to the department's credit) are hired and rewarded. And specific decisions to recruit a particular type of scholar have created some significant changes in department subfield profiles. But this is not a pattern for short-term visibility vis-à-vis other political science departments. In fact, in recent years, the department has lost some visibility. A multitasking, resource-limited department like ours can make substantial, steady contributions to conventional research. It can also produce and reward occasional figural research scholars. It can also do a commendable job of teaching and mentoring its graduate students. But this will not attain for it the highest levels of disciplinary acclaim. The Wisconsin achievement has been laudable, but limited, and almost certainly underexposed and undervalued.

What do the data in this chapter suggest about the *import* dimension of Wisconsin's contribution to the figure/ground model? Where *impact* primarily speaks to the department's role in the discipline, *import* speaks to the question of whether a department's scholarship challenges or legitimates key aspects of American political culture and institutions. How does our department fare in this respect?

Without a detailed knowledge of each Wisconsin scholar's oeuvre, no definitive answers to this question are possible. I possess no such knowledge; other chapters take up the content of research in greater detail. This summary deals mainly with American politics, the area I know best. I offer a tentative interpretation.

The most widely cited Wisconsin author—Murray Edelman—challenges key aspects of American political culture and institutions. His work is highly critical of American capitalism, mass media, and the military. Similarly, Scott, Merelman, Lindberg, Fowler, and Stallings—to varying degrees though not with the insistence or distinctiveness of Edelman—have challenged directly or indirectly American political values and institutions.

By contrast, the bulk of Wisconsin scholars have been essentially reformist rather than radical. That is, their research identifies flaws in the American political system that they believe can be remedied without fundamentally altering the political system. I believe this statement would fairly characterize the work of Epstein and Ranney on parties; Jones on the Presidency and Congress; Gormley, Dresang, and Kettl on public administration; Witte on public education; as well as Jacob, Hinckley, Sharkansky, Peter Eisinger, David Canon, and Kenneth Mayer on diverse political institutions. While all these scholars either explicitly or implicitly criticize certain American political practices and institutions, none envisages a comprehensively transformed system (though Eisinger comes close on occasion). Most confine themselves to particular institutional reforms.

The scholarship of other colleagues is more difficult to characterize. For example, Virginia Sapiro's work takes a powerful feminist approach to American politics, with radical implications. However, her substantive research on women and politics tends to be reformist. The same, I believe, is true of Benjamin Marquez regarding Mexican Americans.

On balance, this pattern suggests that the department mainly reinforces and supports the American political process, while advancing specific institutional reforms. However, there has been a large enough representation of "figural," radical scholarship to provide an ongoing conversation between political reform and radical change in America. And, with few exceptions, the department has not been conservative; that is, it has not resisted political change. Ultimately, in terms of American political culture, the Wisconsin department is probably slightly to the left of most political science departments, a distinctiveness I think uncommon among leading public universities in America.

Works Cited

Ballard, Michael J. and Neil J. Mitchell. 1998. "The Good, the Better, and the Best in Political Science," *PS* 31, 4: 826–29.

Camic, Charles and Neil Gross. 2002. "Alvin Gouldner and the Sociology of Ideas," *Sociological Quarterly* 43, 1: 97–111.

Collins, Randall. 1998. *The Sociology of Philosophies: A Global Theory of Intellectual Change.* Cambridge: Harvard University Press.

DiMaggio, Paul. 1997. "Culture and Cognition," *Annual Review of Sociology* 23: 263–87.

Eisenberg, Avigail. 1995. *Restructuring Political Pluralism.* Albany: State University of New York Press.

Farr, James. 1995. "Remembering the Revolution: Behavioralism in American Political Science," in James Farr, John S. Dryzek and Stephen T. Leonard, eds., *Political Science in History*: 198–225. Cambridge: Cambridge University Press.

Farr, James, John S. Dryzek and Stephen T. Leonard, eds. 1995. *Political Science in History*. Cambridge: Cambridge University Press.

Karl, Barry. 1974. *Charles E. Merriam and the Study of Politics*. Chicago: University of Chicago Press.

Kelly, Donald R. 2002. "Intellectual History and Cultural History: The Inside and the Outside," *History of the Human Sciences* 15, 2: 1–21.

Latour, Bruno and Steve Woolgar. 1986. *Laboratory Life: The Construction of Scientific Facts*. Princeton: Princeton University Press.

Lindblom, Charles E. 1997. "Political Science in the 1940s and 1950s," *Daedalus* 127: 225–53.

Lowi, Theodore J. 1992. "The State in Political Science: How We Become What We Study," *American Political Science Review* 86, 1: 1–7.

Macedo, Stephen, ed. 1997. *Reassessing the Sixties: Debating the Political and Cultural Legacy*. New York: Norton.

Merelman, Richard M. 2003. *Pluralism at Yale: The Culture of American Political Science*. Madison: University of Wisconsin Press.

Miller, Arthur H., Charles Tien and Andrew A. Peebler. 1996. "The American Political Science Review Hall of Fame: Assessments and Implications for an Evolving Discipline," *PS* 29, 1: 73–83.

Miller, Hugh T. and Charles J. Fox. 2001. "The Epistemic Community," *Administration and Society* 38, 6: 668–86.

Nie, Norman, Jane Junn and Carol Stehlke-Barry. 1996. *Education and Democratic Citizenship in America*. Chicago: University of Chicago Press.

Niemi, Richard G. and Jane Junn. 1998. *Civic Education: What Makes Students Learn*. New Haven: Yale University Press.

Rice, Tom W., James M. McCormick and Benjamin D. Bergman. 2002. "Graduate Training, Current Affiliation, and Publishing Books in Political Science," *PS* 35, 4: 751–56.

Savelsberg, Joachim J., Ryan King and Lara Cleveland. 2002. "Politicized Scholarship? Science on Crime and the State," *Social Problems* 49: 3: 327–48.

Smith, Rogers. 1997. "Still Blowing in the Wind: The American Quest for a Democratic, Scientific Political Science," *Daedalus* 127: 253–89.

Ware, Alan. 1998. "Dahl in Perspective: Assessing a Colossus of Political Science," *Public Affairs Report* 39: 14–16.

CHAPTER 14

Conclusions

Crawford Young

Toward the Second Century

Throughout this volume, we have endeavored to sketch a comprehensive portrait of the department: its evolution; its major figures; its place in university, state, and national discipline. In a lineage that traces back beyond the official creation a century ago to the very first days of the University of Wisconsin, 190 scholars have served on the department faculty, whose instruction has left its mark on 11,000 living alumni, and 593 doctorates awarded. In observing the centennial of the formal creation of the department in 1904, we seek not simply a celebration but a balanced representation of its history, foregrounding the accomplishments while acknowledging some shortcomings. The contributions of Jack Dennis and Richard Merelman (chapters 12 and 13) are in different ways critical evaluations of departmental evolution.

In these final pages, I suggest some concluding observations on the culture of the department, which many believe to be an enduring source of its strengths. A few last words on its national standing over time are in order. So also are some parting reflections on departmental achievements.

But there is no better place to begin this concluding chapter than with a return to the centennial conference, attended by nearly 200 alumni, faculty, and friends of the department on 26–27 March 2004. Chair Mark Beissinger closed the event with a memorable keynote address, providing a universally admired centennial summation. The Beissinger address can ably supply the basic framework for the conclusions; we provide extended excerpts.

> We have every reason to celebrate. When you reflect on the fact that this is a Department which has, since its creation a century ago, consistently ranked among the very best political science departments in the country, when you contemplate that it is a Department that has been the home for some of the major

intellectual thinkers about politics over the last hundred years (the John Gauses, Frederic Oggs, Leon Epsteins, Murray Edelmans, John Armstrongs, Charles Jones, Crawford Youngs, James Scotts, and Matthew Holdens of the last several generations), when you think also that it is a Department that has long had a reputation as one of the truly outstanding teaching departments at our University (the legacies of outstanding teachers like Booth Fowler and Melvin Croan), and when you add in that it is a Department that has also been very heavily engaged in service to the community and to the Wisconsin Idea (we are also the Department of Clara Penniman and William Young), it is hard not to conclude that Wisconsin somehow managed to get it right. We have never been a Department that has tried to push a methodological shtick, or that was so caught up with producing prima donna scholars that we didn't care about what kind of instruction we gave to our students. We have never been a Department that sat in its ivory tower without caring what was going on in the world around us, without a sense of duty to the community of which we are a part. We are a Department that has been self-consciously pluralistic, both in terms of the approaches to the study of politics and the ideological positions that we espouse. We are a Department that has cared deeply about both its teaching and its scholarship. And we are a Department that has been very heavily involved in the campus, in the community, and in the world. . . .

As for our 11,000 living alumni, we take great satisfaction in your many achievements. Our former graduates are now lawyers, journalists, professors, congressmen, government officials, businessmen, television and film producers. . . .

I am happy to report that the Wisconsin tradition of political science is still very much alive. Our current faculty's achievements continue to rank our Department among the very best—the top ten or eleven—in the country. Actually, a recent ranking of political science departments based on the publication of books in political science in major presses ranked Wisconsin third in the country (behind Harvard and California-Berkeley). We also continue to be outstanding teachers. On a five-point scale (with a score of 5.0 standing for "excellent" and 4.0 for "good"), the average score on our teaching evaluations for the summary question ("How would you rank the overall performance of this instructor") for all courses we have taught over the last ten years is 4.42. A recent survey of 700 students in the Lakeshore Dormitories identified 63 "Exceptional Professors" across all units of the University. Out of these 63, seven . . . were political science professors—twice as many as any other department or unit at the University. . . . Little wonder that we are the most popular major within the College of Letters and Science (L&S). In terms of community service, our professors continue to remain major sources of advice and expertise for the United Nations, the World Bank, the United State federal government, our own state and local governments, and the media. Besides stem cell research, there is probably no other research at the University that is as widely cited in the press as Kenneth Goldstein's work on campaign advertising, which . . . played an important part in the debates over the McCain-Feingold campaign finance reforms. The name of Donald Kettl . . . is synonymous throughout Wisconsin and across both political parties with the notion of political reform. And our students today are perhaps the best that they have ever been—bright, inquisitive, engaged. If they represent our future, then we have every reason to be optimistic. . . .

But what will the next hundred years be like? . . . There are several things . . . that I think are very exciting, and that will likely help define at least part of the . . . second century of Wisconsin Political Science.

First, I want to mention the wonderful bequest that Doris and Robert Weisberg have made to establish a Weisberg Chair in Liberal Political Thought. . . . This is a splendid gift . . . allowing us to enhance and maintain the excellence of our instruction, and to continue our longstanding reputation in the area of political theory and political thought. . . .

Another important part of our future is the recent establishment of a new Center for the Study of Politics, to be directed by Kenneth Goldstein, under the auspices of the Department. The Center will connect graduate and undergraduate students directly with the research of Department faculty in exciting new ways, allowing students to be involved in some of the most important political research taking place in the country. . . . And it will provide shared technical support for our computer labs, upgrading our currently insufficient computer support capabilities. . . .

> A third major development for the next century is our current Centennial Fellowship Campaign. . . . This has been identified as the major fund-raising goal for the Department, and our primary need . . .
>
> Fourth, what makes me really excited about the next century is our younger faculty. We have been extraordinarily successful in recruiting outstanding younger faculty—indeed, in some cases even wooing people away from Harvard and Yale. . . .
>
> Let me conclude by saying that we should never forget that the past century could have been different. We might not have been able to attract such a distinguished faculty. Those faculty might not have been such excellent teachers and such devoted community members. We might not have produced the Russell Feingolds, David Obeys, Tommy Thompsons, Herbert Kohls, Richard Cheneys, Larry Eaglebergers, Charlene Barshefskys, Ritas Bravers, and others who have made a difference in this world. It took people who cared, people who were both knowledgeable about politics and who could incite passion about it. . . . [1]

The admirable Beissinger peroration requires only a few supplementary observations.

Culture of the Department

The oral histories, the interviews with current faculty, and the responses from doctoral alumni converge upon one crucial defining attribute of the department. Over the years, a unique culture took form in the department, certainly well established by the interwar period. The culture consisted of a set of shared understandings, of informal practices, of social routines, of norms governing interpersonal relations. Its core components were civility, collegiality, and eclecticism.

The civility dimension rests above all upon mutual respect. A department is an intimate community. Though there is slow turnover, the roster of faculty members is relatively stable over time. Thus the investment in interpersonal comity is long-term. Ruptured relationships inflict enduring damage. Even more costly are permanent factional divisions, which bring collateral harm to many ongoing processes: departmental decision-making, graduate student supervision, budget allocations. Civility does not require intimate friendships with all fellow faculty. However, it does rest upon a degree of self-restraint in demands placed upon the department. In a climate of civility, one may rely upon reciprocity of behavior from others.

Collegiality is a second dimension. This involves an internalized ethos of cooperation. Department affairs are a collective undertaking, facilitated by an engagement in mutuality of purpose. The consensual tradition in decision-making is an element in collegiality—not always possible, but still present as a subliminal preference. It requires a modicum of self-restraint in pursuit of goals by any individual or group, and eschewing pursuit of maximal advantage when a temporary majority might exist. A sharing of research interests and teaching concerns is another part. Most faculty have been actively engaged in informal colloquia or discussion groups gathering those interested in a particular theme: mass political behavior, methodology, law and society, cultural pluralism, African politics, among many others that might be cited. One may recollect the stress placed by Matthew Holden in his oral history upon the collegial support he found, uniquely at Wisconsin during his career stops, for his conceptual queries.[2] I would add my own personal witness: both in major research projects covering broad topics, and in teaching, I have derived immense benefit from consultation and critical commentary from colleagues. A walk down the corridor sufficed to unravel many puzzles, or to find direction toward relevant sources.

Third, the legendary eclecticism of conceptual and methodological perspective is both product and precondition for the other two dimensions. In the doctoral alumni survey, no theme resonated more strongly than the value our former graduate students found in their own careers of exposure in their political science training to a diversity of orientations and perspectives. In the postwar period, only behavioralism and rational-choice theory aspired to hegemonical status in the discipline, and achieved it in a number of departments. However, those committed to these perspectives at Wisconsin always accepted a reasonable presence rather than primacy as a goal.

Perhaps the disposition to conflict avoidance, which the culture of the department dictates, is not always conducive to wise decisions. Nor can difference always be set aside. Indeed, there have been conflictual moments in the history this volume recounts: a couple of closely divided tenure cases, the chair succession in 1996. However, the custom of comity associated with the culture of the department is powerful therapy for momentary divisions. At times when events external to the department placed dramatic stress upon it—Cambodia spring or the teaching assistant strikes—the culture of the department insulated the departmental community from the corrosive polarization of the environment.

Another correlate of the culture of the department is an egalitarian ethos. Senior faculty have the same teaching obligations as newly recruited colleagues. Although university statutes restrict voting rights on tenure and budget issues to associate and full professors, since 1987 junior faculty have participated in the debates.[3] At least since the second war, although there has been some difference of generational perspective, seniority has rarely sharply divided older from younger faculty.

The relative absence of a hierarchical environment helped extend the collegial environment to the graduate student community, and surely contributed to their very positive evaluations of their doctoral experience in a survey conducted for this project (see appendix 18 for a summary). On a seven-point scale, in which one stood for excellent, the average rating for quality of the department was 1.66, and for course work in field of specialization, 1.79. In response to a query as to whether they would choose again to attend Wisconsin, with one standing for a definite yes and seven an absolute no, the average was 1.82 (see appendix 18).

Standing and Achievements

The Beissinger address underlines the remarkable stability of department rankings in the top ten nationally.[4] This has been maintained in the past despite the nearly complete faculty turnover following both world wars, examined in chapters 3 and 4. But sustaining national standing is necessarily a major preoccupation. Apprehensions that it may be at risk are perennial, and probably stronger today than at any point since the faculty turnover following World War II. Among those faculty members interviewed, there were some "declinists," a position echoed by Merelman in chapter 12. Recent rankings published by *U.S. News and World Report* provide apparent evidence for the belief that the department has lost standing. The 2005 *U.S. News and World Report* rankings, showing a further drop, seemed to confirm the view that the department has lost ground.[5] Nonetheless, my own reading of the evidence leads to a different conclusion: relatively stable ranking among the leading departments.

The first published ranking of departments in 1925 had ranked Wisconsin fourth. This finding was deconstructed in chapter 3; at the time, the department had only seven members, of whom three were new instructors and a fourth primarily in extension. Thus this high ranking reposed upon the reputations of only three faculty. In all succeeding rankings, based upon much more evident departmental faculty achievement and prestige, until 1995, the department ranked eighth.[6] On that latter occasion, the last ranking of undisputed reliability, by the National Academy of Sciences, the San Diego and Los Angeles campuses of the University of California crept ahead of the department, as did Princeton, displacing the Massachusetts Institute of Technology which dropped to twelfth.

Rather than a marked decline, in my view the small change (and even the larger one reported by *U.S. News and World Report*) reflects above all the growing competition among leading institutions, and in the discipline more broadly. In the 1920s, fewer than 30 doctoral programs existed in the country. At the present time, well over a hundred universities award doctoral degrees. As well, most higher-ranked institutions were located in wealthier universities, a point stressed by Merelman in his arresting "little engine that could" borrowing from Burl Ives in chapter 13. At the time of the 1995 survey, Harvard and Michigan both had 50 faculty members, compared to 37 full-time equivalents for Wisconsin. In a 2002 inquest into departmental rankings on several quality dimensions, a number of institutions which had never enjoyed top ranking in the past appeared in the top ten in at least one measure, a good indication of the growing competition (Washington University, Rutgers University, University of Texas–Austin, Houston University, Texas A&M University, State University of New York–Stony Brook).[7] In this study, Wisconsin ranked third in book production by faculty, and eighth in such output by doctoral alumni.[8]

But the reasons for concern about the future remain. The resource gap between leading private universities and their public counterparts appears to grow. The likelihood of continuing fiscal pressures upon the university is evident, given the hostile environment toward tax increases and other demands upon state resources, especially the runaway costs of prisons and medical assistance. Another factor is a period of unsuccessful recruiting in the latter half of the 1980s, now reflected in the thin ranks in the generation of Mark Beissinger and Donald Downs; the category of midcareer scholars of national note plays an key role in reputational standing. There was also a wave of retirements of the expansion generation of the 1960s around the turn of the century.

Yet the acute pressures on state appropriations for higher education have persisted at least since the 1980s, and the department has managed to maintain its high standing. Better yet, the retirements of the late 1990s were replaced by young scholars of the highest promise. Throughout its history, the department has recruited primarily at the junior level. Through nurture of its newer faculty, and rigorous standards for tenure promotion, the department has reproduced high scholarly quality across the generations. With the exception of the Hawkins Chair, the department would rarely have the opportunity to recruit a senior scholar of high standing; Wisconsin in this respect could not mimic the strategy of Stanford, Harvard, or Yale in preserving its rank. But department-building based upon junior recruitment can succeed in the future as it has in the past. Mark Beissinger, I believe, is well justified in his confidence concerning the future promise of our younger faculty at the centennial mark.

Evidence in support of this hopeful perspective can be found in the array of prizes won by department faculty in the last couple of years. Beissinger won the prestigious APSA Wilson prize and two others for his 2002 book, *Nationalist Mobilization and the Collapse of the Soviet State.* As noted in chapter 5, at the 2004 American Political Science Association annual meetings, no fewer than six younger faculty won prizes for their publications: Charles Franklin, Scott Gehlbach, Kenneth Goldstein, Helen Kinsella, Benjamin Marquez, and Tamir Moustafa.

So I second Beissinger in his auspicious reading of the second century. And my three years of work on this project have greatly deepened my appreciation for the accomplishments of the earlier generations. The richness of this heritage will help propel the department into a future that builds upon and goes beyond its remarkable past.

Notes

1. Mark Beissinger, address to the department centennial conference, 27 March 2004.
2. Matthew Holden, oral history, American Political Science Association, November 1993.
3. The reinterpretation of university statutes to permit junior faculty participation was an innovation of Peter Eisinger as chair; his oral history records that his proposal, although a major change in procedure, won general support and was accepted with good grace by senior faculty. Peter Eisinger, oral history, University Archives, 12 February 2003.
4. A 2001 ranking by *U.S. News and World Report* (included in appendix 12), ranks the department tied for eleventh, and a 2005 tabulation indicated a sharper drop. However, the methodology in this ranking is widely contested; the most recent authoritative ranking by the National Research Center in 1993 (published in 1995) placed the department tenth.

5. The 2005 *U.S. News and World Report* rankings list Wisconsin as 17. Publication of departmental quality-ranking data collected earlier in this decade by the National Academy of Science is long overdue; these findings would merit more serious consideration than the *U.S. News and World Report*, whose methodology is widely criticized.
6. The 1934 ranking listed the top eight only alphabetically, so one is uncertain about the precise placement of the department.
7. Tom W. Rice, James M. McCormick and Benjamin D. Bergmann, "Graduate Training, Current Affiliation and Publishing Books in Political Science," *PS: Political Science & Politics*, 35, 4 (December 2002), 752.
8. Rice, McCormick and Bergmann, "Graduate Training," 752.

Appendixes

Appendix 1

Chronology

1849	John Lathrop named chancellor and professor of civil polity
1858	Lathrop resigns as chancellor, named professor of ethical and political science
1872	John B. Parkinson named professor of civil polity and international law, serves till 1908
1892	Richard T. Ely recruited to found School of Economics, Political Science and History
1896	Samuel Sparling completes first doctorate in political science
1898	Paul Reinsch earns the second doctorate; both Sparling and Reinsch retained on faculty
1900	Sparling helps found Wisconsin League of Municipalities; Reinsch publishes *World Politics at the End of the 19th Century*
1903	Reinsch one of founders of American Political Science Association, first vice president
1904	Official creation of a separate Department of Political Science; Reinsch Chair
1909	Reinsch leads faculty in defending academic autonomy of faculty before regents
1913	Reinsch named ambassador to China, resigns faculty post
1914	Frederic Ogg joins faculty
1917	Ogg named Chair, serves until 1940, then again 1942–44
1923	Arnold Hall, working with Charles Merriam, organizes in Madison the first of three annual National Conferences on the Science of Politics
1926	Governor John Blaine demands firing of Ford MacGregor for writing a pamphlet critical of state tax policy; President Frank refuses

1926	Regent John Cashman calls for firing of Pitman Potter for advocating League of Nations support; no action taken
1927	John Gaus joins faculty to help launch Experimental College
1934–35	Edwin Witte leads team preparing 1935 Social Security Act
1937	Political scientist Clarence Dykstra named president, serves till 1945
1947	Regents reject proposed tenure appointment for Howard McMurray, defeated candidate for U.S. Senate
1947	John Gaus leaves for Harvard, partly because of McMurray case
1948	Ogg retires; nearly complete faculty turnover
1949	William Young named as a top aide to Governor Oscar Rennebohm
1952	William Young begins eight-year term as chair
1960	Leon Epstein replaces Young as chair, initiates three-year-term policy
1961	Rapid expansion begins
1963	Jack Dennis, Joel Grossman, David Tarr and Crawford Young join faculty, all become chairs, serve until retirement
1964	Department moves from South Hall to North Hall
1965	Epstein named dean of the College of Letters & Science, serves till 1969
1969	Clara Penniman leads in founding Center for Public Policy and Administration (later La Follette School of Public Affairs)
1970	Peak of student antiwar protest; first teaching assistant strike, Cambodia spring, Sterling Hall bombing
1980	Second TAA strike
1984	Herbert Jacob named as first Hawkins Professor, followed by Charles Jones and Byron Shafer
1987	Donna Shalala named chancellor, with political science appointment
2004	Department celebrates centennial

Appendix 2

Faculty Roster: Alphabetical

Political Science Faculty 1849–2005*

	Start Year	End Year	Total Years	Start Rank	End Rank
Adamany, David	1972	1978	6	Assoc. Prof.	Professor
Adler, Emanuel	1992	1995	3	Assoc. Prof.	Assoc. Prof.
Adolfson, Lorentz H.	1942	1944	2	Instructor	Assist. Prof.
Anderson, Charles W.	1960	1996	36	Assist. Prof.	Professor
Anderson, Stephen J.	1987	1993	6	Assist. Prof.	Assist. Prof.
Armstrong, John A.	1954	1986	32	Assist. Prof.	Professor
Arneson, Ben A.	1913	1917	4	Assist. Prof.	Assist. Prof.
Bailey, William L.	1909	1912	3	Instructor	Instructor
Barnett, J. D.	1902	1905	3	Assist. Prof.	Instructor
Barnett, Michael	1990	2004	14	Assist. Prof.	Professor
Beard, William	1940	1945	5	Assist. Prof.	Assist. Prof.
Beissinger, Mark	1987	2005	*18*	Assist. Prof.	Professor
Bjorkman, James W.	1976	1985	9	Assist. Prof.	Assist. Prof.
Bonn, Franklyn G. Jr.	1962	1965	3	Instructor	Instructor
Boyd, Richard	2002	2005	*3*	Assist. Prof.	Assist. Prof.
Browning, Rufus P.	1961	1967	6	Assist. Prof.	Assist. Prof.
Canon, David T.	1991	2005	*14*	Assist. Prof.	Professor
Carlisle, Donald P.	1962	1967	5	Assist. Prof.	Assist. Prof.

* Roster includes all persons who held regular faculty appointments from the opening of the University of Wisconsin in February 1849 through the academic year 2004–2005. Lecturers or other temporary appointments are not included. For continuing faculty, 2005 represents the cutoff year for this table, and the length of service (in italics) is calculated from the date of appointment until academic year 2004–2005; the rank is that in 2004–2005.

Carpenter, William S.	1914	1917	3	Instructor	Instructor
Champagne, Richard A.	1985	1990	5	Instructor	Assist. Prof.
Chang, Kelly H.	1998	2002	4	Assist. Prof.	Assist. Prof.
Clarenbach, Fred A.	1945	1962	17	Assoc. Prof.	Professor
Clausen, Aage R.	1966	1971	5	Assist. Prof.	Assist. Prof.
Clough, Michael W.	1985	1987	2	Assist. Prof.	Assist. Prof.
Cnudde, Charles F.	1968	1973	5	Assist. Prof.	Assoc. Prof.
Cohen, Bernard	1959	1990	31	Assist. Prof.	Professor
Coleman, John J.	1992	2005	13	Assist. Prof.	Professor
Croan, Melvin	1967	1996	29	Assoc. Prof.	Professor
Cronin, Bruce L.	1995	2003	8	Assist. Prof.	Assist. Prof.
Dangerfield, Royden J.	1949	1950	1	Professor	Professor
Davis, James W.	1964	1968	4	Assist. Prof.	Assist. Prof.
Deber, Raisa	1974	1978	4	Instructor	Instructor
Dennis, Jack S.	1963	2001	38	Assist. Prof.	Professor
Dolbeare, Kenneth M.	1965	1970	5	Assist. Prof.	Assoc. Prof.
Donald, Carr L.	1958	1960	2	Assist. Prof.	Assist. Prof.
Donoghue, James R.	1948	1984	36	Assist. Prof.	Professor
Downs, Donald A.	1985	2005	20	Assist. Prof.	Professor
Dresang, Dennis L.	1969	2005	36	Assist. Prof.	Professor
Dykstra, Clarence	1937	1945	8	President	President
Ebenstein, William	1938	1946	8	Instructor	Assoc. Prof.
Edelman, Murray J.	1966	1990	24	Professor	Professor
Edgerton, Russel	1965	1969	4	Assist. Prof.	Assist. Prof.
Eisinger, Peter K.	1969	1998	29	Assist. Prof.	Professor
Emmerson, Donald K.	1970	2001	31	Assist. Prof.	Professor
Epstein, Leon D.	1948	1988	40	Assist. Prof.	Professor
Farr, James	1984	1989	5	Assist. Prof.	Assoc. Prof.
Feeley, Malcolm M.	1977	1985	8	Assist. Prof.	Professor
Fellman, David	1947	1978	31	Professor	Professor

Fink, Richard M.	1961	1964	3	Instructor	Instructor
Fioretos, Karl-Orfeo	1999	2005	6	Assist. Prof.	Assist. Prof.
Fogg-Davis, Hawley G.	1999	2005	6	Assist. Prof.	Assist. Prof.
Fowler, R. Booth	1967	2002	35	Assist. Prof.	Professor
Franklin, Charles H.	1991	2005	*14*	Assist. Prof.	Professor
Friedman, Edward	1967	2005	*38*	Assist. Prof.	Professor
Froman, Lewis A. Jr.	1960	1965	5	Assist. Prof.	Assist. Prof.
Gardiner, John A.	1965	1968	3	Assist. Prof.	Assist. Prof.
Gaus, John M.	1927	1947	20	Professor	Professor
Gehlbach, Scott	2003	2005	*2*	Assist. Prof.	Assist. Prof.
Gillespie, Charles	1988	1991	3	Assist. Prof.	Assist. Prof.
Gilliam, Franklin D.	1983	1987	4	Assist. Prof.	Assist. Prof.
Goldstein, Kenneth M.	2000	2005	*5*	Assist. Prof.	Assoc. Prof.
Gormley, William T.	1980	1991	11	Assist. Prof.	Professor
Grant, James A.C.	1927	1930	3	Instructor	Assist. Prof.
Greene, Lee S.	1934	1935	1	Instructor	Instructor
Greffenius, Steven F.	1986	1989	3	Assist. Prof.	Assist. Prof.
Grossman, Joel B.	1963	1996	33	Assist. Prof.	Professor
Hall, Arnold B.	1910	1926	16	Instructor	Professor
Hanson, Donald W.	1967	1971	4	Assist. Prof.	Assoc. Prof.
Harris, Joseph P.	1923	1930	7	Instructor	Assoc. Prof.
Hart, Henry C.	1948	1982	34	Instructor	Professor
Hayward, Fred M.	1968	1991	23	Assist. Prof.	Professor
Hendley, Kathryn	1993	2005	*12*	Assist. Prof.	Professor
Hinckley, Barbara	1972	1988	16	Assoc. Prof.	Professor
Holden, Matthew Jr.	1969	1981	12	Professor	Professor
Hornbeck, Stanley K.	1908, 1914	1909, 1919	6	Instructor	Assoc. Prof.
Howell, William	2000	2002	2	Assist. Prof.	Assist. Prof.
Huitt, Ralph K.	1949	1983	34	Assist. Prof.	Professor

Hutchcroft, Paul D.	1993	2005	12	Assist. Prof.	Assoc. Prof.
Iyenaga, Toyokichi	1902	1904	2	Instructor	Instructor
Jacob, Herbert	1962, 1984	1969, 1986	9	Assist. Prof.	Professor
Jacobson, Jacob M.	1927	1930	3	Instructor	Instructor
Jalal, Ayesha	1987	1989	2	Assist. Prof.	Assist. Prof.
Johnson, Cathy M.	1984	1990	6	Instructor	Assist. Prof.
Jones, Charles O.	1988	1997	9	Professor	Professor
Jones, Chester Lloyd	1910, 1928	1919, 1941	22	Assoc. Prof.	Professor
Kay, David A.	1966	1975	9	Assist. Prof.	Professor
Kettl, Donald F.	1990	2004	14	Professor	Professor
Khademian, Anne	1990	1997	7	Assist. Prof.	Assoc. Prof.
Kinsella, Helen	2004	2005	1	Assist. Prof.	Assist. Prof.
Kirk, Grayson L.	1929	1940	11	Instructor	Professor
Kritzer, Herbert M.	1978	2005	27	Assist. Prof.	Professor
Kronebusch, Karl	1993	1998	5	Assist. Prof.	Assist. Prof.
Lathrop, John	1849	1859	10	Chancellor	Professor
Leavitt, Michael R.	1970	1973	3	Assist. Prof.	Assist. Prof.
Leheny, David	1998	2005	7	Assist. Prof.	Assist. Prof.
Lewis, John D.	1930	1935	5	Instructor	Instructor
Lewis, Steven C.	1986	1993	7	Instructor	Assist. Prof.
Li, Richard P. Y.	1973	1975	2	Assist. Prof.	Assist. Prof.
Lindberg, Leon N.	1962	1997	35	Assist. Prof.	Professor
Lipsky, Michael	1966	1970	4	Assist. Prof.	Assist. Prof.
Lowrie, Seldon G.	1909	1912	3	Instructor	Instructor
MacGilvray, Eric	2003	2005	2	Assist. Prof.	Assist. Prof.
MacGregor, Ford H.	1909	1934	25	Instructor	Assoc. Prof.
Manion, Melanie	2000	2005	5	Assoc. Prof.	Assoc. Prof.
Manley, John F.	1966	1971	5	Assist. Prof.	Assoc. Prof.
Marmor, Theodore R.	1967	1970	3	Assist. Prof.	Assist. Prof.

Marquez, Benjamin	1991	2005	*14*	Assist. Prof.	Professor
Marra, Robin F.	1983	1987	4	Assist. Prof.	Assist. Prof.
Mayda, Jaroslav	1951	1956	5	Instructor	Assist. Prof.
Mayer, Kenneth R.	1989	2005	*16*	Assist. Prof.	Professor
McBain, Harold L.	1910	1914	4	Assoc. Prof.	Assoc. Prof.
McCalla, Robert	1987	1997	10	Assist. Prof.	Assist. Prof.
McCamy, James L.	1947	1971	24	Professor	Professor
McClelland, Glenn B.	1937	1940	3	Instructor	Instructor
McCrone, Donald J.	1965	1971	6	Assist. Prof.	Assist. Prof.
Meier, Kenneth J.	1985	1990	5	Assoc. Prof.	Professor
Menges, Constantine	1964	1967	3	Instructor	Assist. Prof.
Merelman, Richard	1969	2001	32	Assoc. Prof.	Professor
Meyer, E. C.	1908	1910	2	Assist. Prof.	Assist. Prof.
Miller, Jeffrey A.	1974	1979	5	Instructor	Assist. Prof.
Moustafa, Tamir	2003	2005	*2*	Assist. Prof.	Assist. Prof.
Mutz, Diana C.	1988	2000	12	Assist. Prof.	Assoc. Prof.
Ogg, Frederic A.	1914	1948	34	Assoc. Prof.	Professor
Page, Benjamin I.	1977	1979	2	Assoc. Prof.	Assoc. Prof.
Parkinson, J. B.	1872, 1876	1874, 1908	34	Professor	Professor
Parkinson, John M.	1892	1894	2	Assist. Prof.	Assist. Prof.
Payne, Leigh A.	1991	2005	*14*	Assist. Prof.	Professor
Pempel, T. J.	1993	1995	2	Professor	Professor
Penniman, Clara	1953	1984	31	Assist. Prof.	Professor
Pevehouse, Jon C.	2000	2005	*5*	Assist. Prof.	Assist. Prof.
Pfankuchen, Llewellyn	1932	1972	40	Instructor	Professor
Pharr, Susan J.	1977	1987	10	Assist. Prof.	Professor
Pitkin, Hanna	1964	1966	2	Assist. Prof.	Assist. Prof.
Pollack, Mark	1995	2004	9	Assist. Prof.	Assoc. Prof.
Potter, Pitman B.	1920	1931	11	Assist. Prof.	Professor

Rahn, Wendy M.	1991	1995	4	Assist. Prof.	Assist. Prof.
Ranney, J. Austin	1962	1976	14	Professor	Professor
Rapacz, Max P.	1926	1927	1	Instructor	Instructor
Reinsch, Paul S.	1897	1915	18	Assoc. Prof.	Professor
Richardson, Neil R.	1979	2005	*26*	Assist. Prof.	Professor
Riley, Patrick T.	1971	2005	*34*	Assist. Prof.	Professor
Rosenbaum, Allan	1970	1974	4	Assist. Prof.	Assist. Prof.
Rubenstein, Diane S.	1985	1991	5	Assist. Prof.	Assist. Prof.
Salter, John T.	1930	1968	38	Assoc. Prof.	Assoc. Prof.
Sapiro, Virginia	1976	2005	*29*	Assist. Prof.	Professor
Sartori, Anne E.	1997	1999	2	Assist. Prof.	Assist. Prof.
Saunders, Allan F.	1923	1928	5	Instructor	Assist. Prof.
Schatzberg, Michael G.	1991	2005	*14*	Professor	Professor
Scheingold, Stuart A.	1965	1970	5	Assist. Prof.	Assoc. Prof.
Schweber, Howard H.	1999	2005	*6*	Assist. Prof.	Assist. Prof.
Scoble, Harry M. Jr.	1958	1963	5	Assist. Prof.	Assist. Prof.
Scott, James C.	1967	1978	11	Assist. Prof.	Professor
Scott, Robert B.	1906	1910	4	Instructor	Professor
Seidensticker, Ellen	1975	1979	4	Assist. Prof.	Assist. Prof.
Shafer, Byron E.	2001	2005	*4*	Professor	Professor
Shalala, Donna E.	1987	1997	10	Chancellor	Professor
Sharkansky, Ira	1968	1985	17	Assoc. Prof.	Professor
Sharp, Walter R.	1923	1940	17	Instructor	Professor
Sinha, Aseema	1999	2005	*6*	Assist. Prof.	Assist. Prof.
Skilling, Harold G.	1943	1948	5	Assist. Prof.	Assist. Prof.
Smiley, Marion	1989	2002	13	Assist. Prof.	Professor
Soss, Joe	2003	2005	*2*	Assoc. Prof.	Assoc. Prof.
Sparling, Samuel E.	1897	1908	11	Assist. Prof.	Assoc. Prof.
Stallings, Barbara B.	1977	1996	19	Assist. Prof.	Professor
Stiefbold, Rodney P.	1966	1968	2	Assist. Prof.	Assist. Prof.

Stoke, Harold W.	1940	1944	4	Professor	Professor
Stokes, William S.	1946	1958	12	Assoc. Prof.	Professor
Straus, Scott	2004	2005	*1*	Assist. Prof.	Assist. Prof.
Stuart, Graham H.	1917	1923	6	Instructor	Assist. Prof.
Tarr, David W.	1963	1995	32	Assist. Prof.	Professor
Thompson, William R.	1914	1915	1	Instructor	Instructor
Thomson, John S.	1951	1957	6	Instructor	Assist. Prof.
Thorson, Thomas L.	1959	1966	7	Instructor	Assoc. Prof.
Tripp, Aili	1991	2005	*14*	Assist. Prof.	Assoc. Prof.
von der Mehden, Fred R.	1958	1968	10	Assist. Prof.	Professor
Wallace, Benjamin B.	1912	1913	1	Instructor	Instructor
Wallin, Bruce A	1979	1985	6	Assist. Prof.	Assist. Prof.
Walsh, Katherine Cramer	2000	2005	*5*	Assist. Prof.	Assist. Prof.
Weimer, David	2000	2005	*5*	Professor	Professor
Wengert, Herbert	1934	1937	3	Instructor	Assist. Prof.
Wilde, Alexander W.	1969	1976	7	Assist. Prof.	Assist. Prof.
Wilson, Graham K.	1984	2005	*21*	Assoc. Prof.	Professor
Witte, Edwin E.	1933	1957	24	Professor	Professor
Witte, John F.	1977	2005	*28*	Assist. Prof.	Professor
Wittenberg, Jason	2000	2005	*5*	Assist. Prof.	Assist. Prof.
Wolanin, Thomas R.	1971	1977	6	Assist. Prof.	Assist. Prof.
Woodbury, Coleman F.	1958	1962	4	Professor	Professor
Yack, Bernard	1991	2002	11	Assoc. Prof.	Professor
Young, M. Crawford	1963	2001	38	Assist. Prof.	Professor
Young, William H.	1947	1983	36	Assoc. Prof.	Professor
Zolberg, Aristide R.	1961	1963	2	Assist. Prof.	Assist. Prof.

APPENDIX 3

Faculty Roster: Chronological

Political Science Faculty 1849–2005*

	Start Year	End Year	Total Years	Start Rank	End Rank
Lathrop, John	1849	1859	10	Chancellor	Professor
Parkinson, J. B.	1872, 1876	1874, 1908	34	Professor	Professor
Parkinson, John M.	1892	1894	2	Assist. Prof.	Assist. Prof.
Reinsch, Paul S.	1897	1915	18	Assoc. Prof.	Professor
Sparling, Samuel E.	1897	1908	11	Assist. Prof.	Assoc. Prof.
Barnett, J. D.	1902	1905	3	Assist. Prof.	Instructor
Iyenaga, Toyokichi	1902	1904	2	Instructor	Instructor
Scott, Robert B.	1906	1910	4	Instructor	Professor
Hornbeck, Stanley K.	1908, 1914	1909, 1919	6	Instructor	Assoc. Prof.
Meyer, E. C.	1908	1910	2	Assist. Prof.	Assist. Prof.
Bailey, William L.	1909	1912	3	Instructor	Instructor
Lowrie, Seldon G.	1909	1912	3	Instructor	Instructor
MacGregor, Ford H.	1909	1934	25	Instructor	Assoc. Prof.
Hall, Arnold B.	1910	1926	16	Instructor	Professor
Jones, Chester Lloyd	1910, 1928	1919, 1944	22	Assoc. Prof.	Professor

* Roster includes all persons who held regular faculty appointments from the opening of the University of Wisconsin in February 1849 through the academic year 2004–2005. Lecturers or other temporary appointments are not included. For continuing faculty, 2005 represents the cutoff year for this table, and the length of service (in *italics*) is calculated from the date of appointment until academic year 2004–2005; the rank is that in 2004–2005.

McBain, Harold L.	1910	1914	4	Assoc. Prof.	Assoc. Prof.
Wallace, Benjamin B.	1912	1913	1	Instructor	Instructor
Arneson, Ben A.	1913	1917	4	Assist. Prof.	Assist. Prof.
Carpenter, William S.	1914	1917	3	Instructor	Instructor
Ogg, Frederic A.	1914	1948	34	Assoc. Prof.	Professor
Thompson, William R.	1914	1915	1	Instructor	Instructor
Stuart, Graham H.	1917	1923	6	Instructor	Assist. Prof.
Potter, Pitman B.	1920	1931	11	Assist. Prof.	Professor
Harris, Joseph P.	1923	1930	7	Instructor	Assoc. Prof.
Saunders, Allan F.	1923	1928	5	Instructor	Assist. Prof.
Sharp, Walter R.	1923	1940	17	Instructor	Professor
Rapacz, Max P.	1926	1927	1	Instructor	Instructor
Gaus, John M.	1927	1947	20	Professor	Professor
Grant, James A.C.	1927	1930	3	Instructor	Assist. Prof.
Jacobson, Jacob M.	1927	1930	3	Instructor	Instructor
Kirk, Grayson L.	1929	1940	11	Instructor	Professor
Lewis, John D.	1930	1935	5	Instructor	Instructor
Salter, John T.	1930	1968	38	Assoc. Prof.	Assoc. Prof.
Pfankuchen, Llewellyn	1932	1972	40	Instructor	Professor
Witte, Edwin E.	1933	1957	24	Professor	Professor
Greene, Lee S.	1934	1935	1	Instructor	Instructor
Wengert, Herbert	1934	1937	3	Instructor	Assist. Prof.
Dykstra, Clarence	1937	1945	8	President	President
McClelland, Glenn B.	1937	1940	3	Instructor	Instructor
Ebenstein, William	1938	1946	8	Instructor	Assoc. Prof.
Beard, William	1940	1945	5	Assist. Prof.	Assist. Prof.
Stoke, Harold W.	1940	1944	4	Professor	Professor
Adolfson, Lorentz H.	1942	1944	2	Instructor	Assist. Prof.
Skilling, Harold G.	1943	1948	5	Assist. Prof.	Assist. Prof.
Clarenbach, Fred A.	1945	1962	17	Assoc. Prof.	Professor

Stokes, William S.	1946	1958	12	Assoc. Prof.	Professor
Fellman, David	1947	1978	31	Professor	Professor
McCamy, James L.	1947	1971	24	Professor	Professor
Young, William H.	1947	1983	36	Assoc. Prof.	Professor
Donoghue, James R.	1948	1984	36	Assist. Prof.	Professor
Epstein, Leon D.	1948	1988	40	Assist. Prof.	Professor
Hart, Henry C.	1948	1982	34	Instructor	Professor
Dangerfield, Royden J.	1949	1950	1	Professor	Professor
Huitt, Ralph K.	1949	1983	34	Assist. Prof.	Professor
Mayda, Jaroslav	1951	1956	5	Instructor	Assist. Prof.
Thomson, John S.	1951	1957	6	Instructor	Assist. Prof.
Penniman, Clara	1953	1984	31	Assist. Prof.	Professor
Armstrong, John A.	1954	1986	32	Assist. Prof.	Professor
Donald, Carr L.	1958	1960	2	Assist. Prof.	Assist. Prof.
Scoble, Harry M. Jr.	1958	1963	5	Assist. Prof.	Assist. Prof.
von der Mehden, Fred R.	1958	1968	10	Assist. Prof.	Professor
Woodbury, Coleman F.	1958	1962	4	Professor	Professor
Cohen, Bernard	1959	1990	31	Assist. Prof.	Professor
Thorson, Thomas L.	1959	1966	7	Instructor	Assoc. Prof.
Anderson, Charles W.	1960	1996	36	Assist. Prof.	Professor
Froman, Lewis A. Jr.	1960	1965	5	Assist. Prof.	Assist. Prof.
Browning, Rufus P.	1961	1967	6	Assist. Prof.	Assist. Prof.
Fink, Richard M.	1961	1964	3	Instructor	Instructor
Zolberg, Aristide R.	1961	1963	2	Assist. Prof.	Assist. Prof.
Bonn, Franklyn G. Jr.	1962	1965	3	Instructor	Instructor
Carlisle, Donald P.	1962	1967	5	Assist. Prof.	Assist. Prof.
Jacob, Herbert	1962, 1984	1969, 1986	9	Assist. Prof.	Professor
Lindberg, Leon N.	1962	1997	35	Assist. Prof.	Professor
Ranney, J. Austin	1962	1976	14	Professor	Professor

Dennis, Jack S.	1963	2001	38	Assist. Prof.	Professor
Grossman, Joel B.	1963	1996	33	Assist. Prof.	Professor
Tarr, David W.	1963	1995	32	Assist. Prof.	Professor
Young, M. Crawford	1963	2001	38	Assist. Prof.	Professor
Davis, James W.	1964	1968	4	Assist. Prof.	Assist. Prof.
Menges, Constantine	1964	1967	3	Instructor	Assist. Prof.
Pitkin, Hanna	1964	1966	2	Assist. Prof.	Assist. Prof.
Dolbeare, Kenneth M.	1965	1970	5	Assist. Prof.	Assoc. Prof.
Edgerton, Russel	1965	1969	4	Assist. Prof.	Assist. Prof.
Gardiner, John A.	1965	1968	3	Assist. Prof.	Assist. Prof.
McCrone, Donald J.	1965	1971	6	Assist. Prof.	Assist. Prof.
Scheingold, Stuart A.	1965	1970	5	Assist. Prof.	Assoc. Prof.
Clausen, Aage R.	1966	1971	5	Assist. Prof.	Assist. Prof.
Edelman, Murray J.	1966	1990	24	Professor	Professor
Kay, David A.	1966	1975	9	Assist. Prof.	Professor
Lipsky, Michael	1966	1970	4	Assist. Prof.	Assist. Prof.
Manley, John F.	1966	1971	5	Assist. Prof.	Assoc. Prof.
Stiefbold, Rodney P.	1966	1968	2	Assist. Prof.	Assist. Prof.
Croan, Melvin	1967	1996	29	Assoc. Prof.	Professor
Fowler, R. Booth	1967	2002	35	Assist. Prof.	Professor
Friedman, Edward	1967	2005	38	Assist. Prof.	Professor
Hanson, Donald W.	1967	1971	4	Assist. Prof.	Assoc. Prof.
Marmor, Theodore R.	1967	1970	3	Assist. Prof.	Assist. Prof.
Scott, James C.	1967	1978	11	Assist. Prof.	Professor
Cnudde, Charles F.	1968	1973	5	Assist. Prof.	Assoc. Prof.
Hayward, Fred M.	1968	1991	23	Assist. Prof.	Professor
Sharkansky, Ira	1968	1985	17	Assoc. Prof.	Professor
Dresang, Dennis L.	1969	2005	36	Assist. Prof.	Professor
Eisinger, Peter K.	1969	1998	29	Assist. Prof.	Professor
Holden, Matthew Jr.	1969	1981	12	Professor	Professor

Merelman, Richard	1969	2001	32	Assoc. Prof.	Professor
Wilde, Alexander W.	1969	1976	7	Assist. Prof.	Assist. Prof.
Emmerson, Donald K.	1970	2001	31	Assist. Prof.	Professor
Leavitt, Michael R.	1970	1973	3	Assist. Prof.	Assist. Prof.
Rosenbaum, Allan	1970	1974	4	Assist. Prof.	Assist. Prof.
Riley, Patrick T.	1971	2005	34	Assist. Prof.	Professor
Wolanin, Thomas R.	1971	1977	6	Assist. Prof.	Assist. Prof.
Adamany, David	1972	1978	6	Assoc. Prof.	Professor
Hinckley, Barbara	1972	1988	16	Assoc. Prof.	Professor
Li, Richard P. Y.	1973	1975	2	Assist. Prof.	Assist. Prof.
Deber, Raisa	1974	1978	4	Instructor	Instructor
Miller, Jeffrey A.	1974	1979	5	Instructor	Assist. Prof.
Seidensticker, Ellen	1975	1979	4	Assist. Prof.	Assist. Prof.
Bjorkman, James W.	1976	1985	9	Assist. Prof.	Assist. Prof.
Sapiro, Virginia	1976	2005	29	Assist. Prof.	Professor
Feeley, Malcolm M.	1977	1985	8	Assist. Prof.	Professor
Page, Benjamin I.	1977	1979	2	Assoc. Prof.	Assoc. Prof.
Pharr, Susan J.	1977	1987	10	Assist. Prof.	Professor
Stallings, Barbara B.	1977	1996	19	Assist. Prof.	Professor
Witte, John F.	1977	2005	28	Assist. Prof.	Professor
Kritzer, Herbert M.	1978	2005	27	Assist. Prof.	Professor
Richardson, Neil R.	1979	2005	26	Assist. Prof.	Professor
Wallin, Bruce A	1979	1985	6	Assist. Prof.	Assist. Prof.
Gormley, William T.	1980	1991	11	Assist. Prof.	Professor
Gilliam, Franklin D.	1983	1987	4	Assist. Prof.	Assist. Prof.
Marra, Robin F.	1983	1987	4	Assist. Prof.	Assist. Prof.
Farr, James	1984	1989	5	Assist. Prof.	Assoc. Prof.
Johnson, Cathy M.	1984	1990	6	Instructor	Assist. Prof.
Wilson, Graham K.	1984	2005	21	Assoc. Prof.	Professor
Champagne, Richard A.	1985	1990	5	Instructor	Assist. Prof.

Clough, Michael W.	1985	1987	2	Assist. Prof.	Assist. Prof.
Downs, Donald A.	1985	2005	*20*	Assist. Prof.	Professor
Meier, Kenneth J.	1985	1990	5	Assoc. Prof.	Professor
Greffenius, Steven F.	1986	1989	3	Assist. Prof.	Assist. Prof.
Lewis, Steven C.	1986	1993	7	Instructor	Assist. Prof.
Rubenstein, Diane S.	1986	1991	5	Assist. Prof.	Assist. Prof.
Anderson, Stephen J.	1987	1993	6	Assist. Prof.	Assist. Prof.
Beissinger, Mark	1987	2005	*18*	Assist. Prof.	Professor
Jalal, Ayesha	1987	1989	2	Assist. Prof.	Assist. Prof.
McCalla, Robert	1987	1997	10	Assist. Prof.	Assist. Prof.
Shalala, Donna E.	1987	1997	10	Chancellor	Professor
Gillespie, Charles	1988	1991	3	Assist. Prof.	Assist. Prof.
Jones, Charles O.	1988	1997	9	Professor	Professor
Mutz, Diana C.	1988	2000	12	Assist. Prof.	Assoc. Prof.
Mayer, Kenneth R.	1989	2005	*16*	Assist. Prof.	Professor
Smiley, Marion	1989	2002	13	Assist. Prof.	Professor
Barnett, Michael	1990	2004	14	Assist. Prof.	Professor
Kettl, Donald F.	1990	2004	14	Professor	Professor
Khademian, Anne	1990	1997	7	Assist. Prof.	Assoc. Prof.
Canon, David T.	1991	2005	*14*	Assist. Prof.	Professor
Franklin, Charles H.	1991	2005	*14*	Assist. Prof.	Professor
Marquez, Benjamin	1991	2005	*14*	Assist. Prof.	Professor
Payne, Leigh A.	1991	2005	*14*	Assist. Prof.	Professor
Rahn, Wendy M.	1991	1995	4	Assist. Prof.	Assist. Prof.
Schatzberg, Michael G.	1991	2005	*14*	Professor	Professor
Tripp, Aili	1991	2005	*14*	Assist. Prof.	Assoc. Prof.
Yack, Bernard	1991	2002	11	Assoc. Prof.	Professor
Adler, Emanuel	1992	1995	3	Assoc. Prof.	Assoc. Prof.
Coleman, John J.	1992	2005	*13*	Assist. Prof.	Professor
Hendley, Kathryn	1993	2005	*12*	Assist. Prof.	Professor

Hutchcroft, Paul D.	1993	2005	12	Assist. Prof.	Assoc. Prof.
Kronebusch, Karl	1993	1998	5	Assist. Prof.	Assist. Prof.
Pempel, T. J.	1993	1995	2	Professor	Professor
Cronin, Bruce L.	1995	2003	8	Assist. Prof.	Assist. Prof.
Pollack, Mark	1995	2004	9	Assist. Prof.	Assoc. Prof.
Sartori, Anne E.	1997	1999	2	Assist. Prof.	Assist. Prof.
Chang, Kelly H.	1998	2002	4	Assist. Prof.	Assist. Prof.
Leheny, David	1998	2005	7	Assist. Prof.	Assist. Prof.
Fioretos, Karl-Orfeo	1999	2005	6	Assist. Prof.	Assist. Prof.
Fogg-Davis, Hawley G.	1999	2005	6	Assist. Prof.	Assist. Prof.
Schweber, Howard H.	1999	2005	6	Assist. Prof.	Assist. Prof.
Sinha, Aseema	1999	2005	6	Assist. Prof.	Assist. Prof.
Goldstein, Kenneth M.	2000	2005	5	Assist. Prof.	Assoc. Prof.
Howell, William	2000	2002	2	Assist. Prof.	Assist. Prof.
Manion, Melanie	2000	2005	5	Assoc. Prof.	Assoc. Prof.
Pevehouse, Jon C.	2000	2005	5	Assist. Prof.	Assist. Prof.
Walsh, Katherine Cramer	2000	2005	5	Assist. Prof.	Assist. Prof.
Weimer, David	2000	2005	5	Professor	Professor
Wittenberg, Jason	2000	2005	5	Assist. Prof.	Assist. Prof.
Shafer, Byron E.	2001	2005	5	Professor	Professor
Boyd, Richard	2002	2005	3	Assist. Prof.	Assist. Prof.
Gehlbach, Scott	2003	2005	2	Assist. Prof.	Assist. Prof.
MacGilvray, Eric	2003	2005	2	Assist. Prof.	Assist. Prof.
Moustafa, Tamir	2003	2005	2	Assist. Prof.	Assist. Prof.
Soss, Joe	2003	2005	2	Assoc. Prof.	Assoc. Prof.
Kinsella, Helen	2004	2005	1	Assist. Prof.	Assist. Prof.
Straus, Scott	2004	2005	1	Assist. Prof.	Assist. Prof.

Appendix 4

Faculty Profiles

Note: Faculty publications in this list include only those books published before 2005, and which are normally associated with the career at the University of Wisconsin. Edited volumes are not included.

Adamany, David W. (1972–78)

b.	September 23, 1936 Janesville, WI
Degrees:	AB Harvard College, 1958 LLB Harvard Law School, 1961 MS University of Wisconsin, 1963 PhD University of Wisconsin, 1967
Fields:	American Politics, Constitutional Law, Judicial, State and Local Government and Politics
Publications:	Campaign Finance in America, 1972 Campaign Funds as an Intraparty Political Resource, 1972 Political Money: A Strategy for Campaign Financing in America (with George E. Agree), 1975
Career:	Wisconsin Public Service Committee, Commissioner, 1963–65 Administrative Assistant to the Lt. Governor of Wisconsin, 1965 Wisconsin State University Whitewater, Instructor, 1965–67 Wesleyan University, Dean of the College, 1967–72 University of Wisconsin, Associate Professor, 1972–75 Professor, 1975–78 University of Maryland System, Vice President, 1978–82 Wayne State University, President, 1982–2000 Temple University, President, 2000-

Adler, Emmanuel (1992–95)

Degrees:	BA Hebrew University MA Hebrew University PhD University of California–Berkeley
Fields:	International Politics, Comparative Politics, International Law and Organization, International Security, Latin America
Career:	University of Wisconsin, Associate Professor, 1992–95 Hebrew University of Jerusalem, 1995-

Adolfson, Lorentz H. (1942–44)

b.	October 14, 1909 Chicago, IL
d.	July 3, 1985
Degrees:	BA Wabash College, 1933 PhD University of Wisconsin, 1942

Fields: Adult Education, American Politics, Public Administration, Local Government, National Government
Publications: The County Clerk in Wisconsin, 1942
Career: University of Wisconsin, Instructor/Assistant Professor, 1942–44
University of Wisconsin Extension, Dean, 1944–64
Chancellor, Center System, 1964–72

Anderson, Charles W. (1960–96)
b. June 28, 1934
Manitowoc, WI
Degrees: BA Grinnell College, 1955
MA Johns Hopkins University, 1957
PhD University of Wisconsin, 1960
Fields: Comparative Politics, Latin America, Developing Nations, Political Theory and Philosophy
Publications: The Political Economy of Mexico (with William Glade), 1963
Latin American Political Systems, 1963
Politics and Economic Change in Latin America, 1967
Issues of Political Development (with Fred R. von der Mehden and Crawford Young), 1967
Political Economy of Modern Spain, 1970
Statecraft: An Introduction to Political Choice and Judgment, 1977
Pragmatic Liberalism, 1990
Prescribing the Life of the Mind, 1993
Deeper Freedom: Liberal Democracy as an Everyday Morality, 2002
Career: University of Wisconsin, Assistant Professor, 1960–63
Associate Professor, 1963–67
Professor, 1967–96
Chair, Integrated Liberal Studies

Anderson, Stephen (1987–93)
Degrees: PhD MIT, 1987
Fields: Comparative Politics, International Politics, Political Economy, International Political Economy, East Asia, Japan
Career: University of Wisconsin, Assistant Professor, 1987–93
Center for Global Communication, International University of Japan, 1994–98
US Department of Commerce, Foreign Commercial Service, Beijing, China & Nagoya, Japan, 1998-

Armstrong, John A. (1954–86)
b. May 4, 1922
St. Augustine, FL
Degrees: PhB University of Chicago, 1948
MA University of Chicago, 1948
PhD Columbia University, 1953

Fields: Comparative Politics, Western Europe, the Soviet Union, International Relations, American Foreign Policy, International Organizations
Publications: The Soviet Bureaucratic Elite, 1959
The Politics of Totalitarianism, 1961
The European Administrative Elite, 1973
Ideology, Politics, and Government in the Soviet Union, 1962
Nations Before Nationalism, 1982
Ukrainian Nationalism, 1939–45, 1955
Career: University of Denver, Assistant Professor, 1952
University of Wisconsin, Assistant Professor, 1954–57
Associate Professor, 1957–60
Professor, 1960–86
Chair, Russian Area Studies Program, 1959–63, 1964–65

Arneson, Ben A. (1913–17)
b. May 22, 1883
Barneveld, WI
d. February 1958
Degrees: BA University of Wisconsin, 1913
MA University of Wisconsin, 1914
PhD University of Wisconsin, 1916
Fields: Constitutional Law, Public Administration, American Politics, National Government, Civil Service Reform in State Administration
Career: University of Wisconsin, Assistant Professor, 1913–17
Ohio Wesleyan University, 1917
Miami University, 1929 and 1934
Ohio State University, 1932
American University, 1936–38

Bailey, William (1909–12)
Degrees: MA
Fields: Education Policy, Colonial Politics, Political Theory
Career: University of Wisconsin, Assistant Professor, Dept. of Political Science & Dept. of Education, 1908–09
Assistant Professor, Dept. of Political Science, 1909–12

Barnett, James Duff (1902–05)
b. October 25, 1870
Cairo, Egypt
d. 1957
Degrees: BA College of Emporia, Kansas, 1890
PhD University of Wisconsin, 1905
Fields: Constitutional Law, American Politics, National and State Government
Publications: State Administration of Taxation in Wisconsin, 1904
Career: University of Wisconsin, Instructor, 1902–05
University of Oklahoma, 1905–08
University of Oregon, 1908–41

Barnett, Michael (1990–2004)

b. Cincinnati, OH
Degrees: BA University of Illinois, 1982
PhD University of Minnesota, 1989
Fields: International Relations, Comparative Politics, Middle Eastern Politics
Publications: Confronting the Costs of War: Military Power, State and Society in Egypt and Israel, 1992
Dialogues in Arab Politics: Negotiations in Regional Order, 1998
Eyewitness to a Genocide: The United Nations and Rwanda, 2002
Rules for the World: International Organizations in Global Politics (with Martha Finnemore), 2004
Career: Macalester College, Instructor, 1989
Wellesley College, Assistant Professor, 1989–90
University of Wisconsin, Assistant Professor, 1990–94
Associate Professor, 1994–98
Professor, 1998–2004
University of Minnesota, Professor, 2004-present

Beard, William (1940–45)

b. May, 18, 1907
New York City, NY
Degrees: BS MIT, 1928
MA University of California at Los Angeles, 1938
PhD Columbia University, 1941
Fields: American Politics, National Government, State Government, Local Government, Public Administration, Government and Technology
Publications: Regulation of Pipe Lines as Common Carriers, 1941
Government and Liberty- The American System, 1947
American Government and Politics (with Charles A. Beard), 1949
Career: California Institute of Technology, Instructor, 1931–34
TVA Information Division, Chief Publication Section, 1936
University of Wisconsin, Assistant Professor, 1940–45 (on leave 1942–45)
USAAF, Civilian Instructor, 1942–43 (on leave from UW)
Radio Operator, 1943–44 (on leave from UW)
Served with US Army, 1945 (on leave from UW)

Beissinger, Mark R. (1988-present)

b. November 28, 1954
Philadelphia, PA
Degrees: BA Duke University, 1976
PhD Harvard University, 1982
Fields: Comparative Politics, Russia, Post-Soviet Politics, Social Movements
Publications: Scientific Management, Socialist Discipline, and Soviet Power, 1988
Nationalist Mobilization and the Collapse of the Soviet State, 2002

Career: Harvard University, Assistant Professor, 1982–87
Head Tutor, 1984–87
University of Wisconsin, Assistant Professor, 1988–90
Associate Professor, 1990–95
Director, Center for Russia, Eastern Europe, and Central Asia, 1992–98
Professor, 1995-present
Department Chair, 2001–04

Bjorkman, James W. (1976–85)
Degrees: BA University of Minnesota, 1966
MPhil Yale University, 1969
PhD Yale University, 1976
Fields: Public Policy, Comparative Politics, Bureaucracy and Organizational Behavior, Heath Policy, Developing Nations, Federal and Intergovernmental Relations
Publications: <u>Federal-State Health Policies and Imports: The Politics of Implementation</u>
(with C. Altensetter), 1978
<u>Politics of Administrative Alienation in India's Rural Development Programs</u>, 1979
Career: University of Wisconsin, Assistant Professor, 1977–85
International Institute of Comparative Government, Lausanne, Switzerland, Executive Director, 1986–91
America Studies Research Center, Hyderabad, India, Director, 1987–90
Institute of Social Studies, The Hague, Netherlands, and University of Leiden, 1990-

Bonn, Franklyn G. Jr. (1962–65)
b. April 28, 1932
Degrees: BA University of Minnesota, 1954
MA University of Minnesota, 1957
PhD University of Minnesota 1964
Fields: Political Theory, Analytical Political Theory, History of Political Thought, National and State Government, Latin American Government
Career: University of Minnesota, Political Science, Instructor, 1959–61
University of Wisconsin, Instructor, 1962–65
Chatham College, 1965-

Boyd, Richard (2002-present)
b. Taylorville, IL
Degrees: BA University of Chicago, 1992
MA Fordham University, 1994
PhD Rutgers University, 1998
Fields: Political Theory, Comparative Politics, American Politics

Career: University of Chicago, Instructor, 1998–2000
Assistant Professor, 2000–01
University of Pennsylvania, Program in Philosophy, Politics and Economics, Associate Director, 2001–02
Visiting Assistant Professor, Department of Political Science, 2001–02
University of Wisconsin, Assistant Professor, 2002-present

Browning, Rufus (1961–67)
b. March 16, 1934
Cleveland, OH
Degrees: AB Oberlin College, 1954
MA Yale University, 1955
PhD Yale University, 1961
Fields: American Politics, National Government, Public Administration, Statistics
Career: University of Wisconsin, Assistant Professor, 1961–67
Michigan State University, 1967–73
University of California at Davis and San Francisco State University, 1971–74
University of California at Berkeley, Institute of Governmental Studies, Senior Research Political Scientist, 1976–81
San Francisco State University, 1974-

Canon, David T. (1991-present)
b. April 26, 1959
Minneapolis, MN
Degrees: BA Indiana University, 1981
MA Humphrey Institute of Public Affairs, University of Minnesota, 1984
PhD University of Minnesota, 1987
Fields: American Politics, Presidency, Congress, Political Parties, Race and Politics
Publications: Actors, Athletes, and Astronauts: Political Amateurs in the United States Congress, 1990
Race, Redistricting, and Representation: The Unintended Consequences of Black-Majority Districts, 1999
The Dysfunctional Congress? The Individual Roots of an Institutional Dilemma (with Kenneth Mayer), 1999
Career: Duke University, Assistant Professor, 1986–91
University of Wisconsin, Assistant Professor, 1991–94
Associate Professor, 1994–99
Professor, 1999-present
Associate Chair, fall 1997, 1999–2001

Carlisle, Donald P. (1962–67)
b. Sept. 11, 1935
New Haven, CT
d. December 1997
Degrees: BA Brown University, 1958
PhD Harvard University, 1962
Fields: Comparative Politics, Soviet Politics, International Relations, Soviet Foreign Policy and International Communism, Political Philosophy
Career: University of Wisconsin, Assistant Professor 1962–67
University of Toronto, 1967–68
Boston College, 1968–97

Carpenter, William S. (1914–17)
b. Jan. 28, 1890
Wilmington, DE
Degrees: BS University of Pennsylvania, 1911
AM University of Pennsylvania, 1912
PhD Princeton University, 1914
Fields: Political Theory, American Politics
Publications: Judicial Tenure in the US, 1918
Career: University of Wisconsin, Instructor, 1914–17
Princeton University, 1920–46

Champagne, Richard A. (1985–90)
Degrees: JD University of Wisconsin, 1993
PhD Indiana University
Career: University of Wisconsin, Assistant Professor, 1985–90
Wisconsin State Legislature, Legislative Reference Service, 1993-

Chang, Kelly (1998–2002)
Degrees: PhD Stanford University, 1998
Fields: Political Organizations, Formal and Quantitative Methods, Monetary Policy
Publications: Appointing Central Bankers: The Politics of Monetary Policy in the United States and the European Monetary Union, 2003.
Career: University of Wisconsin, Assistant Professor, Joint Appointment in Dept. of Political Science and La Follette Institute of Public Affairs, 1998–2002
Analyst, UBS, 2002-present

Clarenbach, Fred A. (1945–62)
b. April 27, 1909
Jefferson City, MO
d. May 1993
Degrees: BA University of Missouri, 1930
MA University of Missouri, 1932
PhD Cornell University, 1941

Fields: Public Finance, American Politics, National Government, State Government, Local and Regional Planning
Publications: Maintaining Wisconsin: State, Regional, Local Planning Arrangements for Land Development and Environmental Protection, 1972
Career: US Department of Agriculture, Agricultural Economist, 1939–45
University of Wisconsin, Political Science and Agricultural Economics, Assistant Professor, 1945–46
Associate Professor, 1946–53
Professor, 1953–62
Urban and Regional Studies, Professor, 1962–72

Clausen, Aage (1966–71)
b. September 12, 1932
Dannenbrog, Nebraska
Degrees: BA Macalester College, 1957
MA University of Michigan, 1958
PhD University of Michigan, 1964
Fields: American Government, Political Theory, Legislative Behavior, Public Opinion, Survey Methods
Career: University of Wisconsin, Assistant Professor, 1966–71
Ohio State University, 1971-

Clough, Michael (1985–87)
Degrees: PhD University of California–Berkeley, 1985
Fields: International Relations, African International Politics
Career: University of Wisconsin, Assistant Professor, 1985–87
Council on Foreign Relations, Senior Fellow, 1987–96
University of California–Berkeley Institute of International Studies, Research Associate, 1996-

Cnudde, Charles (1968–73)
b. February 12, 1938
Degrees: AB University of Michigan, 1960
PhD University of North Carolina, 1967
Fields: Political Theory, American Politics, Empirical Methods, Public Opinion, Voting Behavior
Publications: Democracy in the American South, 1971
Career: University of California at Irvine, Assistant Professor, 1966–68
University of Wisconsin, Assistant Professor, 1968–70
Associate Professor, 1970–73
Michigan State University, Professor, Chair, 1973–80
University of Texas, Professor, Chair, 1980–87
Florida State University, Dean of Social Science, 1987-

Cohen, Bernard (1959–90)
b. February 22, 1926
Northampton, MA

Degrees:	BA Yale University, 1948 MA Yale University, 1950 PhD Yale University, 1952
Fields:	International Law, Organization and Politics, Foreign Policy, International Politics
Publications:	The Influence of Non-Governmental Groups on Foreign Policy Making, 1959 The Press and Foreign Policy, 1963 The Public's Impact on Foreign Policy, 1972 Democracies and Foreign Policy: Public Participation in the United States and the Netherlands, 1995
Career:	Yale University, Research Associate, Institute for International Studies, 1950–51 Princeton University, Research Associate, Center for International Studies, 1951–59 University of Wisconsin, Assistant Professor, 1959–60 Associate Professor, 1960–63 Professor, 1963–90 Political Science Department Chair, 1966–69 Associate Dean, Graduate School, 1971–75 Provost, 1984–89 Acting Chancellor, 1987

Coleman, John J. (1992-present)

b.	December 5, 1959 Leominster, PA
Degrees:	BA Clark University, 1982 PhD Massachusetts Institute of Technology, 1992
Fields:	American Politics, Political Parties
Publications:	Party Decline in America: Policy, Politics, and the Fiscal State, 1996
Career:	University of Texas at Austin, Instructor, 1990–92 University of Wisconsin, Assistant Professor, 1992–98 Associate Professor, 1998–2001 Professor, 2001-present Associate Chair, 2001–04

Croan, Melvin (1967–96)

b.	November 6, 1931 Boston, MA
Degrees:	AB Harvard College, 1953 MA Harvard University (Regional Studies–Soviet Union Program), 1955 PhD Harvard University, 1960
Fields:	Comparative Politics, Germany, Eastern Europe, Russia and the Ex-Soviet Union, Western Europe, Single Party and

	Authoritarian Systems, Post-Communist Transitions, Comparative Foreign Policy, International Relations, Political Theory, History of Political Thought, Political Sociology
Publications:	East Germany: The Soviet Connection, 1976
Career:	Harvard University, Instructor, 1960–63
	Regional Studies Program (Soviet Union), Assistant Professor and Director, 1963–67
	University of Wisconsin, Associate Professor 1967–70
	Professor, 1970–96
	Associate Chair, 1969–71
	Russian Area Studies Program, Chair, 1972–79
	Russian and Eastern European Studies Program, Chair, 1989–92

Cronin, Bruce (1995–2003)

Degrees:	BA State University of New York at Albany, 1985
	MA New York University, 1990
	PhD Columbia University, 1994
Fields:	International Organization and Institutions, International Law, International Relations Theory, Human and Minority Rights
Publications:	Communities Under Anarchy: Transnational Identity and the Evolution of Cooperation, 1999
Career:	University of Wisconsin, Assistant Professor, 1995–2003
	New York University, 2003-

Dangerfield, Royden J. (1949–50)

b.	Dec. 31, 1902
	Provo, UT
Degrees:	BS Brigham Young University, 1925
	PhD University of Chicago, 1931
Fields:	Foreign Relations, International Relations, Foreign Policy
Career:	University of Oklahoma, Assistant Professor, 1928
	Associate Professor, 1934
	Professor and Associate Dean of Grad School, 1938
	Dean of Faculty, 1942
	Executive Vice President, 1947–48
	University of Wisconsin, Professor, 1949–50
	University of Illinois, Vice President, 1950-

Davis, James W. (1964–68)

b.	September 14, 1935
	Chillicothe, MO
Degrees:	BA Harvard College, 1957
	MPA University of Michigan, 1962
	PhD University of Michigan, 1964
Fields:	American Politics, Urban Politics, Public Administration

Publications:	Little Groups of Neighbors: The Selective Service System (with Kenneth M. Dolbeare), 1968
Career:	University of Wisconsin, Assistant Professor, 1964–68 Washington University, 1968-

Deber, Raisa (1974–78)

b.	October 8, 1949 Toronto, Canada
Degrees:	SB MIT, 1971 SM MIT, 1971 PhD MIT
Fields:	American Politics, Research Methodology, Communications and Human Behavior
Career:	University of Wisconsin, Instructor 1974–78 University of Toronto Department of Health Administration, 1977-

Dennis, Jack S. (1963–2001)

b.	May 24, 1933 Tulsa, OK
Degree:	BA University of Oklahoma, 1955 BA Oxford University, 1957 MA University of Chicago, 1960 PhD University of Chicago, 1962
Fields:	American Politics, Mass Political Behavior, Political Socialization
Publications:	Children in the Political System: Origins of Political Legitimacy (with David Easton), 1969
Career:	University of Wisconsin, Assistant Professor, 1963–68 Associate Professor, 1968–71 Professor, 1971–2001 Chair, 1978–81 Associate Dean for the Social Sciences, College of Letters and Science, 1987–90

Dolbeare, Kenneth (1965–70)

b.	January 25, 1930
Degrees:	BA Haverford College, 1951 LLB Brooklyn Law School, 1958 PhD Columbia University, 1965
Fields:	American Politics, Constitutional Law, National Government, Political Thought
Publications:	American Politics: Policies, Power and Change (with Murray Edelman), 1964 Trial Courts in Urban Politics: State Trial Court Policy Impact and Functions in a Local Political System, 1967 Little Groups of Neighbors: The Selective Service System (with James Davis), 1968

Directions in American Political Thought, 1969
American Ideologies: The Competing Political Beliefs of the 1970's (with Patricia Dolbeare), 1971

Career: Hofstra University, Instructor, 1960–65
University of Wisconsin, Assistant Professor, 1965–68
Associate Professor, 1968–70
University of Washington, 1970-
The Evergreen State University

Donald, Carr L. (1958–60)

b. August 7, 1929
Cedar Rapids, IA

Degrees: BA University of Iowa, 1951
MIA Columbia University, 1955
PhD University of Texas–Austin, 1959

Career: University of Wisconsin, Instructor, 1958–60
Organization of American States

Donoghue, James R. (1948–84)

b. July 3, 1914
Pittsburgh, PA

d. June 1994

Degrees: AB University of Pittsburgh, 1938
MA University of Pittsburgh, 1940
PhD UCLA, 1949

Fields: American Politics, Metro and Urban Government and Politics, State Government, Local Government

Publications: How Wisconsin Voted 1848–1954, 1956
The Local Government System of Wisconsin, 1968

Career: University of Wisconsin, Assistant Professor, 1948–51
Associate Professor, 1951–56
Professor, 1956–84
Institute of Government Affairs, Director, 1956-

Downs, Donald A. (1985-present)

b. Toronto, Canada

Degrees: BA Cornell University, 1971
MA University of Illinois, 1974
PhD University of California–Berkeley, 1983

Fields: American Politics, Public Law

Publications: Nazis in Skokie: Freedom, Community, and the First Amendment, 1985
The New Politics of Pornography, 1989
More the Victims: Battered Women, the Syndrome Society, and the Law, 1996
Cornell '69: Liberalism and the Crisis of the American University, 1999

Career: University of Notre Dame, Instructor and Assistant Professor, 1981–85
University of Wisconsin, Assistant Professor, 1985–89
Associate Professor, 1989–1995
Professor, 1995-present

Dresang, Dennis L. (1969-present)
b. Appleton, WI
Degrees: BA University of Wisconsin, 1964
MA University of California at Los Angeles, 1965
PhD University of California at Los Angeles, 1971
Fields: American Politics, Public Service Management, Public Administration
Publications: <u>The Zambia Civil Service: Entrepreneurialism and Development Administration</u>, 1975
<u>Reforming Civil Service Systems: Special Task Forces and Legislative Processes</u>, 1979
<u>American Politics: The People and the Polity</u> (with Peter K. Eisinger), 2nd edition, 1982
<u>Politics, Policy and Management in American States</u>, 1989
<u>Public Personnel Management and Public Policy</u>, 4th edition, 2001
<u>Politics and Policy in American States and Communities</u> (with James J. Gosling), 3rd edition, 2001
Career: University of Wisconsin, Assistant Professor, 1969–74
Associate Professor, 1974–79
Professor, 1979-present
Associate Chair, 1973–76
Associate Director, Center for Public Policy and Administration, 1977–81
Director Center for Public Policy and Administration, 1981–83
Director, La Follette Institute of Public Affairs, 1983–87
Political Science Chair, 1990–93 and 1999–2001

Dykstra, Clarence Addison (1937–45)
b. February 25, 1883
Cleveland, OH
d. 1950
Degrees: AB State University of Iowa, 1903
LLD, LHD University of Chicago, 1908
Fields: American Government, Municipal Administration
Career: Ohio State University, Assistant Professor, 1908–09
University of Kansas, Associate Professor, 1909–12
Professor, 1912–18
University of California at Los Angeles, Faculty, 1922–30
Cincinnati City Manager, 1930–37
University of Wisconsin, President, 1937–45
University of California at Los Angeles, Provost, 1945–50

Ebenstein, William (1938–46)

b.	May 11, 1910 Vienna, Austria
d.	April 1976
Degrees:	LLD University of Vienna, 1934 PhD University of Wisconsin, 1938
Fields:	Political Theory, Philosophy, Comparative Politics
Publications:	Fascist Italy, 1939 The Law of Public Housing, 1940 The Nazi State, 1943 The German Record: A Political Portrait, 1945 The Pure Theory of Law, 1945
Career:	University of Wisconsin, Instructor, 1938–40 Assistant Professor, 1940–43 Associate Professor, 1943–46 Princeton University, 1946–62 University of California at Santa Barbara, 1964–66

Edelman, Murray J. (1966–90)

b.	November 5, 1919 Nanticoke, PN
d.	January 2001
Degrees:	AB Bucknell College, 1941 MA University of Chicago, 1942 PhD University of Illinois, 1948
Fields:	American Politics, Comparative Politics, Political Psychology, Political Theory
Publications:	Politics as Symbolic Action: Mass Arousal and Quiescence, 1964 American Politics: Policies, Power and Change (with Kenneth Dolbeare), 1971 Political Language: Words That Succeed and Policies That Fail, 1977 The Symbolic Uses of Politics, 1985 Constructing the Political Spectacle, 1988 From Art to Politics: How Artistic Creations Shape Political Conceptions, 1995 Politics of Misinformation, 2001
Career:	University of Illinois, Instructor, 1948–49 Assistant Professor, 1949–54 Associate Professor, 1954–58 Professor, 1958–66 University of Wisconsin, Professor, 1966–90

Edgerton, Russell (1965–69)

b.	May 23, 1938 Los Angeles, CA
Degrees:	BA Stanford University, 1960 PhD Columbia, 1967

Fields: American Politics, American Foreign Policy, Presidency, International Relations, Comparative Politics
Career: University of Wisconsin, Assistant Professor, 1965–69
American Association for Higher Education, President
US Department of Health, Education, and Welfare
Pew Forum on Undergraduate Learning, Director, 2000–04

Eisinger, Peter (1969–98)
b. July 9, 1942
Degrees: BA University of Michigan, 1964
MA University of Michigan, 1965
PhD Yale, 1969
Fields: Urban Politics and Policy, State and Local Economic Development, American Politics, State Politics, Federalism
Publications: The Patterns of Interracial Politics, 1976
The Politics of Displacement: Racial and Ethnic Transition in Three American Cities, 1980
American Politics: The People and the Polity (with Dennis L. Dresang), 2nd Edition, 1982
The Rise of the Entrepreneurial State: State and Local Economic Development Policy in the United States, 1988
The Midwest Response to the New Federalism, 1988
American States and Cities, 2nd Edition, 1997
Career: University of Wisconsin, Assistant Professor, 1969–74
Associate Professor, 1974–79
Professor, 1979–97
Associate Chair, 1976–78
Chair, 1987–1990
La Follette Institute of Public Affairs, Director, 1991–96
Wayne State University, 1997-

Emmerson, Donald K. (1970–2001)
b. July 10, 1940
Tokyo, Japan
Degrees: BA Princeton, 1964
MA Yale, 1966
PhD Yale, 1970
Fields: Comparative Politics, Asia, International Relations
Publications: The Bureaucracy in Indonesia, 1974
Indonesia's Elite: Political Culture and Cultural Politics, 1976
Political Legacies and Prospects for Democratic Governance in Southeast Asia: Burma and Indonesia (with Mary Calahan), 1995
Career: University of Wisconsin, Assistant Professor, 1970–76
Associate Professor, 1976–81
Professor, 1981–2001
Center for Southeast Asia Studies, Director, 1980s
Stanford University, Institute for International Studies, 2001-

Epstein, Leon D. (1948–88)
b. May 29, 1919
Milwaukee, WI
Degrees: BA University of Wisconsin, 1940
MA University of Wisconsin, 1941
PhD University of Chicago, 1948
Fields: Comparative Politics, Western Nations, Political Parties and Elections, Voting Behavior, Foreign Policy, British Politics
Publications: Britain: Uneasy Ally, 1954
Politics in Wisconsin, 1958
British Politics in the Suez Crisis, 1964
Political Parties in Western Democracies, 1967
Governing the University: The Campus and the Public Interest, 1974
Political Parties in the American Mold, 1986
Career: University of Oregon, Assistant Professor, 1947–48
University of Wisconsin, Assistant Professor, 1948–51
Associate Professor, 1951–54
Professor, 1954–88
Chair, 1960–63
College of Letters and Science, Dean, 1965–69

Farr, James (1984–89)
Degrees: PhD University of Minnesota, 1979
Fields: Political Philosophy
Career: Ohio State University
University of Wisconsin, Assistant Professor, 1984–86
Associate Professor, 1986–89
University of Minnesota, 1989-

Feeley, Malcolm (1977–85)
b. November 28, 1942
North Conway, New Hampshire
Degrees: BA Austin College, 1964
MA University of Minnesota, 1967
PhD University of Minnesota, 1969
Fields: American Politics, Public Policy, Law, Empirical Political Theory
Publications: The Process is the Punishment: Handling Cases in a Lower Court, 1979
The Policy Dilemma: Federal Crime Policy and the Law Enforcement Assistance Administration, 1968–1978 (with Austin Sarat), 1980
Court Reform on Trial: Why Simple Solutions Fail, 1983
Career: New York University, Instructor/Assistant Professor, Department of Politics, 1968–72
Yale University, Institution for Social and Policy Studies, Department of Political Science, Research Associate and Lecturer, 1974–77

University of Wisconsin, Assistant Professor, 1977–79
Associate Professor, 1979–85
University of California at Berkeley, 1985-

Fellman, David (**1947–79**)

b.	September 14, 1907
	Omaha, Nebraska
d.	November 23, 2003
Degrees:	AB University of Nebraska, 1929
	MA University of Nebraska, 1930
	PhD Yale University, 1934
Fields:	American Politics, Public Law
Publications:	<u>The Censorship of Books</u>, 1957
	<u>The Defendant's Rights</u>, 1958
	<u>The Limits of Freedom</u>, 1959
	<u>The Constitutional Rights of Association</u>, 1963
	<u>Religion in American Public Law</u>, 1965
	<u>The Defendant's Rights Under English Law</u>, 1966
	<u>The Defendant's Rights Today</u>, 1976
Career:	University of Nebraska, Instructor, 1934–39
	Assistant Professor, 1939–43
	Associate Professor, 1943–47
	University of Wisconsin, Visiting Lecturer, 1942–43, Summer 1946
	Professor, 1947–79
	Vilas Professor of Political Science, 1963–79

Fink, Richard (**1961–64**)

b.	Jan. 23, 1930
	Minneapolis, MN
Degrees:	BA University of Minnesota, 1952
	BPhil. Oxford University, 1955
	PhD Harvard University, 1963
Career:	University of Wisconsin, Instructor, 1961–64
	Private Sector, Minneapolis, 1964-

Fioretos, Orfeo (**1999–2005**)

b.	Kristianstad, Sweden
Degrees:	BA Bennington College, 1990
	MA Columbia University, 1991
	MPhil Columbia University, 1994
	PhD Columbia University, 1998
Fields:	International Relations and Organization, International and Comparative Political Economy, Politics and Society of Advanced Industrial States
Career:	University of California at Berkeley, Visiting Assistant Professor, 1998–99
	University of Wisconsin, Assistant Professor, 1999–2005

Fogg-Davis, Hawley (1999-present)

b. August 23, 1970
Rockford, IL

Degrees: AB Harvard University, 1993
PhD Princeton University, 1998

Fields: Political Theory

Publications: The Ethics of Transracial Adoption, 2002

Career: University of Wisconsin, Assistant Professor, 1999-present

Fowler, R. Booth (1967–2002)

Degrees: BA Haverford College, 1962
PhD Harvard University, 1967

Fields: Political Theory, Religion and Politics, American Political Thought and Politics

Publications: Believing Skeptics: American Political Thought 1945–64, 1978
A New Engagement: Evangelical Political Thought 1966–1976, 1982
Religion and Politics in the United States, 1985
Carrie Chapman Catt: Feminist Politician, 1986
Unconventional Partners: Religion and Liberal Culture in the United States, 1989
The Dance with Community: The Contemporary Debate in American Political Thought, 1991
The Greening of Protestant Thought: 1970–90, 1995
Enduring Liberalism: American Political Thought Since the 1960s, 1999

Career: University of Wisconsin, Assistant Professor, 1967–73
Associate Professor, 1973–78
Professor, 1978–2002
Associate Chair, 1984–87
Chair and Professor in Integrated Liberal Studies, 1999–2002

Franklin, Charles H. (1991-present)

b. June 7, 1954
Philadelphia, PA

Degrees: BA Birmingham–Southern College, 1975
MA University of Michigan, 1979
PhD University of Michigan, 1985

Fields: Political methodology

Career: Washington University, Instructor, 1984–85
Assistant Professor, 1986–92
University of Wisconsin, Assistant Professor, 1991–92
Associate Professor, 1992–97
Professor, 1997-present
Associate Chair, 1993–96

Friedman, Edward (1967-present)

b.	1937
	New York, NY
Degrees:	BA Brandeis University, 1959
	MA Harvard University, 1961
	PhD Harvard University, 1968
Fields:	Comparative Politics, Chinese Politics, International Political Economy
Publications:	Taiwan and American Policy, 1971
	Backward Toward Revolution: The Chinese Revolutionary Party, 1974
	Chinese Village, Socialist State (with Kay Johnson, Paul Pickowicz and Mark Seldon), 1991
	National Identity and Democratic Prospects in Socialist China, 1995
Career:	University of Wisconsin, Assistant Professor, 1967–73
	Associate Professor, 1973–77
	Professor, 1977-present
	Non-academic Employment: US House of Representatives Committee on Foreign Affairs (staff)

Froman, Lewis Acrelius Jr. (1960–65)

b.	December 24, 1935
	Buffalo, NY
Degrees:	BA Yale University, 1957
	PhD Northwestern University, 1960
Fields:	American Politics, National Government, Public Opinion, Public Policy
Publications:	People and Politics, 1962
Career:	University of Wisconsin, Assistant Professor, 1960–65
	University of California, Irvine, 1965-

Gardiner, John A. (1965–68)

b.	July 10, 1937
	Niagara Falls, NY
Degrees:	AB Princeton University, 1959
	MA Yale University, 1962
	LLB Harvard University, 1963
	PhD Harvard University, 1966
Fields:	American Politics, Urban Politics, State Politics, Public Law
Publications:	Police Department Policy-Making: The Case of Traffic Law Enforcement, 1968
Career:	University of Wisconsin, Assistant Professor, 1965–68
	State University of New York, Stony Brook, 1968-

Gaus, John Merriman (1927–47)

b.	September 3, 1894
	Stittville, NY
d.	May 1969
Degrees:	BA Amherst College, 1915
	MA Harvard University, 1917
	PhD Harvard University, 1924

Fields: Administration, American Politics, Regional Planning, Comparative Politics (Europe)

Publications: Great Britain: A Study of Civic Loyalty, 1929
Frontiers of Public Administration (with Leonard D. White and Marshall E. Dimock), 1936
Public Administration and the United States Department of Agriculture (with Leon O. Wolcott), 1940
Reflections on Public Administration, 1947

Career: Amherst College, Instructor, 1920–22
Associate Professor, 1922–23
University of Minnesota, Assistant Professor, 1923–24
Associate Professor, 1924–26
Professor, 1926–27
University of Wisconsin, Professor, 1927–47
Chair, 1940–42
Harvard University, 1947–61

Gehlbach, Scott (2003-present)

b. Lincoln, IL

Degrees: BS University of Illinois, 1989
MBA University of Michigan, 1991
MA University of California–Berkeley (Political Science), 1998
MA University of California–Berkeley (Economics), 2000
PhD University of California–Berkeley, 2003

Fields: Comparative Politics, Methodology, Eastern Europe/Former Soviet Union, Advanced Theory, Industrial Organization

Career: Office of Congressman Thomas W. Ewing, Legislative Assistant, 1992–94
Centre for Economic and Financial Research, Moscow, Visiting Scholar, 2001–03
University of Wisconsin, Assistant Professor, 2003-present

Gillespie, Charles (1988–91)

b. November 5, 1958
London, England

d. 1991

Degrees: BA Magdalen College, Oxford University, 1980
MPhil Yale University, 1985
PhD Yale University, 1987

Fields: Comparative Politics, Latin America, Western Europe, Political Economy

Publications: Negotiating Democracy: Politicians and Generals in Uruguay, 1991

Career: Yale University, Instructor, 1982–86
Amherst College, Visiting Assistant Professor, 1986–88
University of Wisconsin, Assistant Professor, 1988–91

Gilliam, Franklin (1983–87)
Degrees: BA Drake University
PhD University of Iowa
Fields: Modern African-American Politics, Minority Political Empowerment, Politics of Cultural Diversity
Career: University of Wisconsin, Assistant Professor, 1983–87
University of California at Los Angeles, 1987-

Goldstein, Kenneth M. (1996-present)
b. New York, NY
Degrees: BA Haverford College, 1983–87
PhD University of Michigan, 1996
Fields: American Politics, Interest Groups, Research Methods, Political Communication
Publications: Interest Groups, Lobbying, and Participation in America, 1999
Career: CBS News Election and Survey Unit, Researcher, 1987–89
CBS News Nightwatch, Researcher, 1989–90
Arizona State University, Assistant Professor, 1996–2000
University of Wisconsin, Assistant Professor, 2000–02
Associate Professor, 2002-present

Gormley, William T. (1980–91)
Degrees: BA University of Pittsburgh, 1972
PhD University of North Carolina-Chapel Hill, 1976
Fields: Policy Analysis, Regulatory Policy, Social Policy, American Government, Bureaucratic Politics, Federalism and Intergovernmental Relations, Interest Group Politics
Publications: The Politics of Public Utility Regulation, 1983
Taming the Bureaucracy: Muscles, Prayers, and Other Strategies, 1989
Career: State University of New York–Buffalo, Visiting Assistant Professor, 1976–77
State University of New York–Stony Brook, Assistant Professor, 1977–80
University of Wisconsin, Assistant Professor, 1980–83
Associate Professor, 1983–88
Professor, 1988–91
Georgetown University, 1991-

Grant, James Allen Clifford (1927–30)
b. June 19, 1902
Grand Forks, ND
Degrees: AB Stanford University, 1924
MA Stanford University, 1925
PhD Stanford University, 1927
Fields: International Relations, Constitutional Law, American Politics
Career: California Legislature, Assembly Judicial Committee, Clerk, 1927

University of Wisconsin, Instructor, 1927–29
Assistant Professor, 1929–30
University of California at Los Angeles, 1930–69

Greene, Lee Seifert (1935–36)
b. May 31, 1905
Esbon, Kansas
Degrees: AB University of Kansas, 1930
MA University of Wisconsin, 1932
PhD University of Wisconsin, 1934
Fields: American Politics, State and Local Government, Metro and Urban Government and Politics, Administration
Career: University of Wisconsin, Instructor, 1935–36
University of Tennessee-Knoxville, 1937-

Greffenius, Steven (1987–90)
Degrees: BA Reed College, 1976
MA University of Iowa, 1984
PhD University of Iowa, 1987
Fields: International Relations, Political Theory, Comparative Politics
Career: University of Wisconsin, Assistant Professor, 1987–90
Private Sector, Massachusetts

Grossman, Joel B. (1963–96)
b. June 19, 1936
New York, NY
Degrees: BA Queens College, 1957
MA University of Iowa, 1960
PhD, University of Iowa, 1963
Fields: American Politics, Presidency, National Government, US Judicial System, Constitutional Law
Publications: Lawyers and Judges: The ABA and the Politics of Judicial Selection, 1965
Constitutional Law and Judicial Policy Making (with Richard Wells), 1972
Career: University of Wisconsin, Assistant Professor, 1963–67
Associate Professor, 1967–71
Professor, 1971–96
Chair, 1975–78
Johns Hopkins University, 1996-

Hall, Arnold B. (1910–25)
b. July 22, 1881
Franklin, ID
d. May/June 1936
Degrees: BA Franklin College, 1904
JD University of Chicago, 1907

Fields: Law, Political Institutions
Publications: The Past, Present, and Future of the Monroe Doctrine, 1920
Popular Government: An Inquiry Into the Nature and Methods of Representative Government, 1921
Career: University of Chicago, Assistant Instructor, 1907–09
Northwestern University, Instructor, 1909–10
University of Wisconsin, Instructor, 1910–11
Assistant Professor, 1911–16
Associate Professor, 1916–21
Professor, 1921–26
University of Oregon, President, 1926–32
The Brookings Institution, Director of the Institute for Government Research, 1932–36

Hanson, Donald W. (1967–1971)
b. March 6, 1933
Salt Lake City, UT
Degrees: BA University of Utah, 1957
AB Oxford University (Rhodes Scholar), 1959
MA Oxford University, 1963
MA University of Utah, 1961
PhD Harvard University, 1965
Fields: Political Theory, International Politics, International Organization
Publications: From Kingdom to Commonwealth: The Development of Civic Consciousness in English Political Thought, 1970
Political Morality: Some Issues in Contemporary Political Philosophy, 1970
Career: Harvard University, Department of Government, Instructor, 1965–67
University of Wisconsin, Assistant Professor, 1967–70
Associate Professor 1970–71
University of Utah, 1970-

Harris, Joseph Pratt (1923–30)
b. February 18, 1896
Sulphur Springs, NC
Degrees: BA University of Kansas, 1918
PhD University of Chicago, 1923
Fields: Public Administration, Political Parties, Public Opinion, Legislative
Publications: Proportional Representation in the US, 1928
Registration of Voters in the US, 1929
Career: University of Wisconsin, Instructor, 1923–25
Assistant Professor, 1925–28
Associate Professor, 1928–30
University of Washington, 1930–34
University of California at Berkcley, 1941-

Hart, Henry C. (1948–1982)

b. November 17, 1916
Lucknow, India

Degrees: BA Vanderbilt University, 1936
PhD University of Wisconsin, 1950

Fields: Comparative Politics, South Asia: India and Pakistan, Public Administration

Publications: New India's Rivers, 1956
The Dark Missouri, 1957
Administrative Aspects of River Valley Development, 1961

Career: TVA, Administrative Assistant, 1936–43
University of Wisconsin, Instructor, 1948–50
Assistant Professor, 1950–55
Associate Professor, 1955–59
Professor, 1959–1982

Hayward, Fred M. (1968–91)

Degrees: BA University of California at Riverside
PhD Princeton, 1969

Fields: Comparative Politics, African Politics, Ghana, Sierra Leone

Career: University of Wisconsin, Assistant Professor, 1968–73
Associate Professor, 1973–78
Professor, 1978–92
Department Chair 1981–84
College of Letters and Sciences Associate Dean
African Studies, Chair 1973–76
International Studies, Acting Dean 1989–90
American Council on Education, 1991-

Hendley, Kathryn (1993-present)

Degrees: AB Indiana University, 1979
JD UCLA School of Law, 1982
MA Georgetown University, 1987
PhD University of California at Berkeley, 1993

Fields: Public Law, Soviet Politics, Political Economy

Publications: Trying to Make Law Matter: Labor Law and Legal Reform in Russia, 1996

Career: University of Wisconsin, Assistant Professor of Law and Political Science, 1993–97
Associate Professor of Law and Political Science, 1998–2001
Professor of Law and Political Science, 2001-present
Director, Center for Russia, East Europe, and Central Asia, 1998–2001

Hinckley, Barbara (1972–88)

d.	November 21, 1995
	West Lafayette, ID
Degrees:	AB Mt. Holyoke, 1959
	MA Mt. Holyoke, 1961
	PhD Cornell, 1968
Fields:	American politics, Congress
Publications:	The Seniority System in Congress, 1971
	Coalitions & Politics, 1981
	Congressional Elections, 1981
	Stability and Change in Congress, 4th edition, 1987
Career:	University of Massachusetts, Assistant Professor, 1968–70
	Cornell University, Assistant Professor, 1970–72
	University of Wisconsin, Associate Professor, 1972–75
	Professor, 1975–88
	New York University, 1987–92
	Purdue University, 1992–95

Holden Jr., Matthew (1969–81)

b.	September 12, 1931
	Mound Bayou, MS
Degrees:	BA Roosevelt University, 1952
	MA Northwestern University, 1955
	PhD Northwestern University, 1961
Fields:	Public Administration, Urban Politics, African American Politics
Publications:	The Politics of Poor Relief: A Study in Ambiguities, 1973
	The Politics of the Black 'Nation,' 1973
	The White Man's Burden, 1973
	The Divisible Republic, 1973
Career:	Wayne State University, Assistant Professor, 1962–63
	Associate Professor, 1966–68
	Professor, 1968–69
	University of Pittsburgh, Assistant Professor, 1963–66
	University of Wisconsin, Professor, 1969–1981
	Public Service Commissioner, State of Wisconsin, 1975–77
	US Department of Energy, Commissioner, 1978-81
	University of Virginia, 1981-

Hornbeck, Stanley K. (1908–09, 1914–19)

b.	May 4, 1883
	Franklin, MA
d.	December 1966
Degress:	BA University of Denver, 1903
	AB Oxford University, 1907
	PhD University of Wisconsin, 1911

Fields:	Law, Public Administration, Foreign Policy, China
Publications:	The Most Favored Nation Clause, 1910 Contemporary Politics in the Far East, 1916
Career:	University of Wisconsin, Instructor, 1908–09 Assistant Professor, 1914–17 Associate Professor, 1917–19 Chinese Government College, Instructor, 1909–14 US Tariff Commission, Special Expert, 1917–20 Paris Peace Conference, US Delegation Member, 1918–19 Department of State, 1921–44 Ambassador to Netherlands, 1944–47 Paris Peace Conference, US Delegation Member, 1918–19

Howell, William (2000–02)

Degrees:	BA Wesleyan University, 1993 PhD Stanford University, 2000
Fields:	American political institutions, Presidency, Education, Quantitative Methods
Publications:	The Education Gap: Vouchers and Urban Schools, with Paul Peterson, 2002
Career:	University of Wisconsin, Assistant Professor, 2000–2002 Harvard University, 2002-

Huitt, Ralph K. (1949–83)

b.	January 8, 1913 Corsicana, TX
d.	October 1986
Degrees:	AB Southwestern University, 1934 PhD University of Texas, 1950 LLD Southwestern University, 1972
Fields:	American Politics, Legislative, Executive, Public Opinion, Congressional Behavior
Publications:	Congress: Two Decades of Analysis, 1969
Career:	YMCA, Beaumont, TX, Membership Secretary, 1934–35 Boys' Club Secretary, 1935–42 Lamar College, Assistant Professor, 1942–43 University of Wisconsin, Assistant Professor, 1949–54 Associate Professor, 1954–59 Professor, 1959–1983** Staff Aide, Senator Lyndon B. Johnson, 1953–54 Legislative Assistant, Senator William Proxmire, 1959 US Department of Health, Education, Welfare, Assistant Secretary for Legislation, 1965–69 National Association of State Universities and Land Grant Colleges, Executive Director, 1970–78 [**On leave 1965–1978]

Hutchcroft, Paul D. (1993-present)

b. August 15, 1957
Ames, IA

Degrees: BA Macalester College, 1980
MA Yale University, 1986
PhD Yale University, 1993

Fields: Comparative Politics, Political Economy, Southeast Asian Politics

Publications: Booty Capitalism: The Politics of Banking in the Philippines, 1998

Career: Harvard Academy for International and Area Studies, academy scholar, 1991–93
University of Wisconsin, Assistant Professor, 1993–2000
Associate Professor, 2000-present

Iyenaga, Toyokichi (1902–04)

b. 1882

d. 1936

Career: Japanese Administration, Formosa, 1901
University of Wisconsin, Instructor, 1902–04

Publications: Constitutional Development of Japan, 1853–1881, 1891
Japan and the California Problem, 1921

Jacob, Herbert (1962–69, 1984–86)

b. February 10, 1933
Augsburg, Germany

Degrees: AB Harvard University, 1954
MA Yale University, 1955
PhD Yale University, 1960

Fields: American Politics, Judicial, State and Local Government, Methods

Publications: German Administration Since Bismarck, 1963
Debtors in Court: The Consumption of Government Services, 1969
Urban Justice: Law and Order in American Cities, 1973
Elementary Political Analysis (with Robert Weissberg), 2nd edition, 1975
Felony Justice: An Organizational Analysis of Criminal Courts (with James Eisenstein), 1977
The Frustration of Policy: Responses to Crime by American Cities, 1984
Justice in America: Courts, Lawyers, and the Judicial Process, 4th edition, 1984
Silent Revolution: The Transformation of Divorce Law in the United States, 1988

Career: Tulane University, Instructor, 1960–62
University of Wisconsin, Assistant Professor, 1962–64
Associate Professor, 1964–67
Professor, 1967–69
Professor (Hawkins Chair), 1984–1986
Northwestern University, Professor, 1969–84, 1986-

Jacobson, Jacob Mark (1927–31)

b.	January 6, 1905 New York, NY
Degrees:	MA Brown University, 1926 PhD Brown University, 1929
Career:	University of Wisconsin, Instructor, 1927–31

Jalal, Ayesha (1987–90)

Degrees:	BA Wellesley College, 1978 PhD Trinity College, University of Cambridge, 1983
Fields:	Comparative Politics, South Asia
Publications:	The Sole Spokesman: Jinnah, the Muslim League, and the Demand for Pakistan, 1985 State of Martial Law: The Origins of Pakistan's Political Economy of Defence, 1990
Career:	University of Wisconsin, Assistant Professor, 1987–90 Tufts University, 1990-

Johnson, Cathy M. (1984–90)

Degrees:	PhD University of Michigan
Fields:	American Politics, Public Policy
Career:	University of Wisconsin, Instructor, 1984–86 Assistant Professor, 1986–90 Williams College

Jones, Charles O. (1988–97)

b.	October 28, 1931 Worthing, SD
Degrees:	BA University of South Dakota, 1953 MS University of Wisconsin, 1956 PhD University of Wisconsin, 1960
Publications:	Party and Policy-Making: The House Republican Policy Committee, 1965 The Republican Party in American Politics, 1965 Every Second Year: Congressional Behavior and the Two-Year Term, 1967 Minority Party in Congress, 1970 Clean Air: The Policies and Politics of Pollution Control, 1975 The United States Congress: People, Place, and Policy, 1982 An Introduction to the Study of Public Policy, 3rd edition, 1984 The Trusteeship Presidency: Jimmy Carter and the United States Congress, 1988 The Presidency in a Separated System, 1994 Separate But Equal Branches: Congress and the Presidency, 1995 Passages to the Presidency: From Campaigning to Governing, 1998 Clinton and Congress 1993–1996: Risk, Restoration and Reelection, 1999

Career: Wellesley College, Assistant Professor, 1959–62
National Center for Education in Politics, Associate Director, 1962–63
University of Arizona, Associate Professor/Professor, 1963–69
University of Pittsburgh, Maurice Falk Professor of Politics, 1969–81
University of Virginia, Robert Kent Gooch Professor of Government, 1981–88
University of Wisconsin, Professor (Hawkins Chair), 1988–97

Jones, Chester Lloyd (1910–19, 1928–41)
b. March 6, 1881
Hillside, WI
d. January 1941
Degrees: BL University of Wisconsin, 1902
PhD University of Pennsylvania, 1906
Fields: Political Economy, Finance and Industry, Comparative Politics, International Relations
Publications: Caribbean Interests of the US, 1916
Mexico and Its Reconstruction, 1921
Caribbean, 1929
Caribbean Backgrounds and Prospects, 1931
Costa Rica and Civilization in the Caribbean, 1935
The Caribbean Since 1900, 1935
Guatemala, Past and Present, 1940
Career: University of Pennsylvania, Instructor, 1906–10
University of Wisconsin, Associate Professor, 1910–16
Professor, 1916–17, 1928–44
Chair, 1913–18
School of Commerce, Professor and Director, 1929–35
War Trade Board, Director of the Bureau of Foreign Agents, 1918–19
American Embassy Madrid, Commercial Attache, 1919–20
American Embassy Havana, Commercial Attache, 1921
American Embassy Paris, Commercial Attache, 1922–28

Kay, David (1966–75)
b. 1940
Degrees: BBA University of Texas, 1962
MIA Columbia University, 1964
PhD Columbia University, 1967
Fields: International Organization, International Relations, American Foreign Policy, National Security
Policy (American), International Law
Publications: New Nations in the United Nations, 1960–1967, 1970
Career: University of Wisconsin, Assistant Professor, 1966–68
Associate Professor, (rejoined dept.), 1970–73
Professor, 1973–75

Columbia University, Associate Professor, 1968–69
United Nations Weapons Inspector, Iraq, 1991–92
Director, CIA Weapons Search Team, Iraq, 2003–04

Kettl, Donald F. (1990–2004)
b. Philadelphia, PA
Degrees: BA Yale College, 1974
MA Yale University, 1976
MPhil Yale University, 1976
PhD Yale University, 1978
Fields: Public Policy, Public Administration
Publications: The Presidency in a Separated System, 1995
Reinventing Government: A Fifth-Year Report Card, 1998
The Global Public Management Revolution: A Report on the Transformation of Governance, 2000
The Transformation of Governance: Public Administration for the 21st Century, 2002
Career: Columbia University, Assistant Professor, 1978–79
University of Virginia, Assistant Professor, 1979–85
Associate Professor, 1985–89
Vanderbilt University, Associate Professor, 1989–90
University of Wisconsin, Professor, Department of Political Science and La Follette Institute of Public Affairs, 1990–2004
Associate Director, La Follette Institute of Public Affairs, 1992–94
Director, La Follette Institute of Public Affairs, 1996–99
University of Pennsylvania, Professor, 2004-present

Khademian, Anne (1990–97)
Degrees: BA Michigan State University, 1983
MPA Michigan State University, 1985
PhD Washington University, 1989
Fields: Public Administration and Organizational Theory, Public Policy and Political Economy, American Politics
Publications: The SEC and Capital Market Regulation: The Politics of Expertise, 1992
Checking on Banks: Autonomy and Accountability in Three Federal Agencies, 1996
Career: The Brookings Institution, Governmental Studies, Research Fellow, 1989–90
University of Wisconsin, Assistant Professor, 1990–96
Associate Professor, 1996–97
University of Michigan, 1997-

Kinsella, Helen (2004-present)
Degrees: BA, Bryn Mawr College, 1989
MA, University of Minnesota, 1996
PhD University of Minnesota, 2003

Fields: International Relations Theories, International Human Rights Law, International Institutions, International Security, US Foreign Policy, Contemporary Political Theory, Feminist Political Theory

Career: University of Minnesota, Instructor, 2001–2002
Harvard University, Belfer Center International Security Program, Research Fellow, 2003–2004
Stanford University, Center for International Security and Cooperation, Postdoctoral Fellow, 2004–2005
University of Wisconsin, Assistant Professor, 2004-

Kirk, Grayson Lewis (1929–40)

b. October 12, 1903
Jeffersonville, OH

d. November 21, 1997

Degrees: BA Miami University of Ohio, 1924
MA Clark University, 1925
PhD University of Wisconsin, 1931

Fields: International Relations, Foreign Relations, African Politics, International Organization

Publications: Philippine Independence, 1936
Contemporary International Politics (with Walter Sharp), 1940
The Monroe Doctrine Today, 1941

Career: South Park College, Beaumont, Texas, Instructor, 1925–27
University of Wisconsin, Instructor, 1927–30
Assistant Professor, 1930–36
Associate Professor, 1936–38
Professor, 1938–40
Columbia University, 1940-
Provost, 1949–53
Vice President, 1950–53
President, 1959–68

Kritzer, Herbert M. (1977-present)

b. Opelika, AL

Degrees: BA Haverford College, 1969
PhD University of North Carolina, 1974

Fields: Law and Politics, Civil Justice, Research Methodology, Political Analysis and American National Government

Publications: The Justice Broker: Lawyers and Ordinary Civil Litigation, 1990
Let's Make a Deal: Negotiation and Settlement in Ordinary Litigation, 1991
Courts, Law and Politics in Comparative Perspective (with Herbert Jacob, Erhard Blankenburg, Doris Marie Provine, and Joseph Sanders), 1996

	Legal Advocacy: Lawyers and Nonlawyers at Work, 1998
	Risks, Regulations and Rewards: Contingency Fee Legal Practice in the United States, 2004
Career:	Indiana University, Visiting Assistant Professor, 1974–75
	Rice University, Assistant Professor, 1975–78
	University of Wisconsin, Visiting Assistant Professor, 1977–78
	Assistant Professor, 1978–80
	Associate Professor, 1980–85
	Professor, 1985-present
	Chair, 1996–99
	Director, Data and Computation Center, 1982–86

Kronebusch, Karl (**1993–1998**)

Degrees:	BA University of Notre Dame, 1978
	MSc London School of Economics, University of London, 1980
	MPP, Kennedy School of Government, Harvard University, 1990
	PhD Harvard University, 1993
Fields:	Health Policy, Social Policy, Politics of Health and Social Welfare Policy, Public Management
Career:	US Department of Labor, Occupational Safety & Health Administration, Economist, 1979–82
	US Congress, Office of Technology Assessment, Policy Analyst, 1982–87
	University of Wisconsin, Department of Political Science and La Follette Institute of Public Affairs, Assistant Professor, 1993–98
	Yale University, School of Epidemiology and Public Health, 1996-

Lathrop, John (**1849–59**)

b.	1799
d.	1865
Career:	Hamilton College, Professor, ? –1842
	University of Missouri, President, 1842–49
	University of Wisconsin, Chancellor, 1849–58
	Professor, Ethical and Political Science, 1849–59
	University of Missouri, Professor of English Literature, 1859–65
	President, 1865-

Leavitt, Michael R. (**1970–73**)

b.	December 19, 1944
	New York, NY
Degrees:	SB MIT, 1966
	MA Wayne State University, 1968
	PhD Northwestern University, 1971
Fields:	International Politics, Comparative Politics, Applications of Computers to the Study of Politics
Career:	University of Wisconsin, Assistant Professor, 1970–73
	Consolidated Analysis Centers, Inc., Senior Associate, 1972-

Leheny, David (1998-present)

b. October 26, 1967
Danbury, CT

Degrees: BA Wesleyan University, 1989
MA Cornell University, 1994
PhD Cornell University, 1998

Fields: Comparative Politics, Japan

Publications: The Rules of Play: National Identity and the Shaping of Japanese Leisure, 2003

Career: University of Wisconsin, Assistant Professor, 1998–2005
Professor, 2005-

Lewis, John D. (1930–35)

b. October 6, 1905
Paterson, NJ

Degrees: AB Oberlin College, 1928
MA University of Wisconsin, 1929
PhD University of Wisconsin, 1934

Fields: Political Theory and Philosophy, Comparative Politics, Law

Publications: The Genossenschaft Theory of Otto von Gierke, 1935

Career: University of Wisconsin, Instructor, 1930–35
Oberlin College, 1935–72

Lewis, Stephen C. (1986–93)

b. 1957

Degrees: PhD MIT

Fields: Comparative Politics, European Politics, Italian politics

Career: University of Wisconsin, Instructor, 1986–87
Assistant Professor, 1987–94

Li, Richard (1973–75)

Degrees: PhD University of Washington, 1973

Career: University of Wisconsin, Assistant Professor, 1973–75

Lindberg, Leon N. (1962–1997)

b. June 18, 1932
Chicago, IL

Degrees: AB University of California, 1955
MA University of California, 1957
PhD University of California, 1962

Fields: Comparative Politics, Western Europe, European Union, International Political Economy

Publications: The Political Dynamics of European Economic Integration, 1963
Europe's Would-be Polity: Patterns of Change in the European Community (with Stuart A. Scheingold), 1970

Career: University of Wisconsin, Assistant Professor, 1961–65
Associate Professor, 1965–69
Professor, 1969–97

Lipsky, Michael (1966–70)

b.	April 13, 1940 New York, NY
Degrees:	BA Oberlin College, 1961 MPA Woodrow Wilson School of Public and International Affairs, Princeton University, 1964 MA Princeton University, 1964 PhD Princeton University, 1967
Fields:	State and Local Government, American Politics, Party Politics, Modern Political Theory, Comparative Politics
Publications:	Protest in City Politics: Rent Strikes, Housing and the Power of the Poor, 1969
Career:	University of Wisconsin, Assistant Professor, 1966–70 Special Assistant to the Chancellor for Equal Opportunity Programs, 1968–69 MIT, 1969-

Lowrie, Seldon Gale (1909–12)

b.	August 12, 1884
d.	November 1961
Degrees:	AB Knox College, 1907 MA University of Illinois, 1908 PhD University of Wisconsin, 1912
Fields:	Administrative Law, Public Administration, Local Government, International Law, International Relations
Career:	University of Wisconsin, Assistant Professor, 1909–12 Ohio Legislative Reference Bureau, Director, 1912–14 Cincinnati Municipal Reference Bureau, Director, 1912–17 University of Cincinnati, Ohio, 1912–55

MacGilvray, Eric A. (2003-present)

Degrees:	AB Princeton University, 1993 MA University of Chicago, 1995 PhD University of Chicago, 1999
Fields:	Modern and Contemporary Democratic Theory, Modern and Contemporary Liberal Theory, American Pragmatism, History of Political Thought
Publications:	Reconstructing Public Reason, 2004
Career:	University of Chicago, Assistant Professor, 1999–2003 University of Wisconsin, Assistant Professor, 2003-present

MacGregor, Ford H. (1909–34)

Fields:	Municipal Government
Career:	University of Wisconsin, Instructor, 1909–15 Lecturer, 1915–23 Assistant Professor 1923–24 Associate Professor 1924–34

Manion, Melanie Frances (2000-present)

b.	Cold Lake, Alberta, Canada
Degrees:	BA McGill University, 1978
	MA University of London, 1982
	PhD University of Michigan, 1989
Fields:	Comparative Politics, Chinese Politics
Publications:	Retirement of Revolutionaries: Public Policies, Social Norms, Private Interests, 1993
	Corruption by Design: Building Clean Government in Mainland China, 2004
Career:	University of Rochester, Instructor, 1989
	Assistant Professor, 1989–95
	Associate Professor, 1995–2000
	University of Wisconsin, Associate Professor, Political Science and Public Affairs, 2000-present

Manley, John (1966–71)

b.	February 20, 1939
	Utica, NY
Degrees:	BS Le Moyne College, 1961
	MA Syracuse University, 1963
	PhD Syracuse University, 1967
Fields:	American Politics, Legislative Politics
Publications:	The Politics of Finance: The House Committee on Ways and Means, 1970
Career:	University of Wisconsin, Assistant Professor, 1966–69
	Associate Professor, 1969–71
	Stanford University, 1971-

Marmor, Theodore (1967–70)

b.	February 24, 1939
	New York, NY
Degrees:	BA Harvard College, 1960
	PhD Harvard University, 1966
Fields:	Comparative Politics, Political Thought, Politics of Poverty, Health Politics
Publications:	The Politics of Medicare (with Jan S. Marmor), 1970
Career:	University of Wisconsin, Assistant Professor, 1967–70
	University of Minnesota, 1970–73
	University of Chicago, 1973–79
	Yale University, 1979-

Marquez, Benjamin (1991-present)

b.	El Paso, TX
Degrees:	BA University of Texas at El Paso, 1975
	MA University of Wisconsin, 1976
	PhD University of Wisconsin, 1983

Fields:	American Politics, Minority Politics, Political Sociology
Publications:	LULAC: The Evolution of A Mexican American Political Organization, 1993
	Constructing Identities in Mexican-American Political Organizations: Choosing Issues, Taking Sides, 2003
Career:	San Jose State University, Instructor, 1983–84
	University of Kansas, Post-Doctoral Research Fellow, 1984–86
	University of Utah, Assistant Professor, 1986–91
	University of Wisconsin, Assistant Professor, 1991–94
	Associate Professor, 1994–2001
	Professor, 2001-present
	Director, Chicano Studies Program, 1995–97

Marra, Robin F. (1983–1987)

Degrees:	PhD Michigan State University
Career:	University of Wisconsin, Lecturer, 1983–84
	Assistant Professor, 1983–87

Mayda, Jaroslav (1951–56)

b.	December 24, 1918
	Brno, Czechoslovakia
Degrees:	Gymnasium, Brno, Cz., 1937
	Masaryk University, Brno, Cz.
	J.U. Dr. Law Faculty, Masaryk University, Brno, Cz.
Fields:	International Law and Relations
Career:	Engineering Academy, Brno, Teacher, 1943–45
	Shodaworks, Prague, Export Section, Legal Advisor, 1946–48
	US Military Government, Germany, Translator and Research Analyst, 1948–49
	Denison University, Visiting Professor of Government, 1949–50
	Ohio State University, Visiting Professor of International Law and Relations, 1950–51
	University of Wisconsin, Assistant Professor, 1951–56
	Louisiana State University, 1957-

Mayer, Kenneth R. (1989-present)

b.	January 12, 1960
	Auburn, WA
Degrees:	BA University of California at San Diego, 1982
	MA and MPhil Yale University, 1987
	PhD Yale University, 1988
Fields:	American Politics, Presidency, Legislative Politics
Publications:	The Political Economy of Defense Contracting, 1991
	The Dysfunctional Congress? The Individual Roots of an Institutional Dilemma (with David Canon), 1999
	With the Stroke of a Pen: Executive Orders and Presidential Power, 2001

	Debating the Issues in American Politics (with John Coleman and David Canon), 2004
Career:	University of Wisconsin, Assistant Professor, 1989–96
	Associate Professor, 1996–2000
	Professor, 2000-present
	Director, Data and Computation Center, 1996-present

McBain, Harold Lee (1910–14)

Fields:	Public Administration, Municipal Government
Career:	University of Wisconsin, Associate Professor, 1910–14

McCalla, Robert (1987–97)

Degrees:	BA Swathmore College, 1981
	MA University of Michigan, 1984
	PhD University of Michigan, 1987
Fields:	Organizational Politics and National Security, International Conflict and Security, International Organizations and Security Processes, Foreign Policy Decision-making, Organizational Theory
Publications:	Uncertain Perceptions: US Cold War Crisis Decision Making, 1992
Career:	University of Wisconsin, Assistant Professor, 1987–97

McCamy, James L. (1947–71)

b.	1906
	Knoxville, TN
d.	December 1995
Degrees:	BA University of Texas, 1929
	MA University of Texas, 1932
	PhD University of Chicago, 1938
Fields:	Public Administration, American Politics, American Foreign Affairs, Science and Government
Publications:	Government Publications for Citizens, 1949
	The Administration of American Foreign Affairs, 1950
	American Government, 1957
	Science and Public Administration, 1960
	Conduct of the New Diplomacy, 1964
Career:	Bennington College, Teacher, 1934–39, 1941–42
	Assistant to Secretary of Agriculture, Henry A. Wallace, 1939–40
	Assistant to Secretary of Agriculture, Claude A. Wickard, 1940–41
	Assistant to Director, Board of Economic Warfare, 1942–43
	Foreign Economic Administration, Bureau of Areas, Executive Director, 1943–45
	US Forces, Austria, Economic Advisor and US Mission to Austria, Chief Economic Officer, 1945
	US Department of Commerce, World Trade Policy Staff, Chief, 1946
	University of Wisconsin, Professor, 1947–1971
	Chair, 1948–52

McClelland, Glenn (1937–40)
Fields: Political Theory, Constitutional Law
Career: University of Wisconsin, Instructor, 1937–40

McCrone, Donald (1965–71)
b. October 1939
Cambridge, MA
Degrees: BA University of Florida, 1961
PhD University of North Carolina, 1966
Fields: Comparative Politics, Voting Behavior, Latin American Politics, Western European Politics
Career: University of Wisconsin, Assistant Professor, 1965–71
University of Iowa, 1971
University of Washington

Meier, Kenneth J. (1985–90)
Degrees: BA University of South Dakota, 1972
MA Syracuse University, 1974
PhD Syracuse University, 1975
Fields: American Politics, Politics of Regulation
Publications: Regulation: Bureaucracy, Politics, and Economics, 1985
The Political Economy of Regulation: The Case of Insurance, 1988
Race, Class, and Education: The Politics of Second Generation Discrimination (with Joseph Stewart and Robert England), 1989
Career: Rice University, Assistant Professor, 1975–77
University of Oklahoma, Assistant Professor, 1978–81
Associate Professor, 1981–85
University of Wisconsin, Associate Professor, 1985–86
Professor, 1986–89
University of Wisconsin–Milwaukee, Professor, 1989–97
Texas A&M, 1997-

Menges, Constantine C. (1964–67)
b. September 1, 1939
Ankara, Turkey
Degrees: AB Columbia University, 1960
PhD Columbia University 1965
Fields: International Relations; Comparative Politics, Soviet Union and Germany
Career: University of Wisconsin, Instructor, 1964–65
Assistant Professor, 1965–67
US Government, Latin America, Specialist
George Washington University, Professor, 1990–2000
Hudson Institute, Senior Fellow, 2000-

Merelman, Richard (1969–2001)
b. October 10, 1938
Washington DC
Degrees: BA George Washington University, 1960
MA University of Illinois, 1961
PhD Yale University, 1965
Fields: Political Psychology, Political Sociology, Electoral Behavior, Public Opinion, Empirical Political Theory, Political Socialization, Literature and Politics, Culture and Politics
Publications: Political Socialization and Educational Climates: A Study of Two School Districts, 1971
Making Something of Ourselves: On Culture and Politics in the United States, 1984
Partial Visions: Culture and Politics in Britain, Canada, and the United States, 1991
Representing Black Culture: Racial Conflict and Cultural Politics in the United States, 1995
Pluralism at Yale: The Culture of American Political Science, 2003
Career: Wesleyan, Instructor and Assistant Professor, 1964–66
University of California at Los Angeles, Assistant Professor, 1966–69
University of Wisconsin, Associate Professor, 1969–72
Professor, 1972–2001

Meyer, E.C. (1908–10)
Degrees: PhD
Fields: Municipal Government, Administration
Career: University of Wisconsin, Instructor, 1908–09
Assistant Professor, 1909–10

Miller, Jeffrey Allan (1974–79)
Degrees: BA Bowling Green State University, 1970
MA University of Michigan, 1972
PhD University of Michigan, 1975
Fields: Public Policy, Public Administration, Policy Theory, Organizational Theory, American Politics, Legislative, Executive, Elections, Methods
Career: University of Wisconsin, Instructor, 1974–75
Assistant Professor, 1975–1979

Moustafa, Tamir (2003-present)
b. Long Beach, CA
Degrees: BA University of California at San Diego, 1994
MA University of Washington, 1997
PhD University of Washington, 2002
Fields: Comparative Politics, Comparative Law and Society, Political Economy, Middle East Politics

Career: Institute of International Studies, University of California at Berkeley, Post-Doctoral Fellow, 2002–03
University of Wisconsin, Assistant Professor, 2003-present

Mutz, Diana C. (1988–2000)
Degrees: BS Northwestern University, 1984
AM Stanford University, 1985
PhD Stanford University, 1988
Fields: Political Communication, Political Psychology
Publications: Impersonal Influence: How Perceptions of Mass Collectives Affect Political Attitudes, 1998
Career: University of Wisconsin, Assistant Professor, 1988–94
Associate Professor, 1994–2000
Associate Chair, 1996–1999
Ohio State University, 2000-

Ogg, Frederic A. (1914–48)
b. February 8, 1878
Salaberry, Indiana
d. October 1951
Degrees: PhB DePauw University, 1899
AM Indiana University, 1900
AM Harvard University, 1904
PhD Harvard University, 1908
LLD DePauw University, 1928
Fields: Comparative Politics, American Politics, European Politics
Publications: Social Progress in Contemporary Europe, 1912
Daniel Webster, 1914
The Governments of Europe, 1916
National Progress: 1907–17, 1917
Economic Development of Modern Europe, 1917
Germany's Ambition for World Power, 1918
National Governments and the World War, 1919
New Tests of Representative Government, 1925
Recent Advances in Government, 1925
Research in the Humanistic and Social Sciences, 1927
Builders of the Republic, 1927
Essentials of American Government, 1932
European Government and Politics, 1934
English Government and Politics, 1936
The Rise of Dictatorship in France, 1947
Introduction to American Government, 9th Edition (with P. Orban Ray), 1948
Modern Foreign Governments, 1949
Career: Radcliffe College, Instructor, 1907–08
Simmons College, Instructor, Assistant and Associate Professor, 1908–14

University of Wisconsin, Associate Professor, 1914–17
Professor and Acting Chair, 1917–19
Professor and Chair, 1919–40, 1942–44
Professor, 1945–48

Page, Benjamin (**1977–79**)

b.	September 17, 1940 Los Angeles, CA
Degrees:	AB Stanford University, 1960 LLB Harvard University, 1955 PhD Stanford University, 1973
Fields:	American Politics
Publications:	Choices and Echoes in Presidential Elections, 1978
Career:	Dartmouth College, 1971–73 University of Chicago, Assistant Professor, 1973–77 University of Wisconsin, Associate Professor, 1977–79 University of Chicago, Associate Professor, 1978–82 Professor, 1982–83 University of Texas, Professor, 1983-? Northwestern University, Professor

Parkinson, John Barber (**1872–74, 1876–1908**)

b.	April 11, 1834
d.	April 1927
Degrees:	AB University of Wisconsin, 1860 MA University of Wisconsin, 1863 Honorary LLD, 1893
Fields:	Constitutional law, International law, Political economy
Career:	University of Wisconsin, Math, 1867–72 Civil Polity and International Law, 1872–74 Civil Polity and Economics, 1876–92 Vice President, 1885–1908 Professor, Political Science, 1892–1908 Madison Democrat, Editor, 1874–76

Parkinson, John M. (**1892–94**)

Degree:	MA, Johns Hopkins University , 1892
Career:	University of Wisconsin, Assistant Professor, 1892–94

Payne, Leigh Ann (**1991-present**)

b.	Seoul, South Korea
Degrees:	BA New York University, 1980 MA New York University, 1983 MPhil Yale University, 1985 PhD Yale University, 1990
Fields:	Comparative Politics, Politics of Developing Nations, Latin American Politics, US-Latin American Relations, Challenges of Democracy, International Political Economy

Publications: Brazilian Industrialists and Democratic Change, 1994
Uncivil Movements: The Armed Right-Wing and Democracy in Latin America, 2000
Career: Yale University, Lecturer, 1990–91
University of Wisconsin, Assistant Professor, 1991–98
Associate Professor, 1998–2001
Professor, 2001-present
Director, Global Studies Program, 1999–2001

Pempel, T.J. (1993–95)
b. December 15, 1942
Degrees: BS Columbia University, 1966
MA Columbia University, 1969
PhD Columbia University, 1972
Fields: Comparative Politics, East Asia, Japan
Career: Cornell University, Assistant Professor, Department of Government, 1972–1977
Associate Professor, Department of Government, 1977–1981
Professor, Department of Government, 1981–1991
University of Colorado, Professor, Department of Political Science, 1991–93
University of Wisconsin, Professor of Political Science, 1993–1995
Chair, East Asian Studies Program, 1993–1995
University of Washington, 1995–2001
University of California at Berkeley, 2001-

Penniman, Clara (1953–84)
b. April 5, 1914
Steger, IL
Degrees: BA University of Wisconsin, 1950
MA University of Wisconsin, 1951
PhD University of Minnesota, 1954
Fields: American Politics, Public Administration, Budget and Fiscal Management, State and Local Government and Politics
Publications: The Preparation of the Wisconsin State Budget, 1950
Science and State Government in Wisconsin, 1956
State Income Tax Administration (with Walter W. Heller), 1959
State Income Taxation, 1980
Madison: An Administrative History of Wisconsin's Capital City, 1929–1979
(with Paula A. White), 1999
Career: Wisconsin State Employment Service, Administrative Assistant, 1937–47
University of Wisconsin, Institute for Governmental Affairs, Instructor, 1953–54
Department of Political Science, Assistant Professor, 1954–58

Associate Professor, 1958–61
Professor, 1961–84
Chair, 1963–66
Director, Center for Public Policy and Administration, 1969–74

Pevehouse, Jon C. (2000-present)

Degrees:	BA University of Kansas, 1995
	PhD Ohio State University, 2000
Fields:	International Relations, National Security, Political Economy
Publications:	Democracy from Above? Regional Organization and Democratization, 2004
Career:	University of Wisconsin, Assistant Professor, 2000-present

Pfankuchen, Llewellyn E. (1932–72)

b.	May 7, 1904
	Oshkosh, WI
d.	August 1989
Degrees:	BA University of Minnesota, 1924
	MA University of Illinois, 1926
	MA Harvard University, 1927
	PhD Harvard University, 1931
Fields:	International Law, International Organization, International Relations, American Politics
Publications:	Documentary Textbook in International Law, 1940
Career:	New Jersey Law School, Pre-Legal Division, Assistant Professor of Government, 1928–30
	Duke University, Instructor, 1931–32
	University of Wisconsin, Instructor, 1932–34
	Assistant Professor, 1934–38
	Associate Professor, 1938–43
	Professor, 1943–72
	Chair, 1944–48

Pharr, Susan J. (1977–87)

Degrees:	BA Emory University, 1966
	MA Columbia University, 1970
	PhD Columbia University, 1975
Fields:	Comparative Politics, Japan
Publications:	Political Women in Japan: The Search For a Place in Political Life, 1981
	Losing Face: Status Politics in Japan, 1990
Career:	Social Science Research Council, Staff Associate, 1974–76
	University of Wisconsin, Assistant Professor, 1977–80
	Associate Chair, 1979–81
	Associate Professor, 1980–86
	Professor, 1986–87
	Harvard University, 1987-

Pitkin, Hanna (1964–66)

b. July 17, 1931
Berlin, Germany

Degrees: BA University of California at Los Angeles, 1953
MA University of California at Los Angeles, 1954
PhD University of California at Berkeley, 1961

Field: Political Theory, Philosophy, American Politics

Publications: Concept of Representation, 1967

Career: San Francisco State College, Instructor, 1961–62
University of California at Berkeley, Instructor, 1962–64
University of Wisconsin, Assistant Professor, 1964–66
University of California at Berkeley, 1966-

Pollack, Mark A. (1995–2004)

Degrees: BA Rutgers University, 1988
PhD Harvard University, 1995

Fields: International Relations, Comparative Politics, European Politics, European Union, Ethics and International Relations, Environmental Politics

Publications: The Engines of European Integration: Delegation, Agency, and Agenda Setting in the European Union, 2003.

Career: University of Wisconsin, Assistant Professor, 1995–2001
Associate Professor, 2002–2004
Temple University, Associate Professor, 2004-present

Potter, Pitman Benjamin (1920–32)

b. January 1, 1892
Long Branch, NJ

Degrees: AB Harvard University, 1914
AM Harvard University, 1916
PhD Harvard University, 1918

Fields: International Relations, Foreign Policy, American Politics, Public Administration

Publications: An Introduction to the Study of International Organization, 1922
The Freedom of the Seas in History, Law, and Politics, 1924
International Civics, 1927
This World of Nations, Foundations, Institutions, Practices, 1929

Career: Yale University, Instructor, 1916–17
Carnegie Endowment for International Peace, Research Work Division of International Law (State Department Work for Peace Conference), 1918–19
University of Illinois, Associate Professor, 1919–20
University of Wisconsin, Assistant Professor, 1921–23
Associate Professor, 1923–26
Professor, 1926–32
Graduate Institute of International Studies, Geneva, 1932-

Rahn, Wendy M. (1991–95)
Degrees: BA Creighton University, 1984
PhD University of Minnesota, 1990
Fields: American Politics, Political Psychology, Political Behavior
Career: Ohio State University, Instructor, 1989–90
Assistant Professor, 1991
University of Wisconsin, Assistant Professor, 1991–95
University of Minnesota, 1995-

Ranney, J. Austin (1962–76)
b. September 23, 1920
Cortland, NY
Degrees: BS Northwestern University, 1941
MA University of Oregon, 1943
PhD Yale University, 1948
Fields: American Politics, Political Parties, Contemporary Political Systems of Western Developed Nations
Publications: Pathways to Parliament, 1965
The Governing of Man, 3rd edition, 1971
Governing: A Brief Introduction to Political Science, 1971
Curing the Mischiefs of Faction: Party Reform in America, 1975
Career: University of Illinois, Instructor, 1946–51
Assistant Professor, 1951–53
Associate Professor, 1953–59
Associate Dean of Graduate College, 1958–61
Professor, 1959–62
University of Wisconsin, Professor, 1962–76
American Enterprise Institute, 1976–86
University of California at Berkeley, 1986-

Rapacz, Max (1926–27)
b. October 1, 1892
d. August, 1964
Degrees: MA, SJD
Career: University of Wisconsin, Instructor, 1926–27

Reinsch, Paul S. (1897–1915)
b. June 10, 1870
Milwaukee, WI
d. January 1923
Degrees: BA University of Wisconsin, 1892
LLB University of Wisconsin, 1893
PhD University of Wisconsin, 1898
Fields: English and American Law, Jurisprudence, International Politics, Philosophy of the State

Publications: World Politics at the End of the Nineteenth Century, as Influenced by the Oriental Situation, 1900
Colonial Government, 1902
Colonial Administration, 1905
American Legislatures and Legislative Methods, 1907
Intellectual and Political Currents in the Far East, 1911
Public International Unions: Their Work and Organization, A Study in International Administrative Law, 1911
American Legislatures and Legislative Methods, 1913

Career: University of Wisconsin, Instructor and Lecturer, History, 1895–1899
Instructor, Political Science, 1897–98
Assistant Professor, Political Science, 1899–1901
Professor, Political Science, 1901–15
Chair, 1904–08, 1910–11, 1912–13
Ambassador to China, 1913–19
US Delegation, 3rd Pan-American Congress, Rio de Janeiro, 1906
4th Pan-American Congress, Buenos Aires, 1910
Democratic Senate Candidate, Wisconsin, 1920 (defeated)
Government of China, Advisor, 1919–23

Richardson, Neil R. (1979-present)

b. Hamilton, OH

Degrees: BA Miami University, 1965
MA Ohio State University, 1967
PhD University of Michigan, 1974

Fields: International Political Economy, International Relations

Publications: Foreign Policy and Economic Dependence, 1978

Career: University of Texas at Austin, Instructor/Assistant Professor, 1971–79
University of Wisconsin, Assistant Professor, 1979–83
Associate Professor, 1983–95
Professor, 1995-present
Associate Chair, 1982–85
Director, L&S Advising Center

Riley, Patrick T. (1971-present)

b. October 27, 1941

Degrees: BA Claremont College, 1963
MA Harvard University, 1967
PhD Harvard University, 1968

Fields: Political Theory

Publications: Will and Political Legitimacy: A Critical Exposition of Social Contract Theory in Hobbes, Locke, Rousseau, Kant, and Hegel, 1982
Kant's Political Philosophy, 1983
The General Will Before Rousseau, 2nd edition, 1986
Political Philosophy Essays from Journal of History of Ideas, 1940–90, 1992

	Leibniz' Universal Jurisprudence: Justice as the Charity of the Wise, 1996
	The Philosopher's Philosophy of Law: Jurisprudence from Grotius to Rawls and Habermas, 2003
Career:	Harvard University, Assistant Professor, 1968–72
	University of Wisconsin, Assistant Professor, 1971–73
	Associate Professor, 1973–76
	Professor, 1976-present
	Professor of Philosophy, 1996-present

Rosenbaum, Allan (1970–74)

b.	October 5, 1940
	New York, NY
Degrees:	BA University of Miami, 1962
	MS Southern Illinois University, 1964
	MA University of California at Berkeley, 1967
	PhD University of Chicago, 1970
Fields:	American Politics and Public Policy, State and Urban Government, Political Sociology
Career:	University of Wisconsin, Assistant Professor, 1970–74
	Florida International University

Rubenstein, Diane S. (1986–91)

Degrees:	BA University of Wisconsin, 1974
	MA University of Wisconsin, 1975
	MPhil Yale University, 1978
	PhD Yale University, 1985
Fields:	Political Theory, Political Language, American Politics, Comparative Politics of Western Europe, 19th and 20th Century French and German Political Thought
Publications:	What's Left? The Ecole Normale Supérieure and the Right, 1990
Career:	University of Cincinnati, Assistant Professor, 1983–85
	University of Wisconsin, Assistant Professor, 1985–91
	Purdue University, Assistant Professor of Political Science, 1990–1994
	Associate Professor of American Studies and Political Science, 1994–2001
	Cornell University, Visiting Professor, 2000–2002
	Professor of Government and American Studies, 2002-

Salter, John T. (1930–68)

b.	January 17, 1898
	Three Oaks, MI
d.	November 1973
Degrees:	BA Oberlin College, 1921
	PhD University of Pennsylvania, 1928
Fields:	American Politics, Political Parties, State and Local Politics

Publications: Boss Rule: Portraits in City Politics, 1935
The Pattern of Politics: The Folkways of a Democratic People, 1940
The People's Choice: Philadelphia's William S. Vare, 1971
Career: Ursinus College, 1926–27
University of Oklahoma, 1927–30
University of Wisconsin, Associate Professor, 1930–68

Sapiro, Virginia A. (1976-present)
b. East Orange, NJ
Degrees: AB Clark University, 1972
MA University of Michigan, 1976
PhD University of Michigan, 1976
Fields: American Politics, Social Psychology, Women and Politics, Political Socialization
Publications: The Political Integration of Women: Roles, Socialization and Politics, 1983
A Vindication of Political Virtue: The Political Theory of Mary Wollstonecraft, 1992
Women in American Society: An Introduction to Women's Studies, 4th edition, 1998
Career: University of Wisconsin, Assistant Professor, 1976–81
Associate Professor, 1981–86
Professor, 1986-present
Associate Chair Women's Studies Program, 1981–82
Chair Women's Studies Program, 1986–89
Chair Department of Political Science, 1993–96
Director Social Science Data and Computational Center, 1991–94
Associate Vice Chancellor, 2002-present
National Election Studies, Director, 1997–99

Sartori, Anne E. (1997–99)
Degrees: BA Yale College, 1988
PhD University of Michigan, 1998
Fields: International Relations
Career: University of Wisconsin, Assistant Professor, 1997–99
Princeton University, 2000-

Saunders, Allen Frederic (1923–28)
b. December 2, 1897
Crawford, New Jersey
d. 1989
Degrees: BA Amherst College, 1918
MA University of Wisconsin, 1920
PhD University of Wisconsin, 1927
Fields: Political Theory, Comparative Politics, Anthropology, History, Sociology

Publications:	Building America, 1923
Career:	University of Pennsylvania, Instructor, 1920–23
	University of Wisconsin, Instructor, 1923–27
	Assistant Professor, 1927–28
	University of Minnesota, 1928–31
	Scripps and Claremont Colleges, 1932–41
	Deep Springs, 1941–42
	Amherst College, 1942–45
	University of Hawaii, Honolulu, 1945–66

Schatzberg, Michael G. (1991-present)

b.	Brooklyn, NY
Degrees:	BA Tufts University, 1969
	MA University of Wisconsin, 1972
	PhD University of Wisconsin, 1977
Fields:	Comparative Politics, African Politics
Publications:	Politics and Class in Zaire: Bureaucracy, Business, and Beer in Lisala, 1980
	Dialectics of Oppression in Zaire, 1988
	Mobutu or Chaos?: The United States and Zaire, 1960–1990, 1991
	Political Legitimacy in Middle Africa: Father, Family, Food, 2001
Career:	Dalhousie University, Centre for Foreign Policy Studies, Visiting Assistant Professor, 1978–79
	Virginia Polytechnic Institute and State University, Assistant Professor, 1979–81
	The Johns Hopkins University, SAIS, Assistant Professor, 1981–83
	Associate Professor, 1983–90
	University of Wisconsin, Professor, 1991-present

Scheingold, Stuart A. (1965–70)

b.	December 22, 1931
Degrees:	BS Ohio State University, 1953
	MA University of California at Berkeley, 1959
	PhD University of California at Berkeley, 1963
Fields:	International Relations, Law
Publications:	Europe's Would-be Polity; Patterns of Change in the European Community
	(with Leon Lindberg), 1970
Career:	University of California Davis, Assistant Professor, 1962–64
	Harvard University, Center for International Affairs, Research Associate, 1964–65
	University of Wisconsin, Assistant Professor, 1965–1970
	University of Washington, 1969–2000

Schweber, Howard H. (1999-present)

b.	Watertown, MA
Degrees:	BA University of Pennsylvania, 1984
	JD University of Washington Law School, 1989
	MA University of Chicago, 1994
	PhD Cornell University, 1999
Fields:	American Politics, Constitutional Law
Publications:	Speech, Conduct, and the First Amendment, 2003
	The Creation of American Common Law, 1850–1880, 2004
Career:	Graham & James, Associate, 1989–93
	Flynn, Delich & Wise, Contract Attorney, 1993–94
	University of Wisconsin, Assistant Professor, 1999-present

Scoble, Harry M. (1958–63)

b.	August 12, 1926
	East Stroudsberg, PA
Degrees:	BA Williams College, 1949
	MA Yale University, 1953
	PhD Yale University, 1957
Fields:	American Politics, National Government, Constitutional Law
Career:	University of North Carolina, Instructor, 1954–55
	Boston University, Instructor, 1955–57
	University of Wisconsin, Assistant Professor, 1958–63
	University of California at Los Angeles, 1963-
	University of Illinois, Chicago

Scott, James C. (1967–78)

b.	December 2, 1936
	Mt. Holly, NJ
Degrees:	BA Williams College, 1958
	MA Yale University, 1963
	PhD Yale University, 1967
Fields:	Comparative Politics, Southeast Asia, Political Analysis, Research Methods
Publications:	Political Ideology in Malaysia: Reality and the Beliefs of an Elite, 1968
	Comparative Political Corruption, 1971
	Moral Economy of the Peasant: Rebellion and Subsistence in Southeast Asia, 1976
Career:	University of Wisconsin, Assistant Professor, 1967–70
	Associate Professor, 1970–73
	Professor, 1973–78
	Yale University, Professor 1976-

Scott, Robert B. (1906–1910)

Fields:	American Politics, Jurisprudence, Party Government
Career:	University of Wisconsin, Instructor, 1906–07 Associate Professor 1907–08 Professor, 1909–10 Chair, 1908–10

Seidensticker, Ellen (1975–79)

b.	October 6, 1946
Degrees:	BS Ohio State University, 1968 PhD Columbia University, 1975
Fields:	International Relations, World Politics, International Law, International Organization, Statistics, Philosophy of Science, British Politics
Career:	University of Wisconsin, Assistant Professor, 1975–79 Program Manager, Asia and the Pacific Advisory Services, UN Centre for Transnational Corporations, 1977-? Director of Program Development, Harvard Institute for International Development (HIID), Harvard University Global Equity Initiative, Kennedy School of Government, Harvard University

Shafer, Byron E. (2001-present)

b.	January 8, 1947 Hanover, PA
Degrees:	BA Yale University, 1968 PhD University of California at Berkeley, 1979
Fields:	American Politics
Publications:	Quiet Revolution: The Struggle For the Democratic National Party and the Shaping of Post-Reform Politics, 1983 Bifurcated Politics: Evolution and Reform in the National Party Convention, 1988 The End of Realignment? Interpreting American Electoral Eras, 1991 Is America Different? A New Look at American Exceptionalism, 1991 The Two Majorities: The Issue Context of American Politics, 1995 Present Discontents: American Politics in the Very Late Twentieth Century (with Joel H. Sibley), 1997 Partisan Approaches to Postwar American Politics (with Harold E. Bass Jr.), 1998 The Two Majorities and the Puzzle of American Politics, 2003
Career:	Russell Sage Foundation, Resident Scholar, 1977–84 Florida State University, Associate Professor, 1984–85 Oxford University, Professor of American Government, 1985–2001 University of Wisconsin, Professor and Hawkins Chair, 2001-present

Shalala, Donna E. (1987–97)

Degrees: AB Western College for Women, 1962
PhD The Maxwell School of Citizenship and Public Affairs, Syracuse University, 1970

Fields: Public Policy, State and Urban Government and Finance, Political Economy of Education, American Politics

Career: Bernard M. Baruch College of City University of New York, Assistant Professor of Political Science, 1970–72
Columbia University, Teachers College, Program in Politics and Education, Assistant Professor and Chair, 1972–77
Department of Housing and Urban Development, Assistant Secretary for Policy Development and Research, 1977–80
Hunter College of the City University of New York, Professor of Political Science, 1980–87
President of the College, 1980–87
University of Wisconsin, Chancellor, 1987–92
Professor, Political Science and Educational Policy Studies, 1988–97 [on leave, 1993–97]
Department of Health and Human Services, Secretary, 1993–2001
University of Miami, President, 2001-

Sharkansky, Ira (1968–85)

b. November 25, 1938
Fall River, MA

Degrees: BA Wesleyan University, 1960
MS University of Wisconsin, 1961
PhD University of Wisconsin, 1964

Fields: Public Administration, American Politics, Public Enterprise, Policy-Making Process, Israeli Politics

Publications: Spending in the American States, 1968
The Politics of Taxing and Spending, 1969
Policy Analysis in Political Science, 1970
Regionalism in American Politics, 1970
The Routines of Politics, 1970
State and Urban Politics (with Richard I. Hofferbert), 1971
Policy and Politics in American Governments (with Donald Van Meter), 1975
Public Administration: Policy-making in Government Agencies, 4th edition, 1978
The Maligned States: Policy Accomplishments, Problems, and Opportunities, 2nd edition, 1978
The Policy Predicament: Making and Implementing Public Policy (with George C. Edwards III), 1978
The United States: A Study of a Developing Country, 1978
Urban Politics and Public Policy, (with Robert L. Lineberry), 3rd edition, 1978

	Wither the State? Politics and Public Enterprise in Three Countries, 1979
Career:	Ball State University, Assistant Professor, 1964–65
	Florida State University, Assistant Professor, 1965–66
	University of Georgia, Assistant Professor, 1966–68
	University of Wisconsin, Associate Professor, 1968–71
	Professor, 1971–85 (on leave 1975–85)
	Hebrew University of Jerusalem, 1975-

Sharp, Walter Rice (1923–40)

b.	January 25, 1896
	Greenwood, IN
Degrees:	AB Wabash College, 1917
	Doctor en Droit University of Bordeaux, 1920–22
Fields:	International Relations, International Organizations, International Public Administration, Comparative Politics, American Politics
Publications:	The Economic Development of Modern Europe, with Frederic Ogg, 1926
	The French Civil Service: Bureaucracy in Transition, 1931
	The Chief Executive and Auxiliary Agencies in the State of Wisconsin, 1936
	The Government of the French Republic, 1938
	Contemporary International Politics, with Grayson Kirk, 1940
Career:	Washington and Lee University, Assistant Professor, 1922–23
	University of Wisconsin, Instructor, 1923–24
	Assistant Professor, 1924–27
	Associate Professor, 1927–32
	Professor, 1932–40
	City College of New York, 1940–43
	FAO, Chief of Organization, Planning, Interim Commission, 1943–45
	WHO, Senior Administrative Consultant, Geneva, 1946–48
	UNESCO, Chief of Division of International Cooperation, Paris, 1948–50
	Yale University, 1951–64

Sinha, Aseema (1999-present)

b.	Calcutta, India
Degrees:	BA Lady Shri Ram College, 1987
	MA Jawaharlal Nehru University, 1989
	MPhil Jawaharlal Nehru University, 1991
	MA Cornell University, 1997
	PhD Cornell University, 2000
Fields:	Comparative Politics, South Asia
Publications:	Regional Roots of Developmental Politics in India: A Leviathan Divided, 2004
Career:	University of Wisconsin, Assistant Professor, 1999-present

Skilling, Harold G. (1943–48)

Degrees: BA University of Toronto, 1934
BA Oxford University, 1936
MA Oxford University, 1940
PhD University of London, 1940

Fields: Comparative Politics, British Commonwealth, Eastern Europe, Soviet Union, International Organizations

Publications: Canadian Representation Abroad, 1945

Career: University of Wisconsin, Assistant Professor, 1943–48
Dartmouth College, 1948-

Smiley, Marion (1989–2002)

Degrees: BA Mount Holyoke College, 1975
MA Princeton University
PhD Princeton University, 1984

Fields: History of Moral and Political Thought, Analytical Moral and Political Philosophy, Ethics and Public Affairs, Feminist Theory

Publications: Moral Responsibility and the Boundaries of Community: Power and Accountability from a Pragmatic Point of View, 1992

Career: Wellesley College, Visiting Lecturer, 1984–85
Wesleyan University, Visiting Assistant Professor, 1985–86
Princeton University, Visiting Assistant Professor, 1986–87
University of Wisconsin, Assistant Professor, 1989–93
Associate Professor, 1993–98
Professor, 1998–2002
Brandeis University, 2002-

Soss, Joe (2003-present)

Degrees: BA University of Texas-Austin, 1989
PhD University of Wisconsin, 1996

Fields: American Politics, Social Welfare and Poverty Policy, Political Psychology, Political Behavior, Public Opinion, Race and US Politics, Research Methodology

Publications: Unwanted Claims: The Politics of Participation in the US Welfare System, 2000

Career: American University, Assistant Professor, 1997–2000
Associate Professor, 2000–03
University of Wisconsin, Associate Professor, 2003-present

Sparling, Samuel E. (1897–1908)

d. 1941

Degrees: PhD University of Wisconsin, 1896

Fields: Public Administration, Europe and South America, Municipal Government, State and Federal Administration

Publications: Introduction to Business Organization, 1906

Career: University of Wisconsin, Assistant Professor, 1897–98
Instructor, 1900–02
Associate Professor, 1902–08
Farming, Indiana and Alabama, 1908-

Stallings, Barbara B. (1977–96)
Degrees: BA Mt. Holyoke College, 1966
PhD Political Science, Stanford University, 1975
PhD Economics, University of Cambridge, 1985
Fields: Comparative Politics, Latin American Politics, International Political Economy
Publications: Class Conflict and Economic Development in Chile, 1958–1973, 1978
Banker to the Third World: U.S. Portfolio Investment in Latin America, 1900–1986, 1987
Career: Trinity College, University of Cambridge, Instructor, Macroeconomics, 1976–77
University of Wisconsin, Assistant Professor, 1977–82
Associate Professor, 1982–87
Director, Latin American Studies Program, 1985–88
Associate Dean of the Graduate School, 1987–90
Professor, 1987–96
Director, Global Studies Research Program, 1991–93
U.N. Economic Commission for Latin America, Santiago, Chile, Senior Economist, 1993–94
Economic Development Division, U.N. Economic Commission for Latin America, Santiago, Chile, Director, 1994-
Brown University, 2002-

Stiefbold, Rodney (1966–68)
Fields: Comparative Politics
Career: University of Wisconsin, Instructor, 1966–68

Stoke, Harold W. (1940–44)
b. 1903
Bosworth, MO
d. March 1982
Degrees: AB Marion College, 1924
MA University of Southern California, 1925
PhD Johns Hopkins University, 1930
Fields: Comparative Politics, International Relations, Public Administration
Career: University of Nebraska, Assistant and Associate Professor, 1930–37
Dean of the Graduate School, 1939–40
University of Pennsylvania, Associate Professor, 1938–39
University of Wisconsin, Assistant Dean of the Graduate School, 1940–44

Professor, 1940–44
University of New Hampshire, President, 1944–47
Louisiana State University, President, 1947–51
Queens College, President, 1958–64

Stokes, William S. (1946–58)

b.	February 21, 1916 Wilcox, AZ
d.	1967
Degrees:	BA University of California at Los Angeles, 1938 PhD University of California at Los Angeles, 1943
Fields:	Comparative Politics, Latin America, Western Europe, Soviet Union, Far East, Africa, Revolution and Political Violence, National Security Policy, International Relations
Publications:	<u>The Land Law of Honduras</u>, 1947 <u>Honduras: An Area Study in Government</u>, 1950 <u>Latin American Politics</u>, 1952
Career:	Northwestern University, Instructor and Assistant Professor, 1943–46 University of Wisconsin, Associate Professor, 1946–50 Professor, 1950–58 Claremont Men's College, 1958-

Straus, Scott (2004-present)

b.	May 9, 1970 New York, NY
Degrees:	BA, Dartmouth College, 1993 MA, University of California, Berkeley, 1999 PhD, University of California, Berkeley, 2004
Fields:	Comparative Politics, African Politics, Political Economy
Publications:	<u>Africa's Stalled Development: International Causes and Cures</u> (with David Leonard), 2003
Career:	Freelance Journalist, East and Central Africa, 1995–1998 University of Oregon, Faculty Fellow, 2003–2004 University of Wisconsin, Assistant Professor, 2004-present

Stuart, Graham Henry (1917–23)

b.	January 27, 1886 Cleveland, OH
Degrees:	AB Western Reserve University, 1908 MA University of Wisconsin, 1918 PhD University of Wisconsin, 1920
Fields:	International Law, Foreign Relations, Latin American Politics
Publications:	<u>Latin America and the US</u>, 1922 <u>Cuba and Its International Relations</u>, 1923
Career:	University of Wisconsin, Assistant and Instructor, 1917–21 Assistant Professor, 1921–23 Stanford University, 1923–52

Tarr, David (1963–95)
b. July 25, 1931
Melrose, MA
Degrees: BA University of Massachusetts, 1953
MA University of Chicago, 1956
PhD University of Chicago, 1961
Fields: American Foreign Policy, National Security Policy, Arms Control, Civil-Military Relations, International Relations
Publications: American Strategy in the Nuclear Age, 1966
Nuclear Deterrence and International Security: Alternative Nuclear Regimes, 1991
Career: Amherst and Mt. Holyoke Colleges, Instructor, 1958–59
Library of Congress, Legislative Reference Service, National Defense Analyst, 1959
Johns Hopkins, SAIS, Washington Center for Foreign Policy Research, Research Associate, 1962
University of Wisconsin, Assistant Professor, 1963–66
Associate Professor, 1966–69
Professor, 1969–1995
Chair, 1972–75

Thompson, William (1914–15)
Career: University of Wisconsin, Instructor, 1914–15

Thomson, John Seabury (1951–57)
b. March 13, 1921
Nanking, China
d. ca. 1999
Degrees: AB Swarthmore College, 1943
MA Columbia University, 1947
PhD Columbia University, 1953
Fields: Comparative Politics, Southeast Asia, International Relations
Career: Columbia University, Instructor, 1947–50
University of Wisconsin, Instructor, 1951–53
Assistant Professor, 1953–57
US Government, Political Analyst, 1957–63
US Department of State, Foreign Service Institute, Policy Analyst, 1963–66

Thorson, Thomas Landon (1959–66)
b. January 30, 1934
LaPorte, ID
Degrees: AB Indiana University, 1956
MA Indiana University, 1958
MA Princeton University, 1959
PhD Princeton University, 1960

Fields: Political Theory, Political Philosophy, International Relations
Publications: The Logic of Democracy, 1962
Career: University of Wisconsin, Instructor, 1959–61
Assistant Professor, 1961–63
Associate Professor, 1963–66
University of Toronto, 1966–71
Indiana University, South Bend, 1970-

Tripp, Aili Mari (**1992-present**)
b. Market Harborough, Leicestershire, UK
Degrees: BA University of Chicago, 1983
MA University of Chicago, 1985
PhD Northwestern University, 1990
Fields: Comparative Politics, African Politics, Women and Politics
Publications: Changing the Rules: The Politics of Liberalization and the Urban Informal Economy in Tanzania, 1997
Women & Politics in Uganda, 2000
Career: John D. and Catherine T. MacArthur Foundation, Program on Peace and International Cooperation,
Research Associate, 1989–91
University of Wisconsin, Assistant Professor, 1992–99
Associate Professor, 1999-present
Director, Women's Studies Research Center, 2000–2003
Associate Dean, International Studies, 2003-

von der Mehden, Fred R. (**1957–68**)
b. December 1, 1927
San Francisco, CA
Degrees: BA University of Pacific, 1948
MA Claremont Grad School, 1950
PhD University of California at Berkeley, 1957
Fields: Comparative Politics, Southeast Asia, Developing Nations
Publications: Religion and Nationalism in Southeast Asia, 1963
Politics of the Developing Nations, 1964
Issues of Political Development (with Charles W. Anderson and Crawford Young), 1967
Career: University of Wisconsin, Assistant Professor, 1957–63
Associate Professor, 1963–67
Professor, 1967–68
Rice University, 1968-

Wallace, Benjamin B. (**1912–13**)
d. 1947
Degrees: BA Macalester College, 1902
PhD University of Wisconsin, 1911
Fields: International Relations, National Government

Career: University of Wisconsin, Assistant Professor, 1912–13
US Tariff Commission
Advisor, Ministry of Finance, Government of China

Wallin, Bruce A. (1979–85)
Degrees: BA Princeton University, 1970
MA University of California at Berkeley, 1973
PhD University of California at Berkeley, 1983
Fields: American Politics, Budgeting and Public Finance, Federalism, Intergovernmental Relations, Public Administration
Career: University of Wisconsin, Political Science and LaFollette School of Public Affairs, Assistant Professor, 1979–85
California State University, Fullerton, Lecturer, 1986–1990
Northeastern University, 1990-

Walsh, Katherine Cramer (2000-present)
b. Dekalb, IL
Degrees: BA University of Wisconsin, 1994
PhD University of Michigan, 2000
Fields: American Politics, Political Psychology
Publications: Talking About Politics: Informal Groups and Social Identity in American Life, 2004
Career: University of Wisconsin, Assistant Professor, 2000-present

Weimer, David L. (2000-present)
b. Buffalo, NY
Degrees: BA and BS University of Rochester, 1973
MPP University of California at Berkeley, 1975
MA University of California at Berkeley, 1976
PhD University of California at Berkeley, 1978
Fields: American Politics, Public Policy
Publications: Improving Prosecution?: The Inducement and Implementation of Innovations for Prosecution Management, 1980
The Strategic Petroleum Reserve: Planning, Implementation, and Analysis, 1982
Oil Price Shocks, Market Response, and Contingency Planning, (with George Horwich), 1984
Organizational Report Cards (with William T. Gormley, Jr.), 1999
Career: University of Rochester, Instructor, 1977–78
Assistant Professor, 1978–82
Associate Professor, 1982–86
Professor of Political Science and Public Policy, 1986–2000
University of Wisconsin, Professor of Political Science and Public Policy, 2000-present

Wengert, Egbert Semman (1934–37)

b.	July 7, 1912 Bloomington, IL
d.	February 1964
Degrees:	BA University of Wisconsin, 1933 LLB University of Wisconsin, 1936 PhD University of Wisconsin, 1936
Fields:	Law, Public Administration, Administrative Planning
Career:	University of Wisconsin, Instructor 1934–36 Assistant Professor, 1936–37 Wayne University, 1937–41 Sweetbriar College, 1941–47 University of Wyoming, 1947–48 University of Oregon, 1948–64

Wilde, Alexander (1969–76)

b.	August 29, 1940
Degrees:	BA Lawrence University, 1962 PPE Oxford University (Keble College), 1964 PhD Columbia University, 1972
Fields:	Comparative Politics, Latin America
Career:	University of Wisconsin, Assistant Professor, 1969–76 Ford Foundation, Santiago

Wilson, Graham K. (1984-present)

b.	August 22, 1949 Liverpool, UK
Degrees:	BA Oxford University, 1970 MA University of Essex, 1971 DPhil Oxford University, 1975
Fields:	American Politics, Interest Groups, American Presidency, British Politics
Publications:	The Politics of Safety and Health, 1985 Business and Politics, A Comparative Introduction, 2nd edition, 1990 The End of Whitehall: Death of A Paradigm? (with Colin Campbell), 1995 Interest Groups, 1995 Only in America? American Politics in Comparative Perspective, 1998
Career:	University of Oxford, Keble College, College Lecturer, 1972–73 University of Essex, Lecturer, 1973–84 University of Wisconsin, Visiting Associate Professor, 1978–79, 1981–82 Associate Professor, 1984–86 Professor, 1986-present Associate Chair, 1990–93 Chair, European Studies Program, 1992–95

Professor, La Follette Institute for Public Policy, 1999-present
Assoc. Director, La Follette Institute for Public Policy, 1999–2003
Chair, Political Science, 2004-

Witte, Edwin E. (1933–57)

b.	January 4, 1887 Ebenezer, WI
d.	May 1960
Degrees:	BA University of Wisconsin, 1909 PhD University of Wisconsin (Economics), 1927
Fields:	Labor Relations, Social Security
Publications:	The Government in Labor Disputes, 1932 Development of Social Security, 1962
Career:	University of Wisconsin, Professor, Political Science, 1933–48 Professor, Economics, 1933–57 Chair, Economics, 1936–41, 1946-53 Wisconsin Industrial Commission, Executive Secretary, 1917–22 Wisconsin Legislative Reference Library, Chief, 1922–33 Social Security Act, Major Drafter, 1934–35 State Planning Board, 1935–38 Wisconsin Labor Relations Board, 1937–39

Witte, John F. (1977-present)

b.	June 12, 1946
Degrees:	BA University of Wisconsin, 1968 MPhil Yale University, 1974 PhD Yale University, 1978
Fields:	Public Policy and Administration, Education Policy, American Politics, Democratic Theory, Budget and Tax Policy, Methodology
Publications:	Democracy, Authority and Alienation in Work: Workers' Participation in an American Corporation, 1980 The Politics and Development of the Federal Income Tax, 1985 The Market Approach to Education: An Analysis of America's First Voucher Program, 2001
Career:	Yale University School of Organization and Management, Instructor, 1976 University of Wisconsin, Assistant Professor, Political Science and La Follette, 1977–84 Associate Professor, 1984–89 Associate Director, La Follette Institute of Public Affairs, 1985–86 Associate Chair, Political Science, 1987–90 Professor, Political Science and La Follette, 1989-present Professor, School of Education, 1998-present Associate Director, La Follette Institute of Public Affairs, 1998–99 Director, Industrial Relations Research Institute, 2001–2002 Director, La Follette Institute of Public Affairs, 1999–2002

Wittenberg, Jason (2000-present)

b.	Torrance, CA
Degrees:	BA University of California at Berkeley, 1985 MA American University, 1988 PhD MIT, 1999
Fields:	Comparative Politics, East Europe
Career:	University of Wisconsin, Assistant Professor, 2000-present

Wolanin, Thomas (1971–77)

b.	December 1, 1942 Detroit, MI
Degrees:	BA Oberlin College, 1965 MA Harvard University, 1970 PhD Harvard University, 1972
Fields:	American Politics, National Government, Presidency
Publications:	Presidential Advisory Commissions, 1975 Congress and the Colleges: The National Politics of Higher Education (with Lawrence E. Gladieux), 1976
Career:	University of Wisconsin, Assistant Professor, 1971–1977 Staff Director, House Subcommittee on Post-Secondary Education, 1978–81, 1985–87, 1991–93 New York University, Executive Assistant to the President, 1981–82 Staff Director, House Subcommittee on Investigations, 1983–85, 1987–91 Deputy Assistant Secretary for Legislation and Congressional Affairs, Department of Education, 1993–96 Institute for Higher Education Policy, Senior Associate, 1996 George Washington University, Professor, Educational Policy and Political Science, 1997–2000

Woodbury, Coleman F. (1958–62)

b.	July 20, 1903 Sandwich, IL
d.	August 1994
Degrees:	BS Northwestern University, 1925 MS Northwestern University, 1926 PhD Northwestern University, 1930
Fields:	Metro and Urban Government and Urban and Regional Planning
Publications:	A Framework for Urban Studies: An Analysis of Urban-Metro Development and Research Needs, 1959 Urban Studies: Some Questions of Outlook and Selections, 1960
Career:	Northwestern University, Institute for Research in Law and Economy and Public Utilities, Research Associate and Assistant Professor, 1927–31 Temporary Illinois State Housing Commission, Executive Director, 1931–33

Illinois State Housing Board, Executive Director, 1933–34
National Association of Housing Officials, Executive Director, 1934–42
National Housing Agency Assistant Administrator, 1942–46
Urban Redevelopment Study, Director, 1948–51
Harvard University, Department of City and Regional Planning, Professor, 1951–53
University of Wisconsin, Political Science, Visiting Professor, 1946–48
Professor, 1958–62
Department of Urban and Regional Planning, Professor, 1962-
Chair, 1962–65

Yack, Bernard (1991–2002)

b. October 16, 1952
Toronto, Ontario

Degrees: BA University of Toronto, 1975
PhD Harvard University, 1981

Fields: Political Theory, History of Political Thought

Publications: The Problems of a Political Animal: Community, Conflict, and Justice in Aristotelian Political Thought, 1993
Fetishism of Modernities: Epochal Self-consciousness in Contemporary Social and Political Thought, 1997

Career: Princeton University, Assistant Professor, 1981–88
University of Michigan, Associate Professor, 1988–91
University of Wisconsin, Associate Professor, 1991–94
Professor 1994–2002
Brandeis University, Professor, 2002-

Young, M. Crawford (1963–2001)

b. November 7, 1931
Philadelphia, PA

Degrees: BA University of Michigan, 1953
PhD Harvard University, 1964

Fields: Comparative Politics, African Politics, Politics of Cultural Pluralism

Publications: Politics in the Congo: Decolonization and Independence, 1965
Issues of Political Development (with Charles Anderson and Fred von der Mehden), 1967
The Politics of Cultural Pluralism, 1976
Cooperatives and Development: Agricultural Politics in Ghana and Uganda (with Neal Sherman and Tim Rose), 1981
Ideology and Development in Africa, 1982
The Rise and Decline of the Zairian State (with Thomas Turner), 1985
The African Colonial State in Comparative Perspective, 1994

Career: University of Wisconsin, Assistant Professor, 1963–66
Associate Professor, 1966–69

Associate Dean of Graduate School, 1968–71
Professor, 1969–2001
Chair, African Studies Program, 1964–65, 66–68
Chair, Political Science Department, 1969–72, 1984–87
Acting Dean, College of Letters and Science, 1992–93
Universite Nationale du Zaire, Dean, Faculty of Social Science, 1973–75

Young, William H. (1947–83)

b.	October 7, 1912 Coriopolis, PA
Degrees:	BA University of Pittsburg, 1933 MA University of Pittsburg, 1937 PhD University of Wisconsin, 1941
Fields:	American Politics, Public Administration, Presidency, Budget and Fiscal Management
Publications:	<u>Essentials of American Government</u>, multiple editions
Career:	University of Pennsylvania, Instructor, 1941–43 Assistant Professor, 1943–47 University of Wisconsin, Associate Professor, 1947–50 Professor, 1950–83 Chair, 1952–60 Assistant to the President, 1954–70 Director, Center for Development, 1967–83 State of Wisconsin, Division of Research, Office of the Governor, Director, 1949–50 Governor of Wisconsin, Executive Secretary, 1950 Wisconsin Welfare Council Board, 1954–57 Oscar Rennebehn Foundation, Inc., Director, 1960-

Zolberg, Aristide R (1961–63)

Degrees:	BA Columbia University, 1953 MA Boston University, 1956 PhD University of Chicago, 1961
Fields:	Comparative Politics, African Politics, Historical Sociology
Publications:	<u>One-Party Government in the Ivory Coast</u>, 1961 <u>Creating Political Order: The Party-States of West Africa</u>, 1966
Career:	University of Wisconsin, Assistant Professor, 1961–63 University of Chicago, Assistant Professor, 1963–84 New School University, 1984-

Appendix 5

Department Chairs

1904–08	Paul Reinsch
1908–10	Robert Scott
1910–11	Paul Reinsch
1911–12	Harold McBain
1912–13	Paul Reinsch
1913–17	Chester Jones
1917–40	Frederic Ogg
1940–42	John Gaus
1942–44	Frederic Ogg
1944–48	Llewellyn Pfankuchen
1948–52	James McCamy
1952–60	William Young
1960–63	Leon Epstein
1963–66	Clara Penniman
1966–69	Bernard Cohen
1969–72	Crawford Young
1972–75	David Tarr
1975–78	Joel Grossman
1978–81	Jack Dennis
1981–84	Fred Hayward
1984–87	Crawford Young
1987–90	Peter Eisinger
1990–93	Dennis Dresang
1993–96	Virginia Sapiro
1996–99	Herbert Kritzer
1999–2001	Dennis Dresang
2001–04	Mark Beissinger
2004–	Graham Wilson

Appendix 6

Department Associate Chairs

1969–71	Melvin Croan
1971–72	David Tarr
1972–73	Booth Fowler
1973–75	Dennis Dresang
1975–78	Peter Eisinger
1978–81	Susan Pharr
1981–84	Neil Richardson
1984–87	Booth Fowler
1987–90	John Witte
1990–93	Graham Wilson
1993–96	Charles Franklin
1996–97, 1998–99	Diana Mutz
1997, 1999–2001	David Canon
2001–04	John Coleman
2004–	Paul Hutchcroft

APPENDIX 7

Faculty: National Recognition and Associational Leadership

Fellows of the American Academy of Arts and Sciences

Elected while members of the department faculty

Austin Ranney (1969)

Leon D. Epstein (1981)

Charles O. Jones (1989)

M. Crawford Young (1998)

Virginia Sapiro (2002)

Elected after leaving department

John M. Gaus (1950)

Grayson Kirk (1959)

Associational Leadership

From the department's earliest days, the faculty participated actively in professional associations. So, too, over the years, have substantial numbers of its doctoral recipients. Such participation includes many positions and activities in a variety of organizations. Only some of these are recorded here. All Wisconsin-connected presidents of the American Political Science Association and the Midwest Political Science Association are noted, as are Wisconsin-connected editors of their journals. But other offices and important positions—convention program chairs, for instance—in those organizations are not taken into account. With respect to more specialized professional associations, an effort has been made to name their Wisconsin-connected presidents and journal editors, but the canvass of these now numerous organizations is probably incomplete.

The department's presence in the American Political Science Association began with the association's founding in 1903. Professor Paul Reinsch was a member of the committee that launched the association, a vice president in 1903–04, and in 1921, after he had left Wisconsin to become ambassador to

China from 1913 to 1919, Reinsch became its president. Subsequently, five faculty members were elected APSA presidents while at Wisconsin: Frederic A. Ogg (1941), John Gaus (1945), Austin Ranney (1975), Leon Epstein (1979), and Charles Jones (1994). One other APSA president, Clarence Dykstra (1938), was nominally a member of the department while serving as university president. More notable is the fact that Professor Ogg edited the *American Political Science Review* from 1926 to 1949. Later, Ranney, while a member of the department, served as editor from 1964 to 1970. And Charles Jones, a Wisconsin Ph.D. (1960), edited the *APSR* from 1977 to 1981 before he returned to teach at Wisconsin in 1988.

In the Midwest Political Science Association, the department's involvement is even more marked. Since that organization's founding in 1939, six of its presidents—almost 10 percent—were members of our faculty at the time they served: Llewellyn Pfankuchen (1949), David Fellman (1956), Clara Penniman (1966), Leon Epstein (1972), Jack Dennis (1983), and Charles Jones (1992). Furthermore, eight Wisconsin Ph.D.'s (besides Jones) were Midwest Association presidents: Jasper Shannon (1959), William Farber (1964), John Lewis (1968), Frank Sorauf (1974), Samuel Patterson (1981), Ada Finifter (1987), John Kingdon (1988), and Marjorie Hershey (1991). Fellman was the first editor of the *Midwest Review of Political Science*, from 1957 to 1959, and Patterson edited the journal from 1971 to 1973, during which time its name was changed to *American Journal of Political Science*.

Among other professional associations, at least three broad interdisciplinary organizations have been headed by Wisconsin faculty members. John Armstrong was president of the American Association for the Advancement of Slavic Studies, 1965–1967; Crawford Young was president of the African Studies Association, 1982–83; and Joel Grossman was president of the Law and Society Association, 1980–82. Another organization, the British Politics Group, much less broadly interdisciplinary and consisting mainly of political scientists, has had a strong Wisconsin link. Its founder and longtime executive secretary, 1974–94, was Jorgen Rasmussen, a departmental Ph.D. (1962) who also served as the president, 1994–96, as had Leon Epstein, 1974–76. Another Wisconsin Ph.D. whose role should be noted is Donald Kommers (1963), who edited the *Review of Politics*, 1991–94. Less related to political science, but of major professional significance, was the participation of David Fellman in the American Association of University Professors. He was first the chair of its Committee A, concerned with academic freedom, from 1959 to 1964, and then the association's president 1965–67. As already observed, there are good reasons to suspect that other faculty members as well as departmental Ph.D.'s have occupied important professional association positions.

Appendix 8

Department Participation in University Administration and Governance

Appropriately, for a department that is large as well as centrally concerned with governance, the Department of Political Science has seen many of its members in significant positions over the years in both university administration and in the structures of shared governance on the campus.

Three department members have worked at the highest levels of the university administration. Clarence Dykstra, who was president from 1937 until he went to Washington to head the Selective Service System in 1940, returned to the university in 1941 and held a professorship in the department until he left for UCLA in 1945. Donna Shalala, who was chancellor from 1988 through 1992, held a joint appointment in political science and in educational policy studies. And Bernard Cohen, who was acting chancellor in 1987, served in the department from 1959 until his retirement in 1990. Cohen was also the vice chancellor for academic affairs from 1984 to 1987, and again from 1988 to 1989 following his period as acting chancellor.

Two other members of the department held high-level posts in the university. William H. Young was the budgetary assistant to the president of the university for a decade, from 1953 to 1963, a position which has evolved into the vice chancellorship of Budget, Planning and Analysis. And Clara Penniman was appointed by then-Governor Patrick Lucey in 1972 as the only faculty member from the old Chapter–36 universities (at Madison, Milwaukee, Green Bay, and Parkside) on the Merger Implementation Study Committee; that committee drafted the language of the present Chapter 36 of the State of Wisconsin Laws, combining the two former systems of higher education in Wisconsin into a single system.

Two members of the department have been deans of the College of Letters and Science. Leon D. Epstein was dean from 1965 to 1969, years of severe turmoil on the campus and especially in the college due to the Vietnam War. And in 1992–93, M. Crawford Young served as acting dean of the college. In addition, Fred Hayward and Jack Dennis held consecutive terms as associate deans of the college (for the social sciences), Hayward from 1982 to 1987, and Dennis from 1987 to 1990.

Crawford Young and Bernard Cohen also served (in succession) as associate deans of the Graduate School responsible for the social sciences (Young from 1968 to 1971 and Cohen from 1971 to 1975), a post subsequently held by Barbara Stallings (1987–90). And Fred Hayward was acting dean of International Studies and Programs from 1989 to 1990.

It is at the committee level, both within the department and campuswide, that faculty governance at the University of Wisconsin is really exercised. Departmental participation in university committees, both elected and appointed, has been extensive over the past century. I will focus on only two of these committees, not because the others are inconsequential but because there are so many of them. The two that matter the most, because the decisions they reach have the greatest consequences for the academic enterprise, are the University Committee and the divisional committees—in this case the Social Studies Divisional Committee, since that is the division to which members of the political science department belong.

The University Committee is the executive committee of the Faculty Senate, and it has a virtually unlimited mandate with respect to issues involving the faculty. Its views have historically been given great weight by both the faculty and the administration, and election to it is regarded as an honor. The records of membership on the committee go back to 1917, just after its 1916 creation; the records as to who served as chair begin only in the early 1970s. In the 86 years between 1917 and 2003, the political science department had a member on the committee nearly one-third of the time (and almost half the time from 1945 to 1995):

1939–42	John M. Gaus
1945–48	Llewellyn Pfankuchen
1951–54	James L. McCamy
1955–57	Llewellyn Pfankuchen
1960–63	David Fellman
1971–74	Clara Penniman*
1978–81	Bernard C. Cohen*
1984–87	M. Crawford Young*
1991–94	Joel B. Grossman*
1998	M. Crawford Young (as replacement)

*served as chairs in the final year of their term

The Social Studies Divisional Committee has several tasks, the most important of which is giving advice to the dean of the college concerning all promotions or appointments to tenure. It is thus the penultimate watchdog over the quality and strength of the faculty. And since the dean very rarely overrides the committee's advice, the committee is in effect the ultimate source of quality control over the faculty. The current divisional committee structure dates formally from 1945, when the faculty confirmed the "experimental" structure put in place in 1942.[1] In the 58 years from 1942 to 2000, the department had an elected member sitting on the Social Studies Divisional Committee in all but five years. The roster follows:

1942–45	Frederick A. Ogg
1944–49	Llewellyn Pfankuchen
1949–52	William S. Stokes
1952–55	David Fellman
1955–58	Leon D. Epstein
1958–61	Ralph K. Huitt
1959–62	Leon D. Epstein (appointed chair by President Elvehjem)
1961–63	Henry C. Hart
1963–65	Bernard C. Cohen
1965–67	John A. Armstrong
1968–71	Murray J. Edelman (elected chair 1970–71)
1971–74	J. Austin Ranney
1974–77	Barbara Hinckley
1979–80, 1981–82	M. Crawford Young
1982–85	Joel B. Grossman (elected chair 1984–85)
1985–88	Charles W. Anderson
1988–91	Herbert M. Kritzer
1991–94	R. Booth Fowler (elected chair 1993–94)
1994–97	John F. Witte
1997–20	Graham K. Wilson (elected chair 1999–2000)
2001–02	Virginia Sapiro

Note

1. E. David Cronon and John W. Jenkins, *The University of Wisconsin: A History, Vol. III, Politics, Depression, and War*, pp. 356–57.

Appendix 9

Faculty Holding Endowed Chairs

Until the 1960s, the university lacked any endowed chairs. When the Vilas estate, bequeathed to the university in 1908, first became available for distribution, the first step was creation of several Vilas professorships, awarded by campuswide competition. David Fellman was among the first group, named in 1962.[1] Other sources of endowed chairs soon followed. The Wisconsin Alumni Research Foundation made available to the Graduate School resources to create a modest number of chairs (colloquially known from the revenue stream sustaining them as "University Houses") whose funding lasted five years, but whose name (chosen by the beneficiary) was permanent. These professorships were awarded by the Graduate School Research Committee, in a very intense competition. Other campus endowed chairs were funded by the Hilldale Foundation. H. Edwin Young, emeritus L&S dean, Madison chancellor and UW System president, with the assistance of William Young, raised the funds for a pair of five-year term chairs in international studies. These chairs were always awarded in a campuswide competition based on departmental nominations. In 1982, a major bequest to the department from Glenn B. Hawkins, a former political science professor at Oklahoma State University, became available, for the purpose of established a distinguished chair. Further detail on the Hawkins Chair is provided below. Thus far, holders of the Hawkins Chair have always been recruited from outside, though the bequest does not require this. The endowment funds have also permitted the creation of a few short-term midlevel chairs with some modest research funding.

Roster of Chair Holders

Vilas—David Fellman
Hawkins—Herbert Jacob, Charles Jones, Byron Shafer
Hilldale—Murray Edelman, Leon Epstein
WARF ("University Houses")—John Armstrong, Bernard Cohen, Murray Edelman, Patrick Riley, Virginia Sapiro, Crawford Young
H. Edwin Young—Crawford Young
John Bascom—Leon Epstein, Crawford Young
Oscar Rennebohm—Clara Penniman

Note

1. E. David Cronon and John W. Jenkins, *The University of Wisconsin: A History, 1945–1971 – Renewal and Revolution* (Madison: University of Wisconsin Press, 1999), IV: 252–53.

Appendix 10
Hawkins Bequest

Glenn Hawkins completed a doctorate in History at the University of Wisconsin in 1927. His dissertation was in the field of frontier military history, titled *Western Pennsylvania in the Revolutionary War.* His primary mentors were Carl Russell Fish, recruited by Frederick Jackson Turner about 1900 as a specialist in New England history, and Frederick Paxson, who succeeded Turner in the field of frontier history.[1] The third member of his doctoral committee, Walter Sharp, was a political scientist, though with no apparent connection to the thesis topic. The dissertation was a detailed account of the Revolutionary War in this frontier outpost, based upon extensive archival material.

The Hawkins itinerary between that date and 1975, when he made contact with the University of Wisconsin Foundation about a possible bequest, can be reconstructed only by surmise. He apparently spent most or all of his career at Oklahoma State University, which until the early postwar years bore the designation of "Oklahoma A&M University." Before the war, the university doubtless had only very small social science departments, and history may well have been a joint unit with political science. Hawkins was doubtless hired as an historian, and at some point began covering political science courses. By the time the University expanded beyond its agricultural and engineering roots to round itself out after World War II, Hawkins appears to have been its leading political scientist, and long served as department chair.

Once he made contact with the UW Foundation, and the staff realized that the bequest might be substantial, several leading foundation executives paid visits to Oklahoma to work with Hawkins in arranging the endowment he wished to make (Robert Rennebohm, Timothy Reilley, Vernon Howard). Completing the transaction proved challenging, since Hawkins had some eccentricities, among them a visceral distrust of lawyers. Finding an intermediary to assist him in preparing a valid will required arduous administrative acrobatics. He was also suspicious of financial institutions; $129,000 of securities were discovered concealed in a coffee tin in his house, and his wife's extensive jewelry collection was taped to the bottom of a bathtub. The childless couple was evidently very frugal, accumulating substantial savings on what must have been meager Oklahoma State salaries. One official speculated that part of the estate may have reflected some inherited money from his wife.

The Hawkins bequest was originally intended for Oklahoma State. However, the president of the institution refused to accede to a Hawkins request to establish a chair for a named individual (a former student and close associate), and in other ways offended him. Thus Hawkins turned to his doctoral alma mater, but did so through the prism of his adopted disciplinary identity rather than his original departmental affiliation.

The Hawkins bequest was officially accepted by the governing board of the UW Foundation in July 1979, after his decease. His widow passed away soon afterwards, and the bequest became available to the department in 1982, by that time valued at approximately $1.1 million. After one unsuccessful search, the Glenn B. and Cleone Orr Hawkins Chair had its first incumbent, Herbert Jacob, in 1984.

Note

1. Merle Curti and Vernon Carstensen, *The University of Wisconsin: A History 1848–1925* (Madison: University of Wisconsin Press, 1949), I: 311, 337–338.

APPENDIX 11
Faculty Awards

Distinguished Teaching Awards

Winners of Distinguished Teaching Awards are selected in a campus-wide competition. The awards were introduced in 1953, initially with only two given annually. After 1963, the number of awards slowly increased, reaching 10 in 2003. A dozen political science faculty have been honored with Distinguished Teaching Awards.

1962	Thomas Thorson
1963	Charles Anderson
1964	Herbert Jacob
1967	Kenneth Dolbeare
1969	Booth Fowler
1985	Patrick Riley
1985	Donald Emmerson
1986	Melvin Croan
1987	James Farr
1988	Joel Grossman
1989	Donald Downs
2001	James Coleman

Hilldale Awards

Hilldale Awards are given annually, one by each of the four divisional committee (Biological Sciences, Physical Sciences, Humanities and Social Studies). The award, initiated in 1986, recognizes distinction in research, teaching and service. Two political science faculty have won Hilldale Awards.

1996–97	Crawford Young
1999–00	Virginia Sapiro

Appendix 12
Department Rankings

It should not be surprising that a field like political science, with its focus on bringing order to an inherently contentious and subjective realm of inquiry, should occasionally be preoccupied with the ordering of the institutions that produce the scholars that shape the field itself. The development of department rankings has had numerous impacts within the academy—from serving as a basis for the choice of graduate programs for potential students, to influencing the evaluation of manuscripts and proposals based upon institutional affiliation.

With so much at stake, some have called for a regular evaluation and diversification of the procedures for ranking political science departments.[1] Traditional methods of evaluating department performance are subjective, and have evolved over time. Beginning with R. H. Hughes's 1925 *Study of the Graduate Schools of America,* most department rankings have been derived by collecting survey or interview data from various samples of political science instructors—usually focusing on department chairs and scholars of academic distinction—who are asked to rank departments based upon their personal evaluation of the "desirability" or "esteem" of each, as well as the quality of publications and training emanating from them.[2] Recently, more "objective" criteria for ranking political science departments have been formulated—usually premised upon some quantification of the research productivity of department faculty in leading political science journals, number of academic books published, or some other readily quantifiable indicator.[3] Such efforts have buttressed the traditional survey approach by providing a more nuanced understanding of different measures of institutional performance. Finally, *U.S. News and World Report* has recently expanded its ranking of American universities to the ranking of departments within those universities. Not conducted under professional academic auspices with a clearly defined methodology, these reports are generally considered less reliable, though Wisconsin continues its strong performance.

Regardless of the methods, the Department of Political Science at the University of Wisconsin–Madison has historically ranked as one of the premier departments in the nation. Amongst the more subjective reputational rankings, Wisconsin has consistently placed within the top ten programs in the country. Various recent "objective" studies have further highlighted the strengths of the Wisconsin program. For instance, when one gauges faculty publishing productivity while controlling for the number of people in the department, Wisconsin ranks fourth overall, while if one computes productivity based upon the output of book manuscripts, Wisconsin ranks third, behind only Harvard and the University of California at Berkeley.[4]

While enlightening, the relatively recent development of such approaches to departmental rankings based upon objective criteria do not easily lend themselves to historical analysis due to the greater temporal fluctuation in many of the indicators. Traditional survey methods have tended to produce a more stable ranking system that can more easily facilitate the analysis of long-term trends, as is evidenced by the table below.

Political Science Department Rankings, 1925–2001

Rank	1925[a]	1934[b]	1957[c]	1964[d]	1969[e]	1978[f]	1983[g]	1995[h]	2001[i]
	Harvard	*Columbia	Harvard	Yale	Yale	Harvard	Yale	Harvard	Harvard
	Chicago	*Harvard	Chicago	Harvard	Harvard	Yale	Michigan	Cal-Berkeley	Stanford (2)
	Columbia	*Princeton	California	Cal-Berkeley	Cal-Berkeley	Cal-Berkeley	Cal-Berkeley	Yale	Cal-Berkeley (2)
	Wisconsin	*California	Columbia	Chicago	Chicago	Michigan	Chicago	Michigan	Michigan (2)
	Illinois	*Chicago	Princeton	Columbia	Michigan	Stanford	Harvard	Stanford	Yale
	Michigan	*Illinois	Michigan	Princeton	MIT (6)	Chicago	MIT	Chicago	Princeton
	Princeton	*Michigan	Yale	MIT (7)	Stanford (6)	Princeton	Stanford	Princeton	UCSD
	JHU	***Wisconsin**	**Wisconsin**	**Wisconsin (7)**	**Wisconsin**	**Wisconsin**	**Wisconsin**	UCLA	Duke (8)
	Iowa	American	Minnesota	Stanford	Princeton	MIT	Minnesota	UCSD	UCLA (8)
	U. Penn.	Cornell	Cornell	Michigan	UNC		Rochester	**Wisconsin**	Chicago (8)
	California	JHU	Illinois	Cornell	Columbia	Cornell	Rochester		**Wisconsin (11)**
		NYU	UCLA	Northwestern	UCLA	Princeton	MIT	MIT (11)	
		Northwestern	Stanford	UCLA	Minnesota		North Carolina	Minnesota	Rochester (11)
		Ohio State	JHU	Indiana	Cornell		Northwestern	Duke	Columbia (11)
		Stanford	Duke	North Carolina	Indiana		Indiana	Cornell	Ohio State (15)
Out of:	36	23	25	64					66

a R. M. Hughes, *A Study of the Graduate Schools of America* (Oxford, OH: Miami University), 1925, pp. 22–23

b American Council on Education, Report of Committee on Graduate Instruction (Washington, DC: American Council on Education), 1934, p. 30.

c Heyward Keniston, *Graduate Study and Research in the Arts and Sciences* (Philadelphia: University of Pennsylvania Press), 1957, p. 142.

d Allan M. Cartter, *An Assessment of Quality in Graduate Education* (Washington, DC: American Council on Education), 1966, p. 40.

e Kenneth Roose and Charles Andersen, *A Rating of Graduate Programs* (Washington, DC: American Council on Education), 1970, pp. 64–65.

f Everett Carll Ladd, Jr. & Robert Kieth MacDonald, "Technical Report: 1977 Survey of the Professoriate," *Chronicle of Higher Education*, January 15, 1979.

g National Research Center Ranking, 1983.

h Marvin Goldberger et al. (eds.), *Research-Doctrine Programs in the United States: Continuity and Change* (Washington, DC: National Academy Press), 1995, p. 196. Also: Tom Rice, James McCormick and Benjamin Bergmann, "Graduate Training, Current Affiliation and Publishing Books in Political Science," *Political Science and Politics*, December, 2002, p.752.

i *US News and World Report*, "Political Science Program Rankings," 2001.

---

* 1934 listings do not rank departments, but rather note "distinguished" political science departments alphabetically.

Notes

1. Tom Rice, James McCormick and Benjamin Bergmann, "Graduate Training, Current Affiliation and Publishing Books in Political Science," *PS: Political Science and Politics,* vol. 35 (2002), pp. 751–755.
2. In particular: R.H. Hughes, *A Study of the Graduate Schools of America* (Miami University Press: Oxford, OH), 1925, pp. 3–5; American Council on Education, *Report of Committee on Graduate Instruction* (American Council on Education: Washington, DC), 1934, pp. 2–3; Hayward Keniston, *Graduate Study and Research in the Arts and Sciences at the University of Pennsylvania* (University of Pennsylvania Press: Philadelphia, PA), 1959, pp. 115–119; Allan M. Cartter, *An Assessment of Quality in Graduate Education* American Council on Education: Washington, DC), 1966, pp. 15–16; Kenneth D. Roose and Charles J. Andersen, *A Ranking of Graduate Programs* (American Council on Education: Washington, DC), 1970, pp. 32–33; Marvin Goldberger, Brendan Maher and Pamela Ebert Flattau, eds., *Research-Doctorate Programs in the United States: Continuity and Change* (National Academy Press: Washington, DC), 1995, p. 147.
3. Lyle V. Jones, Gardner Lindzey and Porter E. Coggeshall, eds., *An Assessment of Research-Doctorate Programs in the United States: Social and Behavioral Sciences* (National Academy Press: Washington, DC), 1982, p. 15; Michael Ballard and Neil Mitchell, "The Good, the Better, and the Best in Political Science," *PS: Political Science and Politics,* vol. 31 (1998), pp. 826–28; Arthur Miller, Charled Tien and Andrew Peebler, "Department Rankings: An Alternative Approach," *PS: Political Science and Politics,* vol. 29 (1996), pp. 704–717; Tom Rice, James McCormick and Benjamin Bergmann, "Graduate Training, Current Affiliation and Publishing Books in Political Science," *PS: Political Science and Politics,* vol. 35 (2002), pp. 751–755.
4. Tom Rice, James McCormick and Benjamin Bergmann, "Graduate Training, Current Affiliation and Publishing Books in Political Science," *PS: Political Science and Politics,* vol. 35 (2002), pp. 752, 754.

APPENDIX 13

American Political Science Review Articles by Faculty and Graduate Students

Failures and Successes at the Second Hague Conference, Paul S. Reinsch, Vol. 2, No. 2. (Feb., 1908).

Diplomatic Affairs and International Law, 1909, Paul S. Reinsch, Vol. 4, No. 1. (Feb., 1910).

Diplomatic Affairs and International Law, 1910, Paul S. Reinsch, Vol. 5, No. 1. (Feb., 1911).

New Forms of the Initiative and Referendum, S. Gale Lowrie, Vol. 5, No. 4. (Nov., 1911).

Diplomatic Affairs and International Law, 1911, Paul S. Reinsch, Vol. 6, No. 1. (Feb., 1912).

Diplomatic Affairs and International Law, 1912, Paul S. Reinsch, Vol. 7, No. 1. (Feb., 1913), pp. 63–86.

Repeal of the Judiciary Act of 1801,William S. Carpenter, Vol. 9, No. 3. (Aug., 1915), pp. 519–28.

Foreign Governments and Politics: **British Parliamentary Elections,** Frederic A. Ogg, Vol. 13, No. 1. (Feb., 1919), pp. 108–14.

The Institute of Politics: **Organization and Methods,** Pitman B. Potter, Vol. 15, No. 4. (Nov., 1921), pp. 534–39.

Foreign Governments and Politics: **Electoral Reform in France and the Elections of 1919,** Graham H. Stuart, Vol. 14, No. 1. (Feb., 1920), pp. 117–23.

Notes on International Affairs: **Sanctions and Guaranties in International Organization,** Pitman B. Potter, Vol. 16, No. 2. (May, 1922), pp. 297–303.

Origin of the System of Mandates under the League of Nations, Pitman B. Potter, Vol. 16, No. 4. (Nov., 1922), pp. 563–83.

Political Science in the International Field, Pitman B. Potter, *The American Political Science Review*, Vol. 17, No. 3. (Aug., 1923), pp. 381–91.

Foreign Governments and Politics: **The Irish Constitution,** Allan F. Saunders, Vol. 18, No. 2. (May, 1924), pp. 340–45.

Foreign Governments and Politics: **The French Elections**, Walter R. Sharp, Vol. 18, No. 3. (Aug., 1924), pp. 533–40.

Report of the Committee on Political Research: **Political Science in France**, W. R. Sharp, Vol. 18, No. 3. (Aug., 1924), pp. 582–92.

Foreign Governments and Politics: **The Canadian Election of 1925**, Walter R. Sharp, Vol. 20, No. 1. (Feb., 1926), pp. 107–17.

The Future of the Consular Office, Pitman B. Potter, Vol. 20, No. 2. (May, 1926), pp. 284–98.

Notes on International Affairs: **The Origin of the System of Mandates under the League of Nations: Further Notes**, Pitman B. Potter, Vol. 20, No. 4. (Nov., 1926), pp. 842–46.

Foreign Government and Politics: **The Canadian Election of 1926**, Walter R. Sharp, Vol. 21, No. 1. (Feb., 1927), pp. 101–13.

The Political Bureaucracy of France Since the War, Walter R. Sharp, Vol. 22, No. 2. (May, 1928), pp. 301–23.

Legislative Notes and Reviews: **Permanent Registration of Voters**, Joseph P. Harris, Vol. 22, No. 2. (May, 1928), pp. 349–53.

Foreign Governments and Politics: **The New French Electoral Law and the Elections of 1928**, Walter R. Sharp, Vol. 22, No. 3. (Aug., 1928), pp. 684–98.

Notes on Administration: **Evaluating State Administrative Structure—the Fallacy of the Statistical Approach**, J. Mark Jacobson, Vol. 22, No. 4. (Nov., 1928), pp. 928–35.

Notes on Judicial Organization and Procedure: **The Judicial Council Movement**, J. A. C. Grant, Vol. 22, No. 4. (Nov., 1928), pp. 936–46.

American Government and Politics: **Marbury v. Madison Today**, J. A. C. Grant, Vol. 23, No. 3. (Aug., 1929), pp. 673–81.

Legislative Notes and Reviews: **The Progress of Permanent Registration of Voters**, Joseph P. Harris, Vol. 23, No. 4. (Nov., 1929), pp. 908–14.

Notes on Judicial Organization and Procedure: Methods of Jury Selection, J. A. C. Grant, Vol. 24, No. 1. (Feb., 1930), pp. 117–33.

Permanent Delegations to the League of Nations, Pitman B. Potter, Vol. 25, No. 1. (Feb., 1931), pp. 21–44.

Notes on Administration: The Present Status of the Study of Public Administration in the United States, John M. Gaus, Vol. 25, No. 1. (Feb., 1931), pp. 120–34.

International Affairs: **The Concept of "International Government"**, Pitman B. Potter, Vol. 25, No. 3. (Aug., 1931), pp. 713–17.

Representative Government in Evolution, Charles A. Beard; **John D. Lewis**, Vol. 26, No. 2. (April, 1932), pp. 223–40.

Legislative Notes and Reviews: **The Wisconsin Unemployment Compensation Law of 1932**, J. Mark Jacobson, Vol. 26, No. 2. (April, 1932), pp. 300–311.

Public Administration and Administrative Law: **The Wisconsin Executive Council**, John M. Gaus, Vol. 26, No. 5. (Oct., 1932), pp. 914–20.

Foreign Governments and Politics: **Direct Legislation in the German Lander, 1919–32**, Lee S. Greene, Vol. 27, No. 3. (June, 1933), pp. 445–54.

American Government and Politics: **Party Organization in Philadelphia: The Ward Committeeman**, John T. Salter, Vol. 27, No. 4. (Aug., 1933), pp. 618–27.

American Government and Politics: **Governor Pinchot and the Late Magistrate Stubbs**, John T. Salter, Vol. 29, No. 2. (April, 1935), pp. 249–56.

Public Administration: **Public Administration in the United States in 1934, John M. Gaus**; Leonard D. White, Vol. 29, No. 3. (June, 1935), pp. 442–51.

Rural Local Government: **The Progress of County Government Reform in Wisconsin**, Lee S. Green, Vol. 30, No. 1. (Feb., 1936), pp. 96–102.

The Popular Front in France: Prelude or Interlude? Walter R. Sharp, Vol. 30, No. 5. (Oct., 1936), pp. 857–83.

The Quest for Responsibility, Clarence A. Dykstra, Vol. 33, No. 1. (Feb., 1939), pp. 1–25.

American Government and Politics: **Personal Attention in Politics**, John T. Salter, Vol. 34, No. 1. (Feb., 1940), pp. 54–66.

Public Administration: **Executive Leadership and the Growth of Propaganda**, Harold W. Stoke, Vol. 35, No. 3. (June, 1941), pp. 490–500.

American Democracy—After War, Frederic A. Ogg, Vol. 36, No. 1. (Feb., 1942), pp. 1–15.

A Job Analysis of Political Science, John M. Gaus, Vol. 40, No. 2. (April, 1946), pp. 217–30.

Britain Begins to Rebuild Her Cities, Coleman Woodbury, Vol. 41, No. 5. (Oct., 1947), pp. 901–20.

Ten Years of the Supreme Court: 1937–1947: **I. Federalism**, David Fellman, Vol. 41, No. 6. (Dec., 1947), pp. 1142–60.

Constitutional Law in 1947–48: The Constitutional Decisions of the Supreme Court of the United States in the October Term, 1947, David Fellman, Vol. 43, No. 2. (April, 1949), pp. 275–308.

The British Labour Left and U. S. Foreign Policy, Leon D. Epstein, Vol. 45, No. 4. (Dec., 1951), pp. 974–95.

Constitutional Law in 1950–1951, David Fellman, Vol. 46, No. 1. (March, 1952), pp. 158–99.

Federal Regulation of the Uses of Natural Gas, Ralph K. Huitt, Vol. 46, No. 2. (June, 1952), pp. 455–69.

Constitutional Law in 1951–1952, David Fellman, Vol. 47, No. 1. (March, 1953), pp. 126–70.

Politics of British Conservatism, Leon D. Epstein, Vol. 48, No. 1. (March, 1954), pp. 27–48.

Constitutional Law in 1952–1953, David Fellman, Vol. 48, No. 1. (March, 1954), pp. 63–113.

The Congressional Committee: A Case Study, Ralph K. Huitt, Vol. 48, No. 2. (June, 1954), pp. 340–65.

The People of the State Department and Foreign Service, James L. McCamy; Alessandro Corradini, Vol. 48, No. 4. (Dec., 1954), pp. 1067–82.

Constitutional Law in 1953–1954, David Fellman, Vol. 49, No. 1. (March, 1955), pp. 63–106.

Constitutional Law in 1954–1955, David Fellman, Vol. 50, No. 1. (March, 1956), pp. 43–100.

Cohesion of British Parliamentary Parties, Leon D. Epstein, Vol. 50, No. 2. (June, 1956), pp. 360–77.

Constitutional Law in 1955–1956, David Fellman, Vol. 51, No. 1. (March, 1957), pp. 158–96.

The Morse Committee Assignment Controversy: A Study in Senate Norms, Ralph K. Huitt, Vol. 51, No. 2. (June, 1957), pp. 313–29.

Constitutional Law in 1956–1957, David Fellman, Vol. 52, No. 1. (March, 1958), pp. 140–91.

Constitutional Law in 1957–1958, David Fellman, Vol. 53, No. 1. (March, 1959), pp. 138–80.

Constitutional Law in 1958–1959: I, David Fellman, Vol. 54, No. 1. (March, 1960), pp. 167–99.

British M.P.S. and Their Local Parties: The Suez Cases, Leon D. Epstein, Vol. 54, No. 2. (June, 1960), pp. 374–90.

Constitutional Law in 1958–1959: II, David Fellman, Vol. 54, No. 2. (June, 1960), pp. 474–93.

Constitutional Law in 1959–1960, David Fellman, Vol. 55, No. 1. (March, 1961), pp. 112–35.

Democratic Party Leadership in the Senate, Ralph K. Huitt, Vol. 55, No. 2. (June, 1961), pp. 333–44.

Inter-Party Constituency Differences and Congressional Voting Behavior, Lewis A. Froman, Jr., Vol. 57, No. 1. (March, 1963), pp. 57–61.

Inter-Constituency Movement of British Parliamentary Candidates, 1951–1959, Austin Ranney, Vol. 58, No. 1. (March, 1964), pp. 36–45.

A Comparative Study of Canadian Parties, Leon D. Epstein, Vol. 58, No. 1. (March, 1964), pp. 46–59.

Hobbes's Concept of Representation—II, Hanna Pitkin, Vol. 58, No. 4. (Dec., 1964), pp. 902–18.

Conditions for Party Leadership: The Case of the House Democrats Lewis A. Froman, Jr., Randall B. Ripley, Vol. 59, No. 1. (March, 1965), pp. 52–63.

Sources of Administrative Behavior: Some Soviet and Western European Comparisons, John A. Armstrong, Vol. 59, No. 3. (Sept., 1965), pp. 643–55.

Obligation and Consent—I, Hanna Pitkin, Vol. 59, No. 4. (Dec., 1965), pp. 990–99.

Obligation and Consent—II, Hanna Pitkin, Vol. 60, No. 1. (March, 1966), pp. 39–52.

The Linkage between Constituency Attitudes and Congressional Voting Behavior: A Causal Model, Charles F. Cnudde; **Donald J. McCrone,** Vol. 60, No. 1. (March, 1966), pp. 66–72.

Support for the Party System by the Mass Public, Jack Dennis, Vol. 60, No. 3. (Sept., 1966), pp. 600–615.

The Child's Acquisition of Regime Norms: Political Efficacy, David Easton; **Jack Dennis,** Vol. 61, No. 1. (March, 1967), pp. 25–38.

Toward a Communications Theory of Democratic Political Development: A Causal Model, Donald J. McCrone; Charles F. Cnudde, Vol. 61, No. 1. (March, 1967), pp. 72–79.

Measurement Identity in the Longitudinal Analysis of Legislative Voting, Aage R. Clausen, Vol. 61, No. 4. (Dec., 1967), pp. 1020–35.

Protest as a Political Resource, Michael Lipsky, Vol. 62, No. 4. (Dec., 1968), pp. 1144–58.

Agency Requests, Gubernatorial Support and Budget Success in State Legislatures, Ira Sharkansky, Vol. 62, No. 4. (Dec., 1968), pp. 1220–31.

Foreign Policy as an Issue Area: A Roll Call Analysis, Stephen J. Cimbala, Vol. 63, No. 1. (March, 1969), pp. 148–56.

Wilbur D. Mills: A Study in Congressional Influence, John F. Manley, Vol. 63, No. 2. (June, 1969), pp. 442–64.

Party Competition and Welfare Policies in the American States, Charles F. Cnudde; Donald J. McCrone, Vol. 63, No. 3. (Sept., 1969), pp. 858–66.

Dimensions of State Politics, Economics, and Public Policy, Ira Sharkansky; Richard I. Hofferbert, Vol. 63, No. 3. (Sept., 1969), pp. 867–879.

The Development of Political Ideology: A Framework for the Analysis of Political Socialization, Richard M. Merelman, Vol. 63, No. 3. (Sept., 1969), pp. 750–67.

Corruption, Machine Politics, and Political Change, James C. Scott, Vol. 63, No. 4. (Dec., 1969), pp. 1142–58.

A Comparative Analysis of Senate House Voting on Economic and Welfare Policy: 1953–1964, Aage R. Clausen; Richard B. Cheney, Vol. 64, No. 1. (March, 1970), pp. 138–52.

Support for the Institution of Elections by the Mass Public, Jack Dennis, Vol. 64, No. 3. (Sept., 1970), pp. 819–35.

The Development of Policy Thinking in Adolescence, Richard M. Merelman, Vol. 65, No. 4. (Dec., 1971), pp. 1033–47.

Turnout and Representation in Presidential Primary Elections, Austin Ranney, Vol. 66, No. 1. (March, 1972), pp. 21–37.

Patron-Client Politics and Political Change in Southeast Asia, James C. Scott, Vol. 66, No. 1. (March, 1972), pp. 91–113.

The Conditions of Protest Behavior in American Cities, Peter K. Eisinger, Vol. 67, No. 1. (March, 1973), pp. 11–28.

The Structure of Policy Thinking in Adolescence: A Research Note, Richard M. Merelman, Vol. 67, No. 1. (March, 1973), pp. 161–66.

Comment on "Changing the Rules Changes the Game," Austin Ranney, Vol. 68, No. 1. (March, 1974), pp. 43–44.

Racial Differences in Protest Participation, Peter K. Eisinger, Vol. 68, No. 2. (June, 1974), pp. 592–606.

Ethnic Politics, Representative Bureaucracy and Development Administration: The Zambian Case, Dennis L. Dresang, Vol. 68, No. 4. (Dec., 1974), pp. 1605–17.

Courts and Conflict Resolution: Problems in the Mobilization of Adjudication, Austin Sarat; **Joel B. Grossman**, Vol. 69, No. 4. (Dec., 1975), pp. 1200–1217.

APSA Presidential Address, 1976: **"The Divine Science": Political Engineering in American Culture**, Austin Ranney, Vol. 70, No. 1. (March, 1976), pp. 140–48.

Mobilized and Proletarian Diasporas, John A. Armstrong, Vol. 70, No. 2. (June, 1976), pp. 393–408.

A Reassessment of Conventional Wisdom About the Informed Public: National Political Information in Ghana, Fred M. Hayward, Vol. 70, No. 2. (June, 1976), pp. 433–51.

Developing Public Policy Theory: Perspectives from Empirical Research, George D. Greenberg; **Jeffrey A. Miller**; Lawrence B. Mohr; Bruce C. Vladeck, Vol. 71, No. 4. (Dec., 1977), pp. 1532–43.

The Place of Principles in Policy Analysis, Charles W. Anderson, Vol. 73, No. 3. (Sept., 1979), pp. 711–23.

What Happened to the British Party Model? Leon D. Epstein, Vol. 74, No. 1. (March, 1980), pp. 9–22.

Democratic Politics and the Culture of American Education, Richard M. Merelman, Vol. 74, No. 2. (June, 1980), pp. 319–32.

A Reply to Jennings, Richard M. Merelman, Vol. 74, No. 2. (June, 1980), pp. 338–41.

The American Voter in Congressional Elections, Barbara Hinckley, Vol. 74, No. 3. (Sept., 1980), pp. 641–50.

Research Frontier Essay: When Are Interests Interesting? The Problem of Political Representation of Women, Virginia Sapiro, Vol. 75, No. 3. (Sept., 1981), pp. 701–16.

Black Employment in Municipal Jobs: The Impact of Black Political Power, Peter K. Eisinger, Vol. 76, No. 2. (June, 1982), pp. 380–92.

Potential Responsiveness in the Bureaucracy: Views of Public Utility Regulation, William Gormley; John Hoadley; Charles Williams, Vol. 77, No. 3. (Sept., 1983), pp. 704–17.

Articles: **U.S. Defense Spending and the Soviet Estimate,** Charles W. Ostrom, Jr.; **Robin F. Marra,** Vol. 80, No. 3. (Sept., 1986), pp. 819–42.

Articles: **Political Science and the Enlightenment of Enthusiasm,** James Farr, Vol. 82, No. 1. (March, 1988), pp. 51–69.

Articles: **American Federalism, Welfare Policy, and Residential Choices,** Paul E. Peterson; **Mark Rom,** Vol. 83, No. 3. (Sept., 1989), pp. 711–28.

Review Essay: **Mistrust But Verify: Memoirs of the Reagan Era Revolution,** Charles O. Jones, Vol. 83, No. 3. (Sept., 1989), pp. 981–88.

Articles: **Race, Sociopolitical Participation, and Black Empowerment, Lawrence Bobo;** Franklin D. Gilliam, Jr., Vol. 84, No. 2. (June, 1990), pp. 377–93.

Articles: **Eschewing Obfuscation: Campaigns and the Perception of U.S. Senate Incumbents,** Charles H. Franklin, Vol. 85, No. 4. (Dec., 1991), pp. 1193–1214.

Articles: **A Way of Life and Law: Presidential Address, American Political Science Association, 1994,** Charles O. Jones, Vol. 89, No. 1. (March, 1995), pp. 1–9.

Unified Government, Divided Government, and Party Responsiveness, John J. Coleman, Vol. 93, No. 4. (Dec., 1999), pp. 821–35.

Jurisprudential Regimes in Supreme Court Decision Making, Mark J. Richards, **Herbert M. Kritzer,** Vol. 96, No. 2. (June, 2002).

APPENDIX 14

Department Secretaries

The chief departmental administrative officer, the department secretary, has long been a crucial player in the daily operation of the political science department. Records do not permit excavating the lineage of incumbents further back than the eve of World War II; before that time, with a much smaller faculty and more limited functions and resources, administrative and clerical staffing of the department was undoubtedly minimal. In the postwar years, this position became central to the efficient functioning of the department; several of the long-standing incumbents have earned a special niche in the departmental memories of faculty and students.

The department secretary has the operational responsibility for the administrative functioning of the department. This general mandate encompasses a multitude of responsibilities: daily management of the budget, supervision of the clerical staff, assuring necessary supplies are in hand, and linkages with the administrative offices of the university. The nature of the administrative burdens placed upon the department has changed over the years; to cite but one example, the advent of computers has all but eliminated the once critical function of supplying typing services to the faculty for manuscripts, reference letters and the like; in place of these tasks have arisen many other responsibilities created by the increasing complexity of university operations. For example, the College of Letters and Science delegated budget management to several large departments in 1994, including political science; this entails many new accounting tasks.

The first department secretary we can identify was Emily Williams, who held the post from 1935 till 1942 She was replaced by Erna Flader (subsequently Erna Cutlip), who served from 1942 till 1947. She had earlier worked for University Hospital and the Wisconsin Alumni Research Foundation (WARF), and resigned her departmental position when she married Scott Cutlip, a graduate student in the department who completed his doctorate in journalism, stayed on to organize the university centennial observation in 1948, and to found the University News Service, then to pursue most of his academic career on the journalism faculty. Both Erna and Scott Cutlip were regulars at the famed John Gaus Saturday afternoon discussion groups at his residence, and leading figures in the university community.

After some short-lived replacements, the next legendary figure as department secretary, Mary Woodring, assumed the post in 1949; James McCamy was then chair. Woodring, universally known as "San," held the position until 1960, when her husband took a position at Columbia. During most of her tenure, she served with William Young, whose tribute to her follows below. She had held a similar position with the Department of Social Relations at Harvard, under Talcott Parsons. After leaving our department, she worked with the Council on Foreign Relations, then as office manager for the John Simon Guggenheim Foundation from 1968 to 1985. Even after her move to New York, then later Texas, she remained in close touch with McCamy, carefully preserving his frequent correspondence which was contributed to the department history archives upon her death in 2003.

Jeanne Burrell served during the chairmanship of Leon Epstein in 1960–63, followed briefly by Sandra Nash in 1963–64, then Elizabeth Pringle, a departmental icon, who held the post from 1964 until her retirement in 1982. There followed Donna Lewis (1982–89), Jean Neiderklopfer (1989–92), and Patricia Whipple (1992–2000). Lewis left for a higher-ranking position in the College of Engineering, Neiderklopfer returned to journalism, later leaving state service, and Whipple became department administrator for sociology. The present department secretary, Tammi Kuhl, assumed her functions in 2000. Each of these women left her mark upon the department; successive chairs have found their administrative knowledge and skills a critical resource.

A word of tribute is also appropriate for the able and dedicated office staff that has served the department over the years. The names are too many for individual recognition, but they richly deserve acknowledgment for their intelligence, competence and skill. The department as an administrative entity in recent decades has always stood out among its campus peers for the efficiency of its operation. The centennial staff of Elizabeth Smith, Deborah Bakke, Diane Morauske, Daun Wheeler, Harriet Allen, and Megan Chard follow in the footsteps of an admirable crew of predecessors.

Biographical material on the two longest-serving department secretaries, and some personal recollections of Burrell, follow below.

Elizabeth Pringle

Elizabeth Pringle was a North Hall fixture for long enough to acquire legendary status. She is the longest-serving department secretary recorded in our archives, serving 18 years from her first appointment by then-Chair Clara Penniman until her retirement in 1982. A favorite of graduate students and faculty alike, she maintained an atmosphere of efficiency and professional dedication which helped sustain a remarkable continuity among our civil service office staff. She cared deeply about the well-being and professional development of the staff she supervised, even when the promotions she helped them obtain required transfer to another office.

She grew up in South Dakota, graduating with honors from South Dakota State. She began her career as a journalist for the Hot Springs (South Dakota) *Star*. After an interlude as homemaker, she resumed her career as an office manager. In this capacity, to the immense benefit of the department, she was discovered by Penniman and hired as department secretary.

She fully participated in the life of the department, and continued to attend the annual holiday parties long after her retirement. In our alumni survey regarding the doctoral experience, a number paid tribute to her; typical was the observation by Joel Margolis that "Mrs. Pringle was the glue that held the Department together and made it work." Bruce Oppenheimer added that he "once dreamt that Mrs. Pringle was grading prelim exams, and that seemed as it should be." Michael Schatzberg, in an obituary recalling her warm and caring persona in the 2002 *Political Science Newsletter*, noted that "she seemed to run the place," and that "in a more formal era . . . I just assumed that her first name was 'Mrs.'"

Another episode attesting to her special role is found in the Patrick Riley annals. Nearly three decades ago, Riley with his wife and two sons were in Amsterdam. A robbery stripped them of all their funds and return tickets. Riley cabled Pringle to report that he and family were stranded penniless in Amsterdam; she at once wired him $1000 of her personal funds to rescue the Riley family.

For years after she left North Hall, she served as a docent for the Elvehjem Museum of Art. She was also an active patron of the Madison Opera. She passed away on 26 July 2002 at the age of 86, survived by her husband, Henry, and son, John.

— *Crawford Young*

Mary "San" Woodring

San Woodring was hired, I believe, by Jim McCamy, and they became and remained, until he died, the very best of friends. Jim was a very caring and smooth operator and it took San a few weeks to become accustomed to my rather more direct and gritty style and my nearly unreadable penmanship. We soon, however, settled into a most amicable pattern of relating to each another.

She ran our small office with such grace and understanding that I could virtually take it for granted. Never did I hear a complaint from staff, students, or higher levels of management. She educated me on the quips and quirks of those with whom I must deal. Her judgment was rarely mistaken. (I agreed with it.) She began and ended most days impeccably garbed, pleasant of disposition, and professional in behavior.

She treated the students as friends, the faculty as superior beings, and the overlords as masters. We became very close friends; her discretion was exemplary and her tact remarkable. I shared with her my thoughts, pleasures, and pains. I tested many ideas and deprecations with her and her responses were usually both apt and useful. She was also very skillful at deflecting persons and propositions that might burden, worry, or upset me.

I have worked with many aides since her departure. I, and the department, have never been better served.

— *William H. Young*

Recollections of Jeanne Burrell, 1960–63

I have always regarded my administrative experience in the Department of Political Science as one of my most profitable and enjoyable work experiences: the atmosphere of faculty members, graduate students, and the office location as the hub of department activity were sympathetic to my nature; but, most of all, my working relationship with Leon Epstein [then chair] was of the highest quality. I learned a great deal from him because of his extraordinary sense of efficiency in decision-making, his ability to focus on the core of a problem quickly, and his high and consistent standard of judgment in departmental affairs, which allowed me to complement his decision-making in carrying forward a particular action. We were fortunate to have a fine secretarial staff in Sandra Nash, Karen Stein, and others, all of whom were bright and pleasant, in addition to being hard workers.

Among other memories: watching Floridian John Armstrong, with his soft smile, agonizing over the cold Wisconsin winters as he walked by my desk; discussing syntactical and grammatical issues with Bernie Cohen; trying to be kindly in refusing a cup of tea from J. T. Salter in not-so-clean Chinese cups; exchanging stories and quips with Llewelyn Pfankuchen; soothing ruffled feathers in the secretarial staff when Coleman Woodbury or Dave Fellman appeared with a long paper carrying a short deadline; trotting downstairs [in South Hall] to see L&S [Associate] Dean Bob Doremus, always gracious, to present a request for typewriters (including my red typewriter), secretarial positions, furniture; being grateful for the support of Clara Penniman, the one woman on the faculty at that time, and getting to know and enjoy Ralph Huitt, Charlie Anderson, Fred von der Mehden, Tom Thorson, Jamie McCamy, Henry Hart, Nelson Polsby, Aristide Zolberg, Rufus Browning, and others, plus a host of graduate students. It was a rich time.

Appendix 15
The Undergraduate Advisor

It is hard to believe, given how vital the undergraduate advisor is to the Department of Political Science today, that this position did not exist before 1964. However, until the rapid enrollment increases beginning at the end of the 1950s, such a position was never contemplated, neither in our department nor in any other of the large College of Letters and Science units. Until then, undergraduate advising was provided by faculty; each member of the department had a small roster of majors for whom they were responsible. At an earlier time, with much smaller university enrollments, this system appears to have functioned well. Prewar undergraduates such as Leon Epstein have very positive recollections of the effectiveness of the faculty advising they experienced. However, by the early 1960s, with rapid addition of new young faculty who lacked knowledge of curricular requirements and advising experience, and the swiftly swelling enrollments, the system had clearly broken down. The earlier requirement of the faculty advisor signature on registration forms had become unenforceable, and many students were left to their own devices in planning their majors and academic programs.

In 1964, Clara Penniman (then chair) recognized the problem, and conceived the innovative response: establishment of a part-time position of undergraduate advisor. Other large L&S departments soon followed. Initially, the pool of potential candidates drew heavily on faculty spouses with an academic background of their own, and a familiarity with the university and in a number of cases the department. Such was the case with the first undergraduate advisor to remain in office long enough to define the position, Ann Nelson; she and her husband, Harold "Bud" Nelson of the School of Journalism and Mass Communication, were close friends with a number of the long-standing members of the Department of Political Science.

From modest beginnings as a half-time academic year appointment, the position has grown into a full-time, year-round function. Its scope and responsibilities have dramatically increased during its four decades of history. The job description today is lengthy on paper, and even longer in practice. The list of what the advisor does for students and for faculty is almost endless, in fact, and the position has always required a person of considerable dedication, high energy, and enthusiasm for students and for the department. The job involves, above all, helping undergraduates (hundreds of them every academic year) hour after hour, day after day. This assistance involves anything and everything in person and via e-mail, matters grand and mundane as students plan their courses, their programs, and their futures or navigate through bureaucratic rules and personal challenges. It also involves daily consultations with faculty members about students and about the undergraduate program, recruiting students for department committees, operating the teaching assistant evaluation process, searching for internships, and much more. The demands are many, impressively many.

What is equally impressive is how extraordinarily fortunate the Department of Political Science has been in the quality of undergraduate advisors it has employed and their dedication to what one advisor, Elaine Davis, called "the best place I have worked in my lifetime." Nelson, the pathbreaker, served from 1965 to 1970, following the brief tenure of Betty Dunn in 1964–65, who had to resign when the family moved away from Madison in 1965. It was Nelson who established the office as a central, ongoing part of the department. Her years were hardly easy ones, especially as they eventually became the famous late 1960s era of student activism and protest. But Nelson, like Davis, loved the job and became much admired in the department for her service. She left when she moved too far away from the university for reasonable daily commuting.

After a brief year of hard work by Mary Ann Ripple in 1970–71, living through the Sterling Hall bombing and its aftermath, Ernestine (Ernie) Vanderlin became undergraduate advisor. Vanderlin held the post for 20 fruitful years, from 1971 to 1990. In the process she transformed the role of undergraduate advisor enormously, placing an indelible stamp on the office. She expanded the functions of the office in numerous creative ways; by 1986, the position had become a full-time, year-round appointment.

Vanderlin was very active in expanding the role of the undergraduate advisor. She introduced special advising services for helping the numerous prelaw majors, as well as being involved in national organizations concerning prelaw and other advising. Vanderlin also eventually became the advisor for the large numbers of international relations majors, a demanding job now handled by a separate advisor. She worked tirelessly to develop internship and other extra-college student opportunities. Above all, she was immersed in daily student advising, which became an ever greater challenge as the department attracted hundreds of majors and as students became increasingly proactive in terms of program, course, and career planning. The job was overwhelming at times, but Vanderlin was equal to the challenge.

When Vanderlin retired in 1990, Elaine Davis replaced her. Davis served for almost a decade, from 1990 to 1998. While Davis and Vanderlin had different personal styles, Davis was equally dedicated and energetic and, like Vanderlin, acquired a reputation as an advisor committed to high academic standards and goals combined with a determination to help students. Davis felt the largest challenge she experienced, beyond coping with the sheer number of political science majors and the complexity of their demands upon her services, was assisting students in planning and preparation for their future careers. More and more, she found, students were intensely concerned about how their major could help them toward a rewarding future occupation. Davis made educating students about career options with their political science major an integral feature of her role as undergraduate advisor.

When Elaine Davis retired in 1998, she was eventually replaced by a recent doctoral alumna, Collette Niland. She came to the post with significant experience in the College of Letters and Science advising services which, along with her background in political science, made her a highly qualified successor to Davis and Vanderlin. Her youthful enthusiasm was also a great asset, but after a short time she received an offer from another university that recognized her talent and accomplishments here, and she left.

Liane Kosaki began as undergraduate advisor in 2002 and was an instant success. Kosaki came to the post with extensive previous advising experience at the University of Wisconsin–Madison. And, like Niland, Kosaki has a political science doctorate and has taught (and continues to teach) in the field. She thus brought to the position unparalleled training and knowledge. Even more, however, Kosaki has brought to her role the same concern for our students and a vast energy for serving them, the faculty, and the department, which has characterized all of her predecessors. This deep concern which has always textured their daily interactions with students has been the secret of such successful political science undergraduate advisors. Since its 1964 creation, the position of undergraduate advisor has become a crucial resource for the department, thanks in large measure to the remarkable skills and talents of successive occupants of this office.

— *Booth Fowler*

Appendix 16

Graduate Advisor Mary Jane Hill

For over fifteen years, Mary Jane Hill played a central role in the life of the students and faculty of the Department of Political Science. That era came to a close at the end of May 2002, when Mary Jane entered retirement. . . .

Among other duties as Graduate Program Coordinator, Mary Jane introduced potential new students to the Department, helping them through the application process and answering their questions along the way. A couple of years ago the Graduate School analyzed the graduate admissions process of many of the departments on campus, and that study found that Mary Jane's cheerful and expert assistance played a large role in creating a positive image for this Department. Applicants appreciated her prompt, accurate, and friendly responses to their questions.

Those qualities would become only more evident once students arrived on campus. Our graduate students found that Mary Jane was available to answer any questions about our program requirements, administrative details, and Graduate School rules. She kept students on their toes by reminding them about deadlines. And perhaps most important, she was a genuine friend to our students, rejoicing with them when times called for celebration and lending a sympathetic ear in more difficult times. Taking a sincere interest in the students not just as students but as individuals, she provided the kind of emotional support that was critical for many students as they navigated the often difficult terrain of graduate education.

Faculty also found Mary Jane indispensable. She was the person who understood rules that seemed to defy understanding. She coordinated dissertation defenses, arranged prelim examinations and kept detailed student records. . . . Mary Jane was our institutional memory.

— *Associate Chair John J. Coleman, in 2002* Political Science Newsletter

Hill joined our Department in 1986, after a previous career in the School of Business. Although the position she filled was created in 1969, simultaneous with the establishment of an associate chair, she was the first incumbent to serve for an extended period. In the process, she defined and institutionalized a crucial staff position for the department.

Appendix 17

Doctoral Alumni Careers

The First Century of Doctors of Philosophy in Political Science, University of Wisconsin–Madison

Llewellyn Pfankuchen (1975)
Revised and updated by Virginia Sapiro with David Green and Paul Martin (1998)
Revised and updated by Crawford Young with Mark Schrad (2005)

Preface to the 2005 Edition

This massive compendium has been brushed-off and updated in order to be put on (hopefully) permanent display on the enlarged Web site chronicling the history of the political science department at the University of Wisconsin–Madison, which culminated in the March 2004 department centennial celebration.Unfortunately, the sheer size of the compendium, coupled with limited research resources, will ensure that many details associated with this list will continue to be omitted, outdated, or otherwise imprecise. Special thanks must be extended to Herbert Kritzer, who has effectively compiled a list of alumni publications in the department newsletter, which has been incorporated into the present list. To submit further updates and revisions, please contact Mark Schrad at schrad@polisci.wisc.edu.

Bringing the list into the 21st century has presented both challenges and opportunities. The list encompasses an ever-growing body of alumni, who are publishing ever more—creating a gargantuan task of keeping up with hundreds of active graduates. On the positive side, the Internet has proved to be a wonderful resource for tracking both the affiliations and publications of active alumni. Finally, the 2004 edition now introduces hyperlinks to save the page-turning of old. (See www.polisci.wisc.edu/phddirectory.)

Madison, May 2005
M.S.

Preface to the 1998 Edition

In 1975, then Professor Emeritus Llewellyn Pfankuchen completed work on a document intended to inform the members and friends of the Department of Political Science of the University of Wisconsin–Madison of a crucial part of our history: the list and accomplishments of the individuals who had received the Ph.D. in Political Science from this Department. It cannot help but strike anyone flipping through those original pages — especially those of us who remember the nature of research before the electronic, cybernetic era — what a labor of love this must have been. Professor Pfankuchen, who served on our faculty from 1932 to 1972, died at the age of 85 in 1989.

During a term of office as chair of a university department, one runs across many little-known documents left behind by those who went before. Most deserve their obscurity. This one, brought to my attention by Professor Emeritus Leon Epstein, surely deserves better. I therefore cobbled together a bit of money and asked two graduate students, David Green, and Paul Martin, to assist me in revising and updating Professor Pfankuchen's work.

We have done a much less systematic job of it than desirable; a better one will have to await more time and, certainly, more money. Despite our access to many helpful sources, it would require more resources than we had at hand to pursue the record further. We have included the most recent affiliation, we could find, and some previous ones if we had records. We listed some book titles. But there are many gaps. It is much easier to track down individuals who are active academics than those who have retired or who are in other professions. We do not have the most recent place of employment for everyone, and we know that many people listed here must now be deceased. We can only make the same plea that Professor Pfankuchen did twenty years ago. Please send us corrections to the record, and celebrate the knowledge we do have rather than cursing what we lack.

We are trying to build more bridges among our alumni; we now publish *Wisconsin Political Science*, an annual newsletter for alumni and friends of the Department of Political Science. We hope this record of our Ph.D.s adds to that connection.

This list includes the first century of UW–Madison Ph.D.'s in Political Science. It is a distinguished list. We are working to make that list ever more distinguished in the next century.

Madison, 1998
V.S.

Exordium

This record was brought together mainly for the use of current staff and graduate students, Department of Political Science, University of Wisconsin at Madison. More generally, it offers a suggestion of what graduate work in political science at a major American institution has meant in the world. It is regrettably an unfinished record, based on Department files, the six editions of the Biographical Directory of the American Political Science Association (1945,

1948, 1953, 1961, 1968, 1973), information from colleagues, and correspondence with those listed, departments of political science, colleges and universities, and persons with probable knowledge. Not all leads have been followed to the end because life and funds are short. Injustices are probable because there is more information in some cases than in others. In some instances it was not possible to include all the information available; in others there was no information at all after the granting of the degree; in still others the information leaves it uncertain whether the person is alive. None the less the time seems to have come to make the present information available. It is hoped that readers who detect important lapses will write. Those seeking more complete data on individuals listed may consult the Biographical Directories mentioned above, and in more than a few instances, *Who's Who in America*.

Political Science teaching at the University of Wisconsin began in the 1850s, well before the Ph.D. era, with instruction in Civil Polity, International Law, Constitutional Law, and Political Economy. These offerings were expanded in the 1880s, and in 1892–93 a School of Economics, Political Science and History was formed in which seminar work was given. Political Science did not become a Department by itself until 1904. The doctorates won by Samuel Sparling in 1896 and Paul S. Reinsch in 1898 preceded the creation of the separate department.

Though not strictly pertinent to a Ph.D. list, the career of John B. Parkinson sheds some light on political science careers before the Ph.D. era. Parkinson was an instructor at Madison in 1861–1862; Lafayette County Superintendent of Schools 1862–1864; University of Wisconsin Regent 1866–1867; Professor of Mathematics 1867–1872; Professor of Civil Polity and Constitutional Law 1872–1874; of Civil Polity and Political Economy 1876–1893; and of Constitutional and International Law 1893–1908. Acting Vice President of the University from 1885, and in 1908 he became Vice President and Professor of Constitutional and International Law Emeritus. In 1874–1876 he was President of the State of Wisconsin's Board of Centennial Managers, charged with organizing the official celebration of the hundredth anniversary of American independence. Until 1885 Parkinson taught all the courses in the University in what has since come to be called Political Science; and though he was never a Doctor of Philosophy, in 1920 the University made him a Doctor of Laws.

My thanks are due to the University of Wisconsin Foundation; to my Madison colleagues, especially Professors William Young and Booth Fowler; to Richard Rue; to Elizabeth Pringle for help with Department records; to Ardella Nelson for typing; to Thompson Webb of the University of Wisconsin

Press; and to my wife and son, Gretchen and David Pfankuchen, both fellow political scientists.

To end, I must say that this enterprise, subject as it has been to delay and error, has been warmly rewarding, in opening the way to renewed communication with many friends and former students.

Madison, December 1975

L.P.

Contents

Browse the index by scrolling or use your browser's search function to find a specific name, then click on the year to access all the biographies under the appropriate year.

A

Abdul Kadir, Suzaina 1999
Abernathy, Mabra Glenn 1953
Abravanel, Martin 1971
Abubakar, Dauda 1986
Adamany, David Walter 1967
Adams, Melinda Jane 2004
Adler, Madeleine 1969
Adler, Norman M. 1971
Adolfson, Lorentz Henning 1942
Agor, Weston Harris 1969
Ajene, Oga 1984
Alfian, Ibrahim 1969
Akridge, Paul B. 1979
Alger, Keith N. 1985
Alswied, Mohammed Y.M. 1988
Altemus, Vaughn 1986
Anderson, Brent Steven 2002
Anderson, Charles William 1960
Anderson, Roger Charles 1971
Anderson, Thornton Hogan 1948
Angerthal, Steven 1999
Aoki, Andrew L. 1994
Arias, Enrique D., 2001
Arneson, Ben Albert 1916
Arnold, Phil Warren 1974
Ayres, Jeffrey McKelvey 1994

B

Backstrom, Charles H. 1956
Bader, John Burkhardt. 1994
Bailey, John J. 1972
Baines, John Matthew 1968
Bajusz, William 1981
Baker, Andrew Benjamin 2001
Barber, Hollis W. 1935
Barkdull, John, L. 1993
Barletta, Michael 2000
Barnett, James Duff 1905
Barrett, Patrick Stephen 1997
Barth, Thomas Emil 1968
Basom, Kenneth 1989
Bauer, Gretchen Mary 1994
Baum, Lawrence Allen 1973
Beck, Linda J. 1996
Beckett, Paul Anthony 1970
Beckman, Peter Roane 1974
Benitez-Nazario, Jorge Alberto 1989
Bennett, Gordon Anderson 1973
Bennion, Elizabeth Anne, 2001
Berkson, Larry Charles 1973
Bianga, Waruzi 1982
Bibby, John F. 1963
Bickers, Kenneth N. 1988
Billingsley, Keith Ray 1972
Blaisdell, Doris Schostal 1953
Boles, Donald Edward 1956
Bollens, John Constantinus 1948
Bossert, Thomas John 1976
Bosworth, Matthew H. 1997
Bower, Lisa Cornell 1991
Bowersox, Joe William 1995
Bowler, Marion Kenneth 1973
Boyer, William Walter 1953
Braithwaite, Karl Royden 1967
Broh, Charles Anthony 1972
Bromall, Irvin 1967
Brown, Don Wallace 1971
Brown, Maynard Wilson 1936
Brown, Sonya Kay 2001
Browning, Robert X. 1981
Bruce, Harold Rozelle 1920
Bruer, Patrick J. 1987
Brumbaugh, Chalmers S., III 1985
Brutus, Calvin Dennis 1996
Bumiller, Kristin 1984
Burant, Stephen Robert 1983
Burger, Angela Sutherland 1966
Burger, Josef 1965
Burke, Christopher Matthew 1996
Bush, Chilton Rowlette 1935

C

Calderwood, Howard Black 1929
Calkins, Howard Andrew 1952
Callan, James J. 1979
Canon, Bradley C. 1967
Carley, Laurie David 1959
Carroll, Daniel Bernard 1930
Carter, Byrum Earl 1951
Cason, Jeffery W. 1993
Cassell, Mark 1998
Chaffey, Douglas Camp 1967
Chaney, Elsa Mae 1971
Chang, Chi Hsien 1933
Chinn, Jeffrey Bernard 1975
Christensen, Scott 1993
Chu, Francis Yu 1936
Cimbala, Joseph Stephen 1969
Cirn, John Thomas 1978
Claibourn, Michele Paige 2002
Clancy, Michael James 1996
Clark, Mary Allison 1993
Cline, Barry Grayson 1980
Cocks, Peter Greenfield 1976
Cohen, Dennis Julius 1975
Cohen, Edward S. 1990
Cohen, Marc 1982
Cohen, Stephen P. 1967
Coleman, Craig 2000
Coleman, Mary DeLorse 1990
Conant, James K. 1983
Cook, Timothy 1982
Corradini, Alessandro Luigi 1955
Cortner, Richard Carroll 1961
Cox, Ronald W. 1991
Crane, George T. 1986
Crane, Wilder Willard 1959
Cranmer, William H.H. 1982
Curtis, Roy Emerson 1912

D

Dahm, Charles William 1978
Daland, Robert Theodore 1953

Daniels, Debra Bendel 2003
Daniels, Stephen 1978
Davidson, John Richard 1976
Davis, John Roland 1986
Dean, Gillian H. 1974
De Soto, William 1990
Den Dulk, Kevin Ronald 2001
Debardeleben, Joan T. 1979
Drogus, Carol A. 1991
Drucker, Julie S. 1987
Druker, Marvin J. 1974
Dubach, Ulysses Grant 1912
Dubois, Philip Leon 1978
Duerst-Lahti, Georgia 1987
Dunn, Delmer Delano 1967

E

Easterday,John T. 1991
Ebenstein, William 1938
Edoh, Anthony (Tony) A. 1979
Edwards, George C. 1973
Eisner, Marc 1989
Elling, Richard Clement 1976
Engelhardt, Michael 1984
Engert, George E. 1936
Engler, Robert 1947
Epp, Charles R. 1995
Espino, Rodolfo III 2004
Estes, William Edwin 1976
Evans, Alfred Burney, Jr. 1972
Evanson, Robert K. 1979
Ewing, Cortez Arthur Milton 1927
Exoo, Calvin 1979

F

Farber, William Ogden 1935
Farmer, Kenneth Calvin 1977
Fernbach, Alfred Philip 1941
Fieno, John Vincent 2004
Finifter, Ada Weintraub 1967
Fischer, Lisa 2000
Fiscus, Ronald Jerry 1982
Fitzgibbon, Russell Humke 1933
Flannery, James Joseph 1956
Flannery, Richard F., Jr. 1974
Flemming, Gregory Newbert 1999
Fletcher, Brian 2000
Forrest, Joshua B. 1987
Fosdick, Anna Watson 1997
Frederick, Kathryn Dorothy (Clarenbach) 1946
Freeman, Gary Pete 1975
Frees, Deirdre Sullivan 1989
Fremstad, John Leroy 1970
Fuller, Richard Allen 1953

G

Gayton, Jeffrey Thomas 2003
Ger, Yeong-Kuang 1985
German, Lawrence Paul 1980
Gerstmann, Evan 1996
Geske, Mary 1991
Geyer, Robert Ralph 1995
Giamo, Susan Marie 1994
Gilberg, Trond 1969
Gill, Jung-Il 1996
Glaudell, Kenneth Ray 1996
Goetcheus, Vernon M. 1967
Goldberg-Hiller, Jonathan C. 1991
Gorham, Eric 1990
Gosling, James John 1980
Grasso, Patrick G. 1977
Graney, Katherine Ellen 1999
Graubart, Jonathan M. 2002
Gray, Richard Butler 1957
Green, David Michael 1999
Greenberg, Edward S. 1969
Greenberg, Milton 1955
Greene, Lee Seifert 1934
Groves, Roderick Trimble 1965
Grovogui, Siba N'Zatioula 1988
Guasti, Laura Maria 1977
Gudger, William Michael 1975
Gugin, David Arthur 1967
Gundersen, Adolf Gutzke 1991
Gunderson, Gregory G. 1997

H

Habbe, Donald Edwin 1957
Hafner-Burton, Emile M. 2003
Ham, Euiyoung 1964
Hamburg, Roger Phillip 1965
Hamilton, Anne Wing 1999
Hammergren, Linn Ann 1974
Handelman, Howard 1971
Harbeson, John Willis 1970
Harman, John David 1978
Harmon, Mont Judd 1953
Harrington, Christine 1982
Harris, Charles Wesley 1959
Harris, Craig Marshall 1975
Harris, Martha Ann (Caldwell) 1981
Harris, Scott Allen 1980
Hart, Henry Cowles 1950
Hart-Bohne, Brenda 1979
Hartigan, Emily Albrink Fowler 1975
Hartwig, Richard E. 1980
Hawk, Beverly Gale 1988
Hawkins, Darren Greg 1996
Heeren, Harry Ewald 1914
Hennessy, Bernard Charles 1955
Heppe, Paul Harry 1956
Herring, Ronald Jackson 1976
Herrnson, Paul S. 1986
Hershberg, Eric M. 1989
Hershey, Marjorie Randon 1972
Hertzke, Allen 1986
Hibbs, Douglas Albert, Jr. 1971
Hill, Alwyn Spencer 1960
Hill, Norman Llewellyn 1924
Hitchner, Dell Gillette 1940
Hoffmann, Susan M. 1998
Hone, Thomas Clyde 1973
Honeck, Jon P. 1998
Hoover, Kenneth Ray 1970
Hornbeck, Stanley Kuhl 1911
Houn, Franklin W. 1953
Howards, Irving 1955

Hsiang, Lirren J. 1932
Hsu, Tun Chang 1931
Huddleston, Mark Wayne 1978
Huo, Shitao 1995

I

Inglot, Tomasz 1994

J

Jackman, Robert William 1972
Jackson, Donald Wilson 1972
Jackson, James Ernest 1934
Jacobitti, Suzanne Duvall 1967
Jacobson, Norman 1951
Jandali, Abdulfattah 1956
Janes, Henry Lorenzo 1906
Jenkins, Laura Dudley 1998
Jenkins, William Oscar 1975
Jernberg, James Everett 1966
Joachim, Jutta Maria 1999
Johnson, Eldon Lee 1939
Johnson, Kay Ann 1976
Johnson, Victor Charles 1975
Jones, C. Herschel 1949
Jones, Charles Oscar 1960
Jones, Walter 1980
Joseph, Lawrence Bruce 1975
Jourde, Cedric 2002
Jozwiak, Joseph 2000
Julian, William Burt 1975

K

Kagey, Michael Ralph 1972
Kaiser, Diane S. 1984
Kandeh, Jimmy David Arthur 1987
Kanervo, David Wayne 1976
Kann, Mark Eliot 1975
Kapil, Rawi L. 1961
Keddell, Joseph 1990
Keech, William Robertson 1966
Keehn, Norman Henry 1971
Keller, Edmond J. 1974
Kelso, William Alton 1974
Kelly, Kristin, 1998
Kendrigan, Mary Lou 1980
Kent, Alan Edward 1957
Keynes, Edward 1967
Khadiagala, Lynn Steckelberg 1999
Kim, Haknoh 1997
Kim, Jin Yeon 1993
King, Daniel E. 1996
King, Gary M. 1984
Kingdon, John Wells 1965
Kirk, Grayson Louis 1931
Kirkvliet, Benedict John 1972
Kirn, Michael Emmet 1972
Kishima, Takako 1987
Knoche (Fulenwider), Claire F. 1978
Kommers, Donald P. 1963
Koppel, Thomas Paul 1972
Koulish, Robert E. 1996
Krimel, Donald William 1955
Krishnan, Jayanth Kumar 2001
Kroeger, Brian J. 1998
Kurvers Spalding, Andrew R. 2000
Kruschke, Earl Roger 1963
Kundanis, George 1982

L

Laba, Roman 1989
Lambert J. Barlett 1998
Lane, Robert Wheeler 1992
Lee, Geun 1996
Lee, Kang Ro 1990
Lee, Nae-Young 1993
Lee, Tosh (To-Shun) 1970
Leeds, Patricia Lee (Giles) 1977
Leichter, Howard Martin 1973
Levin, Daniel 1993
Levy, Jack Steven 1976
Lewis, Jeffrey M. 1998
Lewis, John Donald 1934
Li, Ti Tsun 1929
Liebowitz, Jeremy Brookner 2001
Linford, Orma 1964
Ling, Chun Chi 1935
Linnevold, Bernard Olaf Johan 1949
Lipson, Daniel Nathan 2002
Lipson, Michael Leslie 1999
Littig, David M. 1974
Lockard, Kathleen Goodman 1974
Longman, Timothy 1995
Loomis, Burdett Anderson 1974
Lorch, Robert Stuart 1957
Louscher, David John 1972
Lott, Leo Benjamin 1954
Lovell, John Philip 1962
Lowrie, Selden Gale 1912
Lufler, Henry 1982

M

Machung, Anne Carol 1983
Magill, John Houston, Jr. 1972
Magnusson, Bruce A. 1997
Malekafzali, Farhad 1994
Malley, Michael Sean 1999
Manna, Paul Francis 2003
Manning, Stephen 1990
Manwaring, David Roger 1959
Margolis, Joel Paul 1973
Margulies, Sylvia Ruth (Sipress) 1964
Marquez, Benjamin 1983
Martin, John Wesley 1998
Martin, Paul Sterling 2000
Mason, John Brown 1929
Masters, Nicholas Arthur 1955
Maternoski, Peter J. 1995
Mathieu, Gilbert 1970
Mattusch, Kurt Robert 1928
Maughan, Ralph B., Jr. 1971
May, Catherine Rose 1997
Mayer, Peter B. 1971
McCaffery, Jerry Lee 1972
McCormick, Barrett L. 1985

McCoy, Terry Luther 1968
McCurdy, Karen 1989
McDougal, Stephen 1989
McKeown, Alex Raymond 1990
McLauchlan, William Philip 1968
McLennan, Barbara Nancy 1965
McMurray, Howard Johnstone 1940
McMurtry, Virginia Anne 1974
Means, Ernest Elmer 1958
Melnick, Daniel 1970
Mendelson, Wallace 1940
Merwin, Frederic Eaton 1937
Meyer, John Mark 1997
Miller, Mark James 1978
Miller, Mary Lenn (Dixon) 1976
Milner, Neal A. 1968
Mingst, Karen Ann 1974
Mion, Mario Romano 1975
Mitchell, Stephen Robert 1961
Mock, Richard Pearson 1970
Mooney, Christopher 1990
Morris, Donald R. 1971
Morrison, John Stephen 1987
Morrison, Minion K.C. 1977
Moser, Robert G. 1995
Moses, Joel Charles 1972
Mosher, James Stephen 2001
Mosser, Michael William 2002
Mott, Rodney L. 1922
Mou, Daniel 1986
Mulligan-Hansel, Kathleen M. 1999
Murdock, Clark Anson 1971
Murphy, Andrew Rober 1996
Murphy, Patrick J. 1996
Mucciaroni, Gary A. 1987

N

Nafziger, Ralph Otto 1936
Nanes, Stefanie E. 2003
Navarro, Sharon Ann 2001
Nelsen, Brent F. 1989
Nelson, Lisa Sue 1999
Nelson, Samuel Peter 1997
Newbury, Mary Catherine (Atterbury) 1975
Nigro, Felix Anthony 1948
Niland, Collette Marie 1997
Nilson, Douglas Carlyle Jr. 1976
Nixon, David Lee 1989
Novotny, Kristin M. 1994
Novotny, Patrick John 1995
Nuquist, Andrew Edgerton 1940
Nzongola-Ntalaja, Georges 1975

O

Obler, Jeffrey Lowell 1970
O'Brien, Peter G. 1988
Oculi, Okello 1977
Odegard, Holtan Peter 1959
Odell, John Stephen 1976
O'Donnell, Maurice Emmett 1954
Oleszczuk, Thomas 1977
Oliver, James H. 1967
Olsen, Erik J. 1991
Olson, David John 1971
Olson, Laura Ruth 1996
Omarova, Saule Tarikhovna 1999
Oppenheimer, Bruce I. 1973
Orenstein, Jeffrey Robert 1971
Orvis, Stephen 1989
Ost, David 1986
Owen, Diana 1986

P

Paddock, Frank 1924
Palmer, Monte 1963
Parker, David C.W. 2004
Parks, Ellen Sorge 1947
Parks, William Robert 1948
Parrish, Rick 2004
Patterson, Samuel Charles 1959
Passavant, Paul Andrew 1997
Penikis, Janis John 1974
Peroff, Kathleen A Schmidt 1977
Peroff, Nicholas Carl 1977
Pettit, Lawrence Kay 1965
Pfiffner, James Price 1975
Picard, Louis Alexander 1977
Pickerill, J. Mitchell 2000
Pienkos, Donald Edward 1971
Pika, Joseph A. III 1979
Pinto, Rene Wentworth 1927
Plano, Jack Charles 1954
Pletcher, James 1982
Plummer, Leonard Neil 1940
Portz, John 1988
Powell, John Duncan 1966
Price, Kevin S. 2002
Purcell, Ralph Elliott 1949

Q

Qubain, Fahim I. 1957
Quigley, Harold Scott 1916
Quimby, Peter Howard 1999

R

Rabe, Kenneth N. 2002
Rae, Douglas Whiting 1966
Ragsdale, Lyn 1982
Randall, Richard Stuart 1966
Randall, Ronald R., Jr. 1971
Rapp, John Ardean 1987
Rasmussen, Jorgen Scott 1962
Ray, John Wallace 1974
Raymond, Paul B. 1986
Reading, Reid Roscoe 1971
Reath, Richard Frost Whipple 1944
Reed, Joseph 1985
Reinsch, Paul S. 1898
Reno, William Sampson Klock 1992
Rhodes, Matthew Aaron 1997
Rhynart, Frederick William 1975
Rice, Pamela Hopkinson (Rendeiro) 1952

Richards, Mark James 1999
Ridout, Travis Nelson 2003
Riegel, Robert Edgar 1922
Rigdon, Mark E. 1995
Ringquist, Evan 1990
Robbin, Alice A. 1984
Roberts, Elliott Phirman 1953
Robinson, Robert Reif 2004
Roehrig, Terence Jerome 1995
Roetter, Friedrich 1947
Roherty, James Michael 1957
Rom, Mark Carl 1992
Roman, Peter J. 1989
Rosenthal, Alisa Joy 2001
Rueckert, George Leonard 1962
Rueter, Theodore A. 1993

S

Samoff, Joel 1972
Samudivanija, Chai Anan 1971
Sarat, Austin Dean 1973
Saunders, Allan Frederic 1928
Sbragia, Alberta Mary 1974
Schatz, Edward Aaron 2000
Schatzberg, Michael Gordon 1977
Scheffer, Walter Francis 1955
Scherpereel, John A. 2003
Schier, Steven Edward 1978
Schmeling, Thomas Arthur 1999
Schneider, Carl Jacob 1944
Schneider, Gregory 1983
Schten, Edward Victor 1959
Schumacher, Waldo 1923
Schumaker, Paul David 1973
Schwartz, Donald Victor 1969
Schwarz, Harry Guenter 1963
Schwartz, Katrina Zenta Sarah 2001
Scott, Robert Edwin 1949
Secher, Herbert Pierre 1954
Seitz, John Lewis 1976
Sell, Kathleen R. 1995
Sessions, Andrew 1998
Shannon, Jasper Berry 1934
Sharkansky, Ira 1964
Shelledy, Robert B. 2003
Shelley, Mack Clayton II 1977
Shelvankar, Krishnarao Shivarao 1929
Shen, Yun-Kung (Justin Y. Shen) 1948
Sherman, Dennnis Mark 1978
Sherman, Gail Richardson 1978
Sherman, Neal Philip 1975
Shipman, Gordon D. 1932
Shively, Ruth Lessl 1993
Shockley, John S. 1972
Shore, Sean 1998
Siemers, David J. 1997
Silver, Brian David 1972
Siminoski, Dan 1978
Sirisumpundh, Kasem 1961
Skidmore-Hess, Daniel 1993
Smith, Charles William 1934
Smith, Daniel A. 1994
Smith, Lincoln 1945
Smuckler, Ralph H. 1952
Sorauf, Frank 1953
Soss, Joe Brian 1996
Souza, Isabel R.O. Gomez 1985
Sparling, Samuel Edwin 1896
Spencer, Charles Franklin 1938
Sprout, Harold Hance 1929
Stafford, David Geoffrey 1998
Stanga, John Ellis, Jr. 1971
Staudt, Kathleen Ann 1976
Stavrakis, Peter 1986
Stearns, Willliam P. 1991
Steinberg, Jules 1977
Stephens, Gordon Ross 1961
Stern, Robert William 1962
Stoner, Floyd Eugene 1976
Stover, Robert Vernon 1972
Strach, Patricia Lynn 2004
Streich, Gregory W. 1997
Stuart, Graham Henry 1920
Suleiman, Michael Wadie 1965
Sullivan, Michael Joseph 1995
Sunthraraks, Pisanu 1986
Swanson, John Robert 1969
Swenson, Rinehart John 1918
Sweet, Martin Jay 2003
Sylla, Soriba 1993

T

Thanamai, Patcharee 1985
Tharp, Paul A., Jr. 1969
Thaxton, Ralph A., Jr. 1975
Thawnghmung, Ardeth Maung 2001
Theobald, H. Rupert 1972
Thoeny, Robert Alan 1968
Thompson, Henry Walter 1921
Thompson, Kenneth H., Jr. 1967
Thurston, Roy Leroy 1937
Tien, Hung-Mao Harold 1969
Tillema, Richard Gordon 1974
Tilley, Virginia A. 1997
Tillman, Nathaniel Patrick, Jr. 1961
Titus, James Emerson 1957
Trask, Haunani-Kay 1981
Trice, Robert Holmes, Jr. 1974
Trilling, Richard Jay 1970
Tsuratani, Taketugu 1966
Turner, Margaret J. (Sandie) 1985
Turner, Robert Claggett 1999
Turner, Thomas Edwin 1973

V

Vadi, Jose Miguel 1977
Valdes, Luis 1968
Van Meter, Donald Stuart 1972
Vanderheiden, Steven Jon 2001
Vardys, Vytas Stanley 1958
Vinyard, C. Dale 1964
Vose, Clement Ellery 1952

W

Walch (Bramschreiber), Karen S. 1991
Waldron, Ellis Lee 1953
Waligorski, Conrad Peter 1973
Wallace, Benjamin Bruce 1911
Wang, Tsao Shih 1929
Wanke, Marshall Carter 1973
Watanabe, Morio 1992
Weaver, Catherine Elizabeth 2003
Webb, Raymond P. 1990
Weber, Edward P. 1996
Weissberg, Robert 1969
Weller, Ben Franklin 1997
Weng, Byron Song?Jan 1971
Wenger, Egbert Semman 1936
Wenger, Norman Irving 1947
Wenner, Lettie Marie 1972
Whann, Christopher Alan 1995
Whisler, Marilyn Evon 1972
White, Gregory W. 1993
White, Julie Anne 1996
Wichaidit, Tawat 1973
Wiener, Don Edward 1978
Williams, James Michael 2001
Willoughby, William Reid 1943
Wilson, Harper Hubert 1947
Wolfgram, Mark Allen 2001
Woliver, Laura R. 1986
Wong, John On-Fat 1982
Wong, Joseph Yit-Chong 2001
Wood, Katherine D. Kleuter 1929
Woodruff, Emily 1989
Woolley, John T. 1980
Worsham, Jeffrey S. 1991
Wynia, Gary 1970

Y

Yamvu, Makasu A M'Teba 1980
Yavuz, Hakan 1998
Yeh, Hsia Ti 1944
Yoast, Richard Alan 1975
Young, Brigitta 1990
Young, William Henry 1941
Yuan, I. 1993

Z

Zaffiro, James 1984
Zelin, Richard David 1992
Zernicke, Paul 1989
Zierler, Matthew C. 2003
Zillmer, Raymond Theodore 1914
Zorn, Stephen Alan 1975
Zwier, Robert 1977

1896

Sparling, Samuel Edwin (d. 1941)
Dissertation title: *Municipal History and Present Organization of the City of Chicago.*
Affiliations: Political Science, University of Wisconsin–Madison; Alderman, City of Madison
Publications: *Introduction to Business Organization* (1906); *Municipal History and Present Organization of the City of Chicago* (1898).

1898

Reinsch, Paul Samuel (d. 1923)
Dissertation title: *English Common Law in the Early American Colonies.*
Affiliations: Political Science, University of Wisconsin–Madison; Roosevelt Professor, Universities of Berlin and Leipzig; U.S. Minister to China; U.S. Delegate: Third and Fourth Pan-American Conference, First Pan-American Scientific Conference; Counsellor to Chinese Government; President, American Political Science Association
Publications: *Secret Diplomacy* (1922); *An American Diplomat in China, 1913–1919* (1922); *Readings in American State Government* (1922); *Public International Unions* (1911); *Intellectual Currents in the Far East* (1911); *The Young Citizens Reader* (1909); *Readings in American Federal Government* (1909); *American Legislatures and Legislative Methods* (1907); *Colonial Administration* (1905); *Colonial Government* (1902); *World Politics at the End of the Nineteenth Century as Influenced by the Oriental Situation* (1900); *The Common Law in the Early American Colonies* (1899).

1905

Barnett, James Duff (d.1957)
Dissertation title: *State Administration of Taxation in Wisconsin.*
Affiliations: Political Science, University of Oregon–Eugene
Publications: *A More Cooperative Democracy* (1941); *Operation of the Initiative, Referendum and Recall in Oregon* (1915).

1906

Janes, Henry Lorenzo (d. 1951)
Dissertation title: *The Extension of French Laws to the Colonies.*
Affiliations: David G. Janes Co. (real estate, investments); U.S. diplomatic service: Havana, Santiago, Rio de Janeiro, Constantinople; Assistant Chief, Division of Latin American Affairs

1911

Hornbeck, Stanley Kuhl (d.1966)
Dissertation title: *The Most Favored Nation Clause in Commercial Treaties.*
Affiliations: Political Science, University of Wisconsin–Madison; U.S. Department of State: Chief, Division of Far Eastern Affairs; Ambassador to the Netherlands
Publications: *Certain Fundamentals of Policy* (1942); *China Today* (1927); *Contemporary Politics in the Far East* (1916); *The Most-Favored-Nation Clause* (1910).

Wallace, Benjamin Bruce (d. 1947)
Dissertation title: *Origin and Development of Village Government in New York.*
Affiliations: U.S. Tariff Commission: Chief, Division of International Relations; Advisor on Foreign Trade Policies; Advisor, Ministry of Finance, Government of China
Publications: (co-author) *International Control of Raw Materials* (1930).

1912

Curtis, Roy Emerson (d. 1960)
Dissertation title: *The Law of Hostile Expeditions as Applied by the United States.*
Affiliations: Economics, and Dean, School of Business and Public Administration, University of Missouri–Columbia
Publications: *The Trusts and Economic Control: A Book of Materials* (1931); *The Law of Military Expeditions as Applied by the United States* (1914).

Dubach, Ulysses Grant (d. 1972)
Dissertation title: *State Administration of Health.*
Affiliations: Professor and Dean of Men, Oregon State College (now University)–Corvallis, Oregon; Lewis and Clark College–Portland, Oregon; National Scholarship Chairman, Sigma Phi Epsilon

Lowrie, Selden Gale (d. 1961)
Dissertation title: *The Classification of Industries under the Fourteenth Amendment to the Constitution: A Study in Social Legislation.*
Affiliations: Political Science, University of Cincinnati, Ohio; Director, Ohio Legislative Reference Bureau; Director, Cincinnati Municipal Reference Bureau
Publications: *The Budget* (1913).

1914

Heeren, Harry Ewald
Dissertation title: *Judicial Control over Legislation in Australia and Canada.*

Zillmer, Raymond Theodore (d. 1960)
Dissertation title: *Uniform Legislation in the United States.*

1916

Arneson, Ben Albert (d. 1958)
Dissertation title: *Civil Service Reform in State Administration.*
Affiliations: Political Science, Ohio Wesleyan University, Delaware, Ohio
Publications: *The Democratic Monarchies of Scandinavia* (1929, 1939); *Elements of Constitutional Law* (1928).

Quigley, Harold Scott (d. 1968)
Dissertation title: *The Immunity of Private Property from Capture at Sea.*
Affiliations: Political Science, University of Minnesota–Minneapolis
Publications: *Far Eastern War, 1937–1941* (1942); *Japanese Government and Politics* (1932); *From Versailles to Locarno* (1927).

1918

Swenson, Rinehart John (Retired)
Dissertation title: *River and Harbor Improvements by the United States Government.*
Affiliations: Government, Washington Square College, New York University
Publications: *National Government and Business* (1924); *Public Regulation of Wages* (1916).

1920

Bruce, Harold Rozelle (d.)
Dissertation title: *The Political Activities of Organized Labor in the United States and Great Britain.*
Affiliations: Dartmouth College; New York State College for Teachers; Member, New Hampshire Constitutional Convention
Publications: *A College Text in American National Government* (1959); *The American Political Scene* (co-author, 1936, 1938); *American Parties and Politics* (1927, 1932, 1937).

Stuart, Graham Henry
Dissertation title: *French Foreign Policy from Fashoda to Sarajevo.*
Affiliations: Ret. 1952; University of Wisconsin–Madison; Stanford University; Head Economic Analyst, U.S. Board of Economic Warfare; Head, War History Division, U.S. Department of State
Publications: *The Department of State* (1949); *American Diplomatic and Consular Practice* (1936; with James Tigner, 1952); *The International City of Tangier* (1931); *Latin America and the United States* (1922, 1974).

1921

Thompson, Henry Walter (d. 1938)
Dissertation title: *The Expansion of the Federal Government through the Commerce Clause.*
Affiliations: Political Science, Stanford University
Publications: *Federal Centralization: A Study and Criticism of the Expanding Scope of Federal Legislation* (1923).

1922

Mott, Rodney L. (d. 1971)
Dissertation title: *Due Process of Law: A Historical and Analytical Treatment of the Principles and Methods Followed by the Courts in the Application of the Concept of the "Law of the Land."*
Affiliations: Charles Evans Hughes Professor and Director Division of Social Sciences, Colgate University–Hamilton, New York; University of Chicago; University of Minnesota; U.S. Army Acting Chief of Public Affairs, Berlin, Germany, 1946; Governor's Commission on Non-Competitive Civil Service
Publications: *Home Rule for America's Cities* (1948); *Constitutions of the States and of the United States* (editor, 1938); *Due Process of Law* (1926).

Riegel, Robert Edgar
Dissertation title: *Trans-Mississippi Construction in 1900.*
Affiliations: Ret. History, Dartmouth College
Publications: *United States of America* (with Helen Haugh); *American Women: A Story of Social Change* (1970); *The American Story* (with David Long, 1955); *Young America, 1830–1840* (1949); *America Moves West* (with A.G. Athearn, 1930, 1947, 1956); *The Story of the Western Railroads* (1926).

1923

Schumacher, Waldo (d. 1960)
Dissertation title: *The Direct Primary in Wisconsin.*
Affiliations: Political Science, University of Oregon–Eugene

1924

Hill, Norman Llewellyn
Dissertation title: *Recent Developments in the Law of Unneutral Service.*
Affiliations: Ret. 1963. University of Nebraska–Lincoln; Ohio Wesleyan University; Western Reserve University; University of Rochester; University of Washington; Fulbright Professor, University of Swansea–Wales
Publications: *The New Democracy in Foreign Policy Making* (1970); *Mr. Secretary of State* (1963); *International Politics* (1963); *Contemporary World Politics* (1954); *International Organization* (1952); *International Relations: Documents and Readings* (1950); *Claims to Territory in International Law and Relations* (1945); *Background of European Governments* (with H.W. Stoke, 1935); *International Administration* (1931); *The Public International Conference* (1929).

Paddock, Frank (d. 1959)
Dissertation title: *English Theories of the Functions of Government since 1776.*
Affiliations: Political Science, Temple University–Philadelphia

1927

Ewing, Cortez Arthur Milton (d. 1962)
Dissertation title: *British Labor Party Policy 1918–1925.*
Affiliations: Professor of Government and Director, School of Citizenship and Public Affairs, University of Oklahoma–Norman; President, Southwestern Social Science Association
Publications: *American National Government* (1958); *Source Book in Government and Politics* (with R. Dangerfield, 1931); *Primary Elections in the South* (1953); *Congressional Elections* (1947); *Presidential Elections* (1940); *Supreme Court Judges* (1938).

Pinto, Rene Wentworth
Dissertation title: *The Pan American Union.*

1928

Mattusch, Kurt Robert
Dissertation title: *British Policy Relating to the Administration of India, 1905–1924.*
Affiliations: U.S. Foreign Economic Administration; Briarcliff Junior College; U.S. Consulate-General, Berlin

Saunders, Allan Frederic
Dissertation title: *The Judicial System of Scotland.*
Affiliations: Ret. 1966. Professor of Government and Dean, College of Arts and Sciences, University of Hawaii–Honolulu; Amherst College; Scripps and Claremont Colleges; University of Minnesota; University of Wisconsin; University of Pennsylvania
Publications: *Building America* (1923).

1929

Calderwood, Howard Black
Dissertation title: *International Protection of Minorities in National States.*
Affiliations: U.S. Department of State; University of Michigan–Ann Arbor

Li, Ti Tsun
Dissertation title: *The Political and Economic Theories of Sun Yat Sen.*
Affiliations: Chinese Minister to Iran

Mason, John Brown
Dissertation title: *The Legal Status of the Free City of Danzig.*
Affiliations: Ret. 1974. Political Science, California State University at Fullerton; Georgetown University; Naval War College; University of Florida; Oberlin; U.S. Foreign Economic Administration; Department of State; High Commissioner to Germany; Hoover Food Commission; Hoover War Library
Publications: *Research Resources: International Relations and Recent History* (1968); *The Danzig Dilemma: A Study in Peacemaking and Compromise* (1946); *Hitler's First Foes, A Study in Religion and Politics* (1936).

Shelvankar, Krishnarao Shivarao
Dissertation title: *The Idea of Equality: An Historical and Analytical Study.*
Affiliations: Ambassador of India to the Soviet Union

Sprout, Harold Hance
Dissertation title: *The Status of Customary International Public Law in the Federal Courts of the United States.*
Affiliations: Geography and International Relations, Princeton University; Stanford
Publications: *Ecology and Politics in America* (co-author, 1971); *Towards a Polity of the Planet Earth* (1971); *Ecological Paradigm for the Study of International Politics* (co-author, 1968); *Foundations of National Power* (edited with M. Sprout, 1945 and later editions).

Wang, Tsao Shih
Dissertation title: *Disarmament in the Foreign Policy Programs of the Great Powers since 1919.*

Wood, Katherine D. Kleuter
Dissertation title: *International Regulation of Migration.*
Affiliations: Ret. 1971. Professor and Director, Department of Social Work and Social Research, Bryn Mawr College–Pennsylvania; National War Labor Board; Social Security Board; Federal Emergency Relief Administration.
Publications: *A Study of Negro Adoption Families: A Comparison of a Traditional and an Innovative Program* (1971); *Post-Placement Functioning of Adopted Children* (1969); *Urban Workers on Relief* (1936).

1930

Carroll, Daniel Bernard (d. 1959)
Dissertation title: *The Unicameral Legislative of Vermont*
Affiliations: Political Science, University of Vermont–Burlington
Publications: *The Unicameral Legislature of Vermont* (1933).

1931

Hsu, Tun Chang
Dissertation title: *The Council of the League of Nations.*

Kirk, Grayson Louis (d. 1997)
Dissertation title: *French Administrative Policy in Alsace Lorraine, 1918–1929.*
Affiliations: Professor, Provost, Vice-President, President, Columbia University; University of Wisconsin–Madison; Third Commission Executive Officer, U.N. San Francisco Conference, 1945; U.S. Delegation staff, Dumbarton Oaks Conference 1944; Head Security Section Division of Political Studies, U.S. Department of State; President, Council on Foreign Relations
Publications: *The Study of International Relations in American Colleges and Universities* (1947); *Contemporary International Politics* (with W. Sharp, 1940); *Domestic Factors Influencing U.S. Foreign Policy* (1936); *Philippine Independence* (1936).

1932

Hsiang, Lirren J.
Dissertation title: *The Policy of the British Labour Party Toward the League of Nations.*
Affiliations: Political Science, Central Military Academy–Nanking, China

Shipman, Gordon D.
Dissertation title: *The Inequality of States in International Organization.*
Affiliations: Ret. 1971. Sociology, University of Wisconsin–Stevens Point; Sociology and Anthropology, Wisconsin State College (now University of Wisconsin)–Milwaukee; Shurtleff College–Alton, Illinois

1933

Chang, Chi Hsien
Dissertation title: *International Political Effects of World Colonization and Migration in the 20th Century.*

Fitzgibbon, Russell Humke
Dissertation title: *Cuba and the U.S., 1900–1935.*
Affiliations: University of California–Santa Barbara; University of California–Los Angeles; President, Western Political Science Association; OAS Observer Group member, Dominican Presidential Elections 1962
Publications: *Uruguay: Portrait of a Democracy* (1954); *The Constitutions of the Americas* (editor, 1948); *Cuba and the United States, 1900–1935* (1935).

1934

Greene, Lee Seifert
Dissertation title: *Direct Legislation in Germany, Austria, and Danzig.*
Affiliations: University of Tennessee–Knoxville; Director, Bureau of Public Administration; Chairman, Research Committee, Tennessee Constitutional Convention; President, Southern Political Science Association
Publications: *American Government: Theory, Structure and Process* (co-author, 1969); *American Government: Policies and Functions* (co-author, 1967); *Government in Tennessee* (co-author, 1962); *Metropolitan Harris County* (co-author, 1957); *A Future for Nashville* (co-author, 1952); *Rescued Earth, the Public Administration of Natural Resources in Tennessee* (co-author, 1948).

Jackson, James Ernest
Dissertation title: *Wisconsin's Attitude Toward American Foreign Policy since 1910.*

Lewis, John Donald
Dissertation title: *The Genossenschaft-Theory of Otto von Gierke: A Study in Political Thought.*
Affiliations: Ret. 1972. Oberlin College–Ohio; Oxford University; Case Western Reserve University; Pennsylvania State University; President, Midwest Political Science Association
Publications: *Anti-Federalists v. Federalists* (1967); *Against the Tyrant: Tradition and Theory of Tyrannicide* (co-author, 1957); *The Genossenschaft-Theory of Otto von Gierke* (1935).

Shannon, Jasper Berry
Dissertation title: *Henry Clay as Political Leader.*
Affiliations: Ret. 1971. Western Kentucky University–Bowling Green; University of Nebraska–Lincoln; University of Kentucky–Lexington; University of Wisconsin–Madison; Johns Hopkins University; U.S. Department of Agriculture Graduate School; President, Southern Political Science Association; President, Midwest Conference of Political Scientists
Publications: *Money and Politics* (1960); *Presidential Politics in Kentucky* (1950); *The Study of Comparative Government: Essays in Honor of Frederic Austin Ogg* (editor, 1949).

Smith, Charles William
Dissertation title: *Roger B. Taney: a Study in Political Theory and Public Law.*
Affiliations: U.S. Department of State
Publications: *The Electorate in an Alabama Community* (1942); *Public Opinion in a Democracy* (1939); *Roger B. Taney, Jacksonian Jurist* (1936).

1935

Barber, Hollis W.
Dissertation title: *Development of Some of the Administrative Departments of the Government of Wisconsin from 1850 to 1930.*
Affiliations: University of Illinois at Chicago Circle; Tulane University; University of Cincinnati; University of Alabama
Publications: *United States in World Affairs* (1955, 1957); *Foreign Policies of the U.S.* (1953).

Bush, Chilton Rowlette (d. 1972)
Dissertation title: *State Centralization: General Property Tax Rate Limitation and Its Relation to Municipal Finance.*
Affiliations: Journalism, Stanford University
Publications: *Free Press and Fair Trial* (editor, 1970); *Newswriting and Reporting Public Affairs* (1965); *The Art of News Communication* (1954); *Editorial Thinking and Writing* (1932); *Newspaper Reporting and Public Affairs* (1929, 1940, 1951).

Farber, William Ogden
Dissertation title: *Judicial Self-Limitation: A Study of Those Limitations Imposed by the United States Supreme Court on Its Exercise of the Power of Judicial Review.*
Affiliations: Professor of Government and Director of Government Research Bureau, University of South Dakota–Vermillion; U.S. Office of Price Administration; Director, South Dakota Legislative Research Council; Chairman, Vermillion City Planning Commission; Member, South Dakota Local Government Study Commission; Member, South Dakota Constitutional Revision Commission; President, Midwest Political Science Association
Publications: *Constitutional Comment* (1969); *The Government of South Dakota* (1962, 1968); *Speakers' Resource Book* (1961); *City Manager Government in South Dakota* (co-author, 1958); *Indians, Law Enforcement and Local Government* (co-author, 1957).

Ling, Chun Chi
Dissertation title: *The British Parliament and Treaty-Making.*

1936

Brown, Maynard Wilson (Deceased 1937)
Dissertation title: *American Public Opinion and European Armaments, 1912–1914.*
Affiliations: Professor and Dean of Journalism, Marquette University–Milwaukee

Chu, Francis Yu
Dissertation title: *The American Department of State and the Foreign Service.*
Affiliations: Political Science, National University of Yunnan–China

Engert, George E.
Dissertation title: *The Socialism of the British Labor Party as Tested by Office: A Record of the Party's Legislative Achievements in the Light of Its Earlier Socialist Promises.*

Nafziger, Ralph Otto (Deceased 1973)
Dissertation title: *The American Press and Public Opinion during the World War, 1914–April 1917.*
Affiliations: Professor and Director, School of Journalism, University of Wisconsin–Madison; University of Minnesota; Chief, Media Division, U.S. Office of War Information; President, American Association of Teachers of Journalism
Publications: *Introduction to Mass Communications Research* (editor, with D.M. White, 1958, 1963); *An Introduction to Journalism Research* (editor, with M.W. Wilkerson, 1949); *International News and the Press* (1940).

Wengert, Egbert Semman (d. 1964)
Dissertation title: *The Public Relations of Selected Federal Administrative Agencies.*
Affiliations: Political Science, University of Oregon–Eugene; University of Wyoming; Sweetbriar College; Wayne University–Detroit; University of Wisconsin–Madison; Michigan Tax Study Commission; U.S. Office of Price Administration; Foreign Economic Administration; Atomic Energy Commission; National Security Resources Board; Oregon Constitutional Revision Commission
Publications: *Financial History of Detroit during the Depression* (1941).

1937

Merwin, Frederic Eaton (d.)
Dissertation title: *Public Relations in Selected Wisconsin Administrative Departments.*
Affiliations: Journalism, Rutgers University
Publications: *The Newspaper and Society* (editor, with C.L. Bird, 1942).

Thurston, Roy Leroy
Dissertation title: *The Nile River: a Regional Study in International Relations.*
Affiliations: Director of Program Development and Dean, Chapman College; Foreign Service Officer, U.S. Department of State; National War College; Deputy U.S. Permanent Representative (Minister) to NATO; Ambassador to Somalia

1938

Ebenstein, William
Dissertation title: *The Law of Public Housing in the United States.*
Affiliations: Political Science, University of California–Santa Barbara; Princeton University; University of Wisconsin–Madison; Director, UNESCO Survey, *Contemporary Political Science*
Publications: *American Government in the Twentieth Century* (co-author); *American Democracy in World Perspective* (co-author); *Church and State in Franco Spain*; *Communism in Theory and Practice*; *Two Ways of Life: The Communist Challenge to Democracy*; *Man and the State: Modern Political Ideas*; *Totalitarianism: New Perspectives*; *Fascist Italy*; *The Law of Public Housing*; *The Nazi State*; *The Pure*

Theory of Law; *The German Record, a Political Portrait*; *Today's Isms: Communism, Fascism, Capitalism, Socialism*; *Political Thought in Perspective*; *Introduction to Political Philosophy*; *Great Political Thinkers, Plato to the Present*; *Modern Political Thought: The Great Issues*.

Spencer, Charles Franklin
Dissertation title: *Improvement of Procedure in State Legislatures*.
Affiliations: Professor of Government and Social Sciences, East Central State College–Ada, Oklahoma; Mayor, City of Ada, Oklahoma; Chairman, City Board of Freeholders, Ada, Oklahoma

1939

Johnson, Eldon Lee
Dissertation title: *Unionism in the Federal Service*
Affiliations: Vice President, University of Illiniois, Urbana, 1966–; President, University of New Hampshire, 1955–62; Director, US Department of Agriculture; Graduate School, University of Oregon, Professor and Chair; Dean, Graduate School.
Publications: *The Study of Comparative Government* (1949).

1940

Hitchner, Dell Gillette
Dissertation title: *Civil Liberties in England from 1914 to 1940*.
Affiliations: Professor of Political Science and Acting Executive Officer, University of Washington–Seattle; Wichita State University; Coe College–Cedar Rapids, Iowa
Publications: *Modern Government* (1972).

McMurray, Howard Johnstone (d. 1961)
Dissertation title: *Some Influences of the University of Wisconsin on the State Government of Wisconsin*.
Affiliations: Government, University of New Mexico–Albuquerque; University of Wisconsin– Madison; Member, U.S. House of Representatives, 5th Wisconsin District; Democratic Nominee for U.S. Senate; President, Western Political Science Association

Mendelson, Wallace
Dissertation title: *The Public Services Commission of Wisconsin: a Study in Administrative Procedure*.
Affiliations: Government, University of Texas–Austin; University of Tennessee–Knoxville; University of Illinois–Urbana; University of Missouri
Publications: *Supreme Court Statecraft: The Rule of Law and Men* (1985); *The American Constitution and the Judicial Process* (1980); *The Supreme Court: Law and Discretion* (1967); *Felix Frankfurter* (editor, 1964); *Discrimination* (1962); *Justices Black and Frankfurter: Conflict in the Court* (1961); *Capitalism, Democracy and the Supreme Court* (1959); *The Constitution and the Supreme Court* (1959).

Nuquist, Andrew Edgerton
Dissertation title: *Chinese Legal Codes as Causation and Effect in Chinese Political Thought*.

Affiliations: Ret. 1971. Political Science, University of Vermont–Burlington; Director, Government Clearing House, University of Vermont; Democratic Candidate for Congress; Governor's Advisory Council; President, New England Political Science Association
Publications: *Town Government in Vermont* (1964).

Plummer, Leonard Neil
Dissertation title: *The Political Leadership of Henry Watterson.*
Affiliations: Ret. 1971. Journalism, University of Kentucky–Lexington

1941

Fernbach, Alfred Philip
Dissertation title: *Federal-State Relations in Unemployment Compensation Administration: Illinois and Wisconsin.*
Affiliations: Government and International Relations, University of Virginia–Charlottesville; Fulbright Scholar, Norway and India; President, Southern Division, International Studies Association
Publications: *Soviet Coexistence Strategy: A Case Study in the International Labor Organization* (1966); *Introduction to International Relations* (1957).

Young, William Henry
Dissertation title: *The Present State of Research in Wisconsin Local Government.*
Affiliations: Ret. Political Science, University of Wisconsin–Madison; Budgetary Assistant to President of the University of Wisconsin; Executive Secretary, Research Director, State of Wisconsin Governor's Office
Publications: *The Development of the Budget System of the State of and the University of Wisconsin* (1986); *An Opportunity for Major American Advance Through Higher Education* (co-author, 1967); *Essentials of American Government* (1959, 1961, 1963, 1969); *Introduction to American Government* (1958, 1962, 1966).

1942

Adolfson, Lorentz Henning
Dissertation title: *The County Clerk in Wisconsin.*
Affiliations: Ret. 1972. Chancellor, University of Wisconsin Center System; Professor and Dean, University of Wisconsin Extension; Wisconsin Governor's Commission on Human Rights

1943

Willoughby, William Reid
Dissertation title: *The Impact of the United States upon Canada's Foreign Policy.*
Affiliations: Political Science, University of New Brunswick–Fredericton; St. Lawrence University–Canton, New York; Research Assistant, U.S. Department of State
Publications: *The Joint Organizations of Canada and the United States* (1979); *The St. Lawrence Waterway: A Study in Politics and Diplomacy* (1961); *Canadian Politics* (1951).

1944

Reath, Richard Frost Whipple
Dissertation title: *The Development of International Activity in the Field of Public Health.*
Affiliations: Political Science, Occidental College–Los Angeles; University of Idaho–Moscow

Schneider, Carl Jacob
Dissertation title: *The Political Liberalism of the Progressive Parties in Germany, 1871 to 1914.*
Affiliations: Ret. Political Science, Kirkland College–Clinton, N.Y.; University of Nebraska–Lincoln; University of New Hampshire–Durham; Currently resides in Essex, CT

Yeh, Hsia Ti (Hu)
Dissertation title: *A Study of the Farm Security Administration as Applicable to China's Problems.*
Affiliations: General Secretary, International Student Service; University of Nanking–China

1945

Smith, Lincoln
Dissertation title: *The Evolution of Maine's Public Power Policy.*
Affiliations: Graduate School of Public Administration, New York University; University of California–Los Angeles; University of Pennsylvania; Maine Governor's Commission on Passamaquoddy Bay; Currently resides in Brunswick, ME
Publications: *The Power Policy of Maine* (1951).

1946

Frederick, Kathryn Dorothy (Clarenbach)
Dissertation title: *Recent Anti-Democratic Ideas and Tendencies in American Politics.*
Affiliations: Political Science, University of Wisconsin Extension; Sociology, Olivet College–Olivet, Michigan; Political Science, Purdue University; Chairperson, Wisconsin Governor's Conference on the Status of Women; First President, Interstate Association of Commissions on the Status of Women; Founder and First Chairman of the Board, National Organization for Women; Chairperson, National Organizing Conference, National Political Caucus
Publications: *Wisconsin Women and the Law* (co-editor, 1989); *Educational Needs of Rural Women and Girls: Report of the National Advisory Council on Women's Educational Programs* (1977).

1947

Engler, Robert
Dissertation title: *Some Problems of Military Occupation as Reflected in the Rehabilitation of a German City.*
Affiliations: Political Science, Brooklyn College, City University of New York; Queens College, City University of New York; New School for Social Research; Columbia University; Sarah Lawrence College–Bronxville, N.Y.; University of Wisconsin–Madison; Special Assistant to the President, National Farmers' Union

Publications: *America's Energy: Reports from the Nation on 100 Years of Struggles for the Democratic Control of Our Resources* (editor, 1980); *The Brotherhood of Oil: Energy Policy and the Public Interest* (1977); *The Politics of Oil: A Study of Private Power and Democratic Directions* (1961); *The Farmers' Union in Washington* (co-author, 1948).

Parks, Ellen Sorge
Dissertation title: *Experiment in the Democratic Planning of Public Agricultural Activity.*

Roetter, Friedrich (d. 1953)
Dissertation title: *The Scope of the Jurisdiction of the Permanent Court of International Justice (and of the International Court of Justice) Under Special Treaties.*
Affiliations: Political Science, Upsala College–East Orange, New Jersey; Assistant Public Prosecutor, Berlin, Germany; Attorney, Supreme Court of Prussia

Wengert, Norman Irving
Dissertation title: *TVA and Agriculture: a Study in Regional Administration.*
Affiliations: Political Science, Colorado State University–Fort Collins; Wayne State University–Detroit; University of Maryland–College Park; North Dakota State College; City College of New York; Resides in Stoughton, WI
Publications: *The Political Allocation of Benefits and Burdens: Economic Externalities and Due Process in Environmental Protection* (1976); *The Energy Crisis: Reality or Myth* (co-editor, 1973); *Urban Water Policies and Decision-making in the Detroit Metropolitan Region* (co-author, 1970); *The Economic Impact of TVA* (1967); *The Administration Of Natural Resources: The American Experience* (1961); *Valley of Tomorrow The TVA and Agriculture* (1952).

Wilson, Harper Hubert
Dissertation title: *Congressional Standards and Disciplinary Procedures.*
Affiliations: Princeton University; Politics, University of Massachusetts; Consultant, Connecticut State Reorganization Commission; National Farmers' Union
Publications: *Pressure Group: the Campaign for Commercial Television in England* (1961); *The Problem of Internal Security in England* (with H. Glickman, 1954); *The Roots of Political Behavior* (with R.C. Glickman, 1949); *Congress: Corruption and Compromise.*

1948

Anderson, Thornton Hogan (d. 1998).
Dissertation title: *Brooks Adams, Constructive Conservative.*
Affiliations: Ret. University of Maryland–College Park; University of California; War Production Board; Office of Price Administration
Publications: *Creating the Constitution: The Convention of 1787 and the First Congress* (1993); *Russian Political Thought* (1967); *Masters of Russian Marxism* (editor and author, 1963); *Brooks Adams, Constructive Conservative* (1951).

Bollens, John Constantinus
Dissertation title: *The Problem of Government in the San Francisco Bay Metropolitan Region.*
Affiliations: Political Science, University of California–Los Angeles; Director, Metropolitan Community Studies–Dayton, Ohio; Executive Officer, Metropolitan St. Louis Survey; Research Director, Municipal League of Seattle
Publications: *Political Corruption: Power, Money, and Sex* (co-author, 1979); *A Guide to Participation: Field Work, Role Playing Cases, and Other Forms* (co-author, 1973); *Yorty: Politics of a Constant Candidate* (co-author, 1973); *California Government and Politics* (co-author, 1972); *The Metropolis* (co-author, 1970); *American County Government* (co-author, 1969); *Governing a Metropolitan Region: The San Francisco Bay Area* (co-author, 1968); *Communities and Government in a Changing World* (1966); *The Government of California* (co-author, 1966); *Exploring the Metropolitan Community* (1961); *Special District Governments in the U.S.* (co-author, 1957); *Appointed Executive Local Government* (1952); *The Problem of Government in the San Francisco Bay Region* (1948); *County Government Organization in California* (co-author, 1947).

Nigro, Felix Anthony
Dissertation title: *Senate Confirmation.*
Affiliations: Political Science, University of Georgia–Athens; University of Delaware–Newark; San Diego State University; University of Southern Illinois–Carbondale; Advanced School of Public Administration–Central America; University of Puerto Rico; Institute of Inter-American Affairs; Florida State University–Tallahassee; University of Texas–Austin; Member, City of Newark, Delaware, Board of Ethics
Publications: *The New Public Personnel Administration* (co-author, 1976); *Modern Public Administration* (with L.G. Nigro, 1973); *Management-Employee Relations in the Public Service* (1969); *Modern Public Administration* (1965); *Public Personnel Administration* (1959); *Public Administration Readings and Documents* (1951).

Parks, William Robert
Dissertation title: *The Effort to Synthesize National Programming with Local Administration in Soil Conservation Districts.*
Affiliations: President, Vice President Academic Affairs, Dean of Instruction, Iowa State University –Ames; Agricultural Economics, University of Wisconsin–Madison; U.S. Department of Agriculture; TVA, U.S. Department of Interior
Publications: *Freedom: Study It, Understand It, Maintain It* (co-author, 1955); *Soil Conservation Districts in Action* (1952).

Shen, Yun-Kung
Dissertation title: *American Official Attitudes toward the Government of China, 1898–1947.*

1949

Jones, C. Herschel
Dissertation title: *Public Service Internships in the National Capital.*
Affiliations: Dean, Vice President and Chief Executive Officer, Williamsport Area Community College–Pennsylvania; Bucknell University; Pennsylvania Civil Service Commission; Member, Pennsylvania Governor's Commission on State Employee Legislation and Benefits; Member, President's Committee on Equal Opportunity in Employment

Linnevold, Bernhard Olaf Johan
Dissertation title: *The Wisconsin Cheese Industry and Government.*
Affiliations: University of Connecticut–Storrs; Currently resides in Williamsburg, VA

Purcell, Ralph Elliott
Dissertation title: *Government and Art in the United States.*
Affiliations: George Washington University–Washington, D.C.; University of Delaware–Newark; Naval War College; University of Virginia–Charlottesville; Sweetbriar College–Sweetbriar, Virginia; Emory University–Atlanta; Foreign Service Officer, U.S. Department of State; Director, Overseas Educational Fund
Publications: *Reality and Myth in U.S. Foreign Policy* (1964); *Government and Art* (1956).

Scott, Robert Edwin
Dissertation title: *Some Aspects of Mexican Federalism, 1917–1948.*
Affiliations: Professor of Political Science and Director, Center for International Comparative Studies, University of Illinois–Urbana
Publications: *Latin American Modernization Problems: Case Studies in the Crises of Change* (editor, 1973); *Mexican Government in Transition* (1959, 1963).

1950

Hart, Henry Cowles
Dissertation title: *The Missouri Basin.*
Affiliations: Ret. Professor of Political Science and Indian Studies, University of Wisconsin–Madison; Tennessee Valley Authority
Publications: *Mobilizing Local Resources for Irrigation* (co-author, 1981); *Anarchy, Paternalism, or Collective Responsibility under the Canals* (1978); *Indira Gandhi's India: A Political System Reappraised* (editor, 1976); *The Village and Development Administration* (1967); *Administrative Aspects of River Valley Development* (1961); *Campus India* (1960); *The Dark Missouri* (1957); *New India's Rivers* (1956).

1951

Carter, Byrum Earl
Dissertation title: *The British Prime Minister since 1894.*
Affiliations: Professor, Dean, Chancellor, Vice President, Indiana University–Bloomington
Publications: *The Office of Prime Minister* (1956).

Jacobson, Norman
Dissertation title: *The Concept of Equality in the Assumptions and the Propaganda of Massachusetts Conservatives, 1790–1840.*
Affiliations: Ret. Political Science, University of California–Berkeley; University of Wisconsin–Madison; Mills College; Oregon State University; Consultant, U.S. President's Commission on Intergovernmental Relations

1952

Calkins, Howard Andrew
Dissertation title: *A Survey of Personnel Practices in Selected Texas Administrative Agencies.*
Affiliations: Ret. 1970. Government, University of Texas–Austin
Publications: *Manual of Texas State Government* (1950).

Rice, Pamela Hopkinson (Rendeiro)
Dissertation title: *Racial Discrimination in Education under the United States Constitution.*
Affiliations: Southern Connecticut College–New Haven; Wellesley College; League of Women Voters

Smuckler, Ralph H.
Dissertation title: *Isolationism, 1933–1950: Its Geographic and Socio-Political Centers.*
Affiliations: Ret. Professor of Political Science and Dean of International Studies and Programs, Michigan State University–East Lansing
Publications: *A University Turns to the World: A Personal History of the Michigan State University International Story* (2002); *New Challenges, New Opportunities: U.S. Cooperation for International Growth and Development in the 1990s* (co-author, 1988); *Education and Development Administration* (1966); *Politics in the Press: An Analysis of Press Content in 1952 Senatorial Campaigns* (co-author, 1954); *Politics in the Press* (1953).

Vose, Clement Ellery (d.)
Dissertation title: *Interest Groups before the Supreme Court: the Restrictive Covenant Cases of 1948*
Affiliations: Government, Wesleyan University; Bowdoin College; Western Reserve University–Cleveland, Ohio; Beloit College–Beloit, Wisconsin
Publications: *Constitutional Change* (1972); *Caucasians Only* (1959).

1953

Abernathy, Mabra Glenn
Dissertation title: *The Right of Assembly.*
Affiliations: University of South Carolina; University of Alabama
Publications: *The Carter Years*; *Civil Liberties under the Constitution* (1968); *Organization and Jurisdiction of South Carolina Courts* (1956).

Blaisdell, Doris Schostal
Dissertation title: *The Constitutional Law of Mr. Justice McReynolds.*

Boyer, William Walter
Dissertation title: *Church-State Relations in Wisconsin.*
Affiliations: University of Delaware–Newark; Political Science, Kansas State University–Manhattan; University of Pittsburgh; Grinnell College–Iowa; University of Punjab–India; Assistant to Governor of Wisconsin and Wisconsin Legislative Council
Publications: *The Higher Civil Service in the United States: Quest for Reform* (co-author, 1996); *Rural Development in South Korea: A Socio-political Analysis* (co-author, 1991); *America's Virgin Islands: A History of Human Rights and Wrongs* (1983); *Bureaucracy on Trial: Policy Making by Government Agencies* (1964); *Administrative Rule-Making* (co-author, 1954); *Municipal Zoning: Florida Law and Practice* (co-author, 1950).

Daland, Robert Theodore (d. 1998).
Dissertation title: *Public Health Administration in Alabama.*
Affiliations: University of North Carolina–Chapel Hill; University of Southern California; University of Connecticut; University of Alabama
Publications: *Exploring Brazilian Bureaucracy: Performance and Pathology* (1981); *Bureaucracy in Brazil: Attitudes of Civilian Top Executives Toward Change* (1972); *Latin American Urban Policies and the Social Sciences* (co-author, 1971); *Contemporary Brazil: Issues in Economic and Political Development* (co-author); *Comparative Urban Research* (editor, 1969); *Brazilian Planning* (1967); *A Strategy for Research in Comparative Urban Administration* (1966); *Dixie City: A Portrait of Political Leadership* (1956); *A Brief Survey of Municipal Auditing Practices in Alabama* (1954); *Trends in Wisconsin Legislation* (1947).

Fuller, Richard Allen
Dissertation title: *Case Studies in Bipartisanship in United States Postwar Foreign Policy.*
Affiliations: Foreign Service Officer, U.S. Department of State; Foreign Affairs Officer, Department of the Army

Harmon, Mont Judd
Dissertation title: *Harold L. Ickes: A Case Study in New Deal Thought.*
Affiliations: Professor of Political Science and Dean, College of Humanities, Arts, and Social Sciences, Utah State University–Logan
Publications: *Essays on the Constitution of the United States* (editor, 1978); *The Search for Consensus* (1964); *Political Thought from Plato to the Present* (1964); *The New Deal: A Revolution Consummated* (1956).

Houn, Franklin W.
Dissertation title: *Central Government of China, 1911–1928: An Institutional Study.*
Affiliations: University of Massachusetts–Amherst; University of Nebraska–Lincoln; University of Dubuque–Iowa; Michigan State University–East Lansing; Administrative Secretary, the Presidential Office of China; Press Liaison Secretary, National Assembly of China

Publications: *A Short History of Chinese Communism* (rev., 1972); *Chinese Political Traditions* (1965); *To Change a Nation: Propaganda and Indoctrination in Communist China* (1961); *The Central Government of China, 1912–1928* (1957).

Roberts, Elliott Phirman
Dissertation title: *Relations between the Tennessee Valley Authority and State Governments in Control of the Tennessee River.*

Sorauf, Frank
Dissertation title: *The Voluntary Committee System in Wisconsin: An Effort to Achieve Party Responsibility.*
Affiliations: Ret. Professor of Political Science and Dean, College of Science, Literature and the Arts, University of Minnesota; University of Arizona; Pennsylvania State University; President, Midwest Political Science Association
Publications: *Inside Campaign Finance: Myths and Realities* (1992); *Money in American Elections* (1988); *The Wall of Separation: The Constitutional Politics of Church and State* (1976); *Party Politics in America* (1968); *Perspectives in Political Science* (1966); *Political Science: An Informal Overview* (1964); *Political Parties in the American System* (1964); *Parties and Representation* (1963); *Party and Representation: Legislative Politics in Pennsylvania* (1963); *State Patronage in a Rural County* (1956).

Waldron, Ellis Lee
Dissertation title: *The Public Purpose Doctrine of Taxation.*
Affiliations: Ret. Professor, Director, Bureau of Government Research, Dean of the Graduate School, University of Montana–Missoula; Member, Montana Constitutional Convention Commission; Currently resides in Madison, WI
Publications: *Montana Legislators, 1864–1979: Profiles and Biographical Directory* (1980); *Atlas of Montana Elections, 1889–1976* (co-author, 1978); *Montana Politics since 1864: An Atlas of Elections* (editor, 1958).

1954

Lott, Leo Benjamin
Dissertation title: *Venezuela and Federalism: A Case Study in Frustration.*
Affiliations: Political Science, University of Montana–Missoula; Ohio State University–Columbus
Publications: *Venezuela and Paraguay: Political Modernity and Tradition in Conflict* (1972); *Political Systems of Latin America* (co-author, 1964).

O'Donnell, Maurice Emmett
Dissertation title: *The Growth of Independent Agencies in Foreign Economic Affairs.*
Affiliations: Political Science, University of Southern Florida–Tampa; Professor and Assistant Director, Bureau of Governmental Research, University of Maryland
Publications: *Municipal Revenue Sources in Maryland* (1959).

Plano, Jack Charles (d.)
Dissertation title: *The United Nations and the India-Pakistan Dispute.*
Affiliations: Western Michigan University

Publications: *The American Political Dictionary* (Harcourt Brace, 1997, 2001, 10th ed.); *The United Nations: International Organization and World Politics* (1994); *Pulling the Weeds and Watering the Flowers: Memories of the Professorial Life (1952–1993)* (1993); *Latin America: A Political Dictionary* (co-author, 1992); *Fishhooks, Apples, and Outhouses: Memories of the 1920s, 1930s, and 1940s* (1991); *Life in the Educational Trenches: Memories of College and University Days* (1991); *The Soviet and East European Political Dictionary* (co-author, 1984); *The Public Administration Dictionary* (co-author, 1982); *The Dictionary of Political Analysis* (co-author, 1982); *International Approaches to the Problem of Marine Pollution* (1972); *The International Relations Dictionary* (co-author, 1969); *The United Nations and the India-Pakistan Dispute* (1967); *Forging World Order* (co-author, 1967); *Michigan State Government* (co-author, 1964); *The American Political Dictionary* (co-author, 1962, 1967); *The A.F.L. in World Affairs* (co-author, 1952).

Secher, Herbert Pierre
Dissertation title: *The Problem of the Austrian State: The Post-World War II Experience.*
Affiliations: Ret. Memphis State University; Political Science, Kansas State University–Manhattan; Case Western Reserve University–Cleveland; University of Maryland–College Park
Publications: *Controlling the New Germany's Military Elite* (1965); *Max Weber's Basic Concepts of Sociology* (1962).

1955

Corradini, Alessandro Luigi
Dissertation title: *The Conduct of Foreign Affairs in Great Britain.*
Affiliations: Political Science, University of Wisconsin–Madison; Italian Food Administration; Allied Military Government, Italy

Greenberg, Milton
Dissertation title: *The Loyalty Oath in the American Experience.*
Affiliations: Ret. American University–Washington; Professor of Political Science and Dean, College of Arts and Sciences, Illinois State University–Normal; Western Michigan University– Kalamazoo; Member, Governor's Commission on Reapportionment
Publications: *The GI Bill: The Law that Changed America* (Lickle Publishing, 1997); *The American Political Dictionary* (Harcourt Brace, 1997, 10th ed.); *The American Political Dictionary* (co-author, 1972); *The Political Science Dictionary* (co-author, 1972); *Salient Issues of Constitutional Revision* (1961).

Hennessy, Bernard Charles
Dissertation title: *British Trade Unions and International Affairs, 1945–1953.*
Affiliations: California State University–Hayward; Pennsylvania State University; Politics, New York University School of Law; University of Arizona; Director, National Center for Education in Politics; Member, Pennsylvania Legislative Modernization Commission
Publications: *Essentials of Public Opinion* (1975); *Political Internships: Theory, Practice, Evaluation* (1970); *Public Opinion* (1970); *The Study of Party Organization* (co-author, 1966); *Politics without Power: the National Party Committees* (co-author, 1964); *Dollars for Democrats* (1959).

Howards, Irving
Dissertation title: *The Influence of Southern Senators on American Foreign Policy from 1840-1950.*
Affiliations: Ret. Professor of Political Science and Director, Bureau of Government Research, University of Massachusetts–Amherst

Krimel, Donald William
Dissertation title: *The Public Communications Functions of the Federal Government: An Examination Primarily Directed Toward a More Precise Definition of the Study Area.*

Nicholas Arthur (d. 1998).
Dissertation title: *Father Coughlin and Social Justice: a Case Study of a Social Movement.*
Affiliations: Political Science, University of Illinois–Edwardsville; Pennsylvania State University; Washington University; Wayne State University
Publications: *The Congressional Budget Process, 1974–1993* (1994); *State Politics and the Public Schools* (co-author, 1963); *The Political Attitudes and Preferences of Union Members: The Case of the Detroit Auto Workers* (co-author, 1959).

Scheffer, Walter Francis
Dissertation title: *Some Inter-Governmental Problems in Post-War Highway Financing and Administration in Wisconsin, with Special Reference to the Truck.*
Affiliations: Professor of Political Science and Director of Graduate Program in Public Administration, University of Oklahoma–Norman

1956

Backstrom, Charles H.
Dissertation title: *The Progressive Party of Wisconsin, 1934–1956.*
Affiliations: Ret. Political Science, University of Minnesota–Minneapolis; Director, Minnesota Council on Education in Politics
Publications: *Survey Research* (co-author, 1964); *Recount* (co-author, 1964).

Boles, Donald Edward
Dissertation title: *Administrative Rule Making in Wisconsin Conservation.*
Affiliations: Iowa State University–Ames; member, Iowa Intergovernmental Relations Commission; member, Iowa Civil Rights Commission; member, Iowa Advisory Commission to U.S. Civil Rights Commission; Chairman, Iowa Governor's Commission on Human Rights; Currently resides in Temecula, CA
Publications: *Mr. Justice Rehnquist, Judicial Activist: The Early Years* (1987); *The Two Swords* (1967); *Religion in the Public Schools* (1965); *The Bible, Religion, and the Public Schools* (1965); *Welfare and Highway Functions in Iowa Counties* (co-author, 1961); *An Evaluation of Iowa County Government* (co-author, 1959).

Flannery, James Joseph
Dissertation title: *Water Pollution Control: The Development of State and National Policy.*
Affiliations: Advisor to the Secretary, U.S. Department of Interior; Water Resources Council; Chief Economist, Federal Water Pollution Control Administration; Chief Economist, Water Pollution Control Program, Department of Health, Education and

Welfare; Economist, Public Health Service; Professor of Public Administration and Director, Bureau of Governmental Research, Florida State University–Tallahassee; Research Director, State Senate Finance Committee; Governor's Office; State Supreme Court and Judicial Council

Heppe, Paul Harry
Dissertation title: *The Liberal Party of Canada.*
Affiliations: Professor and Director, January Program of Studies in Eastern Canada, University of Puget Sound–Tacoma; Kansas State University; University of Wisconsin–Madison; Northwestern University; University of Montana; Advisory Committee to Legislative Committee (Washington) on Urban Problems

Jandali, Abdulfattah
Dissertation title: *United Nations Efforts to Set Standards for National Independence.*
Affiliations: University of Puget Sound–Tacoma; University of Nevada–Reno; United Nations Relief and Work Agency, Beirut, Lebanon; Michigan State University–East Lansing

1957

Gray, Richard Butler
Dissertation title: *Jose Marti: His Life, Ideas, Apotheosis, and Significance as a Symbol in Cuban Politics and Selected Social Organizations.*
Affiliations: Professor of Government and Director of International Affairs, Florida State University–Tallahassee; C.W. Post College–Long Island; Villanueva University–Havana, Cuba; Instituto-Cultural Domenico-Americano, U.S. Department of State, Domincan Republic
Publications: *Latin America and the U.S. in the 1970's* (editor, 1971); *International Security Systems* (1969); *Jose Marti, Cuban Patriot* (1962).

Habbe, Donald Edwin
Dissertation title: *Pearl Harbor: A Case Study in Administration.*
Affiliations: Dean, College of Arts and Sciences, University of South Dakota–Vermillion; Foreign Service Officer, U.S. Department of State

Kent, Alan Edward
Dissertation title: *Portrait in Isolationism: The LaFollettes and Foreign Policy.*

Lorch, Robert Stuart
Dissertation title: *Career Development in the Air Force.*
Affiliations: Political Science, University of Colorado–Colorado Springs; California State College–Long Beach; Georgia Institute of Technology
Publications: *Colorado's Government* (1976); *Democratic Process and Administrative Law* (1969).

Qubain, Fahim I.
Dissertation title: *The Impact of the Petroleum Industry on Iraq and Bahrain.*
Affiliations: Director of Research, Middle East Institute; Yale University; University of Wisconsin Extension Division–Madison
Publications: *Education and Science in the Arab World* (1966); *Crisis in Lebanon* (1961); *Inside the Arab Mind: A Bibliographical Survey of Arab Nationalism and Unity* (1960); *The Reconstruction of Iraq, 1950–1957* (1958).

Roherty, James Michael
Dissertation title: *The Legislative Council as Legislative Institution: A Study of the Wisconsin Joint Legislative Council.*
Affiliations: University of South Carolina–Columbia; College of William and Mary; National Defense College of Japan–Tokyo; Foreign Service Institute, U.S. Department of State; Federal Executive Institute, U.S. Civil Service Commission; Mount Mary College–Milwaukee; Marquette University–Milwaukee; consultant, U.S. Congress, House Republican Policy Committee; consultant, National Aeronautics and Space Administration; consultant, Department of Defense; Steering Committee on Science, Technology and Public Policy, Virginia State Council of Higher Education
Publications: *Defense Policy Formation: Towards Comparative Analysis* (editor, 1980); *Decisions of Robert S. McNamara: A Study of the Role of the Secretary of Defense* (1970).

Titus, James Emerson
Dissertation title: *Studies in American Liberalism of the 1930's: John Dewey, Benjamin Cardozo, and Thurman Arnold.*
Affiliations: Political Science, University of Kansas; Texas Tech University–Lubbock; University of Texas–Austin; Research Director, U.S. Commission on Political Activities of Government Personnel; Chairman, Lawrence (Kansas) Human Relations Commission; Executive Assistant to Director, U.S. Wage Stabilization Board

1958

Means, Ernest Elmer
Dissertation title: *Judicial Independence and the Summary Contempt Power over Publications.*
Affiliations: Director, Statutory Revision Division, State of Florida; Research Aide, Supreme Court of Florida; Executive Director, Judicial Council of Florida; Associate Secretary, Florida Commission on Uniform State Laws; Florida State University; The Citadel

Vardys, Vytas Stanley
Dissertation title: *Select Committees of Congress in Foreign Relations: A Case Study in Legislative Process.*
Affiliations: Political Science, University of Oklahoma–Norman; University of Wisconsin–Milwaukee
Publications: *Lithuania: The Rebel Nation* (1997); *The Catholic Church, Dissent, and Nationality in Soviet Lithuania* (1978); *The Baltic States in Peace and War, 1917–1945* (co-editor, 1978); *Lithuania under the Soviets: Portrait of a Nation, 1940–1963* (editor, 1965).

1959

Carley, Laurie David
Dissertation title: *The Wisconsin Governor's Legislative Role: a Case Study in the Administrations of Philip Fox La Follette and Walter J. Kohler, Jr.*
Affiliations: President, Medical College of Wisconsin–Milwaukee; President, Inland Steel Development Corporation; Chairman, Wisconsin Governor's Committee on Health Care; Regent, University of Wisconsin; candidate for Democratic nomination for Governor of Wisconsin

Crane, Wilder Willard, Jr.
Dissertation title: *The Legislative Struggle in Wisconsin: Decision-Making in the 1957 Wisconsin Assembly.*
Affiliations: University of Wisconsin–Milwaukee; Vanderbilt University–Nashville; Assemblyman, Wisconsin Legislature; Member, Chippewa Wisconsin County Board
Publications: *Wisconsin Government and Politics* (co-author, 1987); *The Job of the Wisconsin Legislator* (co-author, 1971); *State Legislative Systems* (co-author, 1968); *The Legislature of Lower Austria* (1961).

Harris, Charles Wesley
Dissertation title: *International Legal and Political Factors in the United States' Disposition of Alien Enemy Assets Seized during World War II: A Case Study on German Assets.*
Affiliations: Howard University; Coppin State College–Baltimore

Manwaring, David Roger
Dissertation title: *The Flag Salute Litigation.*
Affiliations: Political Science, Boston College
Publications: *Render Unto Caesar* (1962).

Odegard, Holtan Peter
Dissertation title: *Administrative Democracy: A Creative Utopia.*
Affiliations: Planning, University of Minnesota–Minneapolis; Planning Director, Souris-Rainy-Red River Basin Commission; Executive Director, Minnesota-Wisconsin Boundary Area Commission; Planning Director, City of Bloomington–Minnesota
Publications: *The Politics of Truth: Reconstruction in Democracy* (1971); *Sin and Science: Reinhold Niebuhr as Political Theologian* (1956).

Patterson, Samuel Charles
Dissertation title: *Toward a Theory of Legislative Behavior: The Wisconsin State Assemblymen as Actors in a Legislative System.*
Affiliations: Ohio State University–Columbus; University of Iowa–Iowa City; Oklahoma State University–Stillwater; University of Essex–England; Editor, Midwest Journal of Political Science; President, Iowa Conference of Political Scientists
Publications: *Parliaments in the Modern World: Changing Institutions* (co-editor, 1994); *Handbook of Legislative Research* (co-editor, 1985); *A More Perfect Union: Introduction to American Government* (co-author, 1982); *Comparative Legislative Behavior* (editor); *Comparing Legislatures: An Analytic Study* (co-author, 1979); *The*

Legislative Process in the U.S. (co-author, 1972); *American Legislative Behavior* (co-author, 1968); *Midwest Legislative Politics* (editor, 1967); *Labor Lobbying and Labor Reform* (1966); *Toward a Theory of Legislative Behavior* (1962); *Oklahoma Goes Wet: The Repeal of Prohibition* (co-author, 1960).

Schten, Edward Victor
Dissertation title: *The Milwaukee Milk Order: Administration and the Public Interest.*
Affiliations: University of Wisconsin; Haile Salassie University–Ethiopia; Professor of Political Science and Director, Institute of Governmental Affairs, University of Wisconsin Extension; Director of Research, Kentucky Legislative Research Commission
Publications: *Housing in Wisconsin* (editor, 1970); *State and Local Government Training in Wisconsin* (1970); *State Planning in Wisconsin* (co-author, 1965); *Administration of State Planning* (1965); *Constitutional Changes Concerning the Milwaukee County Executive* (co-author, 1963); *Equal Representation on Wisconsin County Boards* (co-author, 1963); *Higher Education in the U.S.* (editor, 1962); *Educational Television for Kentucky* (1961); *Kentucky Veterans Bonus Sales and Use Tax* (1961); *Insurance on State Property in Kentucky* (1960); *Professional Licensing in Kentucky* (1960).

1960

Anderson, Charles William
Dissertation title: *Political Ideology and the Revolution of Rising Expectations in Central America: 1944–1958.*
Affiliations: Ret. 1996. Political Science, University of Wisconsin–Madison; University of Essex–England; U.S. Department of State
Publications: *A Deeper Freedom: Liberal Democracy as an Everyday Morality* (2002); *Prescribing the Life of the Mind: An Essay on the Purpose of the University, the Aims of Liberal Education, the Competence of Citizens, and the Cultivation of Practical Reason* (1993); *Pragmatic Liberalism* (1990); *Statecraft: An Introduction to Political Choice and Judgment* (1977); *The Political Economy of Modern Spain* (1970); *Issues of Political Development* (co-author, 1967); *Politics and Economic Change in Latin America* (1967); *Political Factors in Latin American Economic Development* (1966); *Political Development in Latin America* (co-author, 1966); *Toward a Theory of Latin American Politics* (1964); *The Political Economy of Mexico* (co-author, 1963).

Hill, Alwyn Spencer
Dissertation title: *The Group Struggle over Education of the Poor in England and Wales: 1800–1870.*
Affiliations: Political Science, Michigan Technological University–Houghton; University of Nevada–Reno; Eastern New Mexico University; Drury College–Springfield, Missouri; New Mexico Commission on Higher Education; Currently resides in Salt Lake City, UT

Jones, Charles Oscar
Dissertation title: *The Relationship of Congressional Committee Action to a Theory of Representation.*
Affiliations: Ret. 1997. Political Science, University of Wisconsin–Madison; Politics, University of Pittsburgh; University of Arizona–Tucson; Wellesley College; Associate Director, National Center for Education in Politics
Publications: *Preparing To Be President: The Memos of Richard E. Neustadt*, with Richard Neustadt (2000); *Passages to the Presidency: From Campaigning to Governing*; *Separate But Equal Branches: Congress and the Presidency* (1995); *The Presidency in a Separated System* (1994); *The Reagan Legacy: Promise and Performance* (1988); *The Trusteeship Presidency: Jimmy Carter and the United States Congress* (1988); *The United States Congress: People, Place, and Policy* (1982); *Public Policy Making in a Federal System* (1976); *Clean Air: The Policies and Politics of Pollution Control* (1975); *An Introduction to the Study of Public Policy* (1970); *The Minority Party in Congress* (1970); *Every Second Year* (1967); *The Role of Political Parties in Congress: A Bibliography and Research Guide* (co-author, 1966); *Party and Policy Making* (1964); *The Republican Party in American Politics* (1965).

1961

Cortner, Richard Carroll
Dissertation title: *The Wagner Act Cases.*
Affiliations: Political Science, University of Arizona–Tucson; University of Tennessee
Publications: *Civil Rights and Public Accommodations: The Heart of Atlanta Motel and McClung Cases* (2001); *The Iron Horse and the Constitution: The Railroads and the Transformation of the Fourteenth Amendment* (1993); *A Mob Intent on Death: The NAACP and the Arkansas Riot Cases* (1988); *A "Scottsboro" Case in Mississippi: The Supreme Court and Brown v. Mississippi* (1986); *The Bureaucracy in Court: Commentaries and Case Studies in Administrative Law* (1982); *The Supreme Court and the Second Bill of Rights: The Fourteenth Amendment and the Nationalization of Civil Liberties* (1981); *The Supreme Court and Civil Liberties Policy* (1975); *Constitutional Law and Politics: Three Arizona Case-studies* (1971); *The Apportionment Cases* (1971); *The Wagner Act Cases* (co-author, 1964).

Kapil, Rawi L.
Dissertation title: *Territorial Issues in the Horn of Africa with Special Reference to the Ethiopia-Somalia Boundary.*
Affiliations: Service de la Cooperation technique–Paris, France; Country Director, Peace Corps–Somalia; University of Wisconsin–Milwaukee; University of Wisconsin–Racine Center

Mitchell, Stephen Robert
Dissertation title: *Mr. Justice Horace Gray.*
Affiliations: St. Philips College; Professor of Political Science and Dean, College of Science and Arts, Washington State University–Pullman; Dean and Assistant Chancellor, University of Wisconsin–Parkside; University of Calgary–Alberta
Publications: *Washington County Officials: A Political Profile* (1967).

Sirisumpundh, Kasem
Dissertation title: *Emergence of the Modern National State in Burma and Thailand.*
Affiliations: Dean of Journalism, Thammasat University–Bangkok, Thailand; member, Constitutional Committee to draw up a new Thailand Constitution

Stephens, Gordon Ross
Dissertation title: *Metropolitan Reorganization: A Comparison of Six Cases.*
Affiliations: Ret. Political Science, University of Missouri–Kansas City; University of Connecticut–Storrs; member, Missouri Governor's Commission on Local Government Law; Director of Research, Connecticut Legislature's Metropolitan Districts Study Commission; Currently resides in Leawood, KS
Publications: *Mediopolis: a Simple Fiscal Model of the Metropolis* (1968).

Tillman, Nathaniel Patrick, Jr.
Dissertation title: *Walter Francis White: A Study in Interest Group Leadership.*
Affiliations: Oliver Harvey College–Chicago; Delaware State College–Dover

1962

Lovell, John Philip (d. 1998).
Dissertation title: *The Cadet Phase of the Professional Socialization of the West Pointer: Description, Analysis and Theoretical Refinement.*
Affiliations: Indiana University–Bloomington
Publications: *The Challenge of American Foreign Policy: Purpose and Adaptation* (1985); *Neither Athens nor Sparta?: The American Service Academies in Transition* (1979); *The Military and Politics in Five Developing Nations* (editor, 1970); *Foreign Policy in Perspective* (1970).

Rasmussen, Jorgen Scott
Dissertation title: *Retrenchment and Revival: A Study of the Contemporary British Liberal Party and Its Activists.*
Affiliations: Political Science, Iowa State University; Political Science, Vanderbilt University; University of Arizona–Tucson
Publications: *The Process of Politics* (1969); *The Relation of the Profumo Rebels with Their Local Parties* (1966); *Retrenchment and Revival* (1964).

Rueckert, George Leonard
Dissertation title: *Parliamentary Party Cohesion in the West German Bundestag.*
Affiliations: Foreign Service Officer and Department International Relations Officer, U.S. Department of State
Publications: *On-site Inspection in Theory and Practice: A Primer on Modern Arms Control Regimes* (Praeger, 1998); *Global Double Zero: The INF Treaty from Its Origins to Implementation* (1993).

Stern, Robert William
Dissertation title: *An Experiment in Indian Nationalism: The Impact of the Sino-Indian Border Controversy on the Communist Party of India.*

Affiliations: Politics, Macquarie University–New South Wales, Australia; Wells College–Aurora, New York; Parsons College; Marquette University–Milwaukee
Publications: *Democracy and Dictatorship in South Asia: Dominant Classes and Political Outcomes in India, Pakistan, and Bangladesh* (2001); *Changing India: Bourgeois Revolution on the Subcontinent* (1993); *The Cat and the Lion: Jaipur State in the British Raj* (1987); *The Process of Opposition in India: Two Case Studies of How Policy Shapes Politics* (1970).

1963

Bibby, John F.
Dissertation title: *Legislative Oversight of Administration: a Case Study of a Congressional Committee.*
Affiliations: Political Science, University of Wisconsin–Milwaukee; Northern Illinois University–DeKalb; Director of Research, House Republican Conference, U.S. House of Representatives; Administrative Assistant to Chairman, Republican National Committee
Publications: *Politics, Parties, and Elections in America.* 5th ed. (2003); *Two Parties or More? The American Party System* (Westview Press, 1998, 2nd ed. 2003); *Politics, Parties, and Elections in America* (1992); *Governing By Consent: An Introduction to American Politics* (1992); *Congress Off The Record: The Candid Analyses of Seven Members* (1983); *Current Politics: The Way Things Work in Washington* (co-editor, 1973); *On Capitol Hill: Studies in the Legislative Process* (co-author, 1967, 1972); *The Costs of Political Participation: a Study of National Convention Delegations* (co-author, 1968); *Republican Politics* (co-author, 1968); *The Politics of National Convention Arrangements and Finances* (1968).

Kommers, Donald P.
Dissertation title: *Court Reorganization in Wisconsin.*
Affiliations: Professor and Director, Center for Civil Rights, University of Notre Dame; California State College–Los Angeles; University of Cologne–Germany
Publications: *The Federal Constitutional Court* (1994); *Germany and Its Basic Law: Past, Present, and Future: A German-American Symposium* (co-editor, 1993); *The Constitutional Jurisprudence of the Federal Republic of Germany* (1989); *Liberty and Community in American Constitutional Law: Continuing Tensions* (1986); *Human Rights and American Foreign Policy* (co-editor, 1979); *Freedom and Education: Pierce v. Society of Sisters Reconsidered* (co-editor, 1978); *Judicial politics In West Germany: A Study of the Federal Constitutional Court* (1973); *Judicial Politics in Wisconsin: A Case Study in Court Reorganization* (1965); *The Development and Reorganization of the Wisconsin Court System* (1963).

Kruschke, Earl Roger
Dissertation title: *Female Politicals and Apoliticals: Some Measurements and Comparisons.*
Affiliations: Ret. Political Science, California State University–Chico; University of Wisconsin–Milwaukee; University of Puget Sound–Tacoma, Washington; Director, Institute of Community and Regional Research

Publications: *Gun Control: A Reference Handbook* (1995); *Encyclopedia of Third Parties in the United States* (1991); *Nuclear Energy Policy: A Reference Handbook* (1990); *The Public Policy Dictionary* (1987); *The Right to Keep and Bear Arms: A Continuing American Dilemma* (1985); *California Politics in the 1970's* (co-author, 1972); *Introduction to the Constitution of the U.S.* (1968); *Consensus and Cleavage* (co-author, 1967).

Palmer, Monte
Dissertation title: *Arab Unity: Problems and Prospects.*
Affiliations: Florida State University–Tallahassee; Iowa State University–Ames; Western Illinois University–Macomb
Publications: *The Politics of the Middle East* (2002); *Comparative Politics: Political Economy, Political Culture, and Political Interdependence* (2001); *Survey Research in the Arab World: An Analytical Index* (co-author, 1982); *Political Development and Bureaucracy in Libya* (co-author, 1977); *The Interdisciplinary Study of Politics* (co-author, 1974); *Agrarian Reform in Iraq* (1973); *The Dilemmas of Political Development: An Introduction to the Politics of the Developing Areas* (1973).

Schwarz, Harry Guenter
Dissertation title: *Politics and Administration of Minority Areas in Northwest China and Inner Mongolia.*
Affiliations: Professor and Director, Program in East Asian Studies, Western Washington State College–Bellingham; University of Kansas; University of Washington; University of the Philippines; Marquette University; University of Wisconsin Racine Center; Consultant on China, Western White House
Publications: *Chinese Policies Toward Minorities: An Essay and Documents* (1971); *Liu Shao-ch'i and "People's War"* (1969); *China: Three Facets of a Giant* (1966); *Leadership Patterns in China's Frontier Regions* (1964).

1964

Ham, Euiyoung
Dissertation title: *Ideology in the Foreign Policy of Japanese Socialism.*
Affiliations: Yensei University–Korea; Currently resides in Potomoc, MD

Linford, Orma
Dissertation title: *Separation of Church and State in Utah.*
Affiliations: Political Science, Kansas State University–Manhattan

Sipress, Sylvia Ruth (Margulies)
Dissertation title: *The Pilgrimage to Russia, 1925–1937.*
Affiliations: Political Science, University of Wisconsin–Eau Claire; North Dakota State University– Fargo; Executive Assistant to President, Foreign Policy Association
Publications: *The Pilgrimage to Russia, 1924–1937.*

Sharkansky, Ira
Dissertation title: *Four Agencies and an Appropriations Subcommittee: A Comparative Study of Budget Relations.*

Affiliations: Political Science, Hebrew University–Jerusalem; University of Wisconsin–-Madison; University of Georgia; Florida State University–Muncie, Indiana; Ball State University
Publications: *Coping with Terror: An Israeli Perspective* (2003); *Politics and Policymaking: In Search of Simplicity* (2002); *Policy Making in Israel: Routines for Simple Problems and Coping with the Complex*; *Ritual of Conflict: Religion, Politics, and Pulbic Policy in Israel* (1996); *Ancient and Modern Israel: An Exploration of Political Parallels* (1991); *What Makes Israel Tick: How Domestic Policy-makers Cope with Constraints* (1985); *The United States Revisited: A Study of a Still Developing Country* (1982); *Public Administration: Agencies, Policies, and Politics* (1982); *Wither the State?: Politics and Public Enterprise in Three Countries* (1979); *The Maligned States: Policy Accomplishments, Problems, and Opportunities* (1978); *The Policy Predicament: Making and Implementing Public Policy* (co-author, 1978); *The United States: A Study of a Developing Country* (1975); *Policy and Politics in American Government* (with D. Van Meter, 1975); *The Maligned States: Policy Accomplishments, Problems and Opportunities* (1972); *Urban Politics and Public Policy* (with R.L. Lineberry, 1971, 1974); *State and Urban Politics* (with R.I. Hofferbert, 1971); *The Routines of Politics* (1970); *Policy Analysis in Political Science* (1970); *Public Administration: Policy-Making in Government Agencies* (1970, 1972, 1975); *Regionalism in American Politics* (1970); *The Politics of Taxing and Spending* (1969); *Spending in the American States* (1968).

Vinyard, C. Dale
Dissertation title: *Congressional Committees on Small Business.*
Affiliations: Wayne State University–Detroit; Wisconsin State University–Platteville; Managing Editor, Midwest Journal of Political Science
Publications: *The Presidency* (1971).

1965

Burger, Josef
Dissertation title: *Indian Students and American Education: an Evaluation of a New Tool of American Foreign Policy.*
Affiliations: PDC Facilities, Inc.; University of Wisconsin Center System; Republican candidate for Congress, 7th Wisconsin District

Groves, Roderick Trimble
Dissertation title: *Administrative Reform in Venezuela, 1958–1964.*
Affiliations: Deputy Director Academic Planning Board, Illinois Board of Regents; Office of Superintendent of Public Instruction–Illinois; Northern Illinois University–De Kalb; Wisconsin State University–Stevens Point; Currently resides in Albuquerque, NM

Hamburg, Roger Phillip
Dissertation title: *The Soviet Union and Latin America.*
Affiliations: Indiana University–South Bend; University of Wisconsin–Parkside; Marquette University–Milwaukee; Eastern Washington State College–Cheney

Kingdon, John Wells
Dissertation title: *Candidates for Office: A Study in Political Cognition.*
Affiliations: Political Science, University of Michigan–Ann Arbor; Currently resides in Washington, DC
Publications: *Agendas, Alternatives, and Public Policies* (1984, 2003); *Congressmen's Voting Decisions* (1973, 1989); *Candidates for Office* (1968).

McLennan, Barbara Nancy
Dissertation title: *Concepts of Representation in Southeast Asia.*
Affiliations: LeBoeuf, Lamb, Leiby, McRae; Strategic Studies Research Center, Stanford Research Institute–Arlington, Virginia; Political Science, Temple University–Philadelphia; Currently resides in McLean, VA
Publications: *Possible Patterns of Nuclear Proliferation* (co-author, 1974); *Political Opposition and Dissent* (editor, 1973); *Crime in Urban Society* (editor, 1970).

Pettit, Lawrence Kay
Dissertation title: *The Policy Process in Congress: Passing the Higher Education Facilities Act of 1963.*
Affiliations: Indiana University of Pennsylvania; Commissioner of Higher Education, Montana University System; Pennsylvania State University–University Park; Legislative Assistant, U.S. Senator Lee Metcalf and U.S. Senator James E. Murray
Publications: *The Legislative Process in the U.S. Senate* (co-editor, 1969); *European Political Processes: Essays and Readings* (co-author, 1967).

Suleiman, Michael Wadie
Dissertation title: *Political Parties in Lebanon.*
Affiliations: Political Science, Kansas State University–Manhattan
Publications: *U.S. Policy on Palestine: From Wilson to Clinton* (1995); *American Images of Middle East Peoples: Impact of the High School* (1977); *Political Parties in Lebanon* (1967).

1966

Burger, Angela Sutherland
Dissertation title: *Opposition in a Dominant-Party System: A Study of the Jan Sangh and Praja Socialist and Socialist Parties in Uttar Pradesh, India.*
Affiliations: University of Wisconsin Center System–Marathon County (Wausau)
Publications: *Benchmarks in Wisconsin Politics, 1956 and 1972* (1975); *Opposition in a Dominant-Party System: a Study of the Jan Sangh, the Praja Socialist Party, and the Socialist Party in Uttar Pradesh, India* (1969).

Jernberg, James Everett
Dissertation title: *Program Budgeting: The Influence, Effects and Implications of Reform.*
Affiliations: Professor and Associate Director, School of Public Affairs, University of Minnesota–Minneapolis; Budget Officer, City of Madison–Wisconsin
Publications: *Financial Administration* (1971).

Keech, William Robertson
Dissertation title: *The Negro Vote as a Political Resource: The Case of Durham.*
Affiliations: Carnegie-Mellon University; University of North Carolina–Chapel Hill; Brookings Institution
Publications: *Economic Politics: The Costs of Democracy* (1995); *Electoral and Welfare Consequences of Political Manipulation of the Economy* (co-author, 1983); *Elections and Macroeconomic Policy Optimization: Four Models* (1978); *The Party's Choice* (co-author, 1976); *The Impact of Negro Voting* (1968).

Powell, John Duncan
Dissertation title: *The Politics of Agrarian Reform in Venezuela: History, System and Process.*
Affiliations: Tufts University–Medford, Massachusetts; University of Southern California; Land Tenure Center, University of Wisconsin–Madison; Legislative Reference Service, Library of Congress; Currently resides in Scottsdale, AZ
Publications: *The Political Mobilization of the Venezuelan Peasant* (1971); *The Politics of Agrarian Reform in Venezuela: History, System, and Process* (1966).

Rae, Douglas Whiting
Dissertation title: *The Politics of Electoral Law.*
Affiliations: Yale University; Syracuse University; University of Vermont–Burlington; Center for Advanced Studies–Palo Alto, California; Editorial Board, American Political Science Review; Editorial Committee, British Journal of Political Science
Publications: *City: Urbanism and Its End* (2003); *Equalities* (co-author, 1981); *Public Policy and Public Choice* (co-editor, 1979); *The Analysis of Political Cleavages* (1970); *The Political Consequences of Electoral Laws* (1967, 1971).

Randall, Richard Stuart
Dissertation title: *Control of Motion Pictures in the United States.*
Affiliations: Politics, University College, New York University; University of Nebraska–Lincoln
Publications: *American Constitutional Development* (2002); *Freedom and Taboo: Pornography and the Politics of a Self Divided* (1989); *Censorship of the Movies: The Social and Political Control of a Mass Medium* (1968); *Self Regulation in the Film Industry* (1971).

Tsurutani, Taketsugu
Dissertation title: *Tension, Consensus and Political Leadership (A New Look into the Nature and Process of Modernization).*
Affiliations: Political Science, Washington State University–Pullman; University of Maine; Nevada Southern University–Las Vegas
Publications: *Chief Executives: National Political Leadership in The United States, Mexico, Great Britain, Germany, and Japan* (co-editor, 1992); *Japanese Policy and East Asian Security* (1981); *Political Change in Japan: Response to Postindustrial Challenge* (1977); *The Politics of National Development: Political Leadership in Transitional*

Societies (1973); *Rural Development and Political Integration in Japan, Korea and the Philippines: Annotated and General Bibliographies with an Introduction* (1968).

1967

Adamany, David Walter
Dissertation title: *Money in a State Political System: Wisconsin.*
Affiliations: President, Temple University; President, Wayne State University; Secretary, Department of Revenue, State of Wisconsin; University of Wisconsin–Madison; Associate Professor and Dean of the College, Wesleyan University–Middletown, Connecticut; Wisconsin State University–Whitewater; Commissioner, Wisconsin Public Service Commission; Pardon Counsel, Wisconsin Governor's Office
Publications: *Political Money: A Strategy for Campaign Financing in America* (1975); *Campaign Finance in America* (1972); *Campaign Funds as an Intra-Party Resource* (1972); *Financing Politics* (1969).

Braithwaite, Karl Royden
Dissertation title: *Scientists and Public Officials: Relations in Oceanography.*
Affiliations: Legislative Assistant to U.S. Senator Frank E. Moss; Duke University

Bromall, Irvin
Dissertation title: *Wisconsin Lawyers in Politics: an Exploratory Study.*
Affiliations: Urban Mass Transportation Administration; National Urban League; Oakland University; Ohio University–Athens

Canon, Bradley C.
Dissertation title: *The FCC's "Fairness" Doctrine: Its Substance, Enforcement, and Impact.*
Affiliations: Political Science, University of Kentucky–Lexington
Publications: *Judicial Politics: Implementation and Impact* (CQ Press, 1998, 2nd ed.); *Judicial Policies: Implementation and Impact* (co-author, 1984);

Chaffey, Douglas Camp
Dissertation title: *The Functions of the State Legislative Party Leader and His Socialization: A Comparative Analysis.*
Affiliations: Chatham College–Pittsburgh, Pennsylvania; University of Montana

Cohen, Stephen P.
Dissertation title: *The Military in the Indian Constitutional Order: The British Period.*
Affiliations: Political Science, University of Illinois–Urbana; Keio University–Tokyo, Japan
Publications: *Perception, Politics, and Security in South Asia: The Compound Crisis of 1990* with Castles, Chari, P. R., Pervaiz Iqbal Cheema (2003); *India: Emerging Power.* (2001); *Nuclear Proliferation in South Asia: The Prospects for Arms Control* (editor, 1991); *The Security of South Asia: American and Asian Perspectives* (1987); *The Pakistan Army* (1984); *SYMLOG: A System for the Multiple Level Observation of Groups* (co-author, 1979); *The Andhra Cyclone of 1977: Individual and Institutional Responses to Mass Death* (1979); *India, Emergent Power?* (co-author, 1978); *The Military and Politics in Bangladesh, India, and Pakistan* (1973); *Arms and Politics in Bangladesh, India and Pakistan* (1973); *The Indian Army: Its Contribution to the Development of a Nation* (1971).

Dunn, Delmer Delano
Dissertation title: *Interaction between the Press and Wisconsin State Officials.*
Affiliations: Vice President, University of Georgia; Political Science, University of Georgia–Athens; Director, University of Georgia Reapportionment Services Unit
Publications: *Politics and Administration at the Top: Lessons from Down Under* (University of Pittsburgh Press, 1997); *Financing Presidential Campaigns* (1972); *Public Officials and the Press* (1969).

Finifter, Ada Weintraub
Dissertation title: *Dimensions of Political Alienation: a Multivariate Analysis.*
Affiliations: Political Science, Michigan State University–East Lansing; Andrew Bello Catholic University–Caracas, Venezuela; Universidad de Oriente Cimana–Venezuela; Assistant Study Director, Survey Research Center, University of Michigan; Council Member, Inter-University Consortium for Political Research; APSA Council
Publications: *Political Science: The State of the Discipline* (editor, 1993); *Political Science: The State of the Discipline* (editor, 1983); *Alienation and the Social System* (1972).

Goetcheus, Vernon M.
Dissertation title: *Presidential Leadership: Lyndon B. Johnson and Democratic Members of the House of Representatives.*
Affiliations: Director, Alumni Relations, Polytechnic University–Brooklyn, N.Y.; Chief Minority Staff, U.S. Senate Committee on Nutrition and Human Needs; Columbia University–New York City

Gugin, David Arthur
Dissertation title: *Africanization of the Uganda Public Service.*
Affiliations: Director, Urban Studies Center, University of Evansville–Indiana; Assistant to President and Assistant Dean of Administration, University of Massachusetts; University of Georgia–Athens; University of South Dakota–Vermillion

Jacobitti, Suzanne Duvall
Dissertation title: *Political Theory and Comparative Politics: A Critique of the Political Theory of the Committee on Comparative Politics.*
Affiliations: Political Science, Southern Illinois University–Edwardsville; University of Wisconsin–Whitewater

Keynes, Edward
Dissertation title: *The Dirkson Amendment: A Study of Legislative Strategy, Tactics and Public Policy.*
Affiliations: Political Science, Pennsylvania State University–University Park; University of Cologne–Germany; University of Kiel–Germany; Consultant, Committee on Legislative Modernization, General Assembly of Pennsylvania; Consultant, Committee on House Administration, U.S. House of Representatives
Publications: *Liberty, Property, and Privacy: Toward a Jurisprudence of Substantive Due Process* (1996); *The Court vs. Congress: Prayer, Busing, and Abortion* (co-author, 1989); *Undeclared War: Twilight Zone of Constitutional Power* (1982); *The Borzoi*

Anthology of American Politics (editor, with David Adamany, 1971); *Political Power, Community and Democracy* (co-editor, 1970); *The Legislative Process in the U.S. Senate* (co-editor, 1969).

Oliver, James H.
Dissertation title: *Demands of the Soviet Political System: Moscow and Leningrad, a Case Study.*
Affiliations: University of Maryland–College Park; Currently resides in Aberdeen, WA

Thompson, Kenneth H., Jr.
Dissertation title: *Class Change and Party Choice: A Cross-National Study of the Relationship between Intergenerational Social Mobility and Political Party Preference.*
Affiliations: University of Southern California
Publications: *Cross-National Voting Behavior* (1970).

1968

Baines, John Matthew
Dissertation title: *Jose Carlos Mariategui: A Study of Revolutionary Political Thought.*
Affiliations: Government Relations Consultant, JM Baines and Associates–Washington, D.C.; University of Wyoming–Laramie; Wittenburg University–Springfield, Ohio; Consultant, Wyoming Governor's Commission on Criminal Administration
Publications: *Revolution in Peru: Mariategui and the Myth* (1972).

Barth, Thomas Emil
Dissertation title: *Perception and Acceptance of Supreme Court Decisions at the State and Local Level: the Case of Obscenity Policy in Wisconsin.*
Affiliations: Wisconsin State University–Eau Claire
Publications: *Law and Order in a Democratic Society* (co-editor, 1970); *Perception and Acceptance of Supreme Court Decisions at the State and Local Level: The Case of Obscenity Policy in Wisconsin* (1968).

McCoy, Terry Luther
Dissertation title: *Agrarian Reform in Chile, 1962–1968: A Study of Politics and the Development Process.*
Affiliations: University of Florida; Ohio State University–Columbus; Assistant to the Director, Land Tenure Center, University of Wisconsin–Madison
Publications: *The Dynamics of Population Policy in Latin America* (editor, 1974).

McLauchlan, William Philip
Dissertation title: *Federal Hearing Examiners and the Federal Power Commission.*
Affiliations: Political Science, Purdue University; Southern Illinois University–Edwardsville
Publications: *Federal Court Caseloads* (1984); *Privacy and the Presentence Report* (1978); *Hermes Bound: The Policy and Technology of Telecommunications* (co-author, 1978); *American Legal Processes* (1977).

Milner, Neal A.
Dissertation title: *The Impact of the Miranda Decision on Four Wisconsin Cities.*
Affiliations: University of Hawaii–Honolulu; Grinnell College–Iowa
Publications: *The Possibility of Popular Justice: A Case Study of Community Mediation in the United States* (co-editor, 1993); *The Sex Education Controversy: A Study of Politics, Education, and Morality* (co-author, 1975); *The Biases of Police Reform* (editor, 1971); *Police Response to Legal Change* (1971); *Black Politics, the Inevitability of Conflict* (co-editor, 1971); *The Courts and Local Law Enforcement* (1971).

Thoeny, Robert Alan
Dissertation title: *Press Treatment of Crisis and Noncrisis International Politics.*
Affiliations: Memphis State University; U.S. Air Force Academy–Colorado Springs, Colorado
Publications: *Simulation Games in Social Science Teaching and Research* (co-author, 1970).

Valdes, Luis
Dissertation title: *Voting Patterns in Rural and Urban Sao Paulo: Socio-Economic-Demographic Correlates of Voting.*
Affiliations: Professor and Coordinator of Latin American Studies, Rollins College–Winter Park, Florida; Inter-American University–San German, Puerto Rico; Central College–Pella, Iowa

1969

Adler, Madeleine W.
Dissertation title: *Congressional Reform: An Exploratory Case.*
Affiliations: Political Science, Queens College, City University of New York

Agor, Weston Harris
Dissertation title: *The Chilean Senate: Internal Distribution of Influence.*
Affiliations: Political Science, University of Texas–El Paso; University of Florida–Gainesville; Grand Valley State College–Allendale, Michigan; Wisconsin State University–Oshkosh
Publications: *Intuition in Organizations: Leading and Managing Productively* (1989); *Latin American Legislatures: Their Role and Influence* (editor, 1971); *The Chilean Senate: Internal Distribution of Influence* (1971).

Alfian, Ibrahim (d.)
Dissertation title: *Islamic Modernism in Indonesian Politics: the Mumammadijah Movement during the Dutch Colonial Period.*
Affiliations: Widya Chandra I/E–Jakarta, Indonesia; Senior Researcher, LEKNAS (Lembaha Ekonomi dan Kemasjarakatan Nasional)–Djakarta, Indonesia
Publications: *Dari Samudera Pasai ke Yogyakarta: Persembahan Lepada Teuku Ibrahim Alfian.* Jakarta: Yayasan Masyarakat Sejarawan Indonesia: Sinergi Press (2002) with Yayasan Masyarakat Sejarawan; *Politik dan Sistem Politik Indonesia* (1991); *Social Impact of Satellite Television in Rural Indonesia* (1991); *Muhammadiyah: The Political Behavior of a Muslim Modernist Organization Under*

Dutch Colonialism (1989); *Transformasi Sosial Budaya Dalam Pembangunan Nasional* (1986); *Masalah Dan Prospek Pembangunan Politik Indonesia: Kumpulan Karangan* (1986); *Beberapa Masalah Pembaharuan Politik di Indonesia* (1981); *Politik, Kebudayaan dan Manusia Indonesia* (1980); *Political Science in Indonesia* (1979); *Pemikiran dan Perubahan Politik Indonesia: Kumpulan Karangan* (1978); *Kronika Pasai: Sebuah Tinjauan Sejarah* (1973); *Perkembangan Politil Dalam Pembangunan Nasional* (1970); *Masalah Mental, Aliran dan Radikalisme Dalam Jasjarakat Indonesia* (1970); *Islamic Modernism in Indonesian Politics: The Muhammadijab Movement During the Dutch Colonial Period, 1912–1942* (1969); *Militer dan Politik* (1968).

Cimbala, Joseph Stephen
Dissertation title: *American Military Assistance to Pakistan: A Case Study in Military Policy and National Objectives.*
Affiliations: State University of New York–Stonybrook; Currently resides in Drexel Hill, PA

Gilberg, Trond
Dissertation title: *The Relations between the Norwegian Communist Party and the CPSU, 1917–1940.*
Affiliations: Pennsylvania State University–University Park
Publications: *Nationalism and Communism in Romania: The Rise and Fall of Ceausescu's Personal Dictatorship* (1990); *Coalition Strategies of Marxist Parties* (editor, 1989); *Security Implications of Nationalism in Eastern Europe* (co-editor, 1986).

Greenberg, Edward S.
Dissertation title: *Political Socialization to Support of the System: A Comparison of Black and White Children.*
Affiliations: Political Science, University of Colorado; Indiana University; Stanford University–Palo Alto, California
Publications: *The Struggle for Democracy*, with Benjamin Page (1997, 2001, 2002); *Changes in the State: Causes and Consequences* (co-editor, 1990); *The American Political System: A Radical Approach* (1989); *Workplace Democracy: The Political Effects of Participation* (1986); *Capitalism and the American Political Ideal* (1985); *Understanding Modern Government: The Rise and Decline of the American Political Economy* (1979); *Serving the Few: Corporate Capitalism and the Bias of Government Policy* (1974); *Corporate Capitalism and American Public Policy: the Distribution of Benefits in the Modern Positive State* (1974); *American Politics Reconsidered: Readings in Power and Inequity in American Society* (editor, with R. Young, 1973); *Black Politics: the Inevitability of Conflict* (editor, with D. Olson and N. Milner, 1971); *Political Socialization* (editor, 1970); *Children and Government: A Comparison Across Racial Lines* (1970).

Schwartz, Donald Victor
Dissertation title: *Adaptations of Social Control Theory in the Soviet Union.*
Affiliations: Professor of Political Economy and Assistant to Director, Center for Russian and East European Studies, University of Toronto–Canada
Publications: *The Brezhnev Years, 1964–1981* (editor, 1982).

Swanson, John Robert
Dissertation title: *Soviet Views of the Developing Nations: a Study of Ideological Continuity and Change.*
Affiliations: Political Science, University of Missouri–Columbia

Tharp, Paul A., Jr.
Dissertation title: *Systems Analysis and International Law.*
Affiliations: University of Oklahoma–Norman; President, Southwest Region, International Studies Association; Consultant, Federal Aviation Administration; Consultant, U.S. Department of Health, Education, and Welfare

Tien, Hung-Mao Harold
Dissertation title: *Political Development in China, 1927–1937.*
Affiliations: University of Wisconsin–Waukesha
Publications: *Taiwan's Electoral Politics and Democratic Transition: Riding the Third Wave* (editor, 1995); *The Great Transition: Political and Social Change in the Republic of China* (1989); *Mainland China, Taiwan, and U.S. Policy* (1983); *Government and Politics in Kuomintang China, 1927–1937.*

Weissberg, Robert
Dissertation title: *Political Tolerance: Balancing Community and Diversity* (Sage Publications, 1998); *The Political Socialization of Adolescents: the Role of Social, Experimental and Psychological Factors in Political Learning.*
Affiliations: Political Science, University of Illinois–Urbana; Cornell University–Ithaca, New York
Publications: *Flattering the Leviathan: Public Opinion and the Social Welfare State* (2002); *Democracy and the Academy* (2000); *Polling, Policy, and Public Opinion: The Case Against Heeding the "Voice of the People"* (2002); *Public Opinion and Popular Government* (1976); *Political Learning, Political Choice, and Democratic Citizenship* (1974); *American Democracy: Theory and Reality* (co-author, 1972); *Elementary Political Analysis* (1970, 1975).

1970

Beckett, Paul Anthony
Dissertation title: *Revolutionary Systems: a Conceptual Model and Comparative Study of Four African Revolutionary Regimes.*
Affiliations: Associate Director, African Studies Program, and Associate Dean, International Studies, University of Wisconsin–Madison; Ahmadu Bello University–Zaria, Nigeria
Publications: *Education and Power in Nigeria: A Study of University Students* (co-author, 1977); *Dilemmas of Democracy in Nigeria* (co-editor, 1995).

Harbeson, John Willis
Dissertation title: *Nationalism and Nation Building in Kenya: the Role of Land Reform.*
Affiliations: Political Science, City College of New York; University of Wisconsin–Parkside; University of East Africa

Publications: *Civil Society and the State in Africa* (co-author, 1994); *Africa in World Politics* (co-editor, 1991, 1995, 2000); *The Ethiopian Transformation: The Quest for the Post-imperial State* (1988); *The Military in African Politics* (editor, 1987); *Structural Adjustment and Development Reform in Kenya: The Missing Dimension* (1984); *Nation-Building in Kenya: The Role of Land Reform* (1973); *Nationalism and Nation-Building in Kenya* (1972); *American National Government* (1970).

Hoover, Kenneth Ray
Dissertation title: *Liberty and Psyche: An Argument for Liberal Idealism.*
Affiliations: Political Science, Western Washington University–Bellingham; College of Wooster–Ohio; University of Wisconsin–Whitewater
Publications: *Economics as Ideology: Keynes, Laski, Hayek, and the Creation of Contemporary Politics.* (2003); *The Power of Identity: Politics in a New Key* (1997); *Conservative Capitalism in Britain and the United States: A Critical Appraisal* (co-author, 1989); *The Elements of Social Scientific Thinking* (1980, 1995); *A Politics of Identity: Liberation and the Natural Community* (1975).

Lee, Tosh (To-Shun)
Dissertation title: *Members of the Soka Gakkai: A Study in Mass Political Behavior.*
Affiliations: University of Southern California; Wisconsin State University–Superior

Mathieu, Gilbert
Dissertation title: *The French and Belgian Communist Parties in Relation to Soviet Objective toward Western Europe in 1940 and 1944.*

Melnick, Daniel
Dissertation title: *The Dimensions of Politicization: Language, Communication, Social Mobilization and the Generation of Political Attitudes (Report of a Survey in a North Indian District).*
Affiliations: National Science Foundation; Acting Director, Department of Health and Human Services; University of Maryland–College Park

Mock, Richard Pearson
Dissertation title: *Decision Making and Policy Implementation in the Ghana Water and Sewerage Corporation: a Case Study in Development Administration.*
Affiliations: Southwest Missouri State College–Springfield; American University–Cairo, Egypt

Obler, Jeffrey Lowell
Dissertation title: *Candidate Selection in Belgium.*
Affiliations: University of North Carolina–Chapel Hill
Publications: *Decision-making in Smaller Democracies: The Consociational "Burden"* (1977).

Trilling, Richard Jay
Dissertation title: *Coalition Government, Political Parties, and the National Voter: A Formal Analysis.*

Affiliations: Duke University Durham, North Carolina
Publications: *Realignment in American Politics: Toward a Theory* (co-editor, 1980); *Party Image and Electoral Behavior* (1976).

Wynia, Gary
Dissertation title: *Policy and Democracy in Central America: Comparative Study.*
Affiliations: Carleton College; University of Minnesota–Minneapolis
Publications: *Argentina: Illusions and Realities* (1986, 1992); *Argentina in the Postwar Era: Politics and Economic Policy Making in a Divided Society* (1978); *The Politics of Latin American Development* (1978, 1984, 1990); *Politics and Planners* (1972).

1971

Abravanel, Martin
Dissertation title: *Affect, Belief and International Affairs: Soviet-American Competition and the National Images of Mass Publics.*
Affiliations: Political Science, Case Western Reserve University–Cleveland, Ohio; Currently resides in McLean, VA

Adler, Norman M.
Dissertation title: *Ethnics in Politics: Access to Office in New York City.*
Affiliations: Regional Director, New York Assembly Committee on Cities of New York; Hunter College–New York City; Teachers' College, Columbia University–New York; Pennsylvania State University; American University
Publications: *Political Clubs in New York* (co-author, 1975).

Anderson, Roger Charles
Dissertation title: *The Functional Role of Governors and Their States in the Political Development of Mexico, 1940–1964.*
Affiliations: Political Science, Bowling Green State University–Ohio

Brown, Don Wallace
Dissertation title: *Youth and Law: Adolescents' Acquisition of Compliant and Non-Compliant Orientation and Behavior.*
Affiliations: University of California–Riverside; Currently resides in Austin, TX
Publications: *Statistical Process Control: Theory and Practice* (co-author, 1991); *Policy Implementation: Penalties or Incentives?* (co-editor, 1980).

Chaney, Elsa Mae
Dissertation title: *Women in Latin American Politics: the Cases of Peru and Chile.*
Affiliations: University of Iowa–Iowa City; Fordham University–New York City; National Campaign Staff Director, Women for McCarthy; Press Assistant, Office of U.S. Senator William Proxmire; Press Assistant, Office of U.S. Senator Eugene McCarthy
Publications: *Muchachas No More: Household Workers in Latin America and the Caribbean* (co-editor, 1989); *Sellers & Servants: Working Women in Lima, Peru* (co-author, 1985, 1989); *Supermadre: Women in Politics in Latin America* (1979).

Handelman, Howard
Dissertation title: *Struggle in the Andes: Political Mobilization in Peru.*
Affiliations: Political Science, University of Wisconsin–Milwaukee
Publications: *The Challenge of Third World Development* (2000); *Mexican Politics: The Dynamics of Change* (1997); *Paying the Costs of Austerity in Latin America* (co-editor, 1989); *The Politics of Agrarian Change in Asia and Latin America* (editor, 1981); *Military Government and the Movement Toward Democracy in South America* (co- editor, 1981); *Struggle in the Andes: Peasant Political Mobilization in Peru* (1975).

Hibbs, Douglas Albert, Jr.
Dissertation title: *Domestic Mass Violence: a Cross-National Analysis.*
Affiliations: Professor, Trade Union Institute for Economic Research–Stockholm, Sweden; Massachusetts Institute of Technology–Cambridge
Publications: *Solidarity or Egoism?: The Economics of Sociotropic and Egocentric Influences on Political Behavior: Denmark In International and Theoretical Perspective* (1993); *The American Political Economy: Macroeconomics and Electoral Politics* (1987); *The Political Economy of Industrial Democracies* (1987); *Contemporary Political Economy: Studies on the Interdependence of Politics and Economics* (co-editor, 1980); *Mass Political Violence: A Cross-national Causal Analysis* (1973).

Keehn, Norman Henry
Dissertation title: *The Politics of Fiscal and Monetary Stabilization [Latin America].*
Currently resides in McFarland, WI.

Maughan, Ralph B., Jr.
Dissertation title: *Party Identification and Electoral Change in the United States.*
Affiliations: Idaho State University–Pocatello

Mayer, Peter Baldwin
Dissertation title: *Mofussil: Political Change and Community Politics in Two Indian Provincial Cities.*
Affiliations: Politics, University of Adelaide–Australia

Morris, Donald R.
Dissertation title: *Political Violence and Modernization in Mexico (1952–1964).*
Affiliations: University of Miami–Coral Gables

Murdock, Clark Anson
Dissertation title: *A Comparative Analysis of Defense Policy-Making Procedures in the 1950's and the 1960's.*
Affiliations: State University of New York–Buffalo
Publications: *Revitalizing the U.S. Nuclear Deterrent* (co-author 2002); *Defense Policy Formation: A Comparative Analysis of the McNamara Era* (1974).

Olson, David John
Dissertation title: *Racial Violence and City Politics: the Political Response to Civil Disorders in Three American Cities.*

Affiliations: Political Science, University of Washington; Indiana University–Bloomington
Publications: *Black Politics: The Inevitability of Conflict* (editor, 1970).

Orenstein, Jeffrey Robert
Dissertation title: *The Tradition of Individualist Revolt.*
Affiliations: Kent State University–Ohio; Cuyahoga Community College–Cleveland, Ohio; Currently resides in Boca Raton, FL.
Publications: *United States Railroad Policy: Uncle Sam at the Throttle* (1990); *Contemporary Issues in Political Theory* (co-author, 1977, 1985).

Pienkos, Donald Edward
Dissertation title: *Communist Policy and the Polish Peasant: The Impact of Traditional Society upon Revolutionary Goals.*
Affiliations: University of Wisconsin–Milwaukee
Publications: *For Your Freedom Through Ours: Polish American Efforts on Poland's Behalf, 1863–1991* (1991); *One Hundred Years Young: A History of the Polish Falcons of America, 1887–1987* (1987); *PNA, A Centennial History of the Polish National Alliance of the United States of North America* (1984); *Studies In Ethnicity: The East European Experience in America* (co-editor, 1980).

Randall, Ronald R., Jr.
Dissertation title: *Policy Implementation in the Employment Service: Human Resources Development in Wisconsin.*
Affiliations: Political Science, University of Toledo–Ohio

Reading, Reid Roscoe
Dissertation title: *Political Socialization in Colombia and the United States.*
Affiliations: Political Science, University of Pittsburgh–Pennsylvania

Samudivanija, Chai Anan
Dissertation title: *Politics and Administration of the Thai Budgetary Process.*
Affiliations: National Institute of Development Administration, School of Public Administration–Bangkok, Thailand; Member, of Thailand Constituent Assembly

Stanga, John Ellis, Jr.
Dissertation title: *The Press and the Criminal Defendant: Newsmen and Criminal Justice in Three Wisconsin Cities.*
Affiliations: Wichita State University–Kansas; Lamar State College–Beaumont, Texas

Weng, Byron Song-Jan.
Dissertation title: *Continuity and Change in Peking's UN Policy 1949–1969.*
Affiliations: Wright State University–Dayton, Ohio; United College, Chinese University of Hongkong
Publications: *Peking's UN Policy: Continuity and Change* (1972).

1972

Bailey, John J.
Dissertation title: *Government and Educational Policy in Colombia, 1958–1968.*
Affiliations: Government, Georgetown University–Washington, D.C.
Publications: *Organized Crime & Democratic Governability: Mexico and the U.S.-Mexican Borderlands* (co-author, 2000); *Governing Mexico, 1976–88: The Statecraft of Crisis Management* (1988); *Handbook of Latin American Studies* (1971).

Billingsley, Keith Ray
Dissertation title: *A Multi-Disciplinary Approach to the Study of Political Efficacy in Adolescents: A Search for Efficient Predictors.*
Affiliations: Professor of Political Science and Director, Political Data Analysis Center, University of Georgia–Athens
Publications: *A Pilot Experiment in Early Childhood Political Learning* (co-author, 1968).

Broh, Charles Anthony
Dissertation title: *Issue Attitudes, Conceptualization, and Perception: Toward a Theory of Issue Voting.*
Affiliations: Registrar, Princeton University; Hobart and William Smith Colleges; State University of New York–Geneseo; Southern Illinois University–Carbondale

Evans, Alfred Burney, Jr.
Dissertation title: *Political Socialization: Trends in the Content of Soviet Education.*
Affiliations: Political Science, California State University–Fresno

Hershey, Marjorie Randon
Dissertation title: *The Making of Campaign Strategy: How Personality and Attitudes Influence Campaign Decision-Making.*
Affiliations: Political Science, Indiana University–Bloomington
Publications: *Party Politics in America* (co-author, 2003);*Running For Office: The Political Education of Campaigners* (1984); *The Making of Campaign Strategy* (1974).

Jackman, Robert William
Dissertation title: *Politics and Social Equality: A Cross-National Analysis.*
Affiliations: Political Science, University of California–Davis; Michigan State University–East Lansing
Publications: *Power Without Force: The Political Capacity of Nation-states* (1993); *Class Awareness in the United States* (co-author, 1983); *Politics and Social Equality: A Comparative Analysis* (1975).

Jackson, Donald Wilson
Dissertation title: *The Role of the State Trial Judge: An Exploratory Study.*
Affiliations: Political Science, Texas Christian University–Fort Worth; Idaho State University–Pocatello; Southern Methodist University–Dallas, Texas; President, Dallas Junior Bar Association
Publications: *The United Kingdom Confronts the European Convention on Human Rights* (1997); *Comparative Judicial Review and Public Policy* (co-editor, 1992).

Kagay, Michael Ralph
Dissertation title: *Origin and Consequences of Relative Power Deprivation.*
Affiliations: Louis Harris and Associates; News Survey Editor, The New York Times; Princeton University–New Jersey; Institute for Social Research, University of Michigan–Ann Arbor; Currently resides in Princeton, NJ.
Publications: *American Democracy: Theory and Reality* (co-author, 1972).

Kirkvliet, Benedict John
Dissertation title: *Peasant Rebellion in the Philippines: Origin and Growth of the HMB.*
Affiliations: University of Hawaii–Honolulu

Kirn, Michael Emmet
Dissertation title: *The Idea of Social Science: Critical Studies in the Theory of Knowledge.*
Affiliations: Dean, Augsburg College–Illinois; Augustana College; Florida State University–Tallahassee

Koppel, Thomas Paul
Dissertation title: *Sources of Change in West German Ostpolitik: the Grand Coalition 1966–1969.*
Affiliations: State University of New York–Stonybrook

Louscher, David John
Dissertation title: *Foreign Military Sales: an Analysis of a Foreign Affairs Undertaking.*
Affiliations: University of Akron–Ohio
Publications: *Civil Military Interaction in Asia and Africa* (co-editor, 1991); *Arm Sales and the U.S. Economy: The Impact of Restricting Military Export* (co-author, 1988); *Marketing Security Assistance: New Perspectives on Arms Sales* (co-editor, 1987); *Technology Transfer and U.S. Security Assistance: The Impact of Licensed Production* (co-author, 1987).

Magill, John Houston, Jr.
Dissertation title: *Labor Unions and Political Socialization in Bolivia.*
Affiliations: Development Alternatives, Inc.; U.S. Agency for International Development–Quito, Ecuador
Publications: *Labor Unions and Political Socialization: A Case Study of Bolivian Workers* (1974).

McCaffery, Jerry Lee
Dissertation title: *The Politics of Tax Exemption.*
Affiliations: University of Georgia–Athens

Moses, Joel Charles
Dissertation title: *Cross-Sectional Analysis of Soviet Regional Parties, 1960–1970.*
Affiliations: Political Science, Iowa State University–Ames
Publications: *Dilemmas in Post-Soviet Transitions* (2002); *Political Implications of Economic Reform in Communist Systems: Communist Dialectic* (co-editor, 1990).

Samoff, Joel
Dissertation title: *Politics, Politicians, and Party: Moshi, Tanzania, 1968–1969.*
Affiliations: Center for African Studies, Stanford University; University of Michigan–Ann Arbor
Publications: *Coping With Crisis: Austerity, Adjustment and Human Resources* (editor, 1994); *Education and Social Transition in the Third World* (co-author, 1990); *Tanzania: Local Politics and the Structure of Power* (1974).

Shockley, John S.
Dissertation title: *Crystal City, Texas: Mexican Americans and Political Change.*
Affiliations: Western Illinois University–Macomb; Political Science, Earlham College–Richmond, Indiana
Publications: *Chicano Revolt in a Texas Town* (1974); *Crystal City, Texas: Los Cinco Mexicanos* (1972).

Silver, Brian David
Dissertation title: *Ethnic Identity Change among Soviet Nationalities: a Statistical Analysis.*
Affiliations: Political Science, Michigan State University–East Lansing; Florida State University–Tallahassee
Publications: *Soviet Asian Ethnic Frontiers* (co-editor, 1979).

Stover, Robert Vernon (Deceased 1986)
Dissertation title: *A Symbolic Interactionist View of Perceptions of and Attitudes toward Law.*
Affiliations: University of Colorado–Boulder
Publications: *Making It and Breaking It: The Fate of Public Interest Commitment During Law School* (editor, 1989).

Theobald, H. Rupert (d.)
Dissertation title: *Equal Representation in Wisconsin: a Study of Legislative and Congressional Apportionment.*
Affiliations: Chief, Wisconsin Legislative Reference Bureau
Publications: *Equal Representation: A Study of Legislative and Congressional Apportionment in Wisconsin* (1970).

Van Meter, Donald Stuart
Dissertation title: *The Policy Implication of State Legislative Reapportionment: A Longitudinal Analysis.*
Affiliations: The Ohio State University–Columbus; University of Wisconsin

Wenner, Lettie Marie
Dissertation title: *Enforcement of Water Pollution Control Laws in the United States.*
Affiliations: Political Science, Northern Illinois University–De Kalb; University of Illinois–Chicago Circle; Northern Illinois University–De Kalb; U.S. Department of Health, Education and Welfare; Foreign Service Officer, U.S. Department of State

Publications: *U.S. Energy and Environmental Interest Groups: Institutional Profiles* (1990); *The Environmental Decade in Court* (1982); *One Environment Under Law: A Public-policy Dilemma* (1976).

Whisler, Marilyn Evon
Dissertation title: *The Politics of Zoning in Metropolitan Rochester.*
Affiliations: Florida Technological University–Orlando; State University of New York–Brockport

1973

Baum, Lawrence Allen
Dissertation title: *The Puzzle of Judicial Behavior* (University of Michigan Press, 1997); *Judicial Influence on Policy: A Perspective and the Patent Case.*
Affiliations: Political Science, Ohio State University–Columbus
Publications: *American Courts: Process and Policy* (1990, 1994, 2001); *The Supreme Court* (1981, 1985, 1989, 1995, 2001).

Bennett, Gordon Anderson
Dissertation title: *Activists and Professionals: China's Revolution in Bureaucracy 1959–1965, a Case Study of the Finance-Trade System.*
Affiliations: Government, University of Texas–Austin

Berkson, Larry Charles
Dissertation title: *The Concept of Cruel and Unusual Punishment.*
Affiliations: University of Florida–Gainesville; Currently resides in Pittsfield, NH.
Publications: *The Supreme Court and Its Publics: The Communication of Policy Decisions* (1978); *Managing the State Courts: Text and Readings* (co-editor, 1977); *The Concept of Cruel and Unusual Punishment* (1975).

Bowler, Marion Kenneth
Dissertation title: *The Nixon Administration's Guaranteed Income Proposal: a Study of Incremental and Non-Incremental Policy-Making.*
Affiliations: Committee on Ways and Means, House of Representatives; Vice President, Pfizer Inc.; University of Maryland

Edwards, George C.
Dissertation title: *Presidential Influence in Congress: Presidential Prestige as a Source of Presidential Power.*
Affiliations: Political Science, Texas A&M University; Tulane University–New Orleans, Louisiana
Publications: *On Deaf Ears: The Limits of the Bully Pulpit.* (2003); *Reinventing the Presidency?* With Kenneth Meier (2003); *Government in America: People, Politics, and Policy,* with Martin P. Wattenberg, and Robert L. Lineberry (2000, 2001, 2002); *Researching The Presidency: Vital Questions, New Approaches* (co-editor, 1993); *Presidential Leadership: Politics and Policy Making* (co-author, 1985, 1990, 2003); *Presidential Approval: A Sourcebook* (co-author, 1990); *At The Margins: Presidential Leadership of Congress* (1989); *National Security and the U.S. Constitution: The Impact

of the Political System (co-editor, 1988); *The Presidency and Public Policy Making* (co-editor, 1985); *Public Policy Implementation* (editor, 1984); *Studying The Presidency* (co-editor, 1983); *Presidential Influence in Congress* (1980); *Implementing Public Policy* (1980); *The Policy Predicament: Making and Implementing Public Policy* (co-author, 1978).

Hone, Thomas Clyde
Dissertation title: *Political Obligation, Consent, and Political Equality.*
Affiliations: United States Department of Defense; Miami University–Oxford, Ohio; Political Science, University of Wisconsin–Madison; Currently resides in Arlington, VA.

Leichter, Howard Martin
Dissertation title: *Political Regime and Public Policy: Study of Two Philippine Cities.*
Affiliations: University of Houston, Texas
Publications: *Health Policy Reform in America: Innovations from the States* (editor, 1992); *Free To Be Foolish: Politics and Health Promotion in the United States and Great Britain* (1991); *A Comparative Approach to Policy Analysis: Health Care Policy in Four Nations* (1979).

Margolis, Joel Paul
Dissertation title: *The Conservation Coalition in the United States Senate, 1933–1968.*
Affiliations: New York State Legislative Commission; Rutgers University–Newark, New Jersey

Oppenheimer, Bruce I.
Dissertation title: *The Effects of Policy Variation on Interest Group Behavior in the Congressional Process: The Oil Industry in Two Domestic Issues.*
Affiliations: Political Science, Vanderbilt University–Nashville; Brandeis University–Waltham, Massachusetts
Publications: *Senate Exceptionalism* (2002); *Interest Groups and Influence,* with John R. Wright (2003); *Congress Reconsidered* (co-editor, 1977, 1981, 1985, 1989, 2001); *Oil and the Congressional Process: The Limits of Symbolic Politics* (1974).

Sarat, Austin Dean
Dissertation title: *Compliance and the Law: An Attitude.*
Affiliations: Political Science, Amherst College–Massachusetts; Law and Political Science, Yale University Law School
Publications: *Cultural Analysis, Cultural Studies, and the Law: Moving Beyond Legal Realism* (co-author, 2003); *The Place of Law* (co-author, 2003); *Law's Madness* (co-author, 2003); *Lives In the Law* (co-author, 2002); *Looking Back at Law's Century* (co-author, 2002); *History, Memory, and the Law* (co-author, 2002); *Human Rights: Concepts, Contests, Contingencies* (co-author, 2002); *Law, Violence, and the Possibility of Justice* (2002); *Pain, Death, and the Law* (2001); *Legal Rights: Historical and Philosophical Perspectives* (co-editor, 1996); *Divorce Lawyers and Their Clients: Power and Meaning in the Legal Process* (co-author, 1995); *Identities, Politics, and Rights* (co-editor, 1995); *The Rhetoric of Law* (co-editor, 1994); *Law In Everyday Life* (co-editor, 1993); *Law's Violence* (co-editor, 1992); *Narrative, Violence,*

and the Law: The Essays of Robert Cover (co-editor, 1992); *The Fate of Law* (co-editor, 1991); *Sitting In Judgment: The Sentencing of White-Collar Criminals* (co-author, 1988); *The Policy Dilemma: Federal Crime Policy and the Law Enforcement Assistance Administration, 1968–1978* (co-author, 1980); *American Court Systems: Readings in Judicial Process and Behavior* (co-editor, 1978).

Schumaker, Paul David
Dissertation title: *The Power of Protest Groups: System Responsiveness to Citizen Demands.*
Affiliations: Political Science, University of Kansas–Lawrence
Publications: *Choosing a President: The Electoral College and Beyond,* with Burdett Loomis (2001); *Critical Pluralism, Democratic Performance, and Community Power* (1991).

Tripp, Helen Marshall Carter (Wanke)
Dissertation title: *Political Justice: the African Experience: Studies in Nigeria, Uganda and Zambia.*
Affiliations: Ahmadu Bello University–Nigeria; Wayne State University–Detroit; Southwest Missouri State; U.S. Foreign Service; Currently resides in Alexandria, VA.
Publications: *American Government* (co-author).

Turner, Thomas Edwin
Dissertation title: *A Century of Political Conflict in Sankuru (Congo-Zaire).*
Affiliations: Wheeling Jesuit College–West Virginia; National University of Zaire, Lumumbashi; University of Florida–Gainesville; Université Libre du Congo
Publications: *The Rise and Decline of the Zairian State* (co-author, 1985); *Ethnogenèse et Nationalisme en Afrique Centrale. Aux Racines de Patrice Lumemba* (2000).

Waligorski, Conrad Peter
Dissertation title: *Liberal Economics and Democracy: Keynes, Galbraith, Thurow, and Reich* (University Press of Kansas, 1997); *Radical Traditionalism: William Cobbett in the Industrial Revolution.*
Affiliations: Political Science, University of Arkansas–Fayetteville
Publications: *The Political Theory of Conservative Economists* (1990).

Wichaidit, Tawat
Dissertation title: *Provincial Administration in Thailand: Its Development and Present Problems.*
Affiliations: Secretary-General to Prime Minister; Lecturer and Dean of Students, National Institute of Development Administration–Bangkok, Thailand

1974

Arnold, Phil Warren
Dissertation title: *Political Integration in Culturally Plural States: A Comparison of Political Preferences in Canada, Belgium and Argentina.*
Affiliations: San Francisco Recreation and Parks Department; Legislative Reference Bureau, State of Wisconsin

Beckman, Peter Roane
Dissertation title: *The Influence of the American Military Establishment on American Foreign Policy 1946–1970.*
Affiliations: Political Science, Hobart and William Smith Colleges–Geneva, New York
Publications: *Women In World Politics: An Introduction* (co-editor, 1995); *Women, Gender, and World Politics: Perspectives, Policies, and Prospects* (co-editor, 1994); *World Politics in the Twentieth Century* (1984).

Dean, Gillian Hendrika
Dissertation title: *Impact and Feedback Effects: Divorce Policy and Divorce in the American States.*
Affiliations: Vanderbilt University–Nashville, Tennessee; Currently resides in Saratoga, CA.

Druker, Marvin Jay
Dissertation title: *The Development and Structure of Public Attitudes Toward Multiple Levels of American Government.*
Affiliations: Lewiston-Auburn College, University of South Maine–Lewiston; Political Science, Western Michigan University–Kalamazoo

Flannery, Richard F., Jr.
Dissertation title: *Civil-Military Relations in Wartime: U.S. and Soviet Union, 1940–1945.*
Affiliations: University of Vermont–Burlington; Currently resides in Sheboygan, WI.

Hammergren, Linn Ann
Dissertation title: *Politics in the Periphery: A Study in National Integration and the Development of Local Political Organization.*
Affiliations: Vanderbilt University–Nashville, Tennessee; Currently resides in Lima.
Publications: *Development and the Politics of Administrative Reform: Lessons from Latin America* (1983); *The Politics of Justice and Justice Reform in Latin America: The Peruvian Case in Comparative Perspective* (1998).

Keller, Edmond Joseph, Jr.
Dissertation title: *Education, Manpower, and National Development: Secondary Schooling and Socialization in Kenya.*
Affiliations: Political Science, University of California–Los Angeles; University of California–Santa Barbara; Indiana University–Bloomington
Publications: *Africa in the New International Order: Rethinking State Sovereignty and Regional Security* (co-editor, 1996); *South Africa in Southern Africa: Domestic Change and International Conflict* (co-editor, 1989); *Revolutionary Ethiopia: From Empire to People's Republic* (1988); *Afro-Marxist Regimes: Ideology and Public Policy* (co-editor, 1987).

Kelso, William Alton
Dissertation title: *In Defense of Pluralism: A Comparative Study of Democratic Theory.*
Affiliations: Political Science, University of Florida–Gainesville; Thiel College–Greenville, Pennsylvania
Publications: *Poverty and the Underclass: Changing Perceptions of the Poor in America* (1994); *American Democratic Theory: Pluralism and Its Critics* (1978).

Littig, David M.
Dissertation title: *The Politics of Mass Transportation: State and City Policy-Making in a Federal System.*
Affiliations: University of Wisconsin–Green Bay; University of South Dakota

Lockard, Kathleen Goodman
Dissertation title: *Religion and Political Development in Uganda 1962–72.*
Affiliations: West High School; Northwestern University–Evanston, Illinois

Loomis, Burdett Anderson
Dissertation title: *Resources into Results? Congressional Campaigns in Marginal Districts.*
Affiliations: Political Science, University of Kansas–Lawrence; Knox College–Galesburg, Illinois; Indiana University–Bloomington
Publications: *Choosing a President: The Electoral College and Beyond* (co-author, 2001); *The Contemporary Congress* (2000); *American Politics: Classic and Contemporary Readings* (co-editor, 2002); *The Sound of Money: How Political Interests Get What They Want* (1999); *Interest Group Politics* (co-editor, 1983, 1986, 1991, 1995); *Time, Politics, and Policies: A Legislative Year* (1994); *The New American Politician: Ambition, Entrepreneurship, and the Changing Face of Political life* (1988).

McMurtry, Virginia Anne
Dissertation title: *Foreign Aid and Political Development: The American Experience in West Africa.*
Affiliations: Library of Congress

Mingst, Karen Ann
Dissertation title: *The Process of International Policy Making in Regulation of Tropical Agriculture Products: Coffee and Cocoa.*
Affiliations: Political Science, University of Kentucky–Lexington; Louisiana State University–Baton Rouge
Publications: *Essential Readings in World Politics* (co-editor, 2001); *The United Nations in the Post-Cold War Era* (co-author, 1995); *Politics and the African Development Bank* (1990); *The United States and Multilateral Institutions: Patterns of Changing Instrumentality and Influence* (co-editor, 1990).

Penikis, Janis John
Dissertation title: *Foreign Opinion and American Foreign Policy: the Orientation of American Foreign Policy Makers Toward Non-Governmental Opinion Abroad.*
Affiliations: University of Indiana–South Bend; University of Minnesota–Minneapolis
Publications: *Latvia: Independence Renewed* (1997).

Ray, John Wallace
Dissertation title: *Immanuel Kant and George Hegel on Will, Freedom, and the State.*
Affiliations: Montana Tech

Sbragia, Alberta Mary
Dissertation title: *Urban Autonomy Within the Unitary State: A Case Study on Public Housing Politics in Milan, Italy.*
Affiliations: Political Science, West European Studies Program, University of Pittsburgh
Publications: *Euro-Politics: Institutions and Policymaking in the New European Community* (editor, 1991); *The Municipal Money Chase: The Politics of Local Government Finance* (editor, 1983).

Tillema, Richard Gordon
Dissertation title: *Apartheid in South African Education.*
Affiliations: Budget Analyst, Department of Health Services, State of Wisconsin

Trice, Robert Holmes, Jr.
Dissertation title: *Domestic Political Interests and American Policy in the Middle East: Pro-Israel, Pro-Arab and Corporate Non-Governmental Actors and the Making of American Foreign Policy, 1966–71.*
Affiliations: Vice President for Business Development, McDonnell Douglas Aerospace; The Ohio State University–Columbus; Currently resides in St. Louis, MO.
Publications: *Interest Groups and the Foreign Policy Process: U.S. Policy in the Middle East* (1976).

1975

Chinn, Jeffrey Bernard
Dissertation title: *The Socio-Demographic Consequences of Urbanization in the Soviet Union.*
Affiliations: University of Missouri–Columbia; University of Louisville

Cohen, Dennis Julius
Dissertation title: *Poverty and Development in Jakarta.*
Affiliations: The Monterey Institute of Foreign Studies; Currently resides in Lafayette Hill, PA.
Publications: *Political Economy of Africa: Selected Readings* (co-editor, 1981).

Freeman, Gary Pete
Dissertation title: *British and French Policies on Immigration and Race Relations, 1945–1974.*
Affiliations: Government, University of Texas–Austin; University of Pennsylvania
Publications: *Immigrant Labor and Racial Conflict in Industrial Societies: The French and British Experience, 1945–1975* (1979)

Gudger, William Michael
Dissertation title: *The Regulation of Multinational Corporations in the Mexican Automotive Industry.*
Currently resides in Annapolis, MD.

Harris, Craig Marshall
Dissertation title: *The Development of Community Action Agencies in Wisconsin and the Implementation of Federal Social Policy.*
Affiliations: University of Florida–Gainesville; Currently resides in East Setauket, NY.

Hartigan, Emily Albrink Fowler
Dissertation title: *Social Justice: Substance and Procedure.*
Affiliations: Saint Mary's University–San Antonio; Assistant Dean of Students, College of Letters & Science, University of Wisconsin–Madison

Jenkins, William Oscar, Jr.
Dissertation title: *The Role of the Supreme Court in National Merger Policy: 1950–1973.*
Affiliations: U.S. General Accounting Office; University of Mississippi; Wayne State University

Johnson, Victor Charles
Dissertation title: *The House Foreign Affairs and Senate Foreign Relations Committees.*
Affiliations: Association of International Education

Joseph, Lawrence Bruce
Dissertation title: *Social Science, Public Policy, and Political Theory: The Problem of Equality of Educational Opportunity.*
Affiliations: Associate Director, Center for Urban Research and Policy Studies, University of Chicago
Publications: *Affordable Housing and Public Policy: Strategies for Metropolitan Chicago* (editor, 1993); *Paying for Health Care: Public Policy Choices for Illinois* (1992); *Crime Communities and Public Policy* (editor, 1995); *Education Policy for the 21st Century: Challenges and Opportunities in Standards-Based Reforms* (editor, 2001).

Julian, William Burt
Dissertation title: *The United States Senate and Military Spending: An Exploration of the Relationship Between Issues and Coalitions.*
Affiliations: Monmouth College–Illinois; Central College–Pella, Iowa

Kann, Mark Eliot
Dissertation title: *Consent Theory and Social-Democratic Thought: A Comparative Analysis of Intellectual Continuity and Innovation.*
Affiliations: Political Science, University of Southern California
Publications: *A Republic of Men: The American Founders, Gendered Language, and Patriarchal Politics* (1998); *On The Man Question: Gender and Civic Virtue in America* (1991); *Middle Class Radicalism in Santa Monica* (1986); *The Future of American Democracy: Views from The Left* (editor, 1983); *The American Left: Failures and Fortunes* (1982); *The Problem of Authority in America* (co-editor, 1981).

Mion, Mario Romano
Dissertation title: *Citizenship in the American Experience.*
Affiliations: University of Wisconsin–Eau Claire; Columbus College–Georgia

Newbury, Mary Catharine (Atterbury)
Dissertation title: *The Cohesion of Oppression: A Century of Clientship in Kinyaga, Rwanda.*
Affiliations: Political Science, University of North Carolina–Chapel Hill; Dalhousie University; Smith College
Publications: *Cohesion of Oppression: Clientship and Ethnicity in Rwanda, 1860–1960* (1975).

Nzongola-Ntalaja, Georges
Dissertation title: *Urban Administration in Zaire.*
Affiliations: African Studies, Howard Univesity; Université Libre du Congo–Kisangani; National University of Zaire–Lumumbashi; Atlanta University
Publications: *Resistance and Repression in the Congo: Strengths and Weaknesses of the Democracy Movement, 1956–2000* (2002); *The Congo from Leopold to Kabila: A People's History,* (2002); *Nation-Building and State Building in Africa* (1993); *The African Crisis: The Way Out* (1992); *Revolution and Counter-Revolution in Africa: Essays in Contemporary Politics* (1987); *Proletarianization and Class Struggle in Africa* (co-editor, 1983).

Peroff, Kathleen Schmidt
Dissertation title: *A Time-Series Analysis of Health and Social Welfare Expenditure Policy in Canada, The United Kingdom and the United States.*
Currently resides in Washington, DC.

Pfiffner, James Price
Dissertation title: *Presidential Impoundment of Funds and Congressional Control of the Budget.*
Affiliations: Public and International Affairs, George Mason University–Fairfax, Virginia; University of California–Riverside
Publications: *Understanding the Presidency* 3rd ed. (co-author, 2003); *The Modern Presidency* (1994, 1998, 2000); *The Future of Merit: Twenty Years After the Civil Service Reform Act* (co-author, 2000); *The Managerial Presidency* (editor, 1991); *The Strategic Presidency: Hitting the Ground Running* (1988); *The President, The Budget, and Congress: Impoundment and the 1974 Budget Act* (1979);

Rhynart, Frederick William
Dissertation title: *Community Control and Democratic Theory.*
Affiliations: University of Wisconsin–Baraboo; University of Wisconsin–Eau Claire; Currently resides in Newport, KY.

Sherman, Neal Philip
Dissertation title: *A Political-Economic Analysis of Ugandan Dairy Policy.*
Affiliations: Development Studies Center–Ramat-Aviv, Israel; Hebrew University–Jerusalem
Publications: *Cooperatives & Development: Agricultural Politics in Ghana and Uganda* (co-author, 1981).

Thaxton, Ralph A., Jr.
Dissertation title: *When Peasants Took Power: Toward a Theory of Peasant Revolution in China.*
Affiliations: Brandeis University; Rutgers University
Publications: *Salt of the Earth: The Political Origins of Peasant Protest and Communist Revolution in China* (1997); *China Turned Rightside Up: Revolutionary Legitimacy in the Peasant World* (1983).

Yoast, Richard Alan
Dissertation title: *The Development of Argentine Anarchism: A Socio-Ideological Analysis.*
Affiliations: AMA Office of Alcohol and Other Drug Abuse; Wisconsin Clearinghouse

Zorn, Stephen Alan
Dissertation title: *Federal District Judges and School Segregation Cases in the South, 1968–1971.*
Publications: *Financing Mining Projects in Developing Countries: A United Nations Study* (co-author, 1979).

1976

Bossert, Thomas John
Dissertation title: *Political Argument and Policy Issues in Allende's Chile.*
Affiliations: University Research; Independent Consultant, Los Angeles
Publications: *Promise of Development: Theories of Change in Latin America*, ed. (1986).

Cocks, Peter Greenfield
Dissertation title: *Political Integration and the Growth of Capitalism in Western Europe: A Study of Anglo-Scottish Unification, Nineteenth Century German and Post World War II European Unification.*
Affiliations: Faculty of Division of Social Sciences, Simon's Rock College

Davidson, John Richard
Dissertation title: *The Implementation of the Political Development Goals of the Alliance for Progress.*
Currently resides in Chicago, IL.

Elling, Richard Clement
Dissertation title: *State Parties in the Policy Process: A Comparative and Longitudinal Analysis of State Party Platform Issue-Content and Legislative Performance.*
Affiliations: Political Science, Wayne State University
Publications: *Public Management in the States: A Comparative Study of Administrative Performance and Politics* (1992).

Estes, William Edwin.
Dissertation title: *The Kindness of Strangers: A Critique of Majority Rule in Modern Democracy.*
Affiliations: King County–Washington

Herring, Ronald Jackson
Dissertation title: *Redistributive Agrarian Polity: Land and Credit in South Asia.*
Affiliations: Government, Cornell University
Publications: *Carrots, Sticks, and Ethnic Conflict: Rethinking Development Assistance* (co-author, 2001); *Land to the Tiller: The Political Economy of Agrarian Reform in South Asia* (1983).

Johnson, Kay Ann
Dissertation title: *The Politics of Women's Rights and Family Reform in China.*
Affiliations: Social Science, Hampshire College
Publications: *Women, the Family, and Peasant Revolution in China* (1983).

Kanervo, David Wayne
Dissertation title: *Competition, Constituency, and the Welfare Programs in Congress.*
Affiliations: Political Science, Austin Peay State University

Levy, Jack Steven
Dissertation title: *Military Power, Alliances and Technology: An Analysis of Some Structural Determinants of International War among the Great Powers.*
Affiliations: Political Science, Rutgers University
Publications: *Military Power, Alliances, and Technology: An Analysis of Some Structural Determinants of International War among the Great Powers* (1976); *War in the Modern Great Power System, 1485–1975* (1983); *Systems, Stability, and Statecraft : Essays on the International History of Modern Europe* (co-editor, 2004).

Miller, Mary Lenn (Dixon)
Dissertation title: *When the Center Gives: The Impact of the Regionalization of French Planning, 1968–1972.*
Affiliations: Texas A&M University Press

Nilson, Douglas Carlyle Jr.
Dissertation title: *Some Political And Social Psychological Determinants of Perceptions Toward Active Political Dissension.*
Affiliations: Political Science, Idaho State University

Odell, John Stephen
Dissertation title: *The United States in the International Monetary System: Sources of Foreign-Policy Change.*
Affiliations: International Relations, University of Southern California
Publications: *Negotiating the World Economy* (2000); *U.S. International Monetary Policy: Markets, Power, and Ideas as Sources of Change* (1982).

Seitz, John Lewis
Dissertation title: *The Gap Between Expectations and Performance: An Exploration of American Foreign Aid to Brazil, Iran, and Pakistan, 1950–1970.*
Affiliations: Government, Woffard College

Publications: *Global Issues: An Introduction* (2001); *The Politics of Development: An Introduction to Global Issues* (1988).

Staudt, Kathleen Ann
Dissertation title: *Agricultural Policy, Political Power, And Women Farmers in Western Kenya.*
Affiliations: Political Science, University of Texas–El Paso
Publications: *Pledging Allegiance: Learning Nationalism at the El Paso-Juarez Border,* (co-author, 2003); *Rethinking Empowerment: Gender and Development in a Global/Local World* (co-author, 2002); *Fronteras No Mas: Toward Social Justice at the US-Mexico Border,* (co-author, 2002); *Policy, Politics & Gender: Women Gaining Ground* (1998); *Political Science & Feminisms: Integration or Transformation?*(1997); *Women, Foreign Assistance, and Advocacy Administration* (1985); *Managing Development: State, Society, and International Contexts* (1991).

Stoner, Floyd Eugene
Dissertation title: *Implementation of Ambiguous Legislative Language: Title I of the Elementary and Secondary Education Act.*
Affiliations: American Bankers Association

1977

Farmer, Kenneth Calvin (d.)
Dissertation title: *Ukrainian Nationalism and Soviet Nationalities Policy: 1957–1972.*
Publications: *The Soviet Administrative Elite* (1992).

Grasso, Patrick G.
Dissertation title: *State Politics and Economic Growth: The Centralization-Concentration-Regressivity Syndrome.*
Affiliations: Assistant Director, Program Evaluation and Methodology Division, U.S. General Accounting Office; Operations Evaluation, World Bank; Director of Evaluation and Learning Resources, Pew Charitable Trust
Publications: *World Bank Operations Evaluation Department: The First 30 years* (co-author, 2003).

Guasti, Laura Maria
Dissertation title: *State-Capital Relationship in the Context of Industrialization: Peru 1968–1976.*

Leeds, Patricia Lee (Giles)
Dissertation title: *The Conditions for Issue Voting: A Comparison of Presidential and Congressional Elections.*

Morrison, Minion K.C.
Dissertation title: *Ethnicity and Political Integration: Ashanti, Ghana.*
Affiliations: Political Science, University of Missouri–Columbia
Publications: *African Americans and Political Participation: A Reference Handbook* (2003); *Ethnicity and Political Integration: The Case of Ashanti, Ghana* (1982).

Oculi, Okello
Dissertation title: *Colonial Capitalism and Malnutrition: Nigeria, Kenya, and Jamaica.*
Affiliations: Political Science, Ahamada Bello University, Zaria, Nigeria.
Publications: *Discourses on African Affairs* (1997, 2000); *Political Economy of Malnutrition* (1987).

Oleszczuk,Thomas
Dissertation title: *Participation in Yugoslavia Workers' Councils.*
Currently resides in Brooklyn, NY,
Publications: *Political Justice in the USSR: Dissent and Representation in Lithuania, 1969–1987* (1988).

Peroff, Kathleen A. Schmidt
Dissertation title: *A Times Series Analysis of Health and Social Welfare Expenditures Policy in Canada, United Kingdom and the United States.*
Affiliations: Office of Management and Budget, Executive Office of the President; HUD, Washington D.C.

Peroff, Nicholas Carl
Dissertation title: *Menominee Termination and Restoration.*
Affiliations: Public Administration, University of Missouri–Kansas City
Publications: *Menominee Drums: Tribal Termination and Restoration, 1954–1974* (1982).

Picard, Louis Alexander
Dissertation title: *Role Changes Among Field Administrators in Botswana: Administrative Attitudes and Social Change.*
Affiliations: Graduate School of Public and International Affairs, University of Pittsburgh
Publications: *Attitudes and Development: The District Administration in Tanzania* (1980); *Bureaucrats, Cattle and Public Policy: Land Tenure Changes in Botswana* (1980); *The Politics of Development in Botswana: A Model for Success?* (1987); *Policy Reform for Sustainable Development: The Institutional Imperative* (co-editor, 1994); *Policy Reform for Sustainable Development in the Caribbean* (co-editor, 1996); *Subnational Politics in the 1980s: Organization, Reorganization and Economic Development* (1987).

Schatzberg, Michael Gordon
Dissertation title: *Bureaucracy, Business, Beer: The Political Dynamics of Class Formation in Lisala, Zaire.*
Affiliations: Political Science, University Wisconsin–Madison
Publications: *Political Legitimacy in Middle Africa: Father, Family, Food* (2001); *The Dialectics of Oppression in Zaire* (1988). *Politics and Class in Zaire: Bureaucracy, Business, and Beer in Lisala* (1980). *Mobutu or Chaos?: The United States and Zaire, 1960–1990* (1991).

Shelley, Mack Clayton II
Dissertation title: *The Conservative Coalition in the U.S. Congress, 1933–1976: Time Series Analysis of a Legislative Policy Coalition.*

Affiliations: Political Science and Statistics, Iowa State University
Publications: *Readings in American Government,* (co-editor, 4th ed., 2003); *American Government and Politics Today: The Essentials* (co-author, 1986); *Redefining Family Policy: Implications for the 21st Century,* (co-author, 2000); *The Permanent Majority: The Conservative Coalition in the United States Congress* (1989).

Steinberg, Jules
Dissertation title: *An Examination of the Use of the Idea of a Consent Theory Of Political Obligation in Liberal-Democratic Political Thought.*
Affiliations: Political Science, Denison University
Publications: *Hannah Arendt on the Holocaust: A Study of the Suppression of Truth* (2000).

Vadi, Jose Miguel
Dissertation title: *Mobilization Problems of Chicanos in a Southern California City.*
Affiliations: Political Science, California State Polytechnical University–Pomona

Zwier, Robert
Dissertation title: *Decision Making By Legislative Specialists.*
Affiliations: Political Science, Northwestern College
Publications: *Born-again Politics: The New Christian Right in America* (1982).

1978

Cirn, John Thomas
Dissertation title: *The Political Life of Organized Medicine in Wisconsin.*
Currently resides in Crete, IL.

Dahm, Charles William
Dissertation title: *Authority and Power in the Roman Catholic Church: Ideological and Political Constraints on Democratization in the Authoritarian Institution.*
Currently resides in Chicago, IL.
Publications: *Power and Authority in the Catholic Church: Cardinal Cody in Chicago* (co-author, 1981).

Daniels, Stephen
Dissertation title: *The Use of Social Science, the Constitution, and the Rule of Law: An Interpretation and Analysis of the Empirical Justification of Constitutional Policy.*
Affiliations: Senior Research Analyst, American Bar Foundation

Dubois, Philip Leon
Dissertation title: *Judicial Elections in the States: Patterns and Consequences.*
Affiliations: Political Science, University of North Carolina, Charlotte
Publications: *The Analysis of Judicial Reform*, editor (1982). *Administrative Structures in Large District Courts: A Report to the Conference of Metropolitan District Chief Judges* (1981).

Fulenwider (Knoche), Claire F.
Dissertation title: *Social Movements and Political Change: An Empirical Analysis of Feminism.*
Affiliations: A & C Enercom; Currently resides in Madison, Wisconsin

Harman, John David
Dissertation title: *Rights, Obligations and Social Freedom: The Case of Abortion.*
Affiliations: Political Science, St. John Fisher College

Huddleston, Mark Wayne
Dissertation title: *The Road to Somewhere: Transportation Politics and Policy Change in Wisconsin.*
Affiliations: President, Ohio Wesleyan; Political Science, University of Delaware
Publications: *Comparative Public Administration: An Annotated Bibliography* (1984); *The Highest Civil Service in the United States: Quest for Reform* (co-editor, 1996).

Miller, Mark James
Dissertation title: *The Problem of Foreign Worker Participation and Representation in France, Switzerland and the Federal Republic of Germany.*
Affiliations: Political Science, University of Delaware
Publications: *The Age of Migration: International Population Movements in the Modern World* (co-author, 2003); *Administering Foreign-Worker Programs: Lessons from Europe* (1982); *Foreign Workers in Western Europe: An Emerging Political Force* (1981).

Schier, Steven Edward
Dissertation title: *The Rules and the Game: Democratic National Convention Delegate Selection in Iowa and Wisconsin 1968–1976.*
Affiliations: Political Science, Carleton College
Publications: *Congress: Games and Strategies*, 2nd ed. (2003); *By Invitation Only: The Rise of Exclusive Politics in the United States* (2000); *The Postmodern Presidency: Bill Clinton's Legacy in U.S. Politics* (2000); *A Decade of Deficits: Congressional Thought and Fiscal Action* (1992). *Political Economy in Western Democracies* (editor, 1985).

Sherman, Dennnis Mark
Dissertation title: *The National Security Act, A Blueprint for the Congressional Role in Weapons Development: A Case Study of the B-70 Bomber.*
Affiliations: Mobil Oil Corporation; Currently resides in Upperville, VA.

Sherman, Gail Richardson
Dissertation title: *Images of Power, Theoretical Investigations–After Wittgenstein–of "the Multinational Corporation" as a Political Concept.*

Siminoski, Dan
Dissertation title: *The Myth of "Comprehensive Urban Planning:" A Critical Study of the Development of the Los Angeles General Plan.*
Affiliations: Texas Tech University

Wiener, Don Edward
Dissertation title: *Congress and Natural Gas Policy.*
Currently resides in Miami Beach, FL.

1979

Akridge, Paul B.
Dissertation title: *The Politics of Energy Policy: Regulation of Electric Utility Rate Structure Design By the Public Service Commission of Wisconsin.*
Affiliations: Private consultant, IBM; resides in Prince George's County, MD

Callan, James J.
Dissertation title: *Persons and the Governance of Formal Organization: A Contractarian View.*
Affiliations: James J. Callan Inc.; Currently resides Milwaukee, WI.

Debardeleben, Joan T.
Dissertation title: *Theoretical and Ideological Discussion of Environmental Problems in the Soviet Union and East Germany 1965-77.*
Affiliations: Carleton University, Canada
Publications: *The Environment and Marxism-Leninism: the Soviet and East German Experience* (1985); *Esoteric Policy Debate: Nuclear Safety Issues in the USSR and GDR* (1983); *Soviet Politics in Transition* (1992); *Beyond the Monolith: the Emergence of Regionalism in Post-Soviet Russia* (co-editor, 1997).

Edoh, Anthony (Tony) A.
Dissertation title: *Decentralization and Local Government Reforms in Ghana.*
Affiliations: Senior Lecturer of Political Science, Ahamada Bello University, Zaire, Nigeria.
Publications: *Nigeria, a Republic in Ruins* (co-editor, 1986).

Evanson, Robert K.
Dissertation title: *Political Terror in Czechoslovakia and the Soviet Union: A Study of Comparative Communism.*
Affiliations: Political Science, University Missouri–Kansas City

Exoo, Calvin.
Dissertation title: *Ethnic Culture and the Incentives of Political Party Activists in Two Midwestern Cities.*
Affiliations: Government, St. Lawrence University
Publications: *Democracy Upside Down: Public Opinion and Cultural Hegemony in the United States* (1987).

Hart-Bohne, Brenda
Dissertation title: *The Public Defender as Advocate: An Organizational Perspective on Public Defender Representation.*
Currently resides in Germany

Pika, Joseph A. III
Dissertation title: *The White House Office of Congressional Relations: Exploring Institutionalization.*
Affiliations: Political Science, University of Delaware
Publications: *The Politics of the Presidency* (co-author, 2002); *The Presidential Contest: With a Guide to the 1992 Presidential Race* (co-author, 1992).

1980

Cline, Barry Grayson
Dissertation title: *The Area Agency on Aging Concept: Policy Implementation in Pennsylvania.*

German, Lawrence Paul
Dissertation title: *Power and Interdependence: United States Policy Toward Nigeria 1960–78.*
Affiliations: History & Political Science, Belmont College

Gosling, James John
Dissertation title: *The Wisconsin Budgetary Process: A Study of Participant Influence and Choice.*
Affiliations: Dean, University of Utah
Publications: *Budgetary Politics in American Governments* (2002); *Politics and Policy in American States and Communities* (co-author, 2002); *Budgetary Politics in American Governments* (1991); *Politics, Policy, and Management in the American States* (co-author, 1989).

Harris, Scott Allen
Dissertation title: *Domestic Politics and the Formulation of the United States China Policy, 1949–1972.*
Affiliations: SAIC; Office of U.S. Senator Pell

Hartwig, Richard E.
Dissertation title: *"Administrative Responsibility" in Colombian Government: Organization Theory, Transportation Policy and the Ministry of Public Works.*
Affiliations: Political Science, Texas A&M University
Publications: *Roads to Reason: Transportation, Administration, and Rationality in Columbia* (1983).

Jones, Walter
Dissertation title: *On the Basis of Knowledge: The Use of Program Evaluations in Federal Compensatory Education Policymaking.*
Affiliations: Social and Behavioral Sciences, College of DuPage

Kendrigan, Mary Lou
Dissertation title: *Democratic Theory and Equality Between the Sexes.*
Affiliations: Social Science, Lansing Community College
Publications: *Gender Differences: Their Impact on Public Policy* (editor, 1991). *Political Equality in a Democratic Society: Women in the United States* (1984).

Woolley, John T.
Dissertation title: *The Federal Reserve and the Political Economy of Monetary Policy.*
Affiliations: School of Business Administration, Georgetown University–Washington, D.C.
Publications: *Monetary Politics: The Federal Reserve and the Politics of Monetary Policy* (1984).

Yamvu, Makasu A M'Teba (d.)
Dissertation title: *Political Learning: A Study of the Effects of Social Relations upon Political Knowledge, the Case of Ayos (Cameroon).*
Affiliations: University of Kisangani, Zaire.

1981

Bajusz, William.
Dissertation title: *The Collective Management of Defense: Collaborative Weapons Acquisition in NATO.*
Currently resides in Fairfax, VA.
Publications: *Arms Sales and the U.S. Economy: The Impact of Restricting Military Export* (co-author, 1988).

Browning, Robert X.
Dissertation title: *Political and Economic Predictors of Policy Outcomes: U.S. Social Welfare Expenditures, 1947–1977.*
Affiliations: Public Affairs, Purdue University.
Publications: *Politics and Social Welfare Policy in the United States* (1986).

Harris, Martha Ann (Caldwell)
Dissertation title: *Petroleum Politics in Japan: State and Industry in a Changing Political Context.*
Affiliations: National Academy of Sciences; Science and Technology Assessment Office, US Congress
Publications: *Energy Market Restructuring and the Environment: Governance and Public Goods in Globally Integrated Markets* (2002).

Trask, Haunani-Kay
Dissertation title: *Eros and Power: The Promise of Feminist Theory.*
Affiliations: Ethnic Studies Program, University of Hawaii
Publications: *Night Is a Sharkskin Drum* (2002)

1982

Bianga, Waruzi (d. 1992)
Dissertation title: *Peasant, State and Rural Development in Post-independent Zaire: A Case Study of "Reforme Rurale" 1970–1980 and its Implications.*

Cohen, Marc
Dissertation title: *Food for Development: The Carter Administration and United States Food Aid to Southeast Asia.*
Affiliations: Asia Resource Center; Asia Watch, Washington, D.C.
Publications: *Taiwan at the Crossroads: Human Rights, Political Development, and Social Change on the Beautiful Island* (1988).

Cook, Timothy
Dissertation title: *The Politics of Storytelling: Children's Literature and the Renewal of Political Cultures.*

Affiliations: Political Science, Williams College
Publications: *Governing with the News: The News Media as a Political Institution* (1998); *Making Laws and Making News: Media Strategies in the U.S. House of Representatives* (1989).

Cranmer, William H.H.
Dissertation title: *Fiscal Policy-Making in Sri Lanka, 1946–1973: A "Group-Benefit" Analysis.*
Affiliations: College of St. Catherine, St. Paul

Fiscus, Ronald Jerry (d.)
Dissertation title: *Before the Velvet Curtain: The Connecticut Contraceptive Cases as a Study in Constitutional Law and Supreme Court Behavior.*

Harrington, Christine
Dissertation title: *Shadow Courts: A Study of Informal Dispute Processing.*
Affiliations: Politics, New York University
Publications: *Administrative Law and Politics* (co-author, 2000); *Shadow Justice: The Ideology and Institutionalization of Alternatives to Court* (1985); *The Presidency in American Politics* (co-editor, 1989).

Kundanis, George
Dissertation title: *Ardent Advocates of Action: The Idea of Strong Presidential Leadership in the United States 1885–1965.*
Affiliations: House Democratic Steering & Policy Committee, U.S. Congress

Lufler, Henry
Dissertation title: *The Supreme Court Goes to School: Goss v. Lopez and School Suspensions.*
Affiliations: Assistant to the Chancellor of Education, University of Wisconsin–Madison

Pletcher, James
Dissertation title: *Agricultural Policy and the Political Crisis in Zambia.*
Affiliations: Political Science, Denison University/Knapp Hall

Ragsdale, Lyn
Dissertation title: *Presidents and Publics: The Dialogue of Presidential Leadership, 1949–1979.*
Affiliations: Political Science, University of Arizona–Tucson
Publications: *The Elusive Executive: Discovering Statistical Patterns in the Presidency* (co-author, 1988).

Wong, John On-Fat
Dissertation title: *Security Requirements in Northeast Asia.*
Affiliations: Information Processing, University of Wisconsin–Madison

1983

Burant, Stephen Robert
Dissertation title: *A Theory of Revolutionary Conspiracy.*
Affiliations: US Information Agency, US Department of State
Publications: *East Germany: A Country Study* (1988). *Hungary: A Country Study* (1990).

Conant, James K.
Dissertation title: *Executive Decision-Making in the State.*
Affiliations: Eagleton Institute of Politics, Rutgers University; Political Science, University Oklahoma–Norman

Machung, Anne Carol
Dissertation title: *From Psyche to Technic: The Politics of Office Work.*

Marquez, Benjamin
Dissertation title: *Power and Politics in a Chicano Barrio.*
Affiliations: University Wisconsin–Madison; University of Utah.
Publications: *LULAC: The Evolution of a Mexican American Political Organization* (1993); *Power and Politics in a Chicano Barrio: A Study of Mobilization Efforts and Community Power in El Paso* (1985); *Constructing Identities in a Chicano Barrio: Choosing Issues, Taking Sides* (2003).

Schneider, Gregory
Dissertation title: *Ideology, Law and Public Policy.*
Affiliations: Public Defender, State of Wisconsin
Publications: *Conservatism in America Since 1930: A Reader* (2003)

1984

Ajene, Oga
Dissertation title: *Leadership Perception of Issues and Foreign Policy Difference: A Study of Foreign Policy Decisions in Nigeria, Ghana, and Sierra Leone.*
Affiliations: Government, Ahmadu Bello University; Director of Mamser, Plateau State, Nigeria.

Bumiller, Kristin
Dissertation title: *The Deconstruction of Anti-Discrimination Ideology: The Denial of Self-Respect of Victims Without a Cause.*
Affiliations: Political Science, Amherst College
Publications: *The Civil Rights Society: The Social Construction of Victims* (1988).

Engelhardt, Michael
Dissertation title: *The Foreign Policy Constituencies of House Members.*
Affiliations: Political Science, Luther College

Kaiser, Diane S.
Dissertation title: *A Critique of Empirical Voting Behavior Research as a Form of Explanation.*
Currently resides in Vancouver, WA.

King, Gary M.
Dissertation title: *Do Presidents Make a Difference?*
Affiliations: Government, Harvard University
Publications: *A Solution to the Ecological Inference Problem: Reconstructing Individual Behavior from Aggregate Data* (1997); *Designing Social Inquiry: Scientific Inference in Qualitative Research* (co-author, 1994); *The Elusive Executive: Discovering Statistical Patterns in the Presidency* (co-author, 1988); *Unifying Political Methodology* (1989).

Robbin, Alice A.
Dissertation title: *A Phenomenology of Decision-making: Implementing Information Policy in State Health and Welfare Agencies.*
Affiliations: University of Wisconsin–Madison

Zaffiro, James.
Dissertation title: *Broadcasting and Political Change in Zimbabwe, 1931–1984.*
Affiliations: Political Science, Central College
Publications: *Media and Democracy in Zimbabwe, 1931–2001* (2002); *From Police Network to Station of the Nation: A Political History of Broadcasting in Botswana* (1991).

1985

Alger, Keith N.
Dissertation title: *The Political Economy of U.S. Trade Policy: An Evaluation of Theory.*
Currently resides in Brazil.

Brumbaugh, Chalmers S., III
Dissertation title: *Costa Rica: The Making of a Livable Society.*
Affiliations: Political Science, Elon College

Ger, Yeong-Kuang
Dissertation title: *Ethnic Identity and Ethnic Political Development: The Experience of Chinese Americans.*
Affiliations: Political Science, Taiwan University, Taipei, Taiwan

McCormick, Barrett L.
Dissertation title: *Political Reform in Post-Mao China: Democracy and Due Process in a Leninist State.*
Affiliations: Political Science, Marquette University
Publications: *What If China Doesn't Democratize?: Implications for War and Peace* (co-author, 2000); *Political Reform in Post-Mao China: Democracy and Bureaucracy in a Leninist State* (1990); *China after Socialism: In the Footsteps of Eastern Europe or East Asia?* (co-editor, 1996).

Reed, Joseph
Dissertation title: *Financing Municipal Government: Politics and the Administration of Municipal Credit Ratings.*
Affiliations: Cambridge College

Souza, Isabel R.O. Gomez
Dissertation title: *Labor and Politics: An Analysis of the "New Unionism" in Brazil.*
Currently resides in Rio de Janeiro, Brazil.
Publications: *Trabalho e politica: as origens do Partido dos Trabalhadores* (1988).

Thanamai, Patcharee
Dissertation title: *Patterns of Industrial Policy-making in Thailand: Japanese Multinationals and Domestic Actors.*
Affiliations: Political Science, Thamassat University, Bangkok, Thailand

Turner, Margaret J. (Sandie)
Dissertation title: *Housing in Zaire: How the System Works and How the People Cope.*
Affiliations: Carlow College; Belmont-Harrison Vocational District; Wheeling Community College, W. Virgina

1986

Abubakar, Dauda
Dissertation title: *Oil, the State and Power Politics: The Political Economy of Nigeria's Foreign Policy 1960–1980.*
Affiliations: Political Science, University Maiduguri, Nigeria and Secretary to the Chief Executive office Bornu State, Nigeria

Altemus, Vaughn.
Dissertation title: *The Illusion of Strategy: Conflicting Objectives for American Strategic Forces.*
Affiliations: Political Science, University of Vermont

Crane, George T.
Dissertation title: *China' s Special Economic Zones: The Domestic Political Dynamics of International Economic Integration.*
Affiliations: Political Science and East Asian Studies, Williams College
Publications: *Aidan's Way: The Story of a Boy's Life and a Father's Journey* (2003); *The Political Economy of China's Special Economic Zones* (1990).

Davis, John Roland
Dissertation title: *Class Structure and Mode of Production in Javanese Agriculture.*
Affiliations: WCER, University of Wisconsin; Land Tenure Center, University of Wisconsin–Madison.

Herrnson, Paul S.
Dissertation title: *Do Parties Make a Difference: The Role of Party Organizations in Congressional Elections.*
Affiliations: Government & Political Science, University of Maryland, College Park
Publications: *Multiparty Politics in America: Prospects and Performance* 2nd ed *People, Passions, and Power* (co-author, 2002); *Responsible Partisanship? The Evolution of American Political Parties since 1950* (co-author, 2002); *War Stories from Capitol Hill* (co-author, 2002); *Playing Hardball: Campaigning for the U.S.*

Congress (2001); *Congressional Elections: Campaigning at Home and in Washington* (1995). *Party Campaigning in the 1980s* (1988).

Hertzke, Allen Dale
Dissertation title: *Representing God in Washington: The Role of Religious Lobbies in the American Policy.*
Affiliations: Professor of Political Science and Director of Religious Studies Program, University of Oklahoma
Publications: *Echoes of Discontent: Jesse Jackson, Pat Robertson, and the Resurgence of Populism* (1992); *Representing God in Washington: The Role of Religious Lobbies in the American Polity* (1988).

Mou, Daniel
Dissertation title: *State Power, Agrarian Policies, and Peasant Welfare: The Politics of Agricultural Marketing and Commodity Boards in Nigeria, 1945–1985.*
Affiliations: Political Science, University of JOS; Narcotics officer, Presidency, Abuja, Nigeria.
Publications: *New Hopes but Old Seeds: The Political Economy of Capital Accumulation, State, National Development, Agrarian Transformation, and the Nigerian Peasantry* (co-author, 1993).

Ost, David
Dissertation title: *Democratization, Corporatism and the Solidarity Movement in Poland.*
Affiliations: Political Science, Hobart and William Smith Colleges
Publications: *Workers After Workers' States: Labor and Politics in Postcommunist Eastern Europe* (co-author, 2001); *Solidarity and the Politics of Anti-Politics: Opposition and Reform in Poland since 1968* (1990).

Owen, Diana
Dissertation title: *Media Messages and Their Differential Uses and Influence in the 1984 Presidential Election.*
Affiliations: Georgetown University; Rutgers University
Publications: *New Media and American Politics* (Oxford University Press, 1998); *Media Messages in American Presidential Elections* (1991).

Raymond, Paul B.
Dissertation title: *Congressional Candidates' Advertising Strategies in the 1978 Elections.*
Affiliations: Political Science, Hartwick College

Stavrakis, Peter
Dissertation title: *Soviet Policy in Greece, 1944–1949.*
Affiliations: University of Vermont
Publications: *Moscow and Greek Communism 1944–1949* (1989); *State Building in Post-Soviet Russia: The Chicago Boys and the Decline of Administrative Capacity* (1993).

Sunthraraks, Pisanu
Dissertation title: *Luang Wichit Watakan: Hegemony and Literature.*
Currently resides in Bangkok, Thailand.

Woliver, Laura R.
Dissertation title: *Sputtering Interest: Ad Hoc, Grass Roots Interest Groups in the United States.*
Affiliations: Government & International Studies, University of South Carolina
Publications: *The Political Geographies of Pregnancy* (2002); *From Outrage to Action: The Politics of Grass-Roots Dissent* (1993).

1987

Bruer, Patrick J.
Dissertation title: *Faction in Court: A Study of Interest Group Litigation.*
Affiliations: Political Science, University North Carolina–Chapel Hill

Drucker, Julie S.
Dissertation title: *A Longitudinal Model of Leadership in the United States Congress: 1960–1983.*
Affiliations: Political Science, Wellesley College

Duerst-Lahti, Georgia
Dissertation title: *Gender Power Relations in Public Bureaucracies.*
Affiliations: Dean and Professor of Government, Beloit College

Forrest, Joshua B.
Dissertation title: *State, Peasantry and National Power Struggles in Post-Independence Guinea-Bissau.*
Affiliations: Political Science, University of Vermont; International Affairs, Harvard University
Publications: *Lineages of State Fragility: Rural Civil Society in Guinea-Bissau* (2003); *Namibia's Post-Apartheid Regional Institutions: The Founding Year* (1998); *Guinea-Bissau: Power, Conflict, and Renewal in a West African Nation* (1992); *Subnationalism in Africa: Ethnicity, Alliances and Politics* (2004).

Kandeh, Jimmy David Arthur
Dissertation title: *Dynamics of State, Class and Political Ethnicity: A Comparative Study of State-Society Relations in Colonial and Post-Colonial Sierra Leone.*
Affiliations: Political Science, Kalamazoo College; Political Science, University of Richmond
Publications: *Coups from Below: Armed Subalterns and State Power in West Africa* (2004).

Kishima, Takako
Dissertation title: *Surviving and Transforming Political Life: Reflexivity and Marginality in the Three-Dimensional World of Man in Japan.*
Affiliations: Reischauer Institute, Harvard University; Political Science, University of Massachusetts
Publications: *Political Life in Japan: Democracy in a Reversible World* (1991).

Morrison, John Stephen
Dissertation title: *Divergence From State Failure in Africa: The Relative Success of Botswana's Cattle Sector.*
Affiliations: Subcommittee on Africa, U.S. Congress; Center for Strategic and International Studies; Policy Planning Staff, Department of State; USAID.

Mucciaroni, Gary A.
Dissertation title: *Policy-Making for Employment and Training.*
Affiliations: Political Science, Wellesley College; Political Science, Temple University
Publications: *The Political Failure of Employment Policy, 1945–1982* (1990).
Reversals of Fortune: Public Policy and Private Interests (1995).

Rapp, John Ardean
Dissertation title: *Despotism and the Leninist Party-State: The Chinese Asiatic Mode of Production Debates in Comparative Perspective.*
Affiliations: Government, Beloit College
Publications: *Autocracy and China's Rebel Founding Emperors: Comparing Chairman Mao and Ming Taizu.* (co-author, 2000).

1988

Alswied, Mohammed Y.M.
Dissertation title: *The Gulf Cooperation Council: A Model of a Regional International Regime.*
Currently resides in Riyadh, Saudi Arabia

Bickers, Kenneth N.
Dissertation title: *The Politics of Regulatory Design: Telecommunications Regulation in Historical and Theoretical Perspective.*
Affiliations: Political Science, University of Indiana–Bloomington
Publications: *Perpetuating the Porkbarrel: Policy Subsystems and American Democracy* (co-author, 1995).

Grovogui, Siba N'Zatioula
Dissertation title: *Conflicting Selves to International Law: An Analysis of Colonialism and Decolonization in Namibia.*
Affiliations: Political Science, Eastern Michigan University; Johns Hopkins University
Publications: *Sovereigns, Quasi-Sovereigns and Africans: Race and Self-Determination in International Law* (1996).

Hawk, Beverly Gale
Dissertation title: *Africans and the 1965 U.S. Immigration Law.*
Affiliations: Political Science, University Alabama–Birmingham
Publications: *Africa's Media Image* (editor, 1992).

O'Brien, Peter G.
Dissertation title: *The Paradoxical Paradigm: Turkish Migrants and German Policies.*
Affiliations: Trinity University

Portz, John
Dissertation title: *Politics and Policy Making in the American Political Economy: A Comparison of Local Policy Responses to Industrial Plant Closings.*
Affiliations: Political Science, Northeastern University
Publications: *American Government: Conflict, Compromise, and Citizenship* (co-author, 2000); *The Politics of Plant Closings* (1990).

1989

Basom, Kenneth
Dissertation title: *Edvard Kardelj and the Pluralism of Self-Managing Interests.*
Affiliations: Political Science, Middlebury College; Political Science, University of Northern Iowa

Benitez-Nazario, Jorge Alberto
Dissertation title: *Teachers and Politics: A Case Study on Compliance and Resistance.*
Affiliations: Political Science, University of Puerto Rico
Publications: *Reflexiones En Torno a la Cultura Politica de Los Puertorriqueios: Entre Consideraciones Teiricas y la Evidencia Empirica* (2000)

Eisner, Marc
Dissertation title: *Anti-trust and the Triumph of Economics: Institutions, Expertise, and Policy Change.*
Affiliations: Government, Wesleyan University
Publications: *From Warfare State to Welfare State: World War I, Compensatory State-Building, and the Limits of the Modern Order* (2000); *Antitrust and the Triumph of Economics: Institutions, Expertise, and Policy Change* (1991), *Regulatory Politics in Transition* (1993, 2000), *The State in the American Political Economy* (1995), *Contemporary Regulatory Policy* (co-author, 1999).

Frees, Deidre Sullivan
Dissertation title: *House Party Leaders and Interest Groups as Partners: Emerging Patterns of Cooperation and Influence.*
Resides in Madison, Wisconsin.

Hershberg, Eric M.
Dissertation title: *Transition from Authoritarianism and the Eclipse of the Left: Toward a Reinterpretation of Political Change in Spain.*
Affiliations: Executive Director, David Rockefeller Center at Harvard; Social Science Research Council, Program Director. Senior Research Fellow at the Institute for Latin American Studies at Columbia University, Adjunct Professor in the School of International and Public Affairs, Chair of the Board of Directors of the North American Congress on Latin America (NACLA).
Publications: *Critical Views of September 11: Analyses from Around the World* (co-author, 2002); *Economic Governance and the Challenge of Flexibility in East Asia* (co-author, 2001); *Economic Governance and Flexible Production in East Asia* (co-editor, 2000).

Laba, Roman
Dissertation title: *The Roots of Solidarity: A Political Sociology.*
Affiliations: National Security Affairs, Naval Postgraduate School

McCurdy, Karen
Dissertation title: *When Committees Change: The House Interior and Insular Affairs Committee Confronting Environmental Politics (1955–1986).*
Affiliations: Political Science, University of Missouri; Holocaust Museum, Washington, DC

McDougal, Stephen
Dissertation title: *Disputes and Disputing in Modern Society: A Discourse Analysis of Bakke v. Regents.*
Affiliations: Carroll College; Political Science, University Wisconsin–La Crosse

Nelsen, Brent F.
Dissertation title: *The State Offshore: Petroleum, Politics and State Intervention on the British and Norwegian Continental Shelves.*
Affiliations: Political Science, Furman University

Nixon, David Lee
Dissertation title: *The Congressional Connection: Institutional Patterns and Interorganizational Relations Toward an Organizational Approach to U.S. Foreign Trade Policy.*
Affiliations: Oklahoma State University

Orvis, Stephen
Dissertation title: *The Political Economy of Agriculture in Kisii, Kenya: Social Reproduction to Development Policy.*
Affiliations: Notre Dame; Hamilton College
Publications: *The Agrarian Question in Kenya* (1997).

Roman, Peter J.
Dissertation title: *American Strategic Nuclear Force Planning, 1957–1960; The Interaction of Politics and Military Planning.*
Affiliations: University of Alabama; Political Science, Duquesne University
Publications: *People's Power: Cuba's Experience with Representative Government* (2002)

Woodruff, Emily
Dissertation title: *Groups Concerned with Nuclear Strategic Issues.*
Currently resides in Tallahassee, FL.

Zernicke, Paul Haskell
Dissertation title: *Presidential Roles and Rhetoric.*
Affiliations: Holy Cross College; Corporate and Foundation Relations (full-time administrative appointment) Politics Department (part-time Lecturer) Princeton University.

1990

Cohen, Edward S.
Dissertation title: *Political Reason and Market Rationality in the Liberal Polity.*
Affiliations: Political Science, Westminster College
Publications: *The Politics of Globalization in the United States* (2001).

Coleman, Mary DeLores
Dissertation title: *Legislators, Law and Public Policy: Political Change in Mississippi and the South Since Connor v. Johnson.*
Affiliations: Political Science, Jackson State University
Publications: *Legislators, Law and Public Policy: Political Change in Mississippi and the South* (1993).

De Soto, William
Dissertation title: *The Politics of Business Organizations.*
Affiliations: Political Science, South West Texas State

Gorham, Eric
Dissertation title: *National Service, Citizenship and Political Education.*
Affiliations: Political Science, Loyola University
Publications: *The Theater of Politics: Hannah Arendt, Political Science, and Higher Education* (2000); *National Service, Citizenship, and Political Education* (1992).

Keddell, Joseph
Dissertation title: *Defense as a Budgetary Problem: The Minimization of Conflict in Japanese Defense Policymaking: 1976–1987.*
Affiliations: Law, Tohoku University–Kawauchi Campus
Publications: *The Politics of Defense in Japan: Managing Internal and External Pressures* (1993).

Lee, Kang R
Dissertation title: *Democratic Change and Pluralistic Social Movements in South Korea: The Dynamics of a Bureaucratic Mobilization Regime.*
Resides in Seoul, Korea

Manning, Stephen
Dissertation title: *Democratizing the Leninist Party-State: The Political Economy of Reform in China and the Soviet Union.*
Affiliations: Political Science, University of Detroit Mercy

McKeown, Alex Raymond
Dissertation title: *An Analysis of the Conventional Military Balance on the European Central Front: Some Implications for NATO Strategy and Tactics.*
Affiliations: Kenyon College

Mooney, Christopher Z.
Dissertation title: *Pushing Paper: The Flow and Use of Written Information in State Legislative Decision-Making.*

Affiliations: West Virginia University; University of Essex
Publications: *The Public Clash of Private Values: The Politics of Morality Policy* (2001); *Monte Carlo Simulation* (1997).

Ringquist, Evan John
Dissertation title: *Regulating Air and Water Quality: Politics and Progress at the State Level.*
Affiliations: Political Science, Texas Tech University; Political Science, Florida State University
Publications: *Environmental Protection at the State Level: Politics and Progress in Controlling Pollution* (1993).

Webb, Raymond P.
Dissertation title: *State Politics in the Central African Republic.*
Affiliations: Phillips Andover Academy

Young, Brigitta
Dissertation title: *The Emergence and Disintegration of Modes of Regulation in Agriculture: Germany and the United States in a Historical Perspective.*
Affiliations: Government, Wesleyan University

1991

Bower, Lisa Cornell
Dissertation title: *(Trans)forming the Legal Field: The Role of Feminist Theories and Legal Feminism.*
Affiliations: Political Science, Arizona State University.
Publications: *Between Law and Culture: Relocating Legal Studies* (co-author, 2001).

Cox, Ronald W.
Dissertation title: *Business and the State in US Foreign Economic Policy: Case Studies of Central America from the 1950 to the Present.*
Affiliations: Political Science, University Park Campus; Florida International University.

Drogus, Carol A.
Dissertation title: *Religion, Gender and Political Culture: Attitudes and Participation in Brazilian Basic Christian Communities.*
Affiliations: Government, Hamilton College
Publications: *Women, Religion, and Social Change in Brazil's Popular Church* (1997).

Easterday, John T.
Dissertation title: *Politics and the "Sorest of Afflictions": A Comparative Study of State Policies for the Seriously Mentally Ill.*
Affiliations: Meriter Hospital–Madison

Geske, Mary
Dissertation title: *The Baker Initiative: An Analysis of the Domestic and International Sources of U.S. Foreign Economic Policy.*
Affiliations: Political Science, Smith College

Goldberg-Hiller, Jonathan C.
Dissertation title: *Union Justice: A Longitudinal Case Study of Labor Litigation.*
Affiliations: Political Science, University of Hawaii
Publications: *The Limits to Union: Same-Sex Marriage and the Politics of Civil Rights, Law, Meaning, and Violence,* (2002).

Gundersen, Adolf Gutzke
Dissertation title: *Finding the Kosmos in the Agora.*
Affiliations: Political Science, Texas A&M University
Publications: *Political Theory and Partisan Politics* (co-author, 2000); *The Socratic Citizen: A Theory of Deliberative Democracy* (2000); *The Environmental Promise of Democratic Deliberation* (1995).

Olsen, Erik J.
Dissertation title: *Civil Republicanism and the Properties of Democracy: An Inquiry into the Problem of a Commercial Republic.*
Affiliations: Political Science, Seattle University

Stearns, Willliam P.
Dissertation title: *Space and the Place of Harold D. Laswell.*
Affiliations: St. Benedict College

Walch (Bramschreiber), Karen S.
Dissertation title: *International Cooperation and Self-Interest: The CBI Experience.*
Currently resides in Puerto Rico.

Worsham, Jeffrey S.
Dissertation title: *Political Economy of Financial Regulation: Subgovernments, Subtypes, and the Congressional Connection.*
Affiliations: Political Science, West Virginia University
Publications: *This Land Is Your Land, This Land Is My Land: The Property Rights Movement and Regulatory Takings* (co-author, 2003); *Congress: Lobbying, Contributions, and Influence: Other People's Money: Policy Change, Congress, and Bank Regulation* (1997).

1992

Lane, Robert Wheeler
Dissertation title: *Beyond the Schoolhouse Gate: Free Speech and the Inculcation of Values.*
Affiliations: Political Science, Saginaw Valley State University

Reno, William Sampson Klock
Dissertation title: *Political Domination and Discipline: The Official Invasion of Sierra Leone's Informal Markets.*
Affiliations: Political Science, Northwestern University; Florida International University
Publications: *Warlord Politics and African States* (1998); *Corruption and State Politics in Sierra Leone* (1995).

Rom, Mark Carl
Dissertation title: *The Thrift Tragedy: Are Politicians and Regulators to Blame.*
Affiliations: The Brookings Institution; Government, Georgetown
Publications: *Fatal Extraction: The Story Behind the Florida Dentist Accused of Infecting his Patients with HIV and Poisoning Public Health* (1997).

Watanabe, Morio
Dissertation title: *Image Projection at War: Construction and Deconstruction of the Domus Through Films of World War II in the U.S. and Japan.*

Zelin, Richard David
Dissertation title: *Ethnic and Religious Group Politics in the United States: The Case of the American Jewish Committee 1982–1987.*
Affiliations: Jewish Community Relations

1993

Barkdull, John, L.
Dissertation title: *The Formation of the Marine Oil Pollution Regime: A Case of Institutional Bargaining.*
Affiliations: Political Science, Texas Tech University

Cason, Jeffery W.
Dissertation title: *Development Strategy in Brazil: The Political Economy of Industrial Export Promotion, 1964–1990.*
Affiliations: Middlebury College

Christensen, Scott
Dissertation title: *Coalitions and Collective Choice: The Politics of Institutional Change in Thai Agriculture.*
Affiliations: Business Administration, Concordia University

Clark, Mary Allison
Dissertation title: *Transnational Alliances and Development Strategies: The Transition to Export-Lead Growth in Costa Rica, 1983–1990.*
Affiliations: University Wisconsin–La Crosse; Wesleyan University; Tulane University

Kim, Jin Yeon
Dissertation title: *The Tokyo Uni-polar Concentration: Politics and Economics of Regions in Japan.*
Currently resides in Madison, WI.

Lee, Nae-Young
Dissertation title: *The Politics of Industrial Restructuring: A Comparison of the Auto Industry in South Korea and Mexico.*
Currently resides in Seoul, Korea.

Levin, Daniel
Dissertation title: *Ritual and Rights: The Representation of Popular Sovereignty During the Bicentennial of the United States Constitution.*
Affiliations: University of Utah

Rueter, Theodore
Dissertation title: *The Institutionalization of the Minnesota House of Representatives.*
Affiliations: University of California-Los Angeles.
Publications: *The 267 Stupidest Things Republicans Ever Said — The 267 Stupidest Things Democrats Ever Said* (2000); *Carter Vs. Ford: The Counterfeit Debates of 1976* (co-author, 1980); *Teaching Assistant Strategies: An Introduction to College Teaching* (co-author, 1990); *The United States in the World Political Economy* (1993); *The Minnesota House of Representatives and the Professionalization of Politics* (1994); *The Politics of Race: African Americans and the Political System* (editor, 1995).

Shively, Ruth Lessl
Dissertation title: *Compromised Goods: A Realist Critique of Constructionist Moral Politics.*
Affiliations: Political Science, Texas A&M University
Publications: *Political Theory and Partisan Politics* (co-author, 2000).

Skidmore-Hess, Daniel
Dissertation title: *Philosopher-Kings and "Critical Critics:" Technocracy and its Alternatives in Contemporary Political Theory.*
Affiliations: Government, Armstrong State College

Sylla, Soriba
Dissertation title: *The Politics of Agricultural Development in the Republic of Guinea with Emphasis on a Case Study of Agricultural Liberalization.*
Currently resides in Guinea.

White, Gregory W.
Dissertation title: *A Political Economy of Tunisia's Infitah to the European Communities, 1969–1987.*
Affiliations: Government, Smith College
Publications: *A Comparative Political Economy of Tunisia and Morocco: On the Outside of Europe Looking In* (2001).

Yuan, I.
Dissertation title: *The Social Regime and the Chinese Socialist: The Political Roles of the Chinese Peasantry in a Changing Society.*
Affiliations: Research Fellow, Institute for International Relations, Taipei, Taiwan

1994

Aoki, Andrew L.
Dissertation title: *Ideas and Action: Subcultural Pluralism and Sociopolitical Change.*
Affiliations: Political Science, Augsburg College

Ayres, Jeffrey McKelvey
Dissertation title: *Political Process and the Movement Against Free Trade in Canada, 1981–88.*
Affiliations: Political Science, St. Michael's College
Publications: *Defying Conventional Wisdom: Political Movements and Popular Contention against North American Free Trade* (1998).

Bader, John Burkhardt
Dissertation title: *Taking the Initiative: Congressional Priorities, Democratic Leadership and Divided Government.*
Affiliations: Center for American Politics, UCLA; Assistant Dean for Academic Advising, Johns Hopkins University

Bauer, Gretchen Merry
Dissertation title: *The Labor Movement and the Consolidation of Democracy in Namibia*
Affiliations: Political Science, University of Delaware
Publications: *Labor and Democracy in Namibia, 1971–1996* (1998); *Politics in Southern Africa: State and Society in Transition* (co-author, 2005).

Giaimo, Susan Marie
Dissertation title: *Health Care Reform in Britain and Germany: Recasting the Political Bargain Between the State and the Medical Profession.*
Affiliation: Political Science, MIT
Publications: *Markets and Medicine: the Politics of Health Care Reform in Britain, Germany, and the United States* (2002).

Inglot, Tomasz
Dissertation title: *The Communist Legacy and Post-Communist Politics of Welfare: The Origins, Evolution, and Transformation of Social Policy in Poland from the 1920s to 1993.*
Affiliation: Political Science, Mankato State

Malekafzali, Farhad
Dissertation title: *Foreign Policy Position-Taking by the Members of the House of Representatives.*
Affiliation: University of Wisconsin–Whitewater

Novotny, Kristin M.
Dissertation title: *Identity, Exclusion, and Political Theory*
Affiliation: Political Science, St. Michael's College

Smith, Daniel A.
Dissertation title: *Insular Democracy: Labor-Management Councils in the American States.*
Affiliation: Political Science, University of Florida
Publications: *Educated by Initiative: The Effects of Direct Democracy on Citizens and Political Organizations in the American States.* (co-author, 2004); *Tax Crusaders and the Politics of Direct Democracy* (1998).

1995

Bowersox, Joe William
Dissertation title: *The Public Space of Environmentalism: Reason, Values, and Legitimacy in Environmental Ethics and Politics.*
Affiliation: Political Science, Willamette University
Publications: *Forest Futures: Science, Politics, and Policy for the Next Century* (co-author, 2003); *The Moral Austerity of Environmental Decision Making: Sustainability, Democracy, and Normative Argument in Policy and Law* (co-author, 2002).

Epp, Charles R.
Dissertation title: *Constitutional Courts and the Rights Agenda in Comparative Perspective.*
Affiliation: Department of Political Administration, University of Kansas
Publications: *The Rights Revolution: Lawyers, Activists, and Supreme Courts in Comparative Perspective* (1998).

Geyer, Robert Ralph
Dissertation title: *The Uncertain Union: British and Norwegian Social Democrats in an Integrating Europe*
Affiliation: Political Science, University of Liverpool
Publications: *Exploring European Social Policy* (2000); *The Uncertain Union: British and Norwegian Social Democrats in an Integrating Europe* (1997).

Huo, Shitao
Dissertation title: *Political Transition in Economic Decentralization C Bargaining Coalitions between Central and Provincial Government in China 1978–1993.*
Affiliation: Non-academic

Longman, Timothy
Dissertation title: *Christianity and Crisis in Rwanda: Religion, Civil Society, Democratization and Decline.*
Affiliation: Political Science, Vassar College

Maternowski, Peter J.
Dissertation title: *Implementing the Job Training Partnership Act: The Impact of Decentralized Administration on Training Programs and Policy.*
Affiliation: Wisconsin State Department of Administration

Moser, Robert G.
Dissertation title: *The Emergence of Political Parties in Post-Soviet Russia*
Affiliation: Department of Government, University of Texas-Austin
Publications: *Unexpected Outcomes: Electoral Systems, Political Parties, and Representation in Russia* (2001); *Russian Politics: Challenges of Democratization* (co-editor, 2001).

Novotny, Patrick John
Dissertation title: *Framing and Political Movements: A Study of Four Cases from the Environmental Justice Movement.*
Affiliation: Political Science, Georgia Southern

Rigdon, Mark E.
Dissertation title: *The Business of Education Reform: An Analysis of Corporate Involvement and Education Reform Movements in Kentucky, Milwaukee and Chicago.*
Affiliation: Non-academic

Roehrig, Terence Jerome
Dissertation title: *Extended Deterrence in Korea: The U.S. Defense Commitment to South Korea.*
Affiliation: Political Science, Cardinal Stritch University
Publications: *The Prosecution of Former Military Leaders in Newly Democratic Nations: The Cases of Argentina, Greece, and South Korea* (2002)

Sell, Kathleen R.
Dissertation title: *Differentiated, Dialogical and Prophetic Communitarianism: Embracing Action and Accepting Tragedy.*
Affiliation: Administration, University of Wisconsin

Sullivan, Michael Joseph
Dissertation title: *Democracy and Developmentalism: Discourses of Political Change in Post-Mao China, 1978–1995.*
Affiliation: Non-academic

Whann, Christopher Alan
Dissertation title: *The Revenue Imperative and State Management in Lesotho.*
Affiliation: Skidmore College, Academic Advisor

1996

Beck, Linda J.
Dissertation title: *Patrimonial Democrats in a Culturally Plural Society: Democratization and Political Accommodation in the Patronage Politics of Senegal.*
Affiliation: Political Science, Barnard College

Brutus, Calvin Dennis
Dissertation title: *Marketized Media Versus Democracy? A Structuralist Analysis of Media, Their Performance/Outputs, and Implications for Democratic Functioning.*
Affiliation: Department of Life Sciences Communication, University of Wisconsin–Madison

Burke, Christopher Matthew
Dissertation title: *When Appearances Do Matter: The Development of Representation Jurisprudence.*
Affiliation: Non-academic

Clancy, Michael James
Dissertation title: *Export-Led Growth Strategies, the Internationalization of Services, and Third World Development: The Political Economy of Mexican Tourism, 1967–1992.*
Affiliation: Political Science, University of Hartford
Publications: *Exporting Paradise: Tourism and Development in Mexico* (2001).

Gerstmann, Evan
Dissertation title: *At the Constitutional Crossroads: Gays, Lesbians and the Failure of Class Based Equal Protection.*
Affiliation: Political Science, Loyola Marymount University
Publications: *The Constitutional Underclass: Gays, Lesbians, and the Failure of Class-Based Equal Projection* (1999); *Same-Marriage and the Constitution.* (2003).

Gill, Jung-Il
Dissertation title: *Preadult Learning of Democratic Orientations in three Nations, the United States, Korea and Japan.*
Affiliation: Yonsei University

Glaudell, Kenneth Ray
Dissertation title: *An Afghan of Unknown Views: Jamal al-Din al-Afghani and the Role of Shiism in Islamic Political Thought.*
Affiliation: University of Wisconsin–Whitewater

Hawkins, Darren Greg
Dissertation title: *The International and Domestic Strubble for Legitimacy in Authoritarian Chile.*
Affiliation: Political Science, Brigham Young
Publications: *International Human Rights and Authoritarian Rule in Chile* (2002).

King, Daniel E.
Dissertation title: *New Political Parties and Democratization in Thailand: The Case of the Palang Dharma Party and the New Aspiration Party*

Koulish, Robert E.
Dissertation title: *Bordering on Chaos: Ad-Hoc Decision-making in the Immigration Bureaucracy.*
Affiliation: Bentley College

Lee, Geun
Dissertation title: *Sovereignty, Identity, and Power Politics in Inter-state Policy Coordination: Trade Disputes and Resolutions between the United States and Japan in Semiconductors.*

Murphy, Andrew Robert
Dissertation title: *Conscience and Community: Revisiting Toleration and Religious Dissent in Early Modern England and America.*
Affiliation: Villanova University
Publications: *Conscience and Community: Revisiting Toleration and Religious Dissent in Early Modern England and America* (2001); *The Political Writings of William Penn* (editor, 2002).

Murphy, Patrick J.
Dissertation title: *Why Agencies Cannot Work and Play Well Together: Drug Policy at the State and Federal Level.*

Affiliation: Political Science, University of San Francisco
Publication: *Financing California's Community Colleges,* (2004).

Olson, Laura Ruth
Dissertation title: *Filled with Spirit and Power: The Political Involvement of Protestant Clergy.*
Affiliation: Political Science, Clemson University
Publications: *Filled with Spirit and Power: Protestant Clergy in Politics* (2000); *Encyclopedia of American Religion and Politics, Facts on File Library of American History* (2003); *Christian Clergy in American Politics* (co-author, 2001).

Soss, Joe Brian
Dissertation title: *Unwanted Claims: Politics, Participation, and the U.S. Welfare System.*
Affiliation: Political Science, American University; University of Wisconsin–Madison
Publications: *Unwanted Claims: The Politics of Participation in the US Welfare System* (2002); *Race and the Politics of Welfare Reform* (co-editor, 2000).

Weber, Edward P.
Dissertation title: *Pluralism by the Rules: The Emergence of Collaborative Games in National Pollution Control Politics.*
Affiliation: Political Science, Washington State University
Publications: *Bringing Society Back In: Grassroots Ecosystem Management, Accountability, and Sustainable Communities* (2003); *Pluralism by the Rules: Conflict and Cooperation in Environmental Regulation* (1998).

White, Julie Anne
Dissertation title: *The Problem of Paternalism: Social Policy and the Practices of Care.*
Affiliation: Political Science, Ohio University
Publications: *Democracy, Justice, and the Welfare State: Reconstructing Public Care* (2000).

1997

Barrett, Patrick Stephen
Dissertation title: *Forging Compromise: Business, Parties, and the State in Chile.*
Affiliation: Havens Center, University of Wisconsin–Madison

Bosworth, Matthew H.
Dissertation title: *Do Courts Matter? Public School Finance Reform in Texas, Kentucky, and North Dakota.*
Affiliation: Political Science, Winona State University
Publications: *Courts as Catalysts: State Supreme Courts and Public School Finance Equity* (SUNY Press, 2001).

Fosdick, Anna Watson
Dissertation title: *Confused, Pragmatic, Ambitious, or Politically Savvy?: Examinations of Early Post-Cold War Peacekeeping Decisionmaking.*

Gunderson, Gregory G.
Dissertation title: *In Search of Operational Effectiveness: Military Reform in the 1980s.*
Affiliation: Political Science, Central Missouri State; Eastern Kentucky University

Kim, Haknoh
Dissertation title: *Bones Without Soul? Power Relations Between Organized Labor and Business in the European Community.*
Affiliation: Seoul National University

May, Catherine Rose
Dissertation title: *Erecting Edifices: Home, Homelessness in the Absence of Dwelling.*
Affiliation: DePaul University

Meyer, John Mark
Dissertation title: *The Politics of Nature: Political Theory, Environmentalism, and the Evasion of Political Judgment.*
Affiliation: Political Science, Humboldt State
Publications: *American Indians and U.S. Politics: A Companion Reader* (2002); *Political Nature: Environmentalism and the Interpretation of Western Thought* (2001).

Magnusson, Bruce A.
Dissertation title: *The Politics of Democratic Regime Legitimation in Benin: Institutions, Social Policy, and Security.*
Affiliation: Political Science, Whitman College

Nelson, Samuel Peter
Dissertation title: *Standing Back From the First Amendment: A Pluralist Framework for Freedom of Speech.*
Affiliation: Ohio University; University of Toledo

Niland, Collette Marie
Dissertation title: *Who Links: The Roles of Political Parties and the Neighborhood Organizations in Urban Democratic Linkage.*
Affiliation: University of Wisconsin–Madison, non-teaching

Passavant, Paul Andrew
Dissertation title: *No Escape: Boundaries, Identities, and the Politics of Free Speech in America.*
Affiliation: Political Science, Hobart and William Smith College
Publications: *No Escape: Freedom of Speech and the Paradox of Rights* (2002); *The Empire's New Clothes: Reading Hardt and Negri* (co-author, 2003).

Rhodes, Matthew Aaron
Dissertation title: *The Idea of Central Europe and Visegrad Cooperation.*
Affiliation: US Air War College

Siemers, David J.
Dissertation title: *The Birth of the Constitutional State: Federalists and Antifederalists After Ratification.*
Affiliation: Political Science, Colorado College; University of Wisconsin–Oshkosh
Publication: *Ratifying the Republic: Antifederalists and Federalists in Constitutional Time* (2002).

Streich, Gregory W.
Dissertation title: *After the Celebration: Theories of Community and Practice of Interracial Dialogue.*
Affiliation: Central Missouri State

Tilley, Virginia Q.
Dissertation title: *Indigenous People and the State: Ethnic Meta-Conflict in El Salvador.*
Affiliation: Political Science, Hobart and William Smith College

Weller, Ben Franklin
Dissertation title: *The Breakdown of Authoritarian Regimes and the Quest for Democracy: The Case of Sierra Leone.*
Affiliation: Civil Service, State of Wisconsin

1998

Cassell, Mark
Dissertation title: *Public Agencies in a Private World: A Comparison of the Federal Republic of Germany's Treuhandanstalt and the United States' Resolution Trust Corporation*
Affiliation: Kent State University
Publications: *How Governments Privatize: The Politics of Divestment in the United States and Germany* (2002).

Hoffmann, Susan M.
Dissertation title: *Making Money: Ideas and Institutions in U.S. Banking*
Affiliation: Western Michigan University
Publications: *Politics and Banking: Ideas, Public Policy, and the Creation of Financial Institutions*, (2001).

Honeck, Jon P.
Dissertation title: *Industrial Policy in Older Industrial Regions: A Comparison of Ohio and the Basque Region*
Affiliation: Ohio Legislative Service Commission; Policy Matters

Jenkins, Laura Dudley
Dissertation title: *Identity and Identification: Affirmative Action in India and the United States*
Affiliation: University of Cincinnati
Publications: *Identity and Identification in India: Defining the Disadvantages* (2003).

Kelly, Kristin
Dissertation title: *When the Personal Becomes Political: Renegotiating the Boundaries of Public and Private in the Treatment and Prevention of Domestic Violence*
Affiliation: University of Connecticut
Publications: *Domestic Violence and the Politics of Privacy* (2002).

Kroeger, Brian J.
Dissertation title: *The Foundations of Collective Action: Trade Unions, Civil Rights Policy, and Organizational Behavior*

Lambert J. Barlett
Dissertation title: *The Right to Strike in American Political Development*

Lewis, Jeffrey M.
Dissertation title: *Constructing Interests: The Committee of Permanent Representatives and Decision-Making n the European Union*
Affiliation: Oklahoma State University

Martin, John Wesley
Dissertation title: *Economically Motivated Voting Across Regions and Eras in American Presidential Elections: 1932–1992*
Affiliation: Non-academic

Sessions, Andrew
Dissertation title: *Dialogues of Power: Local-Level Negotiations in South Africa, 1985–1990*

Shore, Sean
Dissertation title: *Building Stable Peace: The Development of the North American Security Community, 1814–1940*
Affiliation: Non-academic

Stafford, David Geoffrey
Dissertation title: *Globalization Amid Diversity: Economic Development Policy in Multi-Ethnic Malaysia, 1987–1997.*
Affiliation: Non-Academic

Yavuz, Hakan
Dissertation title: *Islamic Political Identity in Turkey: Movements, Agents, and Processes*
Affiliation: University of Utah
Publications: *Turkish Islam and the Secular State: The Gulen Movement* (co-editor, 2003); *Islamic Political Identity in Turkey* (2003).

1999

Abdul Kadir, Suzaina
Dissertation title: *Traditional Islamic Society and the State in Indonesia: The Nahdlatul Ulama, Political Accommodation and the Preservation of Autonomy (1984–1997).*
Affiliation: Political Science, National University of Singapore

Angerthal, Steven
Dissertation title: *Officer Education and Democracy: A Study of Argentina*
Affiliation: Summit Analytical Associates

Flemming, Gregory Newbert
Dissertation title: *An Agenda-Setting Model of Congressional Campaigns.*
Affiliations: Pew Foundation

Graney, Katherine Ellen
Dissertation title: *Projecting Sovereignty: Statehood and Nationness in Post-Soviet Russia.*
Affiliation: Political Science, Skidmore College

Green, David Michael
Dissertation title: *Who Are "The Europeans"?: European Political Identity in the Context of the Post-War Integration Project.*
Affiliation: Political Science, Hofstra University

Hamilton, Anne Wing
Dissertation title: *Bureaucrat-Bashing in Russia and the United States: A Comparison of the Cultural Construction of Negative Images of Authority.*
Affiliation: Political Science, UW–Whitewater

Joachim, Jutta Maria
Dissertation title: *NGOs, Agenda-Setting, and the UN: Violence Against Women and Reproductive Rights and Health.*
Affiliation: Institut fur Politische Wissenschaft, Universiteit Hannover

Khadiagala, Lynn Steckelberg
Dissertation title: *Law, Power, and Justice: The Adjudication of Women's Property Rights in Uganda.*
Affiliation: Peace Corps; University of William and Mary

Lipson, Michael Leslie
Dissertation title: *International Cooperation on Export Controls: Nonproliferation, Globalization, and Multilateralism.*
Affiliation: Political Science, University of Colorado-Boulder

Malley, Michael Sean
Dissertation title: *Resource Distribution, State Coherence, and the Changing Level of Political Centralization in Indonesia, 1950–1997.*
Affiliation: Ohio University

Mulligan-Hansel, Kathleen Marie
Dissertation title: *The Political Economy of Women's Organizations in Contemporary Tanzania: Hegemony, Participation and Gender in Post-Colonial Politics.*
Affiliations: Institute for Wisconsin's Future

Nelson, Lisa Sue
Dissertation title: *Toward an Understanding of Supreme Court Decisionmaking.*
Affiliation: Legal Studies, University of Pittsburgh

Omarova, Saule Tarikhovna
Dissertation title: *The Political Economy of Oil in Post-Soviet Kazakhstan.*
Affiliation: Non-Academic

Quimby, Peter Howard
Dissertation title: *Constructing States, Constructing Interests: Religion and Politics in Post-Soviet Russia and Ukraine.*
Affiliation: UW–Madison Administration; Yale University Davenport Residential College

Richards, Mark James
Dissertation title: *Doctrines and Attitudes: Deciding the Supreme Court's Free Expression Cases.*
Affiliation: Political Science, Grand Valley State University

Schmeling, Thomas Arthur
Dissertation title: *The Dynamics of Legal Change: A Diffusion of Innovations Perspective*
Affiliation: Political Science, St. Joseph's University; Rhode Island College

Turner, Robert Claggett
Dissertation title: *Public Policies for Manufacturing Revitalization: Competing Models in Three American States.*
Affiliation: Political Science, Skidmore College

2000

Barletta, Michael
Dissertation title: *Ambiguity, Autonomy, and the Atom: Emergence of the Argentine-Brazilian Nuclear Regime.*
Affiliation: Monterey Institute of International Studies

Coleman, Craig
Dissertation title: *Privacy and Property: A Re-examination of the Right to Private Property.*

Fischer, Lisa
Dissertation title: *Women at the Margin: Challenging Boundaries of the Political in Hong Kong, 1982–1997.*

Fletcher, Brian
Dissertation title: *A Sociological Explanation of International Election Engineering from 1989–1998.*

Jozwiak, Joseph
Dissertation title: *Waste Package Recycling and the Internal Market: Environmental Policy and the European Union.*
Affiliation: Political Science, Texas A&M-Corpus Christi

Kurvers Spalding, Andrew Ryan
Dissertation title: *Beyond Family Values: Toward a Progressive Understanding of Civic Education.*

Martin, Paul Sterling
Dissertation title: *News Media as Sentinel: Why Bad News About Issues is Good News for Political Participation.*
Affiliation: Political Science, University of Oklahoma

Pickerill, J. Mitchell
Dissertation title: *Congress and Constitutional Deliberation: The Role of Judicial Review in a Separated System.*
Affiliation: Political Science, Washington State University
Publications: *Constitutional Deliberation in Congress: The Impact of Judicial Review in a Separated System* (2004).

Schatz, Edward Aaron
Dissertation title: *"Tribes" and "Clans" in Modern Power: The State-Led Production of Subethnic Politics in Kazakhstan.*
Affiliation: Southern Illinois University
Publications: *Modern Clan Politics: The Power of "Blood" in a Central Asian State* (2004).

2001

Arias, Enrique D.
Dissertation title: *Crime, Violence and Democracy: The State and Political Order in Brazilian Shantytowns.*

Baker, Andrew Benjamin
Dissertation title: *The Art of Subtle Persuasion: Explaining Mass Responses to Market Reform in Brazil.*

Bennion, Elizabeth Anne
Dissertation title: *Gender, Perception and Policy Priorities in Three Midwestern State Legislatures.*
Affiliation: Indiana University South Bend

Brown, Sonya Kay
Dissertation title: *The Anarchical Society Revisited: An Examination of the Role of Nonstate Actors in Regional Human Rights Regimes and the Implications for the International Society.*
Affiliation: University of Wisconsin–Madison

Den Dulk, Kevin Ronald
Dissertation title: *Prophets in Caesar's Courts: The Role of Ideas in Catholic and Evangelical Rights Advocacy.*
Affiliation: Grand Valley State University

Krishnan, Jayanth Kumar
Dissertation title: *New Politics, Public Interest Groups, and Legal Strategies in the United States and Beyond.*
Affiliation: William Mitchell College of Law

Liebowitz, Jeremy Brookner
Dissertation title: *What Did the Bishop Do with the Cows? The Church of Uganda and Political Culture in Busoga.*
Affiliation: University of Natal

Mosher, James Stephen
Dissertation title: *Labor Power and Wage Equality: The Politics of Supply-Side Equality.*
Affiliation: Ohio University

Navarro, Sharon Ann
Dissertation title: *Las Mujeres Invisibles/Invisible Women: Identities, Globalization and Latina Activists at the U.S.-Mexico Border..*
Affiliation: University of Texas–San Antonio; Carleton College
Publications: *Latino/a Americans and Political Participation: A Reference Handbook* (co-editor, 2004).

Rosenthal, Alisa Joy
Dissertation title: *Disciplining Bodies: Bodily Invasion, State Power, Liberal Theory.*
Affiliation: Rollins College

Schwartz, Katrina Zenta Sarah
Dissertation title: *Wild Horses and Great Trees: National Identity and the Global Politics of Nature in Latvia.*
Affiliation: Penn State University; University of Florida
Publications: *The Politics of Sustainable Forestry in Latvia: Property, Enterprise and the State in Transition from Communism* (1996).

Thawnghmung, Ardeth Maung
Dissertation title: *Paddy Farmers and the State: Agricultural Policies and Legitimacy in Myanmar.*
Affiliation: University of Victoria, Canada; assistant professor in the Department of Political Science, University of Massachusetts, Lowell
Publications: *Behind the Teak Curtain: Authoritarianism, Agricultural Policies, and Political Legitimacy in Rural Burma* (2003).

Vanderheiden, Steven Jon
Dissertation title: *Green Justice: Liberal Egalitarianism and the Challenge of Environmental Aims.*
Affiliation: University of Minnesota–Duluth

Williams, James Michael
Dissertation title: *Blurring the Boundaries of "Tradition": The Transformation and Legitimacy of the Chieftaincy in South Africa.*
Affiliation: University of San Diego

Wolfgram, Mark Allen
Dissertation title: *Visualizing the Imagined Community: History, Memory and Politics in Germany.*
Affiliation: Political Science, Carleton University; Oklahoma State

Wong, Joseph Yit-Chong
Dissertation title: *Democracy and Welfare: Health Policy in Taiwan and South Korea.*
Affiliation: University of Toronto

2002

Anderson, Brent Steven
Dissertation title: *Foundations as Political Actors: Their Efforts to Shape Interest Group Movements, the Policy-Making Process, and Public Policy Outcomes.*

Claibourn, Michele Paige
Dissertation title: *Beyond the Voting Booth: The Persistence of Presidential Campaigns in the Public Agenda.*
Affiliation: Department of Political Science, University of Oklahoma

Graubart, Jonathan M.
Dissertation title: *Transnational Activism and Soft Law Mobilization: Giving Significance to NAFTA's Labor and Environmental Accords.*
Affiliation: San Diego State University

Jourde, Cedric
Dissertation title: *The Dramas of Ethnic Elites' Accommodation: The Authoritarian Restoration in Mauritania.*
Affiliation: University of Ottawa

Lipson, Daniel Nathan
Dissertation title: *Affirmative Action as We Don't Know It: The Evolution of Undergraduate Admissions Policy at UC-Berkeley, UT-Austin, and UW-Madison.*
Affiliation: Department of Political Science, Kalamazoo College

Mosser, Michael William
Dissertation title: *Engineering Influence: The Subtle Power of Smaller States in International Organizations.*
Affiliation: University of Kansas

Price, Kevin S.
Dissertation title: *Accidental Instruments: Plurality Presidents in the Party System.*
Affiliations: University of Washington

Rabe, Kenneth N.
Dissertation title: *Evolutionary Ethics and Moral Idealism: Kropotkin's Theory of Anarchist Communism.*

2003

Daniels, Debra Bendel
Dissertation title: *Evangelical Feminism: The Egalitarian-Complementarian Debate.*

Gayton, Jeffrey Thomas
Dissertation title: *From Here to Extraterritoriality: American Sovereignty Within and Beyond Borders.*
Affiliation: University of Wisconsin–Madison

Hafner-Burton, Emile M.
Dissertation title: *Globalizing Human Rights? How International Trade Agreements Shape Government Repression.*
Affiliation: Stanford University

Manna, Paul Francis
Dissertation title: *Federalism, Agenda Setting, and the Development of Federal Education Policy, 1965–2001.*
Affiliation: Government, College of William and Mary

Nanes, Stefanie E.
Dissertation title: *Citizenship and National Identity in Jordan: A National Dialogue.*
Affiliation: Franklin & Marshall College; Hofstra University

Ridout, Travis Nelson
Dissertation title: *Presidential Primary Front-Loading, the Information Environment, and Voter Leaning and Choice.*
Affiliation: Political Science, Washington State University

Scherpereel, John A.
Dissertation title: *Between State Socialism and European Union: Remaking the State in the Czech Republic and Slovakia.*
Affiliation: University of Wisconsin–Madison, University of Wisconsin–Milwaukee

Shelledy, Robert B.
Dissertation title: *Legions Not Always Visible on Parade: The Vatican's Influence in World Politics.*
Affiliation: Marquette University

Sweet, Martin Jay
Dissertation title: *Supreme Policymaking: Coping with the Supreme Court's Affirmative Action Policies.*
Affiliation: Dickinson College

Weaver, Catherine Elizabeth
Dissertation title: *The Hypocrisy of International Organizations: The Rhetoric, Reality, and Reform of the World Bank.*
Affiliation: University of Kansas

Zierler, Matthew C.
Dissertation title: *Failing to Commit: The Politics of Treaty Nonratification.*
Affiliation: Michigan State University

2004

Adams, Melinda Jane
Dissertation title: *Negotiating the Boundaries of Political Action: Transnational Linkages, Women's Organizations, and the State in Cameroon.*
Affiliation: James Madison University

Espino, Rodolfo III
Dissertation Title: *Minority Agendas, Majority Rules:Latino Representation in Congress.*
Affiliation: Arizona State University

Fieno, John Vincent
Dissertation title: *Federalism, Decentralization and the Welfare State in Comparative Perspective.*
Affiliation: University of Wisconsin–Madison

Parker, David C.W.
Dissertation title: *Resources Rule: Political Parties, Candidates, Interest Groups, and Election Strategies, 1880–2000.*
Affiliation: DePauw University

Parrish, Rick
Dissertation title: *Aporias of Justice: The Play of Violence and Respect in Derrida, Nietzsche, Hobbes, and Berlin.*
Affiliation: Loyola University New Orleans

Robinson, Robert Reif
Dissertation Title: *A Tale of Two Dauberts: The Selective Application of Scientific Scrutiny for the Admissibility of Expert Testimony.*
Affiliation: Rhodes College

Strach, Patricia Lynn
Dissertation title: *All in the Family: Policy Structure, Process, and Change.*
Affiliation: SUNY—Albany
Publications: *The Medium and the Message: Television Advertising and American Elections* (co-editor, 2004).

(Complete up to January, 2005)

Appendix 18

Alumni Survey Report, 2003

by Matthew Dull and Rachel Girshick

Responses to Close-Ended Questions

The table below provides means and standard deviations for a handful of close-ended questions across several categories of survey respondents. Some caution should be used in interpreting these results, as a few outliers may have disproportionately influenced the results.

Close-Ended Questions: Descriptive Statistics

Overall	Pre–1965	1965–80	1980-Pres	Amer.	Comp	IR	Theory	Acad	Non-Aca
N=95	N=9	N=49	N=36	N=35	N=25	N=7	N=8	N=65*	N=16*

1) How would you rate the quality of coursework in your field of specialization during your time in th Political Science Department? 1=Excellent 7=Very Poor

1.66	**1.44**	**1.61**	**1.81**	**1.54**	**1.76**	**1.57**	**1.88**	**1.65**	**1.94**
(.737)	**(.527)**	**(.640)**	**(.889)**	**(.741)**	**(.879)**	**(.787)**	**(.641)**	**(717)**	**(.929)**

2) Overall, how would you assess the quality of the Political Science Department during your time in graduate program? 1=Very High Quality 7= Very low Quality

1.79	**1.78**	**1.69**	**1.97**	**1.79**	**1.72**	**2.00**	**2.25**	**1.75**	**2.13**
(.837)	**(.833)**	**(.619)**	**(1.07)**	**(.923)**	**(.678)**	**(1.15)**	**(1.03)**	**(.791)**	**(1.02)**

3) How well do you believe your graduate work in the Political Science Department and UW–Madisor prepared you for your career? 1=Very Well 7=Very Poorly

2.06	**1.78**	**2.00**	**2.19**	**1.92**	**2.00**	**2.00**	**3.13**	**2.03**	**2.63**
(1.17)	**(1.09)**	**(1.19)**	**(1.14)**	**(1.22)**	**(1.04)**	**(.577)**	**(1.81)**	**(1.08)**	**(1.59)**

4) Thinking back, if you had it to do over again, would you choose to go to graduate school in the UW–Madison Political Science Department? 1=Yes, Definitely 7=Absolutely not

1.82	**1.22**	**1.86**	**1.97**	**1.71**	**1.91**	**1.43**	**2.88**	**1.75**	**2.57**
(1.26)	**(.441)**	**(1.28)**	**(1.38)**	**(1.18)**	**(1.47)**	**(.535)**	**(2.03)**	**(1.13)**	**(1.87)**

Numbers reported are Mean (Standard Deviation).

---

* Those reporting they are retired are omitted from career figures.

Responses to Open-Ended Questions

Below are a handful of broad themes in responses to the graduate student survey.

Currents and Cross-Currents

Among the intellectual currents observed during their times as graduate students, many respondents discussed the dual trends toward positivism and quantitative approaches within the discipline and the tensions these developments created with other perspectives.

- ". . . there was a creative tension between the behavioralist notion that non-normative social science was possible and an alternative view that there would always be a normative dimension to social science research." (Altemus, 1975)
- "There was a quantitative-qualitative division among some of us grad students and we argued about the value of these perspective over beer in the Union, but Wisconsin was a civil place and we, like the faculty . . . tolerated the differences and indeed most of us were committed to pluralism in the discipline." (Kommers, 1962)
- "This in a nutshell is what I consider the greatest collective strength of the department and perhaps its most distinctive trait: eclecticism and an overall strong core of faculty rather than a particular niche or theoretical specialization." (Lewis, 1998)

Collegiality

Easily the most common sentiments expressed by the respondents addressed the department's collegial atmosphere and tolerance for multiple methodological approaches.

- "[There was] an unbending and overriding commitment by the UW faculty to meritocratic grading and fairness . . . regardless of political view, regardless of methodological approach, and regardless of personality. As a result, there was far less competitiveness among grad students (or rather, it was healthy rather than destructive. . . .) To me, this reflected at least to some extent the cultural impact, however subtle, of Wisconsin/Madison 'public school' origins and connections to the state's long history of a solid blue collar work ethic." (Forrest, 1987)
- "[There was a] real appreciation for different kinds of research and building a sense of community in a department where both were important." (Kingdon, 1965)

- "Though things may not always have been as they seemed, the department faculty seemed to be able to work together on a live and let live basis, allowing students to choose direction without undue pressure from faculty to go one way or the other or unseemly competition among professors for students. There are too many departments today for which those very commendable qualities are muted or absent." (Harbeson, 1970)
- "I came to Wisconsin without a clue of what I wanted to do. None of the women in my family have ever had a professional career. . . The reason I became able to visualize myself as a political scientist and to develop a career in the field was that I was lucky enough to have so many good models in the Wisconsin Faculty—people who treated me like someone capable of raising useful questions and learning how to answer them—and so many supportive colleagues among the graduate students." (Hershey, 1972)
- "I am a conservative Christian. I was an outsider, but never an outcast—even among my Marxist friends." (Nelsen, 1989)
- "What stands out in my mind, and it is impossible to exaggerate this contribution, was that the department's atmosphere made professional political science *fun*. This is deceptively complicated and often overlooked when reflecting on a graduate program. It is all too easy to transform graduate education into drudgery and drive the most creative, brightest people out of the academy." (Weissberg, 1969)

The Christmas/holiday party appears in several of the responses.

- "Every Christmas the graduate students would present a musical satire usually involving the faculty. One year, Ed Keynes dressed up as Santa and placed Clara Penniman on his knee." (Anderson, 1971)

Some others disagree with this assessment, particularly regarding the competition among graduate students for funding.

- ". . . there was a lot of competition for funding, which created a tense graduate experience at times." (Ayers, 1994)
- "Too much infighting—over tenure, over money, etc—really took a toll on some grad students." (Gorham, 1990)
- "Too many good people came and went at UW, and the bottom line on 'productive' research I think often got in the way of crafting a department concerned for both its graduate and undergraduate students." (Gorham, 1990)

- "From 1988–94, the department systematically denied assistant professors tenure, which led to a decline in the sociability/cohesion of the department. It had a demoralizing effect on graduate students, the department became an unstable environment for graduate education." (Smith, 1994)
- "Wisconsin loves to talk about tolerance for diverse theories, but I was not impressed by its display of tolerance while I was a student there. The dominant intellectual current, if there was one, seemed to be a kind of methods-envy, which is typically hostile to political theory and political theorists." (Vanderheiden, 2001)

Multiple Methods
Words like *eclecticism* and *breadth* appear frequently in reference to the department.

- "I think most departments offer and encourage a narrow training in political science. They concede that the discipline is fragmented and appear to train students to further that fragmentation. Wisconsin did not. I always felt that we were encouraged to swim upstream against the tide of fragmentation. . . . The other thing that Wisconsin has is community. The two probably reinforce one another—hard to have community when you fight over orthodoxy. The more I talk to others in different departments, the more I find Wisconsin's a rarity." (Martin, 1998)
- "The greatest impact that my education at UW made is that I embrace intellectual diversity, the notion that there are many ways to understand and study politics." (Mucciaroni, 1987)
- "I suspected that the department was tolerant of diverse theories while a student. Later experience confirmed that this was emphatically so. The entire department provided a terrific community and I recall the experience with fondness. I thoroughly enjoyed grad student life at North Hall—absolutely positive and liberating." (Reno, 1992)
- "There is a strong tradition of interdisciplinary research and use of multiple methods. Even the quantitative Americanists used historical methods at times. Students are all very well trained methodologically." (Turner, 1999)

Again, others disagree:

- "One of the things that disappointed me the most was the low degree of tolerance for diverse theories and methodologies among faculty members.

This intolerance filtered down to students as well. I know of one student who had great difficulty with his dissertation because of the different philosophical and methodological orientations of the two primary advisors on his dissertation committee." (Edmonson, 1973)

Professional Preparation

One of the common critiques of the department is the feeling that former graduate students were not well prepared for the "publishing game" (Anderson) and other aspects of the academic profession. Several respondents lament the lack of rigorous methodological training and opportunities to co-author with faculty members.

- "I do wish I had been more exposed to quantitative methods and rational choice approaches, although the 'dominant intellectual trends' were suitable to me and my interests. Nevertheless, the discipline seems to be increasingly dominated by the formal requiring me to bring myself up to speed post-graduation." (Beck, 1996)
- "My major weakness coming out of the program was in methodology, particularly statistical, but in general as well. There was no requirement in this area, and I did not have the foresight or discipline to push myself as far into this area as I should have."(Portz, 1988)

Learning to Teach

There are two contrasting perspectives on the role of teaching in the department's preparation of grad students. Many highlight faculty members who they admired for their attention to teaching and who they say influenced their own teaching style (Crawford Young, Charles Anderson, David Fellman).

- "My experience as a TA and graduate lecturer over the course of numerous semesters was extremely valuable in preparing me to be a professor." (Ayers, 1994)
- ". . . witnessing Booth Fowler lecturing gave me something to aspire to . . . I am no Booth Fowler, but he made me try to approach his level of skill in the classroom." (Kanervo, 1976)
- "The department's emphasis on good teaching—from the intro level up—both assisted my own education and set a valuable example." (Nelsen, 1989)
- "I was and am impressed at the seriousness with which teaching was taken at Madison. Faculty insisted on a minimum threshold of instructional excellence that has stuck with me through the years." (Olson, 1996)

Others feel that the emphasis on publishing—and particularly pursuing a career in a research-oriented atmosphere like the UW department—ran counter to their own interest in teaching.

- "The department, while I was there, pushed a 'model' of what we students should do with our lives—be like us, publish a lot and work in prestigious institutions, and occasionally offer your services to the government. That was good advice for some students, but the academic world is much more complex than that. Some of us even then didn't fit that mold and we were left feeling that we were casting ourselves into the void. I will never forget the tongue-lashing I got from Herb Jacob when I elected to accept a position at the U. of Montana."(Chaffey, 1967)
- "My subsequent career has always required me to balance scholarship with a commitment to teaching. . . . Looking back, the department helped me less than I would have liked with the challenge of striking these balances. Scholarship was always at the forefront. One was predominantly surround by outstanding scholars, some of whom were very poor teachers despite their individual brilliance." (Pika, 1979)

Responding to Turmoil

Many of the respondents remember the campus politics of the time playing an important role in their graduate experience. Most, but not all, of these are graduate students here during the tumultuous late 1960s. Here are a few examples from different eras:

- "The 'Stick Your Neck Out Club' was formed on campus as a reaction against the climate of fear and repression permeating academics. I served on the executive committee of the organization, which was also joined by Professors David Fellman, Henry Hart, and Leon Epstein." (Gray, 1957)
- "I well remember one meeting with my dissertation director which was interrupted as he went to a press conference to defend himself against charges derived from his presidency, a number of years before, of a national student organization that, like a number of other benign activities, had received some funding from the CIA." (Beckett, 1970)
- "It is my sense that the number of graduate students taken in had been greatly expanded fairly recently, and that ways of bringing graduate students together, and graduate students together with faculty (and, perhaps, faculty with faculty) were not well developed, and had not jelled into a rounded comprehensive system of professional formation." (Beckett, 1970)

- One student who was active in the 1979–80 and 1982–83 TAA strikes notes, "In terms of the department, what I most appreciate was the tolerance, taking me back in after the strike and accepting me despite my radicalism at the time, and despite the fact that most professors in the UW political science department opposed the strike." (Forrest, 1987)
- ". . . when Sterling Hall was bombed, I walked past it the next morning on my way to teach a summer session course in the department." (Hershey, 1972)
- "Tear gas, marches, violence, and finally the math building bombing made discussions of politics, revolution, and repression all too real. Particularly given the powerful (if cherubic) presence of Murray Edelman, I found it difficult to buy completely the prevalent theories. Think, for example, of structuring your theoretical world around David Easton and his system. Geesh. In the end, the various strands of polisci at Madison proved richer than any theoretical construct could contain." (Loomis, 1974)

The Wisconsin Idea

Finally, a number of respondents invoked the Wisconsin Idea in their characterization of the department and the work of UW faculty members.

- "The department's connection to the UW and the 'Wisconsin Idea' stand out above all else." (Brown, 1971)
- "I had always felt that the Wisconsin Idea of research in service to the public was well understood and appreciated in the department. Practical policy analysis and assessment was as welcome during my time there as the highly theoretical work that dominated some of the sub-disciplines."(Dubois, 1978)
- "Dennis Dresang was, for me, an example of the Wisconsin Idea in action." (Altemus, 1975)
- "I acquired respect for the 'Wisconsin Idea' that the boundaries of the university were the boundaries of the state."
- ". . . most important, the concept of the 'Wisconsin Idea'—that the university ought to be of some practical use to the government sometimes. This has been very influential in my career and thinking." (Mooney, 1990)
- "I . . . believe the ready link between academe and policy-makers was distinctive, heavily influenced by the 'Wisconsin Idea' whose influence

permeated the university. I admit that I understood this relationship less during my time at Madison than after I had departed, but I believe that my heavy involvement in public service was strongly influenced by the model of professional responsibility and opportunity that I saw at Madison." (Pika, 1979)

- "It was in my time a 'distinctive' department in only one sense . . . its collective heart was a Midwest tradition of empiricism and institutionalism, and particularly for Wisconsin, committed to the Wisconsin Idea of policy commitment and public service." (Sorauf, 1953)

Others feel the emphasis on preparing graduate students for academic careers in political science draws away from preparing others for public service.

- "[The department was] too narrowly focused on preparing students for academic careers. . . . I don't find the political science journals offer much relevance to me in doing my job. Organizational behavior theories, yes. That saddens me because I would like to see political science making a more useful, constructive contribution to public policy formation and implementation." (not for attribution)

Other Comments

- "Gary King was, of course, something of a legend. He lived just down the hill from us at Eagle Heights and had the first PC, which he introduced to my son Patrick, who was about one at the time. . . . I will never forget when a particular candidate for the Hawkins Chair, a rather big name in the behavioral field, was eviscerated in a series of questions by Gary King sitting at the table in the Ogg room. The rest of us graduate students, sitting in the audience chairs behind the table, just watched with somewhat sinful delight." (Hertzke, 1986)
- "The department allowed its graduates to leave with their love of politics still intact." (Kagay, 1972)

And our favorite:

- "I did get a summer job driving the Zamboni machine at Colorado College, which I never would have done other than having to do my academic sojourn." (Siemers, 1997)

Some Notable (Mostly Nonacademic) Careers

- Vaughn Altemus, Education Finance Director, VT Department of Education

- Thomas J. Bossert, Director, Politics and Governance Group, Department of Population and International Health, Harvard School of Public Health
- Don Brown, Commissioner of Higher Education, Texas Higher Education Coordinating Board
- Stephen Burant, Intelligence Research Specialist, U.S. Department of State
- Charles Dahm, Pastor, St. Pious V Parish, Chicago, IL
- Philip Dubois, President, University of Wyoming
- Roderick Groves, Chancellor (Emeritus), Illinois Board of Regents
- Mark Huddleston, Dean, College of Arts and Sciences, University of Delaware; President, Ohio Wesleyan
- William Jenkins, Director, Financial Markets & Community Investment, General Accounting Office
- Michel Kagay, Polling Director, *New York Times*
- Joel Margolis, President, Program Evaluation and Management Research, Inc.
- Dennis M. Sherman, Vice President Global Business Development, Exxon-Mobil Corp. (retired)
- Robert H. Trice, Sr. Vice President Corporate Business Development, Lockheed Martin Corp.
- Chai-Aman Samudavanija; Senator, Thai Parliament; Judge of Constitutional Court

Appendix 19

Political Science Association of Students

The atmosphere of intense activism and protest induced by the Vietnam War and the Martin Luther King assassination in 1968 gave rise to a short-lived but briefly forceful graduate student association, the Political Science Association of Students (PSAS, better known as "Pizazz"). The title, one of the founders, Brian Silver, recollects, was chosen in part because of the appealing acronym it yielded. Interviews with a pair of its main leaders, Michael Kirn (1972, now dean of Augsburg College), and Jules Steinberg (1977, now at Denison University), and the written souvenirs from Silver, confirmed our own recollections that PSAS emerged in 1968, and had vanished by 1970. Its main preoccupations were departmental governance (the demand for a student voice) and the direction of the discipline (challenging its allegedly conservative quantitative and behavioral orientation), plus the perennial issue of preliminary examination reform.

The Political Science Association of Students was the product of a given graduate student generation, those in their pre-dissertation phase in the 1968–70 period, a tumultuous era marked by the February 1969 black student strike, the prolonged 1970 teaching assistant strike, and the massive protest demonstrations triggered by the May 1970 bombing in Cambodia. Activist energies appear to have shifted by 1970 into the vigorous Teaching Assistant Association (TAA) campaign for formal recognition as bargaining agent. The August 1970 Sterling Hall bombing dramatically altered the campus mood; in its wake, PSAS vanished from the scene, but not before having secured some new representation on department committee structures concerned with graduate curriculum, and changes in prelim regulations. The PSAS generation also produced a "New Testament" of practical survival guidance for graduate students, as an offset to the official "Bible" of graduate program regulations. One of its authors, Peter Cocks, contributed a memorable phrase of justification for the document: "If *history* is the word that we use to refer to our mistakes, this essay is designed to help you to avoid making history."

The following extracts from surviving PSAS publications convey the temper of the times.

November 1968

PSAS General Principles

While recognizing the diversity of opinion and political preferences that underlie a number of shared concerns for political science education, the Political Science Association of Students seeks to foster a critical examination of this political science department, its teachers and students, its courses, its internal mechanisms of control, its position in the university, and the society. We base our Association on the following beliefs:

I. Each student has a right to participate in determining the nature of his education:

   A. In order to have a university oriented to critical learning, we believe there should be a community of scholars. Students and faculty should look upon each other as equal members of this community. The present caste-like relationship is archaic and should be replaced by the recognition that we are all students of political science.

   B. Since students are as much a part of the department as the faculty and are as much affected by its policies, we believe it imperative that students and faculty become equal participants in the determination of departmental policy.

   C. The community of scholars should be critically oriented to political science and society. Assumptions, stated or not, underlying courses, lectures, and the writings of fellow political scientists, must be rigorously analyzed. This critical approach should produce more satisfactory analyses and interpretations of contemporary American society and politics.

II. The university, having numerous intellectual resources, has a responsibility to society at large. We see the university presently serving, in large part, to perpetuate the status quo of our society. We want the university to seek actively to change American society—to help achieve a more humanistic society—free from wars, racism, and other unnecessary ills. . . .

[A university] must be governed democratically, with each of its constituent units sharing equally in the decision-making processes. It must be a virtual community of scholars whose policies are formed by groups of individual, each with different social background, and all with varying degrees of education. . . . In departmental decisions of finance, hiring and firing, tenure, curricula, and teaching assignments, all members of the Political Science department should be granted equal participation.

THEREFORE, THE POLITICAL SCIENCE ASSOCIATION OF STUDENTS PROPOSES THE PLACEMENT OF STUDENTS IN AN EQUAL RATIO TO FACULTY ON ALL DEPARTMENTAL COMMITTEES. TO ENSURE THE EXECUTION OF THE POLICIES OF THESE COMMITTEES, THE P.S.A.S. CALLS FOR THE DEPARTMENT TO ESTABLISH A SENATE COMPOSED OF ALL FACULTY MEMBERS AND AN EQUAL NUMBER OF ELECTED STUDENT REPRESENTATIVES. ALL SENATE MEMBERS ARE TO HAVE EQUAL VOTING POWER, AND STUDENT REPRESENTATIVES ARE ACCOUNTABLE TO THE STUDENTS OF THE DEPARTMENT AT LARGE.

POLITICO #3, 14 March 1969

. . . If we are to assume the task of confronting the politics of our discipline and thus make structural challenges and content challenges, we must understand what the pressures are that act upon Political Science, why it is what it is. Why it has been unable to deal not only with racism, but also with war, exploitation, and poverty. We must understand that we are being socialized by a department and by a discipline that cannot in any meaningful way deal with such problems We are being trained to do research over, under, around and through problems, but Political Science is not finding answers because it is financed and for the most part controlled by institutions that oftentimes find themselves in open conflict with the ghetto dwellers, the worker, the peasant and with us.

— *Dave Roloff*

Memorandum from Chair Bernard C. Cohen, 20 March 1969

Contrary to what you may have read in *Politico*, the faculty has not "agreed to set aside one period after 6-week exams to discuss the success of the course, its content, its structure, and its grading procedures." Nor did the Undergraduate Curriculum Committee urge the faculty to do this.

1970 Mass Meeting

On 15 May 1970, at the initiative of some undergraduate majors, though not explicitly by PSAS itself, an invitation was issued to a mass meeting of the "Department of Political Science," which in the summons was announced as consisting of all undergraduate majors, graduate students, and faculty. This followed a model employed in several other large departments, and gave rise to a series of resolutions in the name of these units denouncing the escalation of the Vietnam War. The assembly attracted several dozen participants, mostly students. David Fellman had agreed to chair the session. Then Chair Crawford Young had informed the faculty that, though he had supported student requests for assignment of a large lecture room for the assembly, he did not intend to attend, since those participating could not legitimately claim to speak for the Department of Political Science per se. Selections from the resolution convey the mood of anger, crisis and urgency which attended the wave of mass protests in Cambodia spring.

1. That a campus-wide referendum should be held immediately on whether the University should be closed before the end of this academic year.

2. That U.S. involvement in S.E. Asia be terminated immediately and Congressional proposals to limit funding for this illegal and immoral war be supported.

. . .

4. That the University suspend classes for the two week period prior to the National and State elections of November 3, 1970, to facilitate the legitimate expression of political sentiment and that if the University does not suspend classes the Department of Political Science will do so.

5. That funds be raised to send a delegation of students and faculty working on the election of peace candidates for Congress from the State of Wisconsin and on the National "Movement for a New Congress."

. . .

8. That the Political Science Department as a matter of daily procedure have a moment of reverent silence before each class in memory of those who have died and those who are yet to die in the war in Southeast Asia; furthermore that the Department urge the Chancellor that this practice be made university wide.

9. That all Political Science classes for the rest of the semester be suspended to allow members of the Political Science department to participate in constructive expressions of their political sentiments during this crisis.

Appendix 20

Political Science Courses at 10-Year Intervals

Fall Semester 1916–17

Course #	Course Title	Instructor	Enrollment
1	General Political Science	Hornbeck	22
2	Elementary Law	Hall	43
7	American Government & Politics	Hall	162
109	Roman Law	Carpenter	11
117	Federal Administration	Ogg	17
118	International Law	Hornbeck	10
119	Contemporary International Politics	Hornbeck	63
122	Party Government	Jones	33
126	Legislation	Jones	28
127	European Government	Ogg	22
132	Contemporary Political Problems	Carpenter	28
138	Contemporary International Relations	Jones	14
145	Historical Political Thought	Hornbeck	8
203	Administrative Law III	Hall	19
252	Seminar: Legislation	Jones	5
258	Seminar: Administration	Ogg	2
261	Seminar: Constitutional Law	Hall	4

Spring Semester 1916–17

Course #	Course Title	Instructor	Enrollment
1	General Political Science	Hornbeck	29
7	American Government & Politics	Hall	101
13	Municipal Government	Ogg	37
111	Jurisprudence	Carpenter	15
112	Constitutional Law	Hall	15
114	Municipal Function	Macgregor	13
115	Municipal Problems	Ogg	15
116	State Administration	Ogg	28
119	Contemporary International Politics	Jones, Hornbeck	88
120	Far Eastern Politics	Hornbeck	10
123	Foreign Service	Jones	17
125	Law or the Press	Carpenter	9
126	Legislation	Jones	19
131	Latin American Inst.	Carpenter	90
136	American Diplomacy	Jones	39
204	Administrative Law IV	Hall	14

218	International Law	Hornbeck	9
252	Seminar: Legislation	Jones	5
258	Seminar: Administration	Ogg	6
261	Seminar: Constitutional Law	Hall	5

Political Science Cumulative Enrollment 1916–17 1086

Fall Semester 1919–20

Course #	Course Title	Instructor	Enrollment
7	Government in the United States	Hall	157
13	Municipal Government	MacGregor	61
112	American Constitutional Law	Hall	18
118	International Law	Page	24
125	Modern Imperialism	Ogg	14
127	Government & Politics of England	Ogg	26
129	Problems Of Democracy	Hall	55
145	History of Political Thought	Ogg	23
201	Administrative Law I	Hall	25

Spring Semester 1919–20

Course #	Course Title	Instructor	Enrollment
2	Elementary Law	Hall	282
7	Government & Politics	Hall	165
25	Law of Press	Rundell	18
32	Contemporary Political Thought	Stuart	87
115	Municipal Government	MacGregor	51
117	Federal Administration	Ogg	44
118	International Law	Page	16
122	Party Government	Stuart	55
124	British Colonies	Ogg	43
128	Government Continental Europe	Ogg	28
131	Latin America	Stuart	24
202	Administrative Law II	Hall	31
256	Seminar	Ogg	8

Political Science Cumulative Enrollment 1919–20 1134

Fall Semester 1929–30

Course #	Course Title	Instructor	Enrollment
1	Introduction to Government and Politics	Gaus	255
13	Municipal Government	Kirk	52
101	Elementary Political Science	Grant	35
112	Constitutional Law	Grant	38
114	Problems in Municipal Government	McGregor	28
118	International Law	Mason	13
123	American Diplomacy	Potter	41

125	World Politics	Kirk	65
127	Comparative Government: England	Mason	13
131	US & Latin America	Jones	43
137	League of Nations	Potter	70
139	Government of Wisconsin	Jacobson	15
140	Far Eastern Politics	Ogg	20
165	American Political Ideas	Jacobson	18
180	Reading Course	Grant, Jacobson	3
245	European Political Thought	Gaus	14
250	Advanced Comparative Government	Ogg	17
255	Seminar World Politics	Ogg	17
259	Seminar on International Law	Potter	6

Spring Semester 1929–30

Course #	Course Title	Instructor	Enrollment
1	Introduction to Government and Politics	Gaus	102
2	Elementary Law	Grant	175
110	National Government of the United States	Jacobson	9
112	Constitutional Law	Grant	28
115	Social Problems Of Municipal Government	Macgregor	61
122	Political Parties	Harris	50
125	World Politics	Kirk	73
128	Continental Europe	Mason	14
131	US & Latin America	Jones	38
133	Africa & Near East	Kirk	72
135	Municipal Administration	Harris	26
137	League of Nations	Mason	15
141	Far Eastern Politics	Ogg	16
143	Principles Of Administration	Harris	12
144	Police Power	Grant	17
150	Thesis	Grant	2
165	American Political Ideas	Jacobson	29
180	Reading Course	Harris, Grant	3
245	European Political Thought	Gaus	15
250	Advanced Comparative Government	Ogg	17
255	Seminar on World Politics	Ogg	16
Political Science Cumulative Enrollment 1929–30			1511

Fall Semester 1940–41

Course #	Course Title	Instructor	Enrollment
7	American Government and Politics	Staff	356
13	Municipal Government	Salter	88

101	European Political Thought	Ebenstein	51
103	Fiscal Policies	Groves	25
112	Constitutional Law	Pfankuchen	52
115	Law in Society	Garrison	100
118	International Law	Pfankuchen	17
122	Political Parties & Citizenship	Salter	34
124	Taxation	Groves	115
127	British Commonwealth	Ebenstein	31
134	Rural Local Government	Pfankuchen	17
138	Pro-Seminar	Ebenstein	26
140	Far Eastern Politics	Ogg	31
143	Public Admin	Gaus, Beard	76
147	Government And Technology	Beard	23
148	Pro-Seminar	Salter	12
180	Special Work	Gaus, Pfankuchen	2
200	Graduate Thesis	Salter, Pfankuchen	2
245	European Political Thought	Gaus	11
250	Advanced Comparative Government	Ogg	17
255	Seminar	Ogg, Gaus	14

Spring Semester 1940–41

Course #	Course Title	Instructor	Enrollment
7	American Government and Politics	Stoke, et al	258
119	International Law	Pfankuchen	27
122	Political Parties & Citizenship	Salter	107
126	Legislation	Witte, Salter	79
128	Comparative Government	Ebenstein	97
135	Municipal Administration	Beard	88
140	Far Eastern Politics	Ogg	34
142	Public Utilities	Glaeser	169
143	Public Administration	Gaus, Beard	69
146	Government & Business	Witte	178
148	Pro-Seminar	Salter	17
150	Political Geography	Hartshorne	31
152	Conservation of Natural Resources	Pfankuchen	16
166	Contemporary American Political Thought	Ebenstein	92
180	Special Work	Staff	4
200	Research	Staff	7
245	European Political Thought	Gaus, Stokes	12
250	Advanced Comparative Government	Ogg	11
255	Seminar	Ogg, Gaus, Pfankuchen	22

Political Science Cumulative Enrollment 1940–41 860

Fall Semester 1950–51

Course #	Course Title	Instructor	Enrollment
7	American Government and Politics	Stokes	803
13	Municipal Government	Hart	56
21	Foundations and Problems of International Relations (crosslisted with 121)	Pfankuchen, Hartshorne (geography)	18
100	Senior Thesis	Staff	2
101	Introduction to Political Theory	Epstein	74
112a	Constitutional Law	Fellman	54
118a	Principles of International Law: Law of Peace	Pfankuchen	33
121	Introduction to International Relations (crosslisted with 21)	Pfankuchen, Hartshorne (geography)	50
122	Political Parties and Public Opinion	Salter	75
123	Administration of United States Foreign Policy	McCamy	200
127	Comparative Government: The British Commonwealth	Epstein	23
130	Governments of Latin America	Stokes	36
134	Rural Local Government	Clarenbach	19
137	International Organization and Diplomacy	Thomson	17
140	Far Eastern Politics	Thomson	54
143	Introduction to Public Administration	Hart	54
148	Proseminar: Political Parties and Public Opinion	Salter	8
152	Government and Natural Resources	Clarenbach	5
155	Proseminar: The United States and the Far East	Thomson	14
165	History of American Political Thought	Fellman	68
172	Politics of Pressure Groups	Huitt	16
173	Seminar: Public Opinion	Huitt	52
174	Seminar: Advanced American Government	Stokes	16
180	Special Work	Staff	9
200	Thesis	Staff	13
245a	History of Political Thought	Young	N/A
250	Seminar in European Government	Epstein	N/A
258	Seminar in Public Administration	McCamy	N/A
259	Seminar in International Law and Organization	Pfankuchen	N/A
262	Seminar in Latin American Government, Politics and International Relations	Stokes	N/A
270a	Seminar in Public Planning	Clarenbach	N/A

Spring Semester 1950–51

Course #	Course Title	Instructor	Enrollment
7	American Government and Politics	Stokes	625
21	Foundations and Problems of International Relations (crosslisted with 121)	Pfankuchen	48
101	Introduction to Political Theory	Epstein	66
110	Government and the Problems of Democracy	Hart	53
112b	Constitutional Law	Fellman	43
118b	Principles of International Law: Law of War and Neutrality	Fellman	17
121	Introduction to International Relations (crosslisted with 21)	Pfankuchen	52
122	Political Parties and Citizenship	Salter	66
123	Administration of United States Foreign Policy	McCamy	221
126	Seminar: Legislation	Huitt	67
128	Comparative Government: Continental Europe	Epstein	39
131	International Relations of Latin America	Stokes	60
138	Contemporary Problems in International Relations	Pfankuchen	21
139	State Government	Young	42
140	Far Eastern Politics	Thomson	92
143	Introduction to Public Administration	Hart, Young	99
148	Proseminar: Political Parties and Public Opinion	Salter	N/A
155	Proseminar: the United States and the Far East	Thomson	N/A
156	Proseminar: Prospects and Problems of World Government	Thomson	N/A
159	Seminar: Problems in American Foreign Policy	McCamy, Ellsworth (economics), Hartshorne (geography)	N/A
163	Seminar: Local Planning and Administration	Clarenbach	N/A
166	Seminar: Contemporary American Political Thought	Clarenbach	N/A
170	Seminar: The Civil Service	Hart	N/A
171	Seminar: Civil Liberties in the United States	Fellman	N/A
173	Seminar: Public Opinion	Huitt	N/A
175	Proseminar: Politics of Pressure Groups	Huitt	N/A

187b	Seminar: International Relations of Scandinavia	Kjeldstadli (Scandinavian)	N/A
245b	History of Political Thought	Young	N/A
258	Seminar in Public Administration	McCamy	N/A
270b	Seminar in Public Planning	Clarenbach	N/A
Political Science Cumulative Enrollment 1950–51			**3768**

Fall Semester 1960–61

Course #	Course Title	Instructor	Enrollment
3	Introduction to Political Analysis	Thorson	123
7a	American Government and Politics: The National Government	Staff	1134
7b	American Government and Politics State and Local Government and Intergovernmental Relations	Staff	45
13	Municipal Government	Staff	34
21	International Relations	Pfankuchen, Staff	99
27	Introduction to Foreign Politics	Armstrong	47
101	Introduction to Political Theory	Epstein	N/A
107a	American Government and Politics: The National Government	Cohen, von der Mehden	92
107b	American Government and Politics: State and Local Govt. and Intergovernmental Relations	Clarenbach	29
112a	Constitutional Law	Fellman	82
115	Law in Society	Auerbach, Mermin	21
118a	Principles of International Law: Law of War of Peace	Pfankuchen	27
121	Foundations and Problems in International Relations	Pfankuchen, Hartshorne (geography)	51
122	Political Parties and Citizenship	Salter	64
123	Conduct of American Foreign Affairs	McCamy	82
124a	Public Finance	Groves (econ.)	10
127	British Politics	Epstein	33
131	Latin American International Relations	Donald	28
133	Government and Politics of the Soviet Union	Armstrong	67
137	International Organizations and the United Nations	Cohen	51
140	Far-Eastern Politics	von der Mehden	28
142	Public Utilities	Thatcher	2
143	Introduction to Public Administration	McCamy	68
146	Government and Business	Granick	7

148	Proseminar: Political Parties and Public Opinion	Salter	27
149	Seminar: Government and Natural Resources	Clarenbach	8
151	Seminar: Politics of India	Hart	10
153	Seminar: Politics of Underdeveloped Areas	von der Mehden	31
159	Seminar: Problems in Foreign and Military Policy	Cohen	44
165	Seminar: History of American Political Thought	Fellman	78
166	Seminar: Contemporary American Political Thought	Thorson	25
173	Seminar: Public Opinion	Staff	28
186	Honors Proseminar in Political Problems	Young	2
194	Seminar: Intro to Public Opinion Research	Reiss	3
195a	Seminar in Military Policy and Administration in the Postwar Period	Runge	7
200	Thesis	Staff	11
245a	History of Political Thought	Young	15
250a	Seminar in Comparative Politics	Epstein	16
260a	Seminar in International Relations	Armstrong	6
270a	Seminar in Public Planning	Woodbury	20
278	Methods of Research in Public Administration	Donoghue	8
280	Special Work		15

Spring Semester 1960–61

Course #	Course Title	Instructor	Enrollment
3	Introduction to Political Analysis	Thorson	64
7a	Am Government and Politics: The National Government	Staff	938
7b	American Government and Politics: State and Local Government and Intergovernmental Relations	Staff	146
21	International Relations	Pfankuchen, Staff	169
27	Introduction to Foreign Politics	Armstrong, Anderson, Thorson	212
51b	The Civilization of India	Gore	6
101	Intro to Political Theory	Epstein	96
107a	American Government and Politics: The National Government	von der Mehden	71
112b	Constitutional Law	Fellman	60

118b	Principles of International Law: Law of War and Neutrality	Pfankuchen	29
122	Political Parties and Citizenship	Salter	70
123	Conduct of American Foreign Affairs	Cohen	70
124a	Public Finance—Taxation	Groves	8
124b	Public Finance—Taxes, Debts, Expenditures	Groves	6
126	Seminar: Legislation	Polsby	43
128	Seminar: Continental European Politics	Epstein	75
130	Seminar: Latin-American Politics	Anderson	43
136	Seminar: Soviet Foreign Policy	Armstrong	105
142	Public Utilities	Thatcher	4
143	Introduction to Public Administration	Penniman	30
148	Proseminar: Political Parties and Pub Opinion		Salter
45			
153	Seminar: Politics of Underdeveloped Areas	von der Mehden	60
159	Problems in American Foreign and Military Policy		Cohen
60			
171	Seminar: Civil Liberties in the United States	Fellman	68
172	Seminar: Politics of Pressure Groups	Froman	30
180	Special Work	Staff	4
195b	Seminar in Military Policy and Administrationin the Postwar Period	Runge	10
200	Thesis	Staff	16
245b	History of Political Thought	Young	11
250b	Seminar in Comparative Politics	von der Mehden	14
258	Seminar in Public Administration	Penniman	7
260b	Seminar in International Relations	Cohen	23
270b	Seminar in Public Planning	Woodbury	16
277	Seminar in Comparative Public Administration		Hart
11			
280	Special Work	Staff	13
285	Seminar in River Basin Planning	Clarenbach, Lenz	1
290	Interdepartmental Seminar in Latin-American Problems	Anderson, et al	4
294	Seminar in the Design and Process of Survey Research	Fisher	N/A

Political Science Cumulative Enrollment 1960–61 5154

Fall Semester 1970–71

Course #	Course Title	Instructor	Enrollment
101	Introduction to Politics	Hart; Eisinger; Wilde; Leavitt	767
106	Introduction to Comparative Politics	Hayward	206

175	International Relations	Pfankuchen	98
181	Introduction to Politics-Honors	Hart	36
199	Independent Work	Edelman	1
218	Politics of Poverty & Social Welfare	Rosenbaum	162
252	The Civilization ff India	Elder	150
277	Africa: Introductory Survey	Wiley	135
316	Principles of International Law	Pfankuchen	59
340	Introduction Public Finance & Fiscal Politics	Chao	32
359	Problems in American Foreign Policy	Tarr	83
375	Foundations & Problems of International Relations	Pfankuchen	98
405	State Government & Public Policy	Donoghue	56
411	Constitutional Law	Grossman	185
413	Problems Of Urban Areas	Rosenbaum	36
413	Problems Of Urban Areas	Rosenbaum	23
424	National Parties & Policy	Ranney	65
424	National Parties & Policy	Ranney	60
461	Organization Theory & Practice	Edelman	27
471	Civil Liberties in the United States	Fellman	164
472	Politics of Pressure Groups	Edelman	69
477	Political Socialization	Merelman	43
500	Public Utilities	Fuller	91
501	Development of Ancient & Medieval Western Political Thought	Fowler	49
544	Introduction to Survey Research	Sharp	47
547	Political Future: National, Sub-National, Transnational	Lindberg	45
627	The British Political System	Epstein	31
630	Latin American Politics	Wilde	40
636	Soviet Foreign Policy	Armstrong	34
639	Far Easter Policy – Southeast Asia	Emmerson	20
646	China in World Politics	Friedman	92
653	Politics of Underdeveloped Areas	Emmerson	11
654	Politics of Revolution	Friedman	300
654	Politics of Revolution	Meisner	-
654	Politics of Revolution	Hosking	29
658	Nationalism & Communism Eastern Europe	Hosking	28
660	African Politics	C. Young	19
675	Policy Making in American States	Sharkansky	38
677	Governments of Scandinavia	Hamalainen	17
681	Senior Honors Thesis	Cohen	8
695	Proseminar: Topics in Political Science	Epstein	14

699	Independent Work		13
772	Development Planning & Administration	W. Young	18
815	Urban Government. & Policy	Eisinger	26
817	Empirical Methods of Political Inquiry	Leavitt	37
824	Politics and Social Process	Merelman	29
831	Concepts in Political Theory	Fowler	24
850	Comparative Politics of Western Nations	Lindberg	19
851	Soviet International Policy: Communism and Nation-State System	Armstrong	13
865	Supreme Court & Constitutional American Politics	Grossman	12
868	Seminar: Rationale of Public Planning	Woodbury	40
873	American Party System	Ranney	23
878	Public Administration	Penniman	15
878	Public Administration	Penniman	22
878	Public Administration	W. Young	27
953	Seminar: American Foreign Policy	Cohen	12
954	Seminar: Revolution & Violence	Friedman	15
958	Seminar: Public Admin	Sharkansky	10
961	Seminar: African Politics	Hayward	10
963	Seminar: Public Law	Grossman	7
965	Seminar: River Basin Planning	Born	17
990	Research and Thesis		26
999	Independent Work		27

Spring Semester 1970–71

Course #	Course Title	Instructor	Enrollment
101	Intro to Politics	Lewis; Wilde; Cocks	414
106	Introduction to Comparative Politics	Hayward	228
175	International Relations	Pfankuchen	61
181	Introduction Politics—Honors	Hart	18
218	Poverty & Social Welfare	Rosenbaum	197
277	Africa: Introductory Survey	Wiley	365
316	Principles in International Law	Pfankuchen	22
340	Introduction to Public Finance & Fiscal Policy	Chao	36
352	Role of Government—The Economy	Weiss	48
359	Problems in American Foreign Policy	Tarr	51
365	International Systems & Process	Kay	23
367	Alliance & Security Community—Atlantic	Leavitt	21
375	Foundations & Problems of International Relations	Pfankuchen	61
377	Politics Force-International Relations	Tarr	67
404	American National Government	Cohen	25

405	State Government & Public Policy	Rosenbaum	39
408	The American Presidency	W. Young	92
412	Constitutional Law	Grossman	180
417	American Judicial System	Grossman	140
420	Administrative Law	Fellman	52
423	Conduct of American Foreign Affairs	Cohen	61
463	Evolution of American Planning	T Logan	50
467	Elections & Voting Behavior	McCrone	82
473	Public Opinion	Merelman	36
477	Political Socialization	Merelman	48
500	Public Utilities	Dodge	82
501	Development of Ancient & Medieval Western Political Thought	Fowler	52
502	Development of Modern Western Political Thought	Anderson	65
503	Cont Political Thought	Kirn	75
504	Science & Government	Steinhart	25
620	Western European Political Systems—Germany	Armstrong	24
621	Western European Political Systems—France & Italy	Wilde	44
630	Latin American Politics	Wilde	20
636	Soviet Foreign Policy	Armstrong	48
639	Far East Politics—Southeast Asia	Emmerson	17
644	Administration of Public Policy	Sharkansky	41
651	Politics of South Asia	H Hart	16
653	Politics of Underdeveloped Areas	Dresang	38
662	African International Relations	Hayward	28
678	Scandinavia in International Relations	Hamalainen	8
682	Senior Honors Thesis	Fowler	6
696	Proseminar: Problems in Political Science	Emmerson	12
699	Independent Reading		18
771	Development Planning & Administration	W. Young	32
821	Mass Political Behavior	McCrone	11
832	Concepts in Political Theory	Fowler	22
851	Soviet International Politics—Communism & Nation-State System	Croan	21
877	Comparative Public Administration	Dresang	38
919	Seminar: Advanced Methodology	Clausen	16
935	Seminar: Political Socialization	Dennis	20
943	Seminar: Budget & Tax Administration	W. Young	10
949	Seminar: Soviet Politics	Armstrong	3
950	Seminar: Comparative Politics—Western Nations	Anderson	11

958	Seminar: Public Administration	Penniman	34
959	Seminar: International Organizations	Kay	8
964	Seminar: Design Process Survey Research	Sharp	10
966	Seminar: Water Resource Planning	Clarenbach	12
969	Seminar: Trends & Issues Public Planning	Woodbury	11
974	Seminar: Politics & Public Policy	Sharkansky	12
982	Independent Seminar: Latin-American Area	Denevan; Harvey	8
990	Research and Thesis	Anderson	13
999	Independent Work	Sharkansky	42

Political Science Cumulative Enrollment 1970–71 **7499**

Fall Semester 1980–81

Course #	Course Title	Instructor	Enrollment
101	Introduction to Political Analysis	M. Young; Fulenwider	229
104	Introduction to American National Government	Huitt; Wilson; Gormley	395
106	Introduction to Comparative Politics	Hayward	204
181	Introduction Political Analysis—Honors	Edelman	34
201	Special Topics in Political Science	Wallin; Wilson	128
209	Issues in Political Thought	Fowler	96
213	Urban Politics	Eisinger	72
219	Introduction to Public Policy	Anderson	56
252	The Civilization Of India	Elder	7
275	Introduction to International Relations	Sanders	126
277	Africa- Introductory Survey	Feierman	19
336	Soviet Foreign Policy	Croan	138
340	Public Finance	Lampman	3
352	Role of Government—The Economy	Weiss	9
359	Problems—American Foreign Policy	Armstrong	142
377	Politics of Force—International Relations	Tarr	57
401	Selected Topics—Political Science	Feeley; Bumiller	72
405	State Government & Public Policy	Donoghue	50
408	The American Presidency	W. Young	104
411	Constitutional Law	Grossman	139
417	American Judicial System	Kritzer	109
420	Administrative Law	Gormley	63
427	Legislative Internship	Raymond	18
448	Energy Policy and Politics	Lindberg	32
449	Government & Natural Resources	Hart	55
463	Evolution of Am Planning	Roberts	5
467	Elections & Voting Behavior	Dennis	23
471	Civil Liberties in the United States	Feeley	57

472	Politics of Pressure Groups	Huitt	68
502	Development of Modern Western Political Thought	Riley	80
512	Science & Government	Steinhart	9
544	Introduction to Survey Research	Sharp	1
554	Quantitative Analysis of Political Data	Sanders	37
577	Contemporary Scandinavia: Politics & History	Hamalainen	8
611	Comparative Political Economy	Lindberg	44
651	Politics of South Asia	Hart	11
658	Nationalism & Social Change: Eastern Europe	Armstrong	29
660	African Politics	M. Young	34
665	Religion and Politics	Fowler	93
682/691	Senior Honors Thesis/Senior Thesis		16
695	Proseminar: Topics in Political Science	Grossman	15
698/699	Directed Study		26
772	Development Planning & Administration	W. Young	14
815	Urban Government & Politics	Eisinger	4
820	Urban Political Theory	Edelman	4
821	Mass Political Behavior	Dennis	14
826	The Legislative Process	Hinckley	18
831	Concepts in Political Theory	Riley	16
857	International Relations Theories	Richardson	23
860	Totalitarian Political Systems	Croan	13
877	Comparative Public Administration	Dresang	33
878	Public Administration	Penniman	9
919	Seminar: Advanced Methodology	Kritzer	7
937	Topics: Political Psychology & Sociology	Sapiro	3
943	Seminar: Budget & Tax Administration	Gosling	4
958	Seminar: Public Administration	Penniman	1
990	Research and Thesis		41
999	Independent Work		15

Spring Semester 1980–81

Course #	Course Title	Instructor	Enrollment
101	Introduction to Political Analysis	Emmerson	125
104	Introduction to American Government	Gormley; Huitt; Schneider	375
106	Introduction to Comparative Politics	Armstrong	117
181	Introduction Politics—Honors	Edelman	17
209	Issues in Political Thought	Croan	121
260	Latin America—Introduction	Stern	16
275	Introduction to International Relations	Richardson	123

277	Africa—Introductory Survey	Hunter	16
323	Conduct of American Foreign Affairs	Cohen	100
331	Latin America—International Relations	Stallings	43
352	Role of Government—The Economy	Weiss	16
368	Politics of Underdeveloped Areas	Emmerson	64
375	International Relations	Richardson	144
401	Selected Topics—Political Science	Lindberg	44
405	State Government & Public Policy	Wallin	161
412	Constitutional Law	Grossman	136
413	Problems Urban Areas	Eisinger	54
424	American Parties & Politics	Epstein	117
426	Legislative Process	Hinckley	71
427	Legislative Internship	Linehan	26
463	Evolution of Am Planning	Roberts	9
467	Elections & Voting Behavior	Fowler	62
476	Political Elites & Leadership	Sapiro	35
477	Political Socialization	Merelman	27
479	Political Communications	Edelman	63
502	Development Modern Western Political Thought	Anderson	56
530	Ethics & Values—Policy Making	Anderson	32
565	History of American Political Thought	Fowler	110
570	Literature and Politics	Merelman	44
613	Water Policy—Politics and Institutions	Hart	19
620	Western European Political System—Germany	Croan	42
640	Politics of Japan	Pharr	28
681/682	Senior Honors Thesis	Richardson	6
698/699	Directed Study		17
771	Development Planning & Admin	W. Young	18
818	Topics: Analysis of Political Data	Kritzer	9
819	Quantitative Methods—Public Policy	Browning	2
850	Comparative Politics—Advanced Industrial Nations	Armstrong	15
868	Rationale—Public Planning	Howe	1
871	Public Policy Evaluation	Gormley	9
873	American Party System	Epstein	20
875	Public Personnel Administration	Dresang	4
876	Federalism & Intergovernmental Policy—US	Wallin	5
878	Public Administration	Penniman	6
937	Topics: Political Psychology & Sociology	Dennis	5
945	Seminar: National Security Affairs	Tarr	14

950	Seminar: Comparative Politics—West Nations	Lindberg	11
960	Seminar: International Relations	Stallings	29
963	Seminar: Public Law	Grossman	8
969	Com Sys: Planners & Architects	Orton	-
974	Seminar: Politics & Public Policy	McGown	9
982	Seminar: Latin America Area	Skidmore	3
990	Research and Thesis		39
999	Independent Work		24
Political Science Cumulative Enrollment 1980–81			**5797**

Fall Semester 1990–91

Course #	Course Title	Instructor	Enrollment
101	Introduction to Political Analysis	Merelman; Young	95
102	American National, State & Local Government	Canon	176
104	Introduction American National Government	Canon; Rahn	641
106	Introduction to Comparative Politics	Anderson; Christner; Inglot	471
181	Introduction—Pol Honors Course	Croan	19
201	Special Topics Political Science	Meznaric	8
205	Introduction to State Government	Dresang	171
209	Issues in Political Thought	Riley	110
244	Southeast Asia: Vietnam to Philippines	Streckfuss	18
252	The Civilization of India	Elder	28
271	Introduction to Afro-American Politics	Culverson	45
275	Introduction to International Relations	Julseth; Gunderson	261
277	Africa: Introduction Survey	Delehanty	24
323	Conduct of American Foreign Affairs	Tarr	102
359	Problems in American Foreign Policy	McCalla	208
375	International Relations	Richardson	199
377	Nuclear Weapons & World Politics	Tarr	68
401	Selected Topics- Political Science	Barnett	111
408	The American Presidency	Jones	113
411	Constitutional Law	Grossman	164
420	Administrative Law	Downs	132
426	Legislative Process	Mayer	65
427	Legislative Internship	Novotny	20
444	Administration of Public Policy	Khademian	99
463	Evolution of American Planning	Howe	17
473	Public Opinion	Rahn	54
501	Ancient & Medieval Western Thought	Fowler	98

502	Development of Modern Western Political Thought	Riley	126
503	Contemporary Political Thought	Yack	20
544	Introduction to Survey Research	Kane	4
551	Quantitative Analysis of Political Data	Kritzer	30
553	Lab-Political Science Research	Thorn	15
611	Comparative Political Economy	Lindberg	68
630	Latin American Politics	Payne	85
634	Nationalities/Ethnonationalism USSR	Beissinger	62
640	Politics of Japan	Anderson	39
653	Politics of Developing Areas		67
654	Politics of Revolution	Friedman	77
659	Politics & Society: Contemporary Eastern Europe	Croan	68
660	African Politics	Young	43
665	Religion and Politics	Fowler	89
680	Honors Tutorial	Downs	1
695	Proseminar: Topics in Political Science	Friedman	34
771	Development Planning & Administration	Andreano	3
800	Political Science as a Discipline	Wilson	26
816	Qualitative Methods of Political Research	Kritzer	16
824	Politics and Social Process	Merelman	19
826	The Legislative Process	Canon	15
831	Concepts in Political Theory	Anderson	13
857	International Relations Theories	Barnett	12
865	Supreme Court & Constitutional American Politics	Downs	18
871	Public Policy Evaluation	Holden	7
878	Public Administration	Kettl	3
932	Seminar: Theories of Justice	Yack	16
937	Topics: Political Psychology & Socialization	Dennis	6
943	Seminar: Budget & Tax Administration	Witte	3
945	Seminar: National Security Affairs	Mayer	4
949	Seminar: Soviet Politics	Beissinger	5
960	Seminar: International Political Economy	Stallings	13
961	Seminar: African Politics	Hayward	6
962	Seminar: Latin American Politics	Payne	6
974	Seminar: Politics & Public Policy	Khademian	3
982	Seminar: Latin American Area	Thompson, Salomon	N/A

Spring Semester 1990–91

Course #	Course Title	Instructor	Enrollment
102	American National State & Local Government	Khademian	197
104	Introduction to American National Government	Khademian; Giaimo	423
106	Introduction to Comparative0 Politics	Beissinger; Reno	557
181	Introduction Pol.- Honors Course	Downs	16
209	Issues in Political Thought	Smiley	137
213	Urban Politics	Eisinger	115
222	Intro to East Asian Civilization	Yang	17
244	Southeast Asia—Vietnam to Philippines	Taylor	12
260	Latin America—Introduction	Thome	67
267	Intro to Political Psychology	Dennis	98
275	Introduction to International Relations	Richardson; Kazmierczak	484
277	Africa—Introductory Survey	Sulton	22
312	Politics of World Economy	Barnett; Friedman	194
342	Japan and World Politics	Anderson	96
346	China in World Politics	Friedman	71
359	Problems in American Foreign Policy	McCalla	236
362	African International Relations	Ate	54
368	International Relations—Southeast Asia	Emmerson	66
375	International Relations	Richardson	220
377	Nuclear Weapons & World Politics	Tarr	67
401	Selected Topics—Political Science	Lewis; Welfeld	30
404	American National Government	Bailey	106
408	The American Presidency	Mayer	98
412	Constitutional Law	Grossman	60
426	Legislative Process	Mayer	59
427	Legislative Internship	Merline	25
449	Government and Natural Resources	Born	30
452	Criminal Law and Justice	Downs	443
477	Political Socialization	Dennis	75
506	Topics in Political Philosophy	Smiley	93
512	Science & Government	Steinhart	7
552	Quantitative Analysis of Political Data	Kritzer	15
611	Comparative Political Economy	Lindberg	37
630	Latin American Politics	Carranza	67
633	Government & Politics - Soviet Union	Beissinger	80
653	Politics of Developing Areas	Emmerson	58
655	Cultural Pluralism & National Integration	Young	32
680/682/ 691/692	Senior Honors Thesis / Honors Tutorial		29

695	Proseminar: Topics in Political Science	Lindberg; Fowler	38
698	Directed Study		16
816	Qualitative Methods of Political Research	Kritzer	20
819	Quantitative Methods in Public Policy	Meyer	2
823	Political Psychology	Sapiro	15
827	Interest Groups and American Politics	Wilson	22
832	Political Theory: Kant- Political Thought	Riley	18
850	Comparative Politics: Advanced Industrial Nations	Lewis	10
854	Politics Integration & Nation Building	Young	22
860	Totalitarian Political Systems	Croan	13
863	The Judicial Process	Grossman	14
875	Public Personnel Administration	Dresang	2
878	Public Administration	Khademian	3
885	Advanced Public Management	Kettl	3
932	Seminar: Political Theory	Fowler	15
943	Seminar: Budget & Tax Administration	Witte	
945	Seminar: National Security Affairs	Tarr	11
950	Seminar: Comparative Politics—Western Nations	Anderson	3
953	Seminar: American Foreign Policy	McCalla	9
960	Seminar: International Relations	Barnett	7
969	Seminar: Alternative Dispute Resolution	Kaufman	2
974	Seminar: Politics & Public Policy	Eisinger	6
982	Seminar: Latin American Area	Cardoso; Haller; Falabella, Gonzalo; Seligman	2
990	Research and Thesis		58
999	Independent Work		11
Political Science Cumulative Enrollment 1990–91			**9354**

Fall Semester 2000–01

Course #	Course Title	Instructor	Enrollment
103	Introduction to International Relations	Fioretos	352
104	Introduction to American Politics and Government	Canon; Goldstein	942
106	Introduction to Comparative Politics	Scherpereel; Manion; Fieno	486
184	Introduction to American Politics	Shafer	19
201	Special Topics in Political Science	Walsh; Weimer	44
209	Introduction to Political Theory	Yack	217
217	Law, Politics, and Society	Ator	167
218	Understanding Political Numbers	Franklin	81
222	Introduction to East Asian Civilization	Reed	32

230	Politics in Multi-Cultural Societies	Marquez	96
244	Intro to Southeast Asia—Vietnam to Philippines	Cullinane	9
252	The Civilization of India—Modern Period	Elder	28
277	Africa: An Introduction Survey	Hutchinson	25
312	Politics of the World Economy	Friedman	91
316	Principles of International Law	Cronin	110
338	The EU: Politics and Political Economy	Fioretos	77
359	Problems in American Foreign Policy	Pevehouse	101
362	African International Relations	Schatzberg	36
401	Selected Topics in Political Science	Downs; Manion	57
404	American Politics and Government	Shober	87
408	The American Presidency	Mayer	93
411	Constitutional Law	Schweber	210
426	Legislative Process	Parker	55
427	Legislative Internship	Niemcek	30
464	Mexican-American Politics	Marquez	14
469	Women in Politics	Tripp	34
473	Public Opinions	Walsh	50
477	Political Socialization	Sapiro	22
501	Dev of Ancient & West Political Thought	Yack	60
505	The Challenge of Democratization	Aguilar	11
506	Topics in Political Philosophy	Riley	80
517	Feminist Political Theory	Strach	51
551	Quantitative Analysis of Political Data	Wittenberg	26
617	Comparative Legal Institutions	Hendley	60
634	Nationalities and Ethno nationalism in Soviet and Post Soviet Politics	Beissinger	38
639	Politics of Southeast Asia	Thawnghmung	25
654	Politics of Revolution	Friedman	20
683	Senior Honors Thesis Seminar	Hutchcroft	6
695	Proseminar: Topics in Political Science	Downs; Howell	40
800	Political Science as a Discipline	Coleman, Schatzberg	21
804	Interdisciplinary West Euro Area Studies Seminar	Broman	0
816	Qualitative Methods for Political Research	Kritzer	14
818	Topics in Analysis of Political Data	Franklin	3
826	The Legislative Process	Canon	12
831	Concepts in Political Theory	Riley	11
852	Comparative Politics of Developing Nations	Sinha	16
857	International Relations Theories	Cronin	9
858		Felstehausen	3

860	Totalitarian Political Systems and Post-Totalitarian Transitions	Wittenberg	9
871	Public Program Evaluation	Witte	0
874	Policy-Making Process	Kettl	0
875	Public Personnel Administration	Soglin	0
879	Politics of Health Policy	Noren	0
904	Seminar: American Politics	Goldstein	10
932	Seminar: Political Theory	Schweber	7
935	Seminar: Political Socialization	Sapiro	4
945	Seminar: National Security Affairs	Pevehouse	8
969	Seminar: Trends and Issues in Public Planning	Beard	1
		Lane	1
974	Topics in Public Affairs	Miller	1
982	Interdepartmental Seminar in the Latin American Area	Stern	0
		Figueroa	2

Spring Semester 2000–01

Course #	Course Title	Instructor	Enrollment
103	Introduction to International Relations	Fioretos	267
104	Introduction to American Politics and Government	Canon	521
106	Introduction to Comparative Politics	Hutchcroft	170
184	Introduction to American Politics	Price	18
205	Introduction to State Government	Fieno; Hoslet	126
209	Introduction to Political Theory	Strangl	175
222	Introduction to East Asian Civilization	Rennie	21
244	Introduction to Southeast Asia—Vietnam to Philippines	Cullinane	7
260	Latin America—An Introduction	Stern	44
277	Africa—An Introductory Survey	Drewal	25
312	Politics of the World Economy	Friedman	40
313	Bargaining in the Global Economy	Richardson	9
337	International Institutions and World Order	Cronin	85
359	Problems in American Foreign Policy	Cronin	63
376	Analysis of International Politics	Hurd	37
401	Selected Topics in Political Science	Mayer; Schatzberg	30
404	American Politics and Government	Fisher; Martin	179
408	The American Presidency	Palacios-Sommer	62
426	Legislative Process	Sweet	56
427	Legislative Internship	Lipson	31
430	Ethnic Politics in America	Merelman	71
452	Criminal Law and Justice	Downs	335

464	Mexican-American Politics	Marquez	11
467	Elections and Voting Behavior	Dennis	36
471	Civil Liberties in the United States	Schweber	122
472	Politics of Pressure Groups	Wilson	13
477	Political Socialization	Dennis	17
502	The Development of Modern Western Political Thought	Riley	69
503	Contemporary Political Thought	McCredy	39
505	The Challenge of Democratization	Payne	19
506	Topics in Political Philosophy	Riley	53
519		Fogg-Davis	19
552	Quantitative Analysis of Political Data	Franklin	9
611	Comparative Political Economy	Johnson	33
642	Political Power in Contemporary China	Friedman	40
651	Politics of South Asia	Sinha	7
653	Politics of Developing Areas	Schatzberg	41
684	Senior Honors Thesis Seminar	Wilson	3
695	Proseminar: Topics in Political Science	Downs	17
		Fioretos	16
		Hurd	5
		Mulligan-Hansel	4
		Grabowska	2
804	Interdisciplinary West Euro Area Studies Seminar	Boswell, Bousquet	18
819	Quantitative Methods of Public Policy	Bernstein	1
828	The Contemporary Presidency—Issues and Approaches	Mayer	10
829	Political Communication	Shah	4
832	Concepts in Political Theory	McCready	3
855	Politics and Cult in Comp. Perspective	Merelman	11
869	Workshop in Program and Policy Analysis	Witte	2
900	Topics in Political Science	Chang	6
932	Seminar: Political Theory	Schweber	17
950	Seminar: Comparative Politics of Western Nations	Grabowska	4
952	Seminar: Comparative Politics of Developing Nations	Hutchcroft	19
958	Seminar: Research in Public Affairs	Dresang	1
960	Seminar: International Relations	Fioretos	17
963	Seminar: Law and Politics	Fogg-Davis	5
974	Topics in Public Affairs	Wilson; Chang	6
Political Science Cumulative Enrollment 2000–01			**7204**

Appendix 21
Enrollment Trends

Comparative Letters & Science Undergraduate Majors, 1954–2003*

	1954–59	1959–64	1964–69	1969–74	1974–79	1979–84	1984–89	1989–94	1994–99	1999–03
Political Science	414	952	1880	1592	1632	2047	3459	5206	2475	2534
Sociology	325	493	986	1397	1301	1765	2194	1736	977	1174
Psychology	537	1079	2193	2293	1203	1306	1711	2576	2051	1429
Economics	1647	1421	1629	1077	1503	1384	1870	2222	2055	1625
Zoology	376	778	1451	1610	1188	691	738	1020	1688	1975]
International Relations/Studies								412**	1493	1297

* *Note:* Covers only respective four-year periods.

** International Relations as a major began in 1993–94

Source: UW–Madison Enrollment Reports, 1954–55 through 2002–03.

Appendix 22

The Essex Exchange

The exchange between the Department of Government of the University of Essex, U.K., and the Wisconsin Department of Political Science proved an important influence on the development of both departments and even more so on the lives of some of the participants. Essex was an infant department when the exchange originated in 1967; the University of Essex had been created only in 1964. It was already apparent, however, that the Essex department was intent on achieving the high ranking that is has since maintained being ranked in the regular British Research Assessment Exercises (RAEs) at the very top of political science departments in Britain. Among the exchangees from Essex were David McKay, Ian Budge, John Lewis, Mary MacAulay, Graham Wilson, Anthony Barker (who came on the exchange twice), Hugh Ward, and David Sanders. Wisconsin participants included Jack Dennis, Richard Merelman, Peter Eisinger, Patrick Riley, Virginia Sapiro, Richard Champagne, James Bjorkman, and Charles Cnudde.

Several notable events in the lives of Essex and Wisconsin faculty occurred through the exchange. The fatal illness that afflicted Anthony King's first wife, Vera, was diagnosed in Madison. On a more cheerful note, Virginia Sapiro and Graham Wilson met when, for the first and only time in the history of the exchange, it was staggered; Wilson came to Madison in 1978–79 and Sapiro completed the exchange in 1979–80. They married in 1981 and Wilson moved permanently to Wisconsin in 1984 as a newly appointed member of the department faculty.

There were, of course, a number of notable misunderstandings of the type that might have been used by David Lodge in his comic novel about such an exchange, *Changing Places*. To the delight of Essex students, visiting Wisconsin professors did not know the odd British grading convention in which, presumably because no one is thought to be perfect, a First Class (Summa Cum Laude) grade was expressed in percentage terms as 70 or 75% grade. Essex students of modest ability were delighted to receive grades beyond their wildest dreams from Wisconsin exchangees who had not intended to confer immense distinction by giving an 80% grade. One visiting Wisconsin professor who regularly taught in Cambridge (Massachusetts) during the summer was determined not to allow the fact that the English academic year extended (like Chicago's) well into June to stand in his way. Leaving his final exam books ungraded, the professor was quietly packing for a discreet departure to Boston when the chair of the Essex department, realizing that the Wisconsin exchangee was about to elope without completing his grading for the year, rushed to apprehend the errant Badger at the house he had rented for the year. Pounding on the front door the furious chair shouted through the letter box (which in English houses is in the front door) in his pronounced Scottish accent, "I KNOW yer in there! Come on ooot!" A member of the Essex department who had been brought along as witness finally prevailed upon the Essex chair to acknowledge that the Exchange was more important than the grading of a hundred exam books.

The exchange was negotiated by then-Chair Bernard Cohen with Anthony King in 1967, when the latter was a visiting scholar in Madison under other auspices. The basic formula was that the participants would replace each other as a salary line in their respective institutions. The fly in the ointment was the large discrepancy in US and UK academic salary levels; initially, the Graduate School was persuaded to make up the differential for the American participant.

The Essex exchange continued for the better part of two decades, enriching both departments by helping to maintain intellectual diversity and aiding faculty with modest travel allowances to gain international experience. Essex always acknowledged that Wisconsin provided far more than half the resource required to operate the exchange and it was the refusal of the Graduate School to continue providing these unequal resources that finally ended the scheme. One other factor was the problems for British academics in obtaining health insurance at a reasonable price. Accustomed to comprehensive coverage through the National Health Service, they were shocked to be told that for the first six months of employment at Wisconsin, they would be responsible for their own health care in the land of massive medical bills (a rule that was finally modified only in the late 1990s). Yet another inhibiting factor was the increasing saliency of dual-career households; a number of potential exchangees had spouses who were reluctant or unable to leave their professional positions for an Essex year.

Graham K. Wilson

APPENDIX 23
North Hall

From: Jim Feldman, *The Buildings of the University of Wisconsin* (Madison, WI, 1997), pp. 10–11.

North Hall was the first building of the University of Wisconsin. Construction started in 1851 at a cost of $19,000; it served as the entire physical plant of the university for four years. When the first Science Hall burned in 1884, the university eliminated the dormitory function of North Hall in favor of instructional space. Since then it has housed a series of academic departments, and is listed on the National Register of Historic Places.

The original plan for the University was developed in 1850 by Chancellor Lathrop, regents Mills and Dean, and drawn by architect John Rague. Rague's plan, which has since been lost, called for four dormitory buildings and a "central edifice." . . . The building proceeded under the direction of contractor James Livesey and was built for a total cost of about $19,000. At this time the projected maximum enrollment of the University was 256 young men.

On September 17, 1851, North Hall opened, and for the next four years North Hall contained the entire University. The University comprised about thirty students, three faculty (J.W. Sterling, O. M. Conover, and John H. Lathrop) and a janitor (John Conklin). The students and Conklin were housed on the first three floors, which contained 24 suites, each with a study and two bedrooms. On the fourth floor were the lecture rooms, studies and chapel. The bulk of the resident students were members of Professor Sterling's previous year's preparatory class which had met in a small building in downtown Madison. The following year's preparatory students, who were not yet college students, did not live in North Halt but took their class work and study periods there.

Student pranks and behavior were an issue from the earliest days of the University. The faculty insisted on daily room inspections, rigidly enforced study and class times, including a prompt 6 AM class time enforced by a large bell installed on the second floor. This schedule lasted until the rebellious students removed and hid the clapper until a more reasonable class time was negotiated.

Students could board with residents in town, eat at restaurants, or feed themselves, which was sometimes considerably cheaper. Many financially strapped students, including John Muir, were said to have survived principally on baked potatoes and "involuntary contributions of the surrounding inhabitants many of whom had cows, pigs or poultry who took turns contributing to the rising generation." Later a general mess hall was established on the first floor to lower student costs. The catalogs for the 1860s promise board may be had for less than $3 per week. It is also likely that some students kept cows on the grounds. In 1861 the regents formally banned all pasturing of animals on campus.

The living conditions were quite primitive even for the frontier. One alumnus described the well water as being so hard it was like chewing limestone and "as hard to get as to drink. It's a wonder it didn't kill us all." For sanitation there were privies, which were regularly upset or set afire. The regents were proud to boast that the building was heated by woodburning furnaces, but the contractors were ordered to install two additional furnaces to keep the temperature tolerable for the students. On any cold day with a wind the cry would go up from the windward side of the building for the janitor to stoke the furnace: "Wood up John! Wood up!" Since all students spent hours in the building all were required to contribute to the firewood fund even if they lived off campus. In 1865, as a budgetary step, the furnaces were replaced by stoves in each room, and students had to furnish their own wood. Much damage ensued to the woods surrounding the building.

From: Jay Rath, "North Hall," ***Newsletter: Wisconsin Political Science*** (Fall 2001).

It's old, drafty and probably not the first building you notice on a jaunt through the UW–Madison campus. But North Hall, all 150 years of it, is history. The first building on the University of Wisconsin campus, North Hall opened on Sept. 17, 1851. For its first four years North Hall was the entire UW campus, and it is still in service today. "It was the whole university," says Art Hove, UW special assistant emeritus and author of *The University of Wisconsin: A Pictorial History.* "Until Bascom Hall was built, and shifted the emphasis, it was the cornerstone of the university. Its significance is enormous." On the day of North Hall's anniversary, Monday, Sept. 17 [2001], that significance was celebrated by the UW's Political Science department, North Hall's current tenant. The celebration was attended by about 75 faculty, staff and graduate students. "There was a very large birthday cake with the inscription, 'Happy 150th Birthday, North Hall,' on it," says Prof. Mark Beissinger, chairman of the department.

"After a short speech noting some of the similarities between 150 years ago and today—just like today, back then the heating in the building was unreliable and the air-conditioning didn't work—we then all joined in singing 'Happy Birthday' to our collective home." If the history and a common heritage can provide strength and unity in times of trouble, it's no surprise that the anniversary of the oldest building on campus was celebrated. Besides serious academia, North Hall's early decades saw a series of wild adventures filled with pranks, ghosts, gunfire and the first nature studies of a young student named John Muir. The building is on the National Register of Historic Places. It may be revered now, but when it was new, "it was cold and drafty and full of people," says Jim Feldman, author of *The Buildings of the University of Wisconsin*. Civilization and 14-year-old Madison was a mile away, and to get to campus you had to walk through thick woods unmarred by trails. "It does seem sort of incredible when you go there now," says Feldman. "There were very few amenities of any kind." "And there still are very few amenities," laughs Beissinger. "There is no elevator to the fourth floor, for example." In the beginning, North Hall, atop Bascom Hill, included dormitory, museum, classrooms, mess hall and library, all within four floors. The next building, South Hall, was completed in 1855, and Bascom Hall in 1860. The university itself first received students Feb. 5, 1849, but the first classes were held in borrowed quarters in town, near Wisconsin Avenue, at the Madison Female Academy, until North Hall could be completed. State Street then ended at Broom Street.

As construction for North Hall began, teenager Daniel K. Tenney hiked over and announced to workmen his intention to attend the university as soon as the building was finished. "Young man," said one of the laborers, "if you intend studying here, now is your chance. You may lay the cornerstone." And so he did. Tenney did go to school at the UW, but after a time "the faculty invited him to adopt some other institution as his alma mater," according to a 1906 issue of *Wisconsin Alumni Magazine*. He afterward worked as a printer for the *Wisconsin State Journal* and went on to become a wealthy leading citizen. About 30 students signed up for the first semester in North Hall. The faculty—all three of them—lived in the building, along with the students and janitor. To signal each day's first class at 6 a.m., the instructors rang a large bell on the second floor. In the first of many mysteries surrounding North Hall, the bell's clapper somehow disappeared until a later starting time was set. Curfew was 9 p.m., and a large basket and rope were sometimes secretly flung outside, for students sneaking in late. In front of North Hall were a hitching post and a pump. The water from it was of dubious quality, and one early alumnus recalled in 1906, "It's a wonder it didn't kill us all." Freshmen came to have an intimate knowledge of the pump, since through the 1860's they were "baptized" beneath it by upper-classmen.

With the Civil War came deep cuts in state aid to the university. In 1864, every senior but one had joined the army, and so commencement was not held. A year later funds dwindled to the point where North Hall's wood-fired furnaces were idled. For heat, students had to provide the wood. Some took axes to the surrounding forest. Others simply stole, until several Madisonians took action by filling logs in their woodpiles with gunpowder. One North Hall stove actually exploded, and stealing stopped. As for restrooms, outhouses served that function, though they were often tipped over or burned.

Food was a problem for the first UW students. By the 1860's, the faculty themselves provided board in a mess room within North Hall, for $3 a week. Some students, such as the legendary naturalist, Muir, lived on mush and roasted potatoes, which they cooked themselves. One survivor of those years recalled that others depended on "the involuntary contributions of the surrounding inhabitants, many of whom had cows, pigs or poultry who took turns contributing to the rising generation." Still other students, and at least one faculty member, kept their own livestock right outside North Hall; in 1861 the UW Board of Regents forbade the pasturing of animals on campus.

Still others hunted. "Madison in the 1850's was a paradise for game," recalled Richard W. Hubbell in 1906. He lived in North Hall before graduating in 1858. "One day a nice flock of quail came near the bedroom window in study hours, and the temptation being too great, I fired out the window at them." Chancellor Lathrop was not pleased. But on another occasion when Hubbell aimed at a partridge and instead hit a chicken, Lathrop was more forgiving.

Said the Chancellor, "If this tame hen was so unwise as to try and imitate the peculiar attributes of the wild bird, I think" (and here is where he cleared his throat) "it justly deserves its fate. You may take it back to the kitchen."

Even Muir hunted around North Hall as a student. "In those days before endangered species, Muir wrote about shooting an eagle with a six-foot wingspan," says Feldman.

Muir came to the UW in the fall of 1860, and legend holds that his room was in the northeast corner of the first floor. His room's location is officially uncertain, but it is true that he filled it with specimens, laboratory equipment and strange wooden clocks, which he built himself.

If Muir had not gone on to become America's earliest and foremost naturalist, and father of our national parks system, he perhaps would have become an inventor. The strangest of his North Hall clocks was also a desk and bookshelf. Its elaborate mechanisms would open books for Muir to study, a half hour at a time, one after the other. It also lighted his lamp. The strange desk-clock has been preserved at the State Historical Society, and you can see it displayed at its headquarters, at 816 State St.

Despite his clocks, Muir had trouble waking each morning, so he and the janitor came to an arrangement: at night Muir would tie a string to his big toe and throw the other end out the window. Each morning the janitor would yank it.

Muir stayed at the UW for four years, but left without receiving a degree.

"I was far from satisfied with what I learned, and should have stayed longer," recalled Muir in *The Story of My Boyhood and Youth*. "Anyhow, I wandered away on a glorious botanical and geological excursion, which has lasted nearly 50 years and is not yet completed."

Despite all the pranks, the faculty did try to keep students in line, and not only with required daily prayers. Chancellor Lathrop created the "Excuse Box," which hung in North Hall and, later, Bascom Hall. Into it were placed students' excuses for missed lectures, to avoid demerits. Students began each semester with a credit of 100 points for scholarship and deportment. Missing prayers cost you two points, and a student lost five points for merely entering any Madison saloon.

In 1880 a student awoke and left his second floor room to see an apparition in white—a ghost! It floated apparently in mid-air in the corridor. The student rushed back to awake his roommate, but the ghost had left. They went back to bed. But the ghost reappeared in their room the same night. According to the student newspaper, *The Daily Cardinal*, the specter "floated around the room a moment or so and then departed."

Word quickly spread across the entire campus (by then the UW comprised a handful of buildings besides North Hall) and the phantom satisfied the curious by reappearing several nights. Sometimes it materialized in a corridor, "skipping through the halls and vanishing," said *The Cardinal*. Other times it would enter a room, eerily linger, and then depart. Often it was satisfied with torturing sleepers by taking coal from scuttles and throwing it down stairways.

The *Wisconsin State Journal* even printed an account by student Alvin Hitchcock, who described the ghost's "garments of unearthly whiteness."

A group of terrified students came to UW President John Bascom for help. And Bascom took action in a manner which some might say has become a model: he formed a committee of study. But student Whitney Trousdale stepped forward and claimed responsibility. He had simply covered himself with a bed sheet and romped through the hallways. Trousdale later became a Methodist minister.

North Hall continued to serve at least partly as a dorm until 1884. As the campus grew, North Hall hosted departments including German, Scandinavian, mathematics and the Madison Weather Bureau. Today, as home to the Department of Political Science, at least one real ghost of sorts has turned up.

"We just renovated a room, and in doing so we had to take down the blackboards," says Beissinger. "And behind it was another blackboard, and on it was an old German lesson."

Students and faculty passing by North Hall each day may not realize the building's history, but, says Hove, "one thing I think about is the elegance of its architecture. On the one hand, it looks like a simple rectangular box. But on the other hand, the proportions are just perfect."

It has such a dignity to it. It never ages.

Appendix 24

The Howard McMurray Case

From: George C. Sellery, *Some Ferments at Wisconsin, 1901–1947: Memories and Reflections* (Madison, WI: University of Wisconsin Press, for the University of Wisconsin Library, 1960), pp. 112–24. Reprinted with permission.

R. HOWARD J. McMURRAY was Instructor in political science in the Extension Division of the University, 1936–38, and an assistant professor in that Division, 1938–42. He resigned Sept. 1, 1942, to run for Congress in the fifth district of the State on the democratic ticket. The Hatch Act made the resignation necessary for candidacy. He was successful and served in Congress 1942–44. In the autumn of 1944 he ran for the United States Senate, but was defeated by Senator Wiley. In September, 1945, he was given a one-year appointment as lecturer in political science, College of Letters and Sciences, replacing Professor Salter then on leave, and with no commitment for renewal of appointment thereafter. In June, 1946, the political science department recommended that he be appointed to an associate professorship beginning 1946–47, and that he be given leave for the fall semester of that year in order that he might again seek nomination and election to the U. S. Senate. (The Hatch Act had been revised and would make this arrangement possible.) President Fred and Dean Ingraham decided that the leave could not be granted, as it would get the University into politics. And so the plan was given up.

McMurray ran for the U.S. Senate again in the autumn of 1946 and was rather badly beaten by the Republican candidate. The election took place November 5, 1946. Two days later, November 7, the department of political science unanimously recommended to Dean Ingraham the appointment of Mr. McMurray as an associate professor in the department, beginning with the second semester of 1946–47. "His sincerity and eloquence," the department wrote, "make him an ideal lecturer for the large student groups to which we have become accustomed to at Wisconsin. . . . The resident department this semester has seven and one-half full-time persons, of whom none has had the experience of participation in political life as candidate or legislator. In an effort to establish a well-balanced program, it seems to us that one such person is desired."

"It would, of course," the department continues, "be difficult to find any person who had practical experience in party politics who was not an active member of some political party. The department would equally recommended a person of Mr. McMurray's training, experience, and eloquence in teaching had he been a Republican. During this last year the department does not believe that Mr. McMurray's teaching has been partisan. It is true that he does not conceal the fact, which it would be impossible to conceal, that he is a Democrat of a particular school. At the same time he endeavors to be fair to all points of view. . . . The Department of Political Science believes deeply that the appointment recommended would contribute greatly to the well-rounded character of our work, and we hope very much that the appointment can be made."

The recommendation of the department was supported by the executive committee of the Faculty Division of the Social Studies, and was approved by Dean Ingraham. In his letter to President Fred, December 11, 1946, setting forth the grounds of his approval, Dean Ingraham expressed his confidence in Mr. McMurray's fairness "to both sides of a controversial question in his teaching," and observed that his experience "brought him background for his teaching similar to that background gained by a geologist who goes into the field, or a man in commerce who enters business, or a journalist who has for a period served on a newspaper."

It is evident that the proposed appointment was already a subject of discussion, for Dean Ingraham ends his letter as follows: "The question has been raised as to whether Mr. McMurray was fair last year in running for senator when he had said upon acceptance of his appointment [lecturer] at the University that at that time he had no plans for immediate political activity. I believe that Mr. McMurray was both honest and fair in this matter, that at the time he returned he did not have plans to run for office. As a matter of fact, he postponed his decision to run until the end of the semester. If I remember correctly he announced his candidacy after all his classes and examinations were over."

Newspaper interest in the proposed appointment was much stimulated by a statement given out by President Fred, December 17, 1946. It reads as follows: "There seems to exist a misunderstanding concerning the proposed appointment of Mr. McMurray. The facts are as follows: A recommendation that Mr. McMurray be appointed as Associate Professor in the Department of Political Science was made by that Department and by Dean Mark H. Ingraham, of the College of Letters and Science. This recommendation was discussed at an informal meeting of the Board of Regents on Friday, December 13. After discussing this matter, it was decided that the recommendation for the appointment of Mr. McMurray would not be brought up at the formal meeting of the Regents on Saturday, December 14. It was also decided that the Dean of the College and the Department of Political Science be requested to canvass the field for additional personnel." President Fred sent a copy of this press notice, December 20, to the chairman of the political science department, who had asked what was the status of the recommendation the department had made, and in his covering note the president said: "It is my understanding that the recommended appointment of Mr. McMurray has been neither approved nor disapproved."

The response of the department to the president's note and to the request of the regents for additional personnel is contained in a three page, single-space, letter of December 23, signed by the chairman on behalf of the executive committee of the department. The letter explains why the department needs Mr. McMurray, urges that his service in politics is an asset, not a liability, and makes clear how carefully the staff had canvassed the field.

The letter also speaks of newspaper stories attributing to some of the regents statements indicating "that Mr. McMurray's political activity is essentially the reason for the delay in acting upon his appointment." The comment of the department is crisp: "This University has a lofty tradition of academic freedom. If there is unwillingness to approve Mr. McMurray's appointment because of his political views and experiences, such an attitude, in the opinion of the department, is unworthy of that tradition."

The position of the department is made clear in the final paragraphs of the letter:

> The department has canvassed the field. We therefore stand by our recommendation of Mr. McMurray. We hope that his appointment can be completed speedily, since two important courses in the second semester await upon its completion. Knowing the existing personnel shortage in the profession as it does, the department has no expectation of being able to offer an alternative recommendation for the second semester. While the existing situation [non-appointment of Mr. McMurray?] continues, it is most doubtful whether any reputable political scientist would consider coming to Wisconsin. . . .
>
> You will appreciate that the description of the plans and procedures of the department which we herewith submit throws light upon the professional standards and integrity both of the department and of Mr. McMurray. Our repute here at the University of Wisconsin and among our colleagues at other educational institutions is a matter of university as well as personal concern. We believe, therefore, that it is wise and just that this letter be made public after you have had an opportunity to read it and initiate such action as shall seem to you most appropriate.

The letter was not given to the press by the president; Dean Ingraham had quite wisely recommended that it should not be. The president was of the same opinion. But the letter leaked, and newspaper assertions that academic freedom was violated and that good men would not accept calls to the University very probably stemmed from it.

The proposed appointment of Mr. McMurray came formally before the Board of Regents at its meeting of January 17, 1947, at which it was recommended by President Fred. The individual regents attending the meeting explained why they were for or against the appointment. (Their statements were later transmitted by President Fred to the faculty, in time for the February faculty meetings.) The regents who were against the appointment took the ground that Mr. McMurray was more interested in a political than in an academic career, as shown by his three candidacies for public office since 1942. They asserted that his politics had nothing to do with their opposition to his appointment.

On this topic President Fred testified, in the review of the history of the proposed recommendation which he read at the opening of the meeting of the Board: "As a matter of public record the President of the University wishes to make it clear that in his opinion the Regents of the University are intelligently, seriously, and conscientiously discharging their responsibility"—in the selection of permanent university personnel. Regent Callahan, Superintendent of Public Instruction, in stating his reasons for voting for the McMurray appointment, remarked: "I haven't seen one particle of politics in this affair. I don't think there is any." Regent Werner, a Democrat, who had voted for McMurray in both his candidacies for the U.S. Senate, argued that Mr. McMurray was primarily interested in a political career: "In supporting his appointment [lecturer, September, 1945] at that time I expressed the belief that Mr. McMurray would not again leave, but that if he did it would pretty clearly indicate that his interests were not with the University and that I would then be the first one to oppose his again returning to the University. That is exactly what has happened and I intend to keep that promise."

I continue with significant excerpts from the statements of the other regents at the meeting. Regent Hodgkins was uncertain as to Mr. McMurray's primary interests, but was willing to give him a chance to prove that a university career was his real ambition. Regent Hodgkins broadened the scope of his review of the issue. "There has been so much talk of academic freedom," he remarked, "and 'sifting and winnowing' that I have been forced to ask myself this question, 'Where do the freedom and the sifting and winnowing start and cease?' Many of the criticisms which have been made would lead one to believe that freedom and sifting and winnowing must cease after the first recommendation is made and that all others who, in their judgment, disagree with this recommendation are the foes of academic freedom and are not competent to do any sifting and winnowing to satisfy their own judgments before making a decision.

"I have nothing against Mr. McMurray as a man, nor regarding his ability, beliefs or ambitions. I do feel it is unwise to appoint him permanently as an associate professor at this time, or until such time has passed that we may be reasonably assured that his affiliation with the University is not merely an interim interest between political campaigns. . . . I shall vote to approve the appointment of Mr. McMurray as Associate Professor for the second semester of 1946–47 and for the academic year 1947–48."

"I have received personally," said Regent Sensenbrenner, "a number of letters for or against his appointment. The theme of many of those favoring his appointment contained the implication that the opposition was influenced by political considerations. I deny that absolutely, and it is negatived by the fact that in the 1946 campaign Mr. [William Gorham] Rice of the College of Law was a candidate on the same ticket with Mr. McMurray. . . His record of service on the University staff was upwards of 20 years, and I am informed this was the first instance when he ran for office. The fact that if Mr. McMurray had been elected to the Senate in 1946 he would have been unavailable for teaching on the staff of the University for six years makes the statement that he is the only available man qualified for the position seem ill founded."

". . . I supported the recommendation," said Regent M. J. Cleary, "that he [McMurray] be given a temporary appointment from September, 1945, to the end of the academic year in May, 1946, to meet what was represented to us by the Political Science Department as an emergency. We are now told seventeen months later that there is an emergency—the same one, I suppose. It seems a bit strange to me that in all these months—with the uncertainty of Mr. McMurray's future before them—the Faculty of the Department were unable to locate a single prospect for the position. What if Mr. McMurray had been elected Senator?"

Regent Kleczka opened his statement with these words: "In order to save time and avoid repetition for the purposes of the record, I hereby fully concur in and adopt as my own the reasons given by Regents Cleary and Werner as to why they would not approve of the recommendation made by the Faculty of the Political Science Department in recommending the appointment of Professor Howard J. McMurray to the University teaching staff."

Regent Daniel Grady was the only regent who argued for the appointment of Mr. McMurray. "The facts in this case," he said, "seem to be undisputed; that

Mr. McMurray with this unanimous recommendation of the Department, Dean, and the President is not only qualified for the appointment, but that his selection would be to the great benefit and advantage of this University. . . .The fact that Mr. McMurray has served as a member of Congress and has participated in political affairs seems to me to be a qualifying factor in the teaching of the science of government. You cannot ask a teacher in any department to refrain from participating in those activities that broaden his knowledge and are helpful in the teaching of students along those lines in which he has had the experience. . . . During the existence of this University for nearly one hundred years its ideals in freedom of thought and action have been the proud boast of the people of our State. . . . We think of those who established this University and of those who have steadfastly sought to maintain its ideals and traditions and I may say today as Grattan said, 'They sat beside her cradle—we must march behind her hearse.' I for one refuse to march behind the hearse on its way to the Interment of the cherished ideals of this University. The recommendation of the President should be approved."

Regent Callahan commented: "I am probably going to vote the same way Mr. Grady will, but I do not take the subject so seriously." Then he went on to remark: "We gave Rice a leave of absence to run for Congress about the same time this man was running for the Senate and Rice will come back to his position in the University without any questions asked. I don't think anyone on this Board is raising any political question with cither of them." Then Mr. Callahan explained why he was going to vote for Mr. McMurray's appointment: "Because it is a habit I have had for the last twenty-five years, I have made it a practice to support the President, or the head of this organization, or any of the other Boards that I am connected with." This last statement makes Mr. Callahan's vote for the appointment of McMurray something less than a personally responsible endorsement.

The recommendation of the president for the appointment of Mr. McMurray came to a vote that day, January 17, 1947. Seven regents were present. The three absentees were reported by colleagues who were present as opposed to the election of Mr. McMurray. Four of the regents at the meeting voted against, and two—Grady and Callahan—for it. Regent Hodgkins refrained from the final voting, as his motion for appointment for a year and a half had won no support.

The action of the board of regents in turning down Mr. McMurray was greeted with a shower of abuse in newspapers of the State. The clippings on the McMurray affair prior to January 17 were relatively few compared with those thereafter. The criticisms of the second period, I estimate, are at least ten times as numerous, it seemed to me, as I read those which were published or republished in the local papers at the time, that the University was being injured by the unbridled attacks upon the integrity of the regents, and I accordingly gave to the press, for publication January 26, 1947, the statement which follows.

The Howard McMurray Case

By G. C. Sellery

The most curious feature of the Howard McMurray case is not the failure of the regents to add him to the staff of the university, but the apparent belief in certain uninformed quarters, widely proclaimed, that this constitutes an attack on academic freedom and gives notice to the academic world that the great University of Wisconsin has ceased to be free to search for and disseminate the truth.

The attack upon the motives of the regents has been particularly violent. Unfortunately for the university the present regents are mostly of one political party. The responsibility for that goes back to Governor Heil, who failed to realize that the best way to keep the university out of politics is to have a well-balanced bipartisan board. And so it has been charged that the motives of the present regents are partisan, that their purposes are sinister, and that they are determined to prevent the free examination of economic doctrines and procedures. This sort of charge one is accustomed to in political campaigns, when it seems to be the accepted rule to ascribe dishonorable motives to the opposition. It should not be the practice in university affairs.

I have not communicated, directly or indirectly, with any regent or administrator; I know nothing about the McMurray case except what I have learned from the newspapers. I write off my own bat. Let us look into the situation.

The regents or some of the regents are said to have been against the appointment because they believed that Mr. McMurray is not primarily interested in academic work. They may have other reasons, not disclosed. I think, however, that President Fred's decision, after taking the count, to support the nomination, must be interpreted as signifying that the other reasons, if any, were not solid; and I reach the conclusion that the regents should have followed the practice of canny John Callahan—to go along with the president of the university in such matters—and should have elected Mr. McMurray. In a word, I think that the majority of the regents made a mistake. But have they not the right to make a mistake? Are they required to be infallible?

I have even some little sympathy with the suspicion that Mr. McMurray is primarily interested in having a political career. For I remember that when my friend, the late Professor Paul S. Reinsch, was increasingly taking leave of absence to go on diplomatic missions for the federal government—he ended as ambassador to China—my chief and I, the dean, ruefully observed that Professor Reinsch was in effect using the university as a perch to rest upon momentarily between diplomatic flights.

I conjecture that the attacks made upon the regents during the interval between their request that the political science department restudy its list of possible candidates for the post and the January meeting of the board may very well have got their backs up. It is not unusual for the regents to ask reconsideration of recommendations; it is their right and may at times be their duty. But they were immediately jumped on—and how! Even the political science department, invariably tactful, was made to seem critical of the regents. Asked to restudy its list of eligibles, instead of sending a report to the regents, through channels, for consideration at their January meeting, that it had done so and had found that Mr. McMurray was still the best bet, the department sent a long letter to President Fred which in some way got into the newspapers long before the regent meeting. The letter explained the need for Mr. McMurray and the futility of restudying its list. It was an excellent letter; but it was not the report which the regents had requested, and it added fuel to the flames already encircling the regents.

The regents are men of acknowledged integrity; but they are human, and the attempt to blacken their reputations may very well have led them to decide that they could not yield in the face of such clamor and abuse.

It is my opinion, then, that if the matter had been handled with discretion, if the right of the regents to ask further consideration had been frankly recognized and responded to, Mr. McMurray's appointment would have been made. I may be wrong. And for that matter the regents may have been right in the decision they finally reached. The unanimity of a department is a solid base for action; but it does not absolutely guarantee the soundness of its recommendation. During the close to a quarter

> century of my deanship I joined with more than one unanimous department in securing appointments to the faculty which turned out to be mistakes. We can only do our best. Nor is the adverse decision of the regents in the McMurray case unprecedented. I recall a similar episode under the great Van Hise, at a time when the regents were riding him hard. He took it as part of his job, for he realized that the university is a great trust, and that its increasing service to our people should not be marred by public squabbles over debatable appointments. And it is painful to me, trained in administration by Van Hise and Birge, to read nonsensical assertions in the public press, that the great University of Wisconsin, which I served for over forty years, in fair weather and foul, can no longer attract great teachers, is no longer a home of freedom, because, forsooth, the regents, the other day, declined to add Howard McMurray to the staff of the university. Fortunately the academic world knows better!

Not having before me the statements the regents made on January 17 regarding the proposed appointment of Mr. McMurray when I wrote the foregoing article for the press, I failed to make clear that the regents did not deny the value of practical experience in one's professorial field, but were of the opinion that the three political campaigns of 1942–46 indicated that Mr. McMurray preferred a political to an academic career. Lecturing the regents on the value of practical experience after January 17 was a waste of energy: they were obviously not against it.

I think now that in my statement I made too much of the influence of newspaper abuse on the regents who were opposed to the appointment. Their respective positions were so firm, as their statements show, that the abuse was not needed to stiffen their backs.

If I had seen the full letter the political science department sent to President Fred, December 23, in response to the regents' request "for additional personnel," I could not have written of that department as "invariably tactful." In my quotations from the letter (see above), the department implies—rather than directly says—that the failure to appoint McMurray "because of his political views and experiences" would be in a way a denial of academic freedom. But worse follows in that letter: "While the existing situation continues, it is most doubtful whether any reputable political scientist would consider coming to Wisconsin"! And as if that were not enough the department asks that its letter of December 23 be made public for the information of the Wisconsin faculty and of "our colleagues at other educational institutions." It says a good deal for the tolerant spirit of the regents, I incline to think, that they say nothing about this letter.

The views expressed on "the McMurray case" by the University of Wisconsin Chapter of the American Association of University Professors—the AAUP—dated January 29, 1947, form a valuable document. It was sent out to the faculty with the calendar for the meeting of February 10. The chapter officers received from President Fred, January 18, they say, "a full review of the transactions of the meeting of the Board [of Regents] of the previous day, and subsequently the President's office furnished a copy of the formal statements presented at the meeting by the President and the members of the Board." The chapter of AAUP found "no technical violation of academic freedom" in the disposition of the case by the regents, since Mr. McMurray was not at the time a member of the faculty; but the reasons the regents gave for their individual decisions "seem to reveal attitudes and viewpoints on the selection of faculty members and the activities appropriate for them which we believe contrary to sound university policy."

I do not like that Scottish type of verdict, "no technical violation of academic freedom;" for it may be read as implying that there was, say, a moral violation, and that, I think, is negatived by the statements of the regents which I have excerpted.

The AAUP chapter recognizes that there are two requisites for an academic appointment: academic qualifications and non- academic qualifications. "This case was unusual," they say, "if not unprecedented, in that it raised doubts concerning the desirability of appointing the man recommended that were pertinent even though they did note his academic qualifications. We recognize that in such cases the responsibility of the Board in appointing men to the faculty positions ". . . may properly cause the members of the Board to consider the doubts involved directly and to decide the issue by their own judgment rather than by depending entirely on the judgment of the faculty and administration."

University and college administrators and departments as well as governing boards, I may remark, have long recognized the importance which attaches to the non-academic qualifications of proposed faculty appointments; I permit myself to say that it is usual and precedented.

"It is necessary to remind ourselves," the AAUP chapter observes, of the inescapable fact that faculty and regents are partners in the life of the university, however different our functions and responsibilities are. When partners disagree, it is desirable to recognize the maximum area of agreement as we have endeavored to do in the preceding paragraphs." They might have added, I think, that the regents, by law, are the senior partners and should be so regarded.

The AAUP chapter supports the policy of leaves of absence for other work. "Many of the outstanding men in this faculty have left the campus for periods of a year or more, not merely once or twice but three times or more, to serve within their professional field the needs of other institutions, of industry, of the federal government. In most, if not all, of these cases, these experiences outside the university, but within their professional fields, have increased their value to the university . . ."

The AAUP chapter favors participation in political activities. "While we note that the regents do not consider it improper in principle for a faculty member to take leave of absence to run for political office, we cannot miss the implication that this should be done only in moderation. . . . We would not consider running for political office as an attempt to find a different kind of employment, but rather as the response to an urgent demand, both from within the individual and from his fellow- citizens, that he take the lead in political activities. . . . But whatever the means that are used for measuring the motives that impel a person to run for office, they should not, we believe, depend on any simple rule of counting the number of times he had run."

I submit that the regents, in the case we are considering, did not follow any such simple rule. They did not turn down Mr. McMurray for running for political office three times, but for running for political office three times in four years of his novitiate—a different matter.

The AAUP report—on the whole a masterly statement—ends with a cogent argument for the employment of the regent-faculty committee or some other fit instrument "in the consideration of a complex case that involves judgment of non-academic as well as of academic qualifications." "Effective interplay of minds, interchange of views on policy and on evidence" are necessary. "If, for example, the combined regent-faculty committee had been utilized as a medium for such an informal exchange of views, the divergence of attitudes on personnel policy outlined in the preceding paragraphs could have been clarified and quite possibly dispelled. The unfortunate publicity that followed the first informal consideration of the question by the regents no doubt made such an interchange unusually difficult; at the same time it greatly increased its desirability."

The ideal opportunity for the calling of the regent-faculty conference, in my opinion, was offered by the informal meeting of the regents, the president, and the dean on December 13. Yet the record shows no evidence that any participant in the meeting asked for or suggested such a move. To call for it after the regents had acted would have been too late.

The first formal reaction of a representative faculty group—taken by nine professors—was not so restrained as the AAUP's. It is embodied in draft resolutions, sent out with the calendar for consideration at the faculty meeting of February 3, 1947. They say: "The faculty heartily endorses the President's statements upon the weight to be given on matters of academic qualifications, to the judgment of the department, etc. Similarly with non-academic qualifications: in considering these "we submit that the judgment of the faculty and administrative officers 'should be given the greatest weight and should be allowed unless proved to be clearly wrong'." In this the nine professors go farther than the president had gone, for his generalization related to the academic qualifications. The extreme position which the me professors took is most clearly shown in two paragraphs of their resolutions: "We believe that in the rare cases in which the Regents may incline to reject an academic nomination or resolution [*sic*] of the faculty, they should do so only after consultation with the faculty and with full explanation of the extraordinary and compelling reasons for their action." "Finally, the faculty respectfully asks for assurance by the Regents that they will in future refer to that [regent-faculty] Committee any serious differences that may arise between the Regents and the faculty."

These draft resolutions of a self-appointed committee did not, I must say, treat the regents with the respect due to the senior partners in the University enterprise, and I conclude that on reflection wiser counsels prevailed. For a revised set of resolutions, prepared by another voluntary committee, which included a member of the AAUP committee, was handed out, as a replacement, to the members of the faculty as they assembled for the regular meeting of the faculty on February 3, 1947. I shall speak of these as the revised resolutions.

The first paragraph of the revised resolutions is conciliatory, and was approved unanimously by the faculty without change. It reads: "1. The university faculty, recognizing the duty of the regents to scrutinize faculty appointments and recognizing their responsibility to pass upon them, endorses as sound academic policy, the statement of President Fred to the Board of Regents at its meeting of January 17, 1947: I believe that upon questions of academic qualifications the judgment of the department concerned and of the dean of the respective college should be given the greatest of weight and should be followed unless proved to be clearly wrong."

The second paragraph of the revised resolutions encountered no opposition and was in the end simplified to read: "2. In the judgment of the faculty, the principle that practical experience in his field enhances the value of a teacher and scholar applies to all fields where practical experience is possible."

Paragraph three of the revised resolutions faced trouble just before it was to be taken up at the adjourned faculty meeting of February 20, 1947. The trouble consisted in a motion "that the faculty terminate all discussion of the matter under consideration now." The motion was lost by a narrow margin of 124 to 120. That vote "gives one to think."

The way was now open for the consideration of the third and the remaining five paragraphs of the revised resolutions, including paragraph 5, which does not breathe moderation. It reads: "The faculty urges as sound practice that in the rare case in which the regents find themselves unable to accept an academic nomination or recommendation of the faculty they first consult with the faculty and, in case of final disapproval, accompany their decision with a full explanation of the extraordinary and compelling reasons for their action."

Paragraph 5, however, was effectively obliterated by the passage of a motion, offered by Professor Hartshorne, seconded by Professor Groves (the two men in charge of the revised resolutions), "to substitute for all paragraphs not yet approved, namely 3 to 8, the following two paragraphs:

"3. In considering the effect a man's outside experience and interests may have on his qualifications as a teacher, his prospective continuity of service, and the contribution he may be expected to make to the university, the faculty believes that the judgment of the department, division, and administrative officers should be given the greatest of weight." (This is a slightly softened version of paragraph 3 of the revised resolutions.)

"4. The faculty urges that measures be taken to enable the Regent-Faculty Conference Committee to function more consistently and more effectively, both as an agency to which it would be normal practice to refer for discussion any matters that might lead to serious differences between the regents and the faculty and as a means of continuous inter change of views on policies of mutual concern. In particular, the faculty representatives on the committee are instructed to meet promptly after their election each year, to organize as a group with a chairman and such other officers as may be needed, and to consider possible programs for discussion in the full committee."

A motion to approve the new paragraph three was lost, 127 to 119. The motion to approve paragraph four was carried, various motions to focus the resolutions specifically on the McMurray case etc. having been beaten down, and paragraphs numbered 1, 2 and 4, quoted in full, above, were adopted as a whole. Thus ended the faculty's consideration of the McMurray case.

A few observations growing out of the faculty's evolving position on the McMurray matter should not be out of place. Paragraph one of the three resolutions the faculty finally adopted, which deals with the great weight which should be given to the departmental and administrative judgment on the academic qualifications of a candidate for a professorial post, was and is in no sense critical of the regents. I cannot recall any case, from the Birge era onwards, in which the regents have not accepted the judgment of the academic authorities on a candidate's academic qualifications. What the regents have also been concerned with is the candidate's non-academic qualifications, and their judgment as to the weight to be attached to those qualifications is to be respected. This is not only because the regents alone have the power and the responsibility of appointing and promoting the staff, but also because their workaday-world judgment on a candidate's non-academic qualifications is likely to be more keen than that of faculty folk.

Paragraph two of the final faculty resolutions, on the value of practical experiences must have been quite acceptable to the regents. It does not say or imply that there should be no limit to the leaves of absence a professor may have for the gaining or increasing of practical experience in the field of his specialty. The regents were opposed to Mr. McMurray's excursions into politics, I think, not because they were in politics, but because he had made them so frequently within a short period as to raise doubts in their minds as to his interest in a university career. Of their growing doubts on this score Mr. Mc- Murray himself was cognizant before he decided to run for the U. S. Senate in 1946. He took a calculated risk. If I had seen the statements the regents made at their meeting on January 17, 1947, before I wrote my press release of January 26, I should have been slow to say, as I did, that if the matter had been handled with discretion Mr. McMurray would probably have been appointed.

The third faculty resolution of February 10, in favor of the more effective functioning of the Regent-Faculty Conference Committee, cannot have displeased any regent or faculty member. The resolution is soundly conceived and clearly stated. The committee is a species of fire brigate whose duty it is to see that no combustibles are lying around loose, and to be ready to be called out when fire threatens.

Appendix 25
Richard Cheney

by Crawford Young

By some distance, the most famed historical figure whose career included a period of association with the Department is Richard Cheney, a doctoral candidate from 1966 to 1968. After his departure from Madison, Cheney achieved a remarkably swift ascent to the very summit of national power, winning the post of chief of staff to President Gerald Ford in 1975, at the age of 34. His talents for political leadership were again displayed in his rise during five terms as a Wyoming congressman to number two in the House Republican leadership, followed by appointment as secretary of defense during the first Bush administration. Most dramatic of all was his election as vice president in 2000. In this role, he is widely viewed as the most powerful incumbent of that office in the history of the republic.

His meteoric rise was slow to begin. He was a very good high school student and two-way starter on the high school football team in Casper, an oil town in central Wyoming. But his higher educational career began inauspiciously. He was admitted to Yale on scholarship, enjoying the good offices of a Casper oil executive and Yale alumnus, Thomas Stroock; however, Cheney flunked out twice. For a time, Cheney abandoned college and worked as a power lineman in southwestern Wyoming.

He then made a fresh start, briefly at a community college, then at the University of Wyoming. His fiancee, Lynne Vincent, played a helpful role by making clear to Cheney that her future plans did not include marriage to a power lineman. Once at Laramie, the exceptional promise of Cheney became evident. He amassed a mostly-A record, and wrote a prize-winning paper for a national student political scientist competition run by the National Center for Education and Politics, then directed by Bernard Hennessey, a 1955 Wisconsin political science doctoral alumnus. Cheney also won one of two student internship positions in the Wyoming State Legislature, where he attracted the further attention of Stroock, then a state senator, and future U.S. Senator Alan Simpson. He also had strong backing from John Thompson, chair of the Wyoming political science department. His prize paper came to the notice of Maureen Drummy, then chief aide to a young Wisconsin congressman, William Steiger.

Cheney continued for an M.A. at Wyoming, which he completed in 1966. Thompson urged him to apply for one of the six-month fellowships in a governor's office sponsored by the National Center for Education and Politics; no Wyoming student had ever held one. With the award in hand, he was steered to the office of Wisconsin Governor Warren Knowles with the help of Drummy and Steiger. He also won a fellowship to the Wisconsin political science department. Thus he arrived in Madison in 1966 to take up the internship with Governor Knowles, a moderate Republican, and began doctoral work that fall. Then-Chair Bernard Cohen recalls discovering that Cheney initially intended full-time employment at the Knowles office as well as his doctoral study, which was contrary to Graduate School policy at the time. Cohen intervened with both Knowles and Cheney to limit the gubernatorial work to half time. When the six-month internship ended, Cheney had sufficiently impressed Knowles to earn part-time appointment to his staff.

By the time Cheney came to Madison, he was married to Lynne Cheney and had an infant daughter. Parenthood and graduate enrollment assured his fifth draft deferment, which insulated Cheney from the risk of service in Vietnam, a matter that was to reappear during the 2004 presidential campaign. Though Cheney was a quiet supporter of the war, he felt no inclination to seek military service; as he would later explain, he did not perceive army duty as a priority.[1]

Those who recollect having Cheney in a class—Jack Dennis and Crawford Young—remember him as a very quiet student, rarely participating in discussion, but earning mostly A's in his written work. His student colleagues have similar recollections; he was reserved and self-contained, not an active participant in graduate student life, perhaps partly because he did not share the strongly anti-Vietnam war views of many, but doubtless also because of his time commitments in the governor's office, and his family obligations. His wife was enrolled in an English doctoral program,[2] and there were parenting responsibilities for their infant daughter.

He did serve as a research assistant to Aage Clausen, who was an assistant professor at Wisconsin from 1966 to 1971 and then left for Ohio State. The project involved multiple regression analysis of legislative voting. Such analysis at the time was still carried out through IBM cards, and computing time at the Sterling Hall computer center was often available only late at night; Cheney with his boxes of cards was a frequent customer on the midnight run. Clausen listed Cheney as coauthor in a 1970 article on Senate and

House voting on economic and welfare policy in the *American Political Science Review*. Only two other vice presidents include *APSR* articles on their vitae (Henry Wallace and Hubert Humphrey).[3]

Cheney passed his preliminary examinations in summer 1968. He won departmental nomination for the American Political Science Association (APSA) congressional fellow program, which attests to the support he must have received from those faculty with whom he worked most closely. Only five slots were then available nationally; he was named as an alternate. But a stroke of good fortune at this juncture opened a career door for Cheney. The Tydings Foundation, named after the former Maryland senator and funded by money from the Joseph Davies estate,[4] had for some years provided one fellowship a year to an undergraduate majoring in political science. The foundation had contacted Chair Cohen, indicating they wished to find an alternative outlet for this scholarship. Cohen then suggested that the funds be made available to Cheney to take up the congressional fellowship. Both the Foundation and APSA agreed, and Cheney was on his way to a dazzling Washington career.

Representative Steiger and his staff assistant Drummer remembered Cheney's prize-winning student paper, and invited him to serve his congressional internship on the Steiger staff. One of his assignments was to take part in a delegation to a number of college campuses in early 1969, to make a judgment on the wisdom of a proposal to slash federal funding for campuses with violent antiwar protests. Cheney organized the Madison visit, taking the group to a Students for a Democratic Society (SDS) meeting and a faculty gathering. Steiger opposed the legislation, which was dropped. However, Cheney later explained that this mission was pivotal in his decision not to pursue his doctorate further. In an interview with Lemann, he expressed disgust at what he perceived as the pusillanimous position of the faculty, full of complaints but refusing to "stand up and be counted."[5]

Cheney swiftly attracted notice among a circle of House Republicans with whom Steiger was close: Gerald Ford, George H.W. Bush, and above all, a rising young Illinois congressman, Donald Rumsfeld. Nixon named Rumsfeld to head the Office of Economic Opportunity, with a mandate to curb its role. Rumsfeld at once invited Cheney to be his aide; the APSA granted special permission for Cheney to use the last half of his congressional fellowship in an executive agency rather than as a congressional aide, an unusual favor. Cheney stayed on the Rumsfeld staff after the fellowship expired, then moved with him to run the Cost of Living Council that Nixon established in 1971 to manage the wage and price controls he imposed.

When Nixon resigned in 1974, President Ford chose Rumsfeld as his chief of staff, and he at once brought Cheney on board as his assistant. The following year, Rumsfeld did his first tour as secretary of defense, and Cheney moved up to the chief of staff position, a role he played in a quiet but forceful way. In this early phase of his ascent, Cheney was mostly within a circuit of moderate Republicans; he was the quintessential loyal, discreet, and efficient subordinate. However, by sharp maneuver he assured his ascendancy within the White House, succeeding in marginalizing Vice President Nelson Rockefeller, and persuading President Ford to drop Rockefeller from the 1976 ticket in favor of Robert Dole.[6]

When Ford lost the 1976 election, Cheney returned to Wyoming to organize a campaign for the state's single seat in the House of Representatives. By the end of his five terms, he had risen to second in command to Illinois Minority Leader Robert Michel. Only after his nomination as vice president did close scrutiny reveal a very conservative voting record.

During his congressional career, Cheney found many occasions to mark his appreciation to the APSA for the opportunity that the Congressional Fellowship Program had provided. He served for many years on the Congressional Fellowship Board, and took on a number of APSA congressional fellows. He was always available to speak to groups with an APSA connection, and, as Charles Jones attests, to help research projects by being interviewed or facilitating contacts with members on both sides of the aisle.

Cheney developed an affection for the House and its historical legendry; perhaps his former academic impulses also came to the fore, motivating him to coauthor with his wife, Lynne Cheney (now head of the National Endowment for the Humanities), *Kings of the Hill*, a book capturing rich moments of the House of Representatives past.[7] The Cheneys chose to portray the House through the careers of eight of its most distinguished leaders, such figures as Henry Clay, James Polk, Joe Cannon and Sam Rayburn.[8]

President George H.W. Bush named Cheney secretary of defense in 1989, as a nominee certain of confirmation after the Senate had rejected the nomination of Senator John Tower. Cheney was then in a strategic role in the first Iraq war in 1991. For a time after the Bush defeat in 1992, Cheney toyed with a campaign for the presidency, an ambition abandoned in 1995 to become head of Halliburton. As a vice president who served a president unusually lacking in national policy experience or background in international affairs, Cheney was cast in an exceptionally influential role. For the first time in his long and distinguished career, he became a polarizing figure, especially through his forceful advocacy of the 2003 invasion of Iraq. The final judgment history will place upon this remarkable leader will doubtless hinge in large measure upon the eventual outcome and consequences of the Iraq venture.

Notes

1. For this judgment and many others, I rely on an excellent and sympathetic profile of Richard Cheney by Nicholas Lemann, "The Quiet Man: Dick Cheney's Discreet Rise to Unprecedented Power," *New Yorker*, 7 May 2001, 56–71. For the Madison years, see also David Maraniss, *They Marched into Sunlight: War and Peace Vietnam and America October 1967* (New York: Simon & Schuster, 2003). Both Lemann and Maraniss benefited from extensive interviews with Cheney. Another valuable source is the hard-hitting biography by Madison Capitol-Times staffer John Nichols, *Dick: The Man Who Is President* (New York: New Press, 2004).
2. Lynne Cheney completed her doctorate in 1970, with a dissertation entitled "Matthew Arnold's Possible Perfection: A Study in the Kantian Stream in Arnold's Poetry."
3. I am indebted to Brian Silver for this observation.
4. Joseph Davies was a Wisconsin graduate, with a B.L. degree in 1898, and a law degree in 1901.
5. Lemann, "The Quiet Man," 63. Nichols has a somewhat different explanation of this episode, based on a Capitol-Times interview with Steiger prior to his 1978 death at the age of 40. Nichols, *Dick*, 45–46. Rumsfeld was also involved in this movement.
6. Nichols provides detail on this scheme, designed to appeal to the party right wing. Ford later characterized this decision as the worst mistake of his career. Nichols, *Dick*, 66–71.
7. Richard B. Cheney and Lynne V. Cheney, *Kings of the Hill: Power and Personality in the House of Representatives* (New York: Continuum Publishing Company, 1983).
8. In an eerily prophetic passage, they conclude by choosing Clay as the most signal figure: "Of all the assertions of power we have seen, the most spectacular was Henry Clay's. No one, not even Thaddeus Stevens, managed to do what young Henry Clay did—thrust the nation into war. Audacious and bold, he and his war hawks were exhilarating company as they maneuvered a doubtful president and a divided nation onto a firm and fiery course." Cheney and Cheney, *Kings of the Hill*, 191. Clay, elected from Kentucky in 1810, was immediately chosen Speaker of the House in 1811. The young Clay was driven by frontier fears of an Indian confederation of 30 tribes stitched together by Tecumseh, which was terrorizing trans-Appalachian settlements. Britain was blamed for arming and inciting the Indians; for Clay and his allies, this called for striking the evil at its source by invading and annexing Canada. Though Clay won his declaration of war in 1812, Congress neglected to appropriate money to fight it, and elation soon turned into confusion and fear, as predictions of swift victory proved wrong.

Lynne Cheney was an author in her own right, writing several books. Among them was an inside-Washington political novel co-authored in 1988 with Victor Gold, a press relations writer who had helped draft the 1987 George H.W. Bush campaign biography. Their novel, *The Body Politic* (New York: St. Martin's Press), is a hilarious and slightly salacious tale of a vice president in mortal distress, again a curiously prophetic theme.

Appendix 26

Alumni Recollections

A small number of graduate alumni representing different generations were asked to provide brief recollections of their North Hall experience by way of contributing to a social history of the graduate student community.

William Farber *(Ph.D. 1935)*

[The Farber statement is extracted from an oral history he dictated in July 1984. Farber spent his entire career at the University of South Dakota, and encouraged a number of his best undergraduate students at pursue advanced degrees at Wisconsin, including Charles Jones and Samuel Patterson.]

My two years at Wisconsin from 1933 to 1935 were most delightful, and very significant for my future career. The atmosphere of the 1930s impressed upon the student the importance of applying political science to practical problems, policy change and innovation. Compared to my undergraduate and M.A. years in the conservative Northwestern environment, Wisconsin was a breath of fresh air.

I had a university fellowship plus a tuition waiver. The fellowship was $600; because of the difficult economic situation, we were required to live in a dormitory, Adams Hall, for which $360 was deducted for room and board. I managed to live on the remaining $26 per month. The there were only a small number of graduate students in the department; much of my social contacts were with students from various fields in Adams Hall. There were occasional speakers; I remember one lecture on sex by E.A. Ross of sociology (who had been fired from Stanford for criticizing Leland Stanford), in which he advocated premarital cohabitation.

We were required to take preliminary examinations in four of five fields. The courses in each of the fields were also open to undergraduates, which had no disadvantage. Classes were small, 20 or so students. My second year I volunteered to conduct one section with Grayson Kirk's course, while holding my fellowship, to acquire some teaching experience. Ogg stressed that I was not required to do so. With the fellowship, I was able to finish the degree in two years.

In addition, examinations in two foreign languages were required, plus a course in statistics which I took with Samuel Stouffer, then in sociology. With two years of French, I was able to pass on the second try, but German was difficult, with no prior work. I prepared with a tutor. Of two possible German examiners, one was hard and one easy; students with weak preparation could arrange with those well prepared to be able to take the exam with the indulgent professor.

Ogg was hardworking, methodical, and fair. There was some criticism of Ogg's assertive leadership, which I felt unfair. I preferred a permanent Chair on whose word one could rely; his decisions would not be subject to subsequent faculty debate. His reputation was so overwhelming that he could assure placement. When I look for employment in spring 1935, jobs were scarce. Ogg knew of two—South Dakota and Alabama. Ogg arranged the South Dakota job for me, and my classmate Hollis Barber got the Alabama one. Ogg had regular Sunday dinners for graduate students.

There was not much social structure in the department, nor much socializing with faculty, who were accessible to students but focused on their own research. There was only one woman student, and no Jews or minorities. I went to some cultural events at the Union, partly because Ogg indicated it was important. I also regularly attended Sunday services at the First Congregational church, and valued the social gospel sermons of Reverend Swan.

William Young *(Ph.D. 1941)*

[The Young statement is drawn from an interview by Crawford Young on 16 July 2004. After beginning his academic career at the University of Pennsylvania, William Young returned to Wisconsin in 1947. He served as chair from 1952 to 1960, then as director of the former Center for Development from 1967 until his 1983 retirement.]

I was a graduate student in Madison from 1939 to 1941. I arrived after a couple of years of graduate study at Pittsburgh; during the second of those years, I took on a double teaching load for an enhanced salary; Pitt was economizing by covering courses with TAs rather than faculty. I taught virtually every subject in the field, which made preliminary examinations easy to pass in Madison. Sally and I arrived with $1000 savings; she earned some money typing. Without these funds we could not have survived on the $500 TA stipend, from which resident tuition was deducted.

Compared to Pittsburgh, the easy informality of professional and social relations between faculty and students stood out. The two great men of the department, Frederic Ogg and John Gaus, both maintained close ties with graduate students. Ogg would regularly invite two or three students for Sunday dinner. He and his wife were very hospitable, although he was never comfortable in social conversation with students. We knew his two passions, outside of political science, were football and opera. We felt it unseemly to raise the subject of football, and knew too little about opera to dare pursue this topic.

Gaus was revered. During the academic year, every Saturday afternoon he hosted an informal coffee, at which all graduate students were welcome, and most attended from time to time. Sometimes a campus visitor was present and would be the focus of conversation. This setting was the best opportunity to have access to the wise reflections of Gaus on political science and current political issues. In class his presentations were not very structured, and tended to revert to discussions of *The Education of Henry Adams*. We entertained both the Oggs and the Gauses in our East Johnson Street apartment.

The foreign language requirements were a major obstacle. I passed the French examination without too much difficulty, but German was a major obstacle. I spent a summer memorizing a German-language history of the United States used in Pennsylvania German-language schools. The German department gave the examination only once a year; there were three examiners. Arriving for the exam, I found lines in front of two doors, and no one waiting by the third door, behind which sat an examiner who had the reputation for severity. I decided to risk this third examiner, and somehow survived.

The graduate students in residence were a cohesive community, with a good deal of social interaction. William Ebenstein, an Austrian emigre who was a former student of Harold Laski and had just finished his Wisconsin doctorate and joined the faculty, was a frequent lunch companion with the graduate students. He had opinions on almost everything.

However, I do not recollect graduate student efforts directed at the perennial issue of prelim reform at the time. Although the depression was by no means over, the larger issue looming over all of us was the sense that war was imminent.

Henry Hart *(Ph.D. 1950)*

[Hart was appointed to the faculty in 1948, and spent his entire career at Wisconsin, retiring in 1982.]

We graduate students in the 1950s had a Political Science Club (maybe "Association"). We heard invited speakers monthly, usually in the Memorial Union. We took advantage of visiting political science notables for this purpose, or of other knowledgeable people known to faculty. I remember an occasion when James McCamy was our speaker. We wanted to have an informal interaction with him afterwards in a social setting; the only venue I could think of was the parlor in Lathrop Hall. Reluctantly the Lathrop custodian gave permission. It was a rewarding evening.

But next day the Lathrop custodian called the department secretary and demanded to know who the chair of the graduate student association was. Me. It turned out that one of the Victorian vintage Lathrop chairs had a fractured leg. The department secretary asked what I intended to do about the matter. My response was to invite the association to better behavior. But the Lathrop custodian gave the department formal notice that Lathrop facilities could never again be used.

Clara Penniman *(B.A. 1950, M.A. 1951)*

[After completing her M.A., Penniman transferred to the University of Minnesota, where she earned her doctorate in 1954. She was appointed to the Wisconsin faculty in 1953, retiring in 1984. She was department chair from 1963 to 1966, then became the founding director of the Center for Public Policy and Administration, now the Robert M. La Follette School of Public Affairs.]

My main memories are of teaching assistant service and working on my M.A. thesis, which dealt with the state budget process, supervised by William Young. In some odd way my thesis was later used as a reference by Senator Proxmire.

There were six or seven teaching assistants; Pam Rice and I were the only women. All of the men, as I recollect, were army veterans. The others worked with the American government course, and I assisted Llewellyn Pfankuchen with the international relations course. We received $700 for the two semesters, and normally handled four quiz sections plus grading papers. Although there was no health insurance, I believe we had access to the UW clinics and student infirmary. The veterans, of course, had the GI Bill to supplement the $700 stipend.

The TAs had a room in one of the metal quonset huts at Park and University. We were generally a congenial group. The political argument I recall most clearly revolved around whether the U.S. should have used the atomic bomb. As usual most of us in 1949–50 were Democrats but there were one or two Republicans.

One of the TAs flunked prelims, which seemed to surprise the faculty more than his fellow TAs.

Another incident I remember was once asking the army officer lecturing to a class next to mine to turn down the record he was playing. When I returned to our room, the men were astounded. Apparently they were still close enough to the army that they would not have made such a request to an officer.

We were so physically separated from the office and faculty that there was no easy communication. For reasons I don't recollect, "the office" was the enemy. Therefore all problems were the fault of "the office." However, we were grateful for the money and eager to get ahead. I was the only one going elsewhere (to Minnesota) for my doctorate; the others had all done undergraduate work elsewhere and hoped to complete their doctorates at Wisconsin.

Barbara McLennan *(Ph.D. 1965)*

[This statement is abstracted from a long text McLennan provided in response to the 2003 alumni survey. After resigning the Temple position described in her recollections, McLennan pursued a Washington career, including work as a congressional staff member, government service with the Treasury, Internal Revenue Service, and Department of Commerce, where she held the post of deputy assistant secretary for trade information and analysis from 1989 to 1991. She is a specialist on tax policy and reform.]

I entered the University of Wisconsin in September 1961. President Kennedy had just been elected (November 1960) and the country was embroiled in the early stages of the civil rights struggle. Dr. Martin Luther King was making his greatest speeches, and many graduate students were anxious to be active in support of civil rights, which was at that time a non-violent movement. In fact, in the spring of 1962, I was invited to join a summer trip with some friends to Mississippi to help register black people to vote. I could not go because I was completing my master's thesis (finished by June 1962) and I was to be married in August 1962. As many people probably know, three UW students who went to Mississippi that summer ended up getting killed.

I was admitted to the UW graduate school on the basis of my academic record, which was very strong. I was a graduate of the Bronx High School of Science and had graduated magna cum laude from CCNY with an A/A- average, and received an academic prize at graduation. This was a rare and difficult accomplishment in 1961, when most students everywhere graduated with B-/C+ averages and A's were unusual. There were five or fewer magna cum laude students graduating with me at CCNY, out of a class of 700–800. I had been accepted by numerous graduate schools, but I selected Wisconsin, because the political science department offered the best fellowship—a three-year NDEA fellowship that took care of tuition and living expenses, and to study comparative politics, the field that I had selected as a major.

I was a very successful student at Wisconsin. In my master's program (beginning September 1961) I earned straight A's in all my courses and completed my master's thesis in two semesters, receiving the MS in June 1962. Over the next two years, I completed all of the required Ph.D. courses, mostly with grades of A. I then was awarded an All-University Fellowship for the completion of my dissertation. I received the Ph.D. in August 1965, just two years and one summer after completing the master's degree. I was only 25 years old, and certainly was one of the youngest Wisconsin Ph.D.'s (male or female) to have received the degree.

The political science department faculty in 1961 saw itself as tolerant and liberal (and supportive of the Democratic Party), but many in the faculty did not understand the implications of this liberalism as a practical matter. Other faculty members were not liberal, and had no qualms about engaging in unequal treatment. For example, UW professed not to engage in overt sex discrimination. In the summer of 1965, when I was looking for a job in academia, however, Wisconsin was nowhere to be found on the employment front. Some faculty members were engaged in an organized program to help graduating students find employment. They were writing letters and asking colleagues around the country about the availability of positions. When I made a request to receive this kind of assistance, I was told (very openly) that men had to be placed first and that if I wanted a job, I should look for one myself.

On the strength of my Wisconsin Ph.D., I took this advice. I obtained interviews at a number of colleges and universities in the New York/Philadelphia area. At Douglass College (Rutgers University) I was offered a position that would have required three separate course preparations each semester, and paid $3,500 per year. This was substantially less compensation than would have been received by a beginning kindergarten teacher without a Ph.D. Finally, I found a position at Temple University in Philadelphia where I started as an assistant professor, at a pay rate more than double offered by Douglass, in September 1965.

In 1965, women were very poorly represented on college/university faculties, and as graduate students. Not only was I a woman, but I was very young (and looked younger), and I was married – three good (and legal) reasons to discriminate. Civil rights and equal employment legislation did not apply to women in 1965, and Wisconsin (and probably most other universities) did not feel that it had to treat women graduate students in a manner equal to their male counterparts. When asked, individual professors would write letters of reference, but the department apparatus for finding employment for graduating students could be openly denied to women.

The situation was not better at Temple. I looked so young that the chairman of my department had to write a letter for me indicating that I was a faculty member, so that I could use the Temple library. My youth, however, did not stop them from giving me a teaching load of three separate course preparations each semester. I had large classes, no teaching assistants, and by the end of my first year I had taught courses in comparative politics, European government, European political parties, political development, international law, and international relations.

By 1969, I had published about half a dozen academic articles. I had also taught numerous (and sometimes very large) classes for the department. Temple rewarded me with a grant of tenure and a promotion to associate professor. On the other hand, the promotion came without any increase in pay. I do not know whether it is common practice in academia to promote without increasing pay, but I was married to a professor (with limited income) and by this time we had a house and a child. My inability to increase my compensation caused genuine hardships for us.

Marjorie Hershey *(Ph.D. 1972)*

[A specialist on American electoral politics, Hershey has been a member of the Indiana University faculty since completing her doctoral training.]

A graduate student at Indiana University once told me how much she envied my graduate student experience "in the incredibly dramatic and romantic period of history, during the Vietnam War." Till that point I hadn't really thought of myself as part of a "romantic period of history." In fact, it was a little sobering to think of myself as being a part of any sort of history (though I suppose that's inevitable if you're lucky enough to stick around for any length of time).

Yet it's true that the grad school experience of my cohort in the late 1960s and early 1970s was dramatically different from that of my graduate students today. I came to Madison in the fall of 1966, just as large-scale protests against American involvement in that war were beginning. The following fall, classroom buildings were picketed to protest the on-campus recruiting of Dow Chemical Company (the manufacturer of napalm) and a number of us teaching assistants had to decide whether to cross a picket line for the first time in our lives. Many of my friends and colleagues joined the Teaching Assistants Association a year or two later, and my husband and I (who were not TAs at that time) brought coffee to the "barricades." (Picketing in Madison during the winter, of course, is more of a test of character than is a protest in a warmer climate.) By 1969 uniformed National Guard members, called up by the governor, wandered freely around campus, spending most of their time ogling girls but occasionally throwing tear gas and pepper gas on street corners and into campus buildings. North Hall became almost uninhabitable.

Then the United States invaded Cambodia in 1970 and the antiwar movement entered a new phase. Stunned and unable to watch the news, I sat outside on a blanket in front of our Eagle Heights apartment. Within a short time, I was joined by dozens of others, no one talking, everyone lost in his or her own feelings of frustration and despair. Within days, four students at Kent State University had been killed by National Guardsmen called to campus to quell protests; two students later died at the hands of police at Jackson State University. Later that summer, a late-night explosion rattled windows in Eagle Heights. Sterling Hall, which housed the Army Mathematics Research Center, had been bombed by a small group of people outraged at the center's involvement in Defense Department research. The bombing killed a researcher who was working in the building in the early hours of the morning. The war had been brought home.

How did these events affect those of us who were grad students at the time? The impact was profound. We saw ourselves as part of the world in a way we had never anticipated. We came to understand that public policy is in fact a matter of life and death and that political science can have a meaningful role in public life. We learned that it is not generally helpful to be insufferably self-righteous, even when you know you're right. And we formed a bond among us that remains tight to this day.

Edmond Keller *(Ph.D. 1974)*

[The Keller statement is extracted from a speech he gave at a reunion of alumni of a Ford Foundation minority fellowship program. He is currently a professor of political science at the University of California at Los Angeles, where he is a former Director of the African Studies Center.]

I am very much a product of the civil rights movement. I entered high school in New Orleans, Louisiana, in 1957. The school I attended was a well-known parochial high school, St. Augustine. It is an all-male school, and politically activist priests from the East Coast taught us . . . my high school counselor and English teacher was the famed anti–Vietnam War activist, Philip Berrigan. The priests . . . attempted to instill in us, the students, a sense of achievement motivation, encouraging us to leave home in search of a first-rate college education.

[After military service, I] was discharged in June 1964. I had missed the marches on Selma and Washington . . . and I could hardly recognize the country when I returned. Things were changing at a dizzying pace. As soon as I returned home, I enrolled in . . . the University of New Orleans. The civil rights movement was in full swing as was the war in Vietnam and the Black Power Movement. I became a student activist, and was joined by a number of idealistic young people who felt that we had the responsibility to make the university live up to its responsibility of social justice. At the time, the student body numbered in the neighborhood of 12,000. Only a handful of students were African Americans, and most of them were first-year students who would never make it to the second semester, let alone the second year. The cards of a legacy of racism and discrimination were stacked against them, and the classroom was not immune.

By 1968 the Black Power Movement had engulfed the entire country, and it was most intense on college campuses. . . . I can recall that the main issues for us were the diversification of the curriculum and the integration of the faculty . . . there was not one faculty member on the entire campus who was African American. When we confronted the university administration on the matter we were told that there were just not suitable candidates out there. We insisted that this was not the case and produced a list of some 40 African American Ph.D. political scientists who might be approached. . . . Needless to say, our appeals fell on deaf ears.

As our efforts and those of like-minded Americans of all races who shared our vision of a deracialized society began to succeed, major American universities began to actively recruit students of color into their graduate programs. I chose to go to the University of Wisconsin. I am not sure why, but the reputation of the school as a bastion of liberalism and the offer of financial assistance seem to have had something to do with it. I was married with two small children.

Wisconsin represented a real cultural shock for my small family and me. When I joined the political science department there, I was the only African American graduate student out of some 130. On the whole campus, there were only a few African Americans, and most of them were in the school of law. If we saw a black person on the street this was a major experience for the day. Despite what I considered to be real cultural hardships, I feel that I was fortunate in that my graduate student cohorts, as well as the faculty, seemed genuinely committed to making my family and me feel welcome.

Initially I had intended to study urban politics. I felt that would best prepare me to go back to my community and make a difference. But sometime in my second year of graduate school I came to rationalize that the problems that society faced were so big that no one person could alone make a decisive difference. Instead, what needed to happen was for the socially committed to identify one piece of the problem that they would tackle with all their might. I decided that my fight would be in academe. I further decided that even though I was committed to my people, I could best help by being the best that I could be in a subdiscipline that was different from urban or black politics. I chose to major in comparative politics with a focus on Africa. One of my main reasons for this was the fact that the faculty members at Wisconsin who studied Africa seemed the most supportive of me and this had a profound effect on me.

[On the job market] I interviewed widely. What was ironic about that experience, however, was that possible employers were less interested in my expertise in African politics, than they were in my fulfilling a political role. . . . When I was a graduate student at Wisconsin, I worked to recruit students of color in the political science department's graduate program. One of my first recruits was . . . Bai Akridge, whom I had met in 1972 in Kenya.

In an increasingly sophisticated but hostile environment, it becomes more important for us to remember that "giving back" to society is what sustains the link to enable us to succeed in achieving our goals of justice and equality. A key issue is the shift in the public mood of the majority about the need for diversity and affirmative action. . . . The battle is not over; we have not yet won.

Margaret (Sandie) Turner *(Ph.D. 1985)*

[Since completing her doctorate, Turner has taught at Wheeling Jesuit College and Carlow College, in Pittsburgh. She has been active in developing interdisciplinary adult education programs.]

The year I entered graduate school in political science was 1966. We were a big entering class, including a good number of women. Some of us were very focused on getting a Ph.D., and others were less sure whether we wanted to continue past an M.A. I remember conversations in the TA room that concerned which professors were open to treating women students as seriously as they did male students and giving us as much time as our male colleagues. We traded information on which faculty really helped women students find jobs. The women students who had been at Wisconsin longer were very helpful in giving advice. Willingness to seriously work with female students was one of the criteria we looked for in an advisor and helped some of us choose which area of political science to focus on. For other women students this was less of a consideration, and they chose their advisors thinking more of career ambitions or other factors.

In my second year in the department I was one of eight grad students chosen to teach my own sections of Pol Sci 101. I was the only woman. I was given the unpopular 7:45 a.m. sections. I don't know if that was because I was the minority, but I do know that the cold and the darkness of the Madison mornings contributed to my believing that teaching was NOT the profession for me. Some of my doubts about teaching as a career built because I did not aspire to be an excellent lecturer and that was the primary model I had of teachers at Wisconsin. (Of course, other experiences led me to revise this decision, and I have ended up in college teaching.) There was only one woman on the political science faculty at that time, and I never took a class from her, so all my professors were male.

The most interesting female role models at Wisconsin at that time for me were the professors' wives I met who were leading social agencies such as Virginia Hart and running for local political office such as Becky Young. I was much impressed by Virginia and Becky because they combined a serious involvement in the life of their family with an intellectual and professional life which was very much respected. The same woman who reminded me to put on gloves on a cold Wisconsin morning was also the acknowledged expert in the county and then in the State House on welfare legislation. I had not known women like this before. They helped me see many more possibilities in my life than becoming a lecturer. I did not feel discriminated against, but there was not the awareness of gender issues that would develop in the '70s nor the variety of role models which was to come.

I left the department after my M.A. for a job and returned in 1972 to complete the course work for my Ph.D. I found that there were new dynamics at work in the department. I was part of a grad student group that participated in the search for a woman faculty member, to be shared, I believe, with women's studies. I remember that Jo Freeman was one of the candidates. She did not get chosen, but went on to publish on the subject of the women's movement. Because I had been out of the country, it was new to me that gender issues were really on the agenda both in hiring of faculty and as a legitimate subject to be studied. Gender was no longer just a demographic category, but a complex influence on political perspectives, economic possibilities, and world views that needed to be examined and better understood. It took a few years for this perspective to really show up in my intellectual products, but the seed was planted in the 70s in Madison.

Allen Hertzke *(Ph.D. 1986)*

[Since completing his doctorate, Hertzke has pursued his academic career at the University of Oklahoma.]

For many of us who passed through North Hall in the 1980s a certain elan developed and so endured that a strong cohort from this decade still looks forward to their annual gathering for dinner and drinks at the APSA convention. Among the wonderful cast of characters from that period I can still recognize some 30 alumni Ph.D.'s, a sign of our grad cohort's comradery.

The department's lack of orthodoxy and eclectic approach to political science contributed to a lively social environment. Instead of tunneling in narrow channels of specialization, we were exposed to the grand sweep of intellectual currents in the discipline, fostering a common experience. Epitomizing that common foundation was Murray Edelman's course we all took the first semester. No matter what our background or interest, we shared the epistemological controversies and debates, the exposure to classics, a sense of disciplinary evolution, and the plain fun of discussing Thomas Kuhn. Given this training ground, it's not so surprising that when the "replication" controversy splashed across the pages of *PS*, two key protagonists were Gary King and Paul Herrnson.

The venerable lounge, though dumpier than today, was a hangout where we learned from each other by osmosis. Given the diversity of students and interests, one could overhear Brigitta Young defend secularism, Jimmy Kandeh discourse on Hume, Steve Orvis explain dependency theory, or Andy Aoki illuminate Bruce Springsteen's contribution to political culture.

The era's diverse faculty—Charles Anderson, Mel Croan, Donald Downs, Dennis Dresang, Murray Edelman, Leon Epstein, Booth Fowler, Ed Friedman, Joel Grossman, Barbara Hinckley, Bert Kritzer, Dick Merelman, Neil Richardson, Patrick Riley, Virginia Sapiro, David Tarr, Graham Wilson, John Witte, and Crawford Young—provided real continuity to the "Wisconsin tradition." Of course no one's roots in the profession reached back as far as Leon's—to the 1940s. I remember learning to be careful in book critiques because Leon would say something like, "Well, I know David Truman, and he never meant to say *that*!" Battle-tested from service as dean of the college in the '60s days of rage, Leon also represented a certain breadth of wisdom that served so many. Before he retired, he chaired such diverse dissertators as Gary King, Paul Hernson, Deidre Sullivan Frees, and myself.

Gary King was something of a legend in the early part of the decade. He was treated more as a department methodologist than as a regular graduate student. I will never forget the job talk by a candidate for the Hawkins Chair, a rather big name in the behavioral field, who was eviscerated by Gary sitting at the table in the Ogg room. The rest of us grad students, sitting in the audience chairs behind the table, just watched with sinful delight.

The episode sparked one of the funniest skits at the annual holiday party, back when they were pretty lighthearted. Exhibiting comic genius, Sam Crane led a haughtily accented chant about the Hawkins Chair—"the Hawkins Chair, the Hawkins Chair, the HAW-KINS CHAIR"—represented by a stool, while the distinguished candidate spoke about predicting the party ID of the parents' pets.

And then there was the time that Georgia Duerst Lahti invited everyone to a party at her parents' dairy farm, producing the striking sight of some thirty of us tramping through the milking barn. The Wisconsin political science department was not only a place of excellent graduate training, it was a great fellowship.

Appendix 27

Department Holiday Skits

From time immemorial, the approach of the holiday season has been celebrated with a department party for faculty and graduate students. By long tradition, the students have prepared a satirical skit, performing gentle spoofs on diverse faculty members. Since the early 1990s, the student skits have been matched by faculty performances. A few of the scripts survive, and serve as commentaries on their time. By way of example, we draw from 1969 and 2002 graduate student skits, and a 1993 faculty script. Those whose North Hall memories extend back to the Vietnam War era will recollect the activist mood it evoked in the student community especially, giving rise to the assertive Political Science Association of Students (PSAS) referenced in the 1969 skit. The 1993 faculty script satirizes the controversial budget-cutting Strategic Plan of the College of Letters & Science, formulated during the 1992–93 tenure of Crawford Young as acting dean, which reduced department faculty strength by three positions. We are grateful to Marjorie Hershey and Virginia Sapiro for contributing these texts.

Extracts from 1969 Graduate Student Skit

STAGE DIRECTOR: Many students in the University this semester have shown intense interest in that archaic institutional forum known as the departmental faculty meeting. Graduate students want to attend and participate in the decisions of faculty meetings. No one could probably be more surprised at this development than the faculty themselves, who up to now have viewed faculty meetings as at best a necessary evil of existence—kind of like taking out the garbage or being nice at those always boring graduate student-faculty get-togethers. This wave of graduate student interest in the faculty meeting has not escaped our own department. Led by that clandestine organization, PSAS, graduate students in our department also want to attend our faculty meeting. Few students in our department, though, have ever had the opportunity to attend an actual faculty meeting, even the agenda and minutes of our departmental meetings are not available to graduate students.

Behind me, you can see the setting for our little drama that is about to unfold. The place—our prominent, but anonymous Big Ten university, the political science building; the time—3:30, any Friday afternoon. Seated at the long table are assembled members of the political science faculty who have come to sift and winnow in their own inevitable fashion. Before it begins, we might introduce some of the most prominent personalities in the faculty meeting. First, at the head of the table, presiding over the meeting, is the chairman of the department of political science, Professor Crawford Compromise. When informed that he had been elected chairman of the department, a position he had not even sought, Compromise was heard to say the following: "Why me?" and "This is the most wonderful thing that's happened to me since I renewed by subscription to the *Daily Cardinal* last June." Seated alongside Professor Compromise at the front of the table are the distinguished full professors of the Department. For example, here seated at the immediate right of Professor Compromise is one of the most distinguished and influential men on the field of political science, Professor Austin Canny. As one pundit has noted, professor Canny has as much influence in American and international political science as Joseph Stalin had in Soviet and international communism—that is, before Stalin finally decided to assume full dictatorial powers. At Professor Canny's right sits another distinguished full professor, Professor John Strongarm. Here on Compromise's left sits Professor David Libertarian. He was honored last year by being voted civil libertarian of the year—by the Madison Police Department and the Wisconsin State Legislature. To Professor Libertarian's left sits Professor Dennis Jack. Rumor has it that the department had stiff competition when they were trying to get Professor Jack; at the same time he had been offered full tenure at Boys' Town and a position as full-time political consultant to Romper Room. On Professor Jack's left sits the most recent addition to the faculty, Professor Richard Merryman. Across from Professor Merryman sits the only woman member of the faculty, Professor Clara Pencilwoman. Here, silent and removed from the table, sit the two philosophers in residence of the department. Once many years ago one of them spoke up at a faculty meeting, and we are still trying to figure out what he meant. Near them sits the faculty expert on revolutions and mass movements, Professor Richard Manfried. Finally, at the rear of the table, sits, appropriately, the non-tenured faculty. This rather motley group with their lollipops are as a whole convinced of the particular relevance of one homily in guiding their behavior during faculty meetings. The homily? "If you want to get along, you go along." But I'm delaying—I think I hear Professor Compromise called the meeting to order, so I will go off to the wings and with you watch the unfolding of this momentous drama—a typical faculty meeting at a prominent Big Ten university.

(General stirring among the faculty. Mumbling and talking as action begins. Compromise is pounding on the table.)

COMPROMISE: Gentlemen! Gentlemen! Some quiet please. We have a long meeting today, including an important committee report and a delegation from the student radical group, so I think it best if we can start the meeting now.

(Talking subsides as Compromise begins meeting.)

COMPROMISE: Before the radical student group addresses our meeting on one of their problems, I have an important announcement to make.

STRONGARM: Which radical student group is it this time?

COMPROMISE: This student radical group calls itself COMPOSE—the combined political organization of students enraged. I would like to remind all of you of the colloquium next week. We will hear a research report from a prospective candidate, Mr. Sigma Statistics, who is a graduate student at the California Institute of Technology. Mr. Statistics is just completing his dissertation. He uses a random selection of crossword puzzles from the *New York Times* to construct a political model that accounts for 32% of the variance in the amount of asphalt highways laid in the states. I would like to emphasize full faculty attendance at the colloquium.

MERRYMAN: I don't want to prejudice Mr. Statistics' presentation next week, but it would seem to me that we already have 7 or 8 faculty members at the present time who are doing similar and just as worthwhile research is Mr. Statistics.

LIBERTARIAN: California Institute of Technology—what's that?

CANNY: It is in California, Dave.

COMPROMISE: Well, before we discuss our important business of the day, the committee report, I think it's probably best if we ask the delegation from the radical group COMPOSE to come in. Would you please ask them to come in now?

(COMPOSE delegation comes in from rear . . . walks towards front of table beside COMPROMISE, and stand silently.)

COMPROMISE: Before the delegates from COMPOSE speak, I'd like to emphasize the very responsible nature of these delegates. Both Miss Luxemburg and Mr. Cohn-Bendit subscribe to the *APSR* and *Presbyterian Life*, they watch the Green Bay Packers football games every Sunday, and—

most importantly—they try not to get involved in any meaningful contemporary problems in our society. In other words, gentlemen, they are just like us and are going to make fine, responsible political scientists like us.

(Faculty members grunt in approval, shake their heads.)

COMPOSE DELEGATE NO. 1: Thank you Professor Compromise. You are probably all aware why we of COMPOSE have come here today. We didn't originally object when the University administration required all students to have photo ID, then fingerprints, and then voiceprints; but now we just have to protest the most recent administrative action. The administration can now hold any student in preventive detention in the basement of Bascom Hall for two weeks. We feel that preventive detention is a clear violation of our constitutional rights as students and Americans.

LIBERTARIAN (interrupting and angry): What do you mean a violation of your constitutional rights? What about other people's constitutional rights—like the rights of the janitors who would have to clean up the basement of Bascom Hall?

CANNY: Good constitutional point, Dave!

STRONGARM: Aren't you people being just a little paranoiac? I mean, if the system is going to get you, it is going to get you; and if the system isn't going to get you, it isn't going to get you.

(Murmur of approval among the faculty.)

PENCILWOMAN: I suggest that they send this problem to our committee on preventive detention.

MERRYMAN: Now, now, Clara, maybe we shouldn't be hasty in our actions. After all, whom do you students of COMPOSE represent?

(Another murmur of approval among the faculty; faculty begin to talk with each other in muttered tones.)

COMPROMISE: Gentlemen, I'm sure we all agreed with everyone who has spoken—this delegation is entirely out of order and burdened with value-infested paranoia. And, furthermore, as you all know, I have always been concerned about anyone who would allow himself to belong to clandestine organizations, whose leaders refuse to reveal themselves, and whose funds come from unknown sources. I'm sorry but our time is too valuable to waste on trivial graduate student problems.

Extracts from Faculty Skit, 1993

A MIDSUMMER NIGHT'S DREAM, by W.S. and V.S.

The Original	*The Revision*	*The players*
Theseus, Duke of Athens	Dissertation Chair	Booth John Wilkes Fowler
Titania, Queen of the Fairies	Chair	Virginia Mayo Sapiro
Oberon, King of the Fairies	Associate Chair	Charles Laughton Franklin
Quince, the Player	Dean Quince	Crawford Broderick Young
Bottom, the Player	Dean Bottom	Graham Green Wilson
Puck	Himself	Richard Widmark Merelman

Act I, Scene II. *In South Hall, Dean Quince and Dean Bottom stand deliberating.*

Dean Quince: Are all the Deans here?

Dean Bottom: Perhaps we should list them all, then recategorize them, then refigure them, then line them up, then shuffle them about, then call their names and state the part they shall play in our Strategic Plans for organizing the College and its budget. First you, Dean Quince.

Dean Quince: Our play is—The most lamentable comedy, and most cruel death of the College budget. And we shall each play Deans.

Dean Bottom: And what is a Dean? A lover or a tyrant?

Dean Quince: A lover—of efficiency—who nearly kills himself and everyone else most gallantly for order and efficiency.

Dean Bottom: That will ask some tears in the true performing of it, Dean Quince. Yet my chief humor is for a tyrant. I could play it as a lion; I will roar; that will do any professor's heart good to hear me.

Dean Quince: And should you roar too terribly you would fright the professors and students, that they would shriek; and that were enough to hang us all, Dean Bottom.

Dean Bottom: We will meet tomorrow by the Lincoln Statue, Dean Quince; and there we may rehearse more obscenely and courageously. Take pains; be perfect; adieu.

Act II, Scene I: The main office of North Hall. Puck stands alone.

Puck [to audience]: How now, spirits! Whither wander you?
Take heed! The Chair and Associate Chair now come within each other's sight. Because she wants to appoint the Lecturers,
And, jealous, he would have the task.
And they would place them in the Bascom Room,
Over objections of the grad students, who would design other uses there.
And I, as the department spirit
Appear as their most careful-thought plans
And then slip away the foundations and down they topple.

[Enter Associate Chair]

Associate Chair: My friend the Chair, I shall torment thee for this injury—
My gentle Puck, come hither: thou remember'st
The coffee in the pot in the Grad Lounge?
'Tis a strange brew.
Fetch that potion, and when the Chair is not looking
Pour some in her cup.
And the next thing then she looks upon,
She will think wondrously intelligent.

Puck: Fear not. I shall do so.

Associate Chair: And know you that churlish dissertation topic
Who keeps fleeing the right student?
Pour this brew also into its cup. But only when the right student is near-by.
Thus will be awake and will be struck by the wisdom of the match—
And that will increase our placement rates.

Puck: I'll put a girdle round the earth in 50 minutes.

Act III, Scene I: Bascom Hall. The Chair sits distracted. Enter the Deans.

Dean Quince: Here's a marvelous convenient place for our rehearsal. This green plot shall be our stage, and all the buildings upon it our set.

Dean Bottom: Dean Quince, there are things in this Strategic Plan that will never please. First, all the tenured professors must come up for review every five years. Then, the assistant professors will have to wait until the last possible moment to get tenure. Then, we're taking away all the financial aid from the graduate students. Then, we're suing the lecturers when the undergraduates misbehave. And finally, we'll force the new professors to sit on an airplane with the football team and cheerleaders for 25 hours straight.

Dean Quince: Dean Bottom, I believe you have left the killing out, when all is done.

Dean Bottom: Not a whit, Dean Quince. I have a device to make all well. Write me a prologue, and let the prologue seem to say, we will do no harm and everything will be well and it is for their own good.

Dean Quince: And we will tell them we are not who they think we are, and we really have the same interests, Dean Bottom?

Dean Bottom: Yes, Dear Quince! In my prologue I will say Fair Colleagues! I would wish you, or, I would request you, or I would entreat you, not to fear, not to tremble: my life for yours. If you think I come hither as a lion, it were a pity of my life. No, I am no such thing; I am a dean as other deans are. I will even tell them they should think this a window of opportunity. And I will demonstrate, and show them a window of opportunity like this [shows window with his hand, holds pose until Puck enters and sees] so they understand and aren't afraid.

Enter Puck.

Puck: What is this creature? Why, if it walks like one . . . and it talks like one . . . then . . . *[Moves behind Dean Quince and gives him donkey ears.]*

Dean Quince: O monstrous! O strange! We are haunted *[flees].*

Dean Bottom: I see his knavery; this is to make an ass of me; to fright me, if they could.

Chair [suddenly becoming undistracted]: Why what intelligent being calls me from my distraction? Thou art wise as thou are beautiful.

Dean Bottom: Not so, neither.

Chair: Ah, yes, and I have hears wondrous tales of your Strategic Plan, where we make all the tenured professors come up for review every five years and make the assistant professors wait until the last possible moment to get tenure and take away the financial aid from all the grad students and sue the lecturers when the undergraduates misbehave and force new professors to sit on an airplane with the football team and cheerleaders for 25 hours straight. Oh, can I help? What shall I do?

Act IV: North Hall main office. Chair is letting Dean Bottom borrow her desk. Puck is still giving him donkey ears.

Chair: Will thou hear some of my memos, my most magnificent Dean?

Dean Bottom: I have a tolerable mind for memos, but I have more desire for hay.

[Enter Associate Chair.]

Associate Chair: I begin to worry there is a danger here. Now that I have appointed lecturers, perhaps we should release the Chair for more serious business.

[Puck removes the donkey ears, snaps his fingers, and Chair starts].

Chair: O Associate Chair! "What visions I have seen. Methought the Dean was an ass and that I was wondrously impressed! How came these things to pass? *[Notices Dean Bottom.]* Oh! What is he doing here? Away!

[Exit Dean Bottom.]

Associate Chair: We have yet more business to finish. For the grad students have been chasing after dissertation topics, and the topics pursuing the topics pursuing the students, and yet nothing is written and no one is being placed. But I have set Puck upon it, and by semester's end, when the committee assembles, all will be right.

Epilogue.

Puck: If we faculty have offended,
Think but this—and all will be mended—
That you have but slumber'd here
While these visions did appear.
And this weak and idle theme,
No more yielding but a dream
Even if in these dreams some nightmares call
Normal progress can be had by all.

Extracts from 2002 Graduate Student Skit

Preemptive Strike

[Action news THEME MUSIC plays. ANCHOR runs in and sits at his desk, adjusts tie, basks in his own brilliance]

ANCHOR: [melodramatically] Good evening and welcome to the Channel 6 Super Action News at 10, your home for up-to-the-minute Super Doppler 3-D radar weather and complete high school sports coverage. I'm Jason Brozek. Our top story tonight: this common household product may kill your children instantly, according to UW experts. But first [ANCHOR turns forward to 'camera 2'], an update on a brewing conflict on the university campus. The battle for positivism took a substantial step forward when political science department chair Mark Beissinger announced the formation of the Department of Department Security. We go now to coverage of Beissinger's press conference, held this afternoon in the Ogg Room.

REPORTERS: Mr. Beissinger! Mr. Beissinger!

BEISSINGER: Yes, Helen?

REPORTER I: Mr. Beissinger, could you explain why it was necessary to form the Department of Department Security?

BEISSINGER: It has come to our attention that certain departments on campus may hold a weapon so nefarious that it threatens not only the fine political science research conducted here in North Hall, but jeopardizes the scientific method that underlies all important academic research. That weapon? Postmodernism.

[Gasps]

REPORTERS: Mr. Beissinger! Mr. Beissinger!

BEISSINGER: Wolf?

REPORTER 2: What functions will the Department of Department Security play in stopping the spread of postmodernism?

BEISSINGER: The department will be headed by our own John Witte, who has time and time again demonstrated his commitment to rigorous, *scientific* research. John will be monitoring the actions of the so-called 'Axis of Pomo,' which includes such evildoers as the English Department and the art historians. Secretary Witte will also be in charge of securing the homeland through our PIMPS program—the Postmodemism Information and Management Prevention System—through which department members can anonymously notify Secretary Witte of postmodemist activities.

ANCHOR: Beissinger also announced the institution of a color-coded warning system to make the department aware of potential postmodemist attacks. *[Pulls out chart]*
At the lemon yellow level, the threat of a pomo attack is low. Political scientists are encouraged to carry on with their day-to-day regression analyses and research-design writings. The department will be placed on seafoam alert when the Department of Department Security becomes aware that a student or students from an Axis of Pomo department or a department that is known to harbor postmodernists, such as sociology, has enrolled in a political science course.

The raw number alert will be given if any student or professor in the department cites the work of Foucault and/or Derrida or attempts a research project without a testable hypothesis, an identifiable dependent variable, and a well-operationalized set of independent variables. Finally, the periwinkle level indicates that a devastating postmodemist attack is imminent. The Department of Department Security was unwilling to describe what such an attack might look like. Or where it may occur. Or when. But it assured us that no matter what, or where, or when, it would be very, very bad.

We'll keep you posted with any further developments. Back to this evening's top story—this inexpensive killer is estimated to be in 95 percent of homes in America. How can you save your children? For the only solution, we go now to . . . I'm sorry, it seems we have some breaking news about a tense situation on Observatory Drive. We have Brittany Lords on the scene. Brittany, what can you tell us?

[Delay with ANCHOR and REPORTER 3 both pressing on their ears]

REPORTER 3: Thanks, Jason. I'm standing outside of Helen C. White, which has taken a direct hit tonight. The political science department has taken responsibility for the attack, deeming it a pre-emptive strike against a department that is strongly suspected of holding postmodemism. They're getting shelled hard out here, Jason.

ANCHOR: Tawny, can you describe the situation for us?

REPORTER 3: You can hear the KKV grenades landing behind me, and it seems that the 2x2 Matrix Mountain Division is rolling in now. The interpretivist perimeter was breached moments ago under heavy utility fire.

ANCHOR: Would you say we're seeing the destruction of deconstruction?

REPORTER 3: The English Department is certainly reinterpreting their paradigm, Jason.

ANCHOR: What do you see happening next in this conflict, Candy?

REPORTER 3: Well, the Philosophy Department has planned a 'Rally for Subjective Realities' and candlelight prayer vigil for tomorrow evening. In addition, United Departments Secretary-General Gina Sapiro has stated that she will attempt to broker a peace deal. Tomorrow, Sapiro will officially announce a summit to be held next week on neutral territory. An unnamed source has informed me that the Terrace is the most likely locale.

ANCHOR: Thanks, Mitzi. Stay with us at Super Action News 6 for complete coverage of all new developments in Operation External Validity. After the break, details on an upcoming cooling trend; will there be a white Christmas? And in sports, can the Pack recover from Sunday's close loss? Stay tuned.

Alternate Department History Timeline

Narrator 1: Stacey Pelika
Narrator 2: Travis Nelson

NARRATOR 1: As you are well aware, the department has embarked on a project to compile a history of the department. Although the project may take another year to complete, we are privileged to present to you tonight we some of the preliminary findings.

NARRATOR 2: January 1858: John Muir, famed naturalist and North Hall resident, accidentally spills coffee on the carpet of Room 313, the present location of the computer lab. The spill was never wiped up, and the stain remains to this day.

NARRATOR 1: April 1865: After Union forces declare victory over the Confederacy, North Hall faculty taunt their counterparts in South Hall.

NARRATOR 2: December 1882: After imbibing a little too much ale at the department's holiday party, political science graduate students put on a skit that goes too far in mocking President Chester A. Arthur. Department Chair Richard Ely calls the performance "puerile and in poor taste."

NARRATOR 1: November 1910: Graduate student Roy Emerson Curtis suggests that the department install an electrical outlet in the reading room.

NARRATOR 2: October 1948: Department faculty unanimously predict a big Dewey victory over Truman on Election Day.

NARRATOR 1: October 1962: Two superpowers square off in Cuba, and 95 percent of future Intro to IR students get a topic for their final paper.

NARRATOR 2: March 1970: UW Graduate student Richard B. Cheney rocks the political science world with a piece on congressional voting in the *American Political Science Review* that relies solely on correlation coefficients. [Hold up *APSR*]

NARRATOR 1: January 1974: Junior Faculty member Ed Friedman does a cutting Richard Nixon impersonation at a dinner party hosted by Richard Merelman. [*In Nixon voice with fingers outstretched in a V*] "I am not a crook!"

NARRATOR 2: November 1979: Graduate student Ben Marquez suggests that the department install an electrical outlet in the reading room.

NARRATOR 1: August 1986: Jon Pevehouse is born.

NARRATOR 2: October 1993: After putting up with his antics *for* four weeks, Graham Wilson and Gina Sapiro expel Mark Neumann from their Polisci 800 class. They tell him that he's not cut out *for* political science and suggest that he "run *for* office or something." Thanks Graham and Gina.

NARRATOR 1: December 1996: Associate Professor Ken Mayer interrupts a job talk with a clarifying question.

NARRATOR 2: October 2001: The nation wonders where Vice President Dick Cheney has been, and White House Spokesperson Ari Fleischer explains that Cheney has been holed up in a secure, undisclosed location. What the nation does not know is that Cheney has been locked in the conference room in the basement of North Hall by orders of his wife Lynne, who has demanded that he finish his dissertation.

NARRATOR 1: December 2002: John Witte is satisfied with a candidate's answer at a job talk.

NARRATOR 2: December 2002: Graduate student Paul Schlomer suggests that the department install an electrical outlet in the reading room.

APPENDIX 28

Department External Review Extracts

In the 1970s, the College of Letters and Science adopted a policy of periodic reviews of departmental performance, intended to be undertaken at ten-year intervals. The review committees were appointed by the dean from faculty within the university, but external to the department. Thus far, two such reviews of the department have been completed, in 1980 and 1997. We reproduce here extracts from these two reviews, which constitute searching appraisals of departmental quality. We also include passages from the Department response to the 1997 review.

The 1980 review committee was chaired by Stanley Payne (history), and included Michael Aiken (sociology), Donald Crawford (philosophy), Robert Haveman (economics), and John McNally (journalism). The 1997 review committee, led by Gerald Marwell (sociology), was composed of Michael Carter (agricultural economics), Thomas Archdeacon (history), Allen Buchanan (philosophy), Daniel Doeppers (geography), and Robert Miller (business and statistics).

1980 Review Committee Report Extracts

. . . Our discussions with individuals within the Political Science Department, and with those in the discipline at other universities, have led to an overall favorable view of the academic strength of the department. In most of the important fields there is a strong senior person with an ongoing research program and a national reputation. This is particularly true in the comparative fields and certain of the more traditional areas in political science.

In these areas of strength, research productivity has been steady and at a high level. Given the nature of the discipline, the writing of monographs—as opposed to journal articles—is a more common means of conveying research output than in some other social science disciplines. It is the rare year in the past decade that less than one research monograph has come out of the department. This productivity is reflected in the national ranking of the department, as it appears in reports based on periodic surveys of members of the profession. The department is always ranked within the top 10 nationally, and usually about 7th or 8th. One study ranked the department first in the country in weighted scholarly productivity for an earlier period (1968–74), and another ranked it fourth in participation in professional conferences for the decade 1966–75.

Despite this overall productivity and national ranking, a number of areas for possible improvement in the department can be identified. On the basis of our discussions and evaluations, we would note the following:

- Much of the department's strength is in the bread-and-butter, more traditional areas of political science. It is difficult to make the case that the department is well prepared to make significant contributions to newer fields which some in the discipline judge will be major areas of interest and development in the next decade. These fields include empirical political theory, public choice, and quantitative analysis. Assuming that the political science discipline will evolve as the other social science disciplines — especially economics and sociology — have and are developing, the role of rigorous empirical methods involving statistical hypothesis testing will continue to increase over the next decade. Wisconsin has had difficult in retaining faculty in this area, and it has not been a strong area in either the faculty or the curriculum over the last decade. Currently, the department is not well poised to make a major contribution in this area, either in research or graduate training. The Committee strongly recommends that a junior appointment be made in this area.
- Though the department has a number of unusually accomplished senior scholars, several of whom deservedly hold chairs, it would be significantly strengthened by a key appointment at the highest level of "star quality" — a scholar who would, for example, be ranked among the five or six most prominent people in one of the core areas of the discipline. During the past decade, Professor Austin Ranney was in this category; his loss to the department was a serious one. Not only was this the loss of one of the most visible faculty members, but it also left a gap in the core field of American politics which has not been filled. The Committee feels that this situation suggests placing a high priority in accelerating the search for a person to fill the senior American politics position for which an endowment will be forthcoming, and if necessary making that appointment before the money becomes available.

These gaps and weaknesses, however, have been offset to some extent by the development of the policy studies area in the department. This is one of the newer fields in the discipline, and one with good potential for growth and visibility. The department should be commended for its efforts to foster and develop this area.

The focus on the policy studies area, however, raises a larger issue concerning the relationship between the Political Science Department and the Center for the Study of Public Policy and Administration. At present the two organizations live overlapping but essentially independent, lives. The department emphasizes scholarly research and Ph.D. training; the Center emphasizes Master's level training and applied policy work. Given these rather disparate foci, the degree of mutual reenforcement between the two organizations is perforce limited.

The Committee has noted the success of several major universities in building a larger and more complementary relationship between political science and policy studies. This has been done through a two-fold strategy: 1) a major university commitment to building a substantial School or Institute of Public Policy, and 2) assigning that School or Institute a substantive research and education role involving political science and economics, and requiring a strong methodological base. The John F. Kennedy School at Harvard, the Institution for Social and Policy Studies at Yale, the Graduate School of Public Policy at Berkeley, the Lyndon Johnson School at Texas, and the Hubert Humphrey School of Public Policy at Minnesota are all examples. It seems likely that a strong University commitment in this direction would have the support of the Political Science Department and, in the view of the Committee, could 1) substantially strengthen both the field of political science and policy studies at the University, 2) strengthen the departments of economics and sociology, which already have strong policy-oriented core faculty groups, 3) establish further ties with other social science disciplines, and 4) provide a good deal of national visibility for the University.

In terms of its internal functioning, the department has established a good record during a difficult period. Until the current semester, the major problem has been declining enrollment in political science courses, both here and at other universities. This phenomenon has affected the humanities and less-quantitative social sciences and has been a nation-wide trend. Consistent with the College's policy of responding cautiously to shifting enrollment patterns, the department has maintained the approximate number of full-time-equivalent faculty (an average of about 35) for the past decade. Some faculty have developed ties with other departments, programs, and institutes at the University which have from time to time supported released time or provided adjunct teaching support. The Committee found no evidence of excessively small classes or other signs of excess faculty capacity.

The department's record in affirmative action is excellent. Its faculty now includes five women, three of whom have tenure, and one tenured minority male. The affirmative action goals of the Political Science Department have been fully met, and this deserves commendation.

Again, a few issues of internal operation merit attention, in spite of an overall favorable evaluation:

- The department functions largely as a collection of individuals who coalesce to make decisions on a set of mutually important issues. In making these decisions, a good deal of collegiality and mutual respect exists, and the decision-making appears efficient. Members of the department have usually been able to maintain an atmosphere in which confrontation is avoided and consensus is maximized. On the other hand, one gets little sense that the collegiality at this level is carried over into professional life. For example, there are few joint or multischolar research projects, the level of joint seminars and workshops is low, and there are few efforts to generate funding for a flow of seminars by visiting political scientists from other universities. The relative absence of this activity severely limits opportunities for Ph.D. students to present their research plans and progress to groups involving more than one faculty member, perhaps weakening opportunities for scholarly crossfertilization and planning for research funding.
- Departmental decisions on promotion and tenure are always of concern in a context in which senior appointments are rare – as is the situation at the University of Wisconsin–Madison. In this situation, the quality of promotion and tenure decision is crucial to strengthening the academic standing of the department. Most department members believe that evaluations of junior faculty have been rigorous during the past decade. In that period of time eight (or nine, if one somewhat ambiguous case is added) assistant professors have not been granted tenure. A number of senior department members, however, question the rigor of the department's evaluations and reviews. Though it is difficult to evaluate this set of concerns, it is a matter for continuing departmental vigilance.
- The College's policy of requiring annual reviews of all non-tenured faculty is generally perceived as debilitating and costly. To non-tenured faculty, the annual review process is seen as unnecessarily stressful and as inducing a short-run view of professional activity. Tenured faculty also note the small increment to knowledge gained in any given annual review relative to the costs. The College should therefore consider whether a biennial procedure of some kind may be more efficient and appropriate.

These considerations, then, have led to suggestions for both the Political Science Department and the College. They include:

1. The department should concentrate on newer areas of political and public choice theory and quantitative methodology in making new departmental appointments.

2. The department and the College should accelerate the search for a person of outstanding national reputation to fill the senior position in American politics.
3. The department (together with related departments) and the University should explore the possibility of creating and gaining funding for a major research and training program in Public Policy Studies and Analysis.
4. The department should seek ways to encourage joint, multi-scholar research and seminar activities, hence encouraging collegial activity at the professional level and improving Ph.D. training.
5. The department and the college should review the promotion and tenure process to ensure that high quality standards are met and that the process is not introducing high costs and short-run biases into professional activity.

1997 Review Committee Report Extracts

I. Introduction

Over the past several decades, the College of Letters and Sciences and the University have been very well served by its Political Science Department. Its faculty has been productive in scholarship, respected in the profession, superb in its classroom teaching, willing to teach its share of student hours, serious about its graduate and undergraduate programs, unstinting in its service to the College and University, and humane and civil in its everyday life. The continuity of these characteristics may be seen quite clearly from the last review of the Department. . . Despite the passing of nearly two decades, much of what was said in that report could be said again today.

The Department may be able to continue to perform at this high level for the foreseeable future—or it may not. For a variety of reasons, the prominence of the Department is certainly in danger. The current situation of the Department requires the faculty and the Dean to deal effectively and immediately with two ongoing major changes: (1) most important, an ongoing radical turnover and decline in departmental faculty personnel due to key retirements and other losses; (2) changes in the discipline to which the Department has not fully responded.

The last few years have seen the faculty both decline in number and suffer the loss of an older, well-regarded cohort of scholars. Thus, hiring and other personnel decisions are undoubtedly the most pressing issue confronting the Department and the Dean. The Department must make some appointments that signal its continued vitality and importance to the profession. In addition, judicious hiring could give the Department the opportunity both to meet its own perceived needs and to build in areas which have become prominent in the field but in which the Department is either numerically weak or almost vacant.

Personnel matters are not, of course, the only issues of moment for the Department. In this report we ask questions and make recommendations concerning the undergraduate and graduate teaching programs, the support and mentoring of junior faculty, minority hiring, staff support, joint appointments, and other matters. Some of these are closely related to the nature of the faculty and the areas of its strengths and weaknesses. . . .

II. Faculty Strength and Department Structure

Numbers and Age Composition

From a peak of 42.5 FTE in 1993–94 the Political Science Department will decline to a tenure roster of 31.5 FTE's in 1998–99 if no appointments are made during 1997–98. The latter number does not include several emeritus faculty who teach up to half time. Nevertheless, in only four years the Department has experienced a precipitous decline of 25% in faculty strength. These do not include Peter Eisinger's probable exit (he has taken leave and accepted a position elsewhere). Nor do they include two junior members of the Department whose spousal situations might lead to their loss. In addition, Crawford Young is 66 years old and Jack Dennis is 64.

A large portion of the department's faculty loss has come through retirement. Replacement (to the extent there has been replacement) has been primarily through junior hires. Several junior staff have also been lost through either termination or resignation, and were themselves mostly replaced by other juniors. Thus, when compared with other departments in the College, Political Science is now relatively young. Approximately half the faculty is less than 45 years old. Almost one-third is less than 40.

Target FTE for the Department has been set at 38.5 (or 39) in the strategic plan. Over the past decade the Department has lost an average of about three faculty per year (almost four per year since 1993). Given the change in age structure that has occurred, and the smaller base, somewhat more modest turnover might be expected in the near future. However, even if the Department averages half as many losses (1.5 per year) in the next few years, the hiring of two faculty per year would not allow the Department to reach its target for more than a decade. At one loss per year, two hires would bring the Department to target in approximately 2004.

Areas
Political science is conventionally divided into four areas: American Politics, Political Theory, Comparative Politics and International Relations. This division is institutionalized in practices of the American Political Science Association as well as at the University of Wisconsin. Not all four parts of the discipline are equal in numbers or stature, either nationally or at Wisconsin: with some faculty wearing more than one hat, approximately one third of the members of the faculty are in Comparative Politics; almost half are in American Politics; four members of the faculty are in Political Theory; three (2.5 FTE) are in International Relations. This last figure, which the faculty seems to agree is too small, continues to challenge the Department's ability to staff an area with enormous student interest but relatively sparse faculty supply in the discipline at large.

Of special relevance to the area description above is the subgroup within American Politics whose main interest is in Public Policy and who are associated with the La Follette Institute. If we do not count Peter Eisinger, four members of the faculty are principal participants in the Institute. . . .

Reputation
The Department has long been proud of its "top-ten" ranking in national surveys. It was ranked tenth in faculty quality in the most recent survey (1993), down from eighth in 1982. The faculty believe that the loss of a top-ten ranking would be a major blow to morale, and to their ability to attract graduate students and top faculty. Our best guess, however, is that if the ratings were done today, or in the near future, the Department will have declined even further.

Several factors account for this appraisal:

(1) The decline in the number of faculty. Most analysts of the structure of departmental reputations believe that size is a surprisingly important ingredient. During the expansions of the 1960s, departments that gained in the ratings, at least near the top, tended to be departments that grew quickly; those that declined in reputation had tended to resist growth. The Department's sharp numerical decline since 1993 undoubtedly hurts its ability to compete reputationally. Members of the Department believe that much of their reputation results from being considered a "full service" department, that covers a wide range of areas. Obviously, such coverage is much more difficult with a smaller faculty.

(2) The loss of their most visible faculty. The age shift in the Department means that a number of faculty with established reputations have left, to be replaced by younger faculty whose reputations still must be built.

Charles Jones was a past President of the American Political Science Association and Managing Editor of the *American Political Science Review*. Murray Edelman was an important intellectual figure, an appraisal supported by the fact that he was cited more than 130 times in 1996. No current member of the Department was cited more than 50 times during that year. The two most cited current faculty are Eisinger, who is probably leaving, and Young, who may be expected to retire in a few years.

(3) The rise of competing institutions. Between 1982 and 1993, the Department's *ratings* only declined by a small, and possibly insignificant amount. Its decline in the *rankings* was due to the enhanced standing of competing departments, most importantly California-San Diego, UCLA and Princeton, which moved ahead of Wisconsin. The two California departments made particularly dramatic improvement, based in part on expansion. Rochester and Duke also gained to the point where they are challenging Wisconsin's rank. Among the top departments, only MIT experienced a really precipitous drop in the rankings (from 6 to 12) and ratings, while Minnesota had the anomalous experience of improved ratings, but a fall in the rankings (from 10 to 13).

Reputational lag. There tends to be considerable inertia in the ratings of departments over time. Thus, the effects of retirements such as Edelman, Cohen and Epstein, and losses such as Adler, Pharr and Stallings, may or may not have strongly affected the 1993 ratings. However, these losses and the loss of Jones and Eisinger will certainly have a negative effect in the future.

Quality

Despite their losses, the faculty of Political Science seem genuinely positive in their evaluations of one another as scholars, teachers and colleagues. The Department points with pride to the high level of scholarly productivity achieved by its faculty over the past decade, and the number of prizes that have been won by books the faculty have written.

Particularly promising is the fact that this positive evaluation definitely extends to the younger members of the Department. According to senior faculty, the Department went through a difficult period during the 1980s, during which they did not recruit well, perhaps because of the decline in the number of superior candidates that was experienced throughout the social sciences. The Department feels it achieved much better results in the 1990s. Repeatedly, senior faculty indicated that they thought their Department was actually in "good shape" for the long run, if they could somehow limit the short-run effects of their severe losses, and keep the younger faculty who are now in place.

We do not disagree with this generally positive evaluation. The Department is certainly full of highly active, professional, and scholarly researchers. We are concerned, however, with what seems to be the limited impact and visibility of this scholarly product, and for the effect this visibility problem might have on the Department's future reputation and self-appraisal.

We understand that citation counts are at best rough indicators of the visibility and importance to the field of any individual and his or her work. Citation counts are somewhat more viable for the comparison of aggregates, such as departments. The National Academy of Sciences (NAS) considers them informative enough to include them in their periodic reports on departmental reputation. Still, we must be cautious so as to not over-interpret their message. Nevertheless, a look at some data seemed to us to be instructive.

Our concerns began with a look at the ratings data from the NAS study of 1993, which are provided in the Appendix of the Department's self-study. Besides its various ratings, the study reports on the total number of citations to the faculty and number of citations per faculty member. On these two criteria Wisconsin ranked 27th and 49th, respectively. Only one other highly ranked department (Berkeley) showed a similarly anomalous pattern. Additional appendices included in the self-report further support the conclusion that citations rates for the Political Science faculty are surprisingly low. With the retirements of the past decade, including Edelman, the Department's relative citation statistics are likely to have declined even further. The departure of Eisinger will again diminish these figures.

To some extent, departmental reputations are based on the visibility of their most eminent members. We looked at the citation patterns of some other highly rated departments. Because of limitations in our information about departments other than Wisconsin (without vitae it is difficult to separate citations for individuals who have common names) our data cannot be regarded as definitive, but they might serve for our purposes. The two top-five departments we checked, Stanford (ranked 5) and Michigan (3.5) were similar to one another, and quite different from Wisconsin. Each is "led" by three "stars" with between one hundred and several hundred citations in 1996. In addition, Michigan has two, and Stanford four, faculty in the 45–80 range. Rochester, which was ranked just below Wisconsin, has one star with 200 citations and three others with 40–60 each. This might predict a continuing rise in its status. In comparison, Minnesota, which ranked 13th, was quite similar to Wisconsin in its distribution of citations—with no one over 50.

Publication Patterns

One reason for the lack of fit between productivity and citation for Wisconsin's faculty may be the faculty's chosen pattern of publication. Data provided by the self-report and conversations with the faculty suggest that relative to the social sciences (and, we believe, political science as a discipline) this is more a book-oriented than an article-oriented department. Assistant Professors indicated that they were encouraged to publish books, and that these would be the crucial element in their promotion decisions. Senior faculty would comment on younger faculty by indicating that they were "waiting for the next book." One senior faculty member indicated concern that excellent scholars in the Department eschewed publishing articles where they were obviously available as parts of some larger work. The dominant message may be that publishing an article based on material that later appears in a book is "double-dipping," and not to the scholar's credit.

We do not want our comments here to be taken as an attack on an emphasis on research monographs. Scholars must choose the most appropriate vehicle for the specific work in which they happen to be involved. However, we believe that in contemporary social science such an emphasis carries with it certain costs regarding departmental visibility, which we think is an important issue for the Department at this time. Monographs and books can receive considerable attention, but there is a very high variance among them. In general, chapters in books have the least likelihood of either making an impact or being cited. They also often do not go through the vigorous editorial scrutiny and rewriting that is expected in the best journals. "Double dipping" might actually have some scholarly value.

The data in . . . the self report indicate that among the faculty, refereed journal articles outnumber scholarly books and monographs only by about 2 to 1, which is surprising considering that books typically require perhaps three to ten times the content and work of an article. Faculty-authored chapters in books outnumber refereed articles by 3 to 2. This appears to be a substantial change from the data provided for 1978–80, when Wisconsin ranked second among political science departments in the number of articles published by faculty.

Among current faculty, we could find for the past decade only one article published in the *American Political Science Review*, the discipline's official and leading journal. There are, in addition, a number of papers (perhaps 40) in the next tier of political science journals (roughly defined), but this number seems to us surprisingly small. Most of the faculty's refereed papers are in specialized journals. As we all know, these may be excellent papers. However, one can see that not publishing in the leading journals for general readership, with their wide circulation, might lead to a comparative lack of recognition.

Theoretical and Methodological Preferences

A related issue is the distribution of theoretical and methodological styles represented within the Department. The Payne report saw that a lack of personnel in the "hot" areas of the discipline was an important issue. The areas that the Payne Committee selected as inadequately represented at that time were "empirical political theory, public choice [which in today's parlance is roughly the same as rational choice], and quantitative analysis." The report also emphasized the need for an appointment in "rigorous empirical methods involving statistical hypothesis testing."

Although the Department has attempted to respond to these recommendations, the faculty do not themselves feel that they have been successful. They are now concerned that rectifying the situation in the near future is unlikely because of hiring limitations.

It is the opinion of this Committee that to some extent these issues still characterize the Department. Furthermore, we worry that they constitute an important problem for the Department's reputation. . . . The members of the Department themselves generally use the term "eclectic" to describe the theoretical and methodological approaches of the faculty. By eclectic they seem to mean that neither the Department, nor any subgroup in the Department, attempts to exert pressure on any individual scholar to do his or her research in any given way or from any given perspective. There is no "Wisconsin School" of how to do political science. Such internal tolerance is indeed supportive and can be a valuable asset. It may also involve costs, particularly to reputation.

The faculty contrasts the situation at Wisconsin with that obtaining in several "reference" departments, such as Michigan, or Ohio State, which are seen as having become bastions of a "rational choice" approach, to the exclusion of other views. This uniformity, the faculty feel (with some resentment, and certainly some truth), now typifies many of the departments with high citation counts.

In their self-report, and in our conversations, many, but not all, of the faculty seem to think of "rational choice" as one of several "flavors of the day" that have swept through political science, with a periodicity of about a decade each. Although each of these approaches "has left a lasting imprint," they say in their self-report, "no one approach has stood the test of time." There is considerable debate within the faculty regarding how to deal with this issue. Political science as a discipline seems to be almost emotionally divided regarding the value of formal modeling or "rational choice," and many of the members of the Wisconsin faculty appear to be on the negative, and somewhat defensive, side. Nevertheless, and to its credit, the Department tried to hire in this area once before, and last year hired a junior person who uses a rational choice approach.

The Department's eclecticism has also mostly left out various forms of what the self-report terms "political economy" approaches. These may well include one or more the "empirically grounded theoretical approaches" for which the Payne report was calling.

The Department has been somewhat more successful in responding to the third area stressed in the Payne report. The number of faculty who use quantitative/statistical methods in their research has increased to about one-third of the Department. However, only two members of the faculty, both of them senior, appear to consider themselves expert enough in these techniques to teach them on the graduate level.... The Department cannot be considered as have made an investment in becoming "cutting edge," or even "state-of-the-art," in quantitative analysis.

Looking in from outside, the Department, on balance, appears to value certain kinds of work more than others. Its general preference seems to be for substantive scholarship – deep knowledge of and/or experience with the subject matter – over innovation and risk-taking, both substantive and methodological. Work of the latter kind is often risky; it suffers from being "trendy," from oversimplification and naivete, from boring discussions of technical matters, and from difficulties in communication with non-adepts. But in the discipline as a whole, work of this kind has frequently been considered path-breaking, exciting, and important, and has built star-like reputations for those who do it successfully. Of course, the perfect candidate has it all. There are few perfect candidates.

We do not want to overemphasize these points. We have paid close attention to the Department's hiring procedures and these seem sensible, and have reduced the control over hires which used to rest more completely with faculty in the particular areas being considered. There is some indication that with changes in personnel, Department preferences may also be changing. We are hopeful about current decisions.

Minority Hiring

In its self-report the Department describes itself as relatively unsuccessful in recruiting and/or retaining members of minority groups. The record confirms that evaluation. Since the Payne report the Department has hired two or three minority faculty.... Today only one of those hires remains.

Our committee agrees that the recent minority hiring and retention record of the Department is not what the College would like to see, although it may not be substantially worse than that if many other departments in the College or in the discipline of political science.

Recommendations Regarding Personnel
We recommend that the Dean consider making a serious investment in the Department of Political Science. We assume that the College's interest lies in the creation and maintenance of respected, productive departments that teach well, serve the College and outside institutions, and treat students and faculty in a humane fashion. The Department of Political Science has a history of doing all of these things, but it is possible that neglect could lead it to lose that respect among its peers and, by that loss, lose respect for itself. It is easier to protect the reputation of a department recently considered among the best, than to rebuild that reputation once it has badly faltered. . . .

Extracts from Department Response (Herbert Kritzer)

. . .

As the Marwell Report makes very clear, faculty retirements and resignations (coupled with aggressive moves by some of the department's national competitors) threaten the department's standing. The central issue framed by the Marwell Committee boil down to this: How can the Department of Political Science retain its national research prominence—and its strong contributions to the university's undergraduate and graduate teaching programs—within the range of likely resources? As the Committee notes, it is unlikely that the department will be unable to pursue the strategy it has used in the past: of positioning itself as a full-service department with separate groups of faculty hired to cover all or most of the discipline's major theoretical and geographical issues. It is equally clear that the resources are not likely to be available for the department to carve out and staff a new niche for itself. Even if the Department were to decide that it wanted to abandon large areas of teaching (many of which are important to the University as a whole), in order to create a radically new focus, the relatively youthful age profiles of the department (which means that we have no reason to expect a sudden opening of large numbers of new positions within our strategic plan), would make such a shift difficult to accomplish.

The only realistic course is to build on the department's widely acknowledged strengths while sharpening its focus. Those strengths lie in the ways in which faculty integrate cross-cutting interests and areas of research, as evidenced in part by the extensive commitment to interdisciplinary research and teaching. With this in mind, we take up the Marwell Committee's challenge by proposing:

- *Positions.* We seek authorization to plan to come back up to our strategic plan target of 39.75 (increased temporarily from 39 as part of a strategic hire opportunity (positions over the next three years (by which time all Post Retirement Agreements involving our faculty will have expired). Based on where we expect to stand at the end of the current academic year, this will mean approximately 4 positions not counting any additional departures or retirements and not counting the Hawkins Chair.
- *Focus.* The department will sharpen its focus by hiring faculty in ways that go beyond filling specific niches or boxes (something we believe we have already begun to do in terms of our recruiting over the last two years). Our goal is to find faculty to cover needed areas but, most important, also help us make linkages across specific fields. That is, *we seek people who help to connect the boxes of the discipline rather than simply filling various boxes.*
- *Level.* To provide departmental, and interdisciplinary program, leadership as well national recognition, we seek to fill at least one third of the positions over the next three years at the tenured level (by which we mean young, but already established, scholars perhaps 10–12 years post-Ph.D.). Compared to the College as a whole, the Department is relatively youthful, and this is beginning to create some problems in terms of leadership both within the department and in the larger campus interdisciplinary community. It also has led to a situation that means that we are relatively bottom heavy with relatively few people in the age range most likely to be at the peak of professional prominence.

By allowing the Department of Political Science to pursue this rebuilding, the College will demonstrate that it is possible for a Department to pursue both disciplinary excellence and interdisciplinary commitments envisioned in Dean Certain's "Creating a New College" and Chancellor Ward's "A Vision for the Future." In fact, we believe that failing to do so will undercut these interdisciplinary directions by confirming to the skeptics that interdisciplinary activities can come only at the cost of departmental prestige (a theme that was an undercurrent in at least some of the discussions with members of the Marwell Committee).

. . .

The department is committed to a tradition of intellectual pluralism, which in fact reflect the pluralism of the discipline of political science and inherent in strong interdisciplinary research. The nationally and internationally renowned members of the Department who have brought us—and the university—fame did so with work that is remarkably different. Leon Epstein and Charles Jones (past presidents of the American Political Science Association) had little or nothing in common in their assumptions, methods or conclusions with Murray Edelman who, as noted by the Marwell Committee, remains prominent in the Social Science Citation Index. Out of this tradition of diversity, we propose to concentrate on pursuing the substantive, theoretical, and methodological approaches that follow. This strategy builds on the strengths for which the department has been internationally recognized, and which have been important for recruiting both faculty and students. It also seeks to recognize the critical issues emerging in the discipline—and to chart a strategy for assuring that the Wisconsin department will play a major leadership role.

While some departments have chosen to become niche players in statistical methods or theoretical approaches, like rational choice, it is clear to us that the next generation of critical theoretical problems are the cross-cutting, boundary-spanning issues: how individual political actors affect the behavior of political institutions; how political institutions respond to pressing challenges of changing policy problems; how the behavior of political institutions in some nations—and regions—affect the behavior of others; and how the lasting issues of political theory inform the newly emerging debates. Our existing substantive, theoretical, and methodological strengths provide a firm foundation for capitalizing on these intellectual trends. These strengths include:

- A commitment to in-depth understandings of the political systems of countries and regions throughout the world combined with strong emphases on theoretical approaches that cross country and regional boundaries.
- An emphasis on the role of institutions and institutional structures on both the day to day operation of political systems and on the opportunities for major changes in political systems (i.e., democratization, emergence of new political groupings, sharp deviations from long-standing public policies, the rise of identity politics).
- An emphasis on understanding the role of the individual actor, both at the mass and elite levels, in political systems around the world. Approaches of faculty have ranged from experimental methods in the social psychology tradition to mass survey methodologies to intensive anthropological-style fieldwork in diverse settings around the world.
- A recognition that the central issues of political analysis flow from philosophical questions about politics, communities, and interpersonal obligation. For this reason, unlike some political science departments, we have never marginalized the study of political philosophy, and we are committed to continuing the important role of political philosophy in our undergraduate curriculum and as part of our graduate program.

- A strong commitment, perhaps one of the strongest such commitments among major departments in the discipline, to the role of interdisciplinary analysis. Politics and government do not exist in isolation, and to ignore the interdisciplinary audiences and sources would lessen both our own understandings of and our own contributions to the study of politics.
- A commitment to applying and teaching rigorous research methods, *broadly defined*. We were one of the first, if not the first, political science departments to develop a graduate course in qualitative research methods.

The intellectual pluralism of the Department has emphasized the connections across these areas of strength. **We will move to maintain and enhance our international leadership by charting in yet more prominent ways these connections.**

To accomplish this, the department will seek to hire new faculty in ways that go beyond filling specific niches or boxes. Our goal will be to find faculty to cover needed areas but who also help us make linkages across specific subfields within political science and with colleagues in other disciplines; we want to insure that we do not isolate ourselves into tightly defined specialties. Rather, we value, and will continue to value, colleagues who enjoy interacting with scholars who have widely varying interests.

While reflecting the disciplinary goals, the Department will continue to be committed to its service obligation within the University. This means that we need to cover courses outside areas that we may put at the top of our priorities from the viewpoints of strengths. For example, the Department has for some time struggled to build a viable and strong group of scholars whose interests center on international relations. In response to the Marwell Committee's suggestion that we cease trying to be what we call a "full-service" department, we could propose to abandon international relations and devote resources elsewhere. We believe that to do so would be irresponsible to the University and particularly to undergraduates interested in international studies; it would also be irresponsible to our graduate students in subfields such as comparative politics who often view international relations as an extremely important second field of concentration.

. . .

The Report raises one issue which the Department believes warrants more than a passing response: have faculty members ins the Department directed their publications in ways that best serve to enhance the reputation of the Department within the discipline?

Publications by faculty tend to appear in four different types of outlets: mainstream political science journals, specialized journals (both within political science and interdisciplinary), books published by major university presses, and chapters in edited collections. Many people in the Department share the view that publishing in major refereed journals should be encouraged (particularly as an alternative to chapters in edited volumes which typically do not achieve the same level or breadth of visibility, although we note that some of the most cited works in the discipline have appeared in edited collections).

Generally, in merit evaluations, publications in such journals tend to be recognized more than chapters in edited collections or articles in lower tier or highly specialized journals. We note however that we believe it is important to continue to value highly publication in top-tier interdisciplinary journals as well as top-tier political science journals. In fact, in some subfields, journals other than the *American Political Science Review* are viewed as more prestigious; *World Politics,* for example, is the premier outlet for international relations (and in one prestige rating of journals some years ago was actually more highly rated than APSR).

The report suggests that journal articles are to be preferred to books. . . . Implicitly it suggests that faculty should think in terms of research projects that lend themselves to article length publications rather than books, suggesting that such work would increase citations and hence visibility. Fundamentally, we believe that faculty should pursue high quality research projects, hopefully ones that can be supported by outside research funding. Some projects lend themselves to article-length reports and we share the review committee's position that the best outlet for such work from a reputational viewpoint is top-tier refereed journals. However, much of the research our faculty undertakes does not lend itself to articles, and for such work we encourage faculty to seek outlets among the top university presses. In the last ten years, faculty at Wisconsin have published books (or currently have books in-press with):

University of Chicago Press (9 books)
Yale University Press (5 books)
Cambridge University Press (3 books)
Harvard University Press (2 books)
Oxford University Press (2 books)
University of California Press (2 books)
Princeton University Press (2 books)

Perhaps another dozen books have been published by academic presses with top series in particular fields (Cornell, Johns Hopkins, University of Michigan, Brookings Institution). We doubt that more than half of the other top 10 departments can match this accomplishment!

Nonetheless, the issue of publication outlets is a difficult one. The nature of diversity within the discipline has meant that there is no one "best" place or form to publish in. Some departments have in fact made publishing in the *American Political Science Review* the single highest priority. However, a really major book is going to have greater impact than most articles appearing in *APSR*. This is particularly true in subfields such as comparative politics and political theory (and some specific areas of American politics such as the presidency and the interest groups) where the core work is disseminated primarily through books. (One senior comparativist noted that in the last batch of comparative politics prelims, almost all of the citations made by the examinees were to books.) Even though some subfields are more "journal-oriented" (political behavior is a prominent example), the importance of books across the discipline is evident in the scholarly records of one of the most eminent group of political scientists, recent presidents of the American Political Science Association, who are known primarily for their books, not their journal articles.

Index

***Note:** Material from the appendixes is not included in this index.*